NARRATIVE AND DRAMATIC SOURCES OF SHAKESPEARE

Volume I
EARLY COMEDIES
POEMS
ROMEO AND JULIET

NARRATIVE AND DRAMATIC SOURCES OF SHAKESPEARE

Edited by
GEOFFREY BULLOUGH
Professor of English Language and Literature,
King's College, London

Volume I
EARLY COMEDIES
POEMS
ROMEO AND JULIET

LONDON: Routledge and Kegan Paul
NEW YORK: Columbia University Press
1957

First published 1957
by Routledge and Kegan Paul Ltd
Broadway House, Carter Lane, E.C.1
and Columbia University Press
Columbia University, New York
Made and printed in Great Britain
by William Clowes and Sons, Limited
London and Beccles

Library of Congress Catalog Card Number: 57–9969

'I may boldly say it because I have seene it, that the Palace of pleasure, the Golden Asse, The Œthiopian historie, Amadis of Fraunce, The Rounde Table, bawdie Comedies in Latine, French, Italian and Spanish, have been throughly ransackt to furnish the Playe houses in London.'

[S. GOSSON : *Playes Confuted in Five Actions*, 1582.]

In these histories (which by another terme I shall call *Novelles*) be described the lives, gestes, conquestes and highe enterprises of great Princes, wherein also be not forgotten the cruell actes and tiranny of some. In these be set forth the great valiance of noble Gentlemen, the terrible combates of corageous personages, the vertuous mindes of noble dames, the chaste hartes of constant Ladyes, the wonderfull pacience of puissant Princes, the milde sufferance of well disposed Gentlewomen, and in divers the quiet bearing of adverse fortune. In these histories be depainted in lively colours, the ugly shapes of Insolence and Pride, the deforme figures of Incontinencie and Rape, the cruell aspectes of Spoile, breach of order, treason, ill lucke and mischiefe of States, and other persons. Wherin also be intermixed, pleasant discourses, merie talke, sporting practises, deceytful devises, and nipping tauntes, to exhilarate the readers minds. And although by the first face and view, some of these may seeme to intreate of unlawfull Love, and the foule practises of the same, yet being throughly read and well considered, both olde and yonge may learne how to avoyde the ruine, overthrow, inconvenience, and displeasure, that lascivious desire, and wanton will, doth bring to the suters and pursuers of the same. All which may render good example for all sortes to follow the best, and imbrace the vertuous, contrariwise to reject the worste, and contempne the vicious . . .

[PAINTER: *The Palace of Pleasure*, 1566. The Epistle.]

v

To Audrey and Denis

PREFACE

IN THE PAST two hundred years considerable attention has been given to Shakespeare's indebtedness for elements of his plots and characterization to earlier English and foreign authors. Editors of individual plays (as in the New Variorum and Arden editions) have provided whole texts or extracts from alleged sources and analogues, and Sir Israel Gollancz in his valuable 'Shakespeare Library' printed material bearing on eleven plays with introductions by various scholars to which subsequent students must be gratefully indebted. This collection is now however very rare.

There have been three major works bringing together a large body of parallels. In 1753-4 Mrs Charlotte Lennox, author of *The Female Quixote*, published in three volumes *Shakespeare Illustrated, or the Novels and Histories on which the Plays of Shakespeare are founded, collected and translated from the original authors. With critical remarks.* In these remarks she unwisely tried to show that Shakespeare spoiled many of his stories by complicating the intrigue and introducing absurdities. In Germany K. Simrock produced (1831) a collection of narrative sources. Then came J. P. Collier's *Shakespeare's Library* (1843) (2 vols.) with illustrations for fifteen plays. This work was expanded into six volumes by W. C. Hazlitt in 1875, since when there has been no compendium of equal scope.

That is perhaps not surprising, for though research has since brought to light comparatively few new parallels, it has become increasingly apparent how much more often one can say, 'This is like Shakespeare', than 'This is definitely Shakespeare's source'. Any attempt to bring together all known parallels must fail by reason of the space required, since some of the stories (e.g. the Bond-theme of *The Merchant of Venice*) are found all over the world. On the other hand some probable sources (e.g. the Jew-play mentioned by Stephen Gosson) have disappeared.

ix

Furthermore there must often remain a doubt as to which one
or more of several available sources the dramatist used. To give
only some of the many texts about which scholars have argued,
and are still arguing, is bound to bring more than the usual
criticism encountered by an anthology. But the need of a
working collection of sources and analogues has long been felt
by students of Shakespeare's technique and of comparative
literature.

The work of which this is the first volume will assemble what
the editor believes to be the chief narrative and dramatic
sources and analogues of Shakespeare's plays and poems so as
to assist the reader who, not being a specialist, wishes to explore
the working of Shakespeare's mind. The arrangement of
material will be as follows: Vol. I Early comedies, Poems and
Romeo and Juliet; Vol. II Comedies 1598–1603; Vol. III The
English Histories; Vol. IV Plays on Classical Themes; Vol. V
Major Tragedies and Romances.

In discussing parallels it is always well to bear in mind Dr
Johnson's warning against seeking an external origin for every
phrase, however brilliant or commonplace, in a great author:
'I have found it remarked that, in this important sentence,
Go before, I'll follow, we read a translation of *I prae, sequar*. I
have been told that when *Caliban*, after a pleasing dream, says,
I cry'd to sleep again, the author imitates *Anacreon*, who had, like
every other man, the same wish on the same occasion.' (*Preface
to Shakespeare.*)

Derived phrases, images and the germs of images there are
nevertheless, and the student will have not only the joy of discovering them for himself, but also the deeper pleasure of
realizing how often Shakespeare has transformed them in
weaving them into the texture of his poetry.

Johnson believed that Shakespeare knew less Latin than,
after the work of Professors T. W. Baldwin and V. Whitaker
and Dr Percy Simpson, we now think. Of modern languages
Johnson was 'inclined to believe that he read little more than
English and chose for his fables only such tales as he found
translated.' We can still agree broadly with this though most
scholars now allow Shakespeare some French and Italian. In
the present work, English translations (wherever possible those
which Shakespeare may have seen) are given. Chiefly to make

room for more analogues and also because comparatively few readers today can cope with Plautus, Ovid and Livy in the original, Latin originals are not usually supplied. This decision was made with reluctance, especially for *Venus and Adonis*, where Professor Baldwin has shown that the poet probably used an edition of the *Metamorphoses* with the Latin commentary of Marsus. But to give the latter would have swollen the section inordinately. A separate reprint of Marsus' Ovid is greatly to be desired. For *Lucrece* a sixteenth century Latin text of the *Fasti* is given—with a later translation—because this work had not been Englished when Shakespeare wrote his poem.

During the adulatory phase of Shakespeare criticism it was customary to extol his virtues at the expense of most previous writers, and Johnson, himself no Bardolater, expressed a long-enduring opinion when he wrote: 'except the characters of Chaucer, to whom I think he is not much indebted, there were no writers in English, and perhaps not many in other modern languages, which showed life in its native colours.' Today we may accept Professor C. S. Lewis's division of early sixteenth century literature into 'Drab' and 'Golden' writings—and who can read through Arthur Brooke's *Romeus and Juliet* with sustained delight?—but we realize that Elizabethan readers had not our standards. Shakespeare probably enjoyed many of the 'Drab' writers when he first read them, as well as Lyly's 'transitional' *Euphues*, although he came to laugh at them later. On the whole, the works which we can regard as major sources, Gower, Gascoigne, Golding's *Ovid*, Painter, North, Holinshed, etc., have, *pace* Dr Johnson, something both in matter and manner to commend them, and the plays which Shakespeare remodelled were good of their kind. A collection such as this, therefore, is not without merit as an anthology of Elizabethan reading.

After a quarter-century during which scholars have been preoccupied with Shakespeare's text and Shakespeare's poetry sometimes to the exclusion, or denigration, of character and plot, the pendulum is swinging back to the more purely dramatic side of his art. This work was begun in the conviction that Shakespeare was essentially a poet *in the theatre*, that his imagination worked best when stimulated by a tale or a situation involving a conflict between human beings, and that a full appreciation

must relate his imagery, rhythms and ideas to the dramatic
handling of the stories and personages as he re-made them. To
trace this in detail is not the purpose of these volumes, which
will present mainly what Henry James called the 'données'—for
to Shakespeare part of a romance by Montemayor or a play of
King Leir served as a seminal impulse just as an anecdote at a
dinner-party did to the American novelist. On the whole
Shakespeare kept close to his sources, but his deviations are at
least as significant as his borrowings. Without a knowledge of
the material available to him neither his debts nor the tran-
scendent scope of his creative energy can be assessed. In the
Introduction to each play, after a brief discussion of the date
of composition in which E. K. Chambers's chronology is usually
followed, the general relationship of the play to the sources and
analogues available to the dramatist is described, and quota-
tions are often given from analogues which cannot be cited
fully. The major texts are given in the order in which they are
mentioned in the Introduction, and I have ventured to suggest
in the heading of each whether it is a certain or a probable
source or an analogue only. Original spelling and punctuation
are kept except (rarely) where they cause ambiguity or difficulty in comprehension. No attempt is made to imitate Elizabethan typography: contractions are expanded, and *v, u, i, ∫,*
become *u, v, j, s,* where modern practice would have it so.
Words and letters within square brackets are the editor's inser-
tions. Title pages are given where significant or of rare works.

The Introductions cannot be exhaustive, but it is hoped that
they will stimulate readers to more detailed comparisons and
inquiry. The Bibliography is selective, providing a list of works
especially valuable for the study of Shakespeare's attitude to
plot and characters and his reading; also a list of books and
articles concerning the source-material of individual plays and
poems. This second section is not limited to the authorities cited
in the Introductions but includes supplementary material for
readers who wish to trace more fully, and from other points of
view, the parallels between Shakespeare and other writers.

To select is to oversimplify, but that danger is inseparable
from this undertaking. Professor K. Muir in a book which
appeared while this volume was in press has rightly laid emphasis on the 'multiple sources' of Shakespeare. In the last

volume of the series I hope to discuss this and other problems suggested by a survey of the whole field. A work such as this is bound to owe much to other men's labours, and grateful acknowledgement is here made to predecessors such as J. P. Collier, W. C. Hazlitt, F. J. Furnivall, Sir I. Gollancz, W. H. D. Rouse, Dr F. S. Boas, and Shakespeare's editors, particularly in the New Variorum edition and the Arden (old and new); to editors of other works such as J. Cunliffe (Gascoigne), Sir S. L. Lee (*Huon of Bordeaux*), E. A. Arber and R. W. Bond (Lyly), to translators such as W. G. Waters (Masuccio) and E. H. Sugden (Plautus); as well as to many other critics and writers on sources listed in the Bibliography. References to Shakespeare's works are to the three-volume Oxford edition, ed. W. J. Craig. Permission has been kindly given by the Council of the Malone Society to print passages from Sir W. W. Greg's reprint of *Gesta Grayorum*; by the Delegates of the Clarendon Press to print from G. C. Macaulay's edition of *The Works of John Gower*; and by Messrs Macmillan and Co. Ltd. to print passages from *The Legend of Good Women* and *The Knight's Tale* from the 'Globe' *Chaucer*, edited by A. W. Pollard and others.

I wish to thank the following for their assistance: Mr A. J. J. Ratcliff, late of Thomas Nelson Ltd., and the directors of that firm for the encouragement they gave early in the last war when this project was first conceived; Professor Kenneth Muir whose unselfishness made it possible of fulfilment in its present form; the Librarians of the British Museum, of King's College and the Goldsmith's Library, University of London, of Cornell University and the Huntington Library, California; Miss Rosemary Jackson and Miss Mollie Butcher for secretarial assistance; my wife for her perennial patience and help.

CONTENTS OF VOLUME I

LIST OF ABBREVIATIONS

1. Shakespeare's Works and Apocrypha

Ado	Much Ado about Nothing
AFev	Arden of Feversham
AShrew	The Taming of A Shrew
AYL	As You Like It
CE	Comedy of Errors
Cor	Coriolanus
Cym	Cymbeline
Ham	Hamlet
1H4	Henry the Fourth, Part I
2H4	Henry the Fourth, Part II
H5	Henry the Fifth
1H6	Henry the Sixth, Part I
2H6	Henry the Sixth, Part II
3H6	Henry the Sixth, Part III
H8	Henry the Eighth
KJ	King John
LComp	Lover's Complaint
Lear	King Lear
LLL	Love's Labour's Lost
Luc	The Rape of Lucrece
Mac	Macbeth
MM	Measure for Measure
MND	A Midsummer Night's Dream
More	Sir Thomas More
MV	The Merchant of Venice
MWW	The Merry Wives of Windsor
NobKin	Two Noble Kinsmen
Oth	Othello
Per	Pericles
PhT	The Phoenix and the Turtle
PPil	The Passionate Pilgrim
R2	King Richard the Second
R3	King Richard the Third
RJ	Romeo and Juliet
Son	Sonnets
TA	Titus Andronicus
Tem	The Tempest
TGV	Two Gentlemen of Verona
Tim	Timon of Athens
TN	Twelfth Night
TrC	Troilus and Cressida
TSh	The Taming of The Shrew
VA	Venus and Adonis
WT	The Winter's Tale

2. Modern Editions and Criticism

Arden	The Arden Shakespeare, 1889–1944
Boas	The Taming of A Shrew, edited F. S. Boas
Camb	The Cambridge edition of Shakespeare, edited A. Quiller-Couch and J. Dover Wilson
Coll	Shakespeare's Library, edited J. Payne Collier, 2 vols.
ELH	English Literary History (Johns Hopkins University, Washington D.C.)
ElSt	E. K. Chambers, The Elizabethan Stage, 4 vols.

MedSt	E. K. Chambers, *The Medieval Stage*, 2 vols.	*SAB*	*Shakespeare Association Bulletin* (U.S.A.)
WSh	E. K. Chambers, *William Shakespeare*, 2 vols.	*ShJb*	Jahrbuch der deutschen Shakespeare—Gesellschaft
5ActS	T. W. Baldwin, *Shakespeare's Five-Act Structure*	*ShLib*	*Shakespeare's Library*, 6 vols. 2nd Edn. 1875, edited J. P. Collier and W. C. Hazlitt. (Also Collier-Hazlitt)
Genetics	T. W. Baldwin, *On the Literary Genetics of Shakespeare's Poems and Sonnets*	*SPhil*	*Studies in Philology* (U. of N. Carolina)
JEGP	*The Journal of English and Germanic Philology*	*ShQ*	*Shakespeare Quarterly*
Jest Books	*Shakespeare Jest Books*, edited W. C. Hazlitt	*Sh.Soc. Trans.*	*Transactions of the (New) Shakespeare Society*
Lee	Sir Sidney Lee, *Life of Shakespeare*	*Texas*	*University of Texas Studies in English*
MalSoc	Malone Society Reprints	*TLS*	*The Times Literary Supplement* (London)
MLR	*The Modern Language Review*	*Var.*	*The New Variorum edition*, ed. H. H. Furness, &c.
MPhil	*Modern Philology*		
New Arden	The Arden Edition of Shakespeare, re-edited 1949–	**3. *Other Abbreviations***	
N&Q	*Notes & Queries*	*Arg*	Argument
Oxf.	The Oxford Edition of Shakespeare, text by W. J. Craig; Introductory Studies by E. Dowden	*Chor*	Chorus
		Prol	Prologue
		Rev.	Review
		F	Folio edition
PhilQ	*Philological Quarterly*	Q	Quarto edition
PMLA	Publications of the Modern Language Association of America	n.d.	No date
		S.R.	The Stationer's Register
RES	*The Review of English Studies*	*STC*	*A Short-Title Catalogue of Books printed ... 1475–1640* (1950)

THE COMEDY
OF ERRORS

INTRODUCTION

THE COMEDY OF ERRORS was first printed in F1.
Divided into Acts and some scenes, it was Shakespeare's shortest
play (1,777 lines), and there is little evidence to support Dover
Wilson's argument that it was considerably abridged. The
doggerel in Act III.1 etc. has been taken to show that the play
revised an earlier work, maybe the lost *The historie of Error*
played by Paul's in 1577, or 'A historie of fferrar' played by
Sussex's men in 1583. More probably Shakespeare was, as in
The Taming of the Shrew and *Love's Labour's Lost*, 'consciously
experimenting with an archaistic form for comic effect' (E. K.
Chambers). The date of composition is unknown. The first
recorded performance was at Gray's Inn on 28 December,
1594, but verbal resemblances in Nashe and *Arden of Feversham*
suggest an earlier date, perhaps 1592. There is some likeness in
theme and style to *The Taming of the Shrew*, which maybe it
preceded.

PROBABLE SOURCES

The play is based mainly on the *Menaechmi* of Plautus but it
also draws on his *Amphitruo*. There were many editions of Plautus
in the century, and Shakespeare doubtless knew enough Latin
to read him in the original. The Folio's opening stage-direction
in II.1 calls Antipholus of Ephesus 'Antipholis Sereptus',
obviously recalling Plautus's Prologue to the *Menaechmi*, which
has (l.38) 'puerum surreptum alterum', and (41) 'qui subreptus
est'. In Act I(F) the other twin is called 'Antipholis Erotis', and
in Act II.2 'Errotis', referring to the Plautine courtesan Erotium (Erotium's Antipholus), or misprints perhaps for 'Errans'
or 'Erraticus'. No English translation of the *Menaechmi* was
printed until 1595 when William Warner's version (Entered
S.R. 10 June, 1594) appeared. Shakespeare may possibly have
read this play of 'much pleasant error' in MS, since Warner

3

rendered it and other Plautine comedies 'for the use and delight of his private friends', and presumably it was handed about. Also, Warner, an attorney of the common pleas, wrote his prose tales *Pan his Syrinx or Pipe* (1585) and his long epic *Albion's England* (1586) under the patronage of Henry Carey Lord Hunsdon, who was Lord Chamberlain from 1586 to 1596, and Shakespeare belonged to his company of players, newly formed in 1594, which may have been the 'company of base and common fellows' jestingly described as having played 'a Comedy of Errors' at the lawyers' Revels at Gray's Inn on 28 December, 1594 (cf. inf. p. 431). Warner's reference to 'much pleasant error' in The Argument may have suggested Shakespeare's title, which, in directing attention to the chief comic devices used, recalls Gascoigne's *Supposes* ('mistakes', 'pretences', 'deceptions') (q.v. pp. 112). The Wife's reference to herself as a 'stale' in Warner V.73 is found in Shakespeare (II.1.101, 'poor I am but his stale'). There are few other verbal resemblances.

Warner's version, given here [I], keeps fairly close to the original, scrupulously marking any large deviations. It provides a good example of Tudor translation, worthy of being compared with Shakespeare's more creative adaptation; it is indeed quite actable, and Rouse declares that Warner's 'brisk exchange has often the advantage over Plautus!'[1] *The Comedy of Errors* must, however, be compared directly with Plautus and considered as one of a long line of adaptations.

The *Menaechmi*, itself taken from a Greek play of unknown authorship, was frequently edited in the Renaissance, acted in Latin or in Italian versions, and adapted or pillaged for incidents, e.g. in the *Calandra* of Cardinal Bernardo Bibbiena (acted 1513); the *Moglie* (1550) of G. Cecchi; J. G. Trissino's *I Simillimi* (1547); and Agnolo Firenzuola's *I Lucidi* (1549). A Spanish version by Juan de Timoneda appeared in 1559, and it was worked over in French and German. In England Plautus was popular from Henry VIII's reign at least, and Stephen Gosson was right in asserting that the early comedies 'smelt of Plautus'. *Thersites* (1537) and *Ralph Roister-Doister* (1534 c.) owed much to the *Miles Gloriosus*, and *Jacke Juggler* (1553)

---

[1] *The Menaechmi . . . The Latin text together with the Elizabethan Translation*: ed. W. H. D. Rouse (The Shakespeare Classics) n.d., p. xi.

anticipated Shakespeare in using Mercury's impersonation of Sosia in the *Amphitruo*. It is interesting to find Shakespeare, in what may be his first comedy, going back to the classical source of modern drama; but the remarkable thing is the complexity he wove within the simple outline provided by Plautus's *Menaechmi*.

To the Renaissance Roman comedy seemed a hilarious combination of realism with ingenuity of story and style. Thus the essay *De Carminibus Comicis* prefaced to the 1558 (Basle) edition[1] of Plautus calls Comedy a versified exposition, 'a complete poem intricate in action or knit together by its characters, concerning a fictitious plot, about things, incidents and affairs taken from common life and resembling everyday occurrences.' It discusses the rise of comedy from rude realistic beginnings and asserts that in language and metrical licence it attempted to approximate to real speech. 'It chooses these rhythms as being apt and fitting, and agreeing closely with the sounds of the human voice. What nature produces with the voice should be included in our rhetoric.'

The Latin Prologue to *Menaechmi* promised lavishness of plot 'measured not by the peck or bushel, but by the barnful'. Shakespeare's comedy is an attempt to outdo the Roman by a manifold complication of his effects. He was almost obliged to this by the brevity of the *Menaechmi* (1,162 lines) which must be expanded for the Elizabethan popular stage. Seeing it as a play of errors he increased the number of misadventures, and added other ingredients more English than Roman.

In the Latin play the first Act lays a solid basis in ordinary life, revealing the relationships of Menaechmus the Citizen with Peniculus the Parasite, the Wife, and Erotium. The confusion of identities begins only in II.2, when Cylindrus encounters the Traveller and Messenio his slave. In II.3 Erotium confuses their identity; in III.2.3 Peniculus and the Maid fall into error. Then we see the results of all this on Menaechmus the Citizen, who is confronted with his Wife (IV.2), the Parasite (IV.2) and Erotium (IV.3) in turn. In the fifth Act the Traveller is thought mad by the Wife (V.1), the Father (V.2) and the Doctor (V.5). The Citizen encounters Messenio (V.7) before

---

[1] *M. Acii Plauti comoediae XX diligente cura . . . Joachimi Camerarii . . . editae Basileum per Joannem Hervagium et Bernhardum Brand.* (MDLVIII.)

the two brothers are brought together and all is gradually
explained (V.8). The whole chain of events is so linked as to
give the Traveller as many embarrassing encounters as possible.
He 'has seven such meetings (counting each of the important
characters as one); the Wife, the Father and Messenio have two
each; Peniculus, Erotium, Cylindrus and the Maid one each'.
(Rouse.) The Citizen, though the victim of other folk's errors,
cannot himself make mistakes of identity.

The *Menaechmi* had certain disadvantages for the Tudor
theatre besides brevity. It was slow in starting its main action.
The Prologue (probably spurious) was too long and inefficient.
The manners described were definitely un-English, with the
Parasite, the Courtesan, the cynical treatment of the Wife. The
rarity of her appearance on the stage, and the absence of
another main woman character, were additional drawbacks.
Some of these features had struck previous adapters; for instance, the Italian Berardo brought the Wife on the stage to
argue with her departing husband; so did Firenzuola in *I
Lucidi* (1549) where Lucido Tolto expatiates on his Fiammetta's
shrewishness: 'I thought to have taken into my house a companion, and I find I have got a confessor—what am I saying?
rather a lawyer, who cross-examines me continually with a
thousand torments.' To which his wife answers, 'I thought to
have taken a husband, and to have found a home, and I find
myself in a prison, a slave, continually wounded and abused.'

In freer adaptations the Wife's part is increased, and other
persons are added. Trissino explained his purpose in *I Simillimi*
(1547) as being 'to treat of actions and the manners of men of
middle or base rank, and with jests and laughable words . . .
In Comedy I have tried to follow the manner of Aristophanes,
that is, of the Ancient Comedy. Wherein having taken a festive
fiction from Plautus, I have changed the names and added
personages, and to some extent altered the order of events; and
I have introduced a Chorus . . . I have moreover, according to
the custom of the Ancient Greeks, taken out the Prologue, and
have given the narrative of the Argument to the first persons
who speak in the play.' Cecchi, who in *La Dote* refused to tell
the Argument 'since men today are so intelligent that they
understand without having so many arguments beforehand', in
La Moglie sets the scene in modern Florence, and declares: 'the

two Menaechmi of Plautus have become our two Alfonsi; be warned not to run into error by confusing them as everyone on the stage will do.' Here too the exposition is given in the play. *La Moglie* shows further the tendency to complicate the Plautine plot, for Cecchi has four old men, and the twins have a long-lost sister who finally marries a third young man, but never appears on the stage. In other stories of twins having some dramatic relation to Plautus one twin becomes a girl, and this leads to romantic complications alien to the *Menaechmi*, as in the *Calandra* of Bibbiena, and G. A. G. Rhodigino's *La Cingana* (1545) with its Spanish version *Medora* by Rueda. This deviation would take us away from *The Comedy of Errors* towards *Twelfth Night*, but in one of the analogues of *Twelfth Night*, Nicolo Secchi's *Gl'Inganni* (1549), there is a father, Anselmo, who has been captured by corsairs, and eighteen years later wins his freedom and is reunited (like Aegeon) to the children he lost.

Seeking a way of enlarging the play Shakespeare remembered another Plautine comedy in which an intruding master and slave were the cause of misunderstanding between husband and wife. This was the *Amphitruo*, perhaps the most popular of all Plautus's works. Here Jupiter takes the place of Amphitruo in Alcmena's bed (I.3) and Mercury takes the identity of the slave Sosia, beginning the action by refusing admission to the latter, declaring that *he* is Amphitruo's Sosia. Much fun comes from Alcmena's bewilderment when her real husband returns from the wars only a few moments after the false one has left her (II.2), and from Amphitruo's suspicion that she is betraying him. Jupiter returns as Amphitruo (III), and the climax comes when Amphitruo tries to enter his house while Jupiter is within, and is refused admission by Mercury disguised as Sosia [IV.2].

By transferring the identical slaves to the other play Shakespeare more than doubled the possibility of error, at risk of bewildering the audience as well as the characters. He further developed the situation of the husband locked out while his wife dines with his double, placing it in the middle of the comedy (II.2; III.1). He might have gone further, but the adultery condoned in Jupiter would be less pardonable in a mortal and raise moral issues to which Shakespeare was already sensitive. He omitted the Citizen's theft of the cloak, and he ascribed his visit to the 'hostess' at the Porpentine, with his wife's chain, to the latter's harsh treatment of him in locking him out (III.1.114–121).

> Since mine own doors refuse to entertain me,
> I'll knock elsewhere, to see if they'll disdain me.

Shakespeare's fusion of the Latin incidents has been closely analysed by T. W. Baldwin,[1] and can be summarized in his words: 'The first two acts of *The Comedy* have been adapted from the materials of the first two of *Menaechmi* . . . For the machinery of the third act we . . . turn to *Amphitruo*, (the fourth act of which) has furnished the principal machinery for the third of *The Comedy*.' 'The material of the third and fourth acts of *Menaechmi* . . . furnishes the fourth act of *The Comedy* . . . Then for the fifth act in both *Menaechmi* and *The Comedy* the twins are confronted and all is explained.' As Baldwin proves, Shakespeare learned in this play to shape his material to the 'five-act formula' for which Terence more than Plautus was responsible.

In using Plautine incidents Shakespeare modified the Plautine attitude to life, and here his divergence from the academic dramas which often sought to recreate the Roman scene in scholarly fashion, is noteworthy. He tells his Ephesian tale in terms of the modern *novella*, which usually included some moral touches in an English version. In Plautus the Citizen's Wife is a figure of fun, a 'nagger' whose father blames her for being too ferocious, 'masterful and obstinate', and in the end she is dismissed with a laugh when her husband says he would sell her if he could find a bidder. Shakespeare builds on this considerably; his play deepens from farce, touching on the relations of husbands and wives, parents and children, in a moralizing way reminiscent of recent English and French translators of Italian story (e.g. Belleforest, Painter). His Wife is not merely a butt; she has a point of view to be discussed and reproved. This implies a confidante; the invention of her sister Luciana provides that, gives a bride for the other brother, supplies feminine contrast, and also makes a part for one of the boys who acted women so well. Moreover Luciana introduces, however faintly, a kind of love and wooing not found in Plautus but

---

[1] T. W. Baldwin, *William Shakespeare's Five-Act Structure*. Urbana, 1947. Chs. XXVIII–XXIX.

already popular in England through the works of John Lyly. She also enables Shakespeare to imitate Lyly's symmetry; but euphuistic wit is noticeably absent from this plain-styled comedy.

The twins' name Antipholus is usually derived from ἀντίφιλος, meaning 'mutual affection'; but in Sidney's *Arcadia* Lib. 2 Antiphilus, beloved by Erona and rescued by her from prison, falls in love with someone else. When King he justifies polygamy and is slain by women. Perhaps Shakespeare was thinking ironically of this when he had to name his henpecked and not-very-faithful or affectionate Citizen. The servants' name Dromio may have significance, for Lyly's *Mother Bombie* contains a servant Dromio—and also a character called Accius, the middle name of Plautus. *Mother Bombie* is a play of duplicated effects and symmetry. It has no fewer than four comic servants who are sent on errands and then searched for by their masters (II.2), and it contains mistaken identities and lost children. Though no close analogue to our play, it supplied the name of its genial rogue who says: 'I have nothing to live by but knaverie, and if the world grow honest, welcome beggerie.'

Shakespeare changed the setting from Epidamnum to Ephesus. To the Romans the name Epidamnum suggested bad luck, and the city which bore it became Dyrrachum (Durazzo) when a Roman colony. Maybe it was no jest to Shakespeare when he referred to Epidamnum at I.2.1, IV.1.87, and V.1. 350–354. But why substitute Ephesus?

His choice was, I believe, connected with his interest in family relationships, and also with his desire to make *The Comedy* a play of wonders in which every loose end should finally be tied up. Ephesus was well known to Elizabethans as the capital of Roman Asia, a great seaport, renowned for its Temple of Diana and as the place where St Paul stayed two years (Acts xix). The *Epistle to the Ephesians* includes earnest exhortations to domestic unity. 'Wives, submit yourselves unto your husbands, as unto the Lord. For the husband is the wives head, even as Christ is the head of the Church ... Husbands, love your wives ... let every one love his wife, even as himselfe, and let the wife see that she feare her husband' (v. 22–33).[1]

---

[1] The Bible, that is, the Holy Scriptures contained in the Olde and New Testament ... London. C. Baker, 1587.

The Apostle also writes of relations between children and parents, and urges servants to 'be obedient unto them that are your masters', while masters are to forbear threatening their servants (vi.1–9). Is it fanciful to suggest that Shakespeare saw the aptness of this as he christianized somewhat the ethics of Plautus's comedy. Does the Ephesian locale explain why the Mother becomes an Abbess, in reminiscence of the Temple of Diana with its priestesses?

In addition, Ephesus was a place of sorcerers and exorcists, and 'curious arts' as St Paul states. Of this idea Shakespeare makes good use; for whereas Plautus makes Messenio warn his master that Epidamnum is 'full of Ribaulds, Parasites, Drunkard Catchpoles, Cony-catchers and Sycophants' besides Curtizans, so that the Traveller is on his guard against theft and dishonest snares, Shakespeare insists on the magical tricks of Ephesus:

> They say this town is full of cozenage;
> As, nimble jugglers that deceive the eye,
> Dark-working sorcerers that change the mind,
> Soul-killing witches that deform the body, etc. (I.2.97f.)

The mistakes of identity which befall him therefore seem like a nightmare of supernatural deception (II.2.199–201). This makes good fooling.

The repetitive Prologue of the *Menaechmi* was omitted by Warner. It was a happy stroke of Shakespeare's (though anticipated by some of the Italians) to put his exposition into the mouth of the father of the twins, bringing the narrative into the play, filling it with character and pathos, and giving to the trivial adventures which follow an overtone of tragic import to be picked up again in V.1. To a Tudor audience aware of the enmities between city states in Italy and elsewhere and the perils of sea-traders, Aegeon's predicament was no romantic fancy. Shipwrecks were as common in life as in romances, and the father's graphic account of the loss of his babes and wife excites both sympathy and expectation that we shall meet them soon.

For the 'discovery' of the Mother he took hints from the story of Apollonius of Tyre which had been retold by Gower in *Confessio Amantis* (and was to influence *Pericles* years later).

The tale has more than one storm at sea, a husband separated from his wife and child, and a mother who undergoes strange adventures. (See III below.) Like the Mother in Shakespeare she becomes 'abbesse' of the Temple of Diana in Ephesus and is reunited to her husband and child after many years.

The introduction of the Mother as an Abbess is a touch of supererogation which argues a humorous attitude in the author towards his creation as he piles wonder on wonder. Throughout one feels him laughing gently at the Roman convention of entanglement and discovery, while enjoying it. One more improbability added to the series can but please. Yet the Abbess has her moral aspect as a grave counsellor against nagging and jealousy (V.1.68). Through her and Aegeon the madcap adventures are placed in a setting of emotional earnestness and ethical normality from which the farce may stray but to which it returns in the end. This method, of placing the main action in a separable setting, was to be repeated in *The Taming of the Shrew* and *A Midsummer Night's Dream*, with very different effect.

THE MENAECHMI OF PLAUTUS
translated by William Warner

MENÆCMI. A pleasant and fine Conceited Comædie, taken out of the most excellent wittie Poet Plautus. Chosen purposely from out of the rest, as least harmefull, and yet most delightfull. Written in English, by W. W. London. Printed by Tho. Creede, and are to be sold by William Barley at his shop in Gratious streete. 1595.

THE PRINTER TO THE READERS

The writer hereof (loving Readers) having diverse of this Poettes Comedies Englished, for the use and delight of his private friends, who in Plautus owne words are not able to understand them: I have prevailed so far with him as to let this one go farther abroad, for a publike recreation and delight to all those, that affect the diverse sorts of bookes compiled in this kind, wherof (in my judgment) in harmelesse mirth and quicknesse of fine conceit, the most of them come far short of this. And although I found him very loath and unwilling to hazard this to the curious view of envious detraction, (being as he tels mee) neither so exactly written, as it may carry any name of a Translation, nor such libertie therin used, as that he would notoriously varie from the Poets owne order: yet sith it is onely a matter of meriment, and the litle alteration therof, can breede no detriment of importance, I have over-rulde him so farre, as to let this be offred to your curteous acceptance, and if you shall applaude his litle labour heerein, I doubt not but he will endevour to gratifie you with some of the rest better laboured, and more curiously pollished.　　　　　*Farewell.*

* Where you finde this marke, the Poets conceit is somewhat altred, by occasion either of the time, the country, or the phrase.

THE ARGUMENT

**Two Twinborne sonnes, a* Sicill *marchant had,*
Menechmus *one, and* Sosicles *the other:*

12

The first his Father lost a litle Lad,
The Grandsire namde the latter like his brother.
This (growne a man) long travell tooke to seeke
His Brother, and to Epidamnum *came,*
Where th'other dwelt inricht, and him so like,
That Citizens there take him for the same:
Father, wife, neighbours, each mistaking either,
Much pleasant error, ere they meete togither.

ACT ONE

Scene i Enter Peniculus, a Parasite

[PENICULUS] *Peniculus* was given mee for my name when I was
yong, bicause like a broome I swept all cleane away, where so ere I
become: Namely all the vittels which are set before mee. Now in
my judgement, men that clap iron bolts on such captives as they
would keepe safe, and tie those servants in chaines who they thinke
will run away, they commit an exceeding great folly: my reason is,
these poore wretches enduring one miserie upon an other, never
cease devising how by wrenching asunder their gyves,[1] or by some
subtiltie or other they may escape such cursed bands. If then ye
would keep a man without all suspition of running away from ye,
the surest way is to tie him with meate, drinke and ease: Let him
ever be idle, eate his belly full, and carouse while his skin will hold,
and he shall never, I warrant ye, stir a foote. These strings to tie
one by the teeth, passe all the bands of iron, steele, or what metall
so ever, for the more slack and easie ye make them, the faster still
they tie the partie which is in them. I speake this upon experience
of my selfe, who am now going for *Menechmus*, there willingly to be
tied to his good cheare: he is commonly so exceeding bountifull and
liberall in his fare, as no marveyle though such guestes as my selfe
be drawne to his Table, and tyed there in his dishes. Now because
I have lately bene a straunger there, I meane to visite him at
dinner: for my stomacke mee-thinkes even thrusts me into the
fetters of his daintie fare. But yonder I see his doore open, and himselfe readie to come foorth.

Scene ii Enter Menechmus talking backe to his wife within

[MENECHMUS] If ye were not such a brabling foole and mad-
braine scold as yee are, yee would never thus crosse your husbande
in all his actions. 'Tis no matter, let her serve me thus once more,

---

[1] 1595 gives.

Ile send her home to her dad with a vengeance. I can never go foorth a doores, but shee asketh mee whither I go? what I do? what busines? what I fetch? what I carry? * As though she were a Constable or a toll-gatherer. I have pampered her too much: she hath servants about her, wooll, flax, and all things necessary to busie her withall, yet she watcheth and wondreth whither I go. Well sith it is so, she shall now have some cause, I mean to dine this day abroad with a sweet friend of mine.

PEN. Yea mary now comes hee to the point that prickes me: this last speech gaules mee as much as it would doo his wife; If he dine not at home, I am drest.

MEN. We that have Loves abroad, and wives at home, are miserably hampred, yet would every man could tame his shrewe as well as I doo mine. I have now filcht away a fine ryding cloake of my wives, which I meane to bestow upon one that I love better. Nay, if she be so warie and watchfull over me, I count it an almes deed to deceive her.

PEN. Come, what share have I in that same?

MEN. Out alas, I am taken.

PEN. True, but by your friend.

MEN. What, mine owne *Peniculus*?

PEN. Yours (ifaith) bodie and goods if I had any.

MEN. Why thou hast a bodie.

PEN. Yea, but neither goods nor good bodie.

MEN. Thou couldst never come fitter in all thy life.

PEN. Tush, I ever do so to my friends, I know how to come alwaies in the nicke. Where dine ye to-day?

MEN. Ile tell thee of a notable pranke.

PEN. What, did the Cooke marre your meate in the dressing? Would I might see the reversion.

MEN. Tell me didst thou see a picture, how *Jupiters* Eagle snatcht away *Ganimede*, or how *Venus* stole away *Adonis*?

PEN. Often, but what care I for shadowes, I want substance.

MEN. Looke thee here, looke not I like such a picture?

PEN. O ho, what cloake have ye got here?

MEN. Prethee say I am now a brave fellow.

PEN. But hearke ye, where shall we dine?

MEN. Tush, say as I bid thee man.

PEN. Out of doubt ye are a fine man.

MEN. What? canst adde nothing of thine owne?

PEN. Ye are a most pleasant Gentleman.

MEN. On yet.

PEN. Nay not a word more, unlesse ye tell mee how you and your wife be fallen out.

MEN. Nay I have a greater secret then that to impart to thee.

PEN. Say your minde.

MEN. Come farther this way from my house.

PEN. So, let me heare.

MEN. Nay farther yet.

PEN. I warrant ye man.

* MEN. Nay yet farther.

PEN. Tis pittie ye were not made a water-man to row in a wherry.

MEN. Why?

PEN. Because ye go one way, and looke an other, stil least your wife should follow ye. But what's the matter, Ist not almost dinner time?

MEN. Seest thou this cloake?

PEN. Not yet. Well what of it?

MEN. This same I meane to give to *Erotium*.

PEN. That's well, but what of all this?

MEN. There I meane to have a delicious dinner prepard for her and me.

PEN. And me.

MEN. And thee.

PEN. O sweet word. What, shall I knock presently at her doore?

MEN. Aye,[1] knocke. But staie too *Peniculus*, let's not be too rash. Oh see shee is in good time comming forth.

PEN. Ah, he now lookes against the Sun, how her beames dazell his eyes.

Enter Erotium

EROT. What mine owne *Menechmus*, welcome sweete heart.

PEN. And what am I, welcome too?

EROT. You Sir? ye are out of the number of my welcome guests.

* PEN. I am like a voluntary souldier, out of paie.

MEN. Erotium, I have determined that here shal be pitcht a field this day; we meane to drinke for the heavens: And which of us performes the bravest service at his weopon the wine boll, yourselfe as Captaine shall paie him his wages according to his deserts.

EROT. Agreed.

PEN. I would we had the weapons, for my valour pricks me to the battaile.

MEN. Shall I tell thee sweete mouse? I never looke upon thee, but I am quite out of love with my wife.

[1] 1595 I.

EROT.   Yet yee cannot chuse, but yee must still weare something of hers: whats this same?

MEN.   This? such a spoyle (sweete heart) as I tooke from her to put on thee.

EROT.   Mine owne *Menechmus*, well woorthie to bee my deare, of all dearest.

PEN.   Now she showes her selfe in her likenesse, when shee findes him in the giving vaine, she drawes close to him.

MEN.   I thinke *Hercules* got not the garter from *Hypolita* so hardly, as I got this from my wife. Take this, and with the same, take my heart.

PEN.   Thus they must do that are right Lovers: especially if they mean to [be] beggers with any speed.

MEN.   I bought this same of late for my wife, it stood mee (I thinke) in some ten pound.

PEN.   There's tenne pounde bestowed verie thriftily.

MENECHMUS   But knowe yee what I woulde have yee doo?

EROTIUM   It shall bee done, your dinner shall be readie.

* MEN.   Let a good dinner be made for us three. Harke ye, some oysters, a mary-bone pie or two, some artichockes, and potato rootes, let our other be as you please.

EROT.   You shall Sir.

MEN.   I have a little businesse in this Cittie, by that time dinner will be prepared. Farewell till then, sweete *Erotium*: Come *Peniculus*.

PEN.   Nay I meane to follow yee: I will sooner leese my life, then sight of you till this dinner be done.   [*Exeunt*

EROTIUM   Who's there? Call me *Cylindrus* the Cooke hither.

Enter Cylindrus

Cylindrus, take the Hand-basket, and heere, there's ten shillings is there not?

CYL.   Tis so mistresse.

EROT.   Buy mee of all the daintiest meates ye can get, ye know what I meane: so as three may dine passing well, and yet no more then inough.

CYL.   What guests have ye to-day mistresse?

EROT.   Here will be *Menechmus* and his Parasite, and myselfe.

CYL.   That's ten persons in all.

EROT.   How many?

CYL.   Ten, for I warrant you, that Parasite may stand for eight at his vittels.

EROT.   Go dispatch as I bid you, and looke ye returne with all speed.

CYL.   I will have all readie with a trice.   [*Exeunt*

ACT TWO

Scene i   Enter Menechmus, Sosicles. Messenio his servant, and some
Saylers

MEN.   Surely *Messenio*, I thinke Sea-fairers never take so comfortable a joy in any thing, as when they have bene long tost and turmoyld in the wide seas, they hap at last to ken land.

MESS.   Ile be sworn, I shuld not be gladder to see a whole Country of mine owne, then I have bene at such a sight. But I pray, wherfore are we now come to *Epidamnum*? must we needs go to see everie Towne that we heare off?

MENECH.   Till I finde my brother, all Townes are alike to me: I must trie in all places.

MESS.   Why then let's even as long as wee live seeke your brother: six yeares now have roamde about thus, *Istria*, *Hispania*, *Massylia*, *Ilyria*, all the upper sea, all high *Greece*, all Haven Townes in *Italy*, I think if we had sought a needle all this time, we must needs have found it, had it bene above ground. It cannot be that he is alive; and to seek a dead man thus among the living, what folly is it?

MEN.   Yea, could I but once find any man that could certainly enforme me of his death, I were satisfied; otherwise I can never desist seeking: Litle knowest thou *Messenio* how neare my heart it goes.

MESS.   This is washing of a Blackamore. Faith let's goe home, unlesse ye meane we should write a storie of our travaile.

MEN.   Sirra, no more of these sawcie speeches, I perceive I must teach ye how to serve me, not to rule me.

MESS.   I , so, now it appeares what it is to be a servant. Wel yet I must speake my conscience. Do ye heare sir? Faith I must tell ye one thing, when I looke into the leane estate of your purse, and consider advisedly of your decaying stocke, I hold it verie needful to be drawing homeward, lest in looking your brother, we quite lose ourselves. For this assure your selfe, this Towne *Epidamnum*, is a place of outragious expences, exceeding in all ryot and lasciviousnesse: and (I heare) as full of Ribaulds, Parasites, Drunkards, Catchpoles, Cony-catchers, and Sycophants, as it can hold: then for Curtizans, why here's the currantest stamp of them in the world. Ye must not thinke here to scape with as light cost as in other places. The verie name shews the nature, no man comes hither *sine damno*.

MEN.   Yee say very well indeed: give mee my purse into mine owne keeping, because I will so be the safer, *sine damno*.

MESS.   Why Sir?

MEN. Because I feare you wil be busie among the Curtizans, & so be cosened of it: then should I take great paines in belabouring your shoulders, so to avoid both these harms, Ile keep it my selfe.

MESS. I pray do so sir, all the better.

Enter Cylindrus

[CYLINDRUS] * I have tickling geare here yfaith for their dinners: It grieves me to the heart to think how that cormorant knave *Peniculus* must have his share in these daintie morsels. But what? Is *Menechmus* come alreadie, before I could come from the Market? *Menechmus*, how do ye sir? how haps it ye come so soone?

MENECH. God a mercy my good friend, doest thou know mee?

CYL. Know ye? no not I. Where's mouldichappes that must dine with ye? A murrin on his manners.

MEN. Whom meanest thou good fellow?

CYL. Why *Peniculus* worship, that whorson lick-trencher, your Parasiticall attendant.

MEN. What *Peniculus*? what attendant? My Attendant? Surely this fellow is mad.

MESS. Did I not tell ye what cony-catching villaines you should finde here?

CYL. *Menechmus*, harke ye sir, ye come too soone backe again to dinner, I am but returned from the Market.

MEN. Fellow, here thou shalt have money of me, goe get the priest to sacrifice for thee. I know thou art mad, els thou wouldst never use a straunger thus.

CYL. Alas sir, *Cylindrus* was wont to be no stranger to you, know ye not *Cylindrus*?

MEN. *Cylindrus*, or *Coliendrus*, or what the divell thou art, I know not, neither do I care to know.

CYL. I know you to be *Menechmus*.

MEN. Thou shouldst be in thy wits, in that thou namest me so right, but tell me, where hast thou knowne me?

CYL. Where? even heere, where ye first fell in love with my mistresse *Erotium*.

MEN. I neither have Lover, neither knowe I who thou art.

CYL. Know ye not who I am? who fils your cup & dresses your meate at our house?

MESS. What a slave is this? that I had somewhat to breake the Rascals pate withall.

MEN. At your house, when as I never came in *Epidamnum* till this day.

CYL. Oh thats true. Do ye not dwell in yonder house?

MEN. Foule shame light upon them that dwell there, for my part.

CYL. Questionlesse, hee is mad indeede, to curse himselfe thus. Harke ye *Menechmus*.

MEN. What saist thou?

CYL. If I may advise ye, ye shall bestow this money which ye offred me, upon a sacrifice for your selfe: for out of doubt you are mad that curse your selfe.

MESS. What a verlet art thou to trouble us thus?

CYL. Tush he wil many times jest with me thus. Yet when his wife is not by, tis a ridiculous jest.

MEN. Whats that?

CYL. This I say, Thinke ye I have brought meate inough for three of you? If not, ile fetch more for you and your wench, and Snatchcrust your Parasite.

MEN. What wenches? what Parasites?

MESS. Villaine, Ile make thee tell me what thou meanest by all this talke?

CYL. Away *Jack Napes*, I say nothing to thee, for I know thee not, I speake to him that I know.

MEN. Out drunken foole, without doubt thou art out of thy wits.

CYL. That you shall see by the dressing of your meat. Go, go, ye were better to go in and finde somewhat to do there, whiles your dinner is making readie. Ile tell my mistresse ye be here.

MEN. Is he gone? *Messenio* I thinke uppon thy words alreadie.

MESS. Tush marke I pray, Ile laie fortie pound here dwels some Curtizan to whom this fellow belong.

MEN. But I wonder how he knowes my name.

MESS. Oh ile tell yee. These Courtizans as soone as anie straunge shippe arriveth at the Haven, they sende a boye or a wench to enquire what they be, what their names be, whence they come, wherefore they come, &c. If they can by any meanes strike acquaintance with him, or allure him to their houses, he is their owne. We are here in a tickle place maister, tis best to be circumspect.

MEN. I mislike not thy counsaile *Messenio*.

MESS. I, but follow it then. Soft, here comes somebodie forth. Here sirs, Marriners, keep this same amongst you.

Enter Erotium

[EROTIUM] Let the doore stand so, away, it shall not be shut. Make hast within there ho: maydes looke that all things be readie. Cover the boord, put fire under the perfuming pannes, let all things be very handsome. Where is hee, that *Cylindrus* sayd stood without here? Oh, what meane you sweet heart, that ye come not in? I trust

you thinke yourselfe more welcome to this house then to your owne,
and great reason why you should do so. Your dinner & all things
are readie as you willed. Will ye go sit downe?

MEN.   Whom doth this woman speake to?

EROT.   Even to you sir, to whom else should I speake?

MEN.   Gentlewoman ye are a straunger to me, and I marvell at
your speeches.

EROT.   Yea sir, but such a straunger, as I acknowledge ye for my
best and dearest friend, and well you have deserved it.

MEN.   Surely *Messenio*, this woman is also mad or drunke, that
useth all this kindnesse to mee uppon so small acquaintance.

MESS.   Tush, did not I tell ye right? these be but leaves which
fall upon you now, in comparison of the trees that wil tumble on
your necke shortly. I tolde ye, here were silver tong'de hacsters.
But let me talke with her a litle. Gentlewoman what acquaintance
have you with this man? where have you seene him?

EROT.   Where he saw me, here in *Epidamnum*.

MESS.   In *Epidamnum*? who never till this day set his foote within
the Towne?

EROT.   Go, go, flowting Jack. *Menechmus* what need al this? I
pray go in.

MEN.   She also calls me by my name.

MESS.   She smels your purse.

MEN.   *Messenio* come hither, here take my purse. Ile know
whether she aime at me or my purse, ere I go.

EROT.   Will ye go in, to dinner, sir?

MEN.   A good motion, yea and thanks with all my heart.

EROT.   Never thanke me for that which you commaunded to be
provided for yourselfe.

MEN.   That I commaunded?

EROT.   Yea, for you and your Parasite.

MEN.   My Parasite?

EROT.   *Peniculus*, who came with you this morning when you
brought me the cloake which you got from your wife.

MEN.   A cloake that I brought you, which I got from my wife?

EROT.   Tush what needeth all this jesting? Pray leave off.

MEN.   Jest or earnest, this I tell ye for a truth. I never had wife,
neither have I, nor never was in this place till this instant: for only
thus farre am I come, since I brake my fast in the ship.

EROT.   What ship do ye tell me off?

* MESS.   Marry ile tell ye, an old rotten weather-beaten ship,
that we have saild up and downe in this sixe yeares, Ist not time to
be going homewards thinke ye?

EROT. Come, come, *Menechmus*, I pray leave this sporting and go in.

MEN. Well Gentlewoman, the truth is, you mistake my person, it is some other that you looke for.

EROT. Why, thinke ye I know ye not to be *Menechmus*, the sonne of *Moschus*, and have heard ye say, ye were borne at *Syracusis* where *Agathocles* did raigne, then *Pythia*, then *Liparo*, and now *Hiero*.

MEN. All this is true.

MESS. Either shee is a witch, or else shee hath dwelt there and knew ye there.

MEN. Ile go in with her *Messenio*, Ile see further of this matter.

MESS. Ye are cast away then.

MEN. Why so? I warrant thee, I can loose nothing, somwhat I shall gaine, perhaps a good lodging during my abode heere. Ile dissemble with her an other while. Nowe when you please let us go in, I made straunge with you, because of this fellow here, least he should tell my wife of the cloake which I gave you.

EROT. Will ye staie any longer for your *Peniculus* your Parasite?

MEN. Not I, Ile neither staie for him, nor have him let come in, if he do come.

EROT. All the better. But sir, will ye doo one thing for me?

MEN. What is that?

EROT. To beare that cloake which you gave me to the Dyars, to have it new trimd and altred.

MEN. Yea that will be well, so my wife shall not know it. Let mee have it with mee after dinner. I will but speake a word or two with this fellowe, then ile follow yee in. Ho *Messenio* come aside: goe and provide for thyselfe, and these shipboyes in some Inne, then looke that after dinner you come hither for me.

MESS. Ah maister, will yee be conycatcht thus wilfully?

MEN. Peace foolish knave; seest thou not what a sot she is, I shall coozen her I warrant thee.

MESS. Ay maister.

MEN. Wilt thou be gone?

* MESS. See, see, she hath him safe inough now. Thus he hath escaped a hundreth Pyrates hands at sea; and now one land-rover hath bourded him at first encounter. Come away fellowes.

ACT THREE

Enter Peniculus

[PENICULUS] * Twentie yeares I thinke and more, have I playde the knave, yet never playd I the foolish knave as I have done this morning. I follow *Menechmus*, and he goes to the Hall where now the Sessions are holden: there thrusting our selves into the prease of people, when I was in midst of all the throng, he gave me the slip, that I could never more set eye on him, and I dare sweare, came directly to dinner. That I would he that first devised these Sessions were hang'd, and all that ever came of him: tis such a hinderance to men that have belly businesses in hand. If a man be not there at his call, they amearce him with a vengeance. Men that have nothing else to do, that do neither bid anie man, nor are themselves bidden to dinner, such should come to Sessions, not we that have these matters to looke too. If it were so, I had not thus lost my dinner this day; which I think in my conscience he did even purposely couzen me off. Yet I meane to go see: if I can but light uppon the reversion, I may perhaps get my penyworthes. But how now? is this *Menechmus* comming away from thence? dinner done, and all dispatcht? What execrable lucke have I?

Enter Menechmus the travailer

[MENECHMUS]   Tush I warrant ye, it shall be done as ye would wish. Ile have it so altered and trimd anew, that it shall by no meanes be knowne againe.

PEN.   He carries the cloake to the Dyars, dinner done, the wine drunke up, the Parasite shut out of doores. Well, let me live no longer, but ile revenge this injurious mockerie. But first ile harken awhile what he saith.

MEN.   Good goddes, who ever had such lucke as I? Such cheare, such a dinner, such kinde entertainment? And for a farewell, this cloake which I meane shall go with me.

PEN.   He speakes so softly, I cannot heare what hee saith. I am sure he is now flowting at me for the losse of my dinner.

MEN.   She tels me how I gave it her, and stole it from my wife. When I perceived she was in an error, though I knew not how, I began to sooth her, and to say every thing as she said. Meane while I far'd well, and that a' free cost.

PEN.   Wel, I'le go talke with him.

MEN.   Who is this same that comes to me?

PEN.   O well met fickle-braine, false and treacherous dealer, craftie and unjust promise-breaker. How have I deserved, you should so give me the slip, come before and dispatch the dinner, deale so badly with him that hath reverenst ye like a sonne?

MEN.   Good fellow, what meanest thou by these speeches? Raile not on mee, unlesse thou intendst to receive a Railers hire.

PEN.   I have received the injury (sure I am) alreadie.

MEN.   Prethee tell me, what is thy name?

PEN.   Well, well, mock on sir, mock on; doo ye not know my name?

MEN.   In troth I never sawe thee in all my life, much lesse do I know thee.

PEN.   Fie, awake *Menechmus*, awake; ye oversleepe your selfe.

MEN.   I am awake, I know what I say.

PEN.   Know you not *Peniculus*?

MEN.   *Peniculus*, or *Pediculus*, I know thee not.

PEN.   Did ye filch a cloake from your wife this morning, and bring it hither to *Erotium*?

MEN.   Neither have I wife, neither gave I any cloake to *Erotium*, neither filcht I any from any bodie.

PEN.   Will ye denie that which you did in my company?

MEN.   Wilt thou say I have done this in thy company?

PEN.   Will I say it? yea, I will stand to it.

MEN.   Away filthie mad drivell, away; I will talke no longer with thee.

PEN.   Not a world of men shall staie me, but ile go tell his wife of all the whole matter, sith he is at this point with me. I will make this same as unblest a dinner as ever he eate.

MEN.   It makes mee wonder, to see how every one that meetes me cavils thus with me. Wherefore comes foorth the mayd now?

Enter Ancilla, Erotiums mayd

[ANCILLA]   *Menechmus*, my mistresse commends her hartily to you, and seeing you goe that way to the Dyars, shee also desireth you to take this Chaine with you, and put it to mending at the Gold-smythes, shee would have two or three ounces of gold more in it, and the fashion amended.

MEN.   Either this or any thing else within my power, tell her, I am readie to accomplish.

ANC.   Do ye know this Chaine sir?

MEN.   Yea I know it to be gold.

ANC.   This is the same you once tooke out of your wives Casket.

MEN.   Who, did I?

ANC.   Have you forgotten?

MEN.   I never did it.

ANC.   Give it me againe then.

MEN.   Tarry, yes I remember it: tis it I gave your mistres.

ANC.   Oh, are ye advised?

MEN.   Where are the bracelets that I gave her likewise?

ANC.   I never knew of anie.

MEN.   Faith, when I gave this, I gave them too.

ANG. Well sir, ile tell her this shall be done?

MEN. I, I, tell her so, shee shall have the cloake and this both togither.

ANG. I pray *Menechmus* put a litle jewell for my eare to making for me: ye know I am alwaies readie to pleasure you.

MEN. I will, give me the golde, ile paie for the workemanship.

ANG. Laie out for me, ile paie it ye againe.

MEN. Alas I have none now.

ANG. When you have, will ye?

MEN. I will. Goe bid your mistresse make no doubt of these. I warrant her, ile make the best hand I can of them. Is she gone? Doo not all the gods conspire to loade mee with good lucke? well I see tis high time to get mee out of these coasts, least all these matters should be lewd devises to draw me into some snare. There shall my garland lie, because if they seeke me, they may think that I am gone that way. * I wil now goe see if I can· finde my man *Messenio*, that I may tell him how I have sped.

ACT FOUR

Enter Mulier, the wife of Menechmus the Citizen, and Peniculus

MULIER Thinkes he I will be made such a sot, and to be still his drudge, while he prowles and purloynes all that I have to give his Trulles?

PEN. Nay hold your peace, wee'll catch him in the nicke. This way he came, in his garland forsooth, bearing the cloak to the Dyars. And see I pray where the garland lyes, this way he is gone. See, see, where he comes againe without the cloake.

MUL. What shall I now do?

PEN. What? that which ye ever do; bayt him for life.

MUL. Surely I thinke it best so.

PEN. Stay, wee will stand aside a little, ye shall catch him unawares.

Enter Menechmus the Citizen

MEN. It would make a man at his wittes end, to see how brabbling causes are handled yonder at the Court. If a poore man never so honest, have a matter come to be scand, there is hee outfaste, and overlaide with countenance: If a rich man never so vile a wretch come to speake, there they are all readie to favour his cause. What with facing out bad causes for the oppressors, and patronizing some just actions for the wronged, the Lawyers they pocket up all the gaines. For mine own part, I come not away emptie, though I have bene kept long against my will: For taking in hand to dispatch a matter this morning for one of my acquaintaunce, I was no sooner entered into it, but his adversaries laide so hard unto his charge, and brought such matter against him, that do what I could, I could not winde my selfe out til now. I am sore afrayed *Erotium* thinks much unkindnes in me that I staid so long, yet she will not be angry considering the gift I gave her to day.

PEN.   How thinke ye by that?

MUL.   I thinke him a most vile wretch thus to abuse me.

MEN.   I will hie me thither.

MUL.   Yea go pilferer, goe with shame inough, no bodie sees your lewd dealings and vile theevery.

MEN.   How now wife, what aile yee? what is the matter?

MUL.   Aske yee mee whats the matter? Fye uppon thee.

PEN.   Are ye not in a fit of an ague, your pulses beate so sore? to him I say.

MEN.   Pray wife why are ye so angry with me.

MUL.   Oh you know not?

PEN.   He knowes, but he would dissemble it.

MEN.   What is it?

MUL.   My cloake.

MEN.   Your cloake?

MUL.   My cloake man, why do ye blush?

PEN.   He cannot cloake his blushing. Nay I might not go to dinner with you, do ye remember? to him I say.

MEN.   Hold thy peace *Peniculus.*

PEN.   Ha hold my peace, looke ye, he beckons on mee to hold my peace.

MEN.   I neither becken nor winke on him.

MUL.   Out, out, what a wretched life is this that I live.

MEN.   Why what aile ye woman?

MUL.   Are ye not ashamed to deny so confidently, that which is apparent?

MEN.   I protest unto before all the goddes (is not this inough) that I beckond not on him.

PEN.   Oh sir, this is another matter; touch him in the former cause.

MEN.   What former cause?

PEN.   The cloake man, the cloake, fetch the cloake againe from the Dyars.

MEN.   What cloake?

MUL.   Nay ile say no more, sith ye know nothing of your owne doings.

MEN.   Tell me wife, hath any of your servants abused you? Let me know.

MUL.   Tush, tush.

MEN.   I would not have you to be thus disquietted.

MUL.   Tush, tush.

MEN.   You are fallen out with some of your friends.

MUL.   Tush, tush.

MEN.   Sure I am, I have not offended you.

MUL.   No, you have dealt verie honestly.

MEN.   Indeed wife, I have deserved none of these words, tell me, are ye not well?

PEN.   What shall he flatter ye now?

MEN.   I speak not to thee knave. Good wife come hither.

MUL.   Away, away, keep your hands off.

PEN.   So, bid me to dinner with you againe, then slip away from me, when you have done, come forth bravely in your garland to flout me: Alas you know not me, even now.

MEN.   Why Asse, I neither have yet dined, nor came I there, since we were there together.

PEN.   Who ever heard one so impudent? Did yee not meete me here even now, and would make me beleeve I was mad, and said ye were a straunger, and ye knew me not?

MEN.   Of a truth since wee went togither to the Sessions Hall, I never returned till this very instant, as you two met me.

PEN.   Go too, go too, I know ye well inough. Did ye think I would not cry quittance with you? yes faith, I have tolde your wife all.

MEN.   What hast thou told her?

PEN.   I cannot tell, aske her?

MEN.   Tell me wife, what hath he told ye of me? Tell me I say, what was it?

MUL.   As though you knew not, my cloake is stolne from me?

MEN.   Is your cloake stolne from ye?

MUL.   Do ye aske me?

MEN.   If I knew, I would not aske.

PEN.   O craftie companion, how he would shift the matter. Come, come, deny it not, I tell ye, I have bewrayd all.

MEN.   What hast thou bewrayd;

MUL.   Seeing ye will yeeld to nothing, be it never so manifest, Heare mee, and ye shall know in fewe words both the cause of my griefe, and what he hath told me. I say my cloake is stolne from me.

MEN.   My cloake is stolne from me?

PEN.   Looke how he cavils, she saith it is stolne from her.

MEN. I have nothing to say to thee: I say wife tell me.

MUL. I tell ye, my cloake is stolne out of my house.

MEN. Who stole it?

MUL. He knowes best that carried it away.

MEN. Who was that?

MUL. *Menechmus.*

MEN. T'was very ill done of him. What *Menechmus* was that?

MUL. You.

MEN. I, who will say so?

MUL. I will.

PEN. And I: and that you gave it to *Erotium.*

MEN. I gave it?

MUL. You.

PEN. You, you, you, shall we fetch a kennel of Beagles that may cry nothing but you, you, you. For we are wearie of it.

MEN. Heare me one word wife, I protest unto you by all the gods, I gave it her not, indeed I lent it her to use a while.

MUL. Faith sir, I never give nor lend your apparell out of doores, mee thinkes ye might let mee dispose of mine own garments, as you do of yours. I pray then fetch it mee home againe.

MEN. You shall have it againe without faile.

MUL. Tis best for you that I have: otherwise thinke not to roost within these doores againe.

PEN. Harke ye, what say ye to me now, for bringing these matters to your knowledge?

MEN. I say, when thou hast anie thing stolne from thee, come to me, and I will helpe thee to seek it. And so farewell.

PEN. God a mercy for nothing, that can never be, for I have nothing in the world worth stealing. So now with husband wife and all, I am cleane out of favour. A mischiefe on ye all.   [*Exit*

MEN. My wife thinks she is notably reveng'd on me, now she shuttes me out of doores, as though I had not a better place to be welcome to. If she shut me out, I know who will shut me in. Now will I entreate *Erotium* to let me have the cloake againe to stop my wifes mouth withall, and then will I provide a better for her. Ho who is within there? Some bodie tell *Erotium* I must speake with her.

Enter Erotium

EROT. Who calls?

MEN. Your friend, more then his owne.

EROT. O *Menechmus*, why stand ye here? pray come in.[1]

MEN. Tarry, I must speake with ye here.

EROT. Say your minde.

[1] 1595 it.

MEN. Wot ye what? my wife knowes all the matter now, and my comming is, to request you, that I may have againe the cloake which I brought you, that so I may appease her: and I promise you, ile give ye an other worth two of it.

EROT. Why I gave it you to carry to your Dyars, and my chaine likewise, to have it altered.

MEN. Gave mee the cloake and your chaine? In truth I never sawe ye since I left it heere with you, and so went to the Sessions, from whence I am but now returned.

EROT. Ah then sir, I see you wrought a device to defraude mee of them both, did I therefore put yee in trust? Well, well.

MEN. To defraud ye? No, but I say, my wife hath intelligence of the matter.

EROT. Why sir, I asked them not, ye brought them me of your owne free motion. Now ye require them againe, take them, make sops of them: you and your wife together, think ye I esteeme them or you either. Goe, come to mee againe when I send for you.

MEN. What so angry with mee, sweete *Erotium*? Staie, I pray staie.

* EROT. Staie? Faith sir no: thinke ye I will staie at your request?

MEN. What, gone in chafing, and clapt to the doores? now I am everie way shut out for a very benchwhistler: neither shall I have entertainment heere nor at home. I were best go trie some other friends, and aske counsaile what to do.

ACT FIVE

Enter Menechmus the Traveller, Mulier

MEN. Most foolishly was I overseene in giving my purse and money to *Messenio*, whom I can no where find, I feare he is fallen into some lewd companie.

MUL. I marvaile that my husband comes not yet, but see where he is now, and brings my cloake with him.

MEN. I muse where the knave should be.

MUL. I will go ring a peale through both his eares for this his dishonest behaviour. Oh sir, ye are welcome home with your thee-very on your shoulders, are ye not ashamde to let all the world see and speake of your lewdnesse?

MEN. How now? what lackes this woman?

MUL. Impudent beast, stand ye to question about it? For shame hold thy peace.

MEN. What offence have I done woman, that I should not speake
to you?

MUL. Askest thou what offence? O shamelesse boldnesse!

MEN. Good woman, did ye never heare why the Grecians termed
Hecuba to be a bitch?

MUL. Never.

MEN. Because she did as you do now, on whom soever she met
withall, she railed, and therefore well deserved that dogged name.

MUL. These foule abuses and contumelies, I can never endure,
nay rather will I live a widowes life to my dying day.

MEN. What care I whether thou livest as a widow or as a wife?
This passeth, that I meet with none but thus they vexe me with
straunge speeches.

MUL. What straunge speeches? I say I will surely live a widowes
life, rather than suffer thy vile dealings.

MEN. Prethee for my part, live a widow till the worldes end,
if thou wilt.

MUL. Even now thou deniedst that thou stolest it from me, and
now thou bringest it home openly in my sight. Art not ashamde?

MEN. Woman, you are greatly to blame to charge mee with
stealing of this cloake, which this day an other gave me to carry to
be trimde.

MUL. Well, I will first complaine to my father. Ho boy, who is
within there? *Vecio* go runne quickly to my father, desire him of all
love to come over quickly to my house. Ile tell him first of your
prankes, I hope he will not see me thus handled.

MEN. What a Gods name meaneth this mad woman thus to
vexe me?

MUL. I am mad because I tell ye of your vile actions and lewde
pilfring away my apparell and my Jewels, to carry to your filthie
drabbes.

MEN. For whome this woman taketh mee I knowe not, I know
her as much as I know *Hercules* wives father.

MUL. Do ye not know me? That's well, I hope ye know my
father, here he comes, looke, do ye know him?

MEN. As much as I knew *Calcas* of *Troy*. Even him and thee I
know both alike.

MUL. Doest know neither of us both, me nor my father?

MEN. Faith nor thy grandfather neither.

MUL. This is like the rest of your behaviour.

Enter Senex

SEN. * Though bearing so great a burthen, as olde age, I can
make no great haste, yet as I can, I will goe to my daughter, who

I know hath some earnest businesse with me, that shee sends in such haste, not telling the cause why I should come. But I durst laie a wager, I can gesse neare the matter: I suppose it is some brabble between her husband and her. These yoong women that bring great dowries to their husbands, are so masterfull and obstinate, that they will have their own wils in everie thing, and make men servants to their weake affections. And yoong men too, I must needs say, be naught now a dayes, Well ile go see, but yonder mee thinks stands my daughter, and her husband too. Oh tis even as I gessed.

MUL.   Father ye are welcome.

SEN.   How now daughter? What? is all well? why is your husband so sad? have ye bin chiding? tell me, which of you is in the fault?

MUL.   First father know, that I have not any way misbehaved my selfe, but the truth is, I can by no meanes endure this bad man to die for it: and therefore desire you to take me home to you againe.

SEN.   What is the matter?

MUL.   He makes me a stale and a laughing stocke to all the world.

SEN.   Who doth?

MUL.   This good husband here, to whom you married me.

SEN.   See, see, how oft have I warned you of falling out with your husband?

MUL.   I cannot avoid it, if he doth so fowly abuse me.

SEN.   I alwaies told ye, you must beare with him, ye must let him alone, ye must not watch him, nor dog him, nor meddle with his courses in any sort.

MUL.   Hee hauntes naughtie harlottes under my nose.

SEN.   Hee is the wiser, because hee cannot bee quiet at home.

MUL.   There hee feastes and bancquets, and spendes and spoiles.

SEN.   Wold ye have your husband serve ye as your drudge? Ye will not let him make merry, nor entertaine his friendes at home.

MUL.   Father, will ye take his part in these abuses, and forsake me?

SEN.   Not so, daughter; but if I see cause, I wil as well tel him of his dutie.

MEN.   I would I were gone from this prating father and daughter.

SEN.   Hitherto I see not but hee keepes ye well; ye want nothing, apparell, mony, servants, meate, drinke, all thinges necessarie: I feare there is fault in you.

MUL.   But he filcheth away my apparell and my jewels, to give to his Trulles.

SEN.   If he doth so, tis verie ill done, if not, you doo ill to say so.

MUL.   You may beleeve me father, for there you may see my

cloake which now he hath fetcht home againe, and my chaine which he stole from me.

SEN. Now will I goe talke with him to knowe the truth. Tell me *Menechmus*, how is it, that I heare such disorder in your life? Why are ye so sad man? wherein hath your wife offended you?

MEN. Old man (what to call ye I know not) by high *Jove*, and by all the Gods I sweare unto you, whatsoever this woman here accuseth mee to have stolne from her, it is utterly false and untrue, and if I ever set foote within her doores, I wishe the greatest miserie in the worlde to light uppon me.

SEN. Why fond man, art thou mad to deny that thou ever setst foote within thine owne house where thou dwellest?

MEN. Do I dwell in that house?

SEN. Doest thou denie it?

MEN. I do.

SEN. Harke yee daughter, are ye remooved out of your house?

MUL. Father, he useth you as he doth me, this life I have with him.

SEN. *Menechmus*, I pray leave this fondnesse, ye jest too perversly with your friends.

MEN. Good old father, what I pray have you to do with me? or why should this woman thus trouble me, with whom I have no dealings in the world?

MUL. Father, marke I pray how his eies sparkle, they rowle in his head, his colour goes and comes, he lookes wildly. See, see.

MEN. What? they say now I am mad, the best way for me is to faine my selfe mad indeed, so I shall be rid of them.

MUL. Looke how he stares about, how he gapes.

SEN. Come away daughter, come from him.

* MEN. *Bachus, Appollo, Phoebus*, do ye call mee to come hunt in the woods with you? I see, I heare, I come, I flie, but I cannot get out of these fields. Here is an old mastiffe bitch stands barking at mee, and by her stands an old goate that beares false witnesse against many a poore man.

SEN. Out upon him Bedlam foole.

MEN. Harke, *Appollo* commaunds me that I shoulde rende out hir eyes with a burning lampe.

MUL. O father, he threatens to pull out mine eyes.

MEN. Good gods, these folke say I am mad, and doubtlesse they are mad themselves.

SEN. Daughter.

MUL. Here father, what shall we do?

SEN. What if I fetch my folkes hither, and have him carried in before he do any harme.

MEN.   How now? they will carry mee in if I look not to my selfe: I were best to skare them better yet. Doest thou bid me, *Phoebus*, to teare this dog in peeces with my nayles? If I laie hold on him, I will do thy commandment.

SEN.   Get thee into thy house daughter, away quickly.

MEN.   She is gone: yea *Appollo* I will sacrifice this olde beast unto thee: and if thou commandest mee, I will cut his throate with that dagger that hangs at his girdle.

SEN.   Come not neare me sirra.

MEN.   Yea I will quarter him, and pull all the bones out of his flesh, then will I barrell up his bowels.

SEN.   Sure I am sore afraid he will do some hurt.

MEN.   Many things thou commandest me *Appollo*, wouldst thou have me harnesse up these wilde horses, and then clime up into the Chariot, & so over-ride this old stincking toothlesse Lyon. So now I am in the Chariot, and I have hold on the raines, here is my whip, hait, come ye wilde Jades, make a hideous noyse with your stamping: Hait! I say; will ye not go?

SEN.   What? doth he threaten me with his horses?

MEN.   Harke, now *Appollo* bids mee ride over him that stands there, and kill him. How now? who pulles mee downe from my Chariot by the haires of my head. Oh shall I not fulfill *Appolloes* commandment?

SEN.   See, see, what a sharpe disease this is, and how well he was even now. I will fetch a Physitian strait, before hee grow too farre into this rage.   [*Exit*

MEN.   Are they both gone now? Ile then hie me away to my ship, tis time to be gone from hence.   [*Exit*

Enter Senex and Medicus

SEN.   My loines ake with sitting, and mine eies with looking, while I staie for yonder laizie Phisitian: see now where the creeping drawlatch comes.

MED.   What disease hath hee, said you? Is it a letargie or a lunacie, or melancholie, or dropsie?

SEN.   Wherfore I pray do I bring you, but that you shuld tell me what it is? and cure him of it.

MED.   Fie, make no question of that. Ile cure him I warrant ye. Oh here he comes, staie, let us marke what he doth.

Enter Menechmus the Citizen

MEN.   Never in my life had I more overthwart fortune in one day, and all by the villanie of this false knave the Parasite, my *Ulisses* that workes such mischiefs against mee his king. But let me live no longer but ile be revengde uppon the life of him: his life? nay tis my life, for hee lives by my meate and drinke. Ile utterly withdraw the slaves life from him. And *Erotium* shee sheweth plainly what she is: who because I require the cloake again to carrie to my wife, saith I gave it her, and flatly falles out with me. How unfortunate am I?

SEN.   Do ye heare him?

MED.   He complaines of his fortune.

SEN.   Go to him.

MED.   *Menechmus*, how do ye man? why keepe you not your cloake over your arme? It is verie hurtfull to your disease. Keepe ye warme I pray.

MEN.   Why hang thy selfe, what carest thou?

MED.   Sir can you smell anie thing?

MEN.   I smell a prating dolt of thee.

MED.   Oh I will have your head throughly purged. Pray tell me *Menechmus*, what use you to drinke? white wine or claret?

MEN.   What the divell carest thou?

SEN.   Looke,   his fit now begins.

MEN.   Why doest not as well aske mee whether I eate bread, or cheese, or beefe, or porredge, or birdes that beare feathers, or fishes that have finnes?

SEN.   See what idle talke he falleth into.

MED.   Tarry, I will aske him further. *Menechmus*, tell me, be not your eyes heavie and dull sometimes?

MEN.   What doest thinke I am, an Owle?

MED.   Doo not your guttes gripe ye, and croake in your belly?

MEN.   When I am hungrie they do, else not.

MED.   He speakes not like a mad man in that. Sleepe ye soundly all night?

MEN.   When I have paid my debts I do. The mischiefe light on thee, with all thy frivolous questions.

MED.   Oh now he rageth upon those words, take heed.

SEN.   Oh this is nothing to the rage he was in even now. He called his wife bitch, and all to nought.

MEN.   Did I?

SEN.   Thou didst, mad fellow, and threatenedst to ryde over me here with a Chariot and horses, and to kill mee, and teare me in peeces. This thou didst, I know what I say.

MEN.   I say, thou stolest *Jupiters* Crowne from his head, and thou wert whipt through the Towne for it, and that thou hast kild thy father, and beaten thy mother. Doo ye thinke I am so mad that I cannot devise as notable lyes of you, as you do of me?

3—S.N.D. I

SEN.   Maister Doctor, pray heartily make speede to cure him, see ye not how mad he waxeth?

MED.   Ile tell ye, hee shall be brought over to my house, and there will I cure him.

SEN.   Is that best?

MED.   What else? there I can order him as I list.

SEN.   Well, it shall be so.

MED.   Oh sir, I will make yee take neesing[1] powder this twentie dayes.

MEN.   Ile beate yee first with a bastanado, this thirtie dayes.

MED.   Fetch men to carry him to my house.

SEN.   How many will serve the turne?

MED.   Being no madder than hee is now, foure will serve.

SEN.   Ile fetch them, staie you with him maister Doctor.

MED.   No by my faith, Ile goe home to make readie all things needfull. Let your men bring him hither.

SEN.   I go.   [*Exeunt*

MEN.   Are they both gone? Good Gods what meaneth this? These men say I am mad, who without doubt are mad themselves. I stirre not, I fight not, I am not sicke. I speake to them, I know them. Well what were I now best to do? I would goe home, but my wife shuttes me foorth a doores. *Erotium* is as farre out with me too. Even here I will rest me till the evening, I hope by that time, they will take pittie on me.

Enter Messenio the Travellers servant

* MESS.   The proofe of a good servant, is to regard his maisters businesse as well in his absence, as in his presence: and I thinke him a verie foole that is not carefull as well for his ribbes and shoulders, as for his belly and throate. When I think upon the rewards of a sluggard, I am ever pricked with a carefull regard of my backe and shoulders: for in truth I have no fancie to these blows, as many a one hath: methinks it is no pleasure to a man to be basted with a ropes end two or three houres togither. I have provided yonder in the Towne, for all our marriners, and safely bestowed all my masters Trunkes and fardels: and am now comming to see if he be yet got forth of this daungerous gulfe, where I feare me [he] is over plunged, pray God he be not overwhelmed and past helpe ere I come.

Enter Senex, with foure Lorarii, porters

[SEN.]   Before Gods and men, I charge and commaund you sirs, to execute with great care that which I appoint you: if yee love the safetie of your owne ribbes and shoulders, then goe take me up

---

[1] neesing, sneezing.

my sonne in lawe, laie all hands upon him, why stand ye stil? what do ye doubt? I saie, care not for his threatnings, nor for anie of his words. Take him up and bring him to the Phisitions house: I will go thither before.   [*Exit*

MEN.   What newes? how now masters? what will ye do with me? why do ye thus beset me? whither carrie ye mee? Helpe, helpe, neighbors, friends, Citizens.

MESS.   O *Jupiter*, what do I see? my maister abused by a companie of varlets.

MEN.   Is there no good man will helpe me?

MESS.   Helpe ye maister? yes the villaines shall have my life before they shall thus wrong ye. Tis more fit I should be kild, then you thus handled. Pull out that rascals eye that holds ye about the necke there. I'le clout these peasants, out ye rogue, let go ye varlet.

MEN.   I have hold of this villaines eie.

MESS.   Pull it out, and let the place appeare in his head. Away ye cutthroat theeves, ye murtherers.

LO. OMNES.   O, O, ay, ay.   [*Crie pittifullie*[1]

MESS.   Away, get ye hence, ye mongrels, ye dogs. Will ye be gone? Thou raskall behind there, ile give thee somewhat more, take that. It was time to come maister, you had bene in good case if I had not bene heere now, I tolde you what would come of it.

MEN.   Now as the gods love me, my good friend I thank thee: thou hast done that for me which I shall never be able to requite.

MESS.   I'le tell ye how sir, give me my freedome.

MEN.   Should I give it thee?

MESS.   Seeing you cannot requite my good turne.

MEN.   Thou are deceived man.

MESS.   Wherein?

MEN.   On mine honestie, I am none of thy maister, I had never yet anie servant would do so much for me.

MESS.   Why then bid me be free: will you?

MEN.   Yea surelie, be free, for my part.

MESS.   O sweetly spoken, thanks my good maister.

SERVUS ALIUS.[2]   *Messenio*, we are all glad of your good fortune.

MESS.   O maister, ile call you maister still, I praie use me in anie service as ye did before, ile dwell with you still, & when ye go home, ile wait upon you.

MEN.   Nay, nay, it shall not need.

MESS.   Ile go strait to the Inne and deliver up my accounts, and all your stuffe: your purse is lockt up safely sealed in the casket, as you gave it mee. I will goe fetch it to you.

---

[1] 1595 puts these words in the text.   [2] Another Slave.

MEN. Do, fetch it.

MESS. I will.

MEN. I was never thus perplext. Some deny me to be him that I am, and shut me out of their doores. This fellow saith he is my bondman, and of me he begs his freedome: he will fetch my purse and monie: well if he bring it, I will receive it, and set him free. I would he would so go his way. My old father in lawe, and the Doctor saie I am mad, who ever sawe such straunge demeanors? well though *Erotium* be never so angrie, yet once againe ile go see if by intreatie I can get the cloake from[1] her to carrie to my wife.

[*Exit*

Enter Menechmus the Traveller, and Messenio

MEN. Impudent knave, wilt thou say that I ever saw thee since I sent thee away to day, and bad thee come for mee after dinner?

MESS. Ye make me starke mad: I tooke ye away and reskued ye from foure great bigboand villaines, that were carrying ye away even heere in this place. Heere they had ye up, you cried, Helpe, helpe. I came running to you: you and I togither beate them away by maine force. Then for my good turne and faithfull service, ye gave mee my freedome: I tolde ye I would go fetch your Casket, now in the mean time you ranne some other way to get before me, and so you denie it all againe.

MEN. I gave thee thy freedome?

MESS. You did.

MEN. When I give thee thy freedome, Ile be a bondman my selfe: go thy wayes.

MESS. Whewe, marry I thanke ye for nothing.

Enter Menechmus the Citizen

[MEN.] Forsworne Queanes, sweare till your hearts ake, and your eyes fall out, ye shall never make me beleeve that I carried hence either cloake or chaine.

MESS. O heavens, maister what do I see?

MEN. TRA. What?

MESS. Your ghoast.

MEN. TRA. What ghoast?

MESS. Your Image, as like you as can be possible.

MEN. TRA. Surely not much unlike me as I thinke.

MEN. CIT. O my good friend and helper, well met: thanks for thy late good helpe.

MESS. Sir, may I crave to know your name?

---

[1] 1595 on.

MEN. CIT. I were too blame if I should not tell thee anie thing, my name is *Menechmus.*

MEN. TRA. Nay my friend, that is my name.

MEN. CIT. I am of *Syracusis* in *Sicilia.*

MEN. TRA. So am I.

MESS. Are you a *Syracusan?*

MEN. CIT. I am.

MESS. O, ho, I know ye: this is my maister, I thought hee there had bene my maister, and was proffering my service to him, pray pardon me sir, if I said any thing I should not.

MEN. TRA. Why doating patch, didst thou not come with me this morning from the ship?

MESS. My faith he saies true, this is my maister, you may go looke ye a man: God save ye maister: you sir farewell. This is *Menechmus.*

MEN. CIT. I say that I am *Menechmus.*

MESS. What a jest is this? Are you *Menechmus?*

MEN. CIT. Even *Menechmus* the sonne of *Moschus.*

MEN. TRA. My fathers sonne?

MEN. CIT. Friend, I go about neither to take your father nor your country from you.

MESS. O immortall Gods, let it fall out as I hope, and for my life these are the two Twinnes, all things agree so jump togither. I will speake to my maister. *Menechmus?*

BOTH What wilt thou?

MESS. I call ye not both, but which of you came with me from the ship?

MEN. CIT. Not I.

MEN. TRA. I did.

MESS. Then I call you. Come hither.

MEN. TRA. What's the matter?

MESS. This same is either some notable cousening Jugler, or else it is your brother whom we seeke. I never sawe one man so like an other; water to water, nor milke to milke, is not liker then he is to you.

MEN. TRA. Indeed I thinke thou saiest true. Finde it that he is my brother, and I here promise thee thy freedom.

MESS. Well, let me about it. Heare ye sir, you say your name is *Menechmus.*

MEN. CIT. I do.

MESS. So is this mans. You are of *Syracusis?*

MEN. CIT. True.

MESS. So is he. *Moscus* was your father?

MEN. CIT.   He was.

MESS.   So was he his. What will you say, if I find that ye are brethren and twins?

MEN. CIT.   I would thinke it happie newes.

MESS.   Nay staie maisters both, I meane to have the honor of this exploit. Answere me: your name is *Menechmus*?

MEN. CIT.   Yea.

MESS.   And yours?

MEN. TRA.   And mine.

MESS.   You are of *Syracusis*?

MEN. CIT.   I am.

MEN. TRA.   And I.

MESS.   Well, this goeth right thus farre. What is the farthest thing that you remember there?

MEN. CIT.   How I went with my father to *Tarentum*, to a great mart, and there in the preasse I was stolne from him.

MEN. TRA.   O *Jupiter*!

MESS.   Peace, what exclaiming is this? How old were ye then?

MEN. CIT.   About seven yeare old, for even then I shedde teeth, and since that time, I never heard of anie of my kindred.

MESS.   Had ye never a brother?

MEN. CIT.   Yes, as I remember, I heard them say, we were two twinnes.

MEN. TRA.   O Fortune!

MESS.   Tush, can ye not be quiet? Were ye both of one name?

MEN. CIT.   Nay (as I think) they cald my brother, *Sosicles*.

MEN. TRA.   It is he, what need farther proofe? O Brother, Brother, let me embrace thee.

MEN. CIT.   Sir, if this be true, I am wonderfully glad, but how is it, that ye are called *Menechmus*?

MEN. TRA.   When it was tolde us that you and our father were both dead, our Graundsire (in memorie of my fathers name) chaungde mine to *Menechmus*.

MEN. CIT.   Tis verie like he would do so indeed. But let me aske ye one question more, what was our mothers name?

MEN. TRA.   *Theusimarche*.

MEN. CIT.   Brother, the most welcome man to mee, that the world holdeth.

MEN. TRA.   I joy, and ten thousand joyes the more, having taken so long travaile and huge paines to seeke you.

MESS.   See now, how all this matter comes about. This it was, that the Gentlewoman had ye in to dinner, thinking it had bene he.

MEN. CIT.   True it is, I willed a dinner to be provided for me heere this morning, and I also brought hither closely a cloake of my wives, and gave it to this woman.

MEN. TRA.   Is not this the same, brother?

MEN. CIT.   How came you by this?

MEN. TRA.   This woman met me, had me into dinner, enterteined me most kindly, and gave me this cloake, and this Chaine.

MEN. CIT.   Indeed she tooke ye for mee: and I beleeve I have bene as straungely handled by occasion of your comming.

MESS.   You shall have time inough to laugh at all these matters hereafter. Do ye remember maister, what ye promised me?

MEN. CIT.   Brother, I will intreate you to performe your promise to *Messenio*, he is worthie of it.

MEN. TRA.   I am content.

MESS.   *Io Tryumphe.*

MEN. TRA.   Brother, will ye now go with me to *Syracusis*?

MEN. CIT.   So soone as I can sell away such goods as I possesse here in *Epidamnum*, I will go with you.

MEN. TRA.   Thanks my good brother.

MEN. CIT.   *Messenio*, plaie thou the Crier for me, and make a proclamation.

MESS.   A fit office. Come on. O yes. What day shall your sale be?

MEN. CIT.   This day sennight.

MESS.   All men, women and children in *Epidamnum*, or elsewhere, that will repaire to *Menechmus* house this day sennight, shall there finde all maner of things to sell: servaunts, household stuffe, house, ground and all: so they bring readie money. Will ye sell your wife too sir?

MEN. CIT.   Yea, but I thinke no bodie will bid money for her.

MESS.   Thus Gentlemen we take our leaves, and if we have pleasde, we require a *Plaudite*.

FINIS

II. English Version of Source

From THE AMPHITRUO OF PLAUTUS
translated by Edward H. Sugden

Comedies of T. Maccius Plautus. Translated in the original metres by Edward H. Sugden, 1893.

[Mercury, disguised as Amphitryon's slave Sosia, acts as *Prologue* to the play telling us that Jupiter has taken Amphitryon's place with his wife Alcmena and is now in the house with her. Sosia enters, describes the prowess of Amphitryon in the war, and, seeing Mercury guarding the door, wishes to confront him but is afraid.]

[ACT ONE]
[*From Scene i*]   *Mercury and Sosia*

MERCURY   Whither goest thou, who bearest Vulcan prisoned in thy lamp?

SOSIA   Pray attend to your own business, you bone-smashing, bruising scamp!

MERC.   Are you slave or freeman, eh, sir?

SOS.   Just whichever I desire.

MERC.   Do you say so?

SOS.   Yes, I do, sir!

MERC.   You whipped slave!

SOS.   There you're a liar!

MERC.   Anyway, I'll try to make my words the truth.

SOS.   No need of that!

MERC.   Will you tell me where you're going, who you are, and what you're at?

SOS.   I'm going here, and I'm my master's servant: is that what you want?

MERC.   You take care or else I give your tongue a squeeze, sir!

SOS.   No you can't!

She's a chaste and modest maiden!

MERC.   Stop your chattering and go!

What's your business at this house, sir?

SOS. Mine! what's *yours*, I'd like to know?

MERC. I'm one of King Creon's watchmen, posted here from night to night.

SOS. Oh, I see! whilst we were absent, he took care o' the house. All right!
Now be off, my man, and tell him that the household has come back.

MERC. *You* a member of the household! See, unless you quickly pack,
You'll be welcomed to the household in no hospitable way.

SOS. This, I tell you, is my home, where I'm a slave.

MERC. Mark what I say!
I'll make you a proud man shortly, if you don't be off.

SOS. Pray how?

MERC. You'll be borne off in a litter,[1] if I use my club, I trow.

SOS. I'm a servant in this household; that's what you don't seem to know.

MERC. Well, I know you'll get a thrashing very soon, unless you go!

SOS. Will you shut me out from home, then, when I've been so long away?

MERC. *This* your home?

SOS. Of course it is.

MERC. And what's your master's name, do you say?

SOS. Why, Amphitryon, the general of the Thebans, and his dame
Is the fair and sweet Alcmena.

MERC. Come now, tell me, what's your name?

SOS. Sosia the Thebans call me, good old Davus was my sire.

MERC. Well, I never! You'll repent it, trying this on me, you liar!
O you brazen tower of cheek, you know you've patched up all this story.

SOS. With a *patched-up* shirt I came, but nothing else, I vow to glory!

MERC. There's a patent lie! you came here with your *feet*, not with your *shirt*.

SOS. Certainly.

MERC. Well, *certainly* for that black lie you'll soon get hurt.

SOS. No! I *certainly* object.

MERC. But *certainly* that doesn't matter,

---

[1] i.e. on a stretcher. Of course only rich people used litters. [E.H.S.]

For it's fixed most *certainly* that I your ribs shall soundly batter.

> [*Mercury beats Sosia*

SOS. O have mercy!

MERC. Do you dare to say that you are Sosia, eh?
I am Sosia. [*beats him again*

SOS. Murder! murder!

MERC. O, there's more upon the way!
Whose slave are you *now*, sir?

SOS. Yours, sir! for your fists make good your claim.
Help me, Thebans

MERC. Stop your bawling and just tell me why you came.

SOS. Oh, I came for you to kill me with your fists. O don't! no more!

MERC. *Whose* slave are you?

SOS. Why Amphitryon's Sosia, as I said before.

MERC. Don't I tell you *I* am Sosia? Oh, I'll beat you black and blue!

SOS. [*aside*] O good lord! I wish you were, for then *I* should be beating *you*.

MERC. What's that muttering?

SOS. Nothing, nothing!

MERC. Who's your master?

SOS. Whom you like!

MERC. *Now* what do you say your name is?

SOS. Anything! O please don't strike!

MERC. Why, just now you said you were Amphitryon's Sosia!

SOS. I was wrong.
'Twas *associate*, not *Sosia*, I intended all along.

MERC. Ah, I thought I was the only slave of ours that bore that name.
Sure, you've missed the mark entirely.

SOS. Would your fists had done the same!

MERC. I am that same Sosia you were mentioning just now to me.

SOS. Please make peace and let me say a word, from fear of beating free.

MERC. No, not peace, but truce I'll grant you, if you've anything to say.

SOS. Not a word till peace is made! Your fists have such an awkward way.

MERC. Fire away! I will not hurt you!

SOS. Can I trust you?

MERC. Yes, you may.

sos.   What if you deceive me?

merc.   Then may Mercury blast Sosia!

sos.   Now pray mark me! and remember I have leave to speak
out plain.

I'm Amphitryon's servant, Sosia.

merc.   Come, I say, not that again!

sos.   Peace was made and truce concluded! It's the truth I'm
telling you.

merc.   All the same you'll get a thrashing.

sos.   -   As you please, of course you'll do;

For you've got the strongest fists; but still the truth I'm bound to
say.

merc.   But you never can persuade me that I am not Sosia.

sos.   Well, by Pollux, you sha'n't rob me of my master, all the
same;

None, except myself, amongst our slaves has ever borne my name;

And I went with brave Amphitryon forth to fight the enemy.

merc.   Oh, he's mad!

sos.   The same to you, sir! *You* are mad, it seems to
me.

What the mischief! am I not Amphitryon's servant, Sosia?

Didn't our vessel come to harbour from the Persic port[1] to-day?

Didn't master send me here, as soon as we had reached the land?

Don't I stand before our dwelling with this lantern in my hand?

Aint I speaking? aint I waking? Didn't he beat me with his fists?

Yes, by Jove, he *did*! I know it! for I'm still all aches and twists.

Why then do I tarry longer? Come, into our house I'll go.

merc.   What, *your* house, you say?

sos.   Why, surely!

merc.   O you villain, would you so?

You're a liar! and I tell you *I'm* Amphitryon's Sosia;

It was *our* ship sailed to harbour from the Persic port to-day;

It was *we* who stormed the city where King Pterelas did reign;

We who 'gainst the Teleboians did that famous victory gain;

And Amphitryon beheaded Pterelas their king in fight.

sos.   [*aside*]   Oh, it nearly makes me doubt myself to hear him
thus recite!

Everything that happened there he tells exactly, right straight on—

[*Aloud*]   Tell me, though, what gift was given to my lord Amphitryon?

---

[1] Some port between the islands of the Teleboians and Thebes. [E.H.S.] Did
Shakespeare misconceive this ('portu Persico') when he made a Merchant, in
IV.1.4, say that he was 'bound to Persia'?

MERC. Why, the golden goblet, out of which King Pterelas used to drink.

SOS. Right again! and where's the goblet now?

MERC.   Oh, in a box, I think,

Sealed with Lord Amphitryon's signet.

SOS.   What's upon the signet, pray?

MERC. It's a rising sun and chariot. Did you think you'd caught me, eh?

SOS. [*aside*] Ah, he beats me with his answers! I must find another name.

How *could* he have known? However, now I'll put the scamp to shame.

For what I did when alone (no soul beside was there that day)

In the tent, I rather think he'll find it difficult to say.

[*Aloud*] If you're really Sosia, tell me, when the soldiers were at fight,

What were you at in the tent then? I'll give in, if you tell right.

MERC. I was drawing wine, a jugfull, from a cask.

SOS. [*aside*]   He's started well!

MERC. Then I drained it. How delicious was its flavour and its smell!

SOS. Yes, it's true enough; I must confess I drained that sweet canteen.

Why, the villain must have seen me, lying in the jug unseen!

MERC. Now then, have I satisfied you, that you are not Sosia?

SOS. No, by Jove, I swear I *am* he; I'm not telling lies, I say.

MERC. Well, by Mercury I swear it, Jove will not accept your troth;

Me on my bare word he trusts far more than you upon your oath.

SOS. Who am I then, if not Sosia? Will you tell me that, I pray?

MERC. When I do not wish to be so, you can then be Sosia.

Now, when I *am* he, be off or you'll excite a lively storm.

SOS. [*aside*] True it is, when I behold him, I can recognise *my* form,

Just as like me as myself when in the glass I take a peep;

Leg and foot, and hair and stature, eyes and mouth, and nose and lip,

Cheeks and chin, and beard and neck, and everything! Yes, I agree!

If his back is scarred with whipping, nothing could be more like me.

Still though, when I come to think on't, I'm the same I've always been,

Know our house and know my master; and my mind is sound and
    keen.
No! for all this fellow's talking, I won't yield!

                                    [*He knocks at the door*

MERC.   Whither away?
SOS.   Why, home!
MERC.   Look here, sir, you may run away, nay, more,
Climb up into Jove's own chariot, but you won't escape your doom.
   SOS.   But my master sent me! Mayn't I go into my lady's room?
   MERC.   Yes, *your* lady's, if you like, sir! but not *mine*! Come, off
    you pack!
If you plague me any more, you'll take away a broken back.
   SOS.   No! I'll go first!—Ye immortal gods, to you I humbly pray!
Am I dead? or am I changed? or have I thrown my shape away?
Have I left myself behind and then perchance forgotten it?
For this man's the image of me—well, it comforts me a bit,
That I've got an image *now*, for when I'm dead, I sha'n't, I fear.[1]
But I'll go and tell my master at the port what's happened here.
O, I say perhaps *he* won't know me! May Jove grant me such good
    hap!
Then this very day I'll shave my head and don the freeman's cap.[2]

                               [*Exit Sosia to the harbour*

[ACT ONE]

[Scene ii]

MERCURY

   MERC.   Come, I've not done so badly here to-day.
I've driven a beastly nuisance from the door,
So that my father mightn't be disturbed.
When he gets to his lord, Amphitryon,
He'll say that he, by a slave called Sosia,
Was driven from the door. He'll think he lies,
And never came here, as he'd told him to.
Thus I'll fill full of madness and confusion
Both them and all Amphitryon's household too,

---

[1] The Roman practice of setting up the images of the ancestors of the family in
the house, and carrying them out at funerals is well known. Of course, a slave
like Sosia had not the *jus imaginum*, which was confined to families of official rank.
[E.H.S.]

[2] Slaves when set free shaved their heads and wore a skull-cap till their hair
grew again.

Until my father's ready to depart
And leave his lover. Then, and not till then,
They all shall know the truth; and Jupiter
Shall reconcile Alcmena and her spouse.

. . . .

[ACT THREE]
[*Scene iv*]

[When Amphitryon returns Sosia tells him about meeting his own
double. The general is greeted by his wife as though he had only
just left her. She shows him that she already has the goblet which
he thought he was bringing her, and his bewilderment becomes
distress and anger when he learns that 'he' slept with her the
night before (II.2). In the Third Act Jupiter (as Amphitryon)
confuses Alcmena, Sosia and then Amphitryon, ordering Mercury
(as Sosia) to drive the husband away from the house while he
(Jupiter) spends an hour with her.]

[*Enter Mercury as Sosia*]

MERC.   Give way, make way, good people all! Come, quickly
get out of my way!
And let no man be found so bold to seek my headlong course to
stay.
For haven't I, who am a god, as good a right to say to you,
As slavelings in your comedies, 'Come, clear the way without ado'?
They come to tell a ship is safe, or some irate old man's at hand;
I, in obedience to Jove, have hastened here at his command.
Therefore I have the greater right to bid you quit and clear the
way;
My father summons me, I come, his word and order to obey.
As every good son ought to be, so am I to my worthy sire;
Now he's in love, I back him up, exhort, stand by, advise, admire!
And everything that pleases him, to me is also excellent.
He loves; therein he's wise. He does quite right to follow up his
bent.
And so should everybody do: that is to say, with honesty.
Well, now he wants Amphitryon fooled, so I'll perform the trick;
you'll see!
Under your very eyes, good friends, I'll put him in a mortal funk.
I'll set a garland on my head and then pretend I'm jolly drunk.
Then will I climb upon the roof and there I'll valorously stand,
And when he comes I'll drive him off, for I shall have the upper
hand.

Although he's sober as a judge, I'll swear I will not leave him dry!
Then straightway Sosia his slave will have to pay the penalty.
He'll think that he's done all I do to-day! But what is that to me?
I must obey my father's whims; 'tis mine to serve him zealously.
But here's Amphitryon; he comes! he'll be deluded properly!
    So kindly give your best attention now.
I'll go inside and make up like a drunkard;
Then climb up on the house and warn him off!

                                  [Exit Mercury into the house

[ACT FOUR]
[Scene i]

AMPHITRYON

[Enter Amphitryon from the town]

AMPH. When I went for Naucrates, I found he wasn't on the ship.
No one's seen him in the city; sure he's given me the slip.
I've gone limping through the squares, gymnasiums, perfumeries,
Race course, market place, and shambles, business quarters, where
    you please,
Chemists' shops and barbers' rooms, and temples where the gods
    are shrined;
I'm just tired to death with seeking; Naucrates I nowhere find.
Now I'm going home, determined to discover from my wife,
Who it is for whom she's ruined and disgraced herself for life.
Rather than I'd let that matter rest unsettled one more day, I would
    die. *[Goes to the door and tries to open it.]* What's this? the door's locked!
    Very pretty, I must say!
Yes! it fits in well enough with all the rest. I'll knock and see.
Open here! Hallo, who's there? Just open this door, somebody!

[ACT FOUR]
[Scene ii]

MERCURY AMPHITRYON

[Enter Mercury as Sosia on the roof, crowned with a garland]

MERC. Who is there?
AMPH.   It's I!
MERC.   O is it?
AMPH.   So I said.

MERC.   Then Jupiter
And the gods are surely angry with you, you door-hammerer!
AMPH.   What?
MERC.   Just this, that you're about to have a very warm
    half-hour!
AMPH.   Sosia!
MERC.   Yes, I'm Sosia, unless my memory's lost its power.
What do you want?
AMPH.   You scoundrel, dare you stand and ask me what I want?
MERC.   Yes, I dare. You've smashed the hinges off our door, you
    miscreant!
Did you think we got our doors provided by the Revenue?
What are you staring at, you idiot? What do you want? and who
    are you?
AMPH.   Villain, do you dare to ask me who I am, deathbed of
    rods?
Won't my birches make your back blush for your insolence! Ye
    gods!
MERC.   When you were a youth, I see you must have sent your
    money skipping.
AMPH.   Why?
MERC.   Because in your old age you've come to me to beg—a
    whipping!
AMPH.   Oh, I'll make you suffer, housedrudge, for these words
    so bold and free.
MERC.   I will offer you—
AMPH.   Pray what?
MERC.   A holocaust of misery!

[(Sugden's note) At this point a gap occurs in the MSS. We may
probably fill it up as follows. The present scene concludes by Mercury's emptying a vessel of dirty water over Amphitryon, and driv-
ing him away from the house. In the next scene Sosia returns from
the harbour, and is met by Amphitryon, who thrashes him soundly
for his supposed conduct in the previous scene. Alcmena comes out
to see what the disturbance is about, and is in turn attacked by
Amphitryon. She is convinced that he is mad, and returns into the
house. Then the confusion is brought to a climax by the entry of
Jupiter, still disguised as Amphitryon. The altercation between the
two Amphitryons is broken off by the arrival of Blepharo, to whom
they appeal to say which of them is the true Amphitryon. But
Blepharo is completely puzzled, and refuses to decide. At this point
the play again resumes.]

[ACT FOUR]

[Scene iii]

[Enter from the house Blepharo, Amphitryon, and Jupiter, as Amphitryon]

BLEPH.   Share yourselves among yourselves, for I must go; my
business calls.
Never did I see such marvels as I've seen within these walls.

AMPH.   Blepharo, I beg you, stay and be my advocate!

BLEPH.   Farewell!
I'm no use as advocate, for whose to be I cannot tell.

[Exit Blepharo to the harbour

JUP.   I'm going in. My wife's in labour.

[Exit Jupiter into the house

AMPH.   Woe is me! I'm quite undone!
What am I to do when all my friends and advocates are gone?
Never shall that villain mock me unavenged, whoe'er he be!
I'll betake me to the King and tell him what's befallen me.
Yes, I will take vengeance on him, with his wizard's impudence,
Who has turned quite topsy-turvy all my people's common sense.
Where is he? He's gone inside the house! and doubtless to my wife!
Thebes contains no man so wretched! What's the use of my poor
life?
No one knows me; everybody at his will makes fun of me.
Yes! I'll burst into the house, and every creature that I see,
Be it maid, or man, or wife, or that accursed adulterer,
Or my father, or my grandsire, I will slay him then and there!
Nor shall Jove nor all the gods prevent me, wish it as they may.
I will do what I've resolved! Now then, to burst the door straight-
way!

*[Amphitryon rushes to the door but a flash of lightning strikes
him to the ground. The maid Bromia enters and tells him that
miracles have happened in the house: Alcmena has brought forth
twins (Hercules conceived by Jupiter, and Iphiclus by Amphitryon),
and Hercules has killed two snakes near his cradle. Jupiter appears
to Amphitryon and tells him the truth.]*

III. Probable Source

CONFESSIO AMANTIS
by John Gower[1]

Lib. 8. Lines 1151–1271; 1833–1886

[Apollonius's wife Lucina, having given birth to a daughter on board ship, seems to die, and is put into a chest which floats to Ephesus and is taken up by a physician named Cerimon who revives the lady.]

Bot now to mi matiere ayein,   1151
To telle as olde bokes sein,
This dede corps of which ye knowe
With wynd and water was forthrowe
Now hier, now ther, til ate laste
At Ephesim the See upcaste
The cofre and al that was therinne.
Of gret merveile now beginne
Mai hiere who that sitteth stille;
That god wol save mai noght spille.   1160
Riht as the corps was throwe alonde,
Ther cam walkende upon the stronde
A worthi clerc, a Surgien,
And ek a gret Phisicien,
Of al that lond the wisest on,
Which hihte Maister Cerymon;
Ther were of his disciples some.
This Maister to the Cofre is come,
He peiseth ther was somwhat in,
And bad hem bere it to his In,   1170
And goth himselve forth withal.
Al that schal falle, falle schal;
They comen hom and tarie noght;
This Cofre is into chambre broght,
Which that thei finde faste stoke,
Bot thei with craft it have unloke.

[1] Text from *Works* ed. G. C. Macaulay. O.U.P. 1901.

Thei loken in, where as thei founde
A bodi ded, which was bewounde
In cloth of gold, as I seide er,
The tresor ek thei founden ther 1180
Forth with the lettre, which thei rede.
And tho thei token betre heede;
Unsowed was the bodi sone,
And he, which knew what is to done,
This noble clerk, with alle haste
Began the veines forto taste,
And sih hire Age was of youthe,
And with the craftes whiche he couthe
He soghte and fond a signe of lif.
With that this worthi kinges wif 1190
Honestely thei token oute,
And maden fyres al aboute;
Thei leide hire on a couche softe,
And with a scheete warmed ofte
Hire colde brest began to hete,
Hire herte also to flacke and bete.
This Maister hath hire every joignt
With certein oile and balsme enoignt,
And putte a liquour in hire mouth,
Which is to fewe clerkes couth, 1200
So that sche coevereth ate laste:
And ferst hire yhen up sche caste,
And whan sche more of strengthe cawhte,
Hire Armes bothe forth sche strawhte,
Hield up hire hond and pitously
Sche spak and seide, 'Ha, wher am I?
Where is my lord, what world is this?'
As sche that wot noght hou it is.
Bot Cerymon the worthi leche
Ansuerde anon upon hire speche 1210
And seith, 'Ma dame, yee ben hiere,
Where yee be sauf, as yee schal hiere
Hierafterward; forthi as nou
Mi conseil is, conforteth you:
For trusteth wel withoute faile,
Ther is nothing which schal you faile,
That oghte of reson to be do.'
Thus passen thei a day or tuo;
Thei speke of noght as for an ende,

Til sche began somdiel amende, 1220
And wiste hireselven what sche mente.

Tho forto knowe hire hol entente,
This Maister axeth al the cas,
Hou sche cam there and what sche was.
'Hou I cam hiere wot I noght,'
Quod sche, 'bot wel I am bethoght
Of othre thinges al aboute':
Fro point to point and tolde him oute
Als ferforthli as sche it wiste.
And he hire tolde hou in a kiste 1230
The See hire threw upon the lond,
And what tresor with hire he fond,
Which was al redy at hire wille,
As he that schop him to fulfille
With al his myht what thing he scholde.
Sche thonketh him that he so wolde,
And al hire herte sche discloseth,
And seith him wel that sche supposeth
Hire lord be dreint, hir child also;
So sih sche noght bot alle wo. 1240
Wherof as to the world nomore
Ne wol sche torne, and preith therfore
That in som temple of the Cite,
To kepe and holde hir chastete,
Sche mihte among the wommen dwelle.
Whan he this tale hir herde telle,
He was riht glad, and made hire knowen
That he a dowhter of his owen
Hath, which he wol unto hir yive
To serve, whil thei bothe live, 1250
In stede of that which sche hath lost;
Al only at his oghne cost
Sche schal be rendred forth with hire.
She seith, 'Grant mercy, lieve sire,
God quite it you, ther I ne may.'
And thus thei drive forth the day,
Til time com that sche was hol;
And tho thei take her conseil hol,
To schape upon good ordinance
And make a worthi pourveance 1260
Ayein the day whan thei be veiled.
And thus, whan that thei be conseiled,

In blake clothes thei hem clothe,
This lady and the dowhter bothe,
And yolde hem to religion.
The feste and the profession
After the reule of that degre
Was mad with gret solempnete,
Where as Diane is seintefied;
Thus stant this lady justefied   1270
In ordre wher sche thenkth to dwelle.

    .   .   .   .   .

[After many years, when the daughter Thais has been saved from a brothel and is reunited to her father, Apollonius is told in a vision to go to the Temple of Diana at Ephesus.]

    With worthi knyhtes environed   1833
The king himself hath abandoned
Into the temple in good entente.
The dore is up, and he in wente,
Wher as with gret devocioun
Of holi contemplacioun
Withinne his herte he made his schrifte;
And after that a riche yifte   1840
He offreth with gret reverence,
And there in open Audience
Of hem that stoden thanne aboute,
He tolde hem and declareth oute
His hap, such as him is befalle,
Ther was nothing foryete of alle.
His wif, as it was goddes grace,
Which was professed in the place,
As sche that was Abbesse there,
Unto his tale hath leid hire Ere: 1850
Sche knew the vois and the visage,
For pure joie as in a rage
Sche strawhte unto him al at ones,
And fell aswoune upon the stones,
Wherof the temple flor was paved.
Sche was anon with water laved,
Til sche cam to hirself ayein,
And thanne sche began to sein:
'Ha, blessed be the hihe sonde,

That I mai se myn housebonde,   1860
That whilom he and I were on!'
The king with that knew hire anon,
And tok hire in his Arm and kiste;
And al the toun thus sone it wiste.
Tho was ther joie manyfold,
For every man this tale hath told
As for miracle, and were glade,
Bot nevere man such joie made
As doth the king, which hath his wif.
And whan men herde hou that hir lif   1870
Was saved, and be whom it was,
Thei wondren alle of such a cas:
Thurgh al the Lond aros the speche
Of Maister Cerymon the leche
And of the cure which he dede.
The king himself tho hath him bede,
And ek this queene forth with him,
That he the toun of Ephesim
Wol leve and go wher as thei be,
For nevere man of his degre   1880
Hath do to hem so mochel good;
And he his profit understod,
And granteth with hem forto wende.
And thus thei maden there an ende,
And token leve and gon to Schipe
With al the hole felaschipe.   1886

THE TAMING OF
THE SHREW

INTRODUCTION

THE DATE of this play is in doubt. It was not named by Meres in 1598, but most critics put it earlier; Chambers in 1594, Dover Wilson before 1593. The style and some resemblances to *The Comedy of Errors* in tone and treatment make me believe that it came soon after that play and probably before *Two Gentlemen of Verona* and *A Midsummer Night's Dream*.

The relationship between *The Shrew* and *The Taming of A Shrew* is also disputed. Until 1607 all bibliographical references were apparently to the latter, which was entered in S.R. on 2 May, 1594 to Peter Shorte, who printed it that year (Q I) for Cuthbert Burbie (cf. Chambers, *W.Sh.*, I.322-3). This version is given below [I]. Other editions appeared in 1596 and 1607.[1] *The Shrew*, first mentioned in FI, 1623, used generally to be regarded as a revision of *A Shrew* made by Shakespeare with or without collaboration.[2] Warburton and Farmer denied that he wrote *The Shrew*; Furnivall, E. K. Chambers and T. M. Parrott believed that he had a collaborator who did the Bianca plot. Dover Wilson argued that Shakespeare revised, not the play represented in Q I, but another version since lost, in which maybe Nashe took a hand. P. Alexander (*TLS*. 16 Sept., 1926) suggested that Q I was a 'bad Quarto'. Just as the old 'Contention' was a bad version of *2 Henry VI*, *A Shrew* was a botched-up version of *The Shrew*. My own view is that Q I is a badly printed version of the old play which Shakespeare used as his main source for *The Shrew*. He may have had access to another MS as well. Despite resemblances between the two plays the differences cannot be explained away by any theory of abridgement or piracy by memorizing or by putting together actors' parts.

[1] For variants between these editions see *The Taming of A Shrew*, ed. F. S. Boas, 1908. Our almost exact text of QI will test students' ingenuity.
[2] K. Wentersdorf in *Shakespeare Quarterly* V, 1954, 11-21, makes a good case for 'The Authenticity of the Taming of the Shrew'.

It contains many echoes of Marlowe (cf. *Boas*, 91–8), but it is incredible that Marlowe would mimic himself so crudely. Did Shakespeare have a hand in *A Shrew*? The Sly scenes and others might suggest that; so *A Shrew* may not be so much the source-play as Shakespeare's first shot at the theme. Played by Pembroke's short-lived Company (1592–3) *A Shrew* seems to have been performed for Henslowe on 13 June, 1594, but possibly the Henslowe play was *The Shrew*, and Chambers's summary may be correct, that '*A Shrew* originally belonged to the Alleyn Company, that it was handed by them to Pembroke's in 1592 and recovered in 1593, that it was allocated to the Chamberlain's on the reconstitution of companies in 1594, and that they rather hastily based *The Shrew* upon it, sold the old book to the printers in May, and played the new one in June.' (*W.Sh.* I.327.)

The Taming of the Shrew has three main elements all present in *A Shrew*: 1. The Induction, with the adventures of Sly the Tinker; 2. The Wedding and Taming of Katharina; 3. The Wooing of her sister. These are linked in idea because all contain discussion of the relations of the sexes in marriage. Both plays deal with different ways of wooing and holding a wife, and portray different kinds of wives and husbands. *The Shrew* becomes thereby a drama with more social and intellectual substance than *The Comedy of Errors*, but in presenting shrewishness and preaching household morality it resembles that play. Moreover it develops the device of putting the main action—here the play proper—into a framework of different tone, namely the Sly story.

THE INDUCTION AND SLY-THEME

The theme of the beggar transported into luxury is found in *The Arabian Nights*, where Haroun Al Raschid plays the trick on a sleeper. Philip the Good of Burgundy repeated it, according to Heuterus, *De Rebus Burgundicis*, Lib. iv., p. 150, 1584. Goulart put this version into French in his *Thrésor d'histoires admirables et mémorables* (1606?), translated into English in 1607 by Edward Grimeston. Burton summarized Heuterus in his *Anatomy of Melancholy*, 1621, Pt. II, Sec. ii. Mem. 4. According to Warton's *History of English Poetry* (Sect. LII) the story was printed in a jest-book 'sett forth by Master Richard Edwardes, mayster of her maiesties revels' in 1570. In Sir Richard Barckley's *A Discourse of the Felicitie of Man* (1598), pp. 24–6, the 'pretie experiment' is ascribed to the Emperor Charles the Fifth. Other versions, *The Waking Man's Dreame* and the Percy Ballad 'The Frolicsome Duke, or the Tinker's Good Fortune' are probably after Shakespeare (cf. *Boas* for the former and for other versions). The author of *A Shrew* must have used Heuterus or some version now lost. I give Grimestone's version of Goulart [II].

The Induction to *The Shrew* (282 lines) is almost twice as long as that in *A Shrew* (147). The general outline is alike, but only a dozen or so sentences are very similar; the unusual phrase 'I'll pheeze you!' (I'll drive you off) is the same in each. In *The Shrew* the Tapster becomes the Hostess, and this change of sex suits the general theme of men's difficulties with the female sex. Sly's character is also greatly developed, his toper's humour and hedge-bottom philosophy. The lordly setting to which he is transported is described much more fully, with a wealth of poetry quite absent from *A Shrew*. His gradual assumption of the grand manner is beautifully done, and the visit of the players and preparation for the main play are smoothly managed. In *A Shrew* the title of the play is mentioned, and makes the Lord give Sly a loving 'wife' quite opposite to what he might expect. In *The Shrew* this pleasant touch vanishes, and the wife is just a filling-out of the practical joke. With its elaboration of Sly's possible pleasures, the pictures, the suggestion that he has slept fifteen years (reminding us of the very different fate of Thomas of Erceldoune, cf. p. 372) the two scenes in *The Shrew* are among the richest pieces of comedy ever written by Shakespeare.

In *A Shrew* the Tinker watches almost all the play and interrupts four times (at the end of Sc. v and of Sc. xiv, the beginning of Sc. xv, and in Sc. xvi). At the end of Sc. xvi orders are given for him to be taken out before the testing of the wives. The last scene of all, xix, shows him back where they found him, and talking again with the Tapster. So the whole piece is rounded off. This proof of the Tinker's constant presence is missing from *The Shrew*; he fades out of the text after the end of Act I.i, where he is already falling asleep and wishing the play were done; and he does not reappear at the close. It is hard to believe that Shakespeare left the play so, when one recalls his care to finish the framework of the *Comedy of Errors* and *A Midsummer Night's Dream*. Pope therefore inserted the Sly passages absent from *The Shrew* in his edition of that play, though he did not think Shakespeare wrote most of 'the old play'.

To ask whether the Heuterus-Sly setting came first into the mind of the author of *A Shrew* and the taming-story later is perhaps an idle question; but there is a fitness in bringing together Sly and the antics of Ferando-Petruchio; for these are eminently suited to the humour of the Tudor plebeian; they make a tale for a tinker. The material is fabliau-stuff, a mocking lesson for a henpecked drunkard who at the end calls his experience 'the bravest dreame' and goes off home to try his prowess: 'I know now how to tame a shrew.' This aspect of the piece is stressed by the player: ''Tis a good lesson for us, my lord, for us that are married men.'

No doubt the full text of Shakespeare's play brought out Sly's connection with this, for Shakespeare was interested in the Tinker as typical of a certain class and even of a locality, as he showed by adding many allusions to Warwickshire places and family names.

Whereas the inset play in *A Shrew* is set in Athens that in *The Shrew* moves to Padua. Why the change was made is doubtful, but in *A Shrew* most of the characters had Italian names, and this may have weighed with Shakespeare, as well as his debt to Gascoigne's *Supposes*, set in Italy (Ferrara). Athens was a seat of learning celebrated in Lyly's *Euphues*, and the friendship between Polidor and Aurelius in *A Shrew*, Sc. iii recalls that of Euphues and Philautus. In *The Shrew* Padua is equally apt as being a famous university city, and the Italian setting suits the Bianca story better than a Greek one would have done. But maybe the change was made for some practical reason, e.g. the availability of suitable costumes, or even because Shakespeare was working on *A Midsummer Night's Dream*, which had Athens as its setting, and he did not want to repeat the effect. In Lyly's novel Italy is regarded as the land of courtiers and the courtship of ladies.

Though Katharina's name remained the same in *The Shrew*,

the others were changed. Petruchio's came from Gascoigne, for a Petrucio is a servant of the Sienese in *Supposes*. Grumio and Tranio may come direct from the *Mostellaria* of Plautus where they are respectively a downright countryman and a slippery townsman. They preserve these characteristics, for Grumio is Petruchio's blunt, 'ancient, trusty, pleasant servant', and Tranio is capable of posing without difficulty as his master Lucentio. It is interesting to note that Lucentio in *The Shrew* is descended from the Bentivogli who gave the name of Benvolio in *Romeo and Juliet*.

THE PETRUCHIO-KATHARINA STORY

This is a variant of the Shrew theme common in fabliaux from classical times. In it Shakespeare carries on the idea of marriage which Luciana expounded in *The Comedy of Errors* against the nagging jealousy of Adriana, and makes a minor element from Plautus the main interest of his new play. Humorous discussions about mastery in marriage had enlivened the road to Canterbury in Chaucer (e.g. The Wife of Bath, the Merchant), and the Jest Books of the Tudor age contained many stories of battle between the sexes. *A Hundred Mery Talys* (*c.* 1525), for example, had an anecdote about a man who, when asked why he married so small a woman, answered, 'In accordance with the text, "Among evil things choose the least!" ' In another, three married men sought entrance to heaven. The first got in because he had suffered much in married life; the second because he had married twice and so suffered more. The third thereupon hopefully declared that he had been married thrice. He was turned away because he 'could not beware the third time, but entered willingly into trouble again'. (*Jest Books*, I.39.) *Tales and Quick Answers* (1567) included the story of the man who, when his wife fell into the river and was lost, sought her upstream because 'she was so wayward and so contrary in everything while she lived that I know very well now she is dead she will go against the stream'. With such a view of woman marriage will seem a struggle for mastery, to discover who should 'wear the breeches'. French folk-literature was peculiarly rich in stories of this nature, many of which were collected by Des Périers (cf. *Fabliaux et Contes des 12me et 13me Siècles*,

1781). Their interest often depends on the methods adopted by husband or wife to win supremacy. In a crude specimen, *Sire Hain et Dame Anieuse*, the husband and wife actually fight for a pair of breeches until the husband knocks the wife into a tub of water and she has to beg for mercy. Often the wife tests her husband's patience to see how far she can go. Thus, a young wife who marries an older man is urged by her mother to go gently at first; so she cuts down a favourite tree. This surprises him but he accepts her explanation and her mother advises caution. Next she kills his tame hare for dirtying her frock; the husband forgives her when she weeps. Encouraged by this she tells her mother that she intends to take a lover, and her mother warns her she is running into grave danger. At the tenants' feast she pulls off the tablecloth, catching its fringe in her keys, deliberately. The husband says nothing at the time, but next morning he brings a surgeon and together they hold the wife down and bleed her; for, as the husband says: 'You have bad blood in your veins.' The wife is cured of her contempt for him (*op. cit.* III.178). Nearer to Shakespeare's theme are the tales in which the husband takes the initiative; e.g. a Count marries the arrogant daughter of a henpecked nobleman. The bride is advised by her mother to master her husband from the first, but she gets little chance, for on the way home from the wedding he takes her hunting and terrifies her by his show of fury when he kills a dog which disobeys him. Arriving home, he orders a feast. The wife interferes, giving different instructions, whereat the Count punishes the Cook and strikes the wife. . . . Three months later the parents come to see how their daughter is faring and find her quite obedient. The mother is treated disrespectfully and given meagre service at table, while her husband is honoured; and finally the Count punishes her by indecently exposing her to see whether she really is a woman (*ibid.*, III.204).

Scoggin's *Jests* (licensed 1565–6) contains incidents of this nature. Scoggin was a jester in Henry IV's reign, mentioned in *2 Henry IV*, III.2.29 as having had his head broken by Falstaff at the court gate. He was more fortunate at home, for when his young wife proved a shrew he cured her by treating her as insane, tying her to a bench, and having her bled. When she demanded an attendant to walk before her in state to

Church, he chalked a white line all the way and told her, 'If you follow this chalk it will bring you the right way to the Church close.' (*Jest Books*, II.120.) *The Ballad of the Curst Wife Wrapt in a Morell's Skin* (*c.* 1550) given in *ShLib* iv. 415ff., also shows the interest taken in unusual methods of taming.

In *A Shrew* the fun begins when Ferando announces his method:

> And she and I must woo with skoulding sure,
> And I will hold her too't till she be wearie,
> Or else Ile make her yeeld to graunt me love.   (Sc. iv)

Kate is a worthy adversary, who when he refuses to be put off by her rudeness, is attracted to him despite herself; and will marry him,

> For I methinkes have livde too long a maid—
> And match him too, or else his manhood's good.   (Sc. v)

We see her bad temper when Valeria is sent to teach her the lute while Polidor and Aurelius woo her sisters (Sc. vi). Ferando's method is to match rudeness with rudeness; as when he comes to his wedding 'baselie attired, and a red cap on his head', explaining that he does not want to run the risk of having his best clothes spoiled by Kate in her fury. When she protests, he praises her in exaggerated Marlowesque terms (vii.61–77). Refusing to stay for the feast, he takes her home, leaving his friends wondering if and how he will master her. He does it by treating her like a wild creature to be broken by fear and fasting. Hence he behaves brutally to his servants, throws down the table and meat, and tells the audience that he intends

> To bridle and hold backe my headstrong wife
> With curbes of hunger, want of ease and sleepe . . .
> Ile mew her up as men do mew their hawkes,
> And make her gentlie come unto the lure . . .   (Sc. ix)

His servant Sander also tantalizes her. When her husband brings her some meat on his dagger, as if feeding a wild animal, she almost takes it, but her pride still rebels, thus proving, as Ferando says, 'Your stomack is not yet come downe.' (Sc. xi.)

With mock-consideration he refuses to accept the clothes she needs for her sisters' wedding (Sc. xiii). He frequently tests her obedience, as when he says it is the wrong time of day (Sc. xiii) and threatens, 'Ile have you say as I doo ere you go'. On the journey she learns her lesson and will say anything he likes, whether about the sun or the Duke of Cestus (Sc. xv). His response is immediate and grateful:

> Why thus must we two live,
> One minde, one heart, and one content for both.

Already, whether Shakespeare wrote it or not, we can see Ferando developing out of the generic Tamer of the fabliaux as he meets caprice with caprice, sometimes refusing to be angry, sometimes behaving with brutality, always with calculated effect, imitating all the faults of the generic shrew, which Kate remains until starvation makes her waver. In *The Shrew* the two portraits are more fully drawn. Petruchio is highly individual, blunt, mercenary, a ferocious playboy, a man's man, rough-humoured in his practical joking, not unkind once he has his way. Katharina too comes to life, in her cruelty to Bianca, her wit-bouts with Petruchio, her growing chagrin and bewilderment, and the touch of pathos which heralds her surrender. Until she admits herself a woman, one of the weaker sex, she is refused all womanly rights, though lipservice may be paid to her. 'He kills her in her own humour.' The final relation between them resembles that in Deloney's *Gentle Craft* where Simon Eyre uses his wife's lap as a 'little table' when eating in public; thus proving his domestic felicity. *A Shrew* thus provided ample material on which the creative genius of Shakespeare might work; only the golden touch was needed; and this is true not only of the main figures but also of the transformation of the impudent, lewd Sander into Grumio. The process is one of enrichment and of smoothing; *The Shrew* is as much a social comedy preaching the subjection of women as was *A Shrew*, but its total effect is more witty and civilized. To this the other plot contributes not a little.[1]

---

[1] W. G. Boswell-Stone in 'The Old-Spelling Shakespeare' edn. of *The Shrew* (1907) gave a useful comparative analysis of the plots of the two plays, and Ariosto's *I Suppositi*. *Boas* reprinted it, pp. 113–28.

THE BIANCA PLOT

Here Shakespeare made larger alterations, in some ways to simplify, in others to complicate, the dramatic narrative. Kate in *A Shrew* has two sisters, the youngest Emelye loved by Polidor, the next, Phylena, by Aurelius.

We first see Polidor welcoming to Athens his friend Aurelius, son of the Duke of Cestus. Polidor is already in love with Alfonso's youngest daughter Emelye, and Aurelius soon falls in love with Phylena, but neither girl may be betrothed until the eldest sister, Kate, has been married. Polidor suggests Ferando as the very man for Kate. Aurelius proposes that his servant Valeria should pretend to be the Duke of Cestus' son while he disguises as the heir of a rich merchant, in order apparently to test whether Phylena can love him truly and not only for his rank. But first Valeria is sent by Polidor to teach Kate the lute while the others woo her sisters. Valeria has a sharp reception from Kate; then he is required by Aurelius to bring a merchant (Phylotus) who will say that Aurelius is his son and produce deeds of land to prove the young man's eligibility. All goes satisfactorily; Valeria is now introduced as the son of the Duke, and Aurelius's friend, which pleases Alfonso greatly. Aurelius tests Phylena by asking her if she would not prefer the Duke's son to her commoner suitor; she answers appropriately, and Emelye swears devotion to Polidor. The two couples are married before the Duke of Cestus (bewildered by the behaviour of Ferando and Kate *en route*) arrives and hears Valeria pretending to be his son. His rage increases when he learns that Aurelius has married beneath him, but after the young people have begged forgiveness all ends happily: but not quite, for after supper Aurelius rashly suggests that they make trial of their wives' obedience. All Ferando's friends are sure that he will lose, but when sent for Phylena returns word that 'She is something busy but she'll come anon', while Emelye answers that if Polidor has any business with her he must come to her. Kate expounds the theory of wifely obedience and lays her hand under her husband's feet. The moral is, not only that wives should be subject to their husbands, but that romantic marriages are no more likely to be successful than marriages of convenience. A neat ironic twist is given to this idea, for in Sc. xiv the initial harsh relations between Ferando and his wife are contrasted with the grandiose pretensions of the love expressed by Emelye and Phylena for their lovers just before marriage. The proof of the pudding is in the eating, and at the end we leave Polidor calling his wife a shrew while she calls Kate a sheep.

On the whole this secondary plot of the younger sisters in *A Shrew* is not well carried through. Maybe that made Shakespeare substitute a similar but better organized plot adapted from Gascoigne's *Supposes* which he used to contrast a willing bride wooed romantically under difficulties and the unwilling Katharina wooed unromantically. *The Shrew* gives Baptista (Alfonso) only two daughters, and Bianca is wooed by two main suitors, Lucentio and Hortensio, though another is added, 'Gremio, a Pantelowne'. The story becomes an intricate one of intrigue and the insistence is on action.

Gascoigne's *Supposes* (1566) is a hard, dry classical comedy of subterfuge and misunderstanding. A prose version of Ludovico Ariosto's *I Suppositi* (1509) it was played at Gray's Inn before publication, and probably again at Trinity College, Oxford, on 8 January, 1582; and it was very suitable for an academic audience. By 'Supposes' Gascoigne meant 'nothing else but a mystaking or imagination of one thing for another'. (*Prologue.*) It was an 'Errors' play and the author pointed out the various mistakes of identity, etc., as they arose, by means of marginal notes.[1] It has no Shrew, but a willing bride whose situation (though he did not make full use of it) must have struck Shakespeare by its contrast with that of Kate. For at the beginning the heroine Polynesta (who rarely appears) has been seduced two years ago by her lover Erostrato and is pregnant. Erostrato is known as Dulipo, for he has changed identities with his servant of that name, taking service in the house of Damon to get access to his daughter. The false Erostrato pretends to wish to marry her, and so becomes the rival of an old lawyer Cleander, who longs for a child to replace the son he lost long ago when the Turks took Otranto. There is much fun between the servants; a Nurse who is a bribable go-between and may have given hints for the Nurse in *Romeo and Juliet* (cf. I.1; III.3); and there are plenty of verbal battles. The false Erostrato

---

[1] In the reprint below these are given as footnotes.

(Dulipo) has said that his rich father is coming with a large dowry; to support this he persuades a Sienese merchant that Ferrara is dangerous, that he should pretend to be his father Philogano. When Damon discovers the false Dulipo (Erostrato) with his daughter he casts him into a dungeon. Then the real father of the true Erostrato comes expecting to meet his son, but finds Dulipo in disguise. The latter refuses to recognize him and confusion abounds until the old lawyer Cleander discovers that the false Erostrato (Dulipo) is really his long-lost son. Reconciliation follows; Cleander surrenders his claim to Polynesta; Erostrato is forgiven for his 'amorous offence', and all ends happily.

Obviously Shakespeare has taken over a good deal from this play. Petrucio is one of the servants of the Sienese stranger in II.2 and Litio servant of Philogano likewise provides Hortensio's name when he appears dressed as a musician (*The Shrew*, III.1.54). The 'amorous offence' of Erostrato may have reminded the poet of something in his own youth, but he avoids this inconvenience (as he must for his scheme of wooing); Bianca is a virgin and Lucentio has not met her when the play opens. He falls in love at first sight when he sees her with her father and the two suitors Gremio and Hortensio. Like Berowne in *Love's Labour's Lost* he at once abandons learning for love and changes place with his man Tranio, who woos Bianca as Lucentio while Lucentio takes service under Gremio and gets access to Bianca as Cambio, a young scholar who will teach her languages and philosophy. This ensures some lively fun, since Hortensio, besides bringing Petruchio to marry Katharina, is introduced by him as a musician. Hortensio gets short shrift, we learn, from Kate (II.1.141ff.) but his lesson with Bianca enables us to compare his language of love-through-music with Lucentio's through translation from Latin (*The Shrew*, III.1). Thus themes from *A Shrew* are combined with material from Gascoigne-Ariosto. And at each stage the comedy of disguise and subterfuge is contrasted with the blunt exaggerations of Petruchio's masculinity (e.g. III.1 and 2). The Sienese becomes a Mantuan Pedant who is persuaded to clothe himself as Lucentio's father (IV.2). Meanwhile Kate and Petruchio are at odds over her food and clothes (IV.3). Then the sequence of 'Supposes' goes on swiftly in IV.4 as Biondello persuades the

disguised Lucentio to marry Bianca while 'Baptista is safe, talking with the deceiving father of a deceitful son' and they are
'busied about a counterfeit assurance'; and in IV.5 we see a
quelled Kate accepting her husband's pretence that the sun
is the moon and the true father Vincentio is a woman.

So *The Shrew* goes on copying and adding to the merry 'Supposes' of Gascoigne; as in V.1, modelled on *Supposes*, IV.iv,
recalling the scene in *Amphitruo* already used in *Comedy of Errors*
where the husband cannot get into his house because his place
is already taken. In *The Shrew* Vincentio finds the Pedant in
occupation, and Biondello disowns him, as does Tranio, like
the false Erostrato in Gascoigne, IV.vii. Vincentio is in danger
of imprisonment when his son comes and begs forgiveness,
confessing to Baptista that he has married his daughter, 'While
counterfeit supposes blear'd thine eyne' (V.1.117). The belief
of Lucentio and Hortensio that their wives are more obedient
than Petruchio's is the last (and richest) 'Suppose' of all (V.2).
A mistake in identity is after all less deeply comic than one in
assessing a person's nature. *The Taming of the Shrew* shows that
Shakespeare was already moving from the outer world of
appearances and situation to the inner world of character and
ethical implications.

I. Source

THE TAMING OF A SHREW

A Pleasant Conceited Historie called The taming of a Shrew. As it was sundry times acted by the Right honorable the Earle of Pembrook his servants. Printed at London by Peter Short and are to be sold by Cuthbert Burbie, at his shop at the Royal Exchange. 1594.

[Scene i][1]   *Enter a Tapster, beating out of his doores*
Slie Droonken

TAPSTER You whorson droonken slave, you had best be gone,
And empty your droonken pa[u]nch some where else
For in this house thou shalt not rest tonight.   [*Exit Tapster*
SLIE Tilly vally, by crisee Tapster Ile fese[2] you anon.
Fils[3] the tother pot and alls paid for, looke you
I doo drinke it of mine owne Instegation, *Omne bene*[4]
Heere Ile lie a while, why Tapster I say,
Fils a fresh cushen[5] heere.
Heigh ho, heers good warme lying.   [*He fals asleepe*

Enter a Noble man and his men from hunting

LORD Now that the gloomie shaddow of the night,   10
Longing to view Orions drisling lookes,
Leapes from th'antarticke World unto the skie
And dims the Welkin with her pitchie breath,
And darkesome night oreshades the christall heavens,
Here breake we off our hunting for to night,
Cupple uppe the hounds and let us hie us home,
And bid the huntsman see them meated well,
For they have all deserv'd it well to daie,
But soft, what sleepie fellow is this lies heere?

[1] The Scene headings are those inserted by F. J. Furnivall in the facsimile by
C. Praetorius (1886).   [2] Beat.   [3] Fill us.
[4] Omnia bene sine poena, tempus est ludendi.   [5] Cuskin, a drinking vessel.

69

Or is he dead, see one what he dooth lacke?   20
   SERVINGMAN My lord, tis nothing but a drunken sleepe,
His head is too heavie for his bodie,
And he hath drunke so much that he can go no furder.
   LORD Fie, how the slavish villaine stinkes of drinke.
Ho, sirha arise. What, so sound asleep?
Go take him uppe and beare him to my house,
And beare him easilie for feare he wake,
And in my fairest chamber make a fire,
And set a sumptuous banquet on the boord,
And put my richest garmentes on his backe,   30
Then set him at the Table in a chaire:
When that is doone against he shall awake,
Let heavenlie musicke play about him still,
Go two of you awaie and beare him hence,
And then Ile tell you what I have devisde,
But see in any case you wake him not.   [*Exeunt two with Slie*
Now take my cloake and give me one of yours;
All fellowes now, and see you take me so,
For we will waite upon this droonken man,
To see his countnance when he dooth awake   40
And finde himselfe clothed in such attire,
With heavenlie musicke sounding in his eares,
And such a banquet set before his eies,
The fellow sure will thinke he is in heaven,
But we will be about him when he wakes,
And see you call him Lord, at everie word,
And offer thou him his horse to ride abroad,
And thou his hawkes and houndes to hunt the deere,
And I will aske what sutes he meanes to weare,
And whatsoere he saith see you doo not laugh,   50
But still perswade him that he is a Lord.

                 Enter one

   MES. And it please your honour your plaiers be com
And doo attend your honours pleasure here.
   LORD The fittest time they could have chosen out,
Bid one or two of them come hither straight,
Now will I fit my selfe accordinglie,
For they shall play to him when he awakes.

   Enter two of the players with packs at their backs, and a boy

Now sirs, what store of plaies have you?
   SAN. Marrie my lord you maie have a Tragicall

Or a comoditie, or what you will.   60
    THE OTHER   A Comedie thou shouldst say, souns thou'lt shame
    us all.
    LORD   And whats the name of your Comedie?
    SAN.   Marrie my lord tis calde The taming of a shrew:
Tis a good lesson for us my lord, for us that are maried men
    LORD   The taming of a shrew, thats excellent sure,
Go see that you make you readie straight,
For you must play before a lord to night,
Say you are his men and I your fellow,
Hees something foolish, but what so ere he saies,
See that you be not dasht out of countenance.   70
And sirha go you make you ready straight,
And dresse yourselfe like some lovelie ladie,
And when I call see that you come to me,
For I will say to him thou art his wife,
Dallie with him and hug him in thine armes,
And if he desire to goe to bed with thee,
Then faine some scuse and say thou wilt anon.
Be gone I say, and see thou doost it well.
    BOY   Feare not my Lord, Ile dandell him well enough
And make him thinke I love him mightilie.   80
                                      [Exit boy

    LORD   Now sirs go you and make you ready to,
For you must play assoone as he dooth wake.
    SAN.   O brave, sirha Tom, we must play before
A foolish Lord, come lets go make us ready,
Go get a dishclout to make cleane your shooes,
And Ile speake for the properties, My Lord, we must
Have a shoulder of mutton for a propertie,
And a little vinegre to make our Divell rore.
    LORD   Very well: sirha see that they want nothing.   89
                                      [Exeunt omnes

[Scene ii]

*Enter two with a table and a banquet on it, and two other, with Slie
asleepe in a chaire, richlie apparelled, & the musick plaieng*

    ONE   So: sirha now go call my Lord,
And tel him that all things is ready as he wild it.
    ANOTHER   Set thou some wine upon the boord
And then Ile go fetch my Lord presentlie.   *[Exit*

Enter the Lord and his men

LORD   How now, what is all thinges readie?

ONE   I my Lord.

LORD   Then sound the musick, and Ile wake him straight,
And see you doo as earst I gave in charge.
My lord, My lord, he sleepes soundlie: My lord.

SLIE   Tapster, gis a little small ale. Heigh ho.   10

LORD   Heers wine my lord, the purest of the grape.

SLIE   For which Lord?

LORD   For your honour my Lord.

SLIE   Who I, am I a Lord? Jesus what fine apparell have I got.

LORD   More richer farre your honour hath to weare,
And if it please you I will fetch them straight.

WIL   And if your honour please to ride abroad,
Ile fetch you lustie steedes more swift of pace
Then winged *Pegasus* in all his pride,
That ran so swiftlie over the *Persian* plaines.   20

TOM   And if your honour please to hunt the deere,
Your hounds stands readie cuppeld at the doore,
Who in running will oretake the Row,
And make the long breathde Tygre broken winded.

SLIE   By the masse I thinke I am a Lord indeed,
Whats thy name?

LORD   *Simon* and it please your honour.

SLIE   *Simon*, thats as much to say *Simion* or *Simon*
Put foorth thy hand and fill the pot.
Give me thy hand, *Sim* am I a lord indeed?   30

LORD   I my gratious Lord, and your lovelie ladie
Long time hath moorned for your absence heere,
And now with joy behold where she dooth come
To gratulate your honours safe returne.

Enter the boy in Womans attire

SLIE   *Sim*. Is this she?

LORD   I my Lord.

SLIE   Masse tis a prettie wench, whats her name?

BOY   Oh that my lovelie Lord would once vouchsafe
To looke on me, and leave these frantike fits,
Or were I now but halfe so eloquent,   40
To paint in words what ile performe in deeds,
I know your honour then would pittie me.

SLIE   Harke you mistresse, wil you eat a peece of bread,
Come sit downe on my knee, *Sim* drinke to hir *Sim*,
For she and I will go to bed anon.

LORD   May it please you, your honors plaiers be come
To offer your honour a plaie.

    SLIE   A plaie *Sim*, O brave, be they my plaiers?

    LORD   I my Lord.

    SLIE   Is there not a foole in the plaie?   50

    LORD   Yes my lord.

    SLIE   When wil they plaie *Sim*?

    LORD   Even when it please your honor, they be readie.

    BOY   My lord Ile go bid them begin their plaie.

    SLIE   Doo, but looke that you come againe.

    BOY   I warrant you my lord, I wil not leave you thus.

[Exit boy

    SLIE   Come *Sim*, where be the plaiers? *Sim* stand by
Me and weele flout the plaiers out of their cotes.

    LORD   Ile cal them my lord. Hoe where are you there?   59

Sound Trumpets

[Scene iii]

Enter two yoong Gentlemen, and a man and a boie

    POL.   Welcome to *Athens* my beloved friend,
To *Platoes* schooles and *Aristotles* walkes,
Welcome from *Cestus* famous for the love
Of good *Leander* and his Tragedie,
For whom the *Helespont* weepes brinish teares,
The greatest griefe is I cannot as I would
Give entertainment to my deerest friend.

    AUREL.   Thankes noble *Polidor* my second selfe,
The faithfull love which I have found in thee
Hath made me leave my fathers princelie court,   10
The Duke of *Cestus* thrise renowmed seate,
To come to *Athens* thus to find thee out,
Which since I have so happilie attaind,
My fortune now I doo account as great
As earst did *Casar* when he conquered most,
But tell me noble friend where shal we lodge,
For I am unacquainted in this place.

    POLI.   My Lord if you vouchsafe of schollers fare,
My house, my selfe, and all is yours to use,
You and your men shall staie and lodge with me.   20

    AUREL.   With all my hart, I will requite thy love.

Enter Simon, Alphonsus,[1] and his three daughters

But staie; what dames are these so bright of hew
Whose eies are brighter then the lampes of heaven,
Fairer then rocks of pearle and pretious stone,
More lovelie farre then is the morning sunne,
When first she opes hir orientall gates.
    ALFON. Daughters be gone, and hie you to the church,
And I will hie me downe unto the key,
To see what Marchandise is come ashore.   [*Ex. Omnes*[2]   29

[*Scene iv*]

    POL. Why how now my Lord, what in a dumpe,
To see these damsels passe away so soone?
    AUREL. Trust me my friend I must confesse to thee,
I tooke so much delight in these faire dames,
As I doo wish they had not gone so soone,
But if thou canst, resolve me what they be,
And what old man it was that went with them,
For I doo long to see them once againe.
    POL. I cannot blame your honor good my lord,
For they are both lovely, wise, faire and yong,   10
And one of them the yoongest of the three
I long have lov'd (sweet friend) and she lov'd me,
But never yet we could not find a meanes
How we might compasse our desired joyes.
    AUREL. Why, is not her father willing to the match?
    POL. Yes trust me, but he hath solemnlie sworne,
His eldest daughter first shall be espowsde,
Before he grauntes his yoongest leave to love,
And therefore he that meanes to get their loves,
Must first provide for her if he will speed,   20
And he that hath her shall be fettred so,
As good be wedded to the divell himselfe,
For such a skould as she did never live,
And till that she be sped none else can speed,
Which makes me thinke that all my labours lost,
And whosoere can get hir firme good will,
A large dowrie he shall be sure to have,
For her father is a man of mightie wealth,

---

[1] Elsewhere called Alfonso. Simon is probably an error.
[2] i.e. Alfonso and his daughters.

And an ancient Cittizen of the towne,
And that was he that went along with them.   30
   AUREL. But he shall keepe hir still by my advise,
And yet I needs must love his second daughter
The image of honor and Nobilitie,
In whose sweet person is comprisde the somme
Of natures skill and heavenlie majestie.
   POL. I like your choise, and glad you chose not mine,
Then if you like to follow on your love,
We must devise a meanes and find some one
That will attempt to wed this devilish skould,
And I doo know the man. Come hither boy,   40
Go your waies sirha to Ferandoes house,
Desire him take the paines to come to me,
For I must speake with him immediatlie.
   BOY I will sir, and fetch him presentlie.
   POL. A man I thinke will fit hir humor right,
As blunt in speech as she is sharpe of toong,
And he I thinke will match hir everie waie,
And yet he is a man of wealth sufficient,
And for his person worth as good as she,
And if he compasse hir to be his wife,   50
Then may we freelie visite both our loves.
   AUREL. O might I see the center of my soule
Whose sacred beautie hath inchanted me,
More faire then was the Grecian *Helena*
For whose sweet sake so many princes dide,
That came with thousand shippes to *Tenedos*,
But when we come unto hir fathers house,
Tell him I am a Marchants sonne of *Cestus*,
That comes for traffike unto *Athens* heere,
And heere sirha I will change with you for once,   60
And now be thou the Duke of *Cestus* sonne,
Revell and spend as if thou wert my selfe,
For I will court my love in this disguise.
   VAL. My lord, how if the Duke your father should
By some meanes come to *Athens* for to see
How you doo profit in these publike schooles,
And find me clothed thus in your attire,
How would he take it then thinke you my lord?
   AUREL. Tush feare not *Valeria* let me alone,
But staie, heere comes some other companie.   70

Enter Ferando and his man Saunders[1] with a blew coat

POL.　Here comes the man that I did tel you of.

FERAN.　Good morrow gentlemen to all at once.

How now *Polidor*, what man still in love?

Ever wooing and canst thou never speed,

God send me better luck when I shall woo.

SAN.　I warrant you maister and you take my councell.

FERAN.　Why sirha, are you so cunning?

SAN.　Who I, twere better for you by five marke

And you could tel how to doo it as well as I.

POL.　I would thy maister once were in the vaine,　　80

To trie himselfe how he could woe a wench.

FERAN.　Faith I am even now a going.

SAN.　I faith sir, my maisters going to this geere now.

POL.　Whither in faith *Ferando*, tell me true.

FERAN.　To bonie *Kate*, the patientst wench alive

The divel himselfe dares scarce venter to woo her,

Signior *Alfonsos* eldest daughter,

And he hath promisde me six thousand crownes

If I can win her once to be my wife,

And she and I must woo with skoulding sure,　　90

And I will hold hir too't till she be wearie,

Or else Ile make her yeeld to graunt me love.

POL.　How like you this *Aurelius*, I thinke he knew

Our mindes before we sent to him,

But tell me, when doo you meane to speake with her?

FERAN.　Faith presentlie, doo you but stand aside,

And I will make her father bring hir hither,

And she, and I, and he, will talke alone.

POL.　With al our heartes, Come *Aurelius*

Let us be gone and leave him heere alone.　　100

[*Exit*

[*Scene v*]

FERAN.　Ho Signiour *Alfonso*, whose within there?

ALFON.　Signiour *Ferando* your welcome hartilie,

You are a stranger sir unto my house.

Harke you sir, looke what I did promise you

Ile performe, if you get my daughters love.

FERAN.　Then when I have talkt a word or two with hir,

Doo you step in and give her hand to me,

---

[1] 1594 calls him variously Saunders, Saunder and Sander, with speech-headings always San. 1607 has Sander throughout.

And tell her when the marriage daie shal be,
For I doo know she would be married faine,
And when our nuptiall rites be once performde   10
Let me alone to tame hir well enough,
Now call her foorth that I may speake with hir.

Enter Kate

ALFON.   Ha *Kate*, Come hither wench & list to me,
Use this gentleman friendlie as thou canst.

    FERAN.   Twentie good morrowes to my lovely *Kate*.

    KATE.   You jest I am sure, is she yours alreadie?

    FERAN.   I tell thee *Kate* I know thou lov'st me well.

    KATE.   The devill you doo, who told you so?

    FERAN.   My mind sweet *Kate* doth say I am the man,
Must wed, and bed, and marrie bonnie *Kate*.   20

    KATE   Was ever seene so grose an asse as this?

    FERAN.   I, to stand so long and never get a kisse.

    KATE   Hands off I say, and get you from this place;
Or I wil set my ten commandments in your face.

    FERAN.   I prethe doo *Kate*; they say thou art a shrew,
And I like thee the better for I would have thee so.

    KATE   Let go my hand, for feare it reach your eare.

    FERAN.   No *Kate*, this hand is mine and I thy love.

    KATE   In faith sir no the woodcock wants his taile.

    FERAN.   But yet his bil wil serve, if the other faile.   30

    ALFON.   How now *Ferando*, what saies my daughter?

    FERAN.   Shees willing sir and loves me as hir life.

    KATE   Tis for your skin then, but not to be your wife.

    ALFON.   Come hither *Kate* and let me give thy hand
To him that I have chosen for thy love,
And thou to morrow shalt be wed to him.

    KATE   Why father, what do you meane to do with me,
To give me thus unto this brainsick man,
That in his mood cares not to murder me?

She turnes aside and speakes

But yet I will consent and marrie him,   40
For I methinkes have livde too long a maid,
And match him too, or else his manhoods good.

    ALFON.   Give me thy hand *Ferando* loves thee wel,
And will with wealth and ease maintaine thy state.
Here *Ferando* take her for thy wife,
And sunday next shall be your wedding day.

    FERAN.   Why so, did I not tell thee I should be the man

Father, I leave my lovelie *Kate* with you,
Provide your selves against our mariage daie,
For I must hie me to my countrie house   50
In hast, to see provision may be made,
To entertaine my *Kate* when she dooth come.
   ALFON. Doo so, come *Kate*, why doost thou looke
So sad, be merrie wench thy wedding daies at hand.
Sonne fare you well, and see you keepe your promise.

Exit Alfonso and Kate

   FERAN. So, all thus farre goes well. Ho *Saunder.*

Enter Saunder laughing

   SAN. *Sander*, Ifaith your a beast, I crie God hartilie
Mercie, my harts readie to run out of my bellie with
Laughing, I stood behind the doore all this while,
And heard what you said to hir.   60
   FERAN. Why didst thou think that I did not speake wel to hir?
   SAN. You spoke like an asse to her, Ile tel you what,
And I had been there to have woode hir, and had this
Cloke on that you have, chud have had her before she
Had gone a foot furder, and you talke of Woodcocks
with her, and I cannot tell you what.
   FERAN. Wel sirha, & yet thou seest I have got her for all this.
   SAN. I marry twas more by hap then any good cunning
I hope sheele make you one of the head men of the
     parish shortly.
   FERAN. Wel sirha leave your jesting and go to *Polidors* house, 70
The yong gentleman that was here with me,
And tell him the circumstance of all thou knowst,
Tell him on sunday next we must be married,
And if he aske thee whither I am gone,
Tell him into the countrie to my house,
And upon sundaie Ile be heere againe.   [*Exit Ferando*
   SAN. I warrant you Maister feare not me
For dooing of my businesse.
Now hang him that has not a liverie cote
To slash it out and swash it out amongst the proudest 80
On them. Why looke you now Ile scarce put up
Plaine *Saunder* now at any of their handes, for and any
Bodie have any thing to doo with my maister, straight
They come crouching upon me, I beseech you good M.
Saunder speake a good word for me, and then am I so
Stout and takes it upon me, & stands upon my pantoflles

To them out of all crie, why I have a life like a giant
Now, but that my maister hath such a pestilent mind
To a woman now a late, and I have a prettie wench
To my sister, and I had thought to have preferd my   90
Maister to her, and that would have beene a good
Deale in my waie but that hees sped alreadie.

Enter Polidors boie

BOY   Friend, well met.
SAN.   Souns, friend well met. I hold my life he sees
Not my maisters liverie coat,
Plaine friend hop of my thum, kno you who we are.
BOY   Trust me sir it is the use where I was borne,
To salute men after this manner, yet notwithstanding
If you be angrie with me for calling of you friend,
I am the more sorie for it, hoping the stile   100
Of a foole will make you amends for all.
SAN.   The slave is sorie for his fault, now we cannot be
Angrie, wel whats the matter that you would do with us.
BOY   Marry sir, I heare you pertain to signior
Ferando.
SAN.   I and thou beest not blind thou maist see,
Ecce signum, heere.[1]
BOY   Shall I intreat you to doo me a message to your
Maister?
SAN.   I, it may be, & you tel us from whence you com.
BOY   Marrie sir I serve yong *Polidor* your maisters
friend.
SAN.   Do you serve him, and whats your name?   110
BOY   My name sirha, I tell thee sirha, is cald Catapie.
SAN.   Cake and pie, O my teeth waters to have a peece
of thee.
BOY   Why slave wouldst thou eate me?
SAN.   Eate thee, who would not eate Cake and pie?
BOY   Why villaine my name is Catapie,
But wilt thou tell me where thy maister is.
SAN.   Nay thou must first tell me where thy maister is,
For I have good newes for him, I can tell thee.
BOY   Why see where he comes.

Enter Polidor, Aurelius and Valeria

POL.   Come sweet *Aurelius* my faithfull friend,   120
Now will we go to see those lovelie dames

[1] Here's the proof; pointing to his livery.

Richer in beawtie then the orient pearle,
Whiter then is the Alpine Christall mould,
And farre more lovelie then the terean plant,
That blushing in the aire turnes to a stone.
What *Sander*, what newes with you?

   SAN.   Marry sir my maister sends you word
That you must come to his wedding to morrow.

   POL.   What, shall he be married then?

   SAN.   Faith I, you thinke he standes as long about it as
     you doo.   130

   POL.   Whither is thy maister gone now?

   SAN.   Marrie hees gone to our house in the Countrie,
To make all thinges in a readinesse against my new
Mistresse comes thither, but heele come againe to
     morrowe.

   POL.   This is suddainlie dispatcht belike,
Well, sirha boy, take *Saunder* in with you
And have him to the buttrie presentlie.

   BOY   I will sir: come *Saunder*.

Exit Saunder and the Boy

   AUREL.   *Valeria* as erste we did devise,
Take thou thy lute and go to *Alfonsos* house,   140
And say that *Polidor* sent thee thither.

   POL.   I *Valeria* for he spoke to me,
To helpe him to some cunning Musition,
To teach his eldest daughter on the lute,
And thou I know will fit his turne so well
As thou shalt get great favour at his handes,
Begon *Valeria* and say I sent thee to him.

   VALER.   I will sir and stay your comming at *Alfonsos*
     house.

Exit Valeria

   POL.   Now sweete *Aurelius* by this devise
Shall we have leisure for to courte our loves,   150
For whilst that she is learning on the lute,
Hir sisters may take time to steele abrode,
For otherwise shele keep them both within,
And make them worke whilst she hir selfe doth play,
But come lets go unto *Alfonsos* house,
And see how *Valeria* and *Kate* agreese,
I doute his Musick skarse will please his skoller,
But stay here comes *Alfonso*.

Enter Alfonso

ALFONSO   What M. *Polidor* you are well mett,
I thanke you for the man you sent to me,   160
A good Musition I thinke he is,
I have set my daughter and him togither,
But is this gentellman a frend of youres?
POL.   He is, I praie you sir bid him welcome,
He's a wealthie Marchants sonne of *Cestus*.
ALFONSO   Your welcom sir and if my house aforde
You any thing that may content your mind,
I pray you sir make bold with me.
AUREL.   I thanke you sir, and if what I have got,
By marchandise or travell on the seas,   170
Sattins or lawnes or azure colloured silke,
Or pretious firie pointed stones of Indie,
You shall command both them my selfe and all.
ALFON.   Thanks gentle sir, *Polidor* take him in,
And bid him welcome to unto my house,
For thou I thinke must be my second sonne,
Ferando, Polidor doost thou not know
Must marry *Kate*, and to morrow is the day.
POL.   Such newes I heard, and I came now to know.
ALFON.   *Polidor* tis true, goe let me alone,   180
For I must see against the bridegroome come,
That all thinges be according to his mind,
And so Ile leave you for an houre or two.   [*Exit*
POL.   Come then *Aureleus* come in with me,
And weele go sit a while and chat with them,
And after bring them foorth to take the aire.   [*Exit*

Then Slie speakes

SLIE   *Sim*, when will the foole come againe?
LORD   Heele come againe my Lord anon.
SLIE   Gis some more drinke here, souns wheres
The Tapster, here *Sim* eate some of these things.   190
LORD   So I doo my Lord.
SLIE   Here *Sim*, I drinke to thee.
LORD   My Lord heere comes the plaiers againe,
SLIE   O brave, heers two fine gentlewomen.   194

[*Scene vi*]

Enter Valeria with a Lute and Kate with him

VALE.   The sencelesse trees by musick have bin moov'd
And at the sound of pleasant tuned strings,
6—S.N.D. I

Have savage beastes hung downe their listning heads,
As though they had beene cast into a trance,
Then it may be that she whom nought can please,
With musickes sound in time may be surprisde,
Come lovely mistresse will you take your lute,
And play the lesson that I taught you last?

    KATE   It is no matter whether I doo or no,
For trust me I take no great delight in it.   10

    VALE.   I would sweet mistresse that it laie in me,
To helpe you to that thing thats your delight.

    KATE   In you with a pestlence, are you so kind?
Then make a night cap of your fiddles case,
To warme your head, and hide your filthie face.

    VAL.   If that sweet mistresse were your harts content,
You should command a greater thing then that,
Although it were ten times to my disgrace.

    KATE   Your so kind twere pittie you should be
      hang'd,
And yet methinkes the foole dooth looke asquint.   20

    VAL.   Why mistresse doo you mocke me?

    KATE   No, but I meane to move thee.

    VAL.   Well, will you plaie a little?

    KATE   I, give me the Lute.

She plaies

    VAL.   That stop was false, play it againe.

    KATE   Then mend it thou, thou filthy asse.

    VAL.   What, doo you bid me kisse your arse?

    KATE   How now jack sause, your a jollie mate,
Your best be still least I crosse your pate,
And make your musicke flie about your eares,   30
Ile make it and your foolish coxcombe meet.

She offers to strike him with the lute

    VAL.   Hold mistresse, souns wil you breake my lute?

    KATE   I on thy head, and if thou speake to me,
There take it up and fiddle somewhere else,

She throwes it downe

And see you come no more into this place,
Least that I clap your fiddle on your face.   [*Ex. Kate*

    VAL.   Souns, teach hir to play upon the lute?
The devill shal teach her first, I am glad shees gone,
For I was neare so fraid in all my life,

But that my lute should flie about mine eares,   40
My maister shall teach her his selfe for me,
For Ile keepe me far enough without hir reach,
For he and *Polydor* sent me before
To be with her and teach her on the lute,
Whilst they did court the other gentlewomen,
And heere methinkes they come togither.

Enter Aurelius, Polidor, Emelia,
and Philena

POL.   How now *Valeria*, whears your mistresse?
VAL.   At the vengeance I thinke and no where else.
AUREL.   Why *Valeria*, will she not learne apace?
VAL.   Yes berlady she has learnt too much already,   50
And that I had felt had I not spoke hir faire,
But she shall neare be learnt for me againe.
AUREL.   Well *Valeria* go to my chamber,
And beare him companie that came to daie
From *Cestus*, where our aged father dwels.   *Ex. Valeria*
POL.   Come faire *Emelia* my lovelie love,
Brighter then the burnisht pallace of the sunne,
The eie-sight of the glorious firmament,
In whose bright lookes sparkles the radiant fire,
Wilie *Prometheus* slilie stole from *Jove*,   60
Infusing breath, life, motion, soule,
To everie object striken by thine eies.
Oh faire *Emelia* I pine for thee,
And either must enjoy thy love, or die.
EME.   Fie man, I know you will not die for love.
Ah *Polidor* thou needst not to complaine,
Eternall heaven sooner be dissolvde,
And all that pearseth Phebus silver eie,
Before such hap befall to *Polidor*.
POL.   Thanks faire *Emelia* for these sweet words,   70
But what saith *Phylena* to hir friend?
PHYLE.   Why I am buying marchandise of him.
AUREL.   Mistresse you shall not need to buie of me,
For when I crost the bubling Canibey,
And sailde along the Cristall Helispont,
I filde my cofers of the wealthie mines,
Where I did cause Millions of labouring Moores
To undermine the cavernes of the earth,
To seeke for strange and new found pretious stones,
And dive into the sea to gather pearle,   80

As faire as *Juno* offered *Priams* sonne,
And you shall take your liberall choice of all.
    PHYLE.   I thanke you sir and would *Phylena* might
In any curtesie requite you so,
As she with willing hart could well bestow.   85

[*Scene vii*]

Enter Alfonso

    ALFON.   How now daughters, is *Ferando* come?
    EME.   Not yet father, I wonder he staies so long.
    ALFON.   And wheres your sister that she is not heere?
    PHYLE.   She is making of hir readie father
To goe to church and if that he were come.
    POL.   I warrant you heele not be long awaie.
    ALFON.   Go daughters get you in, and bid your
Sister provide her selfe against that we doo come,
And see you goe to church along with us.   [*Exit Philena and Emelia*
I marvell that *Ferando* comes not away.   10
    POL.   His Tailor it may be hath bin too slacke,
In his apparrell which he meanes to weare,
For no question but some fantasticke sutes
He is determined to weare to day,
And richly powdered with pretious stones,
Spotted with liquid gold, thick set with pearle,
And such he meanes shall be his wedding sutes.
    ALFON.   I carde not I what cost he did bestow,
In gold or silke, so he himselfe were heere,
For I had rather lose a thousand crownes,   20
Then that he should deceive us heere to daie,
But soft I thinke I see him come.

Enter Ferando baselie attired, and a red cap on his head

    FERAN.   Godmorow father, *Polidor* well met,
You wonder I know that I have staid so long.
    ALFON.   I marrie son, we were almost perswaded,
That we should scarse have had our bridegroome heere,
But say, why art thou thus basely attired?
    FERAN.   Thus richlie father you should have said,
For when my wife and I am married once,
Shees such a shrew, if we should once fal out,   30
Sheele pul my costlie sutes over mine eares,
And therefore am I thus attired awhile,
For manie thinges I tell you's in my head,

And none must know thereof but *Kate* and I,
For we shall live like lammes and Lions sure,
Nor lammes to Lions never was so tame,
If once they lie within the Lions pawes
As *Kate* to me if we were married once,
And therefore come let us to church presently.

    POL. Fie *Ferando* not thus atired for shame,   40
Come to my Chamber and there sute thy selfe,
Of twentie sutes that I did never were.

    FERAN. Tush *Polidor* I have as many sutes
Fantasticke made to fit my humor so
As any in Athens and as richlie wrought
As was the Massie Robe that late adornd,
The stately legate of the Persian King,
And this from them have I made choise to weare.

    ALFON. I prethie *Ferando* let me intreat
Before thou goste unto the church with us,   50
To put some other sute upon thy backe.

    FERAN. Not for the world if I might gaine it so,
And therefore take me thus or not at all.

Enter Kate

But soft se where my *Kate* doth come,
I must salute hir: how fares my lovely *Kate*?
What art thou readie? shall we go to church?

    KATE Not I with one so mad, so basely tirde,
To marrie such a filthie slavish groome,
That as it seemes sometimes is from his wits,
Or else he would not thus have come to us.   60

    FERAN. Tush *Kate* these words addes greater love in me
And makes me thinke thee fairrer then before,
Sweete Kate the lovelier then Dianas purple robe,
Whiter then are the snowie Apenis,
Or icie haire that groes on Boreas chin.
Father I sweare by Ibis golden beake,
More faire and Radiente is my bonie *Kate*,
Then silver Zanthus when he doth imbrace,
The ruddie Simies at Idas feete,
And care not thou swete *Kate* how I be clad,   70
Thou shalt have garments wrought of Median silke,
Enchast with pretious Jewells fecht from far,
By Italian Marchants that with Russian stemes,
Plous up huge forrowes in the *Terren Maine*,
And better farre my lovely *Kate* shall weare,

Then come sweet love and let us to the church
For this I sweare shall be my wedding sute.   [*Exeunt omn.*[1]

    ALFON.   Come gentlemen go along with us,
For thus doo what we can he will be wed.   79
                                 [*Exit*

[*Scene viii*]

Enter Polidors boy and Sander

    BOY   Come hither sirha boy.

    SAN.   Boy; oh disgrace to my person, souns boy
Of your face, you have many boies with such
Pickadevantes I am sure, souns would you
Not have a bloudie nose for this?

    BOY   Come, come, I did but jest, where is that
Same peece of pie that I gave thee to keepe?

    SAN.   The pie? I you have more minde of your bellie
Then to go see what your maister dooes.

    BOY   Tush tis no matter man I prethe give it me,   10
I am verie hungry I promise thee.

    SAN.   Why you may take it and the devill burst
You with it, one cannot save a bit after supper,
But you are alwaies readie to munch it up.

    BOY   Why come man, we shall have good cheere
Anon at the bridehouse; for your maisters gone to
Church to be married alreadie, and thears
Such cheere as passeth.

    SAN.   O brave, I would I had eate no meat this week,
For I have never a corner left in my bellie
To put a venson pastie in, I thinke I shall burst my selfe   20
With eating, for Ile so cram me downe the tarts
And the marchpaines, out of all crie.

    BOY   I, but how wilt thou doo now thy maisters
Married, thy mistresse is such a devill, as sheele make
Thee forget thy eating quickly, sheele beat thee so.

    SAN.   Let my maister alone with hir for that, for
Heele make hir tame wel inough ere longe I warent thee
For he's such a churle waxen now of late that and he be
Never so little angry he thums me out of all crie,
But in my minde sirra the yongest is a verie   30
Prettie wench, and if I thought thy maister would
Not have hir Ide have a flinge at hir
My selfe, Ile see soone whether twill be a match

---

[1] This and the next s.d. should be transposed.

Or no: and it will not Ile set the matter
Hard for my selfe I warrant thee.

    BOY Sounes you slave will you be a Rivall with
My maister in his love, speake but such
Another worde and Ile cut off one of thy legges.

    SAN. Oh, cruell judgement, nay then sirra,
My tongue shall talke no more to you, marry my   40
Timber shall tell the trustie message of his maister,
Even on the very forehead on thee, thus abusious
Villaine, therefore prepare thy selfe.

    BOY Come hither thou Imperfecksious slave in
Regard of thy beggery, holde thee theres
Twoshillings for thee? to pay for the
Healing of thy left legge which I meane
Furiously to invade or to maime at the least.

    SAN. O supernodicall foule? well Ile take your
two shillinges but Ile barre striking at legges.   50

    BOY Not I, for Ile strike any where.

    SAN. Here here take your two shillings again
Ile see thee hangd ere Ile fight with thee,
I gat a broken shin the other day,
Tis not, whole yet and therefore Ile not fight
Come come why should we fall out?

    BOY Well sirray your faire words hath something
Alaied my Coller: I am content for this once
To put it up and be frends with thee,
But soft see where they come all from church,   60
Belike they be Married allredy.

Enter Ferando and Kate and Alfonso and Polidor
and Emelia and Aurelius and Philema

    FERAN. Father farwell, my *Kate*, and I must home,
Sirra go make ready my horse presentlie.

    ALFON. Your horse! what son I hope you doo but jest,
I am sure you will not go so suddainly.

    KATE Let him go or tarry I am resolv'de to stay,
And not to travell on my wedding day.

    FERAN. Tut *Kate* I tell thee we must needes go home,
Villaine hast thou saddled my horse?

    SAN. Which horse, your curtall?   70

    FERAN. Sounes you slave stand you prating here?
Saddell the bay gelding for your Mistris.

    KATE Not for me: for Ile not go.

SAN.   The ostler will not let me have him, you owe ten pence
For his meate, and 6 pence for stuffing my mistris saddle.
   FERAN.   Here villaine go pay him straight.
   SAN.   Shall I give them another pecke of lavender.
   FERAN.   Out slave and bring them presently to the dore
   ALFON.   Why son I hope at least youle dine with us
   SAN.   I pray you maister lets stay till dinner be don.   80
   FERAN.   Sounes villaine art thou here yet?   [*Ex. Sander*
Come *Kate* our dinner is provided at home.
   KATE   But not for me, for here I meane to dine.
Ile have my will in this as well as you,
Though you in madding mood would leave your frends
Despite of you Ile tarry with them still.
   FERAN.   I *Kate* so thou shalt but at some other time,
When as thy sisters here shall be espousd,
Then thou and I will keepe our wedding day,
In better sort then now we can provide,   90
For here I promise thee before them all,
We will ere long returne to them againe,
Come *Kate* stand not on termes we will awaie,
This is my day, to morrow thou shalt rule,
And I will doo what ever thou commandes.
Gentlemen farwell, wele take our leves,
It will be late before that we come home.

Exit Ferando and Kate

   POL.   Farwell *Ferando* since you will be gone.
   ALFON.   So mad a cupple did I never see.
   EMEL.   They're even as well macht as I would wish.   100
   PHILE.   And yet I hardly thinke that he can tame her.
For when he has don she will do what she list.
   AUREL.   Her manhood then is good I do beleeve.
   POL.   *Aurelius* or else I misse my marke,
Her toung will walke if she doth hold her handes,
I am in dout ere halfe a month be past
Hele curse the priest that married him so soone,
And yet it may be she will be reclaimde,
For she is verie patient grone of late.
   ALFON.   God hold it that it may continue still,   110
I would be loth that they should disagree,
But he I hope will holde her in a while.
   POL.   Within this two daies I will ride to him,
And see how lovingly they do agree.
   ALFON.   Now *Aurelius* what say you to this,

What have you sent to *Cestus* as you said,
To certifie your father of your love,
For I would gladlie he would like of it,
And if he be the man you tell to me,
I gesse he is a Marchant of great wealth.   120
And I have seene him oft at *Athens* here,
And for his sake assure thee thou art welcome.
    POL.   And so to me whilest *Polidor* doth live.
    AUREL.   I find it so right worthie gentlemen,
And of what worth your frendship I esteme,
    I leve [to][1] censure of your severall thoughts,
But for requitall of your favours past,
Rests yet behind, which when occasion serves
I vow shalbe remembred to the full,
And for my fathers comming to this place,   130
I do expect within this weeke at most.
    ALFON.   Inough *Aurelius*? but we forget
Our Marriage dinner now the bride is gon,
Come let us se what there they left behind.   134
                              [*Exit Omnes*

[*Scene ix*]

Enter Sanders with two or three serving men

    SAN.   Come sirs provide all thinges as fast as you can,
For my Masters hard at hand and my new Mistris
And all, and he sent me before to see all thinges redy.
    TOM   Welcome home *Sander* sirra how lookes our
New Mistris they say she's a plagie shrew.
    SAN.   I and that thou shalt find I can tell thee and thou
Dost not please her well, why my Maister
Has such a doo with hir as it passeth and he's even like a madman.
    WILL   Why *Sander* what dos he say.
    SAN.   Why Ile tell you what: when they should   10
Go to church to be maried he puts on an olde
Jerkin and a paire of canvas breeches downe to the
Small of his legge and a red cap on his head and he
Lookes as thou wilt burst thy selfe with laffing
When thou seest him: he's ene as good as a
Foole for me: and then when they should go to dinner
He made me Saddle the horse and away he came.
And nere tarried for dinner and therefore you had best
Get supper reddy against they come, for

[1] to, emendation by Malone in 1607 Q in Bodleian.

They be hard at hand I am sure by this time.   20
    TOM   Sounes see where they be all redy.

                    Enter Ferando and Kate

    FERAN.   Now welcome Kate: wher'es these villains
Here, what? not supper yet uppon the borde:
Nor table spred nor nothing don at all,
Wheres that villaine that I sent before.
    SAN.   Now, *adsum*, sir.
    FERAN.   Come hether you villaine Ile cut your nose,
You Rogue: helpe me of with my bootes: wilt please
You to lay the cloth? sounes the villaine
Hurts my foote? pull easely I say; yet againe.   30

                    He beates them all
            They cover the bord and fetch in the meate

Sounes? burnt and skorcht who drest this meate?
    WILL   Forsouth John cooke.

    He throwes downe the table and meate and all, and beates them

    FERAN.   Go you villaines bringe you me such meate,
Out of my sight I say and beare it hence,
Come *Kate* wele have other meate provided,
Is there a fire in my chamber sir?
    SAN.   I forsooth.
                                        [*Exit Ferando and Kate*

            Manent servingmen and eate up all the meate

    TOM   Sounes? I thinke of my conscience my Masters
Mad since he was maried.
    WILL   I laft what a boxe he gave *Sander*
For pulling of his bootes.

                    Enter Ferando againe

    SAN.   I hurt his foote for the nonce man.   40
    FERAN.   Did you so you damned villaine.

                He beates them all out againe

This humor must I holde me to a while,
To bridle and hold backe my headstrong wife,
With curbes of hunger: ease: and want of sleepe,
Nor sleepe nor meate shall she injoie to night,
Ile mew her up as men do mew their hawkes,
And make her gentlie come unto the lure,
Were she as stuborne or as full of strength

As were the *Thracian* horse *Alcides* tamde,
That King *Egeus* fed with flesh of men,   50
Yet would I pull her downe and make her come
As hungry hawkes do flie unto there lure.   52

[*Exit*

[*Scene x*]

Enter Aurelius and Valeria

AUREL.   *Valeria* attend: I have a lovely love,
As bright as is the heaven cristalline,
As faire as is the milke white way of Jove,
As chast as *Phoebe* in her sommer sportes,
As softe and tender as the azure downe,
That circles *Cithereas* silver doves.
Her do I meane to make my lovely bride,
And in her bed to breath the sweet content,
That I thou knowst long time have aimed at.
Now *Valeria* it rests in thee to helpe   10
To compasse this, that I might gaine my love,
Which easilie thou maist performe at will,
If that the marchant which thou toldst me of,
Will as he sayd go to *Alfonsos* house,
And say he is my father, and there with all
Pas over certaine deedes of land to me,
That I thereby may gaine my hearts desire.
And he is promised reward of me.
    VAL.   Feare not my Lord Ile fetch him straight to you,
For hele do any thing that you command,   20
But tell me my Lord, is *Ferando* married then?
    AUREL.   He is: and *Polidor* shortly shall be wed,
And he meanes to tame his wife erelong.
    VALE.   He saies so.
    AUREL.   Faith he's gon unto the taming schoole.
    VAL.   The taming schoole: why is there such a place?
    AUREL.   I: and *Ferando* is the Maister of the schoole.
    VAL.   Thats rare: but what *decorum* dos he use?
    AUREL.   Faith I know not: but by som odde devise
Or other, but come *Valeria* I long to see the man,   30
By whome we must comprise our plotted drift,
That I may tell him what we have to doo.
    VAL.   Then come my Lord and I will bring you to him straight.
    AUREL.   Agreed, then lets go.   34

[*Exeunt*

[Scene xi]

Enter Sander and his Mistres

SAN.   Come Mistris.

KATE   *Sander* I prethe helpe me to some meate,
I am so faint that I can scarsely stande.

SAN.   I marry mistris but you know my maister
Has given me a charge that you must eate nothing,
But that which he himselfe giveth you.

KATE   Why man thy Maister needs never know it.

SAN.   You say true indede: why looke you Mistris,
What say you to a peese of beeffe and mustard now?

KATE   Why I say tis excellent meate, canst thou helpe me to
some?   10

SAN.   I, I could helpe you to some but that
I doubt the mustard is too collerick for you,
But what say you to a sheepes head and garlick?

KATE   Why any thing, I care not what it be.

SAN.   I but the garlike I doubt will make your breath
Stincke, and then my Maister will course me for letting
You eate it: But what say you to a fat Capon?

KATE   Thats meate for a King sweet *Sander* helpe
Me to some of it.

SAN.   Nay berlady then tis too deere for us, we must
Not meddle with the Kings meate.

KATE   Out villaine dost thou mocke me,   20
Take that for thy sawsinesse.

She beates him

SAN.   Sounes are you so light fingerd with a murrin,
Ile keepe you fasting for it this two daies.

KATE   I tell thee villaine Ile tear the flesh of
Thy face and eate it and thou prates to me thus.

SAN.   Here comes my Maister now hele course you.

*Enter Ferando with a peece of meate uppon his
daggers point and Polidor with him*

FERAN.   Se here *Kate* I have provided meate for thee,
Here take it: what ist not worthie thankes,
Goe sirra? take it awaie againe you shallbe
Thankefull for the next you have.   30

KATE   Why I thanke you for it.

FERAN.   Nay now tis not worth a pin go sirray and take
It hence I say.

SAN.   Yes sir Ile Carrie it hence: Maister let her
Have none for she can fight as hungrie as she is.

POL.   I pray you sir let it stand, for Ile eate
Some with her my selfe.

FERAN.   Well sirra set it downe againe.

KATE   Nay nay I pray you let him take it hence,
And keepe it for your owne diete for Ile none,
Ile nere be beholding to you for your Meate,
I tell thee flatlie here unto the thy teethe   40
Thou shalt not keepe me nor feede me as thou list,
For I will home againe unto my fathers house.

FERAN.   I, when you'r meeke and gentell but not
Before, I know your stomack is not yet come downe,
Therefore no marvell thou canste not eate,
And I will goe unto your Fathers house,
Come *Polidor* let us goe in againe,
And *Kate* come in with us I know ere longe,
That thou and I shall lovingly agree.   49

                                                    [*Ex. Omnes*

[*Scene xii*]

Enter Aurelius, Valeria and Phylotus the Marchant

AUREL.   Now Senior *Phylotus*, we will go
Unto *Alfonsos* house, and be sure you say
As I did tell you, concerning the man
That dwells in *Cestus*, whose son I said I was,
For you doo very much resemble him,
And feare not: you may be bold to speake your mind.

PHYLO.   I warrant you sir take you no care,
Ile use my selfe so cunning in the cause,
As you shall soone injoie your harts delight.

AUREL.   Thankes sweet *Phylotus*, then stay you here,   10
And I will go and fetch him hither straight.
Ho, Senior *Alfonso*: a word with you.

Enter Alfonso

ALFON.   Whose there? what *Aurelius* whats the matter
That you stand so like a stranger at the doore?

AUREL.   My father sir is newly come to towne,
And I have brought him here to speake with you,
Concerning those matters that I tolde you of,
And he can certefie you of the truth.

ALFON.   Is this your father? you are welcome sir.

PHYLO.   Thankes *Alfonso*, for thats your name I gesse,   20
I understand my son hath set his mind
And bent his liking to your daughters love,
And for because he is my only son,
And I would gladly that he should doo well,
I tell you sir, I not mislike his choise,
If you agree to give him your consent,
He shall have living to maintaine his state,
Three hundred poundes a yeere I will assure
To him and to his heyres, and if they do joyne,
And knit themselves in holy wedlock bande,   30
A thousand massie ingots of pure gold,
And twise as many bares of silver plate,
I freely give him, and in writing straight,
I will confirme what I have said in wordes.

ALFON.   Trust me I must commend your liberall mind,
And loving care you beare unto your son,
And here I give him freely my consent,
As for my daughter I thinke he knowes her mind,
And I will inlarge her dowrie for your sake.
And solemnise with joie your nuptiall rites,   40
But is this gentleman of *Cestus* too?

AUREL.   He is the *Duke* of *Cestus* thrise renowned son,
Who for the love his honour beares to me:
Hath thus accompanied me to this place.

ALFONSO   You weare to blame you told me not before,
Pardon me my Lord, for if I had knowne
Your honour had bin here in place with me,
I would have donne my dutie to your honour.

VAL.   Thankes good *Alfonso*: but I did come to see
When as these marriage rites should be performed;   50
And if in these nuptialls you vouchsafe,
To honour thus the prince of *Cestus* frend,
In celebration of his spousall rites,
He shall remaine a lasting friend to you,
What saies *Aurelius* father.

PHYLO.   I humbly thanke your honour good my Lord,
And ere we parte before your honor here:
Shall articles of such content be drawne,
As twixt our houses and posterities,
Eternallie this league of peace shall last,   60
Inviolat and pure on either part.

ALFONSO   With all my heart, and if your honour please,

To walke along with us unto my house,
We will confirme these leagues of lasting love.
    VAL.   Come then *Aurelius* I will go with you.   65

                                  [*Ex. omnes*

[Scene xiii]

Enter Ferando and Kate and Sander

    SAN.   Master the haberdasher has brought my
Mistresse home her cappe here.[1]
    FERAN.   Come hither sirra: what have you there?
    HABAR.   A velvet cappe sir and it please you.
    FERAN.   Who spoake for it? didst thou *Kate*?
    KATE   What if I did, come hither sirra, give me
The cap, Ile see if it will fit me.

She sets it one hir head

    FERAN.   O monstrous: why it becomes thee not,
Let me see it Kate: here sirra take it hence,
This cappe is out of fashion quite.   10
    KATE   The fashion is good inough: belike you,
Meane to make a foole of me.
    FERAN.   Why true he meanes to make a foole of thee,
To have thee put on such a curtald cappe,
sirra begon with it.

Enter the Taylor with a gowne

    SAN.   Here is the *Taylor* too with my Mistris gowne.
    FERAN.   Let me see it *Taylor*: what with cuts and jagges?
Sounes you villaine, thou hast spoiled the gowne.
    TAYLOR   Why sir I made it as your man gave me direction,
You may reade the note here.
    FERAN.   Come hither sirra: *Taylor* reade the note.   20
    TAYLOR   Item a faire round compast cape.
    SAN.   I thats true.
    TAYLOR   And a large truncke sleeve.
    SAN.   Thats a lie maister, I sayd two truncke sleeves.
    FERAN.   Well sir goe forward.
    TAILOR   Item a loose bodied gowne.
    SAN.   Maister if ever I sayd loose bodies gowne,[2]
Sew me in a seame and beate me to death,
With a bottome of browne thred.

---

[1] The haberdasher should enter here and exit at l. 14.
[2] gown for a loose woman.

TAILOR   I made it as the note bad me.   30

SAN.   I say the note lies in his throate and thou too,
And thou sayst it.

TAYLOR   Nay nay nere be so hot sirra, for I feare you not.

SAN.   Doost thou heare *Taylor*, thou hast braved
Many men: brave not me.
Thou'st faste[1] many men.

TAYLOR   Well sir.

SAN.   Face not me Ile nether be faste nor braved
At thy handes I can tell thee.

KATE   Come come I like the fashion of it well enough,   40
Heres more a do then needs Ile have it,
And if you do not like it hide your eies,
I thinke I shall have nothing by your will.

FERAN.   Go I say and take it up for your maisters use.

SAN.   Souns: villaine not for thy life touch it not,
Souns, take up my mistris gowne to his
Maisters use?

FERAN.   Well sir: whats your conceit of it.

SAN.   I have a deeper conceite in it then you
thinke for, take up my Mistris gowne
To his maisters use?

FERAN.   *Tailor* come hether: for this time take it   50
Hence againe, and Ile content thee for thy paines.

TAYLOR   I thanke you sir.   *[Exit Taylor*

FERAN.   Come *Kate* we now will go see thy fathers house
Even in these honest meane abilliments,
Our purses shallbe rich, our garments plaine,
To shrowd our bodies from the winter rage.
And thats inough, what should we care for more.
Thy sisters *Kate* to morrow must be wed,
And I have promised them thou shouldst be there.
The morning is well up lets hast away,   60
It will be nine a clocke ere we come there.

KATE   Nine a clock, why tis allreadie past two
In the after noone by all the clocks in the towne.

FERAN.   I say tis but nine a clock in the morning.

KATE   I say tis tow a clock in the after noone.

FERAN.   It shall be nine then ere we go to your fathers,
Come backe againe, we will not go to day.
Nothing but crossing of me still,
Ile have you say as I doo ere you go.   *[Exeunt omnes*

---

[1] fac'd; dressed, trimmed; punning with 'face insolently'.

[*Scene xiv*]

Enter Polidor, Emelia, Aurelius and Philema

POL.   Faire *Emelia* sommers sun bright Queene,
Brighter of hew then is the burning clime,
Where *Phoebus* in his bright aequator sits,
Creating gold and pressious minneralls,
What would *Emelia* doo? if I were forst
To leave faire *Athens* and to range the world.

EME.   Should thou assay to scale the seate of Jove,
Mounting the suttle ayrie regions
Or be snacht up as erste was *Ganimed*,
Love should give winges unto my swift desires,   10
And prune my thoughts that I would follow thee,
Or fall and perish as did *Icarus*.

AUREL.   Sweetly resolved faire *Emelia*.
But would *Phylema* say as much to me,
If I should aske a question now of thee,
What if the duke of *Cestus* only son,
Which came with me unto your fathers house,
Should seeke to git *Phylemas* love from me,
And make thee Duches of that stately towne,
Wouldst thou not then forsake me for his love?   20

PHYLE.   Not for great *Neptune*, no nor *Jove* himselfe,
Will *Phylema* leave *Aurelius* love,
Could he install me *Empres* of the world,
Or make me Queene and guidres of the heavens,
Yet would I not exchange thy love for his,
Thy company is poore *Philemas* heaven,
And without thee, heaven were hell to me.

EME.   And should my love as erste did *Hercules*
Attempt to passe the burning valtes of hell,
I would with piteous lookes and pleasing wordes,   30
As once did *Orpheus* with his harmony,
And ravishing sound of his melodious harpe,
Intreate grim *Pluto* and of him obtaine,
That thou mightest go and safe retourne againe.

PHYLE.   And should my love as earst *Leander* did,
Attempte to swimme the boyling helispont
For *Heros* love: no towers of brasse should hold
But I would follow thee through those raging flouds,
With lockes dishevered and my brest all bare,
With bended knees upon *Abidas* shoore,   40

7—S.N.D.I

I would with smokie sighes and brinish teares,
Importune *Neptune* and the watry Gods,
To send a guard of silver sealed *Dolphyns*,
With sounding *Tritons* to be our convoy,
And to transport us safe unto the shore,
Whilst I would hang about thy lovely necke,
Redoubling kisse on kisse upon thy cheekes,
And with our pastime still the swelling waves.

    EME. Should *Polidor* as great *Achilles* did,
Onely imploy himselfe to follow armes, 50
Like to the warlike *Amazonian* Queene,
Pentheselea Hectors paramore,
Who foyld the bloudie *Pirrhus* murderous greeke,
Ile thrust my selfe amongst the thickest throngs,
And with my utmost force assist my love.

    PHYLE. Let *Eole* storme: be mild and quiet thou,
Let *Neptune* swell, be *Aurelius* calme and pleased,
I care not I, betide what may betide,
Let fates and fortune doo the worst they can,
I recke them not: they not discord with me, 60
Whilst that my love and I do well agree.

    AUREL. Sweet *Phylema* bewties mynerall,
From whence the sun exhales his glorious shine,
And clad the heaven in thy reflected raies,
And now my liefest love, the time drawes nie,
That *Himen* mounted in his saffron robe,
Must with his torches waight upon thy traine,
As *Hellens* brothers on the horned Moone,
Now *Juno* to thy number shall I adde,
The fairest bride that ever Marchant had. 70

    POL. Come faire *Emelia* the preeste is gon,
And at the church your father and the reste,
Do stay to see our marriage rites performde,
And knit in sight of heaven this *Gordian* knot.
That teeth of fretting time may nere untwist,
Then come faire love and gratulate with me,
This daies content and sweet solemnity.   [*Ex. Omnes*

    SLIE *Sim* must they be married now?
    LORD I my Lord. 79

[Scene xv]

Enter Ferando and Kate and Sander

    SLIE Looke *Sim* the foole is come againe now.
    FERAN. Sirra go fetch our horsses forth, and bring

Them to the backe gate presentlie.
   SAN.   I will sir I warrant you.

                              [Exit Sander

   FERAN.   Come *Kate* the Moone shines cleere to night methinkes.
   KATE   The moone? why husband you are deceivd.
It is the sun.
   FERAN.   Yet againe: come backe againe it shall be
The moone ere we come at your fathers.
   KATE.   Why Ile say as you say it is the moone.   10
   FERAN.   Jesus save the glorious moone.
   KATE   Jesus save the glorious moone.
   FERAN.   I am glad *Kate* your stomack is come downe,
I know it well thou knowest it is the sun,
But I did trie to see if thou wouldst speake,
And crosse me now as thou hast donne before,
And trust me *Kate* hadst thou not named the moone,
We had gon back againe as sure as death,
But soft whose this thats comming here.

Enter the Duke of Cestus alone

   DUKE   Thus all alone from *Cestus* am I come,   20
And left my princelie courte and noble traine,
To come to *Athens*, and in this disguise,
To see what course my son *Aurelius* takes,
But stay, heres some it may be Travells thether,
Good sir can you derect me the way to *Athens*?

Ferando speakes to the olde man

Faire lovely maide yoong and affable,
More cleere of hew and far more beautifull,
Then pretious *Sardonix* or purple rockes,
Of *Amithests* or glistering *Hiasinthe*,
More amiable farre then is the plain,   30
Where glistering *Cepherus*[1] in silver boures,
Gaseth upon the Giant *Andromede*,
Sweet *Kate* entertaine this lovely woman.
   DUKE   I thinke the man is mad he calles me a woman.
   KATE   Faire lovely lady, bright and Christalline,
Bewteous and stately as the eie-traind bird,
As glorious as the morning washt with dew,
Within whose eies she takes her dawning beames,
And golden sommer sleepes upon thy cheekes,
Wrap up thy radiations in some cloud,   40

  [1] The River Cephisus; but what was *Andromede*?

Least that thy bewty make this stately towne,
Inhabitable like the burning *Zone*,
With sweet reflections of thy lovely face.
    DUKE   What is she mad to? or is my shape transformd,
That both of them perswade me I am a woman,
But they are mad sure, and therefore Ile begon,
And leave their companies for fear of harme,
And unto *Athens* hast to seeke my son.

Exit Duke

    FERAN.   Why so *Kate* this was friendly done of thee,
And kindly too: why thus must we two live,   50
One minde, one heart, and one content for both,
This good old man dos thinke that we are mad,
And glad he is I am sure, that he is gonne,
But come sweet *Kate* for we will after him,
And now perswade him to his shape againe.   55
                                     [*Ex. Omnes*

[*Scene xvi*]

Enter Alfonso and Phylotus and Valeria,
Polidor, Emelia, Aurelius and Phylema

    ALFON.   Come lovely sonnes your marriage rites performed,
Lets hie us home to see what cheere we have,
I wonder that *Ferando* and his wife
Comes not to see this great solemnitie.
    POL.   No marvell if *Ferando* be away,
His wife I think hath troubled so his wits,
That he remaines at home to keepe them warme,
For forward wedlocke as the proverbe sayes,
Hath brought him to his nightcappe long agoe.
    PHYLO.   But *Polidor* let my son and you take heede,   10
That *Ferando* say not ere long as much to you,
And now *Alfonso* more to shew my love,
If unto *Cestus* you do send your ships,
Myselfe will fraught them with *Arabian* silkes,
Rich affrick spices *Arras* counterpoines,
Muske *Cassia*: sweet smelling *Ambergreece*,
Pearle, curroll, christall, jett, and ivorie,
To gratulate the favors of my son,
And friendly love that you have shone to him.
    VALE.   And for to honour him and this faire bride,   20

Enter the Duke of Cestus

Ile yerly send you from my fathers courte,
Chests of refind suger severally,
Ten tunne of tunis wine, sucket, sweet druges,
To celibrate and solemnise this day,
And custome free your marchants shall converse:
And interchange the profits of your land,
Sending you gold for brasse, silver for leade,
Casses of silke for packes of woll and cloth,
To binde this friendship and confirme this league.

DUKE   I am glad sir that you would be so franke,   30
Are you become the *Duke* of *Cestus* son,
And revels with my treasure in the towne,
Base villaine that thus dishonorest me.

VAL.   Sounes it is the *Duke* what shall I doo,
Dishonour thee why, knowst thou what thou saist?

DUKE   Her's no villaine: he will not know me now,
But what say you? have you forgot me too?

PHYLO.   Why sir, are you acquainted with my son?

DUKE   With thy son? no trust me if he be thine,
I pray you sir who am I?   40

AUREL.   Pardon me father: humblie on my knees,
I do intreat your grace to heare me speake.

DUKE   Peace villaine: lay handes on them,
And send them to prison straight.

Phylotus and Valeria runnes away
Then Slie speakes

SLIE   I say wele have no sending to prison.

LORD   My Lord this is but the play, theyre but in jest.

SLIE   I tell thee *Sim* wele have no sending,
To prison thats flat: why *Sim* am not I *Don Christo Vary?*
Therefore I say they shall not go to prison.

LORD   No more they shall not my Lord,   50
They be run away.

SLIE   Are they run away *Sim?* thats well,
Then gis some more drinke, and let them play againe.

LORD   Here my Lord.

Slie drinkes and then falls asleepe

DUKE   Ah trecherous boy that durst presume,
To wed thy selfe without thy fathers leave,
I sweare by fayre *Cintheas* burning rayes,

By *Merops* head and by seaven mouthed *Nile*,
Had I but knowne ere thou hadst wedded her,
Were in thy brest the worlds immortall soule,   60
This angrie sword should rip thy hatefull chest,
And hewd thee smaller then the *Libian* sandes,
Turne hence thy face: oh cruell impious boy,
Alfonso I did not thinke you would presume,
To mach your daughter with my princely house,
And nere make me acquainted with the cause.

    ALFON.   My Lord by heavens I sweare unto your grace,
I knew none other but *Valeria* your man,
Had bin the *Duke* of *Cestus* noble son,
Nor did my daughter I dare sweare for her.   70

    DUKE   That damned villaine that hath deluded me,
Whome I did send guide unto my son,
Oh that my furious force could cleave the earth,
That I might muster bands of hellish feendes,
To rack his heart and teare his impious soule.
The ceaselesse turning of celestiall orbes,
Kindles not greater flames in flitting aire,
Then passionate anguish of my raging brest.

    AUREL.   Then let my death sweet father end your griefe,
For I it is that thus have wrought your woes,   80
Then be revengd on me for here I sweare,
That they are innocent of what I did,
Oh had I charge to cut of *Hydraes* hed,
To make the toplesse *Alpes* a champion field,
To kill untamed monsters with my sword,
To travell dayly in the hottest sun,
And watch in winter when the nightes be colde,
I would with gladnesse undertake them all,
And thinke the paine but pleasure that I felt,
So that my noble father at my returne,   90
Would but forget and pardon my offence.

    PHILE.   Let me intreat your grace upon my knees,
To pardon him and let my death discharge
The heavy wrath your grace hath vowd gainst him.

    POL.   And good my Lord let us intreat your grace,
To purge your stomack of this Melancholy,
Taynt not your princely minde with griefe my Lord,
But pardon and forgive these lovers faults,
That kneeling crave your gratious favor here.

    EMEL.   Great prince of *Cestus*, let a womans wordes,   100

Intreat a pardon in your lordly brest,
Both for your princely son, and us my Lord.

DUKE   *Aurelius* stand up I pardon thee,
I see that vertue will have enemies,
And fortune will be thwarting honour still,
And you faire virgin too I am content,
To accept you for my daughter since tis don,
And see you princely usde in *Cestus* courte.

PHYLE.   Thankes good my Lord and I no longer live,
Then I obey and honour you in all.   110

ALFON.   Let me give thankes unto your royall grace,
For this great honor don to me and mine,
And if your grace will walke unto my house,
I will in humblest maner I can, show
The eternall service I doo owe your grace.

DUKE   Thanks good *Alfonso*: but I came alone,
And not as did beseeme the *Cestian Duke*,
Nor would I have it knowne within the towne,
That I was here and thus without my traine,
But as I came alone so will I go,   120
And leave my son to solemnise his feast,
And ere't belong Ile come againe to you,
And do him honour as beseemes the son
Of mightie *Jerobell* the *Cestian Duke*,
Till when Ile leave you, Farwell *Aurelius*.

AUREL.   Not yet my Lord, Ile bring you to your ship.

Exeunt Omnes
Slie sleepes

LORD   Whose within there? come hither sirs my Lords
Asleepe againe: go take him easily up,
And put him in his one apparell againe,
And lay him in the place where we did find him,   130
Just underneath the alehouse side below,
But see you wake him not in any case.

BOY   It shall be don my Lord come helpe to beare him
    hence.   133
                                                          [*Exit*

[Scene xvii]

Enter Ferando, Aurelius and Polidor
and his boy and Valeria and Sander

FERAN.   Come gentlemen now that suppers donne,
How shall we spend the time till we go to bed?

AUREL. Faith if you will in triall of our wives,
Who will come sownest at their husbands call.

POL. Nay then *Ferando* he must needes sit out,
For he may call I thinke till he be weary,
Before his wife will come before she list.

FERAN. Tis well for you that have such gentle wives,
Yet in this triall will I not sit out,
It may be *Kate* will come as soone as yours.   10

AUREL. My wife comes soonest for a hundred pound.

POL. I take it: Ile lay as much to youres,
That my wife comes as soone as I do send.

AUREL. How now *Ferando* you dare not lay belike.

FERAN. Why true I dare not lay indeede;
But how, so little mony on so sure a thing,
A hundred pound: why I have layd as much
Upon my dogge, in running at a Deere,
She shall not come so farre for such a trifle,
But will you lay five hundred markes with me,   20
And whose wife soonest comes when he doth call,
And shewes her selfe most loving unto him,
Let him injoye the wager I have laid,
Now what say you? dare you adventure thus?

POL. I weare it a thousand pounds I durst presume
On my wives love: and I will lay with thee.

Enter Alfonso

ALFON. How now sons what in conference so hard,
May I without offence, know where abouts.

AUREL. Faith father a waighty cause about our wives,
Five hundred markes already we have layd,   30
And he whose wife doth shew most love to him,
He must injoie the wager to himselfe.

ALFON. Why then *Ferando* he is sure to lose,
I promise thee son thy wife will hardly come,
And therefore I would not wish thee lay so much.

FERAN. Tush father were it ten times more,
I durst adventure on my lovely *Kate*,
But if I lose Ile pay, and so shall you.

AUREL. Upon mine honour if I loose Ile pay.

POL. And so will I upon my faith I vow.   40

FERAN. Then sit we downe and let us send for them.

ALFON. I promise thee *Ferando* I am afraid thou wilt lose.

AUREL. Ile send for my wife first, *Valeria*
Go bid your Mistris come to me.

VAL.   I will my Lord.

Exit Valeria

AUREL.   Now for my hundred pound.
Would any lay ten hundred more with me,
I know I should obtaine it by her love.

FERAN.   I pray God you have not laid too much already.

AUREL.   Trust me *Ferando* I am sure you have,   50
For you I dare presume have lost it all.

Enter Valeria againe

Now sirra what saies your mistris?

VAL.   She is something busie but shele come anon.

FERAN.   Why so, did not I tell you this before,
She is busie and cannot come.

AUREL.   I pray God your wife send you so good an answere
She may be busie yet she sayes shele come.

FERAN.   Well well: *Polidor* send you for your wife.

POL.   Agreed *Boy* desire your mistris to come hither.

BOY   I will sir.   60
                                        [*Ex. Boy*

FERAN.   I so so he desiers her to come.

ALFON.   *Polidor* I dare presume for thee,
I thinke thy wife will not deny to come.
And I do marvell much *Aurelius*,
That your wife came not when you sent for her.

Enter the Boy againe

POL.   Now wheres your Mistris?

BOY   She bad me tell you that she will not come,
And you have any businesse, you must come to her.

FERAN.   Oh monstrous intollerable presumption,
Worse then a blasing starre, or snow at midsommer,   70
Earthquakes or any thing unseasonable,
She will not come: but he must come to her.

POL.   Well sir I pray you lets here what
Answere your wife will make.

FERAN.   Sirra, command your Mistris to come
To me presentlie.   [*Exit Sander*

AUREL.   I thinke my wife for all she did not come,
Will prove most kinde for now I have no feare,
For I am sure *Ferandos* wife, she will not come.

FERAN.   The mores the pittie: then I must lose.

Enter Kate and Sander

But I have won for see where *Kate* doth come.   80
   KATE   Sweet husband did you send for me?
   FERAN.   I did my love I sent for thee to come,
Come hither Kate, whats that upon thy head.
   KATE   Nothing husband but my cap I thinke.
   FERAN.   Pull it of and treade it under thy feete,
Tis foolish I will not have thee weare it.

She takes of her cap and treads on it

   POL.   Oh wonderfull metamorphosis.
   AUREL.   This is a wonder: almost past beleefe.
   FERAN.   This is a token of her true love to me,
And yet Ile trie her further you shall see,   90
Come hither *Kate* where are thy sisters.
   KATE   They be sitting in the bridall chamber.
   FERAN.   Fetch them hither and if they will not come,
Bring them perforce and make them come with thee.
   KATE   I will.
   ALFON.   I promise thee *Ferando* I would have sworne,
Thy wife would nere have donne so much for thee.
   FERAN.   But you shall see she will do more then this,
For see where she brings her sisters forth by force.   99

[Scene xviii]

Enter Kate thrusting Phylema and Emelia before her,
and makes them come unto their husbands call

   KATE   See husband I have brought them both.
   FERAN.   Tis well don *Kate*.
   EME.   I sure and like a loving peece, your worthy
To have great praise for this attempt.
   PHYLE.   I for making a foole of her selfe and us.
   AUREL.   Beshrew thee *Phylema*, thou hast
Lost me a hundred pound to night.
For I did lay that thou wouldst first have come.
   POL.   But thou *Emelia* hast lost me a great deale more.
   EME.   You might have kept it better then,   10
Who bad you lay?
   FERAN.   Now lovely *Kate* before there husbands here,
I prethe tell unto these hedstrong women,
What dutie wives doo owe unto their husbands.
   KATE   Then you that live thus by your pompered wills,

Now list to me and marke what I shall say,
Theternall power that with his only breath,
Shall cause this end and this beginning frame,
Not in time, nor before time, but with time, confusd,
For all the course of yeares, of ages, moneths,   20
Of seasons temperate, of dayes and houres,
Are tund and stopt, by measure of his hand,
The first world was, a forme, without a forme,
A heape confusd a mixture all deformd,
A gulfe of gulfes, a body bodiles,
Where all the elements were orderles,
Before the great commander of the world,
The King of Kings the glorious God of heaven,
Who in six daies did frame his heavenly worke,
And made all things to stand in perfit course.   30
Then to his image he did make a man,
Olde *Adam* and from his side asleepe,
A rib was taken, of which the Lord did make,
The woe of man so termd by *Adam* then,
Woman for that, by her came sinne to us,
And for her sin was *Adam* doomd to die,
As *Sara* to her husband, so should we,
Obey them, love them, keepe, and nourish them,
If they by any meanes doo want our helpes,
Laying our handes under theire feete to tread,   40
If that by that we, might procure there ease,
And for a president Ile first begin,
And lay my hand under my husbands feete.

She laies her hand under her husbands feete

    FERAN.   Inough sweet, the wager thou hast won,
And they I am sure cannot denie the same.
    ALFON.   I *Ferando* the wager thou hast won,
And for to shew thee how I am pleasd in this,
A hundred poundes I freely give thee more,
Another dowry for another daughter,
For she is not the same she was before.   50
    FERAN.   Thankes sweet father, gentlemen godnight
For *Kate* and I will leave you for tonight,
Tis *Kate* and I am wed, and you are sped.
And so farwell for we will to our beds.

Exit Ferando and Kate and Sander

ALFON.   Now *Aurelius* what say you to this?
AUREL.   Beleeve me father I rejoice to see,
Ferando and his wife so lovingly agree.

Exit Aurelius and Phylema and Alfonso and Valeria

EME.   How now *Polidor* in a dump, what sayst thou man?
POL.   I say thou art a shrew.
EME.   Thats better then a sheepe.   60
POL.   Well since tis don let it go, come lets in.

Exit Polidor and Emelia

[Scene xix]

Then enter two bearing of Slie in his
Owne apparrell againe, and leaves him
Where they found him, and then goes out

Then enter the Tapster

TAPSTER   Now that the darkesome night is overpast,
And dawning day apeares in cristall sky,
Now must I hast abroad: but soft whose this?
What *Slie* oh wondrous hath he laine here allnight,
Ile wake him, I thinke he's starved by this,
But that his belly was so stuft with ale,
What how *Slie*, Awake for shame.
SLIE   *Sim* gis some more wine: whats all the
Plaiers gon: am not I a Lord?
TAPSTER   A Lord with a murrin: come art thou dronken still?
SLIE   Whose this? *Tapster*, oh Lord sirra, I have had   10
The bravest dreame to night, that ever thou
Hardest in all thy life.
TAPSTER   I marry but you had best get you home,
For your wife will course you for dreming here to night,
SLIE   Will she? I know now how to tame a shrew,
I dreamt upon it all this night till now,
And thou hast wakt me out of the best dreame
That ever I had in my life, but Ile to my
Wife presently and tame her too
And if she anger me.   20
TAPSTER   Nay tarry *Slie* for Ile go home with thee,
And heare the rest that thou hast dreamt to night.   22

Exeunt Omnes

FINIS

II. Analogue

From S. GOULART: THRÉSOR D'HISTOIRES ADMIRABLES ET MEMORABLES
translated by Edward Grimeston (1607)
pp. 587–9

Vanity of the World as represented in State

Philip called the good Duke of Bourgondy, in the memory of our ancestors, being at Bruxells with his Court and walking one night after supper through the streets, accompanied with some of his favorits: he found lying upon the stones a certaine Artisan that was very dronke, and that slept soundly. It pleased the Prince in this Artisan to make triall of the vanity of our life, whereof he had before discoursed with his familiar friends. Hee therfore caused this sleeper to be taken up and carried into his Pallace: hee commands him to bee layed in one of the richest beds, a riche Night-cap to bee given him, his foule shirt to bee taken off, and to have an other put on him of fine Holland: when as this Dronkard had digested his Wine, and began to awake: behold there comes about his bed, Pages and Groomes of the Dukes Chamber, who draw the Curteines, make many courtesies, and being bare-headed, aske him if it please him to rise, and what apparell it would please him to put on that day. They bring him rich apparrell. The new Monsieur amazed at such curtesie, and doubting whether he dreampt or waked, suffered himselfe to be drest, and led out of the Chamber. There came Noblemen which saluted him with all honour, and conduct him to the Masse, where with great ceremonie they give him the Booke of the Gospell, and the Pixe to Kisse, as they did usually unto the Duke: from the Masse they bring him backe unto the Pallace: hee washes his hands, and sittes downe at the Table well furnished. After dinner, the great Chamberlaine commandes Cardes, to be brought with a great summe of money. This Duke in Imagination playes with the chiefe of the Court. Then they carrie him to walke in the Gardein, and to hunt the Hare and to Hawke. They bring him back unto the Pallace, where hee sups in state. Candles beeing light, the Musitions

begin to play, and the Tables taken away, the Gentlemen and
Gentle-women fell to dancing, then they played a pleasant Comedie,
after which followed a Banket, whereas they had presently store of
Ipocras and precious Wine, with all sorts of confitures, to this Prince
of the new Impression, so as he was drunke, & fell soundlie a sleepe.
Here-upon the Duke commanded that hee should bee disrobed of all
his riche attire. Hee was put into his olde ragges and carried into
the same place, where he had been found the night before, where
hee spent that night. Being awake in the morning, hee began to
remember what had happened before, hee knewe not whether it
were true in deede, or a dreame that had troubled his braine. But in
the end, after many discourses, hee concluds that all was but a
dreame that had happened unto him, and so entertained his wife,
his Children and his neighbors, without any other apprehension.
This Historie put mee in minde of that which Seneca sayth in the
ende of his 59 letter to Lucilius. No man, saies he, can rejoyce and
content himselfe, if he be not nobly minded, just and temperate.
What then? Are the wicked deprived of all joye? they are glad as
the Lions that have found their prey. Being full of wine and luxury,
having spent the night in gourmandise, when as pleasures poored
into this vessell of the bodie (beeing to little to containe so much)
beganne to foame out, these miserable wretches crie with him of
whome Virgill speakes,

> Thou knowest, how in the midest of pastimes false & vaine,
> We cast and past our latest night of paine.

The dissolute spend the night, yea the last night in false joyes. O
man, this stately usage of the above named Artisan, is like unto a
dreame that passeth. And his goodly day, and the years of a wicked
life differ nothing but in more and lesse. He slept foure and twenty
houres, other wicked men some-times foure and twenty thousands
of houres. It is a little or a great dreame: and nothing more.

III. Source

SUPPOSES
by George Gascoigne
[1566]

Printed in *The Posies of George Gascoigne Esquire*. Corrected, perfected, and augmented by the Author. 1575. *Tam Marti quàm Mercurio*. Printed at London for Richard Smith, and are to be solde at the Northweast doore of Paules Church.

The names of the Actors

BALIA, the Nurse.
POLYNESTA, the yong woman.
CLEANDER, the Doctor, suter to *Polynesta*.
PASYPHILO, the Parasite.
CARION, the Doctors man.
DULYPO, fayned servant and lover of *Polynesta*.
EROSTRATO, fayned master and suter to *Polynesta*.
DALIO and CRAPYNO, servantes to fayned *Erostrato*.
SCENAESE, a gentleman stranger.
PAQUETTO and PETRUCIO, his servantes.
DAMON, father to *Polinesta*.
NEVOLA, and two other his servants.
PSYTERIA, an old hag in his house.
PHYLOGANO, a *Scycilian* gentleman, father to *Erostrato*.
LYTIO, his servant.
FERRARESE, an Inkeeper of *Ferrara*.

The Comedie presented as it were in *Ferrara*

THE PROLOGUE OR ARGUMENT

I suppose you are assembled here, supposing to reape the fruite of my travayles: and to be playne, I meane presently to presente you with a Comedie called Supposes: the verye name wherof may perad[v]enture drive into every of your heades a sundry Suppose, to suppose, the meaning of our supposes. Some percase will suppose we meane to occupie your eares with sophisticall handling of subtill Suppositions. Some other wil suppose we go about to discipher unto you

some queint conceiptes, which hitherto have bene onely supposed as it were in
shadowes: and some I see smyling as though they supposed we would trouble
you with the vaine suppose of some wanton Suppose. But understand, this our
Suppose is nothing else but a mystaking or imagination of one thing for an
other. For you shall see the master supposed for the servant, the servant for
the master: the freeman for a slave, and the bondslave for a freeman: the
stranger for a well knowen friend, and the familiar for a stranger. But what?
I suppose that even already you suppose me very fonde, that have so simply dis-
closed unto you the subtilties of these our Supposes: where otherwise in deede
I suppose you shoulde have hearde almoste the laste of our Supposes, before you
coulde have supposed anye of them arighte. Let this then suffise.

Actus primus.   Scena 1.

BALIA, the Nurse.   POLYNESTA, the yong woman.

Here is no body, come foorth *Polynesta*, let us looke about, to be
sure least any man heare our talke: for I thinke within the house
the tables, the plankes, the beds, the portals, yea and the cupbords
them selves have eares.

POL.   You might as well have sayde, the windowes and the
doores: do you not see howe they harken?

BA.   Well you jest faire, but I would advise you take heede, I
have bidden you a thousande times beware: you will be spied one
day talking with *Dulippo*.

PO.   And why should I not talke with *Dulippo*, as well as with
any other, I pray you?

BA.   I have given you a wherfore for this why many times: but
go too, followe your owne advise till you overwhelme us all with
soden mishappe.

PO.   A great mishappe I promise you: marie Gods blessing on
their heart that sette suche a brooche on my cappe.

BA.   Well, looke well about you: a man would thinke it were
inough for you secretly to rejoyce, that by my helpe you have passed
so many pleasant nightes togither: and yet by my trouth I do it
more than halfe agaynst my will, for I would rather you had setled
your fansie in some noble familie yea and it is no small griefe unto
me, that (rejecting the suites of so many nobles and gentlemen) you
have chosen for your darling a poore servaunt of your fathers, by
whome shame and infamie is the best dower you can looke for to
attayne.

PO.   And I pray you whome may I thanke but gentle nourse?
that continually praysing him, what for his personage, his curtesie,
and above all, the extreme passions of his minde, in fine you would

never cease till I accepted him, delighted in him, and at length desired him with no lesse affection, than he earst desired me.

BA. I can not denie, but at the beginning I did recommende him unto you (as in deede I may say that for my selfe I have a pitiful heart) seeing the depth of his unbridled affection, and that continually he never ceassed to fill mine eares with lamentable complaynts.

PO. Nay rather that he filled your pursse with bribes and rewards, Nourse.

BA. Well you may judge of Nourse as you liste. In deede I have thought it alwayes a deede of charitie to helpe the miserable yong men, whose tender youth consumeth with the furious flames of love. But be you sure if I had thought you would have passed to the termes you nowe stand in, pitie nor pencion, peny nor pater noster shoulde ever have made Nurse once to open hir mouth in the cause.

PO. No of honestie, I pray you, who first brought him into my chamber? who first taught him the way to my bed but you? fie Nourse fie, never speake of it for shame, you will make me tell a wise tale anone.

BA. And have I these thanks for my good wil? why then I see wel I shall be counted the cause of all mishappe.

PO. Nay rather the author of my good happe (gentle Nourse) for I would thou knewest I love not *Dulipo*, nor any of so meane estate, but have bestowed my love more worthily than thou deemest: but I will say no more at this time.

BA. Then I am glad you have changed your minde yet.

PO. Nay I neither have changed, nor will change it.

BA. Then I understande you not, how sayde you?

PO. Mary I say that I love not *Dulipo*, nor any suche as he, and yet I neither have changed nor wil change my minde.

BA. I can not tell, you love to lye with *Dulipo* very well: this geare is Greeke to me: either it hangs not well togither, or I am very dull of understanding: speake plaine I pray you.

PO. I can speake no plainer, I have sworne to the contrary.

BA. Howe? make you so deintie to tell it Nourse, least she shoulde reveale it? you have trusted me as farre as may be, (I may shewe to you) in things that touche your honor if they were knowne: and make you strange to tell me this? I am sure it is but a trifle in comparison of those things wherof heretofore you have made me privie.

PO. Well, it is of greater importance than you thinke Nourse: yet would I tell it you under condition and promise that you shall not tell it agayne, nor give any signe or token to be suspected that you know it.

BA.   I promise you of my honestie, say on.

PO.   Well heare you me then: this yong man whome you have always taken for *Dulipo*, is a noble borne *Sicilian*, his right name *Erostrato*, sonne to *Philogano*, one of the worthiest men in that countrey.

BA.   How *Erostrato*? is it not our neighbour, whiche?

PO.   Holde thy talking nourse, and harken to me, that I may explane the whole case unto thee. The man whome to this day you have supposed to be *Dulipo*, is (as I say) *Erostrato*,[1] a gentleman that came from *Sicilia* to studie in this Citie, & even at his first arrivall met me in the street, fel enamored of me, & of suche vehement force were the passions he suffred, that immediatly he cast aside both long gowne and bookes, & determined on me only to apply his study. And to the end he might the more commodiously bothe see me and talke with me, he exchanged both name, habite, clothes and credite with his servant *Dulipo* (whom only he brought with him out of *Sicilia*) and so with the turning of a hand, of *Erostrato* a gentleman, he became *Dulipo* a serving man, and soone after sought service of my father, and obteyned it.

BA.   Are you sure of this?

PO.   Yea out of doubt: on the other side *Dulippo* tooke uppon him the name of *Erostrato* his maister, the habite, the credite, bookes, and all things needefull to a studente, and in shorte space profited very muche, and is nowe esteemed as you see.

BA.   Are there no other *Sicylians* heere: nor none that passe this way, which may discover them?

PO.   Very fewe that passe this way, and fewe or none that tarrie heere any time.

BA.   This hath been a straunge adventure: but I pray you howe hang these thinges togither? that the studente whome you say to be the servant, and not the maister, is become an earnest suter to you, and requireth you of your father in mariage?

PO.   That is a pollicie devised betweene them, to put Doctor Dotipole out of conceite: the olde dotarde, he that so instantly dothe lye upon my father for me. But looke where he comes, as God helpe me it is he, out upon him, what a luskie yonker is this? yet I had rather be a Nunne a thousande times, than be combred with suche a Coystrell.

BA.   Daughter you have reason, but let us go in before he come any neerer.

[*Polynesta goeth in, and Balya stayeth a little whyle after, speaking a worde or two to the doctor, and then departeth*

---

[1] In margin: The first suppose & grownd of all the suposes.

Scena. 2.

CLEANDER, Doctor.   PASIPHILO, Parasite.   BALYA, Nourse.

Were these dames heere, or did mine eyes dazzle?

PA.   Nay syr heere were *Polynesta* and hir no[u]rse.

CLE.   Was my *Polynesta* heere? alas I knewe hir not.

BA.   He muste have better eyesight that shoulde marry your *Polynesta*, or else he may chaunce to oversee the best poynt in his tables sometimes.

PA.   Syr it is no marvell, the ayre is very mistie too day: I my selfe knew hir better by hir apparell than by hir face.

CLE.   In good fayth and I thanke God I have mine eye sighte good and perfit, little worse than when I was but twentie yeres olde.

PA.   How can it be otherwise? you are but yong.

CLE.   I am fiftie yeres olde.

PA.   He telles ten lesse than he is.

CLE.   What sayst thou of ten lesse?

PA.   I say I woulde have thoughte you tenne lesse, you looke like one of six and thirtie, or seven and thirtie at the moste.

CLE.   I am no lesse than I tell.

PA.   You are like inough too live fiftie more: shewe me your hande.

CLE.   Why, is *Pasiphilo* a Chiromancer?

PA.   What is not *Pasiphilo*? I pray you shewe mee it a little.

CLE.   Here it is.

PA.   O how straight and infracte is this line of life? you will live to the yeeres of *Melchisedech*.

CLE.   Thou wouldest say, *Methusalem*.

PA.   Why is it not all one?

CLE.   I perceive you are no very good Bibler, *Pasiphilo*.

PA.   Yes sir an excellent good Bibbeler, specially in a bottle: Oh what a mounte of Venus here is? but this lighte serveth not very well, I will beholde it an other day, when the ayre is clearer, and tell you somewhat, peradventure to your contentation.

CLE.   You shal do me great pleasure: but tell me, I pray thee *Pasiphilo*, whome doste thou thinke *Polynesta* liketh better, *Erostrato* or me?

PA.   Why? you out of doubt: She is a gentlewoman of a noble minde, and maketh greater accompte of the reputation she shall have in marrying your worship, than that poore scholer, whose birthe and parentage God knoweth, and very fewe else.

CLE.   Yet he taketh it upon him bravely in this countrey.

PA.   Yea, where no man knoweth the contrarie: but let him

brave it, bost his birth, and do what he can, the vertue and knowledge that is within this body of yours, is worth more than all the
countrey he came from.

CLE. It becommeth not a man to praise him selfe: but in deede
I may say, (and say truely,) that my knowledge hath stoode me in
better steade at a pinche, than coulde all the goodes in the worlde.
I came out of *Otranto* when the Turkes wonne it, and first I came to
Padua, after hither, where by reading, counsailing, and pleading,
within twentie yeares I have gathered and gayned as good as ten
thousande Ducats.

PA. Yea mary, this is the righte knowledge: Philosophie,
Poetrie, Logike, a[n]d all the rest, are but pickling sciences in
comparison to this.

CLE. But pyckling in deede, whereof we have a verse:

The trade of Lawe doth fill the boystrous bagges,
They swimme in silke, when others royst in ragges.

PA. O excellent verse, who made it? *Virgil?*

CLE. *Virgil?* tushe, it is written in one of our glosses.

PA. Sure who soever wrote it, the morall is excellent, and worthy
to be written in letters of golde. But to the purpose: I thinke you
shall never recover the wealth that you loste at *Otranto.*

CLE. I thinke I have dubled it, or rather made it foure times as
muche: but in deed, I lost mine only sonne there, a childe of five
yeres olde.[1]

PA. O great pitie.

CLE. Yea, I had rather have lost al the goods in the world.

PA. Alas, alas: by God and grafts of suche a stocke are very
gayson in these dayes.

CLE. I know not whether he were slayne, or the Turks toke him
and kept him as a bond slave.

PA. Alas, I could weepe for compassion, but there is no remedy
but patience, you shall get many by this yong damsell with the
grace of God.

CLE. Yea, if I get hir.

PA. Get her? why doubt you of that?

CLE. Why? hir father holds me off with delayes, so that I must
needes doubt.

PA. Content your selfe sir, he is a wise man, and desirous to
place his Daughter well: he will not be too rashe in hys determination, he will thinke well of the matter: and lette him thinke, for the

---

[1] In margin: An other supose.

longer he thinketh, the more good of you shall he thinke: whose welth? whose vertue? whose skill? or whose estimation can he compare to yours in this Citie?

CLE. And hast thou not tolde him that I would make his Daughter a dower of two thousand Ducates?

PA. Why, even now, I came but from thence since.

CLE. What said he?

PA. Nothing, but that *Erostrato* had profered the like.

CLE. *Erostrato*? how can he make any dower, and his father yet alive?

PA. Thinke you I did not tell him so? yes I warrant you, I forgot nothing that may furder your cause: & doubte you not, *Erostrato* shal never have hir unlesse it be in a dreame.

CLE. Well gentle *Pasiphilo*, go thy wayes and tell *Damon* I require nothing but his daughter: I wil none of his goods: I shal enrich hir of mine owne: & if this dower of two thousand Ducates seem not sufficient, I wil make it five hundreth more, yea a thousand, or what so ever he wil demand rather then faile: go to *Pasiphilo*, shew thy selfe frendly in working this feate for me: spare for no cost, since I have gone thus farre, I wilbe loth to be out bidden. Go.

PA. Where shall I come to you againe?

CLE. At my house.

PA. When?

CLE. When thou wilte.

PA. Shall I come at dinner time?

CLE. I would byd thee to dinner, but it is a Saincts even which I have ever fasted.

PA. Faste till thou famishe.

CLE. Harke.

PA. He speaketh of a dead mans faste.

CLE. Thou hearest me not.

PA. Nor thou understandest me not.

CLE. I dare say thou art angrie I byd the not to dinner: but come if thou wilte, thou shalt take such as thou findest.

PA. What? think you I know not where to dine?

CLE. Yes *Pasiphilo* thou art not to seeke.

PA. No be you sure, there are enowe will pray me.

CLE. That I knowe well enough *Pasiphilo*, but thou canst not be better welcome in any place than to me, I will tarrie for thee.

PA. Well, since you will needes, I will come.

CLE. Dispatche then, and bring no newes but good.

PA. Better than my rewarde by the rood.

[Cleander exit, Pasiphilo restat.

Scena. iii.

PASIPHILO. DULIPO.

[PAS.]   O miserable covetous wretche, he findeth an excuse by
S. Nicolas fast, bicause I should not dine with him, as though I
should dine at his owne dishe: he maketh goodly feasts I promise
you, it is no wonder though hee thinke me bounde unto him for my
fare: for over and besides that his provision is as skant as may be,
yet there is great difference betweene his diet and mine. I never so
much as sippe of the wine that he tasteth, I feede at the bordes ende
with browne bread: Marie I reach always to his owne dishe, for
there are no more but that only on the table. Yet he thinks that for
one such dinner I am bound to do him al the service that I can,
and thinks me sufficiently rewarded for all my travell, with one suche
festivall promotion. And yet peradventure some men thinke I have
great gaines under him: but I may say and sweare, that this dosen
yeere I have not gayned so muche in value as the points at my hose
(whiche are but three with codpeece poynt and al): he thinkes that
I may feede upon his favour and faire wordes: but if I could not
otherwise provide for one, *Pasiphilo* were in a wyse case. *Pasiphilo*
hath mo pastures to passe in than one, I warrant you: I am of housholde with this scholer *Erostrato*, (his rivale) as well as with *Domine
Cleander*: nowe with the one, and then with the other, according as I
see their Caters provide good cheere at the market: and I finde the
meanes so to handle the matter, that I am welcome too bothe. If
the one see me talke with the other, I make him beleeve it is to
harken newes in the furtherance of his cause: and thus I become a
broker on bothe sides. Well, lette them bothe apply the matter as
well as they can, for in deede I will travell for none of them bothe:
yet will I seeme to worke wonders on eche hande. But is not this
one of *Damons* servants that commeth foorth? it is: of him I shall
understand where his master is. Whither goeth this jolly gallant?

DU.   I come to seeke some body that may accompany my Master
at dinner, he is alone, and woulde fayne have good company.

PA.   Seeke no further, you coulde never have found one better
than me.

DU.   I have no commission to bring so many.

PA.   How many? I will come alone.

DU.   How canst thou come alone, that hast continually a legion
of ravening wolves within thee?

PA.   Thou doest (as servants commonly doe) hate al that love to
visite their maisters.

DU.   And why?

PA. Bicause they have too many teeth as you thinke.

DU. Nay bicause they have to many tongues.

PA. Tongues? I pray you what did my tongue ever hurt you?

DU. I speake but merily with you *Pasiphilo,* goe in, my maister is ready to dine.

PA. What? dineth he so earely?

DU. He that riseth early, dineth early.

PA. I would I were his man, maister doctor never dineth till noone, and how dilicately then God knoweth. I wil be bolde to goe in, for I count my selfe bidden.

DU. You were best so.   [*Pasiphilo intrat. Dul. restat.*

Hard hap had I when I first began this unfortunate enterprise: for I supposed the readiest medicine to my miserable affects had bene to change name, clothes, & credite with my servant, & to place my selfe in *Damons* service: thinking that as shevering colde by glowing fire, thurst by drinke, hunger by pleasant repasts, and a thousande suche like passions finde remedie by their contraries, so my restlesse desire might have founde quiet by continuall contemplation. But alas, I find that only love is unsatiable: for as the flie playeth with the flame till at last she is cause of hir owne decay, so the lover that thinketh with kissing and colling to content his unbrideled apetite, is commonly seene the only cause of his owne consumption. Two yeeres are nowe past since (under the colour of *Damons* service) I have bene a sworne servant to *Cupid*: of whom I have received as much favour & grace as ever man founde in his service. I have free libertie at al times to behold my desired, to talke with hir, to embrace hir, yea (be it spoken in secrete) to lie with hir. I reape the fruites of my desire: yet as my joyes abounde, even so my paines encrease. I fare like the covetous man, that having all the world at will, is never yet content: the more I have, the more I desire. Alas, what wretched estate have I brought my selfe unto, if in the ende of all my farre fetches, she be given by hir father to this olde doting doctor, this buzard, this bribing villaine, that by so many meanes seeketh to obtain hir at hir fathers hands? I know she loveth me best of all others, but what may that prevaile when perforce she shalbe constrained to marie another? Alas, the pleasant tast of my sugred joyes doth yet remaine so perfect in my remembrance, that the least soppe of sorow seemeth more soure than gall in my mouth. If I had never knowen delight, with better contentation might I have passed these dreadful dolours. And if this olde *Mumpsimus* (whom the pockes consume) should win hir, then may I say, farewell the pleasant talke, the kind embracings, yea farewel the sight of my *Polynesta*: for he like a jelouse wretch will pen hir up, that I thinke the birdes of the aire shall not winne the sighte of hir. I hoped to have caste a blocke in his waie, by the meanes that my servaunt (who is supposed to be *Erostrato*, and with my habite and credite is wel esteemed) should proffer himself a suter, at the least to countervaile the doctors proffers. But my maister knowing the wealth of the one, and doubting the state of the other, is determined to be fed no longer with faire wordes, but to accept the doctor, (whom he right well knoweth) for his sonne in law. Wel, my servant promised me yesterday to devise yet againe some newe conspiracie to drive maister doctor out of conceite, and to laye a snare that the foxe himselfe might be caughte in: what it is, I knowe not, nor I saw him not since he went about it: I will goe see if he be within, that at least if he helpe me not, he maye yet prolong my life for this once. But here commeth his lackie: ho Jack pack, where is *Erostrato?*

> [*Here must Crapine be comming in with a basket and a sticke in his hand.*]

Scena. iiii.

CRAPINO the Lackie.   DULIPO.

Erostrato? mary he is in his skinne.

DU.   Ah hooreson boy, I say, howe shall I finde *Erostrato?*

CRA.   Finde him? howe meane you, by the weeke or by the yeere?

DU.   You cracke halter, if I catche you by the eares, I shall make you answere me directly.

CRA.   In deede?

DU.   Tarry me a little.

CRA.   In faith sir I have no leisure.

DU.   Shall we trie who can runne fastest?

CRA.   Your legges be longer than mine, you should have given me the advauntage.

DU.   Go to, tell me where is *Erostrato?*

CRA.   I left him in the streete, where he gave me this Casket, (this basket I would have sayde) and bad me beare it to *Dalio*, and returne to him at the Dukes Palace.

DU.   If thou see him, tell him I must needes speake with him immediatly: or abide awhyle, I will go seeke him my selfe, rather than be suspected by going to his house.

> [*Crapino departeth, and Dulipo also: after Dulipo commeth in agayne seeking Erostrato.*]

Finis Actus. 1.

Actus. ii. Scena. i.

DULIPO. EROSTRATO.

I thinke if I had as many eyes as *Argus*, I coulde not have sought a man more narrowly in every streete and every by lane, there are not many Gentlemen, scholers, nor Marchauntes in the Citie of *Ferrara*, but I have mette with them, excepte him: peradventure hee is come home an other way: but looke where he commeth at the last.

ERO. In good time have I spied my good maister.

DU. For the love of God call me *Dulipo* (not master,) maintayne the credite that thou haste hitherto kepte, and let me alone.

ERO. Yet sir let me sometimes do my duetie unto you, especially where no body heareth.

DU. Yea, but so long the Parat useth to crie knappe in sporte, that at the last she calleth hir maister knave in earnest: so long you will use to call me master, that at the last we shall be heard. What newes?

ERO. Good.

DU. In deede?

ERO. Yea excellent, we have as good as won the wager.

DU. Oh, how happie were I if this were true?

ERO. Heare you me, yesternight in the evening I walked out, and founde *Pasiphilo*, and with small entreating I had him home to supper, where by suche meanes as I used, he became my great friend, and tolde me the whole order of our adversaries determination: yea and what *Damon* doth intende to do also, and hath promised me that from time to time, what he can espie he will bring me word of it.

DU. I can not tel whether you know him or no, he is not to trust unto, a very flattering and a lying knave.

ERO. I know him very well, he can not deceive me: and this that he hath told me I know must needes be true.

DU. And what was it in effect?

ERO. That *Damon* had purposed to give his daughter in mariage to this doctor, upon the dower that he hath profered.[1]

DU. Are these your good newes? your excellent newes?

ERO. Stay a whyle, you will understande me before you heare me.

DU. Well, say on.

ERO. I answered to that, I was ready to make hir the lyke dower.

DU. Well sayde.

ERO. Abide, you heare not the worst yet.

[1] In margin: Another supose.

DU.   O God, is there any worsse behinde?

ERO.   Worsse? why what assurance coulde you suppose that I might make without some speciall consent from *Philogano* my father?

DU.   Nay you can tell, you are better scholer than I.

ERO.   In deede you have lost your time: for the books that you tosse now a dayes, treate of smal science.

DU.   Leave thy jesting, and proceede.

ERO.   I sayd further, that I receyved letters lately from my father, whereby I understoode that he woulde be heere very shortly to performe all that I had profered: therefore I required him to request *Damon* on my behalf, that he would stay his promise to the doctor for a fourtnight or more.

DU.   This is somewhat yet, for by this meanes I shal be sure to linger and live in hope one fourtnight longer: but, at the fourth-nights ende when *Philogano* commeth not, how shall I then do? yea and though he came, howe may I any way hope of his consent, when he shall see, that to follow this amorous enterprise, I have set aside all studie, all remembraunce of my duetie, and all dread of shame. Alas, alas, I may go hang my selfe.

ERO.   Comforte your selfe man, and trust in me: there is a salve for every sore, and doubt you not, to this mischeefe we shall finde a remedie.

DU.   O friend revive me, that hitherto since I first attempted this matter have bene continually dying.

ERO.   Well harken a while then: this morning I tooke my horse and rode into the fieldes to solace my self, and as I passed the foorde beyonde *S. Anthonies* gate, I met at the foote of the hill a gentleman riding with two or three men: and as me thought by his habite and his lookes, he should be none of the wisest. He saluted me, and I him: I asked him from whence he came, and whither he would? he answered that he had come from *Venice*, then from *Padua*, nowe was going to *Ferrara*, and so to his countrey, whiche is *Scienna*: As soone as I knewe him to be a *Scenese*, sodenly lifting up mine eyes, (as it were with an admiration) I sayd unto him, are you a *Scenese*, and come to *Farrara*? why not, sayde he: quoth I, (halfe and more with a trembling voyce) know you the daunger that should ensue if you be knowne in *Ferrara* to be a *Scenese*? he more than halfe amased, desired me earnestly to tell him what I ment.

DU.   I understande not wherto this tendeth.

ERO.   I beleeve you: but harken to me.

DU.   Go too then.

ERO.   I answered him in this sorte: Gentleman, bycause I have heretofore founde very curteous entertaynement in your countrey, (beeing a student there,) I accompt my self as it were bounde to a *Scenese*: and therefore if I knewe of any mishappe towards any of that countrey, God forbid but I should disclose it: and I marvell that you knewe not of the injurie that your countreymen offered this other day to the Embassadours of Counte *Hercules*.

DU. What tales he telleth me: what appertayne these to me?

ERO. If you will harken a whyle, you shall finde them no tales, but that they appertayne to you more than you thinke for.

DU. Foorth.

ERO. I tolde him further, these Ambassadoures of Counte *Hercules* had dyvers Mules, Waggons, and Charettes, laden with divers costly jewels, gorgeous furniture, & other things which they caried as presents, (passing that way) to the king of *Naples*: the which were not only stayd in *Sciene* by the officers whom you cal Customers, but serched, ransacked, tossed & turned, & in the end exacted for tribute, as if they had bene the goods of a meane marchaunt.

DU. Whither the divell wil he? is it possible that this geare appertaine any thing to my cause? I finde neither head nor foote in it.

ERO. O how impacient you are: I pray you stay a while.

DU. Go to yet a while then.

ERO. I proceeded, that upon these causes the Duke sent his Chauncelor to declare the case unto the Senate there, of whome he had the moste uncurteous answere that ever was heard: wherupon he was so enraged with all of that countrey, that for revenge he had sworne to spoyle as many of them as ever should come to *Ferara*, and to sende them home in their dublet and their hose.

DU. And I pray thee how couldest thou upon the sudden devise or imagine suche a lye? and to what purpose?

ERO. You shall heare by and by a thing as fitte for our purpose, as any could have happened.

DU. I would fayne heare you conclude.

ERO. You would fayne leape over the stile, before you come at the hedge: I woulde you had heard me, and seene the gestures that I enforced to make him beleeve this.

DU. I beleeve you, for I knowe you can counterfet wel.

ERO. Further I sayde, the duke had charged upon great penalties, that the Inholders and vitlers shoulde bring worde dayly of as many *Sceneses* as came to their houses. The gentleman beeing (as I gessed at the first) a man of smal *sapientia*, when he heard these newes, would have turned his horse an other way.

DU. By likelyhoode he was not very wise when hee would beleeve that of his countrey, which if it had bene true every man must needes have knowen it.

ERO. Why not? when he had not beene in his countrey for a moneth paste, and I tolde him this had hapned within these seven dayes.

DU. Belike he was of small experience.

ERO. I thinke, of as litle as may be: but beste of all for our purpose, and good adventure it was, that I mette with such an one. Now harken I pray you.

DU. Make an ende I pray thee.

ERO. He, as I say, when he hard these words, would have turned the bridle: and I fayning a countenance as though I were somewhat pensive and carefull for him, paused a while, & after with a great sighe saide to him: Gentleman, for the curtesie that (as I said) I have found in your countrey, & bicause your affaires shall be the better dispatched, I will finde the meanes to lodge you in my house, and you shal say to every man, that you are a *Sicilian* of *Cathanea*, your name *Philogano*, father to me that am in deede of that countrey and citie, called here *Erostrato*. And I (to pleasure you) will (during your abode here) do you reverence as you were my father.

DU. Out upon me, what a grosse hedded foole am I? now I perceive whereto this tale tendeth.

ERO. Well, and how like you of it?

DU. Indifferently, but one thing I doubt.

ERO. What is that?

DU. Marie, that when he hath bene here twoo or three dayes, he shal heare of every man that there is no such thing betwene the Duke and the Towne of *Sciene*.

ERO. As for that let me alone, I doe entertaine and will entertaine him so well, that within these two or three daies I will disclose unto him all the whole matter, and doubte not but to bring him in for performance of as muche as I have promised to *Damon*: for what hurte can it be to him, when he shall binde a strange name and not his owne?

DU. What, thinke you he will be entreated to stande bounde for a dower of two thousand Ducates by the yeere?

ERO. Yea why not, (if it were ten thousande) as long as he is not in deede the man that is bound?

DU. Well, if it be so, what shall we be the neerer to our purpose?

ERO. Why? when we have done as muche as we can, how can we doe any more?

DU. And where have you left him?

ERO. At the Inne, bicause of his horses: he and his men shall lie in my house.

DU. Why brought you him not with you?

ERO. I thought better to use your advise first.

DU. Well, goe take him home, make him all the cheere you can, spare for no cost, I will alowe it.

ERO. Content, looke where he commeth.

DU. Is this he? goe meete him, by my trouthe he lookes even lyke a good soule, he that fisheth for him, mighte bee sure to catche a cods heade: I will rest here a while to discipher him.

> [*Erostrato espieth the Scenese and goeth towards him: Dulipo standeth aside.*]

Scena. ii.

The SCENESE. PAQUETTO & PETRUCIO his servants.
EROSTRATO.

[SCENESE] He that travaileth in this worlde passeth by many perilles.

PA. You saye true sir, if the boate had bene a little more laden this morning at the ferrie, wee had bene all drowned,[1] for I thinke, there are none of us that could have swomme.

SC. I speake not of that.

PA. O you meane the foule waye that we had since wee came from this *Padua*, I promise you, I was afraide twice or thrice, that your mule would have lien fast in the mire.

SC. Jesu, what a blockehead thou art, I speake of the perill we are in presently since we came into this citie.

PA. A great peril I promise you, that we were no sooner arived, but you founde a frende that brought you from the Inne, and lodged you in his owne house.

SC. Yea marie, God rewarde the gentle yong man that we mette, for else we had bene in a wise case by this time. But have done with these tales, and take you heede, & you also sirra, take heede that none of you saie we be *Sceneses*, and remember that you call me *Philogano* of *Cathanea*.[2]

PA. Sure I shal never remember these outlandish words, I could well remember *Haccanea*.

SC. I say, *Cathanea*, and not *Haccanea*, with a vengeance.

PA. Let another name it then when neede is, for I shall never remember it.

SC. Then holde thy peace, and take heede thou name not *Scene*.

PA. Howe say you, if I faine my selfe dum as I did once in the house of *Crisobolus*?

---

[1] In margin: An other supose.   [2] In margin: A doltish supose.

sc.   Doe as thou thinkest best: but looke where commeth the gentleman whom we are so much bounde unto.

ero.   Welcome, my deare father *Philogano*.

sc.   Gramercie my good sonne *Erostrato*.

ero.   That is well saide, be mindefull of your toung, for these *Ferareses* be as craftie as the Devill of hell.

sc.   No, no, be you sure we will doe as you have bidden us.

ero.   For if you should name *Scene* they would spoile you immediatly, and turne you out of the towne, with more shame, than I woulde shoulde befall you for a thousande Crownes.

sc.   I warant you, I was giving them warning as I came to you, and I doubt not but they will take good heede.

ero.   Yea and trust not the servauntes of my housholde to far, for they are *Ferareses* all, and never knew my father, nor came never in *Silicia*: this is my house, will it please you to goe in? I will follow.

> [*They goe in.*
> *Dulipo tarieth and espieth the Doctor comming in with his man.*

Scena. iii.

DULIPO alone.

This geare hath had no evill beginning, if it continue so and fall to happie ende. But is not this the silly Doctor with the side bonet, the doting foole, that dare presume to become a suter to such a peerlesse Paragone? O how covetousnesse doth blind the common sort of men. *Damon* more desirous of the dower, than mindfull of his gentle & gallant daughter, hath determined to make him his Sonne in law, who for his age may be his father in law: and hath greater respect to the abundance of goods, than to his owne naturall childe. He beareth well in minde to fill his owne purse, but he litle remembreth that his daughters purse shalbe continually emptie, unlesse Maister Doctour fill it with double ducke egges. Alas: I jest and have no joy, I will stand here aside and laugh a litle at this lobcocke.

> [*Dulippo espieth the Doctor and his man comming.*

Scena. iiii.

CARION the doctors man.   CLEANDER.   DULIPO.

[ca.]   Maister, what the Divel meane you to goe seeke guestes at this time of the day? the Maiors officers have dined ere this time, which are alway the last in the market.

CLE.   I come to seeke *Pasiphilo*, to the ende he may dine with mee.

CA.   As though six mouthes and the cat for the seventh, bee not sufficient to eate an harlotrie shotterell, a pennieworth of cheese, and halfe a score spurlings: this is all the dainties you have dressed for you and your familie.

CLE.   Ah greedie gut, art thou afearde thou shalt want?

CA.   I am afearde in deede, it is not the first time I have founde it so.

DU.   Shall I make some sporte with this gallant? what shall I say to him?

CLE.   Thou arte afearde belike that he will eate thee and the rest.

CA.   Nay, rather that he will eate your mule, both heare and hyde.

CLE.   Heare and hyde? and why not flesh and all?

CA.   Bicause she hath none. If she had any flesh, I thinke you had eaten hir your selfe by this time.

CLE.   She may thanke you then, for your good attendance.

CA.   Nay she may thanke you for your small allowance.

DU.   In faith now let me alone.

CLE.   Holde thy peace drunken knave, and espie me *Pasiphilo*.

DU.   Since I can doe no better, I will set such a staunce betweene him and *Pasiphilo*, that all this towne shall not make them friendes.

CA.   Could you not have sent to seeke him, but you must come your selfe? surely you come for some other purpose, for if you would have had *Pasiphilo* to dinner, I warant you he would have taried here an houre since.

CLE.   Holde thy peace, here is one of *Damons* servaunts,[1] of him I shall understand where he is: good fellow art not thou one of *Damons* servaunts?

DU.   Yes sir, at your knamandement.[2]

CLE.   Gramercie, tell me then, hath *Pasiphilo* bene there this day or no?

DU.   Yes sir, and I thinke he be there still, ah, ah, ah.

CLE.   What laughest thou?

DU.   At a thing, that every man may not laugh at.

CLE.   What?

DU.   Talke, that *Pasiphilo* had with my master this day.

CLE.   What talke I pray thee?

DU.   I may not tell it.

CLE.   Doth it concerne me?

---

[1] In margin: An other supose.   [2] commandment.

DU. Nay I will say nothing.

CLE. Tell me.

DU. I can say no more.

CLE. I woulde but knowe if it concerne mee, I pray thee tell mee.

DU. I would tell you, if I were sure you would not tell it againe.

CLE. Beleve me I will kepe it close: *Carion* give us leave a litle, goe aside.

DU. If my maister shoulde know that it came by me, I were better die a thousand deaths.

CLE. He shall never know it, say on.

DU. Yea, but what assurance shall I have?

CLE. I lay thee my faith and honestie in paune.

DU. A pretie paune, the fulkers will not lend you a farthing on it.

CLE. Yea, but amongst honest men it is more worth than golde.

DU. Yea marie sir, but where be they? but will you needes have me tell it unto you?

CLE. Yea I pray thee if it any thing appertaine to me.

DU. Yes it is of you, and I would gladly tell it you, bicause I would not have suche a man of worship so scorned by a villaine ribaulde.

CLE. I pray thee tell me then.

DU. I will tell you so that you will sweare never to tell it to *Pasiphilo*, to my maister, nor to any other bodie.

CA. Surely it is some toye devised to get some money of him.

CLE. I thinke I have a booke here.

CA. If he knew him as well as I, he woulde never goe aboute it, for he may as soone get one of his teeth from his jawes with a paire of pinchers, as a pennie out of his purse with such a conceite.

CLE. Here is a letter wil serve the turne: I sweare to thee by the contents hereof never to disclose it to any man.

DU. I will tell you, I am sorie to see how *Pasiphilo* doth abuse you, perswading you that alwayes he laboureth for you, where in deede, he lieth on my maister continually, as it were with tooth and naile for a straunger, a scholer, borne in *Sicilia* they call him *Roscus* or arskisse, he hathe a madde name I can never hit upon it.

CLE. And thou recknest it as madly: is it not *Erostrato*?

DU. That same I should never have remembred it: and the villany speaketh al the evill of you that can be devised.

CLE. To whom?

DU. To my maister, yea and to *Polynesta* hirselfe sometimes.

CLE. Is it possible, Ah slave, and what saith he?

DU. More evill than I can imagine: that you are the miserablest and most nigardly man that ever was.

CLE. Sayeth *Pasiphilo* so by me?

DU. And that as often as he commeth to your house, he is like to die for hunger, you fare so well.

CLE. That the Devill take him else.

DU. And that you are the testiest man, & moste divers to please in the whole worlde, so that he cannot please you unlesse he should even kill himselfe with continuall paine.

CLE. O devilish tong.

DU. Furthermore, that you cough continually and spit, so that a dogge cannot abide it.

CLE. I never spitte nor coughe more than thus, vho, vho, and that but since I caughte this murre, but who is free from it?

DU. You saye true sir, yet further he sayth, your arme holes stincke, your feete worse than they, and your breathe worst of all.

CLE. If I quite him not for this geare.

DU. And that you are bursten in the cods.

CLE. O villaine, he lieth, and if I were not in the streete thou shouldest see them.

DU. And he saith, that you desire this yong gentlewoman, as much for other mens pleasure as for your owne.

CLE. What meaneth he by that?

DU. Peradventure that by hir beautie, you woulde entice many yong men to your house.

CLE. Yong men? to what purpose?

DU. Nay, gesse you that.

CLE. Is it possible that *Pasiphilo* speaketh thus of me?

DU. Yea, and much more.

CLE. And doth *Damon* beleeve him?

DU. Yea, more than you would thinke: in such sort, that long ere this, he woulde have given you a flat repulse, but *Pasiphilo* intreated him to continue you a suter for his advantage.

CLE. How for his advantage?

DU. Marie, that during your sute he might still have some rewarde for his great paines.

CLE. He shall have a rope, and yet that is more than he deserveth: I had thought to have given him these hose when I had worne them a litle nearer, but he shall have a. &c.

DU. In good faith sir, they were but loste on him. Will you any thing else with me sir?

CLE. Nay, I have heard to much of thee already.

DU. Then I will take my leave of you.

9—S.N.D. I

CLE.   Farewell, but tell me, may I not know thy name?

DU.   Sir, they call me Foule fall you.

CLE.   An ill favored name by my trouthe: arte thou this countrey man?

DU.   No sir, I was borne by a castle men cal Scabbe-catch-you: fare you well sir.

CLE.   Farewel. O God how have I bene abused? what a spokesman? what a messanger had I provided?

CAR.   Why sir, will you tarie for *Pasiphilo* till we die for hunger?

CLE.   Trouble me not, that the Devill take you both.

CAR.   These newes what so ever they be, like him not.

CLE.   Art thou so hungrie yet? I pray to God thou be never satisfied.

CAR.   By the masse no more I shal as long as I am your servaunt.

CLE.   Goe with mischaunce.

CAR.   Yea, and a mischiefe to you, and to al such covetous wretches.

Finis Actus. 2.

Actus. iii.   Scena. i.

DALIO the cooke.   CRAPINE the lackie.
EROSTRATO, DULIPO.

[DA.] By that time we come to the house, I truste that of these xx. egges in the basket we shall find but very few whole. But it is a folly to talke to him. What the devill, wilt thou never lay that sticke out of thy hande? he fighteth with the dogges, beateth the beares, at every thing in the streate he findeth occasion to tarie: if he spie a slipstring by the waye such another as himself, a Page, a Lackie or a dwarfe, the devill of hell cannot holde him in chaynes, but he will be doing with him: I cannot goe two steppes, but I muste looke backe for my yonker: goe to halter sicke, if you breake one egge I may chance breake, &c.

CRA.   What will you breake? your nose in mine &c?

DA.   Ah beast.

CRA.   If I be a beast, yet I am no horned beast.

DA.   Is it even so? is the winde in that doore? If I were unloden I would tel you whether I be a horned beast or no.

CRA.   You are alway laden either with wine or with ale.

DAL.   Ah spitefull boy, shall I suffer him?

CRA.   Ah cowardely beast, darest thou strike and say never a woorde?

DAL. Well, my maister shall know of this geere, either he shall redresse it, or he shall lose one of us.

CRA. Tel him the worst thou canst by me.

[*Erostra. & Du. ex improviso.*

ERO. What noise, what a rule is this?

CRA. Marie sir, he striketh mee bicause I tell him of his swearing.

DAL. The villaine lieth deadly, he reviles me bicause I bid him make hast.

ERO. Holla: no more of this. *Dalio,* doe you make in a readinesse those Pigeons, stock Doves, and also the breast of Veale: and let your vessell be as cleare as glasse against I returne, that I may tell you which I will have roasted, & which boyled. *Crapine,* lay downe that basket and followe me. Oh that I coulde tell where to finde *Pasiphilo,* but looke where he commeth that can tell me of him.

[*Dulipo is espied by Erostrato.*

DUL. What have you done with *Philogano* your father?

ERO. I have left him within, I would faine speake with *Pasiphilo,* can you tell me where he is?

DU. He dined this day with my maister, but whether he went from thence I know not, what would you with him?

ERO. I woulde have him goe tell *Damon* that *Philogano* my father is come and ready to make assurance of as much as he wil require. Now shall I teach maister doctor a schole point, he travaileth to none other end but to catche *Cornua,* and he shall have them, for as old as he is, and as many subtilties as he hath learned in the law, he can not goe beyond me one ace.

DU. O deere friend, goe thy wayes seeke *Pasiphilo,* finde him out, and conclude somewhat to our contentation.

ERO. But where shall I finde him?

DU. At the feasts if there be any, or else in the market with the poulters or the fishmongers.

ERO. What should he doe with them?

DU. Mary he watcheth whose Caters bie the best meat. If any bie a fat Capon, a good breast of Veale, fresh Samon or any suche good dishe, he followeth to the house, and either with some newes, or some stale jest he will be sure to make himselfe a geast.

ERO. In faith, and I will seeke there for him.

DU. Then muste you needes finde him, and when you have done I will make you laughe.

ERO. Whereat?

DU. At certaine sport I made to day with master doctor.

ERO. And why not now?

DU.   No it asketh further leysure, I pray thee dispatche, and finde out *Pasiphilo* that honest man.

[*Dulipo tarieth.   Erostrato goeth out.*

Scena. ii.

DULIPO alone.

This amorous cause that hangeth in controversie betwene *Domine doctor* & me, may be compared to them that play at primero: of whom some one peradventure shal leese a great sum of money before he win one stake, & at last halfe in anger shal set up his rest: win it: & after that another, another, & another, till at last he draw the most part of the money to his heape: the other by litle & litle stil diminishing his rest, til at last he be come as neere the brinke, as earst the other was: yet again peradventure fortune smiling on him, he shal as it were by peece meale, pull out the guts of his fellows bags, & bring him barer than he himselfe was tofore, & so in play continue stil, (fortune favoring now this way, now that way) til at last the one of them is left with as many crosses as God hath brethren. O howe often have I thoughte my selfe sure of the upper hande herein? but I triumphed before the victorie. And then how ofte againe have I thoughte the fielde loste? Thus have I beene tossed nowe over, nowe under, even as fortune list to whirle the wheele, neither sure to winne nor certayne to loose the wager. And this practise that nowe my servaunte hath devised, although hitherto it hath not succeeded amisse, yet can I not count my selfe assured of it: for I feare still that one mischance or other wyll come and turne it topsie turvie. But looke where my mayster commeth.

[*Damon comming in, espieth Dulipo and calleth him.*

Scena. iii.

DAMON.   DULIPO.   NEVOLA, and two mo servants.

[DA.]   Dulipo.

DU.   Here sir.

DA.   Go in and bid *Nevola* and his fellowes come hither that I may tell them what they shall goe about, and go you into my studie: there upon the shelfe you shall find a roule of writings which John of the Deane made to my Father, when he solde him the Grange ferme, endorced with bothe their names: bring it hither to me.

DU.   It shall be done sir.

DA.   Go, I wil prepare other maner of writings for you than you are aware of. O fooles that trust any man but themselves now adaies: oh spiteful fortune, thou doest me wrong I thinke, that from the depth of Hell pitte thou haste sente mee this servaunt to be the subversion of me and all mine.

[*The servants come in.*

Come hither sirs, and heare what I shal say unto you: go into my studie, where you shall finde *Dulipo*, step to him all at once, take him and (with a corde that I have laide on the table for the nonce) bind him hande and foote, carie him into the dungeon under the stayres, make faste the dore & bring me the key, it hangeth by upon a pin on the wall. Dispatche and doe this geare as privily as you can: and thou *Nevola* come hither to me againe with speede.

NE.   Well I shall.

DA.   Alas how shall I be revenged of this extreme despite? if I punishe my servant according to his divelishe deserts, I shall heape further cares upon mine owne head: for to suche detestable offences no punishment can seeme sufficient, but onely death, and in such cases it is not lawful for a man to be his owne carver. The lawes are ordeyned, and officers appoynted to minister justice for the redresse of wrongs: and if to the potestates I complayne me, I shall publishe mine owne reproche to the worlde. Yea, what should it prevayle me to use all the puinishments that can be devised? the thing once done can not be undone. My daughter is defloured, and I utterly dishonested: how can I then wype that blot off my browe? and on whome shall I seeke revenge? Alas, alas I my selfe have bene the cause of all these cares, and have deserved to beare the punishment of all these mishappes. Alas, I should not have committed my dearest darling in custodie to so carelesse a creature as this olde Nurse: for we see by common proofe, that these olde women be either peevishe, or pitifull: either easily enclined to evill, or quickly corrupted with bribes and rewards. O wife, my good wife (that nowe lyest colde in the grave) now may I well bewayle the wante of thee, and mourning nowe may I bemone that I misse thee: if thou hadst lived (suche was thy governement of the least things) that thou wouldest prudently have provided for the preservation of this pearle. A costly jewell may I well accompte hir, that hath been my cheefe comforte in youth, and is nowe become the corosive of mine age. O *Polynesta*, full evill hast thou requited the clemencie of thy carefull father: and yet to excuse thee giltlesse before God, and to condemne thee giltie before the worlde, I can count none other but my wretched selfe the caytife and causer of all my cares. For of al the dueties that are requisite in humane lyfe, onely obedience is by the parents to be required of the childe: where on the other side the parents are

bound, first to beget them, then to bring them foorth, after to nourish them, to preserve them from bodily perils in the cradle, from
daunger of soule by godly education, to matche them in consort
enclined to vertue, too banish them all ydle and wanton companie,
to allow them sufficiente for their sustentation, to cut off excesse
the open gate of sinne, seldome or never to smile on them unlesse
it be to their encouragement in vertue, and finally, to provide them
mariages in time convenient, lest (neglected of us) they learne to
sette either to much or to litle by themselves. Five yeares are past
since I might have maried hir, when by continuall excuses I have
prolonged it to my owne perdition. Alas, I shoulde have considered,
she is a collop of my owne flesh: what shold I think to make hir a
princesse? Alas alas, a poore kingdome have I now caught to endowe
hir with: It is too true, that of all sorowes this is the head source and
chiefe fountaine of all furies: the goods of the world are incertain,
the gaines to be rejoyced at, and the losse not greatly to be lamented:
only the children cast away, cutteth the parents throate with the
knife of inward care, which knife will kill me surely, I make none
other accompte.

[Damons servants come to him againe.

Scena. iiii.

NEVOLA. DAMON. PASIPHILO.

[NE.]   Sir, we have done as you badde us, and here is the key.

DA.   Well, go then *Nevola* and seeke master *Casteling* the jayler,
he dwelleth by S. Antonies gate, desire him to lend me a paire of the
fetters he useth for his prisoners, and come againe quickly.

NE.   Well sir.

DA.   Heare you, if he aske what I would do with them, say you
can not tell, and tell neither him nor any other, what is become of
Dulipo.   *[Damon goeth out.*

[NE.]   I warant you sir. Fye upon the Devill, it is a thing almost
unpossible for a man nowe a dayes to handle money, but the mettal
will sticke on his fingers[1]: I marvelled alway at this fellowe of mine
Dulipo, that of the wages he received, he could maintaine himselfe
so bravely apparelled, but nowe I perceive the cause, he had the
disbursing and receit of all my masters affaires, the keys of the
granair, *Dulippo* here, *Dulippo* there, [in] favoure with my maister,
in favoure with his daughter, what woulde you more, he was
Magister factotum: he was as fine as the Crusadoe, and wee silly

---

[1] In margin: An other suppose.

wretches as course as canvas: wel, behold what it is come to in the ende, he had bin better to have done lesse.

[*Pasi. subito & improviso venit.*[1]

PA.   Thou saist true *Nevola*, he hath done to much in deed.

NE.   From whence commest thou in the devils name?

PA.   Out of the same house thou camest from, but not out of the same dore.

NE.   We had thought thou hadst bene gone long since.

PA.   When I arose from the table, I felte a rumbling in my belly, whiche made me runne to the stable, and there I fell on sleepe uppon the strawe, and have line there ever since: And thou whether goest thou?

NE.   My master hath sent me on an errand in great hast.

PA.   Whether I pray thee?

NE.   Nay I may not tell: Farewell.

PA.   As though I neede any further instructions: O God what newes I heard even now, as I lay in the stable: O good *Erostrato* and pore *Cleander*, that have so earnestly stroven for this damsel, happie is he that can get hir I promise you,[2] he shall be sure of mo than one at a clap that catcheth hir, eyther Adam or Eve within hir belie. Oh God, how men may be deceived in a woman? who wold have beleeved the contrary but that she had bin a virgin? aske the neighbours and you shall heare very good report of hir: marke hir behaviors & you would have judged hir very maydenly: seldome seene abroade but in place of prayer, and there very devout, and no gaser at outwarde sightes, no blaser of hir beautie above in the windowes, no stale at the doore for the bypassers: you would have thought hir a holy yong woman. But muche good doe it *Domine Doctor*, hee shall be sure to lacke no CORNE in a deare yere, whatsoever he have with hir else: I beshrewe me if I let the mariage any way. But is not this the old scabbed queane that I heard disclosing all this geere to hir master, as I stoode in the stable ere nowe? it is shee. Whither goeth *Psiteria*?

[*Pasiphilo espieth Psiteria comming.*

Scena. v.

PSITERIA, PASIPHILO.

[PS.]   To a Gossip of myne heereby.

PA.   What? to tattle of the goodly stirre that thou keptst concerning *Polynesta*.

PS.   No no: but how knew you of that geere?

---

[1] P. enters suddenly.   [2] In margin: An other suppose.

PA.   You tolde me.

PS.   I? when did I tell you?

PA.   Even now when you tolde it to *Damon*, I both sawe you and heard you, though you saw not me: a good parte I promise you, to accuse the poore wenche, kill the olde man with care, over and besides the daunger you have brought *Dulipo* and the Nursse unto, and many moe, fie, fie.

PS.   In deed I was to blame, but not so much as you think.

PA.   And how not so muche? did I not heare you tell?

PS.   Yes, But I will tell you how it came to passe: I have knowen for a great while, that this *Dulipo* and *Polynesta* have lyen togither, and all by the meanes of the nurse: yet I held my peace, and never tolde it. Now this other day the Nursse fell on scolding with me, and twyce or thryce called me drunken olde whore, and suche names that it was too badde: and I called hir baude, and tolde hir that I knew well enoughe howe often she had brought *Dulipo* to *Polynestas* bed: yet all this while I thought not that anye body had heard me, but it befell cleane contrarye: for my maister was on the other side of the wall, and heard all our talke, whereupon he sent for me, and forced me to confesse all that you heard.

PAS.   And why wouldest thou tell him? I woulde not for. &c.

PS.   Well, if I had thought my maister would have taken it so, he should rather have killed me.

PAS.   Why? how could he take it?

PS.   Alas, it pitieth me to see the poore yong woman how she weepes, wailes, and teares hir heare: not esteming hir owne life halfe so deare as she doth poore *Dulipos*: and hir father, he weepes on the other side, that it would pearce an hart of stone with pitie: but I must be gone.

PAS.   Go that the gunne pouder consume thee olde trotte.

Finis. Actus. 3.

Actus. iiii.   Scena. i.

EROSTRATO fained.

What shall I doe? Alas what remedie shall I finde for my ruefull estate? what escape, or what excuse may I now devise to shifte over our subtile supposes? for though to this day I have usurped the name of my maister, and that without checke or controll of any man, now shal I be openly discyphred, and that in the sight of every man: now shal it openly be knowen, whether I be *Erostrato* the gentleman, or *Dulipo* the servaunt. We have hitherto played our parts in abusing others: but nowe commeth the man that wil not be abused, the right *Philogano* the right father of the right *Erostrato*: going to seke *Pasiphilo*, and hearing that he was at the water gate, beholde I espied my fellowe *Litio*, and by and by my olde maister *Philogano* setting forth his first step on land: I to fuge and away hither as fast as I could to bring word to the right *Erostrato*, of his right father *Philogano*, that to so sodaine a mishap some subtile shift might be upon the sodaine devised. But what can be imagined to serve the turne, although we had [a] monethes respite to beate oure braines about it, since we are commonly knowen, at the least supposed in this towne, he for *Dulipo*, a slave & servant to *Damon*, & I for *Erostrato* a gentleman & a student? But beholde, runne *Crapine* to yonder olde woman before she get within the doores, & desire hir to call out *Dulipo*: but heare you? if she aske who would speake with him, saye thy selfe and none other.

> [*Erostrato espieth Psiteria comming, and sendeth his lackey to hir.*

Scena. ii.

CRAPINE. PSITERIA. EROSTRATO fained.

[CRA.] Honest woman, you gossip, thou rotten whore, hearest thou not olde witche?

PS. A rope stretche your yong bones, either you muste live to be as old as I, or be hanged while you are yong.

CRA. I pray thee loke if *Dulipo* be within.

PS. Yes that he is I warrant him.

CRA. Desire him then to come hither and speake a word with me, he shall not tarie.

PS. Content your selfe, he is otherwise occupied.

CRA. Yet tell him so gentle girle.

PS. I tell you he is busie.

CRA. Why is it such a matter to tell him so, thou crooked Crone?

PS. A rope stretche you, marie.

CRA. A pockes eate you, marie.

PS. Thou wilt be hanged I warant thee, if thou live to it.

CRA. And thou wilt be burnt I warant thee, if the canker consume thee not.

PS. If I come neere you hempstring, I will teache you to sing sol fa.

CRA. Come on, and if I get a stone I will scare crowes with you.

PS. Goe with a mischiefe, I thinke thou be some devill that woulde tempte me.

ERO.   *Crapine*: heare you? come away, let hir goe with a vengeance, why come you not? Alas looke where my maister *Philogano*
commeth: what shall I doe? where shall I hide me? he shall not see
me in these clothes, nor before I have spoken with the right *Erostrato*.

> [*Erostrato espyeth Phylogano comming, and runneth
> about to hide him.*

Scena. iii.

PHILOGANO.   FERRARESE the Inne keper.
LITIO a servant.

[PHI.]   Honest man it is even so: be you sure there is no love to
be compared like the love of the parents towards their children. It
is not long since I thought that a very waightie matter shoulde not
have made me come out of *Sicilia*, and yet now I have taken this
tedious toyle and travaile upon me, only to see my sonne, and to
have him home with me.

FER.   By my faith sir, it hath ben a great travaile in dede, and
to much for one of your age.

PHI.   Yea be you sure: I came in companie with certaine gentlemen of my countrey, who had affaires to dispatche as far as to
An[c]ona, from thence by water to *Ravenna*, and from *Ravenna* hither,
continually against the tide.

FER.   Yea & I think that you had but homly lodging by the way.

PHI.   The worst that ever man had: but that was nothing to the
stirre that the serchers kept with me when I came aborde the ship:
Jesus how often they untrussed my male,[1] & ransaked a litle capcase[2]
that I had, tossed & turned al that was within it, serched my
bosome, yea my breeches, that I assure you I thought they would
have flayed me to searche betwene the fell and the fleshe for fardings.

FER.   Sure I have heard no lesse, and that the marchants bobbe
them somtimes, but they play the knaves still.

PHI.   Yea be you well assured, suche an office is the inheritance
of a knave, and an honest man will not meddle with it.

FER.   Wel, this passage shal seme pleasant unto you when you
shall finde your childe in health and well: but I praye you sir why
did you not rather send for him into *Sicilia*, than to come your selfe,
specially since you had none other businesse? peradventure you
had rather endanger your selfe by this noysome journey, than
hazard to drawe him from his studie.

PHI.   Nay, that was not the matter, for I had rather have him
give over his studie altogither and come home.

---

[1] mail, bag.   [2] travelling case.

FER. Why? if you minded not to make him learned, to what ende did you send him hither at the first?

PHI. I will tell you: when he was at home he did as most yong men doe, he played many mad prankes and did many things that liked me not very well: and I thinking, that by that time he had sene the worlde, he would learne to know himselfe better, exhorted him to studie, and put in his election what place he would go to. At the last he came hither, and I thinke he was scarce here so sone as I felt the want of him, in suche sorte, as from that day to this I have passed fewe nightes without teares. I have written to him very often that he shoulde come home, but continually he refused stil, beseching me to continue his studie, wherein he doubted not (as he said) but to profite greatly.

FER. In dede he is very much commended of al men, and specially of the best reputed studentes.

PHI. I am glad he hath not lost his time, but I care not greatly for so muche knowledge. I would not be without the sighte of hym againe so long, for all the learning in the worlde. I am olde nowe, and if God shoulde call mee in his absence, I promise you I thinke it woulde drive me into disperation.

FER. It is commendable in a man to love his children, but to be so tender over them is more womanlike?

PHI. Well, I confesse it is my faulte: and yet I will tell you another cause of my comming hither, more waightie than this. Divers of my countrey have bene here since hee came hither, by whome I have sente unto him, and some of them have bene thrice, some foure or five times at his house, and yet could never speake with him. I feare he applies his studie so, that he will not leese the minute of an houre from his booke. What, alas, he might yet talke with his countrymen for a while: he is a yong man, tenderly brought up, and if he fare thus continually night & day at his booke, it may be enough to drive him into a frenesie.

FER. In dede, enough were as good as a feast. Loe you sir here is your sonne *Erostratoes* house, I will knocke.

PHI. Yea, I pray you knocke.

FER. They heare not.

PHI. Knocke againe.

FER. I thinke they be on slepe.

LY. If this gate were your Grandefathers soule, you coulde not knocke more softly, let me come: ho, ho, is there any body within?

[*Dalio commeth to the wyndowe, and there maketh them answere.*]

Scena. iiii.

DALIO the cooke. FERARESE the inholder.
PHILOGANO. LITIO his man.

[DAL.]　What devill of hell is there? I thinke hee will breake the gate in peeces.

LI.　Marie sir, we had thoughte you had beene on sleepe within, and therefore we thought best to wake you: what doth *Erostrato*?

DA.　He is not within.

PHI.　Open the dore good fellow I pray thee.

DA.　If you thinke to lodge here, you are deceived I tell you, for here are guestes enowe already.

PHI.　A good fellow, and much for thy maister honesty by our Ladie: and what guestes I pray thee?

DA.　Here is *Philogano* my maisters father, lately come out of *Sicilia*.[1]

PHI.　Thou speakest truer than thou arte aware of, he will be, by that time thou hast opened the dore: open I pray thee hartily.

DA.　It is a small matter for me to open the dore, but here is no lodging for you, I tell you plaine, the house is full.

PHI.　Of whome?

DA.　I tolde you: here is *Philogano* my maisters father come from *Cathanea*.

PHI.　And when came he?

DA.　He came three houres since, or more, he alighted at the Aungell, and left his horses there: afterwarde my maister brought him hither.

PHI.　Good fellow, I thinke thou hast good sport to mocke mee.

DA.　Nay, I thinke you have good spor[te] to make me tarry here, as though I have nothing else to doe: I am matched with an unrulye mate in the kitchen. I will goe looke to him another while.

PHI.　I thinke he be drunken.

FER.　Sure he semes so: see you not how redde he is about the gilles?

PHI.　Abide fellow, what *Philogano* is it whome thou talkest of?

DA.　An honest gentleman, father to *Erostrato* my maister.

PHI.　And where is he?

DA.　Here within.

PHI.　May we see him.

DA.　I thinke you may if you be not blind.

PHI.　Go to, go tel him here is one wold speake with him.

DA.　Mary, that I will willingly doe.

[1] In margin: An other suppose.

PHI.   I can not tell what I shoulde say to this geere, *Litio*, what thinkest thou of it?

LI.   I cannot tell you what I shoulde say sir, the worlde is large and long, there maye be moe *Philoganos* and moe *Erostratos* than one, yea and moe *Ferraras*, moe *Sicilias*, and moe *Cathaneas*: peradventure this is not that *Ferrara* whiche you sent your sonne unto.[1]

PHI.   Peradventure thou arte a foole, and he was another that answered us even now. But be you sure honest man, that you mistake not the house?

FER.   Nay, then god helpe, thinke you I know not *Erostratos* house? yes, and himselfe also: I sawe him here no longer since than yesterday. But here comes one that wil tell us tydings of him, I like his countenaunce better than the others that answered at the windowe erewhile.

> [*Dalio draweth his hed in at the wyndowe, the Scenese commeth out.*

Scena. v.

SCENESE.   PH[I]LOGANO.   DALIO.

[SCE.]   Would you speake with me sir?

PHI.   Yea sir, I would faine knowe whence you are.

SCE.   Sir I am a *Sicilian*, at your commaundement.

PHI.   What part of *Sicilia*?

SCE.   Of *Cathanea*.

PHI.   What shall I call your name?

SCE.   My name is *Philogano*.

PHI.   What trade doe you occupie?

SCE.   Marchandise.

PHI.   What marchandise brought you hither?

SCE.   None, I came onely to see a sonne that I have here whom I sawe not these two yeares.

PHI.   What call they your sonne?

SCE.   *Erostrato*.

PHI.   Is *Erostrato* your sonne?

SCE.   Yea verily.

PHI.   And are you *Philogano*?

SCE.   The same.

PHI.   And a marchant of *Cathanea*?

SCE.   What neede I tell you so often? I will not tell you a lye.

PHI.   Yes, you have told me a false lie, and thou arte a vilaine and no better.

---

[1] In margin: An other suppose.

SCE.   Sir, you offer me great wrong with these injurious wordes.

PHI.   Nay, I will doe more than I have yet proffered to doe, for I will prove thee a lyer, and a knave to take upon thee that thou art not.

SCE.   Sir I am *Philogano* of *Cathanea*, out of all doubte,[1] if I were not I would be loth to tell you so.

PHI.   Oh, see the boldnesse of this brute beast, what a brasen face he setteth on it?

SCE.   Well, you may beleve me if you liste: what wonder you?

PHI.   I wonder at thy impudencie, for thou, nor nature that framed thee, can ever counterfaite thee to be me, ribauld villaine, and lying wretch that thou arte.

DA.   Shall I suffer a knave to abuse my maisters father thus?[2] hence villaine, hence, or I will sheath this good fawchion in your paunch: if my maister *Erostrato* find you prating here on this fashion to his father, I wold not be in your coate for mo conney skins than I gat these twelve monethes: come you in againe sir, and let this Curre barke here till he burst.

> [*Dalio pulleth the Scenese in at the dores.*

Scena. vi.

PHILOGANO.   LITIO.   FERARESE.

[PHI.]   *Litio*, how likest thou this geere?

LI.   Sir, I like it as evill as may be: but have you not often heard tell of the falsehood of *Ferara*, and now may you see, it falleth out accordingly.

FER.   Friend, you do not well to slaunder the Citie, these men are no *Ferrareses* you may know by their tong.

LI.   Well, there is never a barrell better herring, beetwene you both: but in deed your officers are most to blame, that suffer such faultes to escape unpunished.

FER.   What knowe the officers of this? thinke you they know of every fault?

LI.   Nay, I thinke they will knowe as little as may bee, specially when they have no gaines, by it, but they ought to have their eares as open to heare of such offences, as the Ingates be to receive guests.

PHI.   Holde thy peace foole.

LI.   By the masse I am afearde that we shall be proved fooles both two.

PHI.   Well, what shall we doe?

---

[1] In margin: A stoute suppose.   [2] In margin: A pleasant suppose.

LI. I would thinke best we should go seeke *Erostrato* him selfe.

FER. I will waite upon you willingly, and either at the schooles, or at the convocations, we shall find him.

PHI. By our Lady I am wery, I will run no longer about to seke him, I am sure hither he will come at the last.

LI. Sure, my mind gives me that we shall find a new *Erostrato* ere it be long.[1]

FE. Looke where he is, whether runnes he? stay you awhile, I will goe tell him that you are here: *Erostrato, Erostra[t]o*, ho *Erostrato*, I would speake with you.

> [*Erostrato is espied uppon the stage running about.*

Scena. vii.

Fained EROSTRATO. FERARESE.
PHILOGANO. LITIO. DALIO.

[ERO.] Nowe can I hide me no longer. Alas what shall I doe? I will set a good face on, to beare out the matter.

FERA. O *Erostrato, Philogano* your father is come out of *Sicilia*.

ERO. Tell me that I knowe not, I have bene with him and seene him alredy.

FERA. Is it possible? and it seemeth by him that you know not of his comming.

ERO. Why, have you spoken with him? when saw you him I pray you?

FERA. Loke you where he standes, why go you not too him? Looke you *Philogano*, beholde your deare son *Erostrato*.

PHI. *Erostrato*? this is not *Erostrato*: thys seemeth rather to be *Dulipo*, and it is *Dulipo* in deede.

LI. Why, doubte you of that.

ERO. What saith this honest man?

PHI. Mary sir, in deede you are so honorably cladde, it is no marvell if you looke bigge.

ERO. To whome speaketh he?

PHI. What, God helpe, do you not know me?

ERO. As farre as I remember Sir, I never sawe you before.

PHI. Harke *Litio*, here is good geere, this honest man will not know me.

ERO. Gentleman, you take your markes amisse.[2]

LI. Did I not tell you of the falsehood of *Ferrara* master? *Dulipo* hath learned to play the knave indifferently well since he came hither.

---

[1] In margin: A true suppose.   [2] In margin: A shameless suppose.

PHI.   Peace I say.

ERO.   Friend, my name is not *Dulipo*, aske you thorough out this towne of great and small, they know me: aske this honest man that is with you, if you wyll not beleeve me.

FERRA.   In deede, I never knewe him otherwise called than *Erostrato*: and so they call him, as many as knowe him.

LI.   Master, nowe you may see the falsehood of these fellowes[1]: this honest man your hoste, is of counsaile with him, and would face us down that it is *Erostrato*: beware of these mates.

FERA.   Friende, thou doest me wrong to suspect me, for sure I never hearde hym otherwise called than *Erostrato*.

ERO.   What name could you heare me called by, but by my right name? But I am wise enough to stand prating here with this old man; I thinke he be mad.

PHI.   Ah runnagate, ah villaine traitour, doest thou use thy master thus? what hast thou done with my son villain?

DA.   Doth this dogge barke here still? and will you suffer him master thus to revile you?

ERO.   Come in, come in, what wilt thou do with thys pestil?

DA.   I will rap the olde cackabed on the costerd.

ERO.   Away with it, & you sirra, lay downe these stones: come in at dore every one of you, beare with him for his age, I passe not of his evill wordes.

[*Erostrato taketh all his servantes in at the dores.*

Scena. viii.

PHILOGANO. FERARESE. LITIO.

[PHI.]   Alas, who shall relieve my miserable estate? to whome shall I complaine? since he whome I brought up of a childe, yea and cherished him as if he had bene mine owne, doth nowe utterly denie to knowe me: and you whome I toke for an honest man, and he that should have broughte me to the sighte of my sonne, are compacte with this false wretch, and woulde face me downe that he is *Erostrato*.[2] Alas, you might have some compassion of mine age, to the miserie I am now in, and that I am a stranger desolate of all comforte in this countrey: or at the least, you shoulde have feared the vengeaunce of God the supreme judge (whiche knoweth the secrets of all harts) in bearing this false witnesse with him, whome heaven and earth doe knowe to be *Dulipo* and not *Erostrato*.

LI.   If there be many such witnesses in this countrey, men may go about to prove what they wil in controversies here.

[1] In margin: A needelesse suppose.   [2] In margin: An other suppose.

FER.   Well sir, you may judge of me as it pleaseth you: & how the matter commeth to passe I know not, but truly, ever since he came first hither, I have knowen him by the name of *Erostrato* the sonne of *Philogano* a *Cathanese*: nowe whether he be so in deede, or whether he be *Dulipo*, (as you alledge) let that be proved by them that knewe him before he came hether. But I protest before God, that whiche I have said, is neither a matter compact with him, nor any other, but even as I have hard him called & reputed of al men.

PHI.   Out and alas, he whom I sent hither with my son to be his servaunt, and to give attendance on him, hath eyther cut his throate, or by some evill meanes made him away[1]: and hath not onely taken his garmentes, his bookes, his money, and that whiche he brought out of *Sicilia* with him, but usurpeth his name also, and turneth to his owne commoditie the bills of exchaunge that I have alwayes allowed for my sonnes expences. Oh miserable *Philogano*, oh unhappie old man: oh eternall God, is there no judge? no officer? no higher powers whom I may complaine unto for redresse of these wrongs?

FER.   Yes sir, we have potestates, we have Judges, and above al, we have a most juste prince: doubt you not, but you shall have justice if your cause be just.

PHI.   Bring me then to the Judges, to the potestates, or to whome you thinke best: for I will disclose a packe of the greatest knaverie, a fardell of the fowlest falsehoode that ever was heard of.

LI.   Sir, he that wil goe to the lawe, must be sure of foure things: first, a right and a just cause: then a righteous advocate to pleade: nexte, favour *coram Iudice*: and above all, a good purse to procure it.

FER.   I have not heard, that the law hath any respect to favour: what you meane by it I cannot tell.

PHI.   Have you no regard to his wordes, he is but a foole.

FER.   I pray you sir, let him tell me what is favour.

LI.   Favour cal I, to have a friend neere about the judge, who may so sollicite thy cause, as if it be right, speedie sentence may ensue without any delayes: if it be not good, then to prolong it, till at the last, thine adversarie being wearie, shal be glad to compound with thee.

FER.   Of thus much (although I never heard thus muche in this countrey before) doubt you not *Philogano*, I will bring you to an advocate that shall speede you accordingly.

PHI.   Then shall I give my selfe, as it were a pray to the Lawyers, whose insatiable jawes I am not able to feede, although I had here all the goods and landes which I possesse in mine own countrey:

---

[1] In margin: A shrewde suppose.

10—S.N.D. I

much lesse being a straunger in this miserie. I know their cautels of old: at the first time I come they wil so extoll my cause, as though it were already won: but within a sevennight or ten daies, if I do not continually feede them as the crow doth hir brattes, twentie times in an houre, they will begin to waxe colde, and to finde cavils in my cause, saying, that at the firste I did not well instructe them, till at the last, they will not onely drawe the stuffing out of my purse, but the marrow out of my bones.

FER.   Yea sir, but this man that I tell you of, is halfe a Saincte.

LI.   And the other halfe a Devill, I hold a pennie.

PHI.   Well sayd *Litio*, in deede I have but smal confidence in their smothe lookes.

FER.   Well sir, I thinke this whom I meane, is no suche manner of man: but if he were,[1] there is such hatred and evil wil betwene him & this gentleman (whether he be *Erostrato* or *Dulipo*, what so ever he be) that I warrant you, he will doe whatsoever he can do for you, were it but to spite him.

PHI.   Why? what hatred is betwixt them?

FER.   They are both in love and suters to one gentlewoman, the daughter of a welthie man in this citie.

PHI.   Why? is the villeine become of such estimation that he dare presume to be a suter to any gentlewoman of a good familie?

FER.   Yea sir out of all doubt.

PHI.   How call you his adversarie?

FER.   *Cleander*, one of the excellentest doctors in our citie.

PHI.   For Gods love let us goe to him.

FER. . Goe we then.

Finis Actus. 4.

Actus. v.   Scena. i.

Fayned EROSTRATO.

What a mishappe was this? that before I could meete with *Erostrato*, I have light even ful in the lap of *Philogano*: where I was constrained to denie my name, to denie my master, & to faine that I knew him not, to contend with him, & to revile him, in such sort, that hap what hap can, I can never hap well in favour with him againe. Therefore if I could come to speake with the right *Erostrato*, I will renounce unto him both habite and credite, and away as fast as I can trudge into some strange countrey, where I may never see *Philogano* againe. Alas, he that of a litle childe hath brought me up unto this day, and nourished me as if I had bene his owne[1]: &

---

[1] In margin: An other suppose.   [2] In margin: An other suppose.

indeede (to confesse the trouth) I have no father to trust unto but
him. But looke where *Pasiphilo* commeth, the fittest man in the world
to goe on m[y] message to *Erostrato*.

> [*Erostrato espieth Pasiphilo comming towards him.*

Scena. ii.

PASIPHILO. EROSTRATO.

[PAS.]　Two good newes have I heard to day alreadie: one that
Erostrato prepared a great feast this night: the other, that he seeketh
for me. And I to ease him of his travaile, least he shoulde runne up
and downe seeking me, and bicause no man loveth better than I
to have an erand where good cheere is, come in post hast even
home to his owne house: and loke where he is.

ERO.　*Pasiphilo*, thou muste doe one thing for me if thou love me.

PAS.　If I love you not, who loves you? commaunde me.

ERO.　Go then a litle there, to *Damons* house, aske for *Dulipo*,
and tell him.

PAS.　Wot you what? I cannot speake with him, he is in prison.

ERO.　In prison? how commeth that to passe? where is he in
prison?

PAS.　In a vile dungeon there within his masters house.

ERO.　Canst thou tell wherefore?

PAS.　Be you content to know he is in prison, I have told you too
muche.

ERO.　If ever you will doe any thing for me, tell me.

PAS.　I pray you desire me not, what were you the better if you
knew?

ERO.　More than thou thinkest, *Pasiphilo*, by God.

PAS.　Well, and yet it standes me upon more than you thinke,
to keepe it secrete.

ERO.　Why *Pasiphilo*, is this the trust I have had in you? are these
the faire promises you have a[l]wayes made me?

PAS.　By the masse I would I had fasted this night with maister
doctor, rather than have come hither.

ERO.　Wel *Pasiphilo*, eyther tel me, or at few woordes never
thinke to be welcome to this house from hence forthe.

PAS.　Nay, yet I had rather leese all the Gentlemen in this
towne. But if I tell you any thing that displease you, blame no
body but your selfe now.

ERO.　There is nothing can greve me more than *Dulipoes* mishappe, no not mine owne: and therfore I am sure thou canst tell
me no worsse tidings.

PA. Well, since you would needes have it, I wil tell you: he was taken a bed with your beloved *Polynesta*.[1]

ERO. Alas, and doth *Damon* knowe it?

PA. An olde trotte in the house disclosed it to him, wherupon he tooke bothe *Dulipo* and the Nurse which hath bene the broker of all this bargayne, and clapte them bothe in a cage, where I thinke they shall have so[wr]e soppes too their sweete meates.

ERO. *Pasiphilo*, go thy wayes into the kitchin, commaund the cooke to boyle and roast what liketh thee best, I make thee supra visour of this supper.

PA. By the masse if you should have studied this sevennight, you could not have appointed me an office to please me better. You shall see what dishes I will devise.

[*Pasiphilo goeth in, Erostrato tarieth.*

Scena. iii.

Fayned EROSTRATO alone.

I was glad to rid him out of the way, least he shoulde see me burst out of these swelling teares, which hitherto with great payne I have prisoned in my brest, & least he shoulde heare the Eccho of my doubled sighes, whiche bounce from the botome of my hevy heart. O cursed I, O cruell fortune, that so many dispersed griefes as were sufficient to subvert a legion of Lovers, hast sodenly assembled within my carefull carkase to freat this fearfull heart in sunder with desperation. Thou that hast kepte my master all his youthe within the realme of *Sicilia*, reserving the wind and waves in a temperate calme (as it were at his commaunde) nowe to convey his aged limmes hither, neither sooner nor later: but even in the worst time that may be. If at any time before thou haddest conducted him, this enterprise had bene cut off without care in the beginning: and if never so little longer thou hadst lingred his jorney, this happie day might then have fully finished our drifts & devises. But alas, thou hast brought him even in the very worst time, to plunge us al in the pit of perdition. Neither art thou content to entangle me alone in thy ruinous ropes, but thou must also catch the right *Erostrato* in thy crooked clawes, to reward us both with open shame & rebuke. Two yeeres hast thou kept secrete our subtill Supposes, even this day to discipher them with a sorowfull successe. What shall I do? Alas what shift shall I make? it is too late now to imagine any further deceite, for every minute seemeth an houre til I find some succour for the miserable captive *Erostrato*. Wel, since there is no other reme-

[1] In margin: Another plain and homely suppose.

die, I wil go to my master *Philogano*, & to him will I tell the whole truth of the matter, that at the least he may provide in time, before his sonne feele the smart of some sharpe revenge and punishment. This is the best, and thus wil I do. Yet I know, that for mine owne parte I shal do bitter penance for my faults forepassed: but suche is the good will and duetie that I beare to *Erostrato*, as even with the losse of my life I must not sticke to adventure any thing which may turne to his commoditie. But what shall I do? shal I go seeke my master about the towne, or shall I tarrie his returne hither? If I meete him in the streetes, he wil crie out upon me, neither will he harken to any thing that I shall say, till he have gathered all the people wondring about me, as it were at an Owle. Therefore I were better to abide here, and yet if he tarrie long I will goe seeke him, rather than prolong the time to *Erostratos* perill.

[Pasiphilo returneth to Erostrato.

Scena. iiii.

PASIPHILO. Fayned EROSTRATO.

[PAS.]   Yea dresse them, but lay them not to the fire, till they will be ready to sit downe. This geere goeth in order: but if I had not gone in, there had fallen a foule faulte.

ERO.   And what fault I pray thee?

PA.   Marie, *Dalio* would have layd the shoulder of mutton and the Capon bothe to the fire at once like a foole: he did not consider, that the one woulde have more roasting than the other.

ERO.   Alas, I would this were the greatest fault.

PA.   Why? and either the one should have bene burned before the other had bene roasted, or else he muste have drawne them off the spitte: and they would have bene served to the boorde either colde or rawe.

ERO.   Thou hast reason, *Pasiphilo*.

PA.   Now sir, if it please you I will goe into the towne and buye oranges, olives, and caphers, for without suche sauce the supper were more than halfe lost.

ERO.   There are within already, doubt you not, there shal lacke nothing that is necessarie.   *[Erostrato exit.*

PA.   Since I told him these newes of *Dulipo*, he is cleane beside himself: he hath so many hammers in his head, that his braynes are ready to burst: and let them breake, so I may suppe with him to night, what care I?[1] But is not this *Dominus noster Cleandrus* that commeth before? well sayde, by my truth we will teache maister

---

[1] In margin: A knavishe suppose.

Doctor to weare a cornerd cappe of a new fashion. By God *Polynesta* shal be his, he shall have hir out of doubt, for I have tolde *Erostrato* such newes of hir, that he will none of hir.

> [*Cleander and Philogano come in, talking of the matter in controversie.*

Scena. v.

CLEANDER. PHILOGANO. LITIO. PASIPHILO.

Yea, but howe will ye prove that he is not *Erostrato*, having such presumptions to the contrarie? or how shall it be thought that you are *Philogano*, when an other taketh upon him this same name, and for proofe bringeth him for a witnesse, which hath bene ever reputed here for *Erostrato*?

PHI.   I will tel you sir, let me be kept here fast in prison, & at my charges let there be some man sent into *Sicilia*, that may bring hither with him two or three of the honestest men in *Cathanea*, and by them let it be proved if I or this other be *Philogano*, and whether he be *Erostrato* or *Dulipo* my servant: & if you finde me contrarie, let me suffer death for it.

PA.   I will go salute master Doctour.

CLE.   It will aske great labour & great expences to prove it this way, but it is the best remedie that I can see.

PA.   God save you sir.

CLE.   And reward you as you have deserved.

PA.   Then shall he give me your favour continually.

CLE.   He shall give you a halter, knave and villein that thou arte.

PA.   I knowe I am a knave, but no villein. I am your servaunt.

CLE.   I neither take thee for my servant, nor for my friend.

PA.   Why? wherein have I offended you sir?

CLE.   Hence to the gallowes, knave.

PA.   What softe and faire sir, I pray you, *I praesequar*,[1] you are mine elder.

CLE.   I will be even with you, be you sure, honest man.

PA.   Why sir? I never offended you.

CLE.   Well, I will teach you: out of my sight knave.

PA.   What? I am no dogge, I would you wist.

CLE.   Pratest thou yet villein? I will make thee.

PA.   What will you make me? I see wel the more a man doth suffer you, the worse you are.

CLE.   Ah villein, if it were not for this gentleman, I wold tell you what I.

---

[1] *I praesequar*, Go; I follow.

PA. Villein? nay I am as honest a man as you.

CLE. Thou liest in thy throate, knave.

PHI. O sir, stay your wisedome.

PAS. What will you fight? marie come on.

CLE. Well knave, I will meete with you another time, goe your way.

PAS. Even when you list sir, I will be your man.

CLE. And if I be not even with thee, call me cut.

PAS. Nay by the Masse, all is one, I care not, for I have nothing: if I had either landes or goods, peradventure you would pull me into the lawe.[1]

PHI. Sir, I perceive your pacience is moved.

CLE. This villaine: but let him goe, I will see him punished as he hath deserved. Now to the matter, how said you?

PHI. This fellow hath disquieted you sir, peradventure you would be loth to be troubled any further.

CLE. Not a whit, say on, & let him go with a vengeance.

PHI. I say, let them send at my charge to *Cathanea*.

CLE. Yea I remember that wel, & it is the surest way as this case requireth: but tel me, how is he your servant? and how come you by him? enforme me fully in the matter.

PHI. I will tell you sir: when the Turkes won *Otranto*.

CLE. Oh, you put me in remembrance of my mishappes.

PHI. How sir?

CLE. For I was driven among the rest out of the towne (it is my native countrey) and there I lost more than ever I shall recover againe while I live.

PHI. Alas, a pitifull case by S. Anne.

CLE. Well, proceede.

PHI. At that time (as I saide) there were certaine of our countrey that scoured those costes upon the seas, with a good barke, well appointed for the purpose, and had espiall of a Turkey vessell that came laden from thence with great aboundance of riches.

CLE. And peradventure most of mine.[2]

PHI. So they boarded them, & in the end over came them, & brought the goods to *Palermo*, from whence they came, and amongst other things that they had, was this villeine my servaunt, a boy at that time, I thinke not past five yeeres olde.

CLE. Alas, I lost one of that same age there.

PHI. And I beyng there, and liking the Childes favour well, proffered them foure and twentie ducates for him, and had him.

----

[1] In margin: Lawyers are never weary to get money.

[2] In margin: A gentle suppose.

CLE.   What? was the childe a Turke? or had the Turkes brought him from *Otranto*?

PHI.   They saide he was a Childe of *Otranto*, but what is that to the matter? once xxiiii. Ducattes he cost me, that I wot well.

CLE.   Alas, I speake it not for that sir, I woulde it were he whome I meane.

PHI.   Why, whom meane you sir?

LITI.   Beware sir, be not too lavish.[1]

CLE.   Was his name *Dulipo* then? or had he not another name?

LITI.   Beware what you say sir.

PHI.   What the devill hast thou to doe? *Dulipo*? no sir his name was *Carino*.

LITI.   Yea, well said, tell all and more to, doe.

CLE.   O Lord, if it be as I thinke, how happie were I? & why did you change his name then?

PHI.   We called him *Dulipo*, bycause when he cryed as Ch[i]ldren doe sometimes, he woulde alwayes cry on that name *Dulipo*.

CLE.   Well, then I see well it is my owne onely Childe, whome I loste, when I loste my countrie: he was named *Carino* after his grandfather, and this *Dulipo* whome he alwayes remembred in his lamenting, was his foster father that nourished him and brought him up.

LI.   Sir, have I not told you enough of the falshood of *Ferara*? this gentleman will not only picke your purse, but beguile you of your servaunt also, & make you beleve he is his son.

CLE.   Well goodfellow, I have not used to lie.

LITI.   Sir no, but every thing hath a beginning.

CLE.   Fie, *Philogano* have you not the least suspecte that may be of me.

LITI.   No marie, but it were good he had the most suspecte that may be.

CLE.   Well, hold thou thy peace a litle good f[e]llow. I pray you tell me *Philogano* had the child any remembrance of his fathers name, his mothers name, or the name of his familie?

PHI.   He did remember them, and could name his mother also, but sure I have forgotten the name.

LITI.   I remember it well enough.

PHI.   Tell it then.

LITI.   Nay, that I will not marie, you have tolde him too much al ready.

PHI.   Tell it I say, if thou can.

LITI.   Can? yes by the masse I can wel enough: but I wil have

---

[1] In margin: A crafty suppose.

my tong pulled out, rather than tell it, unlesse he tell it first: doe you not perceive sir, what he goeth about?

CLE. Well, I will tell you then, my name you know alredy: my wife his mothers name was *Sophronia*, the house that I came of, they call *Spiagia*.

LITI. I never heard him speake of *Spiagia* but in deede I have heard him say, his mothers name was *Sophronia*: but what of that? a great matter I promise you. It is like enoughe that you two have compact together to deceive my maister.

CLE. What nedeth me more evident tokens? this is my sonne out of doubt whom I lost eighteen yeares since, and a thousand thousand times have I lamented for him: he shuld have also a mould on his left shoulder.

LI. He hath a moulde there in deede: and an hole in an other place to, I would your nose were in it.

CLE. Faire wordes fellow *Litio*: oh I pray you let us goe talke with him, O fortune, howe much am I bounde to thee if I finde my sonne?

PHI. Yea how little am I beholden to fortune, that know not where my sonne is become, and you whome I chose to be mine advocate, will nowe (by the meanes of this *Dulipo*) become mine adversarie?

CLE. Sir, let us first goe find mine: and I warrant you yours will be founde also ere it be long.[1]

PHI. God graunt: goe we then[.]

CLE. Since the dore is open, I will ne'er knocke nor cal, but we will be bolde to goe in.

LI. Sir, take you heede, least he leade you to some mischiefe.

PHI. Alas *Litio*, if my sonne be loste what care I what become of me?

LI. Well, I have tolde you my minde Sir, doe you as you please.

[Exeunt: Damon and Psiteria come in.

Scena sexta.

DAMON. PSITERIA.

[DA.] Come hither you olde kallat,[2] you tatling huswife, that the devill cut oute your tong: tell me, howe could *Pasiphilo* know of this geere but by you?

PSI. Sir, he never knewe it of me, he was the firste that tolde me of it.

---

[1] In margin: A right suppose.   [2] callet, scold.

DA.   Thou liest, old drabbe, but I would advise you tel me the truth, or I wil make those old bones rattle in your skin.

PSI.   Sir, if you finde me contrarie, kill me.

DA.   Why? where should he talke with thee?

PSI.   He talked with me of it here in the streete.

DA.   What did you here?

PSI.   I was going to the weavers for a webbe of clothe you have there.

DA.   And what cause coulde *Pasiphilo* have to talke of it, unlesse thou began the mater first?

PSI.   Nay, he began with me sir, reviling me, bycause I had tolde you of it: I asked him how he knewe of it, and he said he was in the stable when you examined me ere while.

DA.   Alas, alas, what shall I doe then? in at dores olde whore, I wil plucke that tong of thine out by the rootes one day. Alas it greeveth me more that *Pasiphilo* knoweth it, than all the rest. He that will have a thing kept secrete, let him tell it to *Pasiphilo*: the people shall knowe it, and as many as have eares and no mo. By this time he hath tolde it in a hundreth places. *Cleander* was the firste, *Erostrato* the seconde, and so from one to another throughout the citie. Alas, what dower, what mariage shall I nowe prepare for my daughter? O poore doloro[u]s *Damon*, more miserable than miserie it selfe, would God it were true that *Polynesta* tolde me ere while[1]: that he who hathe deflowred hir, is of no servile estate, (as hitherto he hath bene supposed in my service) but that he is a gentleman borne of a good parentage in *Sicilia*. Alas, small riches shoulde content me, if he be but of an honest familie: but I feare that he hathe devised these toyes to allure my daughtres love. Well I wil goe examine hir againe, my minde giveth me that I shall perceive by hir tale whether it be true or not. But is not this *Pasiphilo* that commeth out of my neighbours house? what the devill ayleth him to leape and laughe so like a foole in the high way?

[*Pasiphilo commeth out of the [house] laughing.*

Scena septima.

P[ASIPHIL]O.   DAMON.

[PA.]   O God, that I might finde *Damon* at home.

DA.   What the divill would he with me?

PAS.   That I may be the firste that shall bring him these newes.

DA.   What will he tell me, in the name of God?

PAS.   O Lord, how happie am I? loke where he is.

---

[1] In margin: The first suppose brought to conclusion.

DA.   What newes *Pasiphilo*, that thou arte so merie?

PAS.   Sir I am mery to make you glad: I bring you joyfull newes.

DA.   And that I have nede of *Pasiphilo*.

PAS.   I knowe sir, that you are a sorowfull man for this mishap that hath chaunced in your house, peradventure you thoughte I had not knowen of it. But let it passe, plucke up your sprits, and rejoyce: for he that hath done you this injurie is so well borne, and hath so riche parents, that you may be glad to make him your sonne in law.

DA.   How knowest thou?

PAS.   His father *Philogano* one of the worthiest men in all *Cathanea*, is nowe come to the citie, and is here in your neighbours house.

DA.   What, in *Erostratos* house?

PAS.   Nay in *Dulipos* house: for where you have alwayes supposed this gentleman to be *Erostrato*, it is not so, but your servaunt whom you have emprisoned hitherto, supposed to be *Dulipo*, he is in dede *Erostrato*: and that other is *Dulipo*. And thus they have alwayes, even since their first arival in this citie, exchaunged names, to the ende that *Erostrato* the maister, under the name of *Dulipo* a servant, might be entertained in your house, & so winne the love of your daughter.

DA.   Wel, then I perceive it is even as *Polinesta* told me.

PAS.   Why, did she tell you so?

DA.   Yea: But I thought it but a tale.

PAS.   Well, it is a true tale: and here they will be with you by and by: both *Philogano* this worthie man, and maister doctor *Cleander*.

DA.   *Cleander*? what to doe?

PAS.   *Cleander*? Why therby lies another tale, the moste fortunate adventure that ever you heard: wot you what? this other *Dulipo*, whome all this while we supposed to be *Erostrato*, is founde to be the sonne of *Cleander*, whome he lost at the losse of *Otranto*, and was after solde in *Sicilia* too this *Philogano*: the strangest case that ever you heard: a man might make a Comedie of it. They wil come even straight, and tell you the whole circumstance of it themselves.

DA.   Nay I will first goe heare the storie of this *Dulipo*, be it *Dulipo* or *Erostrato* that I have here within, before I speake with *Philogano*.

PAS.   So shall you doe well sir, I will goe tell them that they may stay a while, but loke where they come.

[*Damon goeth in, Scenese, Cleander and Philogano come upon the stage.*]

Scena. viii.

SCENESE.   CLEANDER.   PHILOGANO.

[SCE.]   Sir, you shal not nede to excuse the matter any further, since I have received no greater injurie than by words, let them passe like wind, I take them well in worthe: and am rather well pleased than offended: for it shall bothe be a good warning to me another time howe to trust every man at the first sighte, yea, and I shall have good game here after to tel this pleasant story another day in mine owne countrey.

CLE.   Gentleman, you have reason: and be you sure, that as many as heare it, will take great pleasure in it. And you *Philogano* may thinke, that god in heaven above, hath ordained your comming hither at this present to the ende I mighte recover my lost sonne, whom by no other meanes I coulde ever have founde oute.

PHI.   Surely sir I thinke no lesse, for I think that not so much as a leafe falleth from the tree, without the ordinance of god. But let us goe seke *Damon*, for me thinketh every day a yeare, every houre a daye, and every minute to much till I see my *Erostrato*.

CLE.   I cannot blame you, goe we then. *Carino* take you that gentleman home in the meane time, the fewer the better to be present at such affaires.

[Pasiphilo stayeth their going in.

Scena. ix.

P[ASIPHILO.]   CLEANDER.

[PAS.]   Maister doctor, will you not shew me this favour, to tell me the cause of your displeasure?

CLE.   Gentle *Pasiphilo*, I muste needes confesse I have done thee wrong, and that I beleved tales of thee, whiche in deede I finde now contrary.

PAS.   I am glad then that it proceeded rather of ignorance than of malice.

CLE.   Yea beleve me *Pasiphilo*.

PAS.   O sir, but yet you shoulde not have given me suche foule wordes.

CLE.   Well, content thy selfe *Pasiphilo*, I am thy frende as I have alwayes bene: for proofe whereof, come suppe with me to night, & from day to day this seven night be thou my guest. But beholde, here commeth *Damon* out of his house.

Here they come all togither.

Scena decima.

CLEANDER PHILOGANO. DAMON. EROSTRATO.
PASIPHILO. POLINESTA. NEVOLA.
and other servaunts.

[CLE.] We are come unto you sir, to turne you[r] sorowe into joy and gladnesse: the sorow, we meane, that of force you have sustained since this mishappe of late fallen in your house. But be you of good comforte sir, and assure your selfe, that this yong man which youthfully and not maliciously hath commited this amorous offence, is verie well able (with consent of this worthie man his father) to make you sufficient amendes: being borne in *Cathanea* of *Sicilia*, of a noble house, no way inferiour unto you, and of wealth (by the reporte of suche as knowe it) farre exceeding that of yours.

PHI. And I here in proper person, doe presente unto you sir, not onely my assured frendship and brotherhoode, but do earnestly desire you to accepte my poore childe (though unworthy) as your sonne in lawe: and for recompence of the injurie he hath done you, I proffer my whole lands in dower to your daughter: yea and more would, if more I might.

CLE. And I sir, who have hitherto so earnestly desired your daughter in mariage, doe now willingly yelde up and quite claime to this yong man, who both for his yeares and for the love he beareth hir, is most meetest to be hir husband. For wher I was desirous of a wife by whom I might have yssue, to leave that litle which god hath sent me: now have I litle neede, that (thankes be to god) have founde my deerely beloved sonne, whom I loste of a childe at the siege of *Otranto*.

DA. Worthy gentleman, your friendship, your alliaunce, and the nobilitie of your birthe are suche, as I have muche more cause to desire them of you than you to request of me that which is already graunted. Therfore I gladly, and willingly receive the same, and thinke my selfe moste happie now of all my life past, that I have gotten so toward a sonne in lawe to my selfe, and so worthye a father in lawe to my daughter: yea and muche the greater is my contentation, since this worthie gentleman maister *Cleander*, doth holde himselfe satisfied. And now behold your sonne.

ERO. O father.

PAS. Beholde the naturall love of the childe to the father: for inwarde joye he cannot pronounce one worde, in steade wherof he sendeth sobbes and teares to tell the effect of his inward in[t]ention. But why doe you abide here abrode? wil it please you to goe into the house sir?

DA. *Pasiphilo* hath saide well: will it please you to goe in sir?

NE. Here I have brought you sir, bothe fetters & boltes.

DA. Away with them now.

NE. Yea, but what shal I doe with them?

DA. Marie I will tell thee *Nevola*: to make a righte ende of our supposes, lay one of those boltes in the fire, and make thee a suppositorie as long as mine arme, God save the sample. Nobles and gentlemen, if you suppose that our supposes have given you sufficient cause of delighte, shewe some token, whereby we may suppose you are content.

Et plauserunt.[1]

FINIS

[1] And they applauded.

VENUS AND ADONIS

Adonis, The name of a childe, which was sonne of Cynare king of Cypres, whome Venus had for hir derling, which was slaine with a Bore: whome the Poets feigned, that Venus turned into a purple flower: some saye into a Rose.

[T. COOPER: *Thesaurus Linguae.* 1565]

INTRODUCTION

ENTERED IN S.R. on 18th April 1593 for Richard Field who printed it in that year, *Venus and Adonis* was the first work admitted to be Shakespeare's own, 'the first heire of my invention' as he termed it in his Dedication to Henry Wriothesley, Third Earl of Southampton, who was then not quite twenty years old. It was the poet's most popular work, going into 16 editions before 1640. It has been suggested that he wrote it in 1592 when the theatres were shut because of plague, but doubtless even a busy actor-dramatist had some 'idle houres'. The style, so much richer and more glowing than that of the earliest Histories and comedies, suggests either a new literary discipleship or some recent enrichment of personal experience, perhaps both. In the nineties mythological story came to be associated, as in Thomas Lodge's *Scillaes Metamorphosis* (1589) and Marlowe's fragmentary *Hero and Leander* (not published till 1598), with ornate imagery and erotic expansiveness. Shakespeare seems to be making a bid for court approval by writing in the lavish manner of the urbaner classicists who took Ovid for a model; hence his prefatory couplet from the *Amores*: 'Let the mob admire base things; may golden Apollo serve me full goblets from the Castalian Fount',[1] and there can be no doubt that Shakespeare read Ovid in the original for he draws on Ovidian pieces of which no translation had been published; in the main he goes to Golding's translation of the *Metamorphoses* (1565–7) but he also knew the *Ars Amatoria* and the *Fasti*.

He had already touched on the Venus-Adonis theme in *The Taming of the Shrew*, Ind. II.47, where, after referring to Sly as a huntsman with swift greyhounds, a servant asks:

> Dost thou love pictures? We will fetch thee straight
> Adonis painted by a running brook,

[1] *Vilia miretur vulgus; mihi flavus Apollo Pocula Castalia plena ministret aqua.*

And Cytherea all in sedges hid,
Which seem to move and wanton with her breath
Even as the moving sedges play wi' th' wind.

Here as in the poem itself we see Shakespeare's confluent
imagination at work, combining elements from two stories:
Venus and Adonis (*Met.* X. 519–59; 705–39) and Salmacis and
Hermaphroditus (*Met.* IV. 285–388). T. W. Baldwin in his
detailed examination of the sources of *Venus and Adonis* argues
that four sonnets in 'The Passionate Pilgrim' (IV, VI, IX, XI)
represent 'a kind of first handling of the Venus and Adonis
story, out of which the poem of Venus and Adonis grew'
(*Genetics*, p. 44). The fourth sonnet, in which Venus watches
Adonis undressing to bathe, resembles somewhat the *Shrew*
passage, but it is difficult to say which was written first.

Ovid's Adonis story [I] is a short account of Venus's love
for the great hunter which made her dress as Diana and take
up the sport. She advises Adonis to beware of lions, boars and
other dangerous beasts, and when he asks the reason, tells him
the story of Atalanta and Hippomenes who were changed into
lions for profaning the grove of Cybele with their love. After
Venus leaves him Adonis hunts a boar which wounds him
fatally. In all this the young man shows no great bashfulness.
Shakespeare however has intermingled part of the story of
Salmacis and Hermaphroditus [II] in which the young son of
Mercury and Venus is wooed by a water-nymph. When he
modestly refuses her a kiss she hides to spy on him, and when
he strips to bathe she follows and embraces him in the water.
He struggles to escape, whereat she begs the gods not to separate
them. They become one, and Hermaphroditus, having now
both sexes, asks that all who bathe in the spring may be made
effeminate. This tale caused quite a cult of the hermaphrodite
in Renaissance literature. Shakespeare draws on the first part
of it for the forwardness of Venus, Adonis blushing (*VA* 49–50;
76–8), the begging and refusal of a kiss (*VA* 84–9; 115–28, &c),
the female's amorous embraces (*VA* 55–72; 225–30), the male's
continued reluctance (379; 710), the image of union when he
bids her goodnight (539–40).

A third Ovidian love-story on which Shakespeare draws is
that of Narcissus, another hunter, pursued by the nymph

Echo [III]. This provides a direct reference in *VA* 157–62,[1] the accusation of self-love which Venus uses as a weapon; and maybe the echoes of Venus's moans which inspire her to a nightlong echo song (830–40).

Other Ovidian touches include the reference (*VA* 211–15) to Adonis as a 'Statue contenting but the eye alone', which recalls that Ovid's Pygmalion (*Met.* X, 243–6)

> Offended with the vice, whereof great store is packed within
> The nature of the womankind, he led a single life,
> And long it was ere he could find in heart to take a wife.

In addition there are the description of the boar (*VA* 616–36) which owes something to Meleager's enemy in *Met.* VIII, 281–427 (which Atalanta, unlike Venus, is bold to encounter); and Venus's allusion to her conquest of Mars (*VA* 97–112) giving an Anacreontic turn, with its 'rose-red chain' to *Ars Amatoria*, ii. 563–4:

> Great Mars, submitting unto Venus' love,
> Of a blunt soldier did an amorist prove.
> (Wolferston's trans. 1661)

Also from the *Art of Love* may come Adonis's plea that he is too young to love (*VA* 523–27) though the image in Ovid is not of plums but 'Wine drunk too new is sour'; and maybe some of Venus's arguments for loving in youth.

The bringing together of the major Ovidian elements throws light on Shakespeare's purpose. Both Hermaphroditus and Narcissus are hostile to female blandishments, the one from youthful unreadiness, the other from self-engrossment. Shakespeare used these attributes in discussing Adonis because his poem was conceived as a study in the coyness of masculine adolescence, the frenzy of female longing, with a debate on physical love and procreation. Adonis is made a boy of sixteen or so, unripe for love, not merely a sturdy huntsman impatient of other sports, like Silvio in Guarini's *Pastor Fido*. From the first Venus insists that, though immature, Adonis should 'be tasted', and 'Make use of time, let not advantage slip' (128–9). The wonderful description of the courser with the 'breeding jennet' (289–

---

[1] The idea that Narcissus was drowned while kissing his own reflection is not in Ovid, but was common in the Renaissance. It recurs in *Lucrece* 265–6.

322), which may owe a little to Virgil's *Georgic* III (75–94), excites Venus more and lends force to her argument that physical love is natural and inevitable (385–408). Similarly her description of the boar introduces a plea that the best way of countering mortality is procreation (721–68), which Adonis answers by accusing her of lust, and differentiating between heavenly and earthly love (769–810). Adonis however is not an allegory of 'Beauty or true love refusing to be won by Venus's love to propagation' (Baldwin). The poem is anything but a Platonic piece; the poet's sympathy is primarily with Venus and the coupling animals, though he also states a point of view which the Spenserians would accept. *Venus and Adonis* is indeed closely related to the first seventeen Sonnets in which Shakespeare urges his friend to marry and have children and uses Venus's arguments among others. These sonnets were probably written about the same time as the narrative poem, and if Southampton were the friend in the Sonnets the Dedication of *Venus and Adonis* to him would have special point.

The poem is not merely or mainly a praise of sexual love; it is a pictorial and psychological study of the physical and emotional attitudes of wooing and revulsion, lust and coyness, pursued with a voluptuous delight (not found in Ovid or his English translator) which is extended after Adonis's death to the goddess's anguish—portrayed in 45 or more stanzas of postures sweet and sad. That *Venus and Adonis* is full of rhetoric has often been shown. It is the rhetoric of the Renaissance treatises rather than of Ovid himself, but undoubtedly the prince of Roman oratorical poets inspired Shakespeare to new flights of patterned speech infused with a colour and warmth greater than his source. The Ovidian influence, coming as the Sonnets suggest at a time of emotional disturbance, urged Shakespeare to fresh verbal flights and was one cause of the freedom, wit, allusiveness and elegance which accompany the emotional enrichment of the next plays. At the end of *Venus and Adonis* the goddess puts a curse on love, saying that it shall be full of paradoxes:

> It shall be waited on with jealousy
> Find sweet beginning, but unsavoury end . . .

> It shall be sparing, and too full of riot,
> Teaching decrepit age to tread the measures, . . .

It shall be raging mad, and silly mild,
Make the young old, the old become a child . . . &c.

(*VA* 1133–64)

So the poem turns not only, like so many of Ovid's episodes, into an explanation of a floral phenomenon, how the anemone got its colour, but into an explanation of love's urgencies, perversities and contrarieties; and these were the subject of Shakespeare's next plays.

I. Source

OVID: METAMORPHOSES
translated by Arthur Golding (1567)
Lib. X. Lines 585–651; 826–63.[1] (Venus and Adonis)

The XV Bookes of P. Ovidius Naso, entytuled Metamorphosis, translated oute of Latin into English meeter, by Arthur Golding Gentleman . . . 1567.

Book X

[Myrrha, having committed incest with her father Cinyra, flees and prays to be changed so that she will be neither with the living nor with the dead. She becomes a tree, but her son Adonis is born with the aid of the goddess Lucina.]

Lucina to this wofull tree came gently downe, and layd
Her hand theron, and speaking woordes of ease, the midwife playd.
The tree did cranye, and the barke deviding made away,
And yeelded out the chyld alyve, which cryde and wayld streyght
    way.
The waternymphes uppon the soft sweete hearbes the chyld did
    lay,
And bathde him with his mothers teares. His face was such, as
    spyght
Must needes have praysd. For such he was in all condicions right,
As are the naked *Cupids* that in tables picturde bee.
But too th'entent he may with them in every poynt agree,
Let eyther him bee furnisshed with wings and quiver light,
Or from the *Cupids* take theyr wings and bowes and arrowes quight.
    Away slippes fleeting tyme unspyde and mocks us too our face,
    And nothing may compare with yeares in swiftnesse of theyr
        pace.

---

[1] The Latin lines are 510–562; 705–739.

That wretched imp whom wickedly his graundfather begate,
And whom his cursed suster bare, who hidden was alate
Within the tree, and lately borne, became immediatly
The beawtyfullyst babe on whom man ever set his eye.
Anon a stripling hee became, and by and by a man,
And every day more beawtifull than other he becam.
That in the end Dame *Venus* fell in love with him: wherby
He did revenge the outrage of his mothers villanye.
For as the armed *Cupid* kist Dame *Venus*, unbeware
An arrow sticking out did raze hir brest uppon the bare.
The Goddesse being wounded, thrust away her sonne. The wound
Appeered not too bee so deepe as afterward was found.
It did deceyve her at the first. The beawty of the lad
Inflam'd hir. To *Cythera* Ile no mynd at all shee had,
Nor unto *Paphos* where the sea beats round about the shore,
Nor fisshy *Gnyde*, nor *Amathus* that hath of mettalls store:
Yea even from heaven shee did absteyne. Shee lovd *Adonis* more
Than heaven. To him shee clinged ay, and bare him companye.
And in the shadowe woont shee was too rest continually,
And for too set her beawtye out most seemely to the eye
By trimly decking of her self. Through bushy grounds and groves,
And over Hills and Dales, and Lawnds and stony rocks shee roves,
Bare kneed with garment tucked up according to the woont
Of *Phebe*, and shee cheerd the hounds with hallowing like a hunt,
Pursewing game of hurtlesse sort, as Hares made lowe before,
Or stagges with loftye heades, or bucks. But with the sturdy Boare,
And ravening woolf, and Bearewhelpes armd with ugly pawes, and
    eeke
The cruell Lyons which delyght in blood, and slaughter seeke,
Shee meddled not. And of these same shee warned also thee
Adonis for too shoonne them, if thou wooldst have warned bee.
Bee bold on cowards (*Venus* sayd) for whoso dooth advaunce
Himselfe against the bold, may hap to meete with sum mischaunce.
Wherfore I pray thee my sweete boy forbeare too bold to bee,
For feare thy rashnesse hurt thy self and woork the wo of mee.
Encounter not the kynd of beastes whom nature armed hath,
For dowt thou buy thy prayse too deere procuring thee sum scath.
Thy tender youth, thy beawty bryght, thy countnance fayre and
    brave
Although they had the force to win the hart of *Venus*, have
No powre ageinst the Lyons, nor ageinst the bristled swyne.
The eyes and harts of savage beasts doo nought to these inclyne.
The cruell Boares beare thunder in theyr hooked tushes, and

Exceeding force and feercenesse is in Lyons to withstand,
And sure I hate them at my hart. To him demaunding why?
A monstrous chaunce (quoth *Venus*) I will tell thee by and by,
That hapned for a fault. But now unwoonted toyle hath made
Mee weerye: and beholde, in tyme this Poplar with his shade
Allureth, and the ground for cowch dooth serve to rest uppon.
I prey thee let us rest us heere. They sate them downe anon,
And lying upward with her head uppon his lappe along,
She thus began: and in her tale shee bussed him among.
    Perchaunce thou hast or this tyme hard of one that overcame
    The swiftest men in footemanshippe: no fable was that same.
She overcame them out of dowt. And hard it is to tell
Thee whither she did in footemanshippe or beawty more excell.

                    (ll. 585–651)

[Venus tells the story of the swift-footed Atalanta who refused love
until Hippomenes beat her in a race; and how they profaned the
grove of Cybele by making love there, and were changed into lions.
The goddess then advises Adonis:]

                                      Shonne
These beastes, deere hart: and not from these alonely see thou ronne,
But also from eche other beast that turnes not backe to flight,
But offreth with his boystrous brest to try the chaunce of fyght:
Anemis[1] lest thy valeantnesse bee hurtfull to us both.
    This warning given, with yoked swannes away through aire she
        goeth.
    But manhood by admonishment restreyned could not bee.
By chaunce his hounds in following of the tracke, a Boare did see,
And rowsed him. And as the swyne was comming from the wood
Adonis hit him with a dart a skew, and drew the blood.
The Boare streyght with his hooked groyne the huntingstaffe out
    drew
Bestayned with his blood, and on *Adonis* did pursew,
Who trembling and retyring back to place of refuge drew,
And hyding in his codds his tuskes as farre as he could thrust
He layd him all along for dead uppon the yellow dust.
Dame *Venus* in her chariot drawen with swannes was scarce arrived
At *Cyprus*, when shee knew afarre the sigh of him depryved
Of lyfe. Shee turnd her Cygnets backe, and when shee from the skye
Beheld him dead, and in his blood beweltred for to lye,
Shee leaped downe, and tare at once hir garments from her brist,
And rent her heare, and beate uppon her stomack with her fist,

    [1] Animous? hot-tempered.

And blaming sore the dest'nyes, sayd: Yet shall they not obteine
Their will in all things. Of my greefe remembrance shall remayne
(*Adonis*) whyle the world doth last. From yeere to yeere shall growe
A thing that of my heavinesse and of thy death shall showe
The lively likenesse. In a flowre thy blood I will bestowe.
Hadst thou the powre *Persephonee* rank-scented Mints to make
Of womens limbes? and may not I lyke powre upon mee take
Without disdeine and spyght, too turne *Adonis* to a flowre?
This sed, shee sprinckled Nectar on the blood, which through the
        powre
Therof did swell like bubbles sheere that ryse in weather cleere
On water. And before that full an howre expyred weere,
Of all one colour with the blood a flowre[1] she there did fynd,
Even like the flowre of that same tree whose frute in tender rynde
Have pleasant graynes inclosde. Howbeit the use of them is short.
For why the leaves doo hang so loose through lightnesse in such sort,
As that the windes that all things perce, with every little blast
Doo shake them off and shed them so, as that they cannot last.

                                                          (ll. 826–63)

II. Source

OVID: METAMORPHOSES
translated by Arthur Golding (1567)
Lib. IV. Lines 347–481 (Salmacis and Hermaphroditus)

Book IV

[In this book the daughters of Minyas, refusing to take part in
Bacchus' festival, stay at home and beguile the time while working
by telling stories. One relates the tale of Pyramus and Thisbe; the
next, Leuconoë, tells of Leucothoë changed into a shoot of frankin-
cense and Clytie into the heliotrope; the third, Alcithoë, tells the
following for its 'charming novelty'. Lines 285–388 in original.]

Learne why the fountaine *Salmacis* diffamed is of yore,
Why with his waters overstrong it weakneth men so sore

---

[1] Usually supposed to be the anemone.

That whoso bathes him there, commes thence a perfect man
     no more.
The operation of this Well is knowne to every wight:
But few can tell the cause thereof, the which I will recite.
     The waternymphes did nurce a sonne of *Mercuries* in *Ide*
     Begot on *Venus*, in whose face such beautie did abide,
As well therein his father both and mother might be knowne,
Of whome he also tooke his name. Assoone as he was growne
To fiftene yeares of age, he left the Countrie where he dwelt
And *Ida* that had fostered him. The pleasure that he felt
To travell Countries, and to see straunge rivers with the state
Of forren landes, all painfulnesse of travell did abate.
He travelde through the lande of *Lycie* to *Carie* that doth bound
Next unto *Lycia*. There he saw a Poole which to the ground
Was Christall cleare. No fennie sedge, no barren reeke,[1] no reede
Nor rush with pricking poynt was there, nor other moorish weede.
The water was so pure and shere, a man might well have seene
And numbred all the gravell stones that in the bottome beene.
The utmost borders from the brim environd were with clowres[2]
Beclad with herbes ay fresh and greene and pleasant smelling flowres.
A Nymph did haunt this goodly Poole: but such a Nymph as neyther
To hunt, to run, nor yet to shoote, had any kinde of pleasure.
Of all the Waterfa[i]ries she alonly was unknowne
To swift *Diana*. As the bru[i]te of fame abrode hath blowne,
Hir sisters oftentimes would say: take lightsome Dart or bow,
And in some painefull exercise thine ydle time bestow.
But never could they hir persuade to runne, to shoote or hunt,
Or any other exercise as *Phebes* knightes are wont.
Sometime hir faire welformed limbes shee batheth in hir spring:
Sometime she downe hir golden haire with Boxen combe doth bring.
And at the water as a glasse she taketh counsell ay
How every thing becommeth hir. Erewhile in fine aray
On soft sweete hearbes or soft greene leaves hir selfe she nicely
     layes
Erewhile again a gathering flowres from place to place she
     strayes.
And (as it chaunst) the selfe same time she was a sorting gayes[3]
To make a Posie, when she first the yongman did espie,
And in beholding him desirde to have his companie.
But though she thought she stoode on thornes untill she went to him,
Yet went she not before she had bedec[k]t hir neat and trim,
And pri'de and peerd upon hir clothes that nothing sat awrie,

---

[1] marsh-vapour?   [2] swelling banks.   [3] gay flowers.

And framde hir countnance as might seeme most amrous to the eie
   Which done shee thus begon: O childe most worthie for to
      bee
   Esteemde and taken for a God, if (as thou seemste to mee)
   Thou be a God, to *Cupids* name thy beautie doth agree.
Or if thou be a mortall wight, right happie folke are they,
By whome thou camste into this worlde, right happy is (I say)
Thy mother and thy sister too (if any bee:) good hap
That woman had that was thy Nurce and gave thy mouth hir pap.
But farre above all other, far more blist than these is shee
Whome thou vouchsafest for thy wife and bedfellow for too bee.
Now if thou have alredy one, let me by stelth obtaine
That which shall pleasure both of us. Or if thou doe remaine
A Maiden free from wedlocke bonde, let me then be thy spouse,
And let us in the bridelie bed our selves togither rouse.
   This sed, the Nymph did hold hir peace, and therewithall the
      boy
   Waxt red: he wist not what love was: and sure it was a joy
To see it how exceeding well his blushing him became.
For in his face the colour fresh appeared like the same
That is in Apples which doe hang upon the Sunnie side:
Or Ivorie shadowed with a red: or such as is espide
Of white and scarlet colours mixt appearing in the Moone
When folke in vaine with sounding brasse would ease unto hir done.
When at the last the Nymph desirde most instantly but this,
As to his sister brotherly to give hir there a kisse,
And therewithall was clasping him about the Ivorie necke:
Leave off (quoth he) or I am gone, and leave thee at a becke
With all thy trickes. Then *Salmacis* began to be afraide,
And to your pleasure leave I free this place my friend shee sayde.
With that she turnes hir backe as though she would have gone hir
      way:
But evermore she looketh backe, and (closely as she may)
She hides her in a bushie queach,[1] where kneeling on hir knee
She always hath hir eye on him. He as a childe and free,
And thinking not that any wight had watched what he did,
Romes up and downe the pleasant Mede: and by and by amid
The flattring waves he dippes his feete, no more but first the sole
And to the ancles afterward both feete he plungeth whole.
And for to make the matter short, he tooke so great delight
In cooleness of the pleasant spring, that streight he stripped quight
His garments from his tender skin. When *Salmacis* behelde

[1] thicket.

His naked beautie, such strong pangs so ardently hir helde,
That utterly she was astraught. And even as *Phebus* beames
Against a myrrour pure and clere rebound with broken gleames;
Even so hir eyes did sparcle fire. Scarce could she tarriance make:
Scarce could she any time delay hir pleasure for to take.
She wolde have run, and in hir armes embraced him streight way:
She was so far beside hir selfe, that scarsly could she stay.
He clapping with his hollow hands against his naked sides,
Into the water lithe and baine[1] with armes displayed glydes.
And rowing with his hands and legges swimmes in the water cleare:
Through which his bodie faire and white doth glistringly appeare,
As if a man an Ivorie Image or a Lillie white
Should overlay or close with glasse that were most pure and bright.
    The prize is won (cride *Salmacis* aloud) he is mine owne.
    And therewithall in all post hast she having lightly throwne
Hir garments off, flew to the Poole and cast hir thereinto,
And caught him fast betweene hir armes for ought that he could doe.
Yea maugre all his wrestling and his struggling to and fro,
She held him still, and kissed him a hundred times and mo.
And willde he nillde he with hir handes she toucht his naked brest:
And now on this side now on that (for all he did resist
And strive to wrest him from hir gripes) she clung unto him fast,
And wound about him like a Snake, which snatched up in hast
And being by the Prince of Birdes borne lightly up aloft,
Doth writhe hir selfe about his necke and griping talants oft,
And cast hir taile about his wings displayed in the winde:
Or like as Ivie runnes on trees about the utter rinde:
Or as the Crabfish having caught his enmy in the Seas,
Doth claspe him in on every side with all his crooked cleas.
    But *Atlas* Nephew still persistes, and utterly denies
    The Nymph to have hir hoped sport: she urges him likewise,
And pressing him with all hir weight, fast cleaving to him still,
Strive, struggle, wrest and writhe (she said) thou froward boy thy
    fill:
Doe what thou canst thou shalt not scape. Ye Goddes of Heaven
    agree
That this same wilfull boy and I may never parted bee.
The Gods were pliant to hir boone. The bodies of them twaine
Were mixt and joyned both in one. To both them did remaine
One countnance. Like as if a man should in one barke beholde
Two twigges both growing into one and still togither holde:
Even so when through hir hugging and hir grasping of the tother

---

[1] limber.

The members of them mingled were and fastned both togither,
They were not any longer two: but (as it were) a toy
Of double shape: Ye could not say it was a perfect boy,
Nor perfect wench: it seemed both and none of both to beene.
Now when *Hermaphroditus* saw how in the water sheene
To which he entred in a man, his limmes were weakened so
That out from thence but halfe a man he was compelde to go:
He lifteth up his hands and said (but not with manly reere)
O noble father *Mercurie*, and *Venus* mother deere,
This one petition graunt your son which both your names doth
        beare,
That whoso commes within this Well may so bee weakened there,
That of a man but halfe a man he may from thence retire.
Both Parentes mooved with the chaunce did stablish this desire
The which their doubleshaped sonne had made, and thereupon
Infected with an unknowne strength the sacred spring anon.

III. Source

OVID: METAMORPHOSES
translated by Arthur Golding (1567)
Lib. III. Lines 427–542; 635–42 (Narcissus)

Book III

[Tiresias, who had been both man and woman, was blinded by Juno
for supporting Jupiter's assertion that the female got more pleasure
in the embraces of love than the male. Jupiter however gave him the
power to know the future. Latin text, lines 341–510.]
        The first that of his soothfast wordes had proofe in all the
            Realme,
        Was freckled *Lyriop*, whom sometime surprised in his streame,
The flood *Cephisus* did enforce. This Lady bare a sonne
Whose beautie at his verie birth might justly love have wonne.
Narcissus did she call his name. Of whom the Prophet sage
Demaunded if the childe should live to many yeares of age,
Made aunswere, yea full long, so that himselfe he doe not know.
The Soothsayers wordes seemde long but vaine, untill the end did
        show

His saying to be true indeede by straungenesse of the rage,
And straungenesse of the kinde of death that did abridge his age.
For when yeares three times five and one he fully lyved had,
So that he seemde to stande beetwene the state of man and Lad,
The hearts of divers trim yong men his beautie gan to move,
And many a Ladie fresh and faire was taken in his love.
But in that grace of Natures gift such passing pride did raigne,
That to be toucht of man or Mayde he wholy did disdaine.
A babling Nymph that *Echo* hight: who hearing others talke,
By no meanes can restraine hir tongue but that it needes must walke,
Nor of hir selfe hath powre to 'ginne to speake to any wight,
Espyde him dryving into toyles the fearefull stagges of flight.
This *Echo* was a body then and not an onely voyce,
Yet of hir speach she had that time no more than now the choyce,
That is to say of many wordes the latter to repeate.
The cause thereof was *Junos* wrath. For when that with the feate
She might have often taken *Jove* in daliance with his Dames,
And that by stealth and unbewares in middes of all his games,
This elfe would with hir tatling talke deteine hir by the way,
Untill that *Jove* had wrought his will and they were fled away.
The which when *Juno* did perceyve, she said with wrathfull mood,
This tongue that hath deluded me shall doe thee little good:
For of thy speach but simple use hereafter shalt thou have.
The deede it selfe did straight confirme the threatnings that she
     gave.
Yet *Echo* of the former talke doth double oft the ende
And backe againe with just report the wordes erst spoken sende.
    Now when she sawe *Narcissus* stray about the Forrest wyde,
    She waxed warme and step for step fast after him she hyde.
The more she followed after him and neerer that she came,
The hotter ever did she waxe as neerer to hir flame.
Lyke as the lively Brimstone doth which dipt about a match,
And put but softly to the fire, the flame doth lightly catch.
O Lord how often would she faine (if nature would have let)
Entreated him with gentle wordes some favour for to get?
But nature would not suffer hir nor give hir leave to ginne.
Yet (so farre forth as she by graunt at natures hande could winne)
Ay readie with attentive eare she harkens for some sounde,
Whereto she might replie hir wordes, from which she is not bounde.
By chaunce the stripling being strayde from all his companie,
Sayde: is there any bodie nie? straight *Echo* answerde: I.
Amazde he castes his eye aside, and looketh round about,
And come (that all the Forrest rung) aloud he calleth out.

And come (sayth she:) he looketh backe, and seeing no man followe,
Why fli'st, he cryeth once againe: and she the same doth hallowe.
He still persistes, and wondring much what kinde of thing it was
From which that answering voyce by turne so duely seemde to passe,
Sayd: let us joyne. She (by hir will desirous to have said,
In fayth with none more willingly at any time or stead)
Sayd: let us joyne. And standing somewhat in hir owne conceit,
Upon these wordes she left the Wood, and forth she yeedeth streit,[1]
To coll the lovely necke for which she longed had so much.
He runnes his way, and will not be imbraced of no such.
And sayth: I first will die ere thou shalt take of me thy pleasure.
She answerde nothing else thereto, but Take of me thy pleasure.
Now when she saw hir selfe thus mockt, she gate hir to the Woods,
And hid hir head for verie shame among the leaves and buddes.
And ever since she lyves alone in dennes and hollow Caves.
Yet stucke hir love still to hir heart, through which she dayly raves
The more for sorrowe of repulse. Through restlesse carke and care
Hir bodie pynes to skinne and bone, and waxeth wonderous bare.
The bloud doth vanish into ayre from out of all hir veynes,
And nought is left but voyce and bones: the voyce yet still remaynes:
Hir bones they say were turnde to stones. From thence she lurking
      still
In Woods, will never shewe hir head in field nor yet on hill.
Yet is she heard of every man: it is hir onely sound,
And nothing else that doth remayne alive above the ground.
Thus had he mockt this wretched Nymph and many mo beside,
That in the waters, Woods, and groves, or Mountaynes did abide.
Thus had he mocked many men. Of which one, miscontent
To see himselfe deluded so, his handes to Heaven up bent,
And sayd: I pray to God he may once feele fierce *Cupids* fire
As I doe now, and yet not joy the things he doth desire.
The Goddesse R[h]amnuse [2](who doth wreake on wicked people take)
Assented to his just request for ruth and pities sake.
      There was a Spring withouten mudde as silver cleare and still,
      Which neyther sheepeheirds, nor the Goates that fed upon the
          hill,
Nor other cattell troubled had, nor savage beast had styrd,
Nor braunch, nor sticke, nor leafe of tree, nor any foule nor byrd.
The moysture fed and kept aye fresh the grasse that grew about,
And with their leaves the trees did keepe the heate of *Phoebus* out.
The stripling wearie with the heate and hunting in the chace,
And much delighted with the spring and coolenesse of the place,

---

[1] goeth directly.   [2] Nemesis.

Did lay him downe upon the brimme: and as he stooped lowe
To staunche his thurst, another thurst of worse effect did growe.
For as he dranke, he chaunst to spie the Image of his face,
The which he did immediately with fervent love embrace.
He feedes a hope without cause why. For like a foolishe noddie
He thinkes the shadow that he sees, to be a lively boddie.
Astraughted like an ymage made of Marble stone he lyes,
There gazing on his shadow still with fixed staring eyes.
Stretcht all along upon the ground, it doth him good to see
His ardent eyes which like two starres full bright and shyning bee,
And eke his fingers, fingers such as *Bacchus* might beseeme,
And haire that one might worthely *Apollos* haire it deeme.
His beardlesse chinne and yvorie necke, and eke the perfect grace
Of white and red indifferently bepainted in his face.
All these he woondreth to beholde, for which (as I doe gather)
Himselfe was to be wondred at, or to be pitied rather.
He is enamored of himselfe for want of taking heede.
And where he lykes another thing, he lykes himselfe in deede.
He is the partie whome he wooes, and suitor that doth wooe,
He is the flame that settes on fire, and thing that burneth tooe.
O Lord how often did he kisse that false deceitfull thing?
How often did he thrust his armes midway into the spring,
To have embraste the necke he saw and could not catch himselfe?
He knowes not what it was he sawe. And yet the foolishe elfe
Doth burne in ardent love thereof. The verie selfe same thing
That doth bewitch and blinde his eyes, encreaseth all his sting.

[He realises that 'The thing I seek is in myself', but wastes away and
dies.]

The water Nymphes his sisters wept and wayled for him sore,
And on his bodie strowde their haire clipt off and shorne therefore.
The Woodnymphes also did lament. And *Echo* did rebound
To every sorrowfull noyse of theirs with like lamenting sound.
The fire was made to burne the corse, and waxen Tapers light.
A He[a]rse to lay the bodie on with solemne pompe was dight.
But as for bodie none remaind: In stead thereof they found
A yellow floure with milke white leaves new sprong upon the ground.

THE RAPE OF LUCRECE

INTRODUCTION

ENTERED IN S.R. on 9 May, 1594, to 'Master Harrison' as a book 'intituled the Ravyshement of Lucrece', the poem was printed in Quarto 'by Richard Field for Iohn Harrison'. Eight editions appeared before 1640. *The Rape* was dedicated to Southampton in more intimate terms than *Venus and Adonis*, and must be the 'graver labour' mentioned in the Epistle to the earlier work. It is a companion piece to the other, for, having described desire unaccomplished against reluctance, Shakespeare now gives desire accomplished by force. The rape which Venus, like Salmacis, wished to perform but could not because of feminine weakness, is here effected with masculine brutality. Whereas Adonis was chaste because inexperienced, ignorant, immature and devoted to the chase, Lucrece is chaste in marriage, experienced, mature and devoted to her husband, the first of Shakespeare's faithful suffering wives.

As 'the grand example of conjugal fidelity throughout the Gothic Ages' (Warton), Lucrece was praised in *Le Roman de la Rose* and included by Chaucer in his *Legend of Good Women* (fifth tale), which Shakespeare certainly knew [Text I]. Chaucer referred to 'Ovyde and Titus Lyvius', and these authorities were used by the Elizabethan poet. It has been proved by Ewig and Baldwin that he probably used an edition of Ovid's *Fasti* with Latin annotations by Paulus Marsus of which there were many reprints from 1508 onwards. To give these notes and explain them would occupy too much space, but I supply the Latin text [II] and a translation by J. Gower (1640), whose homespun lines throw into relief the splendour of Shakespeare's [III].

The dramatist seems to have had before him a copy of Titus Livy's *History of Rome* (Chapters LVII–LX), represented here by the fairly close version made by Painter for his *Palace of Pleasure* (1566) [IV].

Ovid remains the chief source, and Shakespeare's handling recalls *Venus and Adonis*. Here too he begins *in medias res* with one character going to meet the other. There is an apparent discrepancy between the Argument and the first three stanzas, which say nothing of the test by which Collatine proved his wife's virtue, but suggest that he boasted of her chastity a second time, on the night before Tarquin stole away from Ardea (15). Maybe the poem was written without regard to the first journey and test, and the Argument was written later with the full story in mind. The poem can stand on its own feet without the Argument, since it implies (Lines 78–9) that Tarquin had not seen her before but was inflamed by Collatine's praise of her chastity and beauty which he wished to prove

> Haply that name of 'chaste' unhap'ly set
> This bateless edge on his keen appetite   (8–9)

As Baldwin points out, Collatine in Ovid makes no reference to Lucrece's chastity, and Tarquin is excited by the memory of her beauty; but the reference to chastity might be inspired by one of Marsus' notes.

Throughout Shakespeare is expanding Ovid's brief account, swelling 73 lines into 1855, and filling out the outline of the Roman's sophisticated simplicity with long disquisitions on the physical and emotional states of the two main figures as they occur, disquisitions conducted with ritualistic stylization as the contrast between virtue and vice, innocence and lust, hospitality and betrayal, is enforced with rhetorical antithesis and paradox. Lucrece is presented as 'This earthly saint adored by this devil' (85), and we see Tarquin 'Hiding base sin in plaits of majesty' (93). Her innocence could not 'moralize his wanton sight' (104), i.e. interpret his desirous looks, but Shakespeare moralizes always, e.g. when Tarquin lies waiting for dead of night, 'Pawning his honour to obtain his lust' (156). When Tarquin tries to control 'his thoughts unjust' he does so in set debate as reason fights will, desire opposes dread, in terms developed from Ovid, 779–83, who succinctly suggests antitheses, e.g.

(Hostis ut hospes init penetralia Collatini
An enemy in guise of a guest enters the home of Collatine)

to be expanded with all the tricks of Renaissance amplification. Lucrece's pleading is rightly described as 'modest eloquence' and 'oratory' (563–6), in which she uses 'periods' and 'sentences'. The moral of the poem is enforced after the deed by the inflation of Ovid's 'Quid victor gaudes? haec te victoria perdet' in Lines 687–728. The display of oratory continues in Lucrece's great speech on Night, Honour, Opportunity and Time (764–1036) with its addendum promising suicide, which is developed later (1158–1211) into a 'plot of death', as two lines in Ovid (II.813–14) on the coming of day are drawn out from 1082 to 1288. So it continues, as Shakespeare draws parallels with other legends of sexual woe to dilate his theme. The end of night takes Lucrece's mind back to the nightingale (which had ended 'The well-tun'd warble of her nightly sorrow (1080)) and the likeness between Tarquin and Tereus (1133–4). Having written to her husband, she (like the poet himself no doubt) 'Pausing for means to mourn some newer way', recalls in great detail a painting of the Greeks before Troy which excites her dislike of Helen, 'the strumpet that began this stir', raises the apt question

> Why should the private pleasure of some one
> Become the public plague of many moe? (1478–9),

and leads her to connect Tarquin with the false Sinon (1520–68). The main idea of this painting is from Virgil's *Aeneid*, I.456–95, for a picture of the Siege of Troy hangs in the palace of Dido (herself betrayed by a man). The wily Sinon is taken from *Aeneid*, II.76ff; but the descriptions of Ajax and Ulysses (*Luc.* 1398ff) and Nestor (*Luc.* 1401ff) come from Ovid's *Metamorphoses*, XIII.

With the arrival of Collatine and his friends the slow-motion film of stylized gestures and language approaches its catastrophe. Shakespeare continues to work on hints from the Latin. Thus

> Ter conata loqui: ter destitit: ausaque quarto
> Non oculos ideo sustulit illa suos [Cf. Gower 103–5]

becomes a whole stanza:

> Three times with sighs she gives her sorrow fire,
> Ere once she can discharge one word of woe:

> At length address'd to answer his desire,
> She modestly prepares to let them know
> Her honour is ta'en prisoner by the foe;
> While Collatine and his consorted lords
> With sad attention long to hear her words.
>
>   (1604–10)

This deliberate suspense is lingered out while Lucrece 'Begins the sad dirge of her certain ending'. Unlike Ovid's heroine who slays herself speedily:

> Nec mora, caelato fixit sua pectora ferro,

Shakespeare's Lucrece teases the reader and extorts from the lords a protest that 'Her body's stain her mind untainted clears' before naming Tarquin and stabbing herself (1709–29).

The self-conscious modesty of Ovid's (and Chaucer's) Lucrece who falls so carefully, though dying, is omitted, but the grief of the mourners is carefully managed. So that her father may mourn first, Collatine stands as in a dream, from which he starts 'And bids Lucretius give his sorrow place'. Each in his due order, and with attention to climax!

We see then that Shakespeare used Ovid's terse and clear-cut tale as a series of suggestions for a full-scale exercise in lyrical and descriptive dilation. As Wyndham wrote[1]: 'Excepting in the last speech and in the death of Lucrece, the Poem is nowhere dramatic. It tells a story, but at each situation the Poet pauses to survey and to illustrate the romantic and emotional values of the relation between his characters, or to analyse the moral passions and the mental debates in any one of them, or even the physiological perturbations responding to these storms and tremors of the mind and soul.'

In Shakespeare's development as a poet *Venus and Adonis* and *Lucrece* are of supreme importance. After so much practice in the devices of rhetoric, the invention of similitudes and contrasts, the 'production' of moral attitudes and postures of emotion, the accumulation of rich and varied images, the poet could scarcely return to the manner of *The Comedy of Errors*, for his mind was changed by what it worked on. His danger would be to become a mere euphuist like Lyly. Shakespeare

---

[1] *The Poems of Shakespeare, edited . . . by George Wyndham.* 1898. p. xcvi.

was saved from this by three things: his sense of humour, which made him in his next plays react against rhetoric while revelling in it; the growing seriousness and depth of his curiosity about human passions (which may have been due in part to a wealth of new experiences in love, business and social life); and the opportunity, nay the necessity, which his work in the popular theatre brought, for a swifter, more selective and economical presentation of situation, emotion and moral comment. The Ovidian poems, in which he transformed the Roman style and matter with such rich if tedious eloquence, were not only a springboard to his imagination but gave him topics, myths and allusions to which he often returned in afterdays.

I. Probable Source

THE LEGENDE OF GOOD WOMEN
by Geoffrey Chaucer
Lines 1680–1885

Incipit Legenda Lucrecie, Rome, Martiris

Now mote I sayne the exilynge of kynges   1680
Of Rome, for hir[1] horrible doynges;
Of the laste kynge Tarquinius
As sayth Ovyde, and Titus Lyvius.
But for that cause telle I nat this story,
But for to preyse, and drawen to memory
The verray wife, the verray trewe Lucresse,
That for hir wifehode, and hir stedfastnesse,
Nat only that these payens hir com[m]ende,
But he that y-cleped is in oure legende
The grete Austyne[2] hath grete compassyoun   1690
Of this Lucresse that starf at Rome toun.
And in what wise I wol but shortly trete,
And of this thynge I touche but the grete.[3]
    Whan Ardea beseged was aboute
With Romaynes, that ful sterne were and stoute,
Ful longe lay the sege, and lytel wroghte,
So that they were halfe ydel, as hem thoghte.
And in his pley Tarquinius the yonge
Gan for to jape, for he was lyghte of tonge,
And sayde that hyt was an ydel lyfe,   1700
No man dide ther no more than his wife.
'And lat us speke of wives that is best;
Preise every man his owne, as him lest,
And with oure speche let us ease oure herte.'
    A knyght, that highte Colatyne, up sterte,
And sayde thus: 'Nay, for hit is no nede

[1] their.   [2] St. Augustine, *The City of God*. I. xviii.
[3] the summary, outline.

184

To trowen on the worde, but on the dede.
I have a wife,' quod he, 'that as I trowe
Is holden good of al that ever hir knowe.
Go we to Rome, to nyght, and we shul se.'   1710
Tarquinius answerde, 'That lyketh me.'
    To Rome be they come, and faste hem dighte
To Colatynes house, and doun they lyghte,
Tarquinius, and eke this Colatyne.
The housbonde knewe the estres[1] wel and fyne,
And ful prevely into the house they goon,
For at the gate porter was there noon:
And at the chambre dore they abyde.
This noble wyfe sat by hir beddys syde
Disshevele, for no malice she ne thoghte,   1720
And softe wolle saith our boke[2] that she wroghte,
To kepen hir fro slouthe and ydilnesse;
And bad hir servauntes doon hir besynesse;
And axeth hem, 'What tydynges heren ye?
How sayne men of the sege? how shal it be?
God wolde the walles weren falle adoun!
Myn housbonde is to longe out of this toun,
For which the drede doth me so to smerte;
Ryght as a swerde hyt styngeth to myn herte,
Whan I thenke on the sege, or of that place.   1730
God save my lorde, I pray him for his grace!'
    And therwithal ful tendirly she wepe,
And of hir werke she toke no more kepe,
But mekely she let hire eyen falle,
And thilke semblant sat hir wel withalle.
And eke the teeres ful of honeste
Embelysshed hire wifely chastitee.
Hire countenance is to her herte digne,
For they acordeden in dede and signe.
And with that worde hir husbonde Colatyne,   1740
Or she of him was ware, come stertyng ynne,
And sayede, 'Drede the noght, for I am here!'
And she anon up roos, with blysful chere,
And kyssed hym, as of wyves is the wone.
    Tarquinius, this prowde kynges sone,
Conceyved hath hir beaute and hir chere,
Hire yelow heer, hir shap, and hire manere,
Hir hewe, hir wordes that she hath compleyned,

---

[1] the inner parts.   [2] Ovid, *Fasti.* ii. 741–2.

And by no craft hire beaute was not feyned;
And kaughte to this lady suche desire,
That in his herte brent as any fire
So wodely[1] that his witte was forgeten,
For wel thoghte he she shulde nat be geten.
And ay the more that he was in dispaire,
The more he covetyth, and thoght hir faire;
His blynde lust was al his covetynge.

1750

On morwe, whan the brid began to synge,
Unto the sege he cometh ful pryvely,
And by himselfe he walketh sobrely,
The ymage of hir recordyng alwey newe:
'Thus lay hir heer, and thus fressh was hir hewe;
Thus sate, thus spake, thus spanne, this was hir chere;
Thus faire she was, and thys was hir manere.'
Al this conceyte his herte hath new y-take,
And as the see, with tempeste al to-shake,
That after, whan the storme is al ago,
Yet wol the watir quappe[2] a day or two,
Ryght so, thogh that hir forme were absent,
The plesaunce of hir forme was present.

1760

But natheles, nat plesaunce, but delyte,
Or an unryghtful talent with dispite,—
'For mawgree hir, she shal my lemman be:
Happe helpeth hardy man alway,' quod he,
'What ende that I make, hit shal be so!'
And gyrt hym with his swerde, and gan to go,
And forth he rit til he to Rome is come,
And al alone his way than hath he nome
Unto the hous of Colatyne ful ryght.

1770

Doun was the sonne, and day hath lost his lyght,
And inne he come, unto a prevy halke,[3]
And in the nyght ful thefely gan he stalke,
Whan every wyght was to his reste broght,
Ne no wyghte had of tresoun suche a thoght.
Whether by wyndow, or by other gynne,
With swerde y-drawe, shortly he cometh ynne
There as she lay, thys noble wyfe Lucresse,
And as she woke, hir bed she felte presse.
'What be[a]st is that,' quod she, 'that weyeth thus?'
'I am the kynges sone, Tarquinius,'
Quod he, 'but and thow crye, or noyse make,

1780

1790

[1] madly.   [2] ripple.   [3] private corner.

Or if thou any creature awake,
Be thilke God that formede man on lyve,
This swerd thurghout thyn herte shal I ryve.'
And therwithal unto hir throte he sterte,
And sette the swerde al sharpe unto hir herte.

No worde she spake, she hath no myght therto;
What shal she sayne? hir wytte is al ago!
Ryght as a wolfe that fynt a lamb alone,
To whom shal she compleyne or make mone?
What! shal she fyghte with an hardy knyghte?   1800
Wel wote men a woman hath no myghte.
What! shal she crye, or how shal she asterte
That hath hir by the throte, with swerde at herte?
She axeth grace, and seyde al that she kan.

'Ne wolt thou nat?' quod tho this cruelle man,
'As wisly Jupiter my soule save,
As I shal in the stable slee thy knave,
And lay him in thy bed, and lowde crye,
That I the[e] fynde in suche avowtrye[1];
And thus thou shalt be ded, and also lese   1810
Thy name, for thou shalt non othir chese.'

Thise Romaynes wyfes loveden so hir name
At thilke tyme, and dredden so the shame,
That, what for fere of sklaundre, and drede of dethe,
She lost attones bothe wytte and brethe;
And in a swowgh she lay, and woxe so ded,
Men myghten smyten of hir arme or hed,
She feleth nothinge, neither foule ne feyre.

Tarquinius, thou art a kynges eyre,
And sholdest, as by lynage and by ryght,   1820
Doon as a lorde and as a verray knyght;
Why hastow doon dispite to chevalrye?
Why hastow doon thys lady vylanye?
Allas, of the[e] thys was a vilenous dede!

But now to the purpose; in the story I rede
Whan he was goon and this myschaunce is falle.
Thys lady sent aftir hir frendes alle,
Fader, moder, housbonde, alle y-fere,
And al dysshevelee with hir heere clere,
In habyte suche as wymmen usede tho   1830
Unto the buryinge of hir frendes go,
She sytte in halle with a sorowful syghte.

---

[1] adultery.

Hir frendes axen what hir aylen myghte,
And who was dede, and she sytte aye wepynge.
A worde for shame ne may she forthe out brynge,
Ne upon hem she durste nat beholde,
But atte laste of Tarquyny she hem tolde
This rewful case, and al thys thing horryble.
    The wo to telle hyt were an impossible
That she and al hir frendes made attones.   1840
Al hadde folkes hertys ben of stones,
Hyt myght have maked hem upon hir rewe,
Hire herte was so wyfely and so trewe.
She sayde that for hir gylt, ne for hir blame,
Hir housbonde shulde nat have the foule name,
That nolde she nat suffren by no wey.
And they answerde alle upon hir fey,
That they forgaf hyt hyr, for hyt was ryght;
Hyt was no gilt; hit lay not in hir myght,
And seyden hire ensamples many oon.   1850
But al for noght, for thus she seyde anoon:
'Be as be may,' quod she, 'of forgifynge;
I wol not have no forgift for nothinge.'
But pryvely she kaughte forth a knyfe,
And therwithal she rafte hir-selfe hir lyfe;
And as she felle adoun she kaste hire loke,
And of hir clothes yet she hede toke;
For in hir fallynge yet she hadde care,
Lest that hir fete or suche thynge lay bare,
So wel she lovede clennesse, and eke trouthe!   1860
    Of hir had al the toun of Rome routhe,
And Brutus by hir chaste bloode hath swore,
That Tarquyn shulde y-banysshed be therfore,
And al his kynne; and let the peple calle,
And openly the tale he tolde hem alle;
And openly let cary her on a bere
Thurgh al the toun, that men may see and here
The horryble dede of hir oppressyoun.
Ne never was ther kynge in Rome toun
Syn thilke day; and she was holden there   1870
A seynt, and ever hir day y-halwed dere,
As in hire lawe. And thus endeth Lucresse
The noble wyfe, as Titus beryth wittnesse.
    I telle hyt, for she was of love so trewe,
Ne in hir wille she chaungede for no newe;

And for the stable herte, sadde and kynde,
That in these wymmen men may al day fynde;
Ther as they kaste hire herte, there it dwelleth.
For wel I wot that Criste himselfe telleth,
That in Israel, as wyde as is the londe,   1880
Nat so grete feythe in al that londe he fonde,
As in a woman; and this is no lye.
And as for men, loketh which tirannye
They doon al day,—assay hem whoso lyste,
The trewest is ful brotil[1] for to triste.

Explicit Legenda Lucrecie, Rome, Martiris

II. Source

OVID: FASTI

Lib. II. Lines 721–852

Text as in *P. Ovidii Nasonis fastorum libri diligenti emendatione . . . commentatoribus Antonio Constantio fanensi: Paulo Marso piscinate.* Venetiis. Joh. Tacuinus de Tridino, 1520.

Liber II

Cingitur interea Romanis Ardea signis   721
  Et patitur longas obsidione moras.
Dum vacat, & metuunt hostes committere pugnam
  Luditur in castris ocia miles agit:
Tarquinius juvenes socios dapibusque meroque
  Accipit ex illis rege creatus ait:
Dum nos solicitos pigro tenet Ardea bello
  Nec sinit ad patrios arma referre deos:
Ecquid in officio thorus est socialis & ecquid
  Conjugibus nostris mutua cura sumus: 730
Quisque suam laudant. studiis certamina crescunt
  Et fervent multo linguaque corque mero:

[1] brittle.

Surgit cui dederat clarum Collatia nomen;
  Non opus est verbis credite rebus ait:
Nox superest: tollamur equis, urbemque petamus:
  Dicta placent: frenis impediuntur equi:
Pertulerant dominos regalia, protinus ipsi
  Tecta petunt custos in fore nullus erat
Ecce nurum regis fusis per colla coronis
  Inveniunt posito pervigilare mero:
Inde cito passu petitur Lucretia: cujus
  Ante thorum calathi lanaque mollis erant:
Lumen ad exiguum famulae data pensa trahebant
  Inter quas tenui sic ait illa sono:
Mittenda est domino (nunc, nuncuperate) puellae
  Quamprimum nostra facta lacerna manu:
Quid tamen audistis (nam plura audire potestis)
  Quantum de bello dicitur esse super:
Postmodo victa cades melioribus Ardea restas
  Improba: quae nostros cogis abesse viros:
Sint tantum reduces. sed enim temerarius ille
  Est meus & stricto qualibet ense ruit:
Mens abit & morior quotiens pugnantis imago
  Me subit & gelidum pectora frigus habet:
Desinit in lachrymas inceptaque fila remisit
  In gremio vultum deposuitque suo.
Hoc ipsam decuit: lachrymae decuere pudicam,
  Et facies animo dignaque parque fuit.
Pone metum venio conjux ait: illa revixit
  Deque viri collo dulce pependit onus
Interea juvenis furiales regius ignes
  Concipit & caeco raptus amore fuit:
Forma placet, niveusque color flavique capilli
  Quique aderat nulla factus ab arte decor:
Verba placent, & vox & quod corrumpere non est:
  Quoque minor spes est: hoc magis ille cupit
Jam dederat cantum lucis praenuntius ales
  Cum referunt juvenes in sua castra pedem:
Carpitur attonitos absentis imagine sensus
  Ille: recordanti plura magisque placent:
Sic sedit: sic culta fuit sic stamina nevit
  Neglectae collo sic jacuere comae:
Hos habuit vultus haec illi verba fuerunt
  Hic color haec facies hic decor oris erat:
Ut solet a magno fluctus languescere flatu:

740

750

760

770

Sed tamen a vento, qui fuit, unda tumet:
Sic, quamvis aberat placitae praesentia formae:
  Quem dederat praesens forma: manebat amor.
Ardet: & injusti stimulis agitatus amoris
  Comparat indigno vimque metumque toro.   780
Exitus in dubio est: audebimus ultima dixit.
  Viderit: audentes forsque Venusque juvant.
Cepimus audendo Gabios quoque talia fatus
  Ense latus cinxit: tergaque pressit equi.
Accipit aerata juvenem Collatia porta,
  Condere jam vultus Sole parante suos.
Hostis ut hospes init penetralia Collatini:
  Comiter excipitur: sanguine junctus erat.
Quantum animis erroris inest. parat inscia rerum
  Infelix epulas hostibus illa suis.   790
Functus erat dapibus: poscunt sua tempora somnum:
  Nox erat: & tota lumina nulla domo.
Surgit: & auratum vagina liberat ensem:
  Et venit in thalamos nupta pudica tuos,
Utque torum pressit ferrum, Lucretia mecum est,
  Natus ait regis, Tarquiniusque vocor.
Illa nihil: neque enim vocem viresque loquendi
  Aut aliquid toto pectore mentis habet.
Sed tremit, ut quondam stabulis deprensa relictis,
  Parva sub infesto cum jacet agna lupo.   800
Quid faciat? pugnet? vincetur foemina pugnans.
  Clamet? at in dextra, qui vetet, ensis erat:
Effugiat? positis urgentur pectora palmis:
  Tunc primum externa pectora tacta manu.
Instat amans hostis, pretio, precibusque minisque:
  Nec prece, nec pretio, nec movet ille minis.
Nil agis, eripiam dixit per crimina vitam:
  Falsus adulterii testis adulter ero.
Interimam famulum: cum quo deprensa fereris.
  Succubuit famae victa puella metu.   810
Quid victor gaudes? haec te victoria perdet.
  Heu quantum regnis nox stetit una tuis.
Jamque erat orta dies: sparsis sedet illa capillis,
  Ut solet ad nati mater itura rogum
Grandaevumque patrem fido cum conjuge castris
  Evocat: & posita venit uterque mora.
Utque vident habitum: quae luctus causa requirunt:
  Cui paret exsequias, quove sit icta malo.

Illa diu reticet, pudibundaque caelat amictu
Ora: fluunt lachrymae more perennis aquae.   820
Hinc pater, hinc conjux lachrymas solantur: & orant,
Indicet: & caeco flentque paventque metu.
Ter conata loqui: ter destitit: ausaque quarto:
Non oculos ideo sustulit illa suos.
Hoc quoque Tarquinio debebimus: eloquar, inquit,
Eloquar infelix dedecus ipsa meum.
Quodque potest narrat: restabant ultima: flevit:
Et matronales erubuere genae.
Dant veniam genitor facto conjuxque coacto,
Quam dixit veniam vos datis, ipsa nego.   830
Nec mora, caelato fixit sua pectora ferro:
Et cadit in patrios sanguinolenta pedes.
Tunc quoque jam moriens, ne non procumbat honeste:
Respicit: haec etiam cura cadentis erat.
Ecce super corpus communia damna gementes
Obliti decoris virque paterque jacent.
Brutus adest: tandemque animo sua nomina fallit:
Fixaque semianimi corpore tela rapit.
Stillantemque tenens generoso sanguine cultrum,
Edidit impavidos ore minante sonos: 840
Per tibi ego hunc juro fortem, castumque cruorem:
Perque tuos manes, qui mihi numen erunt:
Tarquinium profuga poenas cum stirpe daturum:
Jam satis est virtus dissimulata diu.
Illa jacens ad verba oculos sine lumine movit:
Visaque concussa dicta probare coma.
Fertur in exequias animi matrona virilis:
Et secum lachrymas, invidiamque trahit.
Vulnus inane patet: Brutus clamore Quirites
Convocat, & regis facta nefanda refert.   850
Tarquinius cum prole fugit: capit annua Consul
Jura: dies regnis illa suprema fuit.   852

III. Translation of Source

OVID: FASTI
translated by John Gower (1640)
Lib. II. Lines 721–852

Ovids Festivalls, or Romane Calendar, Translated into English verse equinumerically, By John Gower Master of Arts, and sometimes of Jesus Colledge in Cambridge. Roger Daniel. Cambridge, 1640.

Romes conquering Eagles in the meantime over
The city *Ardea* in a long siege hover.
The foe, not daring battel, couch'd in forts:
Our souldiers revel in their tents with sports.
Young *Tarquine* makes a feast to all his lords;
'mongst whom in mirth he falls unto these words:
Whilst in dull warre this *Ardea* us deteins,
From carrying tropheys to our countrey fanes,
Do any of our wives mind us? or are
They carefull of us who for them take care?   10
Each prais'd his own, and very earnest grow:
The frollick bowls make lungs and tongues to glow.
Up starts Lord Collatine, Few words are best.
But come to triall; night's not yet deceast:
Mount we our steeds and to the citie all
Career. Content: They for their horses call,
And straight were gallop'd by their speedy feet
To th' royall court. No watch was in the street:
Lo there the King's sonnes joviall wives they find
With garlands crown'd, at midnight up well win'd: 20
Thence to fair *Lucrece* post they out of hand;
By whose bedside the wool and baskets stand.
At little lights their task her maidens spun;
To whom she softly thus these words begun;
Maids, we must make (plie, plie your bus'nesse faster)
A coat to send in haste unto your master.

What news heare you? for more than I you heare:
How long will't be e're warres be ended there?
Well, Ardea, thou that keepest our Lords from home,
Thy betters thou affront'st, thy fall will come.   30
Be they but safe! but my Lord's bloud's so high,
That with his sword he anywhere doth flie.
My heart doth fail quite chill'd with frozen fear
Whene're I think of his encounters there.

Tears were the period: She lets fall her thread,
And in her bosome hangeth down her head,
This was a grace; her tears became her well:
Her beauty was her mind's true parallel.
Fear not, sweet wife; I'm come, cries he. She meets
And hangs on's neck, a burden full of sweets.   40
Meanwhile the young Prince furiall lust doth move;
His boyling spirits are fir'd in secret love.
Her lilie-skin, her gold-deluding tresses,
Her native splendour slighting art him pleases.
Her voice, her stainless modesty, h'admires:
And hope's decay still strengthens his desires.
Day's horn-mouth'd harbinger proclaim'd the morn;
The frollick gallants to their tents return.
His mazing fansie on her picture roves;
The more he muses still the more he loves: 50
Thus did she sit, thus drest, thus did she spin,
Thus plai'd her hair upon her necks white skin;
These looks she had, these rosie words still'd from her;
This eye, this cheek, these blushes did become her.
As billows fall down after some great blast,
Yet make some swelling when the wind is past:
So though her person from his sight was tane,
Yet did that love her person bred remain.
He burns; and prick'd with spurs of basest lust,
Against her chast bed plots attempts unjust.   60
Th'events ambiguous, yet we'll throughly try't:
That she shall see. Fate helps the vent'rous sprite.
We slav'd the Gabines by a daring deed.
Thus girts he on his sword and mounts his steed.
Into *Collatia's* brasen ports he came
About the time *Sol* hides his glowing flame.
A foe the Court doth enter as a friend,
And there was welcome: For they were akind.[1]

---

[1] akin.

Ah blind mankind! she thinking nought, good woman!
Provides good chear to entertain her foeman.   70
The supper's ended: time to sleep invites;
In all the housen now are seen no lights.
Up starts he, and draws forth his gilded blade,
And chast *Lucretia's* chamber doth invade.
Laid on the bed; *Lucretia, no deniall:*
Here is my sword: I'm Tarquine *of bloud royall.*
Nought she replies; nor had she power to say
Or plead, but stupid and quite senselesse lay.
And like a lamb that from the sheepfold rambles,
Now caught in claws of ravening wolf, she trembles.   80
What dares she? fight? ah, he could overmatch her!
Cry out? alas! his sword would soon dispatch her.
Fly? how? his arm is link'd about her wa[i]st:
Her wa[i]st then first by strangers hand embrac'd!
The Lecher pleads with proffers, threats, intreats:
She's no whit mov'd with gifts, intreats, nor threats.
Yield, or I'll damne thee for a whore, cries he,
And thee acuse for base adulterie:
I'll kill the man, with whom I'll bruit thy shame.
She yielded, conquer'd by the fear of fame.   90
Why triumph'st thou? thy conquest is thy fall:
Ah, what a price bought'st thou that night withall!
Now day appear'd: with scatter'd hairs she lies,
As doth a mother when her deare sonne dies.
For her old father and deare husband home
She sends: To her without delay they come.
Whose grief they seeing ask the cause of it,
Whom she laments, and with what evil smit.
She veils her modest face, nor any thing
Would utter; tears as from a fountain spring.   100
Her sire, her husband comfort her sad tears,
Pray her to speak, and weep in hidden fears.
Thrice she assay'd to speak, thrice stopt; yet tries
Once more, but shamed to lift up her eyes.
Shall we owe Tarquine *this too? ah! shall I,*
Shall I here publish my own infamie?
Something she tells, and for the period weeps,
And her grave cheeks in pure vermilion steeps.
They both forgive her forc'd adultery.
That pardon you give, I, cries she, *deny.*   110
Forthwith her self she stabs with hidden knife,

And at their feet pours forth her crimson life;
And even in Fate's last act, as she did die,
Express'd a care to fall with modestie.
Her Sire, her Lord self-carelesse both fall down,
And o're her corpse their common losse bemone.
Brute came, whose mind at length his name deceiv'd,
And from her dying breast the knife repriev'd:
There holds it spuing of her noble bloud,
And dauntlesse threatnings breath'd forth as he stood;
By this chaste noble bloud I vow to thee   [120
And thy dear ghost, which as my God shall be,
Proud Tarquine *with his seed for this shall pay:*
No longer I the counterfeit will play.
She at his words her sightlesse eyes doth move,
And shook her head as seeming to approve.
The manly matrone's exequies are done,
Endow'd with tears and emulation.
The wound lies open: *Brute* calls all the States,
And to their ears the King's base act relates.   130
Proud *Tarquine's* house all flie. Two Consuls sway:
And that became the last *Monarchick* day.

IV. Translation of Source

THE PALLACE OF PLEASURE
by William Painter (1566)
THE SECOND NOVELL
[a translation of T. Livius: Historia I, LVII–LX]

The Pallace of Pleasure Beautified, adorned and Well furnished, with Pleasant Histories and excellent Novelles, selected out of divers good and commendable Authors. By William Painter, Clerke of the Ordinaunce and Armarie. 1566. Imprinted at London, by Henry Denham, for Richard Tottell and William Iones.

Sextus Tarquinius ravished Lucrece. And she bewayling the losse of her chastitie, killed her selfe.

Great preparation was made by the Romaines, against a people called Rutuli, who had a citie named Ardea, excelling in wealth and riches which was the cause that the Romaine king, being exhausted and quite voyde of money, by reason of his sumptuous buildinges, made warres uppon that countrie. In the time of the siege of that citie the yonge Romaine gentlemen banqueted one another, amonges whom there was one called Collatinus Tarquinius, the sonne of Egerius. And by chaunce they entred into communication of their wives, every one praysing his several spouse. At length the talke began to grow hot, whereupon Collatinus said, that words were vaine. For within few houres it might be tried, how much his wife Lucretia did excel the rest, wherefore (quoth he) if there be any livelihood in you, let us take our horse, to prove which of oure wives doth surmount. Wheruppon they roode to Rome in post. At their comming they found the kinges doughters, sportinge themselves with sondrye pastimes: From thence they went to the house of Collatinus, where they founde Lucrece, not as the others before named, spending time in idelnes, but late in the night occupied and busie amonges her maydes in the middes of her house spinning of wool. The victory and prayse wherof was given to Lucretia, who when she saw her husband, gentlie and lovinglie intertained him, and curteouslye badde the Tarquinians welcome. Immediately Sextus Tarquinius the sonne of Tarquinius Superbus (that time the Romaine king) was incensed wyth a libidinous desire, to construpate and defloure Lucrece. When the yonge gentlemen had bestowed that night pleasantly with their wives, they retourned to the Campe. Not long after, Sextus Tarquinius with one man retourned to Collatia unknowen to Collatinus, and ignorant to Lucrece and the rest of her housholde, for what purpose he came. Who being well intertayned, after supper was conveighed to his chamber. Tarquinius burninge with the love of Lucrece, after he perceived the housholde to be at reste, and all thinges in quiet, with his naked sworde in his hande, wente to Lucrece being a sleepe, and keeping her downe with his left hande, saide: 'Holde thy peace Lucrece, I am Sextus Tarquinius, my sworde is in my hand, if thou crie, I will kill thee.' The gentlewoman sore afrayed, being newely awaked oute of her sleepe, and seeing imminent death, could not tell what to do. Then Tarquinius confessed his love, and began to intreate her, and therewithall used sundry menacing wordes, by all meanes attempting to make her quiet: when he saw her obstinate, and that she woulde not y[i]elde to his request, notwithstanding his cruell threates, he added shameful and villanous speach, saying: That he would kill her, and when she was slaine, he woulde also kill his slave, and place him by her, that it might be reported howe she was slaine, being taken in adulterie. She vanquished with his terrible and infamous threate, his fleshlye and licentious enterprice overcame the puritie of her chaste and honest hart, which done he departed. Then Lucrece sent a post to Rome to her father, and an other to Ardea to her husbande, requiringe them that they would make speede to come unto her, with certaine of their trustie frendes, for that a cruell facte was chaunced. Then Sp. Lucretius with P. Valerius the sonne of Volesius, and Collatinus with L. Junius Brutus, made hast to Lucrece: where they founde her sitting, very pensive and sadde, in her chamber. So sone as she sawe them she began pitiously to weepe. Then her husband asked her, whether all thinges were well: unto whome she sayde these wordes:

'No, deare husbande, for what can be wel or safe unto a woman, when she hath lost her chastitie? Alas Collatine, the steppes of an other man be now fixed in thy bed. But it is my bodye onely that is violated, my minde God knoweth is guiltles, whereof my death shalbe witnesse. But if you be men give me your handes and trouth, that the adulterer may not escape unrevenged. It is Sextus Tarquinius whoe being an enemie, in steede of a frende, the other night came unto mee, armed with his sword in his hand, and by violence caried away from me (the Goddes know) a woful joy.'

Then every one of them gave her their faith, and comforted the pensive and languishing lady, imputing the offence to the authour and doer of the same, affirming that her bodye was polluted, and not her minde, and where consent was not, there the crime was absente. Whereunto shee added: 'I praye you consider with your selves, what punishmente is due for the malefactour. As for my part, though I cleare my selfe of the offence, my body shall feele the punishment; for no unchast or ill woman shall hereafter impute no dishonest act to Lucrece.'

Then she drewe out a knife, which she had hidden secretely, under her kirtle, and stabbed her selfe to the harte. Which done, she fell downe grouelinge uppon her wound and died. Whereupon her father and husband made great lamentation, and as they were bewayling the death of Lucrece, Brutus plucked the knife oute of the wound, which gushed out with abundance of bloude, and holding it up, said: 'I sweare by the chast bloud of this body here dead, and I take you the immortall Gods to witnes, that I will drive and extirpate oute of this Citie, both L. Tarquinius Superbus, and his wicked wife, with all the race of his children and progenie, so that none of them, ne yet any others shall raigne anye longer in Rome.' Then hee delivered the knife to Collatinus, Lucretius and Valerius, who marveyled at the strangenesse of his words; and from whence he should conceive that determination. They all swore that othe. And followed Brutus, as their captaine, in his conceived purpose. The body of Lucrece was brought into the market place, where the people wondred at the vilenesse of that facte, every man complayning uppon the mischiefe of that facinorous rape, committed by Tarquinius. Wherupon Brutus perswaded the Romaynes, that they should cease from teares and other childishe lamentacions, and to take weapons in their handes, to shew themselves like men. . . .

[At Rome] the people out of all places of the citie, ranne into the market place. Where Brutus complained of the abhominable Rape of Lucrece, committed by Sextus Tarquinius. And thereunto he added the pride and insolent behaviour of the king, the miserie and drudgerie of the people, and howe they, which in time past were victors and conquerours, were made of men of warre, Artificers, and Labourers. He remembred also the infamous murder of Servius Tullius their late kinge. These and such like he called to the people's remembraunce, whereby they abrogated and deposed Tarquinius, banishing him, his wife, and children. . . .

When Tarquinius was come to Rome, the gates were shutte against him, and he himselfe commaunded to avoide into exile. The campe received Brutus with great joye and triumphe, for that he had delivered the citie of such a tyraunte. Then Tarquinius with his children fledde to Caere, a Citie of the Hetrurians. And as Sextus Tarquinius was going, he was slaine by those that premeditated revengemente, of olde murder and injuries by him done to their predecessours. This L. Tarquinius Superbus raigned XXV yeares. The raigne of the kings from the first foundation of the Citie continued CCXLIV yeares. After which governmente two Consuls were appointed, for the order and administration of the Citie. And for that yeare L. Junius Brutus and L. Tarquinius Collatinus.

THE TWO GENTLEMEN OF VERONA

INTRODUCTION

NO PRINTED EDITION of this play exists before the Folio of 1623, and Francis Meres's reference in *Palladis Tamia* helps little to date it, since the play is obviously early in part and probably as a whole. Since it replaces the dry hardness of *A Comedy of Errors* and *The Shrew* with some of the warmth and eloquence, the surplusage of word-play, found in *A Midsummer Night's Dream* and *Love's Labour's Lost*, the play probably belongs to the same group, though it may be earlier than these, for it treats its romantic theme with a somewhat jejune absence of self-criticism hardly possible after their delighted mockery of love. As in *The Shrew* Shakespeare begins with an idea or at least a situation illustrating current ideas, which he develops with a wit and lyricism plainly owing much to John Lyly, the adept in the court comedy of romantic ethics and pastoral motifs.

The main basis of *The Two Gentlemen of Verona* is the conflict between the duties of friendship and love. This favourite theme had been used by Boccaccio in his *La Teseide* and in the tale of Tito and Gisippo (*Decamerone* X.8), and by Chaucer in *The Knight's Tale* (which helped the incubation of *A Midsummer Night's Dream* (q.v.)). The friendship of Titus and Gisippus had been celebrated by Sir Thomas Elyot in *The Governour* (1531) and Edward Lewicke in a verse tale (1562). Part of Elyot's version is given here [Text I]. The generous act of Gisippus in resigning his bride to the friend who had fallen in love with her may account for what, like the swooning Julia, I take to be Valentine's Quixotic generosity when he says

> And that my love may appear plain and free,
> All that was mine in Silvia I give thee (*V*.4.82,3)

Valentine thus emphasizes the contrast between true and false friendship which such stories involved.

From Lyly's *Euphues. The Anatomy of Wit* (1579) Shakespeare may have taken hints for the theme of the disloyal friend and the right ethical attitudes, but Lyly has also an unfaithful mistress [II] and his thin tale ends suddenly when Lucilla abandons Euphues for someone else, leaving Euphues to bid 'a farewell to women' and the world and to make peace with Philautus in complete disillusion. Shakespeare's debt to Lyly was probably more one of technique than of matter, and he worked out any suggestions got from *Euphues* in accordance with the symmetrical balance of character found more in Lyly's plays than in his moral romance.

The pervasive influence of Lyly's plays cannot be adequately illustrated in a selective work of this kind. But some close anticipations of Shakespeare must be noted. *Endimion* has the love-friendship conflict when Eumenides wishes to free the hero from his enchanted sleep but hesitates because it means leaving his cruel mistress Semele. He reveals his struggle to Geron (III.4) who praises friendship at love's expense:

'Eumenides, release Endimion, for all things (friendship excepted) are subject to fortune: love is but an eye-worme, which only tickleth the head with hopes, and wishes; friendship the image of eternitie, in which there is nothing movable, nothing mischievous. As much difference as there is between beautie and vertue, bodies and shadowes, colours and lignes— so great oddes is there between love and friendship. . . .'

Again, the passage in *The Two Gentlemen* where Valentine naively gives advice to the Duke on winning a lady (III.1.89– 105) recalls the scene in *Sapho and Phaon* (II.4) in which Phao gets counsel from Sibylla:

'I would wish thee first to be diligent: for that women desire nothing more than to have their servants officious. Be alwayes in sight, but never slothfull. Flatter, I meane lie; little things catch little minds, and fancie is a worme, that feedeth first upon fennell . . . It is unpossible for the brittle mettle of women to withstand the flattering attempts of men . . . Bee prodigall in prayses and promises; beautie must have a trumpet, and pride a gift . . . Chuse such times to breake thy suit as thy lady is pleasant. . . . When thou talkest with her, let thy speech bee pleasant but not incredible . . . Chuse such words as may (as many may) melt her mind . . . Write, and persist in writing;

they reade more than is written to them, and write lesse than they thinke. In conceit studie to be pleasant; in attire brave, but not too curious . . . Can you sing, show your cunning; can you dance, use your legges; can you lay upon any instrument, practise your fingers to please her fancie; seek out qualities. If shee seeme at the first cruell, bee not discouraged. I tell thee a strange thing, women strive, because they would be overcome . . . Looke pale, and learne to be leane, that who so seeth thee may say, the gentleman is in love . . . He that hath wit enough, can give enough. Dumbe men are eloquent if they be liberall. Beleeve me, great gifts are little gods. If thou have a rival be patient; arte must winde him out, not malice; time, not might; her change, and thy constancie. . . .'

The lovers, serious and comic, in many of Shakespeare's later comedies owe much to such teaching, for Lyly served Shakespeare as a master in the dramatic use of the courtly and amorous code. He also gave him many comic tricks. Thus Launce and Speed are foreshadowed by the two waggish servants, Dares and Samias in *Endimion*, who jest about their masters; and the grammatical quips and logic-chopping which begin in this play come from Lyly's jesting, e.g. in the dialogue between Licio and Petulus in *Midas* I.2, and that between Sir Tophas and Epiton in *Endimion* III.3. Lylyan too is the device by which the servant's adventures parody his master's. Hence after Proteus says goodbye to Julia (*TGV* II.2) Launce tells how *he* said goodbye to his family. When Valentine and Proteus are in love with Silvia, Launce tells us about his love for a milkmaid, and so on. Especially like Lyly is the badinage between Valentine and Speed in II.1. And Sir Thurio, the foolish suitor, owes something to Sir Tophas in *Endimion*, though he is not so rich a character as that lover of old matrons.

Lyly was fond of a sprightly romantic heroine, but it was Shakespeare's primary source for the story of Julia which made him switch the main interest from Proteus to a woman in love and thus start a practice which produced so many later triumphs in comedy. In the *Diana Enamorada* of the Portuguese Jorge de Montmayor (Valencia, 1542) he found a story in which treachery to a male friend is accompanied by a detailed account of treachery to a former mistress. Instead of the pallid villainy of Euphues the *Diana* gives a lively story of adventure, suspense and pathos, with elements of chivalric and pastoral romance which had already endeared themselves to Sidney. Shakespeare may have known enough Spanish to read the original; there was also a French translation by Nicolas Collin (1578, 1587). He may have seen a manuscript copy of Bartholomew Yonge's English version, which, though not published till 1598, was completed sixteen years earlier.[1] And he may have used a play now lost, *The History of Felix and Felio(s?)-mena* which was played 'by her majesty's servants on the Sunday next after New Year's Day' (1585) and was probably a pastoral based on Montemayor. Perusal of the extract given from Montemayor [III] will show that Shakespeare used many ingredients in *The Two Gentlemen,* including Don Felix's use of a maid as a go-between and the capricious coyness of Felismena about his letter until on a second occasion her maid lets it fall; in Shakespeare Julia tears up the letter, then tries hard to decipher it—a charming stroke. Montemayor's lover goes away too grieved to inform her; in Shakespeare *she* finds it hard to speak when they part. In both she follows him, and being urged by the Host of an inn to hear some brave music, hears her lover serenading her unknown rival. Shakespeare omits Fabius and the means by which Felismena becomes Don Felix's page. He compresses time; she takes the ring in order to get Silvia's picture, not a month later, but next day. (IV.2.134; IV.4.97ff.) In *Diana* Celia falls in love with the page (Valerius) and dies of chagrin when he fails to respond. Shakespeare does not use either of these motifs (though the first appears in *Twelfth Night*) but makes Silvia faithful to Valentine, whom she follows into exile as Julia has followed Proteus. Montemayor's Felismena is an Amazonian shepherdess who slays savages and knights and after Celia's death searches long for Felix, saves his life and wins him back. In Shakespeare the disguised Julia follows Proteus to the forest in pursuit of Silvia and Eglamour. Certainly no Amazon, she swoons when she thinks that Valentine is surrendering to Proteus his rights in Silvia.

---

[1] Partial translations were made by Edward Paston and Thomas Wilson. Barnabe Googe's *Eglogs, Epytaphes and Sonnettes* (1563) drew on the *Diana* in telling how a Knight (Faustus) uses his (male) page (Valerius) to woo a court lady (Claudia). She falls in love with the page and dies,

An English parallel to the sex disguise of Felismena may have come to Shakespeare's mind from Sir Philip Sidney's *Arcadia*, where the Amazon Zelmane (probably derived from Montemayor) serves Pyrocles as a page, falls ill and is revealed to her master when she lies at the point of death. [IV.]

The sudden election of Valentine to be king of the 'wild faction' of outlaws has been compared with the appearance of Sidney's Pyrocles as captain of the Helots in *Arcadia* I.6. The resemblance is slight, though there is a hint in *TGV* V.4. 1–12 of Pyrocles's praise (in *Arc.* I.9) of meditation and the country life against Musidorus's attack on 'solitariness, the slye enimie, that doth most separate a man from well doing': 'The workings of the minde I finde much more infinite' (says Pyrocles) 'then can be led unto by the eye, or imagined by any, that distract their thoughts without themselves. And in such contemplation, or as I thinke more excellent, I enjoye my solitarines; and my solitarines perchaunce is the nurse of these contemplations. Eagles we see fly alone; and they are but sheepe, which alwaies heard together; condemne not therefore my minde sometime to enjoy it selfe; nor blame not the taking of such times as serve most fitte for it. And alas, deere *Musidorus*, if I be sadde, who knowes better than you the just causes I have of sadnes?' To which Musidorus replies by praising action, ending that he will give his friend leave 'ever to defend solitarines; so long as, to defende it, you ever keep companie.'

Other sources for the greenwood adventures have been suggested, including Anthony Munday's two-part play *The Downfall and The Death of Robert, Earl of Huntington, Otherwise called Robin Hoode of merrie Sherwodde* (1601), but these were paid for by Henslowe and licensed for performance in 1598. Munday (*Downfall*, III.2) makes Little John read the 'articles' by which Robin Hood rules his men. Compare Valentine's 'I have much to do/ To keep them from uncivil outrages' (*TGV* V.4.16–17). Perhaps both Shakespeare and Munday owed something to a play now lost, *The Pastoral Comedy of Robin Hood and Little John*, which was entered in S.R. on 14 May, 1594, as well as to the Robin Hood ballads.

Miss D. F. Atkinson (*S. Phil.* XLI, 1944, pp. 223–34) sees 'The Source of *Two Gentlemen of Verona*'—apart from the Julia story—in the fifth story in Henry Wotton's *A Courtlie controversie of Cupid's Cautels . . . translated out of French as neare as our English phrase will permit, by H. W. Gentleman*(1578), which is taken from Jacques d'Yver's *Le Printemps d'Yver* (1572), a work whose popularity rivalled Bandello's in France. In this tale Floradine falls in love with his friend Claribel's wife Margarite, and visits her in Claribel's absence. Returning home the latter finds Floradine's letters, and disappears for years. Meeting accidentally the two men renew their friendship and have picaresque adventures. After dressing a miller's wife as a page they become outlaws. Finally Claribel and Margarite are reunited.

This seems an analogue rather than a source of Shakespeare. Parallels of great interest occur in a collection[1] of fifty 'subjects for dramatic works' (i.e. scenarii) by the Duke of Mantua's comedian Flaminio Scala (otherwise called Flavio), printed in 1611 but probably used on the stage long before. The Argument and other extracts from the scenario in question, *Flavio Tradito*, are given below [V]. They include the infidelity of a friend and the passing of letters by a servant.

The plot is not close to Shakespeare's but most of it is translated here since it is an interesting illustration of the mixture of Commedia dell' arte elements which Shakespeare may have got to know about this time and which he possibly drew on in *Love's Labour's Lost* and elsewhere.[2]

Among other analogues which have been described as sources is the German play of *Julio and Hyppolita* derived from one played by the English comedians in Germany early in the seventeenth century and published with a translation in A. Cohn's *Shakespeare in Germany* (1865). The version now extant is very debased, and has only slight resemblance to Shakespeare's plot. Romulus is betrothed to Hyppolita and leaves her in his friend Julius's care while he goes to inform his parents at Rome of his approaching marriage to her. Julius falls in love with her and discredits his friend by getting his servant, disguised as a postboy, to bring forged letters as if from Romulus stating that he no longer loves Hyppolita or respects her father. Letters are torn here, as in Shakespeare, but they are the forged letters, which lie on the stage until Romulus returns to read

---

[1] *Il Teatro delle Favole rappresentative . . . composta da Flaminio Scala detto Flavio Comico del Sereniss. Sig. Duca di Mantova.* Venetia. MDCXI.

[2] Cf. O. J. Campbell, '*TGV* and Italian comedy', in *Michigan Studies*, 1925.

them! This he does on the wedding morning after Julius by long siege and despite Hyppolita's accusations of disloyalty has persuaded her to marry him. Romulus swears revenge on discovering the truth, and disguises himself as a Masker. While he is dancing in a Tragic Dance he slays Julius; whereupon Hyppolita, not recognizing him, slays herself, and Romulus follows suit, leaving the Duke to become a hermit. The passages printed here [VI] in the translation by Georgina Archer (which do no wrong to the original) give little idea of the original English play, which may or may not have preceded *The Two Gentlemen of Verona*. There are one or two resemblances to Shakespeare, e.g. the character of the disloyal friend, his attempt to get rid of his rival, and the servant Grobianus who, like Launce, speaks about a dog (how differently, though!). Grobianus acts as Julius's messenger to Hyppolita (as Julia does for Proteus in IV.4.68ff., and he gets a ducat for bringing back her refusal (cp. the reference to a ducat in *TGV* I.1.139). The device by which Julius discredits Romulus has nothing in common with Proteus's, which comes nearer to *Romeo and Juliet* or Brooke's poem on that theme, with its use of a cord ladder by which Valentine is to climb to Silvia's window for their elopement (*TGV* II.4.180–84). Valentine's outburst against banishment resembles that in Brooke, and Proteus's hypocritical consolation to him recalls Friar Laurence's to Romeus (cp. *infra* p. 321). Later Eglamour meets Silvia by Friar Patrick's cell, where she should go to Confession; and as they run through the wood, going, as she says, 'To Mantua, where I hear, he makes abode', we learn from the Duke, 'Friar Laurence met them both/As he in penance wandered through the forest.' Obviously Shakespeare had been reading Brooke's poem before writing *The Two Gentlemen of Verona*; and maybe the Verona setting may be ascribed to this.

There are interesting parallels to *The Merchant of Venice*. The proposed elopement of Silvia has something in common with that of Jessica. Julia with her waiting-woman pass in review her suitors (I.2) much as Portia does with Nerissa (*MV* I.2). There are also references to Jews. Launce says that 'a Jew would have wept' to see his parting from his dog; and tells Speed that, if he will not go with him to an alehouse 'thou art a Hebrew, a Jew, and not worth the name of Christian . . . Because thou

14—S.N.D. I

hast not so much charity in thee as to go to the ale with a Christian' (II.5.56–60)—which reminds one of Shylock's refusal to eat with Christians. Probably Shakespeare was already turning over the Jew story in his mind. When he wrote it he repeated some ideas, and Launce became Lancelot Gobbo.

The Two Gentlemen of Verona is a dramatic laboratory in which Shakespeare experimented with many of the ideas and devices which were to be his stock-in-trade and delight for years to come. Thus we have the story of betrayal in love, of an intriguing villain and a trusting friend, of a woman forlorn but pursuing; the sex-disguise; the movement of major characters from court to country. We see the heroine with her confidante, with a parent, young men discussing love together, the disguised lady describing herself to her rival; the villain soliloquizing in moral conflict; scenes of parting, despair, forgiveness. Moreover in this play Shakespeare carries forward the development of the servant as a comic character in relation to his fellows and his master begun in *The Comedy of Errors* and *The Shrew*. We must not overlook some weaknesses, the hasty ending during which Silvia never speaks despite Valentine's astonishing offer to give her up; the disappearance of Sir Eglamour, who is anything but 'a valiant knight'. Did Shakespeare name him in jest?

It is a play of technical experiment in which the endstopped lines and neatness of movement suggest a mind not yet 'possessed' by the theme. The style is rhetorical and adorned at times with conscious artifice: 'A sea of melting pearl which some call tears', &c.

This new style goes with the new source-material which probably suited a new mood in the poet. Instead of the classical farce and the modern fabliau in which life was treated conventionally from the outside, we have a sympathetic exploration of the difficulties of young people in love and friendship. By now Shakespeare has himself had bitter experience of both, in circumstances which evoke a new awareness of the potentialities of words and story. Valentine's renunciation, however unprepared for, is paralleled by Sonnet 40, 'Take all my loves, my love, yea, take them all', while the wounds caused by treachery bleed in Sonnets 34, 42, 93. The play may even have been written as a gesture of renewed friendship to Shakespeare's own

betrayer before the poison had taken full effect. However that
may be, Shakespeare began in 1593–4 to regard the world of
Renaissance story as an opportunity for lyrical treatment and
ethical exploration. Montemayor's *Diana* became his text-book
of amorous entanglements and sentiment as Lyly's comedies
were for a time his handbook to witty converse and artificial
balance of character.

From THE GOVERNOUR
by Sir Thomas Elyot (1531)
Book II. Chapter XII (Titus and Gisippus)

XII. *The wonderful history of Titus and Gisippus, and whereby is fully declared the figure of perfet amitie*

But nowe in the middes of my labour, as it were to pause and take brethe, and also to recreate the reders, which, fatigate with longe preceptes, desire varietie of mater, or some newe pleasaunt fable or historie, I will reherce a right goodly example of frendship. Whiche example, studiousely reade, shall ministre to the redars singuler pleasure and also incredible comforte to practise amitie.

There was in the citie of Rome a noble senatour named Fulvius, who sent his sone called Titus, beinge a childe, to the citie of Athenes in Greece (whiche was the fountaine of al maner of doctrine), there to lerne good letters, and caused him to be hosted with a worshipfull man of that citie called Chremes. This Chremes hapned to have also a sone named Gisippus, who nat onely was equall to the said yonge Titus in yeres, but also in stature, proporcion of body, favour, and colour of visage, countenaunce and speche. The two children were so like, that without moche difficultie it coulde nat be discerned of their propre parentes, whiche was Titus from Gysippus, or Gysippus from Titus. These two yonge gentilmen, as they semed to be one in fourme and personage, so, shortely after acquaintaunce, the same nature wrought in their hartes suche a mutuall affection, that their willes and appetites daily more and more so confederated them selfes, that it semed none other, whan their names were declared, but that they hadde onely chaunged their places, issuinge (as I mought saye) out of the one body, and entringe in to the other. They together and at one tyme went to their lerninge and studie, at one tyme to their meales and refection; they delited bothe in one doctrine, and profited equally therein; finally they to gether so increased in doctrine, that within a fewe yeres, fewe within Athenes mought be compared unto them. At the laste died Chremes, which

212

was nat only to his sone, but also to Titus, cause of moche sorowe and hevinesse. Gysippus, by the goodes of his father, was knowen to be a man of great substaunce, wherfore there were offred to hym great and riche mariages. And he than beinge of ripe yeres and of an habile and goodly parsonage, his frendes, kynne, and alies exhorted hym busely to take a wyfe, to the intent he mought increase his lygnage and progenie. But the yonge man, havinge his hart all redy wedded to his frende Titus, and his mynde fixed to the studie of Philosophie, fearinge that mariage shulde be the occasion to sever hym bothe from thone and thother, refused of longe tyme to be perswaded; untill at the last, partly by the importunate callynge on of his kynnesmen, partly by the consent and advise of his dere frende Titus, therto by other desired, he assented to mary suche one as shulde lyke hym. What shall nede many wordes? His frendes founde a yonge gentilwoman, whiche in equalitie of yeres, vertuous condicions, nobilitie of blode, beautie, and sufficient richesse, they thought was for suche a yonge man apte and convenient. And whan they and her frendes upon the covenauntes of mariage were throughly accorded, they counsailed Gysippus to repayre unto the mayden, and to beholde howe her parsone contented hym. And he so doinge founde her in every fourme and condicion accordinge to his expectation and appetite; wherat he moche rejoysed and became of her amorouse, in so moche as many and often tymes he leavinge Titus at his studie secretely repayred unto her. Nat withstandyng the fervent love that he had to his frende Titus, at the last surmounted shamefastnes. Wherfore he disclosed to him his secrete journayes, and what delectacion he toke in beholdinge the excellente beautie of her whom he purposed to mary, and howe, with her good maners and swete entretaynement, she had constrained hym to be her lover. And on a tyme he, havynge with hym his frende Titus, went to his lady, of whom he was resceyved most joyously. But Titus furthwith, as he behelde so hevenly a personage adourned with beautie inexplicable, in whose visage was moste amiable countenaunce, mixte with maydenly shamefastnesse, and the rare and sobre wordes, and well couched, whiche issued out of her pratie mouthe, Titus was therat abasshed, and had the harte through perced with the firy darte of blinde Cupide. Of the whiche wounde the anguisshe was so excedinge and vehement, that neither the study of Philosophie, neyther the remembraunce of his dere frende Gysippus, who so moche loved and trusted hym, coulde any thinge withdrawe hym from that unkynde appetite, but that of force he must love inordinately that lady, whom his said frende had determined to mary. All be it with incredible paynes he kepte his thoughtes secrete, untyll that he and Gysippus were retourned unto their lodgynges. Than the miserable Titus withdrawynge hym as it were to his studie, all turmented and oppressed with love, threwe hym selfe on a bedde, and there rebukyng his owne moste despitefull unkyndnesse, whiche, by the sodayne sight of a mayden, he had conspired agayne his moste dere frende Gysippus, agayne all humanitie and reason, he cursed his fate or constellation, and wisshed that he had never comen to Athenes. And there with he sent out from the botome of his harte depe and colde sighes, in suche plentie that it lacked but litle that his harte ne was riven in peces. In dolour and anguisshe tossed he hym selfe by a certayne space, but to no man wolde he discover it. But at the last the payne became so intollerable, that, wolde he or no, he was inforced to kepe his bedde, beinge, for lacke of slepe and other naturall sustenaunce, brought in suche feblenesse, that his legges mought nat sustayne his body. Gysippus missyng his dere frende Titus was moche abasshed, and heringe that he laye sicke in his bedde had furthwith his harte perced with hevinesse, and with all spede came to hym where he laye, . . . and with a comfortable countenaunce demaunded of Titus what was the cause of his disease, blamynge him of unkyndenesse that he so longe had sustayned it without geving him knowledge, that he mought for him have provided some remedie, if any mought have ben goten, though it were with the dispendinge of all his substaunce. With whiche wordes the mortall sighes renewed in Titus, and the salte teares brast out of his eien in suche habundaunce, as it had ben a lande flode runnynge downe of a mountayne after a storme. That beholdinge Gysippus, and beinge also resolved in to teares moste hartely desired hym and (as I mought saye) conjured him that for the fervent and entier love that had ben, and yet was, betwene them, he wolde no lenger hyde from him his griefe, and that there was nothing to him so dere or precious (all though it were his owne life) that mought resture Titus to helthe, but that he shulde gladly and without grutchinge employe it. With whiche wordes, obtestations, and teares of Gysippus, Titus constrayned, all blusshinge and ashamed, holdinge downe his hedde, brought furthe with great difficultie his wordes in this wyse. My dere and moste lovynge frende, withdrawe your frendely offers, cease of your courtaisie, refrayne your teares and regrettinges, take rather your knyfe and slee me here where I lye, or otherwise take vengeaunce on me, moste miserable and false traytour unto you, and of all other moste worthy to suffre moste shamefull dethe. . . . Alas, Gysippus, what envious spirite meved you to bringe me with you to her whom ye have chosen to be your wyfe, where I receyved this poison? I saye,

Gysippus, where was then your wisedom, that ye remembred nat the fragilitie of our commune nature? What neded you to call me for a witnesse of your private delites? Why wolde ye have me see that, whiche you youre selfe coulde nat beholde without ravisshinge of mynde and carnall appetite? Alas, why forgat ye that our myndes and appetites were ever one? And that also what so ye lyked was ever to me in lyke degree pleasaunt? What will ye more? Gysippus, I saye your trust is the cause that I am intrapped; the rayes or beames issuinge from the eyen of her whom ye have chosen, with the remembraunce of her incomparable vertues, hath thrilled throughout the middes of my hart, and in suche wise brenneth it, that above all thinges I desire to be out of this wretched and moste unkinde lyfe, whiche is nat worthy the company of so noble and lovynge a frende as ye be. And therewith Titus concluded his confession with so profounde and bitter a sigh, receyved with teares, that it semed that al his body shulde be dissolved and relented in to salt dropes.

But Gysippus, as he were there with nothynge astonyed or discontented, with an assured countenaunce and mery regarde, imbrasinge Titus and kissynge him, answered in this wyse. Why, Titus, is this your onely sickenesse and griefe that ye so uncurtesely have so longe counceiled, and with moche more unkyndnesse kept it from me than ye have conceyved it? I knowlege my foly, wherwith ye have with good right imbrayded me, that, in showing to you her whom I loved, I remembred nat the commune astate of our nature, ne the agreablenesse, or (as I mought saye) the unitie of our two appetites, suerly that defaulte can be by no reason excused. Wherfore it is onely I that have offended. For who may by right prove that ye have trespased, that by the inevitable stroke of Cupides darte are thus bitterly wounded? Thinke ye me suche a fole or ignorant persone that I knowe nat the powar of Venus, where she listeth to shewe her importable violence? Have nat ye well resisted agayne suche a goddesse, that for my sake ye have striven with her all moste to the dethe? What more loyaltie or trouthe can I require of you? Am I of that vertue that I may resiste agayne celestiall influence preordinate by providence divine? If I so thought, what were my wittes? Where were my studie so longe tyme spent in noble Philosophie? I confesse to you, Titus, I love that mayden as moche as any wise man mought possible, and toke in her companye more delite and pleasure than of all the treasure and landes that my father lefte to me, whiche ye knowe was right abundaunt. But nowe I perceyve that the affection of love towarde her surmounteth in you above measure, what, shal I thinke it of a wanton lust or sodayne appetite in you, whome I have ever knowen of grave and sadde disposition, inclyned alway to honest doctrine, fleinge all vayne daliaunce and dishonest passetyme? Shall I imagine to be in you any malice or fraude, sens from the tendre tyme of our childhode I have alway founden in you, my swete frende Titus, suche a conformitie with all my maners, appetites, and desires, that never was sene betwene us any maner of contention? Nay god forbede that in the frendshippe of Gysippus and Titus shulde happen any suspition, or that any fantasie shulde perce my hedde, whereby that honorable love betwene us shulde be the mountenaunce of a cromme perisshed. Nay, nay, Titus, it is (as I have said) the onely providence of god. She was by hym from the beginnynge prepared to be your lady and wife. For suche fervent love entreth nat in to the harte of a wise man and vertuous, but by a divine disposition; whereat if I shulde be discontented or grudge, I shulde nat onely be injuste to you, withholdinge that from you whiche is undoughtedly youres, but also obstinate and repugnaunt agayne the determination of god; whiche shall never be founden in Gysippus. Therfore, gentill frende Titus, dismay you nat at the chaunce of love, but receyve it joyously with me, that am with you nothinge discontented, but mervailous gladde, sense it is my happe to finde for you suche a lady, with whome ye shall lyve in felicitie, and receyve frute to the honour and comfort of all your linage. Here I renounce to you clerely all my title and interest that I nowe have or mought have in that faire mayden. Call to you your pristinate courage, wasshe clene your visage and eyen thus biwept, and abandone all hevinesse. The day appointed for our mariage approcheth; let us consult howe without difficultie ye may holy attayne your desires. Take hede, this is myne advise; ye knowe well that we two be so like, that, beinge a parte and in one apparayle, fewe men do knowe us. Also ye do remember that the custome is, that, natwithstandinge any ceremony done at the tyme of the spousayles, the mariage natwithstandinge is nat confirmed, untyll at night that the husbande putteth a rynge on the finger of his wyfe, and unloseth her girdell. Therfore I my selfe will be present with my frendes and perfourme all the partes of a bride. And ye shall abyde in a place secrete, where I shall appoint you, untill it be nyght. And than shall ye quickely convaye your selfe in to the maidens chambre, and for the similitude of our parsonages and of our apparaile, ye shall nat be espied of the women, whiche have with none of us any acquaintaunce, and shortely gette you to bedde, and put your owne rynge on the maydens fynger, and undo her gyrdell of virginitie, and do all other thinge that shall be to your pleasure. Be nowe of good chere, Titus, and comfort your selfe with good refections and solace, that this wan and pale colour, and your chekes meigre and leane, be nat the cause of your discoveringe. I knowe well that, ye havinge your purpose, I shall be in obloquy and derision of all men, and so hated of all my kynrede, that they shall seke occasion to expulse me out of this citie, thinkyng me to be a notable reproche to al my familie. But let god therin warke. I force nat what payne that I abyde, so that ye, my frende Titus, may be saulfe, and pleasauntly enjoy your desires, to the increasinge of your felicitie. . . .

[Titus does as his friend suggests, then publicly announces that he has married the lady. Gisippus is scorned and leaves home, but after many adventures and misunderstandings is restored to his lands and friend.]

This example in the affectes of frendshippe expresseth (if I be nat deceyved) the description of frendship engendred by the similitude of age and personage, augmented by the conformitie of maners and studies, and confirmed by the longe continuaunce of company.

II. Analogue

From EUPHUES, THE ANATOMY OF WIT
by John Lyly (1579)

[Euphues, a rich young Athenian, 'of more wit than wealth, and yet of more wealth than wisdom', comes to Naples ('a place of more pleasure than profit, and yet of more profit than piety') where his education in human nature begins.]

Euphues having sojourned by the space of two monethes in *Naples* whether he were moved by the courtesie of a young gentleman named *Philautus*, or inforced by destiny: whether his pregna[n]t wit, or his pleasant conceits wrought the greater lyking in the minde of *Euphues*, I know not for certeintie: But *Euphues* showed such entyre love towards him, that he seemed to make small accompt of any others, determining to enter into such an inviolable league of friendship with him, as neither time by peecemeale should impaire, neither fancie utterly desolve, nor any suspition infringe. I have read (saith he) and well I beleeve it, that a friend is in prosperitie a pleasure, a solace in adversitie, in griefe a comfort, in joy a merry companion, at al times an other I, in all places the expresse Image of myne owne person: insomuch that I cannot tell wether the immortall Gods have bestowed any gift upon mortall men, either more noble [able] or more necessary then friendship. Is there any thing in the world to be reputed (I will not say compared) to friendship? Can any treasure in this transitory pilgrimage be of more valew then a friend? in whose bosome thou maist sleepe secure without feare, whom thou maist make partner of al thy secrets without suspition of fraude, and partaker of all thy misfortune without mistrust of fleeting, who will accompt thy bale his bane, thy mishap his misery, the pricking of thy finger the percing of his heart. But whether am I caryed? Have I not also learned that one should eate a bushel of salt with him whom he meaneth to make his friend? that tryal maketh trust? that ther is falshood in felowship? and what then? Doth not the simpathy of manners make the conjunction of mindes? Is it not a by word lyke will to lyke? Not so common as commendable it is, to see young Gentlemen choose them such friendes, with whom they may seeme being absent to be present, being a sunder to be conversant, being dead to be alive. I will therefore have *Philautus* for my pheere, and by so much the more I make my selfe sure to have *Philautus*, by how much the more I view in him the lively image of *Euphues*.

Although there be none so ignoraunt that doth not know, neither any so impudent that will not confesse, friendship to be the jewell of humaine joye: yet whosoever shal see this amitie grounded upon a little affection, will soone conjecture that it shall be dissolved upon a light occasion: as in the sequele of *Euphues* and *Philautus* you shall see, whose hot love waxed soone colde: For as the best Wine doth make the sharpest vineger, so the deepest love turneth to the deadlyest hate. Who deserved the most blame, in mine opinion, it is doubtful and so difficult, that I dare not presume to give verdict. For love being the cause for which so many mischiefes have ben attempted, I am not yet perswaded, whether of them was most to be blamed, but certeinely neither of them was blamelesse. I appeale to your judgement Gentlemen, not that I thinke any of you of the lyke disposition, able to decide the question, but being of deeper discretion then I am, are more fit to debate the quarrell. . . .

[Euphues asks Philautus for his friendship.]

'Which if I may obteine, assure your selfe, that *Damon* to his *Pythias*, *Pilades* to his *Orestes*, *Tytus* to his *Gysippus*, *Thesius* to his

Pirothus, Scipio to his *Laelius*, was never founde more faithfull, then *Euphues* will bee to *Philautus*.' . . .

But after many embracings and protestations one to an other, they walked to dinner, wher they wanted neither meat, neither Musicke, neither any other pastime: and having banqueted, to digest their sweete confections, they daunced all that after noone. they used not onely one boorde but one bed, one booke (if so be it they thought not one too many). Their friendship augmented every day, insomuch that the one could not refraine the company of the other one minute, all things went in common betweene them, which all men accompted commendable.

Phila[u]tus being a towne borne childe, both for his owne countenaunce, and the great countenaunce which his father had while he lived, crept into credit with *Don Ferardo* one of the chiefe governours of the citie, who although he had a courtly crew of gentlewomen sojourning in his pallaice, yet his daughter, heire to his whole revenewes stayned the beautie of them al, whose modest bashfulnes caused the other to looke wanne for envie, whose Lilly cheekes dyed with a Vermilion red, made the rest to blush for shame. For as the finest Ruby staineth the coulour of the rest that be in place, or as the Sunne dimmeth the Moone, that she cannot be discerned, so this gallant girle more faire then fortunate, and yet more fortunate then faithful, eclipsed the beautie of them all, and chaunged their colours. Unto hir had *Philautus* accesse, who wan hir by right of love, and should have worne hir by right of law, had not *Euphues* by straunge destenie broken the bondes of mariage, and forbidden the banns of Matrimony.

It happened that *Don Ferardo* had occasion to goe to *Venice* about certeine [of] his owne affaires, leaving his daughter the onely steward of his household, who spared not to feast *Philautus* hir friend, with al kinds of delights and delycates, reserving only hir honestie as the chiefe stay of hir honour. Hir father being gone she sent for hir friend to supper, who came not as hee was accustomed solitarilye alone, but accompanyed with his friend *Euphues*. The Gentlewoman whether it were for nicenesse, or for nigardnesse of courtesie, gave him such a colde welcome, that he repented that he was come.

Euphues though he knewe himselfe worthy everye way to have a good countenaunce, yet coulde he not perceive hir willing any way to lende him a friendly looke. Yet least he should seeme to want gestures, or to be dashed out of conceipt with hir coy countenaunce, he addressed him to a Gentlewoman called *Livia*. . . .

Supper was set on the bord, then *Philautus* spake thus unto

Lucilla. Yet Gentlewoman, I was the bolder to bring my shadow with me, (meaning *Euphues*) knowing that he should be the better welcome for my sake: unto whom the Gentlewoman replyed: Sir, as I never when I saw you, thought that you came without your shadow, so now I cannot a lyttle mervaile to see you so overshot in bringing a new shadow with you. *Euphues*, though he perceived hir coy nippe, seemed not to care for it, but taking hir by the hand said.

Faire Lady, seeing the shade doth [so] often shield your beautie from the parching Sunne, I hope you will the better esteeme of the shadow, and by so much the lesse it ought to be offensive, by how much the lesse it is able to offende you, and by so much the more you ought to lyke it, by how the more you use to lye in it.

Well Gentleman, aunswered *Lucilla*, in arguing of the shadow, we forgoe the substaunce: pleaseth it you therefore to sit downe to supper. And so they all sate downe, but *Euphues* fed of one dish, which ever stoode before him, the beautie of *Lucilla*.

Heere *Euphues* at the first sight was so kindled with desire, that almost he was like to burn to coales. Supper beeing ended, the order was in *Naples*, that the Gentlewomen would desire to heare some discourse, either concerning love, or learning: And although *Philautus* was requested, yet he posted it over to *Euphues*, whome he knewe most fit for that purpose: *Euphues* beeing thus tyed to the stake by their importunate intreatie, began as followeth.

[He discusses the question whether graces of mind are more to be loved than those of the body.]

And seeing we are even in the bowells of love, it shal not be amisse, to examine whether man or woman be soonest allured, whether be most constant the male or the female. And in this poynte I meane not to be mine owne carver, least I should seeme either to picke a thanke with men, or a quarel with women. If therefore it might stand with your pleasure (Mistres *Lucilla*) to give your censure, I would take the contrarie: for sure I am though your judgement be sound, yet affection will shadow it.

Lucilla seeing his pretence, thought to take advauntage of his large profer, unto whom she saide. Gentleman in my opinion, women are to be wonne with every wind, in whose sexe ther is neither force to withstand the assaults of love, neither constancy to remaine faithfull. And bicause your discourse hath hetherto bred delight, I am loth to hinder you in the sequele of your devises. *Euphues*, perceiving himselfe to be taken napping, aunswered as followeth.

Mistres *Lucilla*, if you speake as you thinke, these gentlewomen present have little cause to thanke you, if you cause me to commend women, my tale will be accompted a meere trifle, and your wordes the plaine truth: Yet knowing promise to be debt, I will paye it with performance. . . .

. . . .

Touching the yeelding to love, albeit their heartes seeme tender, yet they harden them lyke the stone of *Sicilia*, the which the more it is beaten the harder it is: for being framed as it were of the perfection of men, they be free from all such cogitations as may any way provoke them to uncleanenesse, insomuch as they abhorre the light love of youth, which is grounded uppon lust, and dissolved, upon every light occasion. When they see the folly of men turne to fury, their delyght to doting, their affection to frencie, when they see them as it were pine in pleasure, and to wax pale through their own peevishnes, their sutes, their service, their letters, their labours, their loves, their lives, seeme to them so odyous, that they harden their hearts against such concupysence, to the ende they might convert them from rashnesse to reason: from such lewde disposition, to honest discretion. Heereoff it commeth that men accuse woemen of cruelty, bicause they themselves want civility: they accompt them full of wyles, in not yeelding to their wickednes: faithlesse for resisting their filthynes. But I had almost forgot my selfe, you shal pardon me Mistres *Lucilla* for this time, if [thus] abruptlye, I finish my discourse: it is neither for want of good wil, or lack of proofe, but yat I feele in my self such alteration, yat I can scarcely utter one worde. Ah *Euphues, Euphues*.

The gentlewomen were strooke into such a quandary with this sodeine chaunge, that they all chaunged coulour. But *Euphues* taking *Philautus* by the hande, and giving the gentlewomen thankes for their patience and his repast, bad them al farewell, and went immediatly to his chamber.

[Lucilla falling in love with Euphues is conscious of her disloyalty to Philautus.]

But suppose that *Euphues* love thee, that *Philautus* leave thee, wil thy Father thinkest thou give thee libertie to lyve after thine owne lust? Wil he esteeme him worthy to enherite his possessions, whome he accompeth unworthy to enjoy thy person? Is it lyke that hee will match thee in mariage with a straunger, with a *Grecian*, with a meane man? I, but what knoweth my father whether he be wealthy whether his revenews be able to countervaile my fathers landes,

whether his birth be noble yea, or no? Can any one make doubt of
his gentle bloud, that seeth his gentle conditions? . . .

. . . .

Let my father use what speaches he lyst, I will follow mine owne
lust. Lust *Lucilla*, what sayst thou? No no, mine owne love I should
have sayd, for I am as farre from lust, as I am from reason, and as
neere to love as I am to folly. Then sticke to thy determination, and
shew thy selfe, what love can doe, what love dares doe, what love
hath done. Albeit I can no way quench the coales of desire with
forgetfulnesse, yet will I rake them up in the ashes of modestie:
Seeing I dare not discover my love for maidenly shamefastnesse, I
will dissemble it till time I have opportunitie. And I hope so to
behave my selfe, as *Euphues* shall thinke me his owne, and *Philautus*
perswade himself I am none but his. But I would to God *Euphues*
would repaire hether that the sight of him might mitigate some parte
of my martirdome.

She having thus discoursed with hir selfe hir owne miseries, cast
hir selfe on the bedde and there lette hir lye, and retourne we to
Euphues, who was so caught in the ginne of folly, that he neither could
comfort himselfe, nor durst aske counsaile of his friend, suspecting
that which in deede was true, that *Philautus* was corrival with him
and cooke-mate with *Lucilla*. Amiddest therefore these his extremities, betweene hope and feare, he uttered these or the lyke speaches.

What is he *Euphues*, that knowing thy witte, and seeing thy folly,
but will rather punish thy leaudnesse, then pittie thy heavinesse?
Was ther ever any so fickle so soone to be allured? any ever [ever
anie] so faithlesse to deceive his friend? ever any so foolish to bathe
himselfe in his owne misfortune? Too true it is, that as the sea Crab
swimmeth alwayes against the streame, so wit alwayes striveth
against wisedome: And as the Bee is oftentimes hurt with hir
owne Honny, so is witte not seldome plagued with his owne
conceipt. . . .

Ah my *Lucilla*, would thou wer either lesse faire, or I more fortunate: either I wiser, or thou milder: either I would I were out of
this mad moode, either I would we wer both of one minde. But how
should she be perswaded of my loyaltie, that yet had never one
simple proofe of my love? will she not rather imagine me to be
entangled with hir beautie, then with hir vertue. That my fancie
being so lewdly chaunged at the first, will be as lyghtly chaunged at
the last: that nothing violent, can bee permanent. Yes, yes, shee
must needes conjecture so, although it bee nothing so: for by howe
much the more my affection commeth on the sodeine, by so much
the lesse will she thinke it certeine. The ratling thunderbolt hath

but his clap, the lightning but his flash, and as they both come in a moment, so doe they both ende in a minuite.

[He decides to woo her gradually.]

In battayles there ought to be a doubtfull fight, and a desperat ende, in pleadinge a diffyculte enteraunce, and a defused determination, in love a lyfe wythout hope, and a death without feare. Fyre commeth out of the hardest flynte wyth the steele. Oyle out of the dryest Jeate by the fyre, love out of the stoniest hearte by fayth, by trust, by tyme. Hadde *Tarquinus* used his love with coulours of countenuaunce, *Lucretia* woulde eyther wyth some pitie have aunswered hys desyre, or with some perswasion have stayed hir death. It was the heate of hys lust, that made hyr hast to ende hir lyfe, wherefore love in neyther respecte is to bee condempned, but hee of rashnesse to attempte a Ladye furiouslye, and shee of rygor to punishe hys follye in hir owne fleshe, a fact (in myne opinion) more worthy the name of crueltie then chastitie, and fitter for a Monster in the desartes, then a Matrone of *Rome*. *Penelope* no lesse constaunt then shee, yet more wyse, woulde bee wearie to unweave that in the nyght, shee spunne in the daye, if *Ulysses* hadde not come home the sooner. There is no woeman, *Euphues*, but shee will yeelde in time, bee not therefore dismaied either with high lookes or frowarde wordes.

Euphues having thus talked with himselfe, *Philautus* entered the chamber, and finding him so worne and wasted with continuall mourning, neither joying in hys meate, nor rejoycing in his friend, with watry eyes uttered this speach.

Friend and fellow, as I am not ignoraunt of thy present weakenes, so I am not privie of the cause: and although I suspect many things, yet can I assure my self of no one thing. Therfore my good *Euphues*, for these doubts and dumpes of mine, either remove the cause, or reveale it. Thou hast hetherto founde me a cheerefull companion in thy myrth, and nowe shalt thou finde me as carefull with thee in thy moane. If altogether thou maist not be cured, yet maist thou bee comforted.

[Euphues pretends that he loves Livia, and is taken by Philautus to the house of Ferardo, who welcomes him for Philautus' sake and leaves him with Lucilla when he and Philautus go away on business. This gives Euphues a chance to woo Lucilla, who finally admits:]

Tush, *Philautus* was liked for fashion sake, but never loved for fancie sake: and this I vowe by the faith of a Virgin, and by the love I beare thee, (for greater bands to confirme my vow I have not) that my father shall sooner martir mee in the fire then marye mee to *Philautus*. No no, *Euphues*, thou onely hast wonne me by love, and shalt onely weare me by law: I force not *Philautus* his fury, so I may have *Euphues* his friendship: neither wil I prefer his possessions before thy person, neither esteme better of his lands, then of thy love. *Ferardo* shal sooner disherite me of my patrimony, then dishonour me in breaking my promise? It is not his great mannors, but thy good manners, that shal make my mariage. In token of which my sincere affection, I give thee my hande in pawne, and my heart for ever to be thy *Lucilla*.

.   .   .   .

But as *Ferardo* went in post, so hee retourned in hast having concluded with *Philautus*, that the mariage should immediatly be consummated, which wrought such a content in *Philautus*, that he was almost in an extasie through the extremitie of his passions: such is the fulnesse and force of pleasure, that ther is nothing so daungerous as the fruition, yet knowing that delayes bring daungers, although hee nothing doubted of *Lucilla* whome hee loved, yet feared he the ficklenesse of olde men, which is always to be mistrusted.

Hee urged therefore *Ferardo* to breake with his Daughter, who beeing willyng to have the matche made, was content incontinentlye to procure the meanes: finding therefore his daughter at leasure, and having knowledge of hir former love, spake to hir as followeth.

Deere daughter as thou hast long time lived a maiden, so now thou must learne to be a Mother, and as I have bene carefull to bring thee up a Virgin, so am I now desirous to make thee a Wife. Neither ought I in this matter to use any perswasions, for that maidens commonly now a dayes are no sooner borne, but they beginne to bride it: neither to offer any great portions, for that thou knowest thou shalt enherite al my possessions. Mine onely care hath bene hetherto, to match thee with such an one, as shoulde be of good wealth, able to mainteine thee: of great worship, able to compare with thee in birth: of honest conditions, to deserve thy love: and an *Italian* borne to enjoy my landes. At the last I have found one aunswerable to my desire, a Gentleman of great revenewes, of a noble progenie, of honest behaviour, of comly personage, borne and brought up in *Naples*, *Philautus* (thy friend as I gesse) thy husband *Lucilla* if thou lyke it, neither canst thou dislike him, who wanteth nothing that should cause thy liking, neither hath any thing that should breede thy loathing.

And surely I rejoyce the more that thou shalt bee linked to him in mariage, whom thou hast loved, as I heare beeing a maiden, neither can there any jarres kindle betweene them, wher the mindes

be so united, neither any jealousie arise, where love hath so long bene
setled. Therefore *Lucilla*, to the ende the desire of either of you may
now be accomplyshed to the delyght of you both, I am heere come
to finishe the contract by giving handes, which you have already
begunne betweene your selves by joyning of hearts, that as GOD
doth witnesse the one in your consciences, so the world may testifie
the other, by your conversations, and therefore *Lucilla* make such
aunswere to my request, as may lyke me and satisfie thy friende.

[Lucilla refuses to marry Philautus, and finally, in his presence,
confesses that she loves his friend Euphues. Raging against them
both Philautus writes a furious letter to Euphues, who answers in
'gibing termes'. Almost at once however we learn that Lucilla has
turned again, accepting the suit of 'one Curio, a gentleman of
Naples of little wealth and lesse wit.' So Euphues has to lament the
loss of his mistress and of 'that which I shall hardlye finde againe, a
faithfull friende.']

   Philautus having intellygence of *Euphues* his [ill] successe, and the
falsehoode of *Lucilla*, although he began to rejoyce at the miserie of
his fellow, yet seeing hir ficklenesse, coulde not but lament hir folly,
and pitie his friends misfortune. Thinking that the lyghtnesse of
Lucilla enticed *Euphues* to so great lyking.

   Euphues and *Philautus* having conference between themselves,
casting discourtesie in the teeth each of the other, but chiefely
noting disloyaltie in the demeanor of *Lucilla*, after much talke
renewed their old friendship, both abandoning *Lucilla*, as most
abhominable.

III. Translation of Source

From DIANA ENAMORADA
by J. de Montemayor
translated by B. Yonge (1598)

Diana of George of Montemayor: Translated out of
Spanish into English by Bartholomew Yong of the
Middle Temple, Gentleman. At London, Printed by
Edm. Bollifant, Impensis G.B. 1598.

[In the Second Book of Part One the Shepherdess Selvagia and her friends Sylvanus and Syrenus wander through the woodland towards the Fountain of the Sycamores.]

'Let us go,' said Selvagia; and so step by step, they went towards the place where they heard that singing, and hiding themselves behind certaine trees neere unto the brook, they saw three Nymphes sitting upon the golden flowers, of such excellent beauty that (it seemed) nature had made a manifest proofe of that she was able to do. They were apparelled with upper garments of white silke, wrought all above with fringe of gold, their haire, (which in brightnes obscured the sunnie beames) was tied about their heads with fillets of oriental pearle, whose curled lockes upon their christalline foreheads made a fine periwig; just in the midst whereof hung downe an Eagle of gold, holding betweene her talons a rich and pretious Diamond. All three with marvellous good consent so sweetly plaied on their instruments whereunto they joyned their Angelicall voices, that it seemed no lesse then celestiall musicke, and the first thing they sung, was this fancie.

> Contents of love,
> That come with so great paine,
> If that you come, why go you hence againe? . . .

[The Shepherdesses are Doria, Cynthia, and Polydora. First Cynthia sings a song, then Syrenus and Diana.]

But now the faire Nymphes tooke up their instruments, and went walking up and downe the greene meadow, least of all suspecting that which happened unto them, for having gone but a little way from the place, where the Shepherdes were secretly abiding, three monstrous and foule Savages came out of a thicket of high broome and bushes on the right hande of the woode, armed with corselets and morions of tygres skins, and so ugley to behold, that to the fearefull Nymphes it was a strange and terrible sight. [The savages accost and attack the nymphs, and though the shepherds try to help them by throwing stones they would have been lost if] a certaine strange Shepherdesse (of such singular beautie and comely feature, as made both the Savages and the rest amazed at her goodly personage) had not come out of the thicke wood neere unto the fountaine, where they before were singing. She had her bowe hanging on her left arme, and a quiver of arrowes at her shoulder, in her hand a fine staffe of wilde oke, armed at the end with a long and well steeled pike.

[She kills two of the wild men.]

But setling her selfe to shoote at the third, that was keeping the
three Nymphes, she could not so soone effect it, but that he came
running in to her, within the length of his club, and had surely
dispatched her with one blowe, if the faire Shepherdesse, by lifting
up her knottie staffe (as he was discharging upon her) had not taken
it upon the iron point (whereby his club brake in two peeces) and
immediately requited him with another upon the top of his crowne,
wherewith she made him stagger on his knees, and then running a
thrust at his face (and with such force and aime it was) that pearcing
his eies, her staffe made speedie passage thorow his braines, so that
the fierce Savage, yelling out a horrible and lowde grone, fell downe
dead to the ground.

[After this they sit down by the fountain and the Shepherds go off
to get food at the nearest town, leaving the three Nymphs with the
unknown Shepherdess. They tell her who they are and that they
dwell 'in *Diana's* wood, where sage *Felicia* keeps her stately court,
whose course of life and only exercise is to cure and remedie the
passions of love'. Encouraged by this the Shepherdess tells the story
of her life.]

You shall therefore knowe (faire Nymphes) that great *Vandalia*
is my native countrie, a province not far hence, where I was borne,
in a citie called *Soldina*, my mother called *Delia*, my father *Andronius*,
for linage and possessions the chiefest of all that province. It fell
out that as my mother was married many yeeres, and had no
children, (by reason whereof she lived so sad and malecontent that
she enjoyed not one merry day) with teares and sighes she daily
importuned the heavens, and with a thousand vowes and devout
offerings besought God to grant her the summe of her desire: whose
omnipotencie it pleased, beholding from his imperiall throne her
continuall orisons, to make her barren bodie (the greater part of
her age being now spent and gone) to become fruitfull. What infinite
joy she conceived thereof, let her judge, that after a long desire
of any thing, fortune at last doth put it into her handes. Of which
content my father *Andronius* being no lesse partaker, shewed such
tokens of inward joy, as are impossible to be expressed. My mother
Delia was so much given to reading of ancient histories, that if, by
reason of sicknes or any important businesse, she had not bene
hindred, she would never (by her will) have passed the time away
in any other delight; who (as I said) being now with childe, and
finding herselfe on a night ill at ease, intreated my father to reade
something unto her, that her minde being occupied in contemplation
thereof, she might the better passe her greefe away. My father, who
studied for nothing els but to please her in all he might, began to

reade unto her the historie of *Paris*, when the three Ladies referred their proude contention for the golden Apple to his conclusion and judgement. But as my mother held it for an infallible opinion that *Paris* had partially given that sentence, (perswaded thereunto by a blinde passion of beautie) so she said, that without all doubt he did not with due reason and wisedome consider the Goddesse of battels; for, as martiall and heroicall feates (saide she) excelled all other qualities, so with equitie and justice the Apple should have bene given to her. My father answered, that since the Apple was to be given to the fairest, and that *Venus* was fairer than any of the rest, *Paris* had rightly given his judgement, if that harme had not ensued thereof, which afterwardes did. To this my mother replied, that, though it was written in the Apple, *That it should be given to the fairest*, it was not to be understood of corporall beautie, but of the intellec- tuall beautie of the mind. And therefore since fortitude was a thing that made one most beautiful, and the exercise of arms an exterior act of this vertue, she affirmed, that to the Goddesse of battels this Apple should be given, if *Paris* had judged like a prudent and un- appassionate judge. So that (faire Nymphes) they spent a great part of the night in this controversie, both of them alledging the most reasons they could to confirme their owne purpose. They per- sisting in this point, sleepe began to overcome her, whom the reasons and arguments of her husband coulde not once moove; so that being very deepe in her disputations, she fell into as deepe a sleepe, to whom, (my father being now gone to his chamber) appeered the Goddesse *Venus*, with as frowning a countenance as faire, and saide, I marvell, *Delia*, who hath mooved thee to be so contrarie to her, that was never opposite to thee? If thou hadst but called to minde the time when thou wert so overcome in love for *Andronius*, thou wouldest not have paide me the debt (thou owest me) with so ill coine. But thou shalt not escape free from my due anger; for thou shalt bring forth a sonne and a daughter, whose birth shall cost thee no lesse than thy life, and them their contentment, for uttering so much in disgrace of my honour and beautie: both which shall be as in- fortunate in their love as any were ever in all their lives, or to the age wherein, with remedylesse sighes, they shall breath forth the summe of their ceaselesse sorrowes. And having saide thus, she vanished away: when, likewise, it seemed to my mother that the Goddesse *Pallas* came to her in a vision, and with a merry counten- ance saide thus unto her: With what sufficient rewardes may I be able to requite the due regarde (most happie and discreete *Delia*) which thou hast alleaged in my favour against thy husbands obstin- ate opinion, except it be by making thee understand that thou shalt bring foorth a sonne and a daughter, the most fortunate in armes that have bene to their times. Having thus said, she vanished out of her sight, and my mother, thorow exceeding feare, awaked immediately. Who, within a moneth after, at one birth was delivered of me, and of a brother of mine, and died in childebed, leaving my father the most sorrowfull man in the world for her sudden death; for greefe whereof, within a little while after, he also died. And bicause you may knowe (faire Nymphes) in what great extremities love hath put me, you must understand, that (being a woman of that qualitie and disposition as you have heard) I have bene forced by my cruell destinie to leave my naturall habit and libertie, and the due respect of mine honour, to follow him, who thinkes (perhaps) that I do but leese it by loving him so extremely. Behold, how bootelesse and unseemely it is for a woman to be so dextrous in armes, as if it were her proper nature and kinde, wherewith (faire Nymphes) I had never bene indued, but that, by meanes thereof, I should come to doe you this little service against these villaines; whiche I account no lesse then if fortune had begun to satisfie in part some of those infinite wrongs that she hath continually done me. The Nymphes were so amazed at her words, that they could neither aske nor answere any thing to that the faire Shepherdesse tolde them, who, prosecuting her historie, saide:

My brother and I were brought up in a Nunnerie, where an aunt of ours was Abbesse, until we had accomplished twelve yeeres of age, at what time we were taken from thence againe, and my brother was caried to the mightie and invincible *King of Portugall* his Court (whose noble fame and princely liberalitie was bruted over all the world) where, being growen to yeeres able to manage armes, he atchieved as valiant and almost incredible enterprises by them, as he suffered unfortunate disgraces and foiles by love. And with all this he was so highly favoured of that magnificent king, that he would never suffer him to depart from his Court. Unfortunate I, reserved by my sinister destinies to greater mishaps, was caried to a grandmother of mine, which place I would I had never seene, since it was an occasion of such a sorrowfull life as never any woman suffered the like. And bicause there is not any thing (faire Nymphes) which I am not forced to tell you, as well for the great vertue and desertes which your excellent beauties doe testifie, as also for that for my minde doth give me, that you shall be no small part and meanes of my comfort, knowe, that as I was in my grandmothers house, and almost seventeene yeeres olde, a certaine yoong Gentleman fell in love with me, who dwelt no further from our house then the length of a garden Terrasse, so that he might see me every sommers night when I walked in the garden. When as therefore ingratefull *Felix* had beheld in that place the unfortunate *Felismena* (for this is the name of the wofull woman that tels you her mishaps) he was extremely enamoured of me, or else did cunningly dissemble it, I not knowing then whether of these two I might beleeve, but am now assured, that whosoever beleeves lest, or nothing at all in these affaires, shall be most at ease. Many daies *Don Felix* spent in endeavouring to make me know the paines which he suffered for me, and many more did I spende in making the matter strange, and that he did not suffer them for my sake. And I know not why love delaied the time so long by forcing me to love him, but onely that (when he came indeed) he might enter into my hart at once, and with greater force and violence. When he had, therefore, by sundrie signes, as by Tylt and Tourneyes, and by prauncing up and downe upon his proude Jennet before my windowes, made it manifest that he was in love with me (for at the first I did not so well perceive it) he determined in the end to write a letter unto me; and having practised divers times before with a maide of mine, and at length, with many gifts and faire promises, gotten her good will and furtherance, he gave her the letter to deliver to me. But to see the meanes that *Rosina* made unto me, (for so was she called) the dutifull services and unwoonted circumstances, before she did deliver it, the othes that she sware unto me, and the subtle words and serious protestations she used, it was a pleasant thing, and woorthie the noting. To whom (neverthelesse) with an angrie countenance I turned againe, saying, If I had not regard of mine owne estate, and what hereafter might be said, I would make this shamelesse face of thine be knowne ever after for a marke of an impudent and bolde minion: but bicause it is the first time, let this suffice that I have saide, and give thee warning to take heed of the second.

Me thinkes I see now the craftie wench, how she helde her peace, dissembling very cunningly the sorrow that she conceived by my angrie answer; for she fained a counterfaite smiling, saying, Jesus, Mistresse! I gave it you, bicause you might laugh at it, and not to moove your patience with it in this sort; for if I had any thought that it would have provoked you to anger, I praie God he may shew his wrath as great towards me as ever he did to the daughter of any mother. And with this she added many wordes more (as she could do well enough) to pacifie the fained anger and ill opinion that I had conceived of her, and taking her letter with her, she departed from me. This having passed thus, I began to imagine what might ensue thereof, and love (me thought) did put a certaine desire into my minde to see the letter, though modestie and shame forbad me to

ask it of my maide, especially for the wordes that had passed betweene us, as you have heard. And so I continued all that day untill
night, in varietie of many thoughts; but when *Rosina* came to helpe
me to bedde, God knowes how desirous I was to have her entreat me
againe to take the letter, but she woulde never speake unto me about
it, nor (as it seemed) did so much as once thinke thereof. Yet to trie,
if by giving her some occasion I might prevaile, I saide unto her:
And is it so, *Rosina*, that *Don Felix*, without any regard to mine
honour, dares write unto me? These are things, mistresse, (saide she
demurely to me againe) that are commonly incident to love, wherefore I beseech you pardon me, for if I had thought to have angred
you with it, I would have first pulled out the bals of mine eies. How
cold my hart was at that blow, God knowes, yet did I dissemble the
matter, and suffer my selfe to remaine that night onely with my
desire, and with occasion of little sleepe. And so it was, indeede, for
that (me thought) was the longest and most painfull night that ever
I passed. But when, with a slower pace (then I desired) the wished
day was come, the discreet and subtle *Rosina* came into my chamber
to helpe me to make me readie, in dooing whereof, of purpose she
let the letter closely fall, which, when I perceived, What is that that
fell downe? (saide I), let me see it. It is nothing, Mistresse, saide she.
Come, come, let me see it (saide I): what! moove me not, or else tell
me what it is. Good Lord, Mistresse (saide she), why will you see it:
it is the letter I would have given you yesterday. Nay, that it is not
(saide I) wherefore shewe it me, that I may see if you lie or no. I
had no sooner said so but she put it into my handes, saying, God
never give me good if it be anie other thing; and although I knewe it
well indeede, yet I saide, what, this is not the same, for I know that
well enough, but it is one of thy lovers letters: I will read it, to see in
what neede he standeth of thy favour. And opening it, I founde it
conteined this that followeth.

'I ever imagined (deere Mistresse) that your discretion and wisedome woulde have taken away the feare I had to write unto you,
the same knowing well enough (without any letter at all) how much
I love you, but the very same hath so cunningly dissembled, that
wherein I hoped the only remedie of my griefes had been, therein
consisted my greatest harme. If according to your wisedome you
censure my boldnes, I shall not then (I know) enjoy one hower of
life; but if you do consider of it according to loves accustomed effects,
then will I not exchange my hope for it. Be not offended, I beseech
you, (good Ladie) with my letter, and blame me not for writing
unto you, untill you see by experience whether I can leave of to
write: and take me besides into the possession of that which is yours,

since all is mine doth wholly consist in your hands, the which, with all reverence and dutifull affection, a thousand times I kisse.'

When I had now seene my *Don Felix* his letter, whether it was for reading it at such a time, when by the same he shewed that he loved me more than himselfe, or whether he had disposition and regiment over part of this wearied soule, to imprint that love in it whereof he wrote unto me, I began to love him too well, (and, alas, for my harme!) since he was the cause of so much sorrow as I have passed for his sake. Whereupon, asking *Rosina* forgivenes of what was past (as a thing needfull for that which was to come) and committing the secrecie of my love to her fidelitie, I read the letter once againe, pausing a little at every worde (and a very little indeede it was) bicause I concluded so soone with my selfe, to do that I did, although in verie truth it lay not otherwise in my power to do. Wherefore, calling for paper and inke, I answered his letter thus.

'Esteeme not so slightly of mine honour, *Don Felix*, as with fained wordes to thinke to enveagle it, or with thy vaine pretenses to offend it any waies. I know wel enough what manner of man thou art, and how great thy desert and presumption is; from whence thy boldnes doth arise (I gesse), and not from the force (which thing thou wouldst faine perswade me) of thy fervent love. And if it be so (as my suspicion suggesteth) thy labor is as vaine as thy imagination presumptuous, by thinking to make me do any thing contrarie to that which I owe unto mine honour. Consider (I beseech thee) how seldome things commenced under suttletie and dissimulation have good successe; and that it is not the part of a Gentleman to meane them one way and speak them another. Thou praiest me (amongst other things) to admit thee into possession of that that is mine: but I am of so ill an humour in matters of this qualitie, that I trust not things experienced, how much lesse then thy bare wordes; yet, neverthelesse, I make no small account of that which thou hast manifested to me in thy letter; for it is ynough that I am incredulous, though not unthankfull.'

This letter did I send, contrarie to that I should have done, because it was the occasion of all my harmes and greefes; for after this, he began to waxe more bolde by unfolding his thoughts, and seeking out the meanes to have a parly with me. In the end, (faire Nymphes) a few daies being spent in his demaunds and my answers, false love did worke in me after his wonted fashions, every hower seasing more strongly upon my unfortunate soule. The Tourneies were now renewed, the musicke by night did never cease; amorous letters and verses were re-continued on both sides; and thus passed I away almost a whole yeere, at the end whereof, I felt my selfe so far in his

love, that I had no power to retire, nor stay my selfe from disclosing
my thoughts unto him, the thing which he desired more then his
owne life. But my adverse fortune afterwardes would, that of these
our mutuall loves (when as now they were most assured) his father
had some intelligence, and whosoever revealed them first, perswaded
him so cunningly, that his father (fearing lest he would have married
me out of hand) sent him to the great Princesse *Augusta Caesarinas*
court, telling him, it was not meete that a yoong Gentleman, and of
so noble a house as he was, should spende his youth idly at home,
where nothing could be learned but examples of vice, whereof the
verie same idlenes (he said) was the onely Mistresse. He went away
so pensive, that his great greefe would not suffer him to acquaint me
with his departure; which when I knew, how sorrowfull I remained,
she may imagine that hath bene at any time tormented with like
passion. To tell you now the life that I led in his absence, my sadnes,
sighes, and teares, which every day I powred out of these wearied
eies, my toong is far unable: if then my paines were such that I
cannot now expresse them, how could I then suffer them? But being
in the mids of my mishaps, and in the depth of those woes which the
absence of *Don Felix* caused me to feele, and it seeming to me that
my greefe was without remedie, if he were once seene or knowen
of the Ladies in that Court (more beautifull and gracious then my
selfe), by occasion whereof, as also by absence (a capitall enemie to
love) I might easily be forgotten, I determined to adventure that,
which I think never any woman imagined; which was to apparell
my selfe in the habit of a man, and to hye me to the Court to see
him, in whose sight al my hope and content remained. Which
determination I no sooner thought of then I put in practise, love
blinding my eies and minde with an inconsiderate regarde of mine
owne estate and condition. To the execution of which attempt I
wanted no industrie; for, being furnished with the helpe of one of my
approoved friends, and treasouresse of my secrets, who bought me
such apparell as I willed her, and a good horse for my journey, I
went not onely out of my countrie, but out of my deere reputation,
which (I thinke) I shall never recover againe; and so trotted directly
to the Court, passing by the way many accidents, which (if time
would give me leave to tell them) woulde not make you laugh a
little to heare them. Twenty daies I was in going thither, at the ende
of which, being come to the desired place, I took up mine Inne in a
streete less frequented with concurse of people: and the great desire
I had to see the destroier of my joy did not suffer me to thinke of
any other thing, but how or where I might see him. To inquire of
him of mine host I durst not, lest my comming might (perhaps)

have bene discovered; and to seeke him foorth I thought it not best, lest some inopinate mishap might have fallen out, whereby I might have bene knowen. Wherefore I passed all that day in these perplexities, while night came on, each hower whereof (me thought) was a whole yeere unto me. But midnight being a little past, mine host called at my chamber doore, and told me if I was desirous to heare some brave musicke, I should arise quickly, and open a window towards the street. The which I did by and by, and making no noise at all, I heard how *Don Felix* his Page, called *Fabius* (whom I knew by his voice) saide to others that came with him, Now it is time, my Masters, bicause the Lady is in the gallerie over her garden, taking the fresh aire of the coole night. He had no sooner saide so, but they began to winde three Cornets and a Sackbot, with such skill and sweetenesse, that it seemed celestiall musicke; and then began a voice to sing, the sweetest (in my opinion) that ever I heard. And though I was in suspence, by hearing *Fabius* speake, whereby a thousand doubtes and imaginations (repugnant to my rest) occurred in my minde, yet I neglected not to heare what was sung, bicause their operations were not of such force that they were able to hinder the desire, nor distemper the delight that I conceived by hearing it. That therefore which was sung were these verses:

> Sweete mistresse, harken unto me,
> (If it greeves thee to see me die)
> And hearing though it greeveth thee,
> To heare me yet, do not denie.

> O grant me then this short content,
> For forc'd I am to thee to flie:
> My sighes do not make thee relent,
> Nor teares thy hart do mollifie.

> Nothing of mine doth give thee payne,
> Nor thou think'st of no remedie:
> Mistresse how long shall I sustaine
> Such ill, as still thou dost applie?

> In death there is no helpe, be sure,
> But in thy will, where it doth lie:
> For all those illes which death doth cure,
> Alas, they are but light to trie:

> My troubles to not trouble thee,
> Nor hope to touch thy soule so nie:
> O! from a will that is so free,
> What should I hope when I do crie?

How can I mollifie that brave
   And stony hart, of pittie drie?
Yet Mistresse, turne those eies (that have
   No peeres) shining like stars in skie;

But turne them not in angrie sort,
   If thou wilt not kill me thereby:
Though yet in anger, or in sport,
   Thou killest onely with thine eie.

After they had first, with a concert of musicke, sung this song, two plaied, the one upon a Lute, the other upon a silver sounding Harpe, being accompanied with the sweete voice of my *Don Felix.* The great joy that I felt in hearing him cannot be imagined, for (me thought) I heard him nowe, as in that happie and passed time of our loves. But after the deceit of this imagination was discovered, seeing with mine eies, and hearing with mine eares, that this musicke was bestowed upon another, and not on me, God knowes what a bitter death it was unto my soule: and with a greevous sigh, that caried almost my life away with it, I asked mine host if he knew what the Ladie was for whose sake the musicke was made? He answered me, that he could not imagine on whom it was bestowed, bicause in that streete dwelled manie noble and faire Ladies. And when I saw he could not satisfie my request, I bent mine eares againe to heare my *Don Felix,* who now, to the tune of a delicate harpe, whereon he sweetely plaied, began to sing this Sonnet following:—

A SONNET

My painefull yeeres impartiall Love *was spending*
   In vaine and booteles hopes my life appaying,
And cruell Fortune *to the world bewraying*
Strange samples of my teares that have no ending.
Time everie thing to truth at last commending,
   Leaves of my steps such markes, that now betraying,
   And all deceitfull trusts shall be decaying,
And none have cause to plaine of his offending.
Shee, whom I lov'd to my obliged power,
   That in her sweetest love to me discovers
Which never yet I knew (those heavenly pleasures),
And I do saie, exclaiming every hower,
   Do not you see what makes you wise, O Lovers?
Love, Fortune, Time, *and my faire Mystresse treasures.*

The Sonnet being ended, they paused awhile, playing on fower Lutes togither, and on a paire of Virginals, with such heavenly melodie, that the whole worlde (I thinke) could not affoord sweeter musick to the eare nor delight to any minde, not subject to the panges of such predominant greefe and sorrow as mine was. But then fower voices, passing well tuned and set togither, began to sing this song following:

A SONG

That sweetest harme I doe not blame,
First caused by thy fairest eies,
But greeve, bicause too late I came,
To know my fault, and to be wise.

I never knew a worser kinde of life,
To live in feare, from boldnesse still to cease:
Nor woorse then this, to live in such a strife,
Whether of bothe, to speake, or holde my peace?

And so the harme I do not blame,
Caused by thee or thy faire eies;
But that to see how late I came,
To know my fault, and to be wise.

I ever more did feare that I should knowe
Some secret things, and doubtfull in their kinde,
Bicause the surest things doe ever goe
Most contrarie unto my wish and minde.

And yet by knowing of the same
There is no hurt; but it denies
My remedie, since late I came,
To knowe my fault, and to be wise.

When this song was ended, they began to sound divers sorts of instruments, and voices most excellently agreeing togither, and with such sweetnes that they could not chuse but delight any very much who were so farre from it as I. About dawning of the day the musicke ended, and I did what I could to espie out my *Don Felix*, but the darknes of the night was mine enimie therein. And seeing now that they were gone, I went to bed againe, where I bewailed my great mishap, knowing that he whom most of al I loved, had so unwoorthily forgotten me, whereof his musicke was too manifest a

witnes. And when it was time, I arose, and without any other consideration, went straight to the Princesse her pallace, where (I
thought) I might see that which I so greatly desired, determining
to call my selfe *Valerius*, if any (perhaps) did aske my name. Comming therefore to a faire broad court before the pallace gate, I
viewed the windowes and galleries, where I sawe such store of
blazing beauties, and gallant Ladies, that I am not able now to
recount, nor then to do any more but woonder at their graces, their
gorgeous attyre, their jewels, their brave fashions of apparell, and
ornaments wherewith they were so richly set out. Up and downe
this place, before the windowes, roade many lords and brave gentlemen in rich and sumptuous habits, and mounted upon proud jen-
nets, every one casting his eie to that part where his thoughts were
secretly placed. God knowes how greatly I desired to see *Don Felix*
there, and that his injurious love had beene in that famous pallace;
bicause I might then have beene assured that he should never have
got any other guerdon of his sutes and services, but onely to see and
to be seene, and sometimes to speake to his Mistresse, whom he
must serve before a thousand eies, bicause the privilege of that place
doth not give him any further leave. But it was my ill fortune that
he had settled his love in that place where I might not be assured of
this poore helpe. Thus, as I was standing neere to the pallace gate, I
espied *Fabius*, *Don Felix* his page, comming in great haste to the
pallace, where, speaking a word or two with a porter that kept the
second entrie, he returned the same waie he came. I gessed his
errant was, to knowe whether it were fit time for *Don Felix* to come to
dispatch certaine business that his father had in the court, and that
he could not choose but come thither out of hand. And being in this
supposed joy which his sight did promise me, I saw him comming
along with a great traine of followers attending on his person, all of
them being bravely apparelled in a liverie of watchet silke, garded
with yellow velvet, and stitched on either side with threedes of
twisted silver, wearing likewise blew, yellow, and white feathers in
their hats. But my lorde *Don Felix* had on a paire of ash colour hose,
embrodered and drawen foorth with watchet tissue; his dublet was
of white satten, embrodered with knots of golde, and likewise an
embrodered jerkin of the same coloured velvet; and his short cape
cloke was of blacke velvet, edged with gold lace, and hung full of
buttons of pearle and gold, and lined with a razed watchet satten:
by his side he ware, at a paire of embrodered hangers, a rapier and
dagger, with engraven hilts and pommell of beaten golde. On his
head, a hat beset full of golden stars, in the mids of everie which a
rich orient pearle was enchased, and his feather was likewise blew,

yellow and white. Mounted he came upon a faire dapple graie Jennet, with a rich furniture of blew, embrodered with golde and seede pearle. When I sawe him in this rich equipage, I was so amazed at his sight, that how extremely my sences were ravished with sudden joye I am not able (faire Nymphes) to tell you. Truth it is, that I could not but shed some teares for joy and greefe, which his sight did make me feele, but, fearing to be noted by the standers by, for that time I dried them up. But as *Don Felix* (being now come to the pallace gate) was dismounted, and gone up a paire of staires into the chamber of presence, I went to his men, where they were attending his returne; and seeing *Fabius*, whom I had seene before amongst them, I tooke him aside, and saide unto him, My friend, I pray you tell me what Lord this is, which did but even now alight from his Jennet, for (me thinkes) he is very like one whom I have seene before in an other farre countrey. *Fabius* then answered me thus: Art thou such a novice in the court that thou knowest not *Don Felix?* I tell thee there is not any Lord, knight, or gentleman better knowne in it than he. No doubt of that (saide I), but I will tell thee what a novice I am, and how small a time I have beene in the court, for yesterday was the first that ever I came to it. Naie then, I cannot blame thee (saide *Fabius*) if thou knowest him not. Knowe, then, that this gentleman is called *Don Felix*, borne in *Vandalia*, and hath his chiefest house in the antient cittie of Soldina, and is remaining in this court about certaine affaires of his fathers and his owne. But I pray you tell me (said I) why he gives his liveries of these colours? If the cause were not so manifest, I woulde conceale it (saide *Fabius*), but since there is not any that knowes it not, and canst not come to any in this court who cannot tell thee the reason why, I thinke by telling thee it I do no more then in courtesie I am bound to do. Thou must therefore understand, that he loves and serves a Ladie heere in this Citie named *Celia*, and therefore weares and gives for his liverie an azure blew, which is the colour of the skie, and white and yellow, which are the colours of his Lady and Mistresse. When I heard these words, imagine (faire Nymphes) in what a plight I was; but dissembling my mishap and griefe, I answered him: This Ladie certes is greatly beholding to him, bicause he thinkes not enough, by wearing her colours, to shew how willing he is to serve her, unlesse also he beare her name in his liverie; whereupon I gesse she cannot but be very faire and amiable. She is no lesse, indeede, (saide *Fabius*) although the other whom he loved and served in our owne countrey in beautie farre excelled this, and loved and favoured him more then ever this did. But this mischievous absence doth violate and dissolve those thinges which men thinke to be most strong and

firme. At these wordes (faire Nymphes) was I faine to come to some
composition with my teares, which, if I had not stopped from issuing
foorth, *Fabius* could not have chosen but suspected, by the alteration
of my countenance, that all was not well with me. And then the
Page did aske me, what countreyman I was, my name and of what
calling and condition I was: whom I answered, that my countrey
where I was borne was Vandalia, my name *Valerius*, and till that
time served no Master. Then by this reckoning (saide he) we are
both countrey-men, and may be both fellowes in one house if thou
wilt; for *Don Felix* my Master commanded me long since to seeke
him out a Page. Therefore if thou wilt serve him, say so. As for meate,
drinke, and apparell, and a couple of shillings to play away, thou
shalt never want; besides pretie wenches, which are not daintie in
our streete, as faire and amorous as Queenes, of which there is not
anie that will not die for the love of so proper a youth as thou art.
And to tell thee in secret (because, perhaps, we may be fellowes),
I know where an old Cannons maide is, a gallant fine girle, whom
if thou canst but finde in thy hart to love and serve as I do, thou
shalt never want at her hands fine hand-kerchers, peeces of bacon,
and now and then wine of *S. Martyn*. When I heard this, I could not
choose but laugh, to see how naturally the unhappie Page played
his part by depainting foorth their properties in their lively colours.
And because I thought nothing more commodious for my rest, and
for the enjoying of my desire, then to follow *Fabius* his counsel, I
answered him, thus: In truth, I determined to serve none; but now,
since fortune hath offered me so good a service, and at such a time,
when I am constrained to take this course of life, I shall not do
amisse if I frame myselfe to the service of some Lord or Gentleman
in this Court, but especially of your Master, because he seemes to
be a woorthy Gentleman, and such an one that makes more reckoning of his servants then an other. Ha, thou knowest him not so well
as I (said *Fabius*); for I promise thee, by the faith of a Gentleman (for
I am one indeede, for my father comes of the *Cachopines* of *Laredo*),
that my Master *Don Felix* is the best natured Gentleman that ever
thou knewest in thy life, and one who useth his Pages better then
any other. And were it not for those troublesome loves, which makes
us runne up and downe more, and sleepe lesse, then we woulde,
there were not such a Master in the whole worlde againe. In the
end (faire Nymphes) *Fabius* spake to his Master, *Don Felix*, as soone
as he was come foorth, in my behalfe, who commanded me the same
night to come to him at his lodging. Thither I went, and he entertained me for his Page, making the most of me in the worlde; where,
being but a few daies with him, I sawe the messages, letters, and

gifts that were brought and caried on both sides, greevous wounds (alas! and corsives to my dying hart), which made my soule to flie sometimes out of my body, and every hower in hazard to leese my forced patience before every one. But after one moneth was past, *Don Felix* began to like so well of me, that he disclosed his whole love unto me, from the beginning unto the present estate and forwardnes that it was then in, committing the charge thereof to my secrecie and helpe; telling me that he was favoured of her at the beginning, and that afterwards she waxed wearie of her loving and accustomed entertainment, the cause whereof was a secret report (whosoever it was that buzzed it into her eares) of the love that he did beare to a Lady in his owne countrey, and that his present love unto her was but to entertaine the time, while his business in the Court were dispatched. And there is no doubt (saide *Don Felix* unto me) but that, indeede, I did once commence that love that she laies to my charge; but God knowes if now there be any thing in the world that I love and esteeme more deere and precious then her. When I heard him say so, you may imagine (faire Nymphes) what a mortall dagger pierced my wounded heart. But with dissembling the matter the best I coulde, I answered him thus: It were better, sir (me thinkes), that the Gentlewoman should complaine with cause, and that it were so indeed; for if the other Ladie, whom you served before, did not deserve to be forgotten of you, you do her (under correction, my Lord) the greatest wrong in the world. The love (said *Don Felix* againe) which I beare to my *Celia* will not let me understand it so; but I have done her (me thinkes) the greater injurie, having placed my love first in an other, and not in her. Of these wrongs (saide I to my selfe) I know who beares the woorst away. And (disloyall) he, pulling a letter out of his bosome, which he had received the same hower from his Mistresse, reade it unto me, thinking he did me a great favour thereby, the contents whereof were these:

Celias letter to Don Felix

Never any thing that I suspected, touching thy love, hath beene so farre from the truth, that hath not given me occasion to beleeve more often mine owne imagination then thy innocencie; wherein, if I do thee any wrong, referre it but to the censure of thine owne follie. For well thou mightest have denied, or not declared thy passed love, without giving me occasion to condemne thee by thine owne confession. Thou saiest I was the cause that made thee forget thy former love. Comfort thy selfe, for there shall not want another to make thee forget thy second. And assure thy selfe of this (Lord

Don Felix) that there is not any thing more unbeseeming a Gentleman, then to finde an occasion in a Gentlewoman to leese himselfe for her love. I will saie no more, but that in an ill, where there
is no remedie, the best is not to seeke out any.

After he had made an end of reading the letter, he said unto me,
What thinkest thou, *Valerius*, of these words? With pardon be it
spoken, my Lord, that your deedes are shewed by them. Go to,
said *Don Felix*, and speake no more of that. Sir, saide I, they must
like me wel, if they like you, because none can judge better of their
words that love well then they themselves. But that which I thinke
of the letter is, that this Gentlewoman would have beene the first,
and that Fortune had entreated her in such sort, that all others might
have envied her estate. But what wouldest thou counsell me? said
Don Felix. If thy griefe doth suffer any counsell, saide I, that thy
thoughts be divided into this second passion, since there is so much
due to the first. *Don Felix* answered me againe, sighing, and knocking
me gently on the shoulder, saying, How wise art thou, *Valerius*, and
what good counsell dost thou give me if I could follow it. Let us
now go in to dinner, for when I have dined, I will have thee carie
me a letter to my Lady *Celia*, and then thou shalt see if any other
love is not woorthy to be forgotten in lieu of thinking onely of her.
These were wordes that greeved *Felismena* to the hart, but bicause
she had him before her eies, whom she loved more than her-selfe,
the content, that she had by onely seeing him, was a sufficient
remedie of the paine, that the greatest of these stings did make her
feele. After *Don Felix* had dined, he called me unto him, and giving
me a speciall charge what I should do (because he had imparted
his griefe unto me, and put his hope and remedie in my hands), he
willed me to carie a letter to *Celia*, which he had alreadie written,
and, reading it first unto me, it said thus:—

Don Felix *his letter to* Celia

The thought, that seekes an occasion to forget the thing which it
doth love and desire, suffers it selfe so easily to be knowne, that
(without troubling the minde much) it may be quickly discerned.
And thinke not (faire Ladie) that I seeke a remedie to excuse you
of that, wherewith it pleased you to use me, since I never came to
be so much in credit with you, that in lesser things I woulde do it.
I have confessed unto you that indeede I once loved well, because
that true love, without dissimulation, doth not suffer any thing to
be hid, and you (deere Ladie) make that an occasion to forget me,
which should be rather a motive to love me better. I cannot per-

swade me, that you make so small an account of your selfe, to thinke
that I can forget you for any thing that is, or hath ever been, but
rather imagine that you write cleane contrarie to that, which you
have tried by my zealous love and faith towards you. Touching all
those things, that, in prejudice of my good will towards you, it
pleaseth you to imagine, my innocent thoughts assure me to the
contrarie, which shall suffice to be ill recompenced besides being so
ill thought of as they are.

After *Don Felix* had read this letter unto me, he asked me if the
answer was correspondent to those words that his Ladie *Celia* had
sent him in hers, and if there was any thing therein that might be
amended; whereunto I answered thus: I thinke, Sir, it is needlesse
to amende this letter, or to make the Gentlewoman amendes, to
whom it is sent, but her, whom you do injurie so much with it.
Which under your lordships pardon I speake, bicause I am so
much affected to the first love in all my life, that there is not any
thing that can make me alter my minde. Thou hast the greatest
reason in the world (said *Don Felix*) if I coulde perswade my selfe
to leave of that, which I have begun. But what wilt thou have me
do, since absence hath frozen the former love, and the continuall
presence of a peerelesse beautie rekindled another more hot and
fervent in me? Thus may she thinke her selfe (saide I againe) unjustly deceived, whom first you loved, because that love which is
subject to the power of absence cannot be termed love, and none can
perswade me that it hath beene love. These words did I dissemble
the best I could, because I felt so sensible griefe, to see myselfe forgotten of him, who had so great reason to love me, and whom I did
love so much, that I did more, then any would have thought, to
make my selfe still unknowen. But taking the letter and mine
errant with me, I went to *Celias* house, imagining by the way the
wofull estate whereunto my haplesse love had brought me; since I
was forced to make warre against mine owne selfe, and to be the
intercessour of a thing so contrarie to mine owne content. But
comming to *Celias* house, and finding a Page standing at the dore,
I asked him if I might speake with his Ladie: who being informed of
me from whence I came, tolde *Celia* how I would speake with her,
commending therewithall my beautie and person unto her, and
telling her besides, that *Don Felix* had but lately entertained me into
his service; which made *Celia* saie unto him, What, *Don Felix* so
soone disclose his secret loves to a Page, but newly entertained?
he hath (belike) some great occasion that mooves him to do it. Bid
him com in, and let us know what he would have. In I came, and to

the place where the enimie of my life was, and, with great reverence
kissing her hands, I delivered *Don Felix* his letter unto her. *Celia*
tooke it, and casting her eies upon me, I might perceive how my
sight had made a sudden alteration in her countenance, for she was
so farre besides herselfe, that for a good while she was not able to
speake a worde, but, remembring her selfe at last, she saide unto
me, What good fortune hath beene so favourable to *Don Felix* to
bring thee to this Court, to make thee his Page? Even that, faire
Ladie, saide I, which is better then ever I imagined, bicause it hath
beene an occasion to make me behold such singular beautie and
perfections as now I see cleerely before mine eies. And if the paines,
the teares, the sighes, and the continuall disquiets that my Lord
Don Felix hath suffred have greeved me heeretofore, now that I have
seene the source from whence they flow, and the cause of all his ill,
the pittie that I had on him is now wholly converted into a certaine
kinde of envie. But if it be true (faire Lady) that my comming is
welcome unto you, I beseech you by that, which you owe to the
great love which he beares you, that your answer may import no
lesse unto him. There is not anie thing (saide *Celia*) that I would
not do for thee, though I were determined not to love him at all,
who for my sake hath forsaken another. For it is no small point of
wisedome for me to learne by other womens harmes to be more
wise, and warie in mine owne. Beleeve not, good lady (saide I),
that there is any thing in the worlde that can make *Don Felix* forget
you. And if he hath cast off another for your sake, woonder not
thereat, when your beautie and wisedome is so great, and the others
so small that there is no reason to thinke that he will (though he hath
woorthelie forsaken her for your sake) or ever can forget you for
any woman else in the worlde. Doest thou then know *Felismena* (said
Celia), the Lady whom thy Master did once love and serve in his
owne countrey? I know her (saide I), although not so well as it was
needfull for me to have prevented so many mishaps, (and this I
spake softly to my selfe). For my fathers house was neere to hers; but
seeing your great beautie adorned with such perfections and wisedome, *Don Felix* can not be blamed, if he hath forgotten his first love
only to embrace and honour yours. To this did *Celia* answer, merily
and smiling, Thou hast learned quickly of thy Master to sooth. Not
so, faire Ladie, saide I, but to serve you woulde I faine learne: for
flatterie cannot be, where (in the judgement of all) there are so manifest signes and proofes of this due commendation. *Celia* began in
good earnest to ask me what manner of woman *Felismena* was, whom
I answered, that, touching her beautie, Some thought her to be very
faire; but I was never of that opinion, bicause she hath many daies

since wanted the chiefest thing that is requisite for it. What is that? said *Celia*. Content of minde, saide I, bicause perfect beautie can never be, where the same is not adjoyned to it. Thou hast the greatest reason in the world, said she, but I have seene some Ladies whose lively hewe sadnes hath not one whit abated, and others whose beautie anger hath encreased, which is a strange thing me thinkes. Haplesse is that beauty, saide I, that hath sorrow and anger the preservers and mistresses of it, but I cannot skill of these impertinent things: And yet that woman, that must needes be molested with continuall paine and trouble, with greefe and care of minde and with other passions to make her looke well, cannot be reckoned among the number of faire women, and for mine owne part I do not account her so. Wherein thou hast great reason, said she, as in all things else that thou hast saide, thou hast showed thy selfe wise and discreete. Which I have deerely bought, said I againe: But I beseech you (gracious Lady) to answer this letter, because my Lord *Don Felix* may also have some contentment, by receiving his first well emploied service at my hands. I am content, saide *Celia*, but first thou must tell me if *Felismena* in matters of discretion be wise, and well advised? There was never any woman (saide I againe) more wise then she, bicause she hath beene long since beaten to it by her great mishaps: but she did never advise her selfe well, for if she had (as she was accounted wise) she had never come to have bene so contrarie to her selfe. Thou speakest so wisely in all thy answeres, said *Celia*, that there is not any that woulde not take great delight to heare them: which are not viands (said I) for such a daintie taste, nor reasons for so ingenious and fine a conceit (faire Lady), as you have, but boldly affirming, that by the same I meane no harme at all. There is not any thing, saide *Celia*, whereunto thy wit cannot attaine, but because thou shalt not spende thy time so ill in praising me, as thy Master doth in praying me, I will reade thy letter, and tell thee what thou shalt say unto him from me. Whereupon unfolding it, she began to read it to her selfe, to whose countenance and gestures in reading of the same, which are oftentimes outwarde signes of the inwarde disposition and meaning of the hart, I gave a watchfull eie. And when she had read it, she said unto me, Tell thy Master, that he that can so well by wordes expresse what he meanes, cannot choose but meane as well as he saith: and comming neerer unto me, she saide softly in mine eare, And this for the love of thee, *Valerius*, and not so much for *Don Felix* thy Master his sake, for I see how much thou lovest and tenderest his estate. And from thence, alas (saide I to my selfe), did all my woes arise. Whereupon kissing her hands for the great curtesie and favour she shewed me, I hied me to *Don Felix* with this answer, which was no small joy to him to heare it, and another death to me to report it, saying manie times to my selfe (when I did either bring him home some joyfull tydings or carrie letters or tokens to her), O thrise unfortunate *Felismena*, that with thine owne weapons art constrained to wounde thy ever-dying hart, and to heape up favours for him, who made so small account of thine. And so did I passe away my life with so many torments of minde, that if by the sight of my *Don Felix* they had not beene tempered, it coulde not have otherwise beene but that I must needes have lost it. More then two monethes togither did *Celia* hide from me the fervent love she bare me, although not in such sort, but that by certaine apparant signes I came to the knowledge thereof, which was no small lighting and ease of that griefe, which incessantly haunted my wearied spirites; for as I thought it a strong occasion, and the onely meane to make her utterly forget *Don Felix*, so likewise I imagined, that, perhaps, it might befall to him as it hath done to many, that the force of in-gratitude, and contempt of his love, might have utterly abolished such thoughtes out of his hart. But, alas, it happened not so to my *Don Felix*; for the more he perceived that his Ladie forgot him, the more was his minde troubled with greater cares and greefe, which made him leade the most sorowfull life that might be, whereof the least part did not fall to my lot. For remedie of whose sighes and pitious lamentations, poore *Felismena* (even by maine force) did get favours from *Celia*, scoring them up (whensoever she sent them by me) in the catalogue of my infinite mishaps. For if by chaunce he sent her anie thing by any of his other servants, it was so slenderly accepted, that he thought it best to send none unto her but my selfe, perceiving what inconvenience did ensue thereof. But God knowes how many teares my messages cost me, and so many they were, that in *Celias* presence I ceased not to powre them foorth, earnestly beseeching her with praiers and petitions not to entreat him so ill, who loved her so much, bicause I would binde *Don Felix* to me by the greatest bonde, as never man in like was bounde to any woman. My teares greeved *Celia* to the hart, as well for that I shed them in her presence, as also for that she sawe if I meant to love her, I woulde not (for requitall of hers to me) have sollicited her with such diligence, nor pleaded with such pittie, to get favours for another. And thus I lived in the greatest confusion that might be, amids a thousand anxieties of minde, for I imagined with my selfe, that if I made not a shew that I loved her, as she did me, I did put it in hazard lest *Celia*, for despite of my simplicitie or contempt, woulde have loved *Don Felix* more then before, and by loving him that mine coulde not have any good successe; and if I fained my selfe, on the other side, to be in love with her, it might have beene an occasion to have made her reject my lord *Don Felix*, so that with the thought of his love neglected, and with the force of her contempt, he might have lost his content, and after that, his life, the least of which two mischiefes to prevent I would have given a thousand lives, if I had them. Manie daies passed away in this sort, wherein I served him as a thirde betweene both, to the great cost of my contentment, at the end whereof the successe of his love went on woorse and woorse, bicause the Love that *Celia* did beare me was so great, that the extreme force of her passion made her leese some part of that compassion she should have had of her selfe. And on a day after that I had caried and recaried many messages and tokens betweene them, sometimes faining some my selfe from her unto him, bicause I could not see him (whom I loved so deerly) so sad and pensive, with many supplications and earnest praiers I besought Lady *Celia* with pittie to regard the painfull life that *Don Felix* passed her for sake, and to consider that by not favouring him, she was repugnant to that which she owed to her selfe: which thing I entreated, bicause I saw him in such a case, that there was no other thing to be expected of him but death, by reason of the continuall and great paine which his greevous thoughts made him feele. But she with swelling teares in her eies, and with many sighes, answered me thus: Unfortunate and accursed *Celia*, that nowe in the end dost know how thou livest deceived with a false opinion of thy great simplicitie (ungratefull *Valerius*) and of thy small discretion. I did not beleeve till now that thou didst crave favours of me for thy Master, but onely for thy selfe, and to enjoy my sight all that time, that thou diddest spende in suing to me for them. But now I see thou dost aske them in earnest, and that thou art so content to see me use him well, that thou canst not (without doubt) love me at all. O how ill dost thou acquite the love I beare thee, and that which, for thy sake, I do nowe forsake? O that time might revenge me of thy proude and foolish minde, since love hath not beene the meanes to do it. For I cannot thinke that Fortune will be so contrarie unto me, but that she will punish thee for contemning that great good which she meant to bestow on thee. And tell thy Lord *Don Felix*, that if he will see me alive, that he see me not at all: and thou, vile traitour, cruell enemie to my rest, com no more (I charge thee) before these wearied eies, since their teares were never of force to make thee knowe how much thou art bound unto them. And with this she suddenly flang out of my sight with so many teares, that mine were not of force to staie her. For in the greatest haste in the worlde she got her into her chamber, where, locking the dore after her, it availed me not to call and crie unto her, requesting her with amorous and sweete words to open me the dore, and to take such satisfaction on me as it pleased her: nor to tell her many other things, whereby I declared unto her the small reason she had to be so angrie with me, and to shut me out. But with a strange kinde of furie she saide unto me, Come no more, ungratefull and proud *Valerius*, in my sight, and speake no more unto me, for thou art not able to make satisfaction for such great disdaine, and I will have no other remedie for the harme which thou hast done me, but death it selfe, the which with mine owne hands I will take in satisfaction of that, which thou deservest: which words when I heard, I staied no longer, but with a heavie cheere came to my *Don Felix* his lodging, and, with more sadnes then I was able to dissemble, tolde him that I could not speake with *Celia*, because she was visited of certaine Gentlewomen her kinsewomen. But the next day in the morning it was bruted over all the citie, that a certaine trance had taken her that night, wherein she gave up the ghost, which stroke all the court with no small woonder. But that, which *Don Felix* felt by her sudden death, and how neere it greeved his very soule, as I am not able to tell, so cannot humane intendement conceive it, for the complaints he made, the teares, the burning sighes, and hart-breake sobbes, were without all measure and number. But I saie nothing of my selfe, when on the one side the unlucky death of *Celia* touched my soule very neere, the teares of *Don Felix* on the other did cut my hart in two with greefe: and yet this was nothing to that intollerable paine which afterwards I felt. For *Don Felix* heard no sooner of her death, but the same night he was missing in his house, that none of his servants nor any bodie else could tell any newes of him.

Whereupon you may perceive (faire Nymphes) what cruell torments I did then feele: then did I wish a thousand times for death to prevent all these woes and myseries, which afterwards befell unto me: for Fortune (it seemed) was but wearie of those which she had but till then given me. But as all the care and diligence which I emploied in seeking out my *Don Felix* was but in vaine, so I resolved with my selfe to take this habite upon me as you see, wherein it is more then two yeeres since I have wandred up and downe, seeking him in manie countryes: but my Fortune hath denied me to finde him out, although I am not a little now bounde unto her by conducting me hither at this time, wherein I did you this small piece of service. Which (faire Nymphes) beleeve me, I account (next after his life in whom I have put all my hope) the greatest content that might have fallen unto me. . . .

When the Nymphes had heard faire *Felismena's* tale, and understood what a great Lady she was, and how love had made her forsake her naturall habite, and take upon her the weedes and life of a shepherdesse, they were no lesse amazed at her constancie and zeale, then at the great power of that cruel tyrant, who absolutely commands so many liberties to his service. And they were mooved besides to no small pittie, to see the teares and burning sighes wherewith the Ladie did solemnize the historie of her love. *Doria* therefore, whose tender soule *Felismena's* greefe did most transpierce, and who was more affected to her, then to any woman, with whom she had ever conversed before, tooke her by the hand, and began to say to her in the manner following: What can we do (faire Lady) against the blowes of Fortune, what place is there so strong, where one may be safe from the mutabilities of time? What harneys so impenetrable, or steele so well tempered, that may serve for a defence against the violence of this tyrant, whom so unjustly they call *Love*? And what hart (though it be harder then diamond) which an amorous thought can not mollifie and make tender? Certes, this beautie, this valour, and this wisedome, deserve not to be forgotten of him, who had but once seene and knowne them. But we live now in such an age, that the deserts of any thing, are the meanes and occasions of not obtaining it. And cruell love is of so strange a condition, that he bestoweth his contents without any good order and rule, and giveth there greatest favours, where they are least esteemed; but the medicine of so many ills (whereof this tyrant is the cause), is her discretion and courage that suffers them. But whom doth he leave so free, that these may serve her for a remedie? or who can command her selfe so much in this passion, that in other womens affaires she is able to give counsell, how much lesse to take it in her owne. Yet for all this, I beseech thee (faire Ladie) to put before thine eies, and consider what thou art, bicause if women of such high renowne and vertue as thou art, are not able to tolerate his adverse effects, how can they suffer them that are not such.'

[Doria takes Felismena to 'the sage *Felicias* pallace . . . where . . . thou shalt finde great remedies for thy greefes'. There (in the Fourth Book) Felicia discusses the relation between Love and Reason, in response to Syrenus' question: 'They do all affirme (that would seeme to knowe something) *That true Love doth spring of reason*: which if it be so, what is the reason, that there is not a more timorous and unruly thing in the worlde then love and which is least of all governed by it?']

As this Question (answered *Felicia*) is more then a simple Shepherdes conceite, so is it necessarie, that she that must answer it,

ought to have more then a sillie womans wit: But to satisfie thy minde
with that little skill I have, I am of a contrarie opinion, affirming
that Love, although it hath Reason for his mother, is not therefore
limited or governed by it. And it is so unruly, that it resultes oftentimes to the hurt and prejudice of the lover: since true lovers for the
most part fall to hate and neglect themselves, which is not onely
contrarie to reason, but also the lawe of nature. And this is the cause
why they paint him blinde, and void of all reason. And as his mother
Venus hath most faire eies, so doth he also desire the fairest. They
paint him naked, because good love can neither be dissembled with
reason, nor hidden with prudence. They paint him with wings,
because he simply enters into the lovers soule; and the more perfect
he is, with more swiftnes and alienation of himselfe he goeth to
seeke the person of the beloved, for which cause *Euripedes* said: That
the lover did live in the body of the beloved. They paint him also
shooting his arrowes out of his bowe, because he aymes right at the
hart, as at his proper white: And also, because the wound of love is
like that, which an arrow or dart maketh, narrow at the entrance,
and deepe in his inward soule that loveth. This is an inscrutable
and almost incurable wounde, and very slowe in healing: So that
thou must not marvell *Syrenus* that perfect love (though it be the
sonne of reason) is not governed by it, bicause there is nothing, after
it is borne, that doth lesse conforme itselfe to the originall of his
birth, then this doth. Some saie there is no other difference betweene
vertuous and vicious love, but that the one is governed by reason,
and the other not: but they are deceived, because excesse and force
is no lesse proper to dishonest, then to honest love, which is rather a
qualitie incident to everie kinde of love, saving the one doth make
vertue the greater by it, and the other doth the more encrease vice.
Who can denie, but that in true and honest love excessive and
strange effects are sometimes founde? . . .

[In Bk. 7 Felismena brings together the parted lovers Amarillis and
Filemon, and hears Duarda refusing to have more to do with
Danteus.]

The Shepherdesse having made an ende of her sharpe answer and
Felismena beginning to arbitrate the matter between them; they
heard a great noise in the other side of the meadow, like to the
sound of blowes, and smiting of swordes upon harneies, as if some
armed men had fought together, so that all of them with great haste
ranne to the place where they heard the noise, to see what the
matter was. And being come somewhat neere, they saw in a little
Iland (which the river with a round turning had made) three knights

fighting against one. And although he defended himself valiantly, by shewing his approved strength and courage, yet the three knights gave him so much to do, that he was faine to help himselfe by all the force and pollicie he could. They fought on foote, for their horses were tied to little trees, that grew thereabout. And now by this time, the knight that fought all alone and defended himselfe, had laid one of them at his feete with a blowe of his good sword, which ended his life. But the other two that were very strong and valiant, redoubled their force and blowes so thicke on him, that he looked for no other thing then death. The Shepherdesse *Felismena* seeing the knight in so great danger, and if she did not speedily helpe him, that he could not escape with life, was not afraide to put hers in jeopardy by doing that which in such a case she thought, she was bound to performe: wherefore putting a sharpe headed arrowe into her bowe, shee saide unto them: Keepe out knights, for it is not beseeming men that make account of this name and honour, to take advantage of their enimies with so great oddes. And ayming at the sight of one of their helmets, she burst it with such force, that the arrow running into his eies, came out of the other side of his head, so that he fell downe dead to the ground. When the distressed knight sawe two of his enimies dead, he ran upon the third with such force as if he had but then begun the combat; but *Felismena* helped him out of more trouble, by putting another arrow into her bow, the which transpiercing his armour, she left under his left pap, and so justly smot his hart, that this knight also followed his two companions. When the Shepherds and the knight beheld what *Felismena* had done, and how at two shootes she had killed two such valiant knights, they were all in great wonder. The knight therefore taking off his helmet, and comming unto her saide: How am I able (faire Shepherdesse) to requite so great a benefite and good turne as I have received at thy hands this day, but by acknowledging this debt for ever in my gratefull minde. When *Felismena* beheld the knights face, and knew him, her sences were so troubled, that being in such a traunce she could scarce speake, but comming to herselfe againe, she answered him:

Ah my *Don Felix*, this is not the first debt, wherein thou art bound unto me. And I cannot believe, that thou wilt acknowledge this (as thou saiest) no more then thou hast done greater then this before. Beholde to what a time and ende my fortune and thy forgetnesse hath brought me, that she that was woont to be served of thee in the Citie with Tilt and Tourneyes, and honoured with many other things, whereby thou didst deceive me, (or I suffered my selfe to be deceived) doth nowe wander uppe and downe, exiled from her native countrey and libertie, for using thus thine owne. If this brings thee not into the knowledge of that which thou owest me, remember how one whole yeere I served thee as thy Page in the Princesse *Cesarinas* Court: and how I was a solicitor against myselfe, without discovering my selfe, or my thoughts unto thee, but onely to procure thy remedie, and to helpe the griefe, which thine made thee feele. How many times did I get thee favours from thy Mistress *Celia* to the great cost of my teares and greefes: all which account but small *Don Felix* in respect of those dangers (had they beene unsufficient) wherein I would have spent my life for redresse of thy paines, which thy injurious love affoorded thee. And unlesse thou art weary of the great love, that I have borne thee, consider and weigh with thy selfe the strange effects, which the force of love hath caused me to passe. I went out of my native countrey, and came to serve thee, to lament the ill that thou didst suffer, to take upon me the injuries and disgraces that I received therein; and to give thee any content, I cared not to lead the most bitter and painefull life, that ever woman lived. In the habite of a tender and daintie Ladie I loved thee more then thou canst imagine, and in the habite of a base page I served thee (a thing more contrarie to my rest and reputation then I meane now to reherse) and yet now in the habite of a poore and simple Shepherdesse I came to do thee this small service. What remaines then more for me to do, but to sacrifice my life to thy lovelesse soule, if with the same yet I could give thee more content—and if in lieu therof thou wouldest but remember, how much I have loved, and do yet love thee! here hast thou thy sword in thy hand; let none therefore but thy selfe revenge the offence that I have done thee. When the Knight heard *Felismena's* words, and knew them all to be as true as he was disloyall, his hart by this strange and sudden accident recovered some force againe to see what great injurie he had done her, so that the thought thereof, and the plenteous effusion of blood that issued out of his woundes, made him like a dead man fall downe in a swoune at faire *Felismenas* feete. Who with great care, and no lesse feare, laying his head in her lap, with showers of teares that rained from her eies upon the Knights pale visage, began thus to lament: What meanes this cruell Fortune? Is the period of my life come just with the last ende of my *Don Felix* his daies? Ah my *Don Felix* (the cause of all my paine) if the plenteous teares, which for thy sake I have now shed, are not sufficient; and these which I now distill upon thy lovely cheekes, too fewe to make thee come to thy selfe againe, what remedie shall this miserable soule have to prevent, that this bitter joy by seeing thee, turne not to occasion of utter despaire. Ah my *Don Felix*, Awake my love, if thou dost but sleepe, or beest in a traunce, although I would not woonder if thou dost not, since never anything that I could do, prevailed with thee to frame my least content. And in these and other lamentations was faire *Felismena* plunged, whom the Portugall Shepherdesses with their teares and poor supplies endeavoured to incourage, when on the sudden they saw a faire Nymphe comming over the stony causey that lead the way into the Ilande, with a golden bottel in one hand, and a silver one in the other, whom *Felismena* knowing by and by, saide unto her: Ah *Doria*, could any come at this time to succour me, but thou faire Nymph? Come hither then, and thou shalt see the cause of al my troubles, the substance of my sighs, and the object of my thoughts, lying in the greatest danger of death that may be. In like occurrents (saide *Doria*) vertue and a good hart most take place. Recall it then (faire *Felismena*) and revive thy daunted spirits, trouble not thy selfe any more, for nowe is the ende of thy sorrowes, and the beginning of thy contentment come. And speaking these wordes, she besprinkled his face with a certaine odoriferous water which she brought in the silver bottle, whereby he came to his memorie againe, and then saide unto him: If thou wilt recover thy life, Sir Knight, and give it her that hath passed such an ill one for thy sake, drinke of the water in this bottle: The which *Don Felix* taking in his hande, drunke a good draught, and resting upon it a little, founde himselfe so whole of his wounds, which the three knights had given him, and of that which the love of *Celia* had made in his brest, that now he felt the paine no more, which either of them had caused in him, then if he had never had them. And in this sort he began to rekindle the old love, that he bore to *Felismena*, the which (he thought) was never more zealous then now. Where-upon sitting downe upon the greene grasse, hee tooke his Lady and Shepherdesse by the hands, and kissing them manie times saide thus unto her. How small account would I make of my life (my deerest *Felismena*) for cancelling that great bond, wherein (with more then life) I am for ever bound unto thee: for since I enjoy it by thy meanes, I thinke it no more then righte, to restore thee that, which is thine owne. . . . What words are sufficient to excuse the faults, that I have committed against thy faith, and firmest love, and loyaltie? . . . Truth is, that I loved *Celia* well, and forgot thee, but in such sort that thy wisedome and beautie did ever slide out of my minde. . . .

[He knows that her beauty excels *Celia*'s, and begs forgiveness.]

The Shepherdesse *Felismena*, who saw *Don Felix* so penitent for his passed misdeeds, and so affectionately returned to his first thoughts, with many teares told him, that she did pardon him,

because the love, that she had ever borne him, would suffer her to
do no lesse: which if she had not thought to do, she would never have
taken so great paines and so many wearie journeyes to seeke him
out, and many other things, wherewith *Don Felix* was confirmed in
his former love. . . . And *Don Felix* wondred not a little to understand how his Ladie *Felismena* had served him so many daies as his
page, and that he was so far gone out of his wits, and memorie, that
he knew her not all that while. And his joy on the other side to see
that his Ladie loved him so well, was so great, that by no meanes
he could hide it. Thus therefore riding on their way they came to
Dianas Temple, where the sage *Felicia* was looking for their comming: and likewise the Shepherd *Arsileus*, and *Belisa*, *Sylvanus*, and
Selvagia, who were now come thither not many daies before. They
were welcomed on everie side, and with great joy entertained; but
faire *Felismena* especially, who for hir rare vertues and singular
beautie was greatly honoured of them all. There they were all
married with great joy, feasts and triumphes, which were made by all
the goodly Nymphes, and by the sage and noble Ladie *Felicia*. . . .

[After their marriage Lord Felix and his lady take charge of the
pastoral discussions and many stories are told in their presence.]

IV. Analogue

From THE COUNTESSE OF
PEMBROKES ARCADIA
by Sir Philip Sidney (1590)
Book II. Chapter 22

[Zelmane the 'famous Amazon' (daughter of Plexirtus the villainous
bastard son of the old blind King of Paphlagonia[1]) loves Philoclea,
defends her title of beauty against Phalantus, and slays a lion which
endangers Philoclea. She takes service as a page with Pyrocles whom
she loves, and Pyrocles tells of it.]

But the next morning, we (having striven with the Sunnes ear-
liness) were scarcely beyond the prospect of the high turrets of that

[1] The story of this blind king gave the Edmund-Gloster plot in *King Lear*.

building, when there overtoke us a young Gentleman, for so he seemed to us, but indeede (sweete Ladie) it was the faire *Zelmane*, *Plexirtus* daughter; whom unconsulting affection (unfortunately borne to me-wards) had made borrowe so much of her naturall modestie, as to leave her more-decent rayments, and taking occasion of *Andromanas* tumultuous pursuing us, had apparrelled her selfe like a Page, with a pittifull crueltie cutting of her golden haire, leaving nothing, but the short curles, to cover that noble head, but that she ware upon it a faire headpeece, a shielde at her back, and a launce in her hand, els disarmed. Her apparrell of white, wrought upon with broken knots, her horse, faire & lustie, which she rid so, as might shew a fearefull boldnes, daring to doo that, which she knew that she knew not how to doo: and the sweetnes of her countenance did give such a grace to what she did, that it did make hansome the unhansomnes, and make the eye force the minde to beleeve, that there was a praise in that unskilfulnesse. But she straight approached me, and with fewe words (which borowed the help of her countenance to make themselves understood) she desired me to accept her in my service; telling me, she was a noblemans sonne of *Iberia*, her name *Daiphantus*, who having seene what I had done in that court, had stolne from her father, to follow me. I enquired the particularities of the maner of *Andromanas* following me, which by her I understood, she hiding nothing (but her sexe) from me. And still me thought I had seen that face, but the great alteration of her fortune, made her far distant from my memorie: but liking very well the yong Gentleman, (such I tooke her to be) admitted this *Daiphantus* about me: who well shewed, there is no service like his, that serves because he loves. For, though borne of Princes bloud, brought up with tenderest education, unapt to service (because a woman) & full of thoughts (because in a strange estate;) yet Love enjoyned such diligence, that no apprentise, no, no bondslave could ever be by feare more readie at all commaundementes, then that yong Princesse was. How often (alas) did her eyes say unto me, that they loved? and yet, I (not looking for such a matter) had not my conceipt open, to understand them. How often would she come creeping to me, be-tweene gladnes to be neere me, & feare to offend me? Truly I remember, that then I marvailing, to see her receive my commande-ments with sighes, and yet do them with cheerefulnes: sometimes answering me in such riddles, as I then thought childish in experi-ence: but since returning to my remembrance, they have come more neere unto my knowledge: & pardon me (onely deare Lady) that I use many words: for her affection to me deserves of me an affectionate speach.

In such sort did she serve me in that kingdom of *Bythinia*, for two moneths space. In which time we brought to good end, a cruell warre long maintained betweene the King of *Bythinia* and his brother. For my excellent cousin, and I (dividing our selves to either side) found meanes (after some triall we had made of our selves) to get such credite with them, as we brought them to as great peace betweene themselves, as love towards us, for having made the peace.

[Grieved at her father's fault she falls sick.]

Poore *Daiphantus* fell extreme sick, yet would needs conquere the delicacie of her constitution, and force her selfe to waite on me: till one day going towarde *Pontus*, we met one, who in great hast went seeking for *Tydeus* & *Telenor*, whose death as yet was not knowne unto the messenger; who (being their servaunt and knowing how deerely they loved *Plexirtus*) brought them word, how since their departing, *Plexirtus* was in pre[se]nt daunger of a cruel death, if by the valiantnesse of one of the best Knightes of the world, he were not reskewed: we enquired no further of the matter (being glad he should now to his losse finde what an unprofitable treason it had bene unto him, to dismember himselfe of two such friendes) and so let the messenger part, not sticking to make him know his masters destruction, by the falshood of *Plexirtus*.

But the griefe of that (finding a bodie alreadie brought to the last degree of weaknesse) so overwhelmed the little remnant of the spirits left in *Daiphantus*, that she fell sodainely into deadly soundings; never comming to her selfe, but that withall she returned to make most pittifull lamentations; most straunge unto us, because we were farre from ghessing the ground thereof. But finding her sicknesse such, as beganne to print death in her eyes, we made al hast possible to convey her to the next towne: but before we could lay her on a bed, both we, & she might find in herselfe, that the harbinger of over-hastie death, had prepared his lodging in that daintie body, which she undoubtedly feeling, with a weake chearefulnes, shewed comfort therin; and then desiring us both to come neere her, & that no bodie els might be present; with pale, and yet (even in palenes) lovely lippes, Now or never, and never indeed, but now it is time for me (said she) to speake: and I thanke death which gave me leave to discover that, the suppressing whereof perchance hath bene the sharpest spur, that hath hasted my race to this end. Know then my Lords, and especially you my Lord and master, *Pyrocles*, that your page *Daiphantus* is the unfortunat *Zelmane*, who for your sake caused my (as unfortunate) lover, and cosen, *Palladius*, to leave his fathers court, and consequently, both him & my Aunt his mother, to loose their lives. For your sake my selfe have become, of a Princesse a Page: and for your sake have put off the apparell of a woman, & (if you judge not more mercifully) modestie. We were amazed at her speach, and then had (as it were) new eyes given us to perceve that which before had bene a present stranger to our minds. For indeed, we forthwith knew it to be the face of *Zelmane*, whom before we had knowen in the court of *Iberia*. And sorrow and pittie laying her paine upon me, I comforted her the best I could by the tendernes of good-will, pretending indeed better hope then I had of her recovery.

But she that had inward ambassadors from the tyrant that should shortly oppresse her. No, my deere master (said she) I neither hope nor desire to live. I know you would never have loved me (& with that she wept) nor, alas, had it bene reason you should, considering manie wayes my unworthines. It sufficeth me that the strange course I have taken, shall to your remembrance, witnesse my love: and yet this breaking of my harte, before I would discover my paine, will make you (I hope) think I was not altogether unmodest. Thinke of me so, deare Master, and that thought shal be my life: and with that, languishingly looking upon me: And I pray you (said she) even by these dying eies of mine (which are onely sorrie to dye, because they shall lose your sight) and by these pouled lockes of mine (which while they were long, were the ornament of my sex, now in their short curles, the testimonie of my servitude) and by the service I have done you (which God knowes hath beene full of love) thinke of me after my death with kindnes, though ye cannot with love.

V. Analogue

From FLAVIO TRADITO, COMEDIA
by Flaminio Scala (1611)

Il Teatro delle Favole rappresentative, overo La Ricreatione Comica, Boscareccia, e Tragica: . . . Composte da Flaminio Scala detto Flavio Comico del Sereniss. Sig. Duca di Mantova. Venetia. MDCXI.

THE FIFTH DAY

THE ARGUMENT

There were two young men in Florence who loved each other most cordially, and were true and loyal friends to one another; one was named Flavio Alidori, and the other Oratio Belmonte. It happened (as often occurs) that Flavio was fired by the beauty of a young lady, daughter of a Doctor, Gratiano Forbicione; her name was Isabella, and she loved Flavio with reciprocal passion. It came to pass that Oratio too fell in love with the maiden Isabella, having no regard at all to the ancient friendship he shared with Flavio; and he so worked with his deceits that he made Flavio believe that he was betrayed by his mistress and that she loved and desired Oratio only. By which means he reduced Flavio to such despair that the latter gave his word to marry another lady and yielded to Oratio his beloved Isabella. By the astuteness of a servant, however, Oratio's treachery was discovered, and Flavio, when he knew it, was on the point of challenging him. However, going with great caution, he waited for time to bring about some strange accident by reason of the treachery practised against him. Nor had much time passed when Oratio, engaging in a quarrel with one of his enemies, was struck down by his opponent and overcome. At that moment there arrived by chance his friend Flavio (who still loved him), by whose help Oratio was freed from the hands of his enemy. By this he made Oratio realise his error, who confessing it received pardon and yielded to Flavio the lady whom he wished to marry. So once more becoming true and faithful friends they henceforth enjoyed a happy life with their ladies.

Dramatis Personae

PANTALONE, a Venetian.
FLAMINIA, his daughter.
GRATIANO, a doctor.
ISABELLA, his daughter.
PEDROLINO & FRANCESCHINA, servants.

CAPTAIN SPAVENTO
ARLECCHINO, a servant.
FLAVIO, a lover.
ORATIO, a lover.
BURATTINO, host of an inn.

Properties for the Comedy

An inn-sign; a large valise; a bundle of letters.

ACT ONE

Scene: Florence

FLAVIO who enters with Oratio his friend learns from him that he is loved by many ladies and has given his heart to one alone, but that, to his great disgust, she is beloved by one of his greatest friends.

Flavio seeks to learn who this friend is. Oratio says that time will disclose it, whereupon

FRANCESCHINA at the window whispers to Oratio, telling him to take the letter which Isabella has sent him. Flavio comes forward thinking that she is speaking to him, but she goes on talking freely to Oratio, throwing him the letter, which he takes. Franceschina retires. Oratio reads the letter aloud, so that Flavio hears that in it Oratio receives instructions from Isabella to go to her at once, as usual, reminding him that she is pregnant by him. Flavio is silent. Oratio takes leave of him and goes off happily. Flavio inveighs against Isabella and Pedrolino (who knows his love for her), calling them traitors. This

FLAMINIA, at the window, pauses to hear. Loving Flavio she tries to console him, telling him that this trouble has come upon him because he had no compassion for her who loved him; it is an amorous punishment. Flavio turns to her weeping and asking her pardon. Flaminia, interrupted in similar laments, then retires. Flavio remains, desolate; on which

PEDROLINO enters from the house with a letter. He goes to Flavio, who on seeing him sets hand to sword, calling him a traitor. Pedrolino flees, and in doing so drops a letter. Flavio chases him indoors.

CAPTAIN SPAVENTO comes from Naples to marry Isabella, his father Arlecchino (who enters with him) having corresponded with her father Gratiano and made a marriage contract with him. They knock on the inn-door.

BURATTINO the Host receives the strangers and ushers Arlecchino indoors with the luggage. The Captain asks the Host if he knows Doctor Gratiano. He says, yes. The Captain takes from a bundle of letters one intended for Gratiano, and prays the Host to deliver it. He goes out. Burattino sees the letter dropped by Pedrolino, and picks it up, thinking that it has been dropped by Captain Spavento. On this

PEDROLINO enters terrified, looking for his letter. He asks the Host about it, and the Host gives him the letter intended for Gratiano, and also that which he has found. Exit. Pedrolino says that Flavio has almost killed him. Now

ISABELLA enters and asks Pedrolino if he gave her letter to Flavio. Pedrolino says, no, and relates what has befallen him. Isabella marvels, not knowing the cause of it all. Pedro retires to listen when

ORATIO and PANTALONE enter. Oratio says that as Flavio's friend he hopes that Pantalone will give Flavio his daughter Flaminia since Flavio loves and desires her. Moreover he himself wishes to marry Isabella so that the two of them may have their weddings together.

Pantalone says that Gratiano has betrothed Flaminia to a Captain Spavento who is daily expected from Naples. Oratio declares that Isabella is already betrothed to him and is pregnant—showing him the letter which Franceschina gave him. Pantalone is amazed. So are Pedrolino and Isabella (who have been eavesdropping); they come down as Pantalone says that he will discuss matters with Gratiano.

ISABELLA comes forward and, dissimulating, asks Oratio what letter he spoke about with Pantalone, and declares that she has never written anything to him. Oratio, putting on a bold front, says, 'Signora, since you do not wish them to know about our love-affair, I shall be silent.' The furious Isabella calls him a traitor, saying, 'What letter? You are talking about my honour.' . . .

[Other complications about letters follow.]

ACT TWO

[Pedrolino tries to get Captain Spavento to kill Oratio by promising that Isabella will marry him. Thinking that she is doubly unfaithful Flavio apologises to Oratio for setting her above his friend, and agrees to marry Flaminia. He is then accused of treachery by Pedrolino and Isabella.]

ACT THREE

[Pedrolino tells Flavio that the promise of Isabella to marry the Captain was just a ruse to have Oratio slain.]

PEDROLINO gets Franceschina to confess how Oratio bribed her to carry that false letter. Overcome with anger Flavio draws his dagger to kill her. She cries out; Burattino comes in and says he wishes to marry her. Pedrolino pleads for her and she is pardoned by Flavio. . . .

PEDROLINO turns Isabella's rage to grief by telling her that Captain Spavento has killed Flavio. Flavio hears, discovers himself, they embrace, asking pardon one of the other for the offences they have committed and for their suspicions.

FLAMINIA, overhearing this from the window, is plunged into grief. (In the end)

ORATIO quarrels with the Captain and though Pantalone tries to separate them Oratio in hand-to-hand combat is felled to the ground. The Captain leaps on him meaning to kill him. At this

FLAVIO attacks the Captain, frees Oratio, and throws Spavento to the ground, but grants him his life. . . . Oratio kneels and confesses his treachery, regretting that he betrayed Flavio and Isabella because of the great love he bore her, blaming Love and Fortune for what he has done. He asks pardon of Flavio. They forgive him and lift him from the ground; so they are reconciled and their former friendship is restored. Flavio asks Gratiano for Isabella's hand. Captain Spavento expostulates, saying that she is his promised bride. Gratiano excuses himself, declaring that the Captain must put up with it, since Isabella loves Flavio. Flavio marries Isabella and Oratio Flaminia. Burattino marries Franceschina.

VI. Analogue

From TRAGAEDIA VON JULIO UND HYPPOLITA[1]

English version by Georgina Archer

Acts I and II

Persons represented:

THE PRINCE
HYPPOLITA, the princess.
ROMULUS ⎱
JULIUS ⎰ two Romans.
GROBIANUS PICKELHERING (the Clown), servant to Julius.
SERVANT to Romulus.

ACT ONE

Enter the Prince, Romulus, Julius, and Hyppolita. The Prince comes forward. Julius stands a little apart from the others, very melancholy

PRINCE   Noble Roman, you have now waited one month, since you urged your suit for my dear daughter's hand. Tell me now truly, do you love her with all your heart?
ROMULUS   I love her from the bottom of my heart.

---

[1] Printed from A. Cohn: *Shakespeare in Germany in the Sixteenth & Seventeenth Centuries* (1865), pp, 121–34. Cohn took the German text from *Englische Comedien und Tragedien* (1620), Vol.1, in which it is the seventh piece.

PRINCE Dear daughter, say, dost thou love Romulus?

HYPPOLITA Yes, dear father, and an it be your will I have chosen him for my husband.

PRINCE Enough, enough. I wish you a long life, and give you my young daughter, my only hope and comfort upon earth.

ROMULUS My lord, I esteem this beautiful lady, your beloved daughter, more highly than silver and gold, and render you my hearty thanks for this your Jewel.   [*Holds her by the hand*

PRINCE When is it then your pleasure to celebrate your nuptials?

ROMULUS My lord, I should prefer to-day to to-morrow. But it is my duty first to go to Rome to announce my intended marriage to my parents, lest, if they hear nothing of it, they should take offence. I trust shortly to be here again, and therefore I beg your Grace and my best beloved, to grant me leave to go.

PRINCE Noble Roman, cannot this journey be postponed till after the solemnization of the marriage. Pray bethink you, and celebrate your nuptials, ere you undertake this journey.

ROMULUS My lord, I have considered the thing well; but it cannot be, for in such a matter we must not quite neglect our parents. I pray you therefore, grant me leave to go.

PRINCE Since it must be so, I give my consent. But do not suffer yourself to be detained.

HYPPOLITA Sweet my love, an it be possible, remain;—why will ye be so unmerciful as to go from me?

ROMULUS Mine own dear love, you know not how loath I am to go from you; but it must be so. And take comfort for I commit you to the loving care of my faithful friend and brother Julius, who in my absence will delight you with pleasant speech and thus while the hours away. There he stands, let's go to him. Most faithful friend and brother Julius, why so melancholy?

JULIUS Gentle and beloved brother, I am not melancholy.

ROMULUS O brother, disclose to me the cause of thy sadness! thou would'st fain shut it up within thyself, but canst not. I would shed my blood to turn it from thee.

JULIUS In truth, dear brother, thy journey makes me sad. Thou know'st what love I bear thee, and that I account my life as naught to serve thee. O how can I be otherwise than sad?

ROMULUS 'Tis true. From childhood have we been faithful to each other. But, gentle brother, how can I recompense thee?—Here say adieu to thy woman's heart, and grieve not for my journey, for so it must be. Wherefore, my faithful friend and brother, I do commend to thee my fair Hyppolita, my sweet love, and beg thee to entreat her kindly in my absence. And fair Hyppolita, do not afflict yourself, for I trust ere long, again to behold your clear crystal eyes. I'll hasten back to you on the wings of Mercury, and as soon as I have arrived in Rome I will visit you with letters.

PRINCE   Now let us go in, and Julius comes with us, that we may see Romulus on his way.

[*Exeunt the Prince, Romulus and Hyppolita. Julius is sad*

JULIUS   How loath am I to see thee depart!   [*Falls on his knees*
O that thou never would'st return! Then should I be happiest of mortals, and even now I make me etc.

Re-enter ROMULUS   Wherefore didst thou not follow us, dear brother? What means this kneeling?

JULIUS   Gentle brother, I am calling upon the gods to be favourable to thee, and to bring thee soon back again.

ROMULUS   O thou art a true friend to me. Thy like for faithfulness have I nowhere found in all the world. Wherefore once more I pray thee, delight my love in my absence with sweet discourses, and entreat her well for the love thou bear'st me. And for as much as I know thou art of all the most faithful to me, I commend her to thee alone.

JULIUS   O me, faithful! [*Falls on his knees.*] I swear by the sun, moon, and stars etc.

ROMULUS   Rise up, most faithful friend and brother! I crave no oath of thee; think'st thou I cannot trust thee without one? Now farewell,—thou canst not know how loath I am to part from thee. Adieu, adieu, the longer here, the longer there.   [*Exit*

JULIUS   Ay, go,—and so that thou break thy neck and never return. Now must I contrive my plan. Romulus, Romulus! a faithful friend art thou to me, 'tis true; but now must I prove to thee what faithless brotherhood is. O! lovely Hyppolita, what cannot thy fair form effect. O! what cannot love accomplish. O! Hyppolita, thou wonder amongst women, thou must be mine, else I cannot live. Now I must bethink me how to set about it. Men say 'practica est multiplex';—now 'tis for me to try one.   [*Exit*

ACT TWO

JULIUS   Julius, consider well how thou dost act by Romulus. Here have I letters to deliver to fair Hyppolita, his sweet love; but it must not be,—I must keep them back, and in their stead I have writ others. Pause and weigh well, Julius—'tis to a Roman thou play'st the knave, and they seek vengeance on their foes and triumph over all others in the world. Ay, an wert thou the most contentious of all Romans, I would not, could not refrain from being faithless to thee in this matter. I must fulfil my purpose now;—for what will not love do, for whose sweet sake I place my life in jeopardy? Well, it must be so. Ho! my servant Grobianus, ho!

Enter Grobianus, his master whistles. He stands still

GROBIANUS   May-be my master thinks he has a dog before him.
[*Julius whistles again*

GROBIANUS   Whistle away, I am not thy dog.

JULIUS   Boy, hast thou not heard me call?   Wherefore dost thou stand so?

GROBIANUS   My lord, I heard no calling, but whistling, and thought your worship was whistling to his dog.

JULIUS   Come hither, knave, and mark ye well my words. Bear these letters to fair Hyppolita, dress thee as a postboy, and say that Romulus charged thee with these letters from Rome. Here is money, perform thy errand faithfully, and by and by my hands shall be more liberal.

GROBIANUS   My lord, what would I not do for money? An I could get money for't, I'd throw whore at my mother and call my father rogue. A trusty messenger I'll prove to do your bidding.

JULIUS   'Tis well—prepare thee quickly, and go deliver the letters.

GROBIANUS   On the instant.   [*Exit*

JULIUS   So may I hope to possess fair Hyppolita as my own wife. Julius, take heart, ay an iron heart. Thou play'st a high game and must not faint in the midst of it.   [*Stands apart in deep thought*

Enter the Prince. Hyppolita is sad and sits down

PRINCE   How strange are women's ways, how passing strange! When they are in love, crying, weeping, roaring is their food, an their sweetheart is not with them. Daughter, thy folly will cause thee to fall sick, thy Romulus will surely come to thee again; wherefore then grievest thou?

HYPPOLITA   O father, I have cause to weep, for I know not whether my sweet love hath reached Rome in safety, as the time is past in which he swore to write from thence. There I see Julius standing in deep thought. Dear father, let's go to him, and learn whether he has received aught from Rome.   [*They approach Julius*

HYPPOLITA   A good morning, Julius.

JULIUS   Have thanks your worship, and you too, fair lady.

PRINCE   Julius, can you not advise me? My daughter is quite desperate because her love hath left her for a short time.

JULIUS   My lord, no doctor hath a remedy for that, for we mortals are born with it, and ardent love effects it.

HYPPOLITA   Good friend, have you received no writing from Rome?

JULIUS   Fair lady, none whatever.

HYPPOLITA   O the time is already past, in which he swore by his true love to write to me.

JULIUS   Fair lady, do not torment yourself with doubts, for full well I know his heart, that what he has surely promised he will as surely hold. It may be that the messenger whom he has despatched tarries on the way.

Enter Grobianus

GROBIANUS   All happiness and peace to you, fair lady!

HYPPOLITA   I thank thee, messenger, most heartily! O tell me quick, dost thou come from Rome?

GROBIANUS   You have hit it; from Rome I come, and am sent to you by Romulus.

HYPPOLITA   O blessed hour! O blessed messenger! show me quick the letter from Romulus, my heart's treasure!

GROBIANUS   Wait a little. First you must remember the messenger.

HYPPOLITA   Take this;—produce the letter speedily for which I have so yearned.

GROBIANUS   There be the letters, as delivered to me by my master Romulus.   [*She kisses the letter*

HYPPOLITA   Welcome, o welcome! here are two other letters, one to Julius, and one to you, dear father.

PRINCE   For us too, daughter? that is well—very well. Weep now too, daughter, I knew that good Romulus would not fail to write.

[*They read, are one and all astonished, and scratch their heads*

HYPPOLITA   Alas! alas! Eve in Paradise how shamefully wert thou deceived!

PRINCE   O! Troy thou wert taken by stratagem.   [*They read on*

JULIUS   O thou most deceitful amongst men, thou abomination and disgrace, how couldst thou find it in thy heart?

HYPPOLITA   O anguish! O mortal anguish! never have I experienced such sore pain on earth. O! cursed be thou Romulus, cursed be the hour when first I set my eyes on thee! O wherefore have the Gods made and created you men to wring with anguish our poor virgin hearts! O, ye poets! wherefore do you write that women are fickle! O no! you do us wrong, you men, 'tis you who are full of fickleness, the most perfidious, the most unmerciful creatures on earth, who change with every wind. O accursed, o false Romulus, is that the constant love you promised and swore to me?

Ho! ye immortal gods shorten my days, that the troubles of my heart may cease!

PRINCE Dear daughter, be calm, for thy lamentations can avail thee nothing. Fie, thou accursed Romulus! How couldst thou be so false?

JULIUS Ay, full of perfidy and shame! Pity is it that he is born a Roman. Fie, thou accursed treacherous man! Henceforth do I renounce thy friendship, nay more, I will pursue thee with my hate and enmity, that thou hast acted so perfidiously, so mercilessly towards her, who would have given her life for thine. All friendship be henceforth withdrawn from thee, and, trust me, I will call him to account. Therefore, fair Princess, grieve no more, for I will surely call him to account for this. Meanwhile rejoice that you have not become the consort of so vile a man.

PRINCE Dear Julius, pray tell us what this treacherous villain has writ to you.

JULIUS My lord, it is all to the same effect, save the postscript here: 'greet that old fool, that simpleton, Hyppolita's father of whom I have made a laughing-stock. You think I should go to work gently, hm, hm, hm, gently I say'.

PRINCE Hm! Why the devil does he call me an old fool and a simpleton?—the devil thank him for it! But what more does the varlet write?

JULIUS Perhaps you had better read it yourself.

[*He reads, and shakes his head*

PRINCE But how, by all the elements, am I to understand this? Think I should go to work gently, etc.

JULIUS I cannot guess, but should be inclined to think that perchance my lord has been accustomed to employ this manner of speech.

PRINCE Ay, ay, now I understand it. When the varlet used to sit by my daughter and embrace her, it was my custom so to speak; and now he scoffs at us to our hurt! Is this the Deo gratias for all our benefits? It must have been the devil himself that sent the rascal to us. Now I know that while he was pretending such kindness and humility, he was only making a fool of me. Devil take such guests, I'll none of them.

GROBIANUS Fair lady, what answer shall I take to Romulus?

HYPPOLITA [*Tears the letter and throws it on the ground*] That, that is my answer.

PRINCE [*Tears his also*] That is my answer too.

GROBIANUS My lord, what answer from your lordship?

JULIUS What answer? O tell this monster, this abomination of men, this accursed perfidious Romulus, that I am his bitterest enemy, and never to the end of my life will forget it, and so and so [*tearing the letter*] do I answer him.

GROBIANUS   I fully believe, my lord, that you are, and will remain, his bitterest foe. Farewell, I hie me hence.   [*Exit*

JULIUS   Fair lady, do you hold it worth your while to be sad for that accursed false Romulus?

HYPPOLITA   Ay, I am sad, and the saddest woman on earth.

JULIUS   Pray banish him from your thoughts and heart, and let joy restore you.

PRINCE   Such is my counsel too, dear daughter. Banish him quite out of thy heart and never think of him more; else will there be no end of tears and lamentations. Let us go in and never mention him again, for indeed I have reason. But never to the end of my life shall I forget such outrage and dishonour.   [*End of Act II*

ROMEO AND JULIET

INTRODUCTION

THE FIRST QUARTO of *Romeo and Juliet* is a 'bad Quarto' and there is little evidence that it comes from a first draft of the play. Q2 was printed by Thomas Creede for Cuthbert Burby in 1599, but in style the piece goes with the Sonnets, and with *A Midsummer Night's Dream* in which the Pyramus and Thisbe playlet may be a whimsical burlesque of Shakespeare's first experiment in romantic tragedy. It has been pointed out that the dramatist had probably read Arthur Brooke's *Romeus and Juliet* before writing *Venus and Adonis*, since the description of the boar in the latter may owe something to the former[1] (*B* 1023ff). But Shakespeare's grasp of character is so much better in *Romeo and Juliet* that I date it 1594–5—and after *Two Gentlemen of Verona* which also owes something to Brooke.

PREVIOUS VERSIONS OF THE STORY

In the *Ephesiaca* of Xenophon of Ephesus (fifth century A.D.), a story not printed till 1726 and translated into English in 1727,[2] the wife Anthia is separated from her husband and rescued from robbers by Perilaus, to avoid marrying whom she obtains from a physician a draught which she thinks deadly but is only a sleeping potion. She awakes in the tomb and is carried off by tomb-robbers to other adventures.

The theme became popular in Renaissance Italy. Masuccio's *Il Novellino* (1476) includes the story of Mariotto and Giannozza of Siena, who are secretly married by a Friar, after which Mariotto quarrels with a prominent citizen, kills him with a stick, and is exiled to Alexandria. To avoid marrying a suitor chosen by her father, Giannozza obtains a sleeping-potion from the Friar, sends a message to her husband, is buried, delivered

---

[1] See P. A. Daniel's Introduction to the *New Shakespere Society* ed. of Brooke and Painter. 1875. [2] Translated by Rooke.

from the tomb by the Friar, and sails for Alexandria. Her
messenger having been captured by pirates, Mariotto on
hearing of her death returns home disguised as a pilgrim.
Trying to open the tomb, he is seized and beheaded. Giannozza
comes back to Siena and dies in a convent.

With Luigi da Porto's *Istoria novellamente ritrovata di due
Nobili Amanti* (pubd. *c.* 1530) the tale comes near to Shakespeare. The scene is Verona, the lovers are aristocrats, and their
families, the Montecchi and the Cappelletti, are at feud.
Romeo goes, disguised as a nymph, to a Carnival ball at his
enemies' house in hope of seeing a lady who has scorned his
love. Giulietta falls in love with him at first sight and is sad to
see him holding himself aloof; but in the last dance (the Torch),
where the ladies change partners, he is left next to Giulietta,
on the other side of whom is a noble youth named Marcuccio
Guertio ('who by nature had very cold hands, in July as in
January'). She takes Romeo's hands and, to make him speak,
thanks him for coming since at least one hand will be warm
though Marcuccio is freezing the other. She tells him that no
other nymph present appears to her as beautiful as he is. He
soon abandons pursuit of his cruel fair one, and Giulietta hopes
that her marriage to him might reconcile the two houses,
'already tired and sated with their strife.' The lovers see each
other at church, and Romeo haunts her chamber-window,
climbing her balcony to woo her ardently. They meet there
frequently until one night when it is snowing he begs admit-
tance to her room. Giulietta refuses with modest scorn, declaring that once she is his bride she will give herself to him and
follow him anywhere. The Franciscan Friar Lorenzo, a great
philosopher and experimenter in things natural and magical,
and a friend of Romeo's, marries the pair, hoping to bring
peace between their families. 'And things being thus, it happens
that Fortune, enemy of every earthly joy, sowing I know not
what evil seed, revives the almost dead feud.' In a brawl Romeo
avoids harming any of his wife's people, but when his own
party is stricken and vanquished he slays Thebaldo Cappelletti,
'Who appears the fiercest of his enemies'. He leaves for Mantua
after telling his wife's servant to let him know through the Friar
everything that happens in her house. Seeing her grief Giulietta's parents think she wants to be married, since she is now

18. They arrange a marriage with the Count of Lodrone, but she enrages her father by refusing him, while her mother suspects she must be in love with someone else. Her servant Peter tells the Friar, who lets Romeo know; he says that he will come for Giulietta in eight or ten days' time. Giulietta asks the Friar for poison to 'free me from grief and Romeo from shame'; instead he gives her a sleeping potion to last 48 hours, intending to take her from the family vault and hide her in his cell until he can take her to Mantua, disguised as a Friar. All goes as planned until Friar Lorenzo, obliged to leave the city on duty, gives a letter for Romeo to another Friar who goes to Mantua, calls twice or thrice on Romeo, and not finding him at home, keeps the letter for safety. Meanwhile Peter, believing his mistress dead, takes the bad news to Romeo, who dresses as a peasant, and carrying with him some poison which he already has in his chest, goes to the Cappelletti tomb, laments over Giulietta's body, takes the poison, and lies down embracing her. She awakes and they speak to each other before Romeo dies. The Friar arrives and tries to persuade Giulietta to go to a convent, but, resolved on death, she 'drew in her breath and held it long, and then, uttering a great cry, fell dead on the corpse of Romeo.' All being known, the grieving parents 'freely embraced each other . . . so that the long feud . . . was now extinguished by the unhappy and piteous death of the two lovers.'

Adrian Sevin made a free adaptation in French of Masuccio's story in *Halquadrich and Burglipha* (1542), and a poem in *ottava rima* by Clízia was published in Venice in 1553. Here Lady Capulet believes Julietta's grief to be caused by Tebaldo's death. A play by Luigi Groto, *Hadriana* (1578) has a love affair drawn from da Porto in which the nightingale sings when the lovers part (Cp. *RJ* III.5.2), the opiate works as in Shakespeare, and the consolation offered to Capulet on his daughter's supposed death resembles Friar Lawrence's in IV.5.65ff. It is very unlikely that Shakespeare knew this play. More directly in the line from da Porto to Shakespeare are a *novella* by Bandello and its French translation by Boiastuau.

The story of Romeo and Julietta in *Le Novelle del Bandello*, (1554), is intended 'to warn young people that they should govern their desires and not run into furious passion.' It contains interesting variants. The feud is not dormant; more is made of Romeo's calf-love; he attends the ball not as a nymph but 'in a masque after supper with certain other young gentlemen'; he removes his vizard and is recognized, but is so young and handsome that nobody insults him. The man with the icy hands is called Mercutio, 'of audacity among maidens as a lion among lambs'. Romeo gets to know who Julietta is only when he asks a friend on leaving, and Julietta finds out his identity from her old nurse. When he waits under Julietta's window she speaks of his danger; they decide at this first nocturnal meeting to get married, and the Nurse is persuaded to help. Pietro is Romeo's servant, who provides the rope-ladder which Romeo gives to the Nurse; with the aid of this Romeo visits Julietta's room before their marriage, which is consummated in the Capulet garden. Almost at once Romeo comes upon his kinsmen and Julietta's fighting in the street, and although he tries to make peace he is forced to fight and slays Tibaldo, then hides in the Friar's cell, whence he writes to his wife before bidding her goodbye in the garden. Julietta wants to accompany him to Mantua dressed as a page, but he will not allow it; she begs Friar Lawrence to help her flee in disguise, and he suggests the potion-scheme. Before taking the drug she is terrified of awaking in the charnelhouse.

Pietro, Romeo's servant, rushes off to Mantua, finds his master in bed, and breaks the false news of Julietta's death, whereupon Romeo accuses himself of being its cause, and tries to kill himself with a sword but is prevented. So he sends his servant back to Verona, writes a letter to his father confessing everything, and goes off carrying a phial of poison which he has obtained some time before from one Spolentino who loved asps and serpents. He drinks the poison in the tomb, and is still alive when Julietta wakes. Before he dies he regrets the death of Tibaldo and urges Julietta to live. But rather than go to a nunnery as the Friar advises, she embraces her husband's body and dies without another word. The lovers are buried in the same tomb.

The plain, naturalistic style of Bandello's admirable narrative is clouded with moralizing and sentiment in its French adaptation by Pierre Boiastuau in his additions to Belleforest's
— *Histoires Tragiques extraictes des Oeuvres italiens de Bandel* (Paris

1559) which was translated by William Painter in his *Palace of Pleasure* (1567). Some of his variants are noteworthy since they were passed on to Shakespeare.[1] Thus whereas Bandello's hero went to the ball with the idea of distracting his mind from his cruel lady by taking part in social gaieties, the French Romeo goes in hope of seeing her. When he removes his vizard the Capulets are indignant at his presence but conceal their hatred. Boiastuau makes him approach Juliet when she is sitting between dances; but uses the allusion to cold hands. The French heroine is more circumspect than her Italian counterpart; Romeo may not enter her room until after marriage, and the rope-ladder is used then. On the other hand Boiastuau revels in the bedroom-scene, when the lovers indulge in flights of sentiment until the Nurse interrupts, saying:

'He that wasteth time in talk, recovereth the same too late. But forasmuch as either of you hath endured such mutual pains, behold (quoth she) a camp which I have made ready': (showing them the field bed which she had prepared and furnished), whereunto they easily agreed . . .', etc., etc. (Painter's translation.)

Boiastuau loses no chance of bringing rhetoric to the support of narrative. So when Juliet hears of Thibault's death she inveighs against Romeo, then reproves herself for attacking her dear husband, thus presenting 'a situation as original to Boiastuau as it is purely French in quality, the characteristic French dilemma of love and family honour in conflict' (Charlton). Similarly Juliet's father harangues her when she refuses to marry the Count Paris, reminding her of the powers of Roman fathers. Boiastuau also adds one or two incidents to the Italian story, the most important being that of the 'covetous apothecary', which Painter translated thus:

'[Romeo] went out of his chamber, and commanded his man to tarry behind him, that he might walk throughout all the corners of the city to find proper remedy (if it were possible) for his grief. And amongst others, beholding an apothecary's shop of little furniture and less store of boxes and other things requisite for that science, thought that the very poverty of the master apothecary would make him willingly yield to that

[1] Cf. H. B. Charlton, 'France as Chaperone of Romeo & Juliet' in *Studies in French Language & Mediaeval Literature presented to M. K. Pope* (1939), pp. 43–59.

which he pretended to demand: and after he had taken him aside, secretly said unto him: "Sir, if you be the master of the house, as I think you be, behold here fifty ducats, which I give you to the intent you deliver me some strong and violent poison, that within a quarter of an hour is able to procure death unto him that shall use it." The covetous apothecary, enticed by gain, agreed to his request, and feigning to give him some other medicine before the people's face he speedily made ready a strong and cruel poison: afterwards he said unto him softly: "Sir, I give you more than is needful, for the one half is able to destroy the strongest man of the world!" who, after he had received the poison, returned home, where he commanded his man to depart with diligence to Verona, and that he should make provision of candles, a tinder box, and other instruments meet for the opening of the grave of Julietta, and that above all other things, he should not fail to attend his coming besides the churchyard of St. Francis, and upon pain of his life to keep his intent in silence. Which Pietro obeyed in order as his master had required . . .'

On the other hand Boiastuau omits the ironic situation at the close obtained by da Porto and Bandello, who keep Romeo alive until Juliet awakes. He dies, she wakes, kisses his body, and laments, then draws his dagger from its sheath, wounds herself with many blows, and dies after making a sad speech. After this the Friar in Boiastuau explains everything in order to prove his own innocence, which is acknowledged. The apothecary is taken, racked and hanged, and the Nurse banished for concealing the marriage.

Whether or no Shakespeare read Boiastuau is uncertain. But he did not need him, nor indeed Painter's translation, though he surely knew this latter. Undoubtedly his main and perhaps sole source was Arthur Brooke's long poem *The Tragicall Historye of Romeus and Juliet*. Published in 1562, five years before Painter's translation, this piece was based on Boiastuau, whose bedroom-scene, love-conflict, and apothecary it took over. It is unlikely that Shakespeare drew on the imitation of Brooke published in 1563, Bernard Garter's *Two English Lovers*, which put the tale in an English setting.

Little is known of Arthur Brooke except that he died young, in 1563, drowned (according to George Turberville) on his

way to New Haven to serve in the English army overseas.
Turberville's elegy praises his narrative of

> Julyet and her mate;
> For there he shewde his cunning passing well,
> When he the tale to English did translate.

In 1563 appeared ' *An Agreement of sundry places of Scripture seeming in shew to Jarre, serving instead of Commentaryes, not only for
these but others lyke:* Translated out of French, and nowe fyrst
published by Arthur Broke and printed by Lucas Harrison.'
That Brooke was a serious-minded Protestant moralist is suggested by the *Address to the Reader* before his poem (cf. p. 284).
In this he refers to some theatrical production of the story, but
that early play has disappeared. (The Latin fragment *Romeus
et Julietta* in Sloane MS 1775 seems to be post-Shakespearian.)

The story of Romeo and Juliet was popular in the reign of
Elizabeth. Tottell obtained a licence to reprint Brooke in 1582
and it was reissued in 1587 by Robt. Robinson, whose title-
page announced it as containing 'a rare example of true constancie, with the subtill counsells and practises of an old fryer
and their ill event'. George Gascoigne's *Posies* (1575) contained
a Mask written for the double marriage between the son of
Viscount Montacute and the daughter of Sir William Dormer,
and Montacute's daughter with Sir William's son. For this
important day of union between two great Catholic families,
'eight Gentlemen (all of blood or alliaunce to the sayd L.
Mountacute) . . . had determined to present a Maske, . . . and
so farre they had proceeded therein, that they had already
bought furniture of Silkes, &c, and had caused their garmentes to bee cut of the Venetian fashion.' They asked Gascoigne to devise some verses which might explain their Venetian
dress, and he, calling to mind 'that there is a noble House of
the Mountacutes in Italie' decided to bring in a boy-actor
who would declare himself a descendant of the Italian Mountacutes, and that 'his father being slaine at the last warres against
the Turke, and he there taken, hee was recovered by the Venetians in their last victorie, and with them sayling towardes
Venice, they were driven by tempest upon these coastes, and
so came to the marriage upon report as followeth . . .' The

young actor, who was accompanied by four torch-bearers, had 'a token in his cap like to the Mountacutes of Italie':

> This token which the *Mountacutes* dyd beare alwaies, for that
> They covet to be knowne from *Capels* where they passe,
> For ancient grudge which long ago 'twene these two houses
> was.

This fictitious connection between the English and Italian Montagues may have no bearing on Shakespeare's play. But some scholars have argued that the Nurse's reference at I.3.23: 'Tis since the earthquake now eleven years' might suggest that a version of the play was made in 1591, for an earthquake had been felt in England in 1580. It is worth mentioning that Viscount Montague was high in court favour in 1591, when the Queen visited him at Cowdray Park in August and was sumptuously entertained for a week. A Romeo play would have been very suitable for that occasion. But the Nurse may have alluded to the Italian earthquakes of 1570, or to no real event.

SHAKESPEARE'S USE OF BROOKE

In *A Midsummer Night's Dream* Shakespeare discussed love's inevitability and the comic tricks it makes lovers perform. In *Romeo and Juliet* he discusses its tragic misfortunes in the face of external obstacles, and the 'true constancie' of its martyrs.

Da Porto addressed his story to a beautiful and prudent lady, a relative of his, as showing 'what great risks and what rash deeds lovers will commit in the name of love and in some cases their follies lead them even to death itself.' He says that he had the tale from an elderly archer named Peregrino who, seeing him melancholy for love, warned him that 'it is very unbecoming to stay long in the prison of love; so sad are almost all the ends to which Love leads us that to follow him is dangerous.'

Boiastuau and Painter find the story interesting for 'the variety of strange accidents', the 'novelty of so rare and perfect amity', and its illustration of the violence of passion, but they show no moral disapproval. They condone Friar Lawrence's conduct because he loved the young couple and hoped to make peace between their families, and so he is let go in peace 'without any note of infamie'. Brooke is more heavily moral in his

Address to the Reader, accusing the lovers of lust and disobedience, 'abusing the honourable name of lawefull marriage to cloke the shame of stolne contractes', and even, 'by all meanes of unhonest life, hastnyng to most unhappy deathe'. In the poem itself, however, the translator's sympathy is with the lovers. Brooke stresses Juliet's modesty and Romeo's integrity; the Friar is not 'superstitious' but a real sage, of famed virtue, respected by both houses and the Prince.

Shakespeare has followed this sympathetic approach, and only a blind critic could regard 'These violent delights have violent ends' as the moral text of the play.

Brooke rather than Painter led Shakespeare to stress the 'misadventured piteous overthrows' of the 'star-crossed lovers' for his poem insists time and again on the part played by 'false Fortune', 'the blyndfold goddesse', now smiling, now severe. 'Wavering Fortunes wheele' is the engine of the tragedy for Brooke, who pictures Romeo as a man 'so much in heavens grace, of fortune and of nature so beloved' that when 'all his hap turnes to mishap,' the sorrow is the greater; for he is of the unlucky sort 'whose greefe is much increast by myrth that went before'. Ill Fortune is assisted by human agencies. The feud, Tybalt's rage, the parents, the Nurse with her wily willingness, Friar Lawrence with his benevolence, all combine to destroy the lovers' happiness.

In Shakespeare there is less insistence that 'In nothing Fortune constant is, save in unconstancie'; he uses Fortune more consistently as a menace, working it out in terms of premonitions and the stars rather than in explicit statements, and having fate work mainly through the opposition of circumstance, the feud, etc. The play is full of antitheses, between love and hate, youth and age, innocence and cynicism; the Friar's kindness turns out ill; excellent plans fail by mischance. So the tragic conception is not of a flaw in the hero or heroine. We do not disapprove of their love or conduct, though both flout the authority of their parents and Juliet in particular deceives hers. We pity their youth, beauty, lyricism; and we fear for them because the world in which they live is unworthy of them, a place of less generous passions, so that Capulet may well call them 'Poor sacrifices of our enmity'.

Brooke's poem is a leaden work which Shakespeare transmuted to gold. He was one of Mr C. S. Lewis's 'Drab Age' verse writers,[1] yet no doubt Shakespeare enjoyed him. Brooke's poulter's measure is often dreary, but, if he lacked Bandello's racy energy, he had a homely realism, and the full picture he gives of Verona and the people concerned in the tragic history probably irritated and stimulated the dramatist to reinterpret the tale in terms of the new imagery and feeling of the nineties. A patient reading of Brooke will show how much he had to offer: the background of upper-class life, of church customs, of feud and riot; and much detail as the story progresses: the advice of Romeo's friends, Mercutio at the dance, Juliet going to church with her nurse and maid, Friar Lawrence, Tybalt, the Nurse (who helps to bring them together, recovers Juliet from her swoon, and threatens to kill herself should the girl die), the mother's depiction of Paris, the father's anger at Juliet's refusal to marry him, their joy when she agrees, the Nurse's *volte-face*, Juliet's subterfuge to sleep alone, and so on to the end. In Brooke Shakespeare found his subject well laid out and ready for quick dramatization, but told with a turgid emotionalism and pedestrian repetitiveness. The surprising thing is that Shakespeare preserved so much of his source in vitalizing its dead stuff.

Like Brooke he begins with a sonnet, for the *Chorus Prologue* is a sonnet of Shakespearian pattern (Brooke's *Argument* is Italianate). Whereas Brooke tells the main details of his plot, Shakespeare presents the general 'public' outline and the tone of his story. The public aspect of the theme is emphasized in I.1 which, after the comedy of the underlings, presents the whole complex of hate and disorder against which the lovers are to move, showing Tybalt in action, the Prince enforcing peace, and prepares us for a Romeo almost Hamlet-like in melancholy before we see him crying (prophetically), 'Here's much to do with hate but more with love', and revealing its cause, the cruel Rosaline who is a female counterpart (I.1.215–22) of the young friend in Shakespeare's first Sonnets, who likewise 'Cuts beauty off from all posterity'. So Shakespeare modulates from the public to the private theme and makes Romeo's conventional passion express itself in contradictions and paradoxes suited to the pattern of the whole play. It is a

---

[1] C. S. Lewis, *English Literature in the Sixteenth Century*. Book II.ii.259.

great scene, and comparison with Brooke's first 140 lines will show how naturally and with what brilliance it emerged from reading the poem in terms of the lively manners of contemporary English courtly youths. So 'the trustiest of his feeres/ Farre more then he with counsel fild, and ryper of his yeeres' becomes the genial Benvolio, Romeo's cousin, set on by his father to learn the cause of his melancholy.

The early introduction of Tybalt is followed by a similar use of Paris in I.2, who is to be Romeo's rival in love as Tybalt is in hate—and equally also his victim. We know that Paris has Capulet's favour before Benvolio persuades Romeo to go to the feast to seek Capulet's niece (the feud does not seem to matter where she is concerned). Romeo is less easily persuaded than Brooke's Romeus to attend

'At every feast ykept by day and banquet made by night'; for his passion is not gradually cooled, but driven out by a greater love.

Note the vivid and concrete way in which Shakespeare handles even small details from Brooke, whose reference to invitations to Capulet's feast ('by his name in paper sent') becomes the amusing episode in I.2 which Benvolio uses as a means of getting Romeo to compare Rosaline with other ladies. Romeo's assurance about his love makes the speedy introduction of Juliet very fitting, hence I.3 presents her against her domestic background, including a vivid portrait of the Nurse, based on such hints as Brooke's 'This old dame in her youth, had nurst her with her mylke' (Cp. *B* 652–66), and developed into a great humorous creation, her aged bawdiness contrasting with Juliet's purity and inexperience. In Brooke Juliet is 16, in Painter 18; Shakespeare makes her not yet 14, only just ripening for marriage, still more to emphasize the charm of her girlish directness, the pathos of her passion and resolution.[1] By the end of I.3 both Romeo and Juliet are going to a ball, one to see the woman he thinks he loves, the other to see (with favourable eye) the man her parents want her to love. Both are soon to change.

The rich expansion of the Nurse's character is paralleled by Mercutio's, and probably for the same reason, since Mercutio

[1] Other youthful lovers are Marina (14) and Miranda (15).

with his debonair worldliness, assurance and sensuality is a foil to Romeo's romantic idealism. All seems set for comedy till Romeo, melancholy among the masquers, and prevented from telling his dream by Mercutio's delicate mockery, utters his premonition of 'Some consequence yet hanging in the stars' (I.4.107).

At the ball the unmasking occurs in Brooke before Romeo meets Juliet, and 'The Capulets disdayne the presence of theyr foe'. In Shakespeare Romeo is recognized by Tybalt by his voice, and more tension is excited by the latter's violence.

Shakespeare knows well when to spare words. Thus, whereas Brooke tells lengthily how Rosaline is driven from his mind, Shakespeare shows it by altering the direction of the hero's lyricism, by his desire to touch Juliet's hand (not in a dance but between dances, I.5.53) and by the simple decisive question, 'Did my heart love till now?' Mercutio's cold hands are not mentioned, but 'hand' suggests the train of images and compliments when Romeo and Juliet first address each other. Juliet lets him speak first, but answers his prayer to kiss her hand with a charming play on 'pilgrim' and 'palmer'. Brooke has nothing like this, nor the discovery of identities (note Juliet's sly indirections), nor the intensity with which they realize their dilemma. Similarly Brooke has no parallel to the journey back from the ball when the others lose Romeo, nor to the irony of Mercutio's conjuration of Rosaline. Brooke makes 'a week or two' elapse before the lovers meet first by moonlight at her window overlooking the 'garden plot'; Shakespeare has them meet the same night. The jejune fears and long speeches of Julietta are turned to innocent frankness. Brooke lets Romeo swear and call on heaven; Shakespeare's Juliet begs him not to swear. From Brooke's 'But if your thought be chaste' (*B* 535) comes Shakespeare's 'If that thy bent of love be honourable' (II.2.143–8), but Shakespeare's Nurse interrupts the warning against lust which Brooke develops. How delightfully Shakespeare breaks up Brooke's long conversation by making Juliet retire and then return, irresistibly drawn back to her lover!

Brooke's Friar Lawrence, a doctor of divinity learned in Nature's secret ways, is a popular confessor, counsellor to the Prince, and friend to both rival parties. Shakespeare makes him less of a public figure but emphasizes his interest in drugs, building, on Brooke's idea that there is a right and a wrong way of using arcane knowledge, a wider conception of the double nature of all living things including man, who suffers the antithesis of 'grace and rude will' on which the good or evil use of all properties depends (II.3.17–30). The dramatist cuts short the Friar's protests and persuasions to delay, for he does not want us to apply such herbal moralizing to the lovers, but his Friar hopes that the match may end the feud.

As if antithetically to show the vanity of this pious hope, Shakespeare's next scene (II.4) informs us that Tybalt has challenged Romeo, though it is mostly occupied with badinage by which the hero makes Mercutio believe that his passion for Rosaline is cured, and (again note the use of contrast) shows him arranging for the marriage 'this afternoon'. Here and later Shakespeare avoids Brooke's ugly talk how 'To mock the silly mother that suspecteth nothing less' (*B* 640) and minimizes the deceitfulness of Juliet's actions. He elaborates the scene with Juliet in which Brooke's Nurse's delay (because 'I fear your hurt by sudden joy') becomes a deliberate teasing which brings out the girl's anxiety (II.5). This youthful impetuosity the Friar seeks to check in II.6 by asserting once more the duality in things (lines 11–15) and urging them to 'love moderately'. We do not see the wedding or hear the Friar preaching, and Act III begins, as if in deliberate contrast with the peaceful images of Brooke's preliminaries to the wedding night, with an upsurge of violence between the marriage and its consummation. The affrays leading to the death of Tybalt occur in Brooke 'a month or twain' after this. Shakespeare telescopes time again to enforce the conjunction of love and hate. In Brooke Mercutio plays no part in the brawls; Romeo kills Tybalt in self-defence after trying to prevent a general mêlée. In Shakespeare Mercutio thinks to purge his friend's lost honour by fighting for him, and is killed (ironically) through Romeo's attempt to stop the fight. Thus the motif of the play, that even our good deeds confound us when Fortune is against us, is stressed in this new episode, which proves Romeo's 'respective lenity', given up only when his friend has been slain.

When Juliet grieves for Tybalt she expands the antithesis in Brooke (1078–9):

How fares the lover hearing of her lover's banishment?
How wails she Tybalt's death, whom she had loved so well?

and she uses occasional images from the source, e.g. the tongue
(cp. *B* 1145 and *RJ* III.2.90,98); the heart and hand (cp.
B 1128 and *RJ* 71, 73) though Shakespeare adds adornment
of dragons, fiends, dove and raven, for here is quite another
order of imagination than Brooke's pedestrian fancy. Shakespeare rejects the swoon at the climax of Brooke's scene; his
Juliet is made of sterner stuff. A parallel picture of grief follows
in III.3 when Romeo learns he is banished, improving on
Brooke, yet also playing with the fatal word, and falling to the
ground. From Brooke come Lawrence's rebuke, 'Art thou a
man?' (*B* 1353; *RJ* III.3.108), some subsequent images, and
the railing 'on thy birth, the heaven, and earth' which Shakespeare's hero does scarcely at all.[1] Shakespeare's Friar gives
no stoic sermon (Cp. *B* 1359–1480) but calls on Romeo's manly
valour, tells him to count his blessings, and gives him practical
suggestions.

Even now Shakespeare does not let us know that the lovers
consummated their union in mingled joy and despair without
interjecting new suspense and irony by having Capulet discuss
with Paris the date of his marriage to Juliet—at the very time,
as we learn in III.5, when Romeo and Juliet were together in her
room. Shakespeare omits their bridal meeting and the long
preliminaries interrupted by the Nurse with her conventional
salaciousness. In Brooke this came earlier (782ff), so after
Tybalt's death they meet 'in wonted sort' (*B* 1530); they
bewail Fortune's blows; Juliet threatens suicide if she may not
go with Romeo, and he promises to return honourably in four
months' time (*B* 1673). Shakespeare gives us only their parting
at dawn (as in Brooke), letting the situation, the poetry, and
the premonition of Juliet's 'ill-divining soul' do their work. He
takes over the mother's bewilderment at Juliet's grief, and
the scenes with her parents in which the girl refuses to
marry (III.5). He puts here too the brief scene from Brooke
(*B* 2296ff) in which the Nurse praises Paris and reveals her
weathercock dishonesty.

It was a good stroke of Shakespeare's to make Juliet en-

[1] Cf. R. A. Law, in *U. of Texas Bulletin, Studies in English* (1929).

counter Paris at the Friar's cell when she comes to discuss how to avoid marrying him; the irony and pathos here are doubled, since Paris is so likeable. Shakespeare makes Capulet, in his delight when Juliet agrees, put forward the wedding from Thursday to Wednesday (Brooke's day). This has its effect on Friar Lawrence's plan to inform Romeo and to open the tomb. It also increases the tension since Juliet has at once to decide to drug herself. Shakespeare uses some of Brooke's details of horror at thought of the tomb. When Juliet is discovered 'dead', Shakespeare's Capulet, unlike Brooke's, is not speechless, but uses some of Brooke's own antitheses on the change from mirth to moan (*B* 2507ff; *RJ* IV.5.84ff). Relief is obtained in the play by a comic discussion of the power of music by Peter and the musicians of the County Paris. The spectator is surprised when not the Friar's messenger but Balthazar (Peter in Brooke) reaches Romeo and describes Juliet's death and burial. The needy Apothecary is taken over from the poem, but Shakespeare elaborates his shop. Only after this do we learn about the plague and quarantine which have held up Friar John (who is called this also in Brooke, Anselmo in most other analogues). In Brooke Paris does not come to the tomb, and so is not slain by Romeo; in both poem and play Romeo begs pardon of Tybalt's corpse, and dies before the Friar enters or Juliet awakes; she refuses to leave the vault, the Friar tries to escape the watch, and she kills herself with Romeo's dagger. After this Shakespeare compresses greatly both in time and explanations. Whereas Brooke's Friar tells his tale at length Shakespeare says 'short date of breath Is not so long as is a tedious tale'. The tragic effect is not dissipated: 'Some shall be pardoned, and some punished', says the Prince, and so the play ends with our minds focused on the reconciliation of the families and the memorials due to the woeful pair.[1]

---

[1] For a stimulating discussion of the structural and chronological relations of the play see T. W. Baldwin, *5ActS*. Chaps. **XXXI–II**.

I. Source

THE TRAGICALL HISTORYE OF ROMEUS AND JULIET

written first in Italian by Bandell, and nowe in Englishe by Ar. Br.

In aedibus Richardi Tottelli. Cum Privilegio

[1562]

TO THE READER

The God of all glorye created universallye all creatures, to sette forth his prayse, both those whiche we esteme profitable in use and pleasure, and also those, whiche we accompte noysome, and lothsome. But principally he hath appointed man, the chiefest instrument of his honour, not onely, for ministryng matter thereof in man himselfe: but aswell in gatheryng out of other, the occasions of publishing Gods goodnes, wisdome, & power. And in like sort, everye dooyng of man hath by Goddes dyspensacion some thynge, whereby God may, and ought to be honored. So the good doynges of the good, & the evil actes of the wicked, the happy successe of the blessed, and the wofull procedinges of the miserable, doe in divers sorte sound one prayse of God. And as eche flower yeldeth hony to the bee: so every exaumple ministreth good lessons, to the well disposed mynde. The glorious triumphe of the continent man upon the lustes of wanton fleshe, incourageth men to honest restraynt of wyld affections, the shamefull and wretched endes of such, as have yelded their libertie thrall to fowle desires, teache men to witholde them selves from the hedlong fall of loose dishonestie. So, to lyke effect, by sundry meanes, the good mans exaumple byddeth men to be good, and the evill mans mischefe, warneth men not to be evyll. To this good ende, serve all ill endes, of yll begynnynges. And to this ende (good Reader) is this tragicall matter written, to describe unto thee a coople of unfortunate lovers, thralling themselves to unhonest desire, neglecting the authoritie and advise of parents and frendes, conferring their principall counsels with dronken gossyppes, and superstitious friers (the naturally fitte instrumentes of unchastitie) attemptyng all adventures of peryll, for thattaynyng of their wished lust, usyng auriculer confession (the kay of

284

whoredome, and treason) for furtheraunce of theyr purpose, abusyng the honorable name of lawefull mariage, the cloke the shame of stolne contractes, finallye,
by all meanes of unhonest lyfe, hastyng to most unhappye deathe. This president (good Reader) shalbe to thee, as the slaves of Lacedemon, oppressed with
excesse of drinke, deformed and altered from likenes of men, both in mynde,
and use of body, were to the free borne children, so shewed to them by their
parentes, to thintent to rayse in them an hatefull lothyng of so filthy beastlynes.
Hereunto if you applye it, ye shall deliver my dooing from offence, and profit
your selves. Though I saw the same argument lately set foorth on stage with
more commendation, then I can looke for: (being there much better set forth
then I have or can dooe) yet the same matter penned as it is, may serve to lyke
good effect, if the readers do brynge with them lyke myndes, to consider it.
which hath the more incouraged me to publishe it, suche as it is.　　Ar. Br.

TO THE READER

Amid the desert rockes, the mountaine beare.
　　Bringes forth unformd, unlyke her selfe her yong:
　　Nought els but lumpes of fleshe withouten heare,
　　In tract of time, her often lycking tong
Geves them such shape, as doth (ere long) delight
　　The lookers on: Or when one dogge doth shake
　　With moosled mouth, the joyntes too weake to fight.
　　Or when upright he standeth by his stake,
(A noble creast,) or wylde in savage wood,
　　A dosyn dogges one holdeth at a baye,
　　With gaping mouth, and stayned jawes with blood,
　　Or els, when from the farthest heavens, they
The lode starres are, the wery pilates marke,
　　In stormes to gyde to haven the tossed barke.
　　　　　　　　　　　　Right so my muse
Hath (now at length) with travell[1] long brought forth
　　Her tender whelpes, her divers kindes of style,
　　Such as they are, or nought, or little woorth,
　　Which carefull travell, and a longer whyle,
May better shape. The eldest of them loe,
　　I offer to the stake, my youthfull woorke,
　　Which one reprochefull mouth might overthrowe:
　　The rest (unlickt as yet) a whyle shall lurke,
Tyll tyme geve strength, to meete and match in fight
　　with slaunders whelpes. Then shall they tell of stryfe
　　Of noble tryumphes, and deedes of martial might,
　　And shall geve rules of chast and honest lyfe.

[1] travail.

The whyle I pray that ye with favour blame,
Or rather not reprove the laughing game
               Of this my muse.

THE ARGUMENT

Love hath inflamed twayne by sodayn sight.
   And both do graunt the thing that both desyre.
   They wed in shrift by counsell of a frier.
   Yong Romeus clymes fayre Juliets bower by night.
Three monthes he doth enjoy his cheefe delight.
   By Tybalts rage, provoked unto yre,
   He payeth death to Tybalt for his hyre.
   A banisht man he scapes by secret flight.
New mariage is offred to his wyfe:
   She drinkes a drinke that seemes to reve her breath.
   They bury her, that sleping yet hath lyfe.
Her husband heares the tydinges of her death.
   He drinkes his bane. And she with Romeus knyfe,
When she awakes, her selfe (alas) she sleath.

ROMEUS AND JULIET

There is beyonde the Alps, a towne of auncient fame
Whose bright renoune yet shineth cleare, Verona men it name,
Bylt in an happy time, bylt on a fertile soyle,
Maynteined by the heavenly fates, and by the townish toyle.
The fruitfull hilles above, the pleasant vales belowe,
The silver streame with chanell depe, that through the towne doth
    flow,
The store of springes that serve for use, and eke for ease
And other moe commodities which profite may and please,
Eke many certaine signes of thinges betyde of olde,
To fyll the houngry eyes of those that curiously beholde   10
Doe make this towne to be preferde above the rest
Of Lumbard townes, or at the least compared with the best.
In which while Escalus, as prince alone dyd raigne,
To reache rewarde unto the good, to pay the lewde with payne,
Alas (I rewe to thinke) an heavy happe befell
Which Boccace skant (not my rude tong) were able forth to tell.
Within my trembling hande, my penne doth shake for feare
And on my colde amased head, upright doth stand my heare.
But sith she doth commaunde, whose hest I must obaye,
In moorning verse, a wofull chaunce to tell I will assaye.   20

Helpe learned Pallas, helpe, ye muses with your arte,
Helpe all ye damned feendes to tell, of joyes retournd to smart,
Helpe eke ye sisters three, my skillesse penne t'indyte
For you it causd which I (alas) unable am to wryte.
There were two auncient stockes, which Fortune high dyd place
Above the rest, indewd with welth, and nobler of their race,
Loved of the common sort, loved of the Prince alike,
And like unhappy were they both, when Fortune list to strike.
Whose prayse with equall blast, fame in her trumpet blew:
The one was cliped Capelet, and thother Montagew.   30
A wonted use it is, that men of likely sorte
(I wot not by what furye forsd) envye eche others porte.
So these, whose egall state bred envye pale of hew,
And then of grudging envyes roote, blacke hate and rancor grewe.
As of a little sparke, oft ryseth mighty fyre,
So of a kyndled sparke of grudge, in flames flashe out theyr yre,
And then theyr deadly foode, first hatchd of trifling stryfe
Did bathe in bloud of smarting woundes, it re[a]ved breth and lyfe.
No legend lye I tell, scarce yet theyr eyes be drye
That did behold the grisly sight, with wet and weping eye.   40
But when the prudent prince, who there the scepter helde,
So great a new disorder in his common weale behelde,
By jentyl meane he sought, their choler to asswage,
And by perswasion to appease, their blameful furious rage.
But both his woords and tyme, the prince hath spent in vayne
So rooted was the inward hate, he lost his buysy payne.
When frendly sage advise, ne jentyll woords avayle,
By thondring threats, and princely powre their courage gan he
      quayle,
In hope that when he had the wasting flame supprest,
In time he should quyte quench the sparks that boornd within
      their brest.   50
Now whilst these kyndreds do remayne in this estate,
And eche with outward frendly shew dooth hyde his inward hate,
One Romeus, who was of race a Montague,
Upon whose tender chyn, as yet, no manlyke beard there grewe,
Whose beauty and whose shape so farre the rest did stayne,
That from the cheefe of Veron youth he greatest fame dyd gayne,
Hath founde a mayde so fayre (he found so foule his happe)
Whose beauty, shape, and comely grace, did so his heart entrappe,
That from his owne affayres, his thought she did remove,
Onely he sought to honor her, to serve her, and to love.   60
To her he writeth oft, oft messengers are sent:

At length (in hope of better spede) himselfe the lover went
Present to pleade for grace, which absent was not founde,
And to discover to her eye his new receaved wounde.
But she that from her youth was fostred evermore
With vertues foode, and taught in schole of wisdomes skilfull lore,
By aunswere did cutte of[f] thaffections of his love,
That he no more occasion had so vayne a sute to move.
So sterne she was of chere, (for all the payne he tooke)
That in reward of toyle, she would not geve a frendly looke.   70
And yet how much she did with constant mind retyre
So much the more his fervent minde was prickt fourth by desyre.
But when he many monthes, hopelesse of his recure,
Had served her, who forced not what paynes he did endure,
At length he thought to leave Verona, and to prove
If chaunge of place might chaunge awaye his ill bestowed love.
And speaking to himselfe, thus gan he make his mone:
What booteth me to love and serve a fell unthankfull one,
Sith that my humble sute and labour sowede in vayne,
Can reape none other fruite at all but scorne and proude
    disdayne?   80
What way she seekes to goe, the same I seeke to runne,
But she the path wherin I treade, with spedy flight doth shunne.
I can not live, except that nere to her I be,
She is ay best content when she is farthest of from me.
Wherfore henceforth I will farre from her take my flight.
Perhaps mine eye once banished by absence from her sight,
This fyre of myne, that by her pleasant eyne is fed
Shall little and little weare away, and quite at last be ded.
But whilest he did decree this purpose still to kepe,
A contrary repugnant thought sanke in his brest so depe   90
That doutefull is he now which of the twayne is best.
In sighs, in teares, in plainte, in care, in sorow and unrest,
He mones the daye, he wakes the long and wery night,
So deepe hath love with pearcing hand, ygravd her bewty bright
Within his brest, and hath so mastred quite his hart
That he of force must yeld as thrall, no way is left to start.
He can not staye his steppe, but forth still must he ronne,
He languisheth and melts awaye, as snow against the sonne,
His kyndred and al[l]yes do wonder what he ayles,
And eche of them in frendly wise, his heavy hap bewayles.   100
But one emong the rest, the trustiest of his feeres,
Farre more then he with counsel fild, and ryper of his yeeres,
Gan sharply him rebuke, suche love to him he bare

That he was felow of his smart, and partner of his care.
What meanst thou Romeus (quoth he) what doting rage
Dooth make thee thus consume away, the best parte of thine age,
In seking her that scornes, and hydes her from thy sight,
Not forsing all thy great expence, ne yet thy honor bright,
Thy teares, thy wretched lyfe, ne thine unspotted truth
Which are of force (I weene) to move the hardest hart to
    ruthe.   110
Now for our frendships sake, and for thy health I pray
That thou hencefoorth become thyne owne, O geve no more away
Unto a thankeles wight, thy precious free estate.
In that thou lovest such a one, thou seemst thy selfe to hate,
For she doth love els where, (and then thy time is lorne)
Or els (what booteth thee to sue) loves court she hath forsworne.
Both yong thou art of yeres, and high in Fortunes grace,
What man is better shapd than thou? who hath a sweeter face?
By painfull studies meane, great learning hast thou wonne,
Thy parentes have none other heyre, thou art theyr onely
    sonne.   120
What greater griefe (trowst thou?) what wofull dedly smart
Should so be able to distraine thy seely fathers hart?
As in his age to see thee plonged deepe in vyce
When greatest hope he hath to heare thy vertues fame arise.
What shall thy kinsmen thinke, thou cause of all theyr ruthe?
Thy dedly foes do laugh to skorne thy yll employed youth.
Wherfore my counsell is, that thou henceforth beginne
To knowe and flye the errour which to long thou livedst in.
Remove the veile of love, that keepes thine eyes so blynde,
That thou ne canst the ready path of thy forefathers fynde.   130
But if unto thy will so much in thrall thou art,
Yet in some other place bestowe thy witles wandring hart.
Choose out some worthy dame, her honor thou and serve,
Who will geve eare to thy complaint, and pitty ere thou sterve.
But sow no more thy paynes in such a barrayne soyle
As yeldes in harvest time no crop in recompence of toyle.
Ere long the townishe dames together will resort,
Some one of bewty, favour, shape, and of so lovely porte
With so fast fixed eye, perhaps thou mayst beholde,
That thou shalt quite forget thy love, and passions past of
    olde.   140
The yong mans lystning eare receivde the [w]holesome sounde,
And reasons truth yplanted so, within his head had grounde
That now with healthy coole ytempred is the heate

And piecemeale weares away the greefe that erst his heart dyd
    freate.
To his approved frend, a solemne othe he plight:
At every feast ykept by day, and banquet made by night,
At pardons in the churche, at games in open streate,
And every where he would resort where Ladies wont to meete.
Eke should his savage heart lyke all indifferently,
For he would view and judge them all with unallured eye.   150
How happy had he been had he not been forsworne
But twyse as happy had he been had he been never borne,
For ere the Moone could thryse her wasted hornes renew,
False Fortune cast for him poore wretch, a myschiefe newe to
    brewe.
The wery winter nightes restore the Christmas games,
And now the season doth invite to banquet townish dames.
And fyrst in Capels house, the chiefe of all the kyn
Sparth for no cost, the wonted use of banquets to begyn.
No Lady fayre or fowle, was in Verona towne,
No knight or gentleman of high or lowe renowne   160
But Capilet himselfe hath byd unto his feast,
Or by his name in paper sent, appoynted as a geast.
Yong damsels thether flocke, of bachelers a rowte,
Not so much for the banquets sake, as bewties to searche out.
But not a Montagew would enter at his gate,
For as you heard, the Capilets, and they were at debate,
Save Romeus, and he in maske with hidden face,
The supper done, with other five dyd prease into the place.
When they had maskd a whyle, with dames in courtly wise
All dyd unmaske, the rest dyd shew them to theyr ladies eyes. 170
But bashfull Romeus, with shamefast face forsooke
The open prease, and him withdrew into the chambers nooke.
But brighter then the sunne, the waxen torches shone
That mauger what he could, he was espyd of every one.
But of the women cheefe, theyr gasing eyes that threwe
To woonder at his sightly shape, and bewties spotles hewe.
With which the heavens him had and nature so bedect
That Ladies thought the fayrest dames were fowle in his respect.
And in theyr head beside, an other woonder rose,
How he durst put himselfe in throng among so many foes.   180
Of courage stoute they thought his cumming to procede
And women love an hardy hart as I in stories rede.
The Capilets disdayne the presence of theyr foe
Yet they suppresse theyr styrred yre, the cause I do not knowe.

Perhaps toffend theyr gestes the courteous knights are loth,
Perhaps they stay from sharpe revenge, dreadyng the Princes
    wroth,
Perhaps for that they shamd to exercise theyr rage
Within their house, gainst one alone and him of tender age.
They use no taunting talke, ne harme him by theyr deede,
They neyther say, what makst thou here, ne yet they say God
    speede,   190
So that he freely might the Ladies view at ease,
And they also beholding him, their chaunge of fansies please.
Which nature had him taught to doe with such a grace,
That there was none but joyed at his being there in place.
With upright beame he wayd the bewty of eche dame,
And judged who best, and who next her, was wrought in natures
    frame.
At length he saw a mayd, right fayre of perfect shape
Which Theseus, or Paris would have chosen to their rape,
Whom erst he never sawe, of all she pleasde him most.
Within himselfe he said to her, thou justly mayst thee boste   200
Of perfit shapes renoune, and Beauties sounding prayse,
Whose like ne hath, ne shalbe seene, ne liveth in our dayes.
And whilest he fixd on her his partiall perced eye,
His former love, for which of late he ready was to dye,
Is nowe as quite forgotte, as it had never been.
The proverbe saith, unminded oft are they that are unseene
And as out of a planke a nayle a nayle doth drive,
So novell love out of the minde the auncient love doth rive.
This sodain kindled fyre in time is wox so great,
That onely death and both theyr blouds might quench the
    fiery heate.   210
When Romeus saw himselfe in this new tempest tost
Where both was hope of pleasant port, and daunger to be lost,
He doubtefull, ska[r]sely knew what countenance to keepe;
In Lethies floud his wonted flames were quenchd and drenched
    deepe.
Yea he forgets himselfe, ne is the wretch so bolde
To aske her name, that without force hath him in bondage folde.
Ne how tunloose his bondes doth the poore foole devise,
But onely seeketh by her sight to feede his houngry eyes.
Through them he swalloweth downe loves sweete empoysonde
    baite,
How surely are the wareles wrapt by those that lye in wayte?   220
So is the poyson spred throughout his bones and vaines,

That in a while (alas the while) it hasteth deadly paines.
Whilst Juliet (for so this gentle damsell hight)
From syde to syde on every one dyd cast about her sight.
At last her floting eyes were ancored fast on him,
Who for her sake dyd banishe health and fredome from eche
     limme.
He in her sight did seeme to passe the rest as farre
As Phoebus shining beames do passe the brightnes of a starre.
In wayte laye warlike love with golden bowe and shaft,
And to his eare with steady hand the bowstring up he raft.   230
Till now she had escapde his sharpe inflaming darte,
Till now he listed not assaulte her yong and tender hart.
His whetted arrow loosde, so touchd her to the quicke,
That through the eye it strake the hart, and there the hedde did
     sticke.
It booted not to strive, for why, she wanted strength:
The weaker aye unto the strong of force must yeld at length.
The pomps now of the feast her heart gyns to despyse
And onely joyeth when her eyen meete with her lovers eyes.
When theyr new smitten heartes had fed on loving gleames,
Whilst passing too and fro theyr eyes ymingled were theyr
     beames,   240
Eche of these lovers gan by others lookes to knowe
That frendship in their brest had roote, and both would have it
     grow.
When thus in both theyr harts had Cupide made his breache
And eche of them had sought the meane to end the warre by
     speache,
Dame Fortune did assent theyr purpose to advaunce,
With torche in hand a comly knight did fetch her foorth to
     daunce.
She quit her selfe so well, and with so trim a grace,
That she the cheefe prayse wan that night from all Verona race.
The whilst our Romeus, a place had warely wonne
Nye to the seate where she must sit, the daunce once beyng
     donne   250
Fayre Juliet tourned to her chayre with pleasant cheere
And glad she was her Romeus approched was so neere.
At thone side of her chayre, her lover Romeo
And on the other side there sat one cald Mercutio,
A courtier that eche where was highly had in pryce,
For he was coorteous of his speche, and pleasant of devise
Even as a Lyon would emong the lambes be bolde,

Such was emong the bashfull maydes, Mercutio to beholde.
With frendly gripe he ceasd[1] fayre Juliets snowish hand.
A gyft he had that nature gave him in his swathing band,   260
That frosen mountayne yse was never halfe so cold
As were his handes, though nere so neer the fire he dyd them
    holde.
As soone as had the knight the vyrgins right hand raught
Within his trembling hand her left hath loving Romeus caught,
For he wist well himselfe for her abode most payne
And well he wist she loved him best, unles she list to fayne.
Then she with tender hand his tender palme hath prest,
What joy trow you was graffed so in Romeus cloven brest?
The soodain sweete delight hath stopped quite his tong
Ne can he claime of her his right, ne crave redresse of wrong.   270
But she espyd straight waye, by chaunging of his hewe
From pale to red, from red to pale, and so from pale anewe,
That vehment love was cause, why so his tong dyd stay
And so much more she longde to heare what love could teache
    him saye.
When she had longed long, and he long held his peace,
And her desire of hearing him, by sylence dyd encrease,
At last with trembling voyce and shamefast chere, the mayde
Unto her Romeus tournde her selfe, and thus to him she sayde.
O blessed be the time of thy arrivall here:
But ere she could speake forth the rest, to her love drewe so
    nere   280
And so within her mouth, her tong he glewed fast,
That no one woord could scape her more, then what already past.
In great contented ease the yong man straight is rapt,
What chaunce (quoth he) unware to me O lady myne is hapt?
That geves you worthy cause, my cumming here to blisse?
Fayre Juliet was come agayne unto her selfe by this.
Fyrst ruthfully she lookd, then sayd with smylyng cheere
Mervayle no whit my heartes delight, my onely knight and fere,
Mercutio's ysy hande had all to frosen myne
And of thy goodnes thou agayne hast warmed it with thine.   290
Whereto with stayed brow, gan Romeus to replye
If so the gods have graunted me suche favour from the skye,
That by my being here, some service I have donne
That pleaseth you I am as glad, as I a realme had wonne.
O wel bestowed tyme, that hath the happy hyre,
Which I woulde wysh if I might have, my wished harts desire,

----

[1] seiz'd.

For I of God woulde crave, as pryse of paynes forpast,
To serve, obey, and honour you, so long as lyfe shall last.
As proofe shall teache you playne, if that you like to trye
His faltles truth, that nill for ought, unto his lady lye,   300
But if my tooched hand, have warmed yours some dele,
Assure your self the heat is colde, which in your hand you fele
Compard to suche quick sparks and glowing furious gleade
As from your bewties pleasaunt eyne, love caused to proceade
Which have so set on fyre, eche feling parte of myne,
That lo, my mynde doeth melt awaye, my utwerd parts doe pyne
And but you helpe all whole, to ashes shall I toorne,
Wherfore (alas) have ruth on him, whom you do force to boorne.
Even with his ended tale, the torches daunce had ende,
And Juliet of force must part from her new chosen frend.   310
His hand she clasped hard, and all her partes did shake,
When laysureles with whispring voyce thus did she aunswer
          make:
You are no more your owne (deare frend) then I am yours,
(My honor saved) prest tobay your will, while life endures.
Lo, here the lucky lot that seld true lovers finde,
Eche takes away the others hart, and leaves the owne behinde.
A happy life is love if God graunt from above,
That hart with hart by even waight doo make exchaunge of love.
But Romeus gone from her, his heart for care is colde,
He hath forgot to aske her name that hath his hart in holde.   320
With forged careles cheere, of one he seekes to knowe,
Both how she hight, and whence she came, that him enchaunted
          so
So hath he learnd her name, and knowth she is no geast,
Her father was a Capilet, and master of the feast.
Thus hath his foe in choyse to geve him lyfe or death
That scarsely can his wofull brest keepe in the lively breath.
Wherfore with piteous plaint feerce Fortune doth he blame
That in his ruth and wretched plight doth seeke her laughing
          game.
And he reproveth love, cheefe cause of his unrest,
Who ease and freedome hath exilde out of his youthful brest.   330
Twyse hath he made him serve, hopeles of his rewarde.
Of both the ylles to choose the lesse, I weene the choyse were
          harde.
Fyrst to a ruthlesse one he made him sue for grace
And now with spurre he forceth him to ronne an endles race.
Amyd these stormy seas one ancor doth him holde,

He serveth not a cruell one, as he had done of olde
And therfore is content, and chooseth still to serve
Though hap should sweare that guerdonles the wretched wight
    should sterve.
The lot of Tantalus is Romeus lyke to thine
For want of foode amid his foode, the myser styll doth pine.   340
As carefull was the mayde what way were best devise
To learne his name, that intertaind her in so gentle wise,
Of whome her hart received so deepe, so wyde a wounde.
An aunciend dame she calde to her, and in her eare gan rounde.
This olde dame in her youth, had nurst her with her mylke,
With slender nedle taught her sow, and how to spin with silke.
What twayne are those (quoth she) which prease unto the doore,
Whose pages in theyr hand doe beare, two toorches light before?
And then as eche of them had of his housould name,
So she him namde yet once agayne, the yong and wyly
    dame,   350
And tell me who is he with vysor in his hand,
That yonder doth in masking weede besyde the window stand?
His name is Romeus, (said she) a Montegewe
Whose fathers pryde first styrd the strife which both your
    housoldes rewe.
The woord of Montegew, her joyes did overthrow,
And straight in steade of happy hope, dyspayre began to growe.
What hap have I quoth she, to love my fathers foe?
What, am I wery of my wele? what, doe I wishe my woe?
But though her grievous paynes distraind her tender hart
Yet with an outward shewe of joye she cloked inward smart,   360
And of the courtlyke dames her leave so courtly tooke,
That none dyd gesse the sodain change by changing of her looke.
Then at her mothers hest to chamber she her hyde,
So well she faynde, mother ne nurce, the hidden harme descride.
But when she should have slept as wont she was, in bed,
Not halfe a winke of quiet slepe could harber in her hed
For loe, an hugy heape of dyvers thoughtes arise
That rest have banisht from her hart, and slumber from her eyes.
And now from side to side she tosseth and she turnes,
And now for feare she shevereth, and now for love she
    burnes,   370
And now she lykes her choyse, and now her choyse she blames,
And now eche houre within her head, a thousand fansies frames
Sometime in mynde to stop, amyd her course begonne
Sometimes she vowes what so betyde, thattempted race to ronne.

Thus dangers dred and love, within the mayden fought,
The fight was feerce continuyng long by their contrary thought.
In tourning mase of love she wandreth too and fro,
Then standeth doubtfull what to doe, last overprest with woe.
How so her fansies cease, her teares dyd never blyn,[1]
With heavy cheere and wringed hands, thus doth her plaint
    begyn.   380
Ah sily foole (quoth she) ycought in soottill snare,
Ah wretched wench bewrapt in woe, ah caytife clad with care,
Whence come these wandring thoughtes to thy unconstant brest
By straying thus from raysons lore, that re[a]ve thy wonted rest?
What if his suttel brayne to fayne have taught his tong,
And so the snake that lurkes in grasse thy tender hart hath stong?
What if with frendly speache the traytor lye in wayte,
As oft the poysond hooke is hid, wrapt in the pleasant bayte?
Oft under cloke of truth, hath falshod served her lust
And toornd theyr honor into shame, that did so slightly
    trust.   390
What, was not Dido so, a crouned Queene, defamd?
And eke for such an heynous cryme, have men not Theseus
    blamd?
A thousand stories more, to teache me to beware,
In Boccace, and in Ovids bookes too playnely written are.
Perhaps, the great revenge he cannot woorke by strength,
By suttel sleight (my honor staynde) he hopes to worke at length.
So shall I seeke to finde my fathers foe, his game,
So I defylde, Report shall take her trompe of blacke defame,
Whence she with puffed cheeke shall blowe a blast so shrill
Of my disprayse, that with the noyse Verona shall she fill.   400
Then I, a laughing stocke through all the towne becomme,
Shall hide my selfe, but not my shame, within an hollowe toombe.
Straight underneth her foote, she treadeth in the dust
Her troublesom thought, as wholy vaine, ybred of fond distrust.
No, no, by God above, I wot it well quoth shee,
Although I rashely spake before, in no wise can it bee
That where such perfet shape with pleasant bewty restes,
There crooked craft and trayson blacke should be appoynted
    gestes.
Sage writers say, the thoughts are dwelling in the eyne,
Then sure I am, as Cupid raignes, that Romeus is myne.   410
The tong the messenger, eke call they of the mynd;
So that I see he loveth me, shall I then be unkynd?

[1] cease.

His faces rosy hew, I saw full oft to seeke
And straight againe it flashed foorth, and spred in eyther cheeke,
His fyxed heavenly eyne, that through me quite did perce
His thoughts unto my hart, my thoughts they semed to rehearce.
What ment his foltring tunge, in telling of his tale,
The trembling of his joynts, and eke his cooller waxen pale?
And whilst I talkt with him, hym self he hath exylde,
Out of him self (as seemed me) ne was I sure begylde.   420
Those arguments of love, craft wrate not in his face,
But Natures hande when all deceyte was banishd out of place.
What other certayn signes seke I of his good wil?
These doo suffise, and stedfast I will love and serve him still,
Till Attropos shall cut my fatall thread of lyfe,
So that he mynde to make of me his lawfull wedded wyfe.
For so perchaunce this new aliance may procure
Unto our houses such a peace as ever shall endure.
   Oh how we can perswade, our self to what we like,
And how we can diswade our mynd, if ought our mynd
      mislyke.   430
Weake arguments are stronge, our fansies streyght to frame
To pleasing things, and eke to shonne, if we mislike the same.
The mayde had scarsely yet ended the wery warre,
Kept in her heart by striving thoughtes, when every shining starre
Had payd his borowed light, and Phebus spred in skies
His golden rayes, which seemd to say, now time it is to rise.
And Romeus had by this forsaken his wery bed,
Where restles he a thousand thoughts had forged in his hed.
And while with lingring step by Juliets house he past,
And upward to her windowes high his gredy eyes did cast,   440
His love that looked for him there gan he straight espie.
With pleasant cheere eche greeted is, she followeth with her eye
His parting steppes, and he oft looketh backe againe,
But not so oft as he desyres; warely he doth refraine.
What life were lyke to love, if dred of jeopardy
Ysowred not the sweete, if love were free from jelosy.
But she more sure within, unseene of any wight,
When so he comes, lookes after him, till he be out of sight.
In often passing so, his busy eyes he threw,
That every pane and tooting[1] hole the wily lover knew.   450
In happy houre he doth a garden plot espye,
From which, except he warely walke, men may his love descrye,
For lo, it fronted full upon her leaning place,

---

[1] peeping.

Where she is woont to shew her heart by cheerefull frendly face.
And lest the arbors might theyr secret love bewraye,
He doth keepe backe his forward foote from passing there by daye.
But when on earth the night her mantel blacke hath spred,
Well armd he walketh foorth alone, ne dreadfull foes doth dred.
Whom maketh love not bold, naye whom makes he not blynde?
He reveth daungers dread oft times out of the lovers minde.   460
By night he passeth here, a weeke or two in vayne
And for the missing of his marke, his griefe hath him nye slaine.
And Juliet that now doth lacke her hearts releefe,
Her Romeus pleasant eyen (I meene) is almost dead for greefe.
Eche day she chaungeth howres, (for lovers keepe an howre)
When they are sure to see theyr love, in passing by their bowre.
Impacient of her woe, she hapt to leane one night
Within her window, and anon the Moone did shine so bright
That she espyde her love, her hart revived, sprang
And now for joy she clappes her handes, which erst for woe
      she wrang.   470
Eke Romeus, when he sawe his long desired sight,
His moorning cloke of mone cast off, hath clad him with delight.
Yet dare I say, of both, that she rejoyced more:
His care was great, hers twise as great, was all the tyme before,
For whilst she knew not why he dyd himselfe absent,
Ay douting both his health and lyfe, his death she dyd lament.
For love is fearefull oft, where is no cause of feare
And what love feares, that love laments, as though it chaunced
      weare.
Of greater cause alway is greater woorke ybred:
While he nought douteth of her helth, she dreads lest he be
      ded.   480
When onely absence is the cause of Romeus smart:
By happy hope of sight agayne he feedes his fayntting hart.
What woonder then if he were wrapt in lesse annoye?
What marvell if by sodain sight she fed of greater joye?
His smaller greefe or joy no smaller love doo prove
Ne, for she passed him in both, did she him passe in love.
But eche of them alike dyd burne in equall flame,
The welbeloving knight, and eke the welbeloved dame.
Now whilst with bitter teares her eyes as fountaynes ronne,
With whispering voyce, ybroke with sobs, thus is her tale
      begonne.   490
Oh Romeus (of your lyfe) too lavas[1] sure you are,

---

[1] lavish, reckless.

That in this place, and at thys tyme to hasard it you dare,
What if your dedly foes, my kynsmen, saw you here?
Lyke Lyons wylde, your tender partes asonder would they teare.
In ruth and in disdayne, I weary of my life,
With cruell hand my moorning hart would perce with bloudy
    knyfe.
For you myne owne once dead, what joy should I have here?
And eke my honor staynde which I then lyfe doe holde more
    deare.
   Fayre lady myne dame Juliet my lyfe (quod he)
Even from my byrth committed was to fatall sisters three.   500
They may in spyte of foes, draw foorth my lively threed
And they also, who so sayth nay, asonder may it shreed.
But who to reave my lyfe, his rage and force would bende,
Perhaps should trye unto his payne how I it could defende.
Ne yet I love it so, but alwayes, for your sake,
A sacrifice to death I would my wounded corps betake.
If my mishappe were such, that here, before your sight,
I should restore agayne to death, of lyfe my borowde light,
This one thing and no more my parting sprite would rewe:
That part he should, before that you by certaine triall knew   510
The love I owe to you, the thrall I languish in
And how I dread to loose the gayne which I doe hope to win
And how I wishe for lyfe, not for my propre ease,
But that in it, you might I love, you honor, serve and please
Tyll dedly pangs the sprite out of the corps shall send.
And therupon he sware an othe, and so his tale had ende.
   Now love and pitty boyle, in Juliets ruthfull brest,
In windowe on her leaning arme, her weary hed doth rest,
Her bosome bathd in teares, to witnes inward payne,
With dreary chere to Romeus, thus aunswerd she agayne.   520
Ah my deere Romeus, keepe in these woordes (quod she)
For lo, the thought of such mischaunce, already maketh me
For pitty and for dred welnigh to yelde up breath.
In even ballance peysed are my life and eke my death,
For so my hart is knitte, yea, made one selfe with yours
That sure there is no greefe so small, by which your mynde
    endures,
But as you suffer payne, so I doe beare in part,
(Although it lessens not your greefe), the halfe of all your smart.
But these thinges overpast, if of your health and myne
You have respect, or pitty ought my teary weping eyen,   530
In few unfained woords, your hidden mynd unfolde,

That as I see your pleasant face, your heart I may beholde.
For if you doe intende my honor to defile
In error shall you wander still, as you have done this whyle,
But if your thought be chaste, and have on vertue ground,
If wedlocke be the ende and marke which your desire hath found,
Obedience set aside, unto my parentes dewe,
The quarell eke that long agoe betwene our housholdes grewe,
Both me and myne I will all whole to you betake
And following you where so you goe, my fathers house
        forsake.   540
But if by wanton love, and by unlawfull sute,
You thinke in ripest yeres to plucke my maydenho[o]ds dainty
        frute,
You are begylde, and now your Juliet you beseekes
To cease your sute, and suffer her to live emong her likes.
Then Romeus, whose thought was free from fowle desyre
And to the top of vertues haight, did worthely aspyre
Was fild with greater joy, then can my pen expresse
Or, till they have enjoyed the like, the hearers hart can gesse.
And then with joyned hands heavd up into the skies
He thankes the Gods, and from the heavens for vengeance
        downe he cries,   550
If he have other thought, but as his lady spake,
And then his looke he toornd to her, and thus did aunswer make.
Since Lady that you like to honor me so much,
As to accept me for your spouse, I yeld my selfe for such.
In true witnes wherof, because I must depart,
Till that my deede do prove my woord, I leave in pawne my hart.
To morow eke betimes, before the sunne arise,
To fryer Lawrence will I wende, to learne his sage advise.
He is my gostly syre, and oft he hath me taught
What I should doe in things of wayght, when I his ayde have
        sought.   560
And at this selfe same houre, I plyte you here my fayth:
I wil be here (if you thinke good) to tell you what he sayth.
She was contented well, els favour found he none
That night, at lady Juliets hand, save pleasant woordes alone.
    This barefoote fryer gyrt with cord his grayish weede,
For he of Frauncis order was, a fryer as I reede,
Not as the most was he, a grosse unlearned foole,
But doctor of divinitie proceded he in schoole.
The secretes eke he knew, in natures woorkes that loorke,
By magiks arte most men supposd that he could wonders
        woorke.   570

Ne doth it ill beseeme devines those skils to know
If on no harmefull deede they do such skilfulnes bestow.
For justly of no arte can men condemne the use
But right and reasons lore crye out agaynst the lewd abuse.
The bounty of the fryer and wisdom hath so wonne
The townes folks herts, that welnigh all to fryer Lawrence ronne
To shrive them selfe the olde, the yong, the great and small.
Of all he is beloved well, and honord much of all.
And for he did the rest in wisdome farre exceede,
The prince by him (his counsell cravde) was holpe at time of
    neede.   580
Betwixt the Capilets and him great frendship grew:
A secret and assured frend unto the Montegue.
Loved of this yong man more then any other gest,
The frier eke of Verone youth aye liked Romeus best,
For whom he ever hath, in time of his distres,
(As erst you heard) by skilfull lore, found out his harmes redresse.
To him is Romeus gonne, ne stayth he till the morowe,
To him he paynteth all his case, his passed joy and sorow,
How he hath her espyde with other dames in daunce,
And how that first to talke with her, himselfe he did
    advaunce.   590
Their talke and change of lookes he gan to him declare
And how so fast by fayth and troth they both ycoupled are
That neither hope of lyfe, nor dreed of cruel death,
Shall make him false his fayth to her while lyfe shall lend him
    breath.
And then with weping eyes he prayes his gostly syre
To further and accomplish all theyr honest hartes desire.
A thousand doutes and moe in thold mans hed arose,
A thousand daungers like to come, the olde man doth disclose,
And from the spousall rites he redeth him refrayne:
Perhaps he shalbe bet advisde within a weeke or twayne.   600
Advise is banishd quite from those that followe love,
Except advise to what they like theyr bending mynde do move.
As well the father might have counseld him to stay
That from a mountaines top thrown downe, is falling halfe the
    way,
As warne his frend to stop, amyd his race begonne,
Whom Cupid with his smarting whip enforceth foorth to ronne.
Part wonne by earnest sute, the fryer doth graunt at last.
And part, because he thinkes the stormes so lately overpast,
Of both the housholdes wrath, this mariage might apease,

So that they should not rage agayne, but quite for ever cease. 610
The respite of a day, he asketh to devyse
What way were best, unknowne to ende so great an enterprise.
The wounded man, that now doth dedly paines endure,
Scarce pacient tarieth whilst his leeche doth make the salve to
    cure,
So Romeus hardly graunts a short day and a night,
Yet nedes he must, els must he want his onely hearts delight.
    You see that Romeus no time or payne doth spare:
Thinke that the whilst fayre Juliet is not devoyde of care.
Yong Romeus powreth foorth his hap and his mishap,
Into the friers brest, but where shall Juliet unwrap   620
The secretes of her hart? to whom shall she unfolde,
Her hidden burning love, and eke her thought and cares so colde?
The nurce of whom I spake within her chaumber laye,
Upon the mayde she wayteth still; to her she doth bewray
Her new received wound, and then her ayde doth crave.
In her she saith it lyes to spill, in her her life to save.
Not easely she made the froward nurce to bowe
But wonne at length, with promest hyre she made a solemne
    vowe
To do what she commaundes, as handmayd of her hest,
Her mistres secrets hide she will, within her covert brest.   630
    To Romeus she goes; of him she doth desyre,
To know the meane of mariage, by councell of the fryre.
On Saterday, quod he, if Juliet come to shrift,
She shalbe shrived and maried, how lyke you noorse this drift?
Now by my truth (quod she) gods blessing have your hart
For yet in all my life I have not heard of such a part.
Lord how you yong men can such crafty wiles devise,
If that you love the daughter well to bleare the mothers eyes,
An easy thing it is with cloke of holines,
To mocke the sely mother that suspecteth nothing lesse   640
But that it pleased you to tell me of the case.
For all my many yeres perhaps, I should have found it scarse.
Now for the rest let me and Juliet alone.
To get her leave, some feate excuse I will devise anone,
For that her golden lockes by sloth have been unkempt,
Or for unwares some wanton dreame the youthfull damsell
    drempt,
Or for in thoughts of love her ydel time she spent,
Or otherwise within her hart deserved to be shent.
I know her mother will in no case say her nay,

I warrant you she shall not fayle to come on Saterday.   650
And then she sweares to him, the mother loves her well,
And how she gave her sucke in youth she leaveth not to tell.
A prety babe (quod she), it was when it was yong,
Lord how it could full pretely have prated with it tong,
A thousand times and more I laid her on my lappe,
And clapt her on the buttocke soft and kist where I did clappe
And gladder then was I of such a kisse forsooth,
Then I had been to have a kisse of some olde lechers mouth.
And thus of Juliets youth began this prating noorse,
And of her present state to make a tedious long discoorse.   660
For though he pleasure tooke in hearing of his love,
The message aunswer seemed him to be of more behove.
But when these Beldams sit at ease upon theyr tayle,
The day and eke the candle light before theyr talke shall fayle
And part they say is true, and part they do devise,
Yet boldly do they chat of both when no man checkes theyr lyes.
Then he .vi. crownes of gold out of his pocket drew
And gave them her, a slight reward (quod he) and so adiew.
In seven yeres twise tolde she had not bowd so lowe,
Her crooked knees, as now they bowe, she sweares she will
    bestowe   670
Her crafty wit, her time, and all her busy payne,
To helpe him to his hoped blisse, and, cowring downe agayne,
She takes her leave, and home she hyes with spedy pace.
The chaumber doore she shuts, and then she saith with smyling
    face,
Good newes for thee, my gyrle, good tidinges I thee bring,
Leave of thy woonted song of care and now of pleasure sing.
For thou mayst hold thy selfe the happiest under sonne
That in so little while, so well so worthy a knight hast wonne.
The best yshapde is he, and hath the fayrest face,
Of all this towne, and there is none hath halfe so good a
    grace,   680
So gentle of his speche, and of his counsell wise,
And still with many prayses more she heaved him to the skies.
Tell me els what (quod she) this evermore I thought,
But of our mariage say at once, what aunswer have you brought?
Nay, soft, quoth she, I feare your hurt by sodain joye.
I list not play quoth Juliet, although thou list to toye.
How glad trow you was she, when she had heard her say
No farther of then Saterday, differred was the day.
Againe the auncient nurce doth speake of **Romeus**,

And then (said she) he spake to me, and then I spake him
    thus.   690
Nothing was done or said, that she hath left untolde,
Save onely one, that she forgot the taking of the golde.
There is no losse quod she, (sweete wench) to losse of time,
Ne in thine age shalt thou repent so much of any crime.
For when I call to mynde, my former passed youth
One thing there is which most of all doth cause my endles ruth.
At sixtene yeres I first did choose my loving feere,
And I was fully ripe before, (I dare well say) a yere.
The pleasure that I lost, that yere so overpast,
A thousand times I have bewept, and shall while lyfe doth
    last.   700
In fayth it were a shame, yea sinne it were ywisse,
When thou mayst live in happy joy to set light by thy blisse.
She that this mornyng could her mistres mynde disswade,
Is now becomme an Oratresse, her lady to perswade.
If any man be here, whom love hath clad with care,
To him I speake, if thou wilt spede, thy purse thou must not
    spare.
Two sortes of men there are, seld welcome in at doore,
The welthy sparing nigard, and the sutor that is poore
For glittring gold is woont by kynd to moove the hart,
And often times a slight rewarde doth cause a more desart.   710
Ywritten have I red, I wot not in what booke,
There is no better way to fishe, then with a golden hooke.
Of Romeus these two, doe sitte and chat a while,
And to them selfe they laugh, how they the mother shall begyle.
A feate excuse they finde, but sure I know it not
And leave for her to goe to shrift on Saterday she got.
So well this Juliet, this wyly wench dyd know
Her mothers angry houres, and eke the true bent of her bowe.
The Saterday betimes in sober weede yclad,
She tooke her leave, and forth she went with visage grave and
    sad.   720
With her the nurce is sent as brydle of her lust,
With her the mother sendes a mayde, almost of equall trust.
Betwixt her teeth the bytte, the Jenet now hath cought,
So warely eke the vyrgin walkes her mayde perceiveth nought.
She gaseth not in churche, on yong men of the towne,
Ne wandreth she from place to place, but straight she kneleth
    downe
Upon an alters step, where she devoutly prayes:

And there upon her tender knees the wery lady stayes
Whilst she doth send her mayde the certain truth to know,
If fryer Lawrence laysure had, to heare her shrift, or no.   730
Out of his shriving place he commes with pleasant cheere:
The shamefast mayde with bashfull brow to himward draweth
    neere.
Some great offence (quoth he) you have committed late,
Perhaps you have displeasd your frend, by geving him a mate.
Then turning to the nurce, and to the other mayde:
Goe heare a masse or two quod he, which straight way shalbe
    sayde,
For her confession heard, I will unto you twayne
The charge that I receivd of you, restore to you agayne.
What, was not Juliet trow you, right well apayde
That for this trusty fryre hath chaungde her yong mistrusting
    mayde?   740
I dare well say there is in all Verona none
But Romeus, with whom she would so gladly be alone.
Thus to the fryers cell, they both foorth walked bin:
He shuts the doore as soone as he and Juliet were in.
But Romeus her frend was entred in before
And there had wayted for his love, two howers large and more.
Eche minute seemde an howre, and every howre a day:
Twixt hope he lived and despayre, of cumming or of stay.
Now wavering hope and feare, are quite fled out of sight
For what he hopde he hath at hande his pleasant cheefe
    delight   750
And joyfull Juliet is healde of all her smart,
For now the rest of all her parts, have found her straying hart.
Both theyr confessions first the fryer hath heard them make
And then to her with lowder voyce thus fryer Lawrence spake.
Fayre lady Juliet, my gostly doughter deere,
As farre as I of Romeus learne, who by you standeth here,
Twixt you it is agreed that you shalbe his wyfe
And he your spouse in steady truth till death shall end your life.
Are you both fully bent to kepe this great behest?
And both the lovers said it was theyr onely harts request.   760
When he did see theyr myndes in linkes of love so fast:
When in the prayse of wedlocks state somme skilfull talke was
    past.
When he had told at length the wife what was her due:
His duety eke by gostly talke the youthfull husband knew.
How that the wife in love must honor and obay:

What love and honor he doth owe, and dette that he must pay.
The woords pronounced were which holy church of olde
Appointed hath for mariage: and she a ring of golde
Received of Romeus: and then they both arose.
To whom the frier then said, perchaunce a part you will
    disclose   770
Betwixt your selfe alone the bottome of your hart,
Say on at once, for time it is that hence you should depart.
Then Romeus said to her, (both loth to part so soone),
Fayre lady send to me agayne your nurce this after-noone.
Of corde I will bespeake, a ladder by that time,
By which, this night, while other sleepe, I will your window clime.
Then will we talke of love, and of our olde dispayres
And then with longer laysure had, dispose our great affaires.
    These said, they kisse, and then part to theyr fathers house,
The joyfull bryde unto her home, to his eke goth the spouse.   780
Contented both, and yet both uncontented still
Till night and Venus child, geve leave the wedding to fulfill.
The painfull souldiour sore ybet with wery warre,
The merchant eke that nedefull things doth dred to fetch from
    farre,
The plowman that for doute of feerce invading foes,
Rather to sit in ydle ease then sowe his tilt[h] hath chose,
Rejoyce to heare proclaymd the tydinges of the peace.
Not pleasurd with the sound so much, but when the warres do
    cease
Then ceased are the harmes which cruell warre bringes foorth.
The merchant then may boldly fetch, his wares of precious
    woorth,   790
Dredelesse the husband man doth till his fertile feeld,
For welth her mate, not for her selfe, is peace so precious held.
So lovers live in care, in dread, and in unrest
And dedly warre by striving thoughts they kepe within their brest.
But wedlocke is the peace wherby is freedome wonne,
To do a thousand pleasant thinges that should not els be donne.
The newes of ended warre these two have h[e]ard with joy
But now they long the fruite of peace with pleasure to enjoy.
In stormy wind and wave, in daunger to be lost,
Thy stearles ship (O Romeus) hath been long while betost.   800
The seas are now appeasd, and thou by happy starre
Art comme in sight of quiet haven and, now the wrackfull barre
Is hid with swelling tyde, boldly thou mayst resort
Unto thy wedded ladies bed, thy long desyred port.

God graunt no follies mist, so dymme thy inward sight,
That thou do misse the chanell, that doth leade to thy delight.
God graunt no daungers rocke, ylurking in the darke,
Before thou win the happy port, wracke thy sea beaten barke.
A servant Romeus had, of woord and deede so just,
That with his life (if nede requierd) his master would him
    trust.   810
His faithfulnes had oft our Romeus proved of olde
And therfore all that yet was done unto his man he tolde,
Who straight as he was charged, a corden ladder lookes
To which he hath made fast two strong and crooked yron hookes.
The bryde to send the nurce at twylight fayleth not,
To whom the bridegroome geven hath, the ladder that he got,
And then to watch for him appointeth her an howre
For whether Fortune smyle on him, or if she list to lowre,
He will not misse to comme to his appoynted place,
Where wont he was to take by stelth the view of Juliets
    face.   820
How long these lovers thought the lasting of the day,
Let other judge that woonted are lyke passions to assay.
For my part, I do gesse eche howre seemes twenty yere
So that I deeme, if they might have (as of Alcume[1] we heare)
The sunne bond to theyr will, if they the heavens might gyde,
Black shade of night and doubled darke should straight all over
    hyde.
   Thappointed howre is comme, he clad in riche araye,
Walkes toward his desyred home, good Fortune gyde his way.
Approching nere the place from whence his hart had life,
So light he wox, he lept the wall, and there he spyde his
    wife,   830
Who in the windowe watcht the cumming of her lorde,
Where she so surely had made fast the ladder made of corde
That daungerles her spouse the chaumber window climes,
Where he ere then had wisht himselfe above ten thousand times.
The windowes close are shut, els looke they for no gest,
To light the waxen quariers, the auncient nurce is prest,
Which Juliet had before prepared to be light,
That she at pleasure might beholde her husbandes bewty bright.
A Carchef white as snowe, ware Juliet on her hed,
Such as she wonted was to weare, attyre meete for the bed.   840
As soone as she him spyde, about his necke she clong
And by her long and slender armes a great while there she hong.

[1] Alcmena and Zeus.

A thousand times she kist, and him unkist agayne
Ne could she speake a woord to him though would she nere so
    fayne.
And like betwixt his armes to faynt his lady is,
She fettes a sigh, and clappeth close her closed mouth to his
And ready then to sownde she looked ruthfully
That loe, it made him both at once to live and eke to dye.
These piteous painfull panges were haply overpast
And she unto her selfe agayne retorned home at last.   850
Then through her troubled brest, even from the farthest part,
An hollow sigh, a messenger she sendeth from her hart.
O Romeus quoth she, in whome all vertues shyne,
Welcome thou art into this place where from these eyes of myne
Such teary streames dyd flowe, that I suppose welny
The source of all my bitter teares is altogether drye.
Absence so pynde my heart, which on thy presence fed,
And of thy safetie and thy health so much I stood in dred.
But now what is decreed by fatall desteny,
I force it not, let Fortune do and death their woorst to me.   860
Full recompensd am I for all my passed harmes,
In that the Gods have graunted me to claspe thee in myne armes.
The christall teares began to stand in Romeus eyes,
When he unto his ladies woordes, gan aunswere in this wise.
Though cruell Fortune be so much my dedly foe
That I ne can by lively proofe cause thee (fayre dame) to knowe
How much I am by love enthralled unto thee,
Ne yet what mighty powre thou hast by thy desert on me,
Ne tormentes that for thee I did ere this endure,
Yet of thus much (ne will I fayne) I may thee well assure.   870
The least of many paynes, which of thy absence sprong,
More paynefully then death it selfe my tender hart hath wroong,
Ere this one death had reft a thousand deathes away
But lyfe prolonged was by hope, of this desired day,
Which so just tribute payes of all my passed mone
That I as well contented am as if my selfe alone
Did from the Occean reigne unto the sea of Inde.
Wherfore now let us wipe away old cares out of our mynde,
For as the wretched state is now redrest at last,
So is it skill behinde our backe the cursed care to cast.   880
Since Fortune of her grace hath place and time assi[g]nde
Where we with pleasure may content our uncontented minde,
In Lethes hyde we deepe all greefe and all annoy,
Whilst we do bath in blisse, and fill our hungry harts with joye.

And for the time to comme, let be our busy care,
So wisely to direct our love as no wight els be ware,
Lest envious foes by force despoyle our new delight,
And us throwe backe from happy state to more unhappy plight.
Fayre Juliet began to aunswere what he sayde:
But foorth in hast the olde nurce stept, and so her aunswere
    stayde.   890
Who takes not time (quoth she) when time well offred is,
An other time shall seeke for time, and yet of time shall misse,
And when occasion serves, who so doth let it slippe,
Is woorthy sure (if I might judge) of lashes with a whippe.
Wherfore, if eche of you hath harmde the other so,
And eche of you hath been the cause of others wayled woe,
Loe here a fielde, (she shewd a fieeldbed ready dight)
Where you may, if you list, in armes, revenge your selfe by fight.
Wherto these lovers both gan easely assent,
And to the place of mylde revenge with pleasant cheere they
    went,   900
Where they were left alone, the nurce is gone to rest.
How can this be? they restles lye, ne yet they feele unrest.
I graunt that I envie the blisse they lived in:
Oh that I might have found the like, I wish it for no sin.
But that I might as well with pen their joyes depaynt,
As heretofore I have displayd their secret hidden playnt.
Of shyvering care and dred, I have felt many a fit,
But Fortune such delight as theyrs dyd never graunt me yet.
By proofe no certain truth can I unhappy write,
But what I gesse by likelihod, that dare I to endite.   910
The blyndfyld goddesse that with frowning face doth fraye,
And from theyr seate the mighty kinges throwes downe with
    hedlong sway,
Begynneth now to turne, to these her smyling face,
Nedes must they tast of great delight, so much in Fortunes grace.
If Cupid, God of love, be God of pleasant sport,
I thinck O Romeus Mars himselfe envies thy happy sort.
Ne Venus justly might, (as I suppose) repent,
If in thy stead (O Juliet) this pleasant time she spent.
    Thus passe they foorth the night in sport, in joly game:
The hastines of Phoebus steeds in great despyte they blame.   920
And now the virgins fort hath warlike Romeus got,
In which as yet no breache was made by force of canon shot,
And now in ease he doth possesse the hoped place.
How glad was he, speake you that may your lovers parts embrace.

The mariage thus made up, and both the parties pleasd,
The nigh approche of dayes retoorne these seely foles[1] diseasd,
And for they might no while in pleasure passe theyr time,
Ne leysure had they much to blame the hasty mornings crime.
With frendly kisse in armes of her his leave he takes,
And every other night to come, a solemne othe he makes.   930
By one selfe meane, and eke to come at one selfe howre:
And so he doth till Fortune list to sawse his sweete with sowre.
But who is he that can his present state assure
And say unto himselfe, thy joyes shall yet a day endure?
So wavering Frotunes whele her chaunges be so straunge
And every wight ythralled is by fate unto her chaunge,
Who raignes so over all, that eche man hath his part
(Although not aye perchaunce alike) of pleasure and of smart.
For after many joyes, some feele but little payne
And from that little greefe they toorne to happy joy againe.   940
But other somme there are, that living long in woe,
At length they be in quiet ease, but long abide not so.
Whose greefe is much increast by myrth that went before
Because the sodayne chaunge of thinges doth make it seeme the
          more.
Of this unlucky sorte our Romeus is one
For all his hap turnes to mishap, and all his myrth to mone.
And joyfull Juliet an other leafe must toorne
As wont she was (her joyes bereft), she must begin to moorne.
     The summer of their blisse, doth last a month or twayne
But winters blast with spedy foote doth bring the fall agayne.   950
Whom glorious fortune erst had heaved to the skies
By envious fortune overthrowne on earth now groveling lyes.
She payd theyr former greefe with pleasures doubled gayne,
But now for pleasures usery ten folde redoubleth payne.
     The prince could never cause those housholds so agree,
But that some sparcles of their wrath, as yet remaining bee
Which lye this while rak'd up, in ashes pale and ded,
Till tyme do serve that they agayne in wasting flame may spred.
At holiest times, men say most heynous crimes are donne;
The morowe after Easter day the mischiefe new begonne.   960
A band of Capilets did meete (my hart it rewes)
Within the walles, by Pursers gate, a band of Montagewes.
The Capilets as cheefe, a yong man have chose out,
Best exercisd in feates of armes, and noblest of the rowte,
Our Juliets unkles sonne that cliped was Tibalt.

---

[1] 'poor innocents'.

He was of body tall and strong, and of his courage halt.
They neede no trumpet sounde to byd them geve the charge,
So lowde he cryde with strayned voyce and mouth outstretched
    large.
Now, now, (quod he) my frends, our selfe so let us wreake,
That of this dayes revenge, and us, our childrens heyres may
    speake.   970
Now once for all let us their swelling pride asswage,
Let none of them escape alive; then he with furious rage
And they with him gave charge, upon theyr present foes,
And then forthwith a skyrmishe great upon this fray arose.
For loe, the Montagewes thought shame away to flye,
And rather then to live with shame, with prayse did choose to
    dye.
The woordes that Tybalt usd to styre his folke to yre,
Have in the brestes of Montagewes kindled a furious fyre.
With Lyons hartes they fight, warely themselfe defende,
To wound his foe, his present wit and force eche one doth
    bend.   980
This furious fray is long, on eche side stoutly fought,
That whether part had got the woorst full doutfull were the
    thought.
The noyse hereof anon, throughout the towne doth flye
And partes are taken on every side, both kinreds thether hye.
Here one doth gaspe for breth, his frend bestrideth him,
And he hath lost a hand, and he another maymed lim,
His leg is cutte whilst he strikes at an other full
And whom he would have thrust quite through hath cleft his
    cracked skull.
Theyr valiant harts forbode theyr foote to geve the grounde,
With unappauled cheere they tooke full deepe and doutfull
    wounde.   990
Thus foote by foote long while, and shield to shield set fast,
One foe doth make another faynt but makes him not agast.
And whilst this noyse is ryfe in every townes mans eare,
Eke walking with his frendes, the noyse doth wofull Romeus heare.
With spedy foote he ronnes unto the fray apace,
With him those fewe that were with him he leadeth to the place.
They pittie much to see the slaughter made so greate,
That wetshod they might stand in blood on eyther side the streate.
Part frendes (sayd he) part frendes, helpe frendes to part the fray
And to the rest, enough (he cryes) now time it is to staye.   1000
Gods farther wrath you styrre, beside the hurt you feele

And with this new uprore confounde all this our common wele.
But they so busy are in fight so egar and feerce.
That through theyr eares his sage advise no leysure had to pearce.
Then lept he in the throng, to part, and barre the blowes,
As well of those that were his frendes as of his dedly foes.
As soone as Tybalt had our Romeus espyde,
He threw a thrust at him that would have past from side to side,
But Romeus ever went (douting his foes) well armde
So that the swerd (kept out by mayle) hath nothing Romeus
    harmde.   1010
Thou doest me wrong (quoth he) for I but part the fraye,
Not dread, but other waighty cause my hasty hand doth stay.
Thou art the cheefe of thine, the noblest eke thou art:
Wherfore leave of thy malice now, and helpe these folke to parte.
Many are hurt, some slayne, and some are like to dye.
No, coward, traytor boy (quoth he) straight way I mynd to trye
Whether thy sugred talke, and tong so smothely fylde,
Against the force of this my swerd shall serve thee for a shylde.
And then at Romeus hed, a blow he strake so hard,
That might have clove him to the brayne but for his cunning
    ward.   1020
It was but lent to him that could repay agayne
And geve him death for interest, a well forborne gayne.
Right as a forest bore, that lodged in the thicke,
Pinched with dog, or els with speare ypricked to the quicke,
His bristles stiffe upright upon his backe doth set,
And in his fomy mouth, his sharp and crooked tuskes doth whet,
Or as a Lyon wylde that rampeth in his rage,
His whelpes bereft, whose fury can no weaker beast asswage,
Such seemed Romeus in every others sight,
When he him shope, of wrong receavde tavenge himselfe by
    fight.   1030
Even as two thunderboltes, throwne downe out of the skye,
That through the ayre the massy earth and seas have power to
    flye,
So met these two, and while they chaunge a blowe or twayne,
Our Romeus thrust him through the throte and so is Tybalt
    slayne.
Loe here the ende of those that styrre a dedly stryfe:
Who thyrsteth after others death, himselfe hath lost his life.
The Capilets are quaylde, by Tibalts overthrowe,
The courage of the Mountagewes, by Romeus sight doth growe,
The townes men waxen strong, the prince doth send his force,

The fray hath end, the Capilets do bring the brethles corse,   1040
Before the prince and crave that cruell dedly payne
May be the guerdon of his falt, that hath their kinsman slaine.
The Montagewes do pleade, theyr Romeus voyde of falt,
The lookers on do say, the fight begonne was by Tybalt,
The prince doth pawse, and then geves sentence in a while,
That Romeus, for sleying him should goe into exyle.
His foes would have him hangde, or sterve in prison strong,
His frendes do think (but dare not say) that Romeus hath wrong.
Both housholds straight are charged on payne of losing lyfe,
Theyr bloudy weapons layd aside, to cease the styrred stryfe.   1050
This common plag[u]e is spred, through all the towne anon,
From side to syde the towne is fild with murmour and with mone
For Tybalts hasty death, bewayled was of somme,
Both for his skill in feates of armes, and for in time to comme
He should (had this not chaunced) been riche, and of great powre
To helpe his frendes, and serve the state, which hope within an
       howre
Was wasted quite, and he thus yelding up his breath,
More then he holpe the towne in lyfe, hath harmde it by his
       death.
And other somme bewayle, (but ladies most of all)
The lookeles lot by Fortunes gylt, that is so late befall,   1060
(Without his falt) unto the seely Romeus,
For whilst that he from natife land shall live exyled thus,
From heavenly bewties light, and his welshaped parts,
The sight of which, was wont (faire dames) to glad your youthfull
       harts,
Shall you be banishd quite, and tyll he do retoorne
What hope have you to joy? what hope to cease to moorne?
This Romeus was borne so much in heavens grace
Of Fortune, and of nature so beloved, that in his face,
(Beside the heavenly bewty glistring ay so bright
And seemely grace that wonted so to glad the seers sight),   1070
A certain charme was graved by natures secret arte
That vertue had to draw to it, the love of many a hart.
So every one doth wish, to beare a part of payne,
That he released of exyle, might straight retorne agayne.
But how doth moorne emong the moorners Juliet?
How doth she bathe her brest in teares? what depe sighes doth
       she fet?
How doth she tear her heare? her weede how doth she rent?
How fares the lover hearing of her lovers banishment?

How wayles she Tibalts death, whom she had loved so well?
Her hearty greefe and piteous plaint, cunning I want to tell   1080
For delving depely now in depth of depe dispayre,
With wretched sorowes cruell sound she fils the empty ayre
And to the lowest hell, downe falles her heavy crye,
And up unto the heavens haight her piteous plaint doth flye.
The waters and the woods, of sighes and sobs resounde
And from the hard resounding rockes her sorowes do rebounde.
Eke from her teary eyne, downe rayned many a showre
That in the garden where she walkd might water herbe and
          flowre.
But when at length she saw her selfe outraged so,
Unto her chaumber straight she hied, there, overchargd with
     wo,   1090
Upon her stately bed, her painfull parts she threw
And in so wondrous wise began her sorowes to renewe
That sure no hart so hard, (but it of flint had byn,)
But would have rued the pitious plaint that she did languishe in.
Then rapt out of her selfe, whilst she on every side
Did cast her restles eye, at length the windowe she espide,
Through which she had with joy seene Romeus many a time,
Which oft the ventrous knight was wont for Juliets sake to clyme.
     She cryde, O cursed windowe, a[c]curst be every pane,
Through which (alas) too soone I raught the cause of life and
     bane.   1100
If by thy meane I have some slight delight receaved,
Or els such fading pleasure as by Fortune straight was reaved,
Hast thou not made me pay a tribute rigorous
Of heaped greefe, and lasting care, and sorowes dolorous,
That these my tender partes, which nedefull strength do lacke,
To beare so great unweldy lode, upon so weake a backe
Opprest with waight of cares and with these sorowes rife,
At length must open wide to death, the gates of lothed lyfe?
That so my wery sprite, may somme where els unlode
His deadly lode, and free from thrall may seeke els where
     abode   1110
For pleasant quiet ease, and for assured rest,
Which I as yet could never finde, but for my more unrest.
O Romeus, when first we both acquainted were,
When to thy paynted promises I lent my listning eare
Which to the brinkes you fild with many a solemne othe,
And I them judgde empty of gyle, and fraughted full of troth,
I thought you rather would continue our good will,

And seeke tappease our fathers strife which daily groweth still.
I little wend you would have sought occasion how
By such an heynous act to breake the peace, and eke your
    vowe   1120
Wherby your bright renoune, all whole yclipsed is,
And I unhappy, husbandles, of cumfort robde, and blisse.
But if you did so much the blood of Capels thyrst,
Why have you often spared mine? myne might have quencht it
    first,
Since that so many times, and in so secret place,
(Where you were wont with veile of love to hyde your hatreds
    face),
My doutfull lyfe hath hapt by fatall dome to stand,
In mercy of your cruell hart, and of your bloudy hand.
What? seemd the conquest which you got of me, so small?
What? seemd it not enough that I, poore wretch, was made
    your thrall?   1130
But that you must increase it with that kinsmans blood,
Which, for his woorth and love to me, most in my favour stood?
Well, goe henceefoorth els where, and seeke another whyle,
Some other as unhappy as I, by flattry to begyle
And where I comme, see that you shonne to shew your face,
For your excuse within my hart shall finde no resting place.
And I that now too late my former fault repent
Will so the rest of wery life with many teares lament
That soone my joyceles corps, shall yeld up banishd breath,
And where on earth it restles lived, in earth seeke rest by
    death.   1140
    These sayde, her tender hart, by payne oppressed sore,
Restraynd her teares, and forced her tong to keepe her talke in
    store.
And then as still she was, as if in s[w]ownd she lay,
And then agayne, wroth with her selfe, with feble voyce gan say.
    Ah cruell murthering tong, murthrer of others fame,
How durst thou once attempt to tooch the honor of his name?
Whose dedly foes doe yelde him dewe and earned prayse,
For though his fredome be bereft, his honor not decayes.
Why blamst thou Romeus for sleying of Tybalt,
Since he is gyltles quite of all, and Tybalt beares the falt?   1150
Whether shall he (alas), poore banishd man, now flye?
What place of succor shall he seeke beneth the starry skye,
Synce she pursueth him, and him defames by wrong
That in distres should be his fort, and onely rampier strong?
Receive the recompence, O Romeus, of thy wife,

Who, for she was unkind her selfe, doth offer up her lyfe.
In flames of yre, in sighes, in sorow and in ruth,
So to revenge the crime she did commit against thy truth.
These said, she could no more, her senses all gan fayle
And dedly panges began straight way her tender hart
 assayle.   1160
Her limmes she stretched forth, she drew no more her breath,
Who had been there, might well have seene the signes of present
 death.
The nurce that knew no cause, why she absented her,
Did doute lest that some sodain greefe too much tormented her.
Eche where but where she was the carefull Beldam sought,
Last, of the chamber where she lay, she haply her bethought,
Where she with piteous eye, her nurce childe did beholde:
Her limmes stretched out, her utward parts as any marble colde.
The nurce supposde that she had payde to death her det
And then as she had lost her wittes, she cryed to Juliet. 1170
Ah my dere hart (quoth she) how greeveth me thy death?
Alas what cause hast thou thus soone to yelde up living breath?
But while she handled her, and chafed every part,
She knew there was some sparke of life by beating of her hart,
So that a thousand times she cald upon her name.
There is no way to helpe a traunce, but she hath tryde the same.
She openeth wide her mouth, she stoppeth close her nose,
She bendeth downe her brest, she wringes her fingers and her toes,
And on her bosome colde, she layeth clothes hot,
A warmed and a holesome juyce she powreth downe her
 throte.   1180
At length doth Juliet heave fayntly up her eyes,
And then she stretcheth forth her arme, and then her nurce she
 spyes.
But when she was awakde from her unkindly traunce:
Why dost thou trouble me (quoth she) what drave thee (with
 mischaunce)
To come to see my sprite, forsake my brethles corse?
Goe hence, and let me dye, if thou have on my smart remorse.
For who would see her frend to live in dedly payne?
Alas, I see my greefe begoone, for ever will remayne.
Or who would seeke to liue, all pleasure being past?
My myrth is donne, my moorning mone for ay is like to
 last.   1190
Wherfore since that there is none other remedy,
Comme gentle death, and ryve my hart at once, and let me dye.

The nurce with tricling teares, to witnes inward smart,
With holow sigh fetchd from the depth, of her appauled hart,
Thus spake to Juliet, yclad with ougly care.
Good lady myne, I do not know what makes you thus to fare,
Ne yet the cause of your unmeasurde heavines,
But of this one I you assure, for care and sorowes stresse,
This hower large and more, I thought (so god me save)
That my dead corps should wayte on yours, to your untimely
      grave.   1200
Alas my tender nurce, and trusty frend (quoth she)
Art thou so blinde, that with thine eye, thou canst not easely see
The lawfull cause I have, to sorow and to moorne,
Since those the which I hyld most deere I have at once forlorne?
Her nurce then aunswerd thus. Me thinkes it sits you yll,
To fall in these extremities that may you gyltles spill,
For when the stormes of care, and troubles do aryse,
Then is the time for men to know, the foolish from the wise.
You are accounted wise, a foole am I your nurce
But I see not how in like case I could behave me wurse.   1210
Tibalt your frend is ded, what, weene you by your teares,
To call him backe againe? thinke you that he your crying heares?
You shall perceve the falt, (if it be justly tryde)
Of his so sodayn death, was in his rashnes and his pryde.
Would you that Romeus, him selfe had wronged so,
To suffer himselfe causeles to be outraged of his foe
To whom in no respect, he ought a place to geve?
Let it suffise to thee fayre dame, that Romeus doth live,
And that there is good hope that he, within a while,
With greater glory shalbe calde home from his hard exile.   1220
How wel yborne he is, thy selfe I know canst tell,
By kindred strong, and well alyed, of all beloved well.
With patience arme thy selfe, for though that Fortunes cryme,
Without your falt, to both your greefes depart you for a time,
I dare say for amendes of all your present payne
She will restore your owne to you, within a month or twayne,
With such contented ease, as never erst you had.
Wherfore rejoyce a while in hope, and be ne more so sad.
And that I may discharge your hart of heavy care
A certaine way I have found out, my paynes ne will I spare   1230
To learne his present state, and what in time to comme
He mindes to doe, which knowne by me, you shall know all and
      somme.
But that I dread the whilst your sorowes will you quell,

Straight would I hye, where he doth lurke, to frier Lawrence cell.
But if you gyn eftsones (as erst you did) to moorne,
Wherto goe I, you will be ded before I thence retoorne.
So I shall spend in wast, my time and busy payne,
So unto you (your life once lost) good aunswere commes in vayne,
So shall I ridde my selfe with this sharpe pointed knife,
So shall you cause your parents deere wax wery of theyr life,   1240
So shall your Romeus, (despysing lively breath,)
With hasty foote (before his tyme) ronne to untimely death.
Where if you can a while, by reason, rage suppresse,
I hope at my retorne to bring the salve of your distresse.
Now choose to have me here a partner of your payne,
Or promesse me, to feede on hope, till I retorne agayne.
    Her mistres sendes her forth, and makes a grave behest,
With reasons rayne to rule the thoughts that rage within her brest.
When hugy heapes of harmes, are heapd before her eyes,
Then vanish they by hope of scape, and thus the lady lyes,   1250
Twixt well assured trust, and doutfull lewd dispayre,
Now blacke and ougly be her thoughts, now seeme they white and
    fayre.
As oft in summer tide, blacke cloudes do dimme the sonne,
And straight againe in clearest skye his restles steedes do ronne,
So Juliets wandring mynd yclowded is with woe,
And by and by her hasty thought the woes doth overgoe.
    But now is time to tell, whilst she was tossed thus,
What windes did drive or haven did hold her lover, Romeus.
When he had slayne his foe, that gan this dedly strife,
And saw the furious fray had ende, by ending Tybalts life,   1260
He fled the sharpe revenge of those that yet did live,
And douting much what penall doome the troubled prince myght
    gyve,
He sought some where unseene, to lurke a little space,
And trusty Lawrence secret cell, he thought the surest place.
In doutfull happe ay best, a trusty frend is tride,
The frendly fryer in this distresse, doth graunt his frend to hyde.
A secret place he hath, well seeled round about,
The mouth of which, so close is shut, that none may finde it out
But roome there is to walke, and place to sitte and rest,
Beside, a bed to sleape upon, full soft and trimly drest.   1270
The flowre is planked so with mattes, it is so warme,
That neither wind, nor smoky damps have powre him ought to
    harme.
Where he was wont in youth, his fayre frendes to bestowe,

There now he hydeth Romeus whilst forth he goeth to knowe
Both what is sayd and donne, and what appoynted payne
Is published by trumpets sound; then home he hyes agayne.
  By this, unto his cell, the nurce, with spedy pace,
Was comme the nerest way: she sought no ydel resting place.
The fryer sent home the newes of Romeus certain helth
And promesse made (what so befell) he should that night by
    stelth   1280
Comme to his wonted place that they in nedefull wise
Of theyr affayres in time to comme, might thorowly devyse.
Those joyfull newes, the nurce brought home with mery joy
And now our Juliet joyes to thinke, she shall her love enjoye.
The fryer shuts fast his doore, and then to him beneth,
That waytes to heare the doutefull newes of lyfe or els of death,
Thy hap quoth he, is good, daunger of death is none
But thou shalt live, and doe full well, in spite of spitefull fone.
This onely payne for thee was erst proclaymde aloude,
A banishd man, thou mayst thee not within Verona
    shroude.   1290
  These heavy tydinges heard, his golden lockes he tare
And, like a frantike man, hath torne the garmentes that he ware.
And as the smitten deere, in brakes is waltring found,
So waltreth he, and with his brest doth beate the troden grounde.
He rises eft, and strikes his head against the wals,
He falleth downe againe, and lowde for hasty death he cals.
Come spedy death (quoth he) the readiest leache in love,
Since nought can els beneth the sunne the ground of griefe
    remove,
Of lothsome life breake downe the hated staggering stayes,
Destroy, destroy at once the lyfe that faintly yet decayes.   1300
But you (fayre dame) in whome dame nature dyd devise,
With cunning hand to woorke, that might seeme wondrous in our
    eyes,
For you I pray the Gods, your pleasures to increase,
And all mishap, with this my death, for evermore to cease.
And mighty Jove with speede, of justice bring them lowe,
Whose lofty pryde (without our gylt) our blisse doth overblowe.
And Cupide graunt to those theyr spedy wrongs redresse,
That shall bewayle my cruell death, and pity her distresse.
Therewith, a cloude of sighes, he breathd into the skies
And two great streames of bitter teares, ran from his swollen
    eyes.   1310
These thinges, the auncient fryre, with sorow saw, and heard,

Of such begynning eke, the ende, the wise man greatly feard.
But loe, he was so weake, by reason of his age,
That he ne could by force, represse the rigour of his rage.
His wise and frendly woordes, he speaketh to the ayre
For Romeus so vexed is, with care and with dispayre,
That no advise can perce, his close forstopped eares,
So now the fryer doth take his part, in shedding ruthfull teares.
With colour pale, and wan, with armes full hard yfold,
With wofull cheere, his wayling frend, he standeth to
    beholde.   1320
And then, our Romeus, with tender handes ywrong,
With voyce, with plaint made horce, with sobs, and with a foltring
    tong,
Renewd with novel mone the dolours of his hart,
His outward dreery cheere bewrayde, his store of inward smart.
Fyrst, nature did he blame, the author of his lyfe,
In which his joyes had been so scant, and sorowes aye so ryfe;
The time and place of byrth, he fiersly did reprove,
He cryed out (with open mouth) against the starres above;
The fatall sisters three, he said, had done him wrong,
The threed that should not have been sponne they had drawne
    foorth too long.   1330
He wished that he [ne] had before this time been borne,
Or that as soone as he wan light, his life he had forlorne.
His nurce he cursed, and the hand that gave him pappe,
The midwife eke with tender grype that held him in her lappe
And then did he complaine, on Venus cruel sonne,
Who led him first unto the rockes, which he should warely shonne,
By meane wherof he lost, both lyfe and libertie,
And dyed a hundred times a day, and yet could never dye.
Loves troubles lasten long, the joyes he geves are short:
He forceth not a lovers payne, theyr ernest is his sport.   1340
A thousand thinges and more, I here let passe to write,
Which unto love this wofull man, dyd speake in great despite.
On Fortune eke he raylde, he calde her deafe, and blynde,
Unconstant, fond, deceitfull, rashe, unruthfull, and unkynd
And to him self he layd a great part of the falt,
For that he slewe, and was not slayne, in fighting with Tibalt.
He blamed all the world, and all he did defye
But Juliet, for whom he lived, for whom eke would he dye.
When after raging fits, appeased was his rage,
And when his passions (powred forth) gan partly to
    asswage,   1350

So wisely did the fryre unto his tale replye,
That he straight cared for his life, that erst had care to dye.
Art thou, quoth he, a man? thy shape saith so thou art:
Thy crying and thy weping eyes, denote a womans hart,
For manly reason is quite from of thy mynd outchased,
And in her stead affections lewd, and fansies highly placed,
So that I stoode in doute this howre (at the least)
If thou a man, or woman wert, or els a brutish beast.
A wise man in the midst of troubles and distres,
Still standes not wayling present harme, but seeks his harmes
    redres   1360
As when the winter flawes, with dredfull noyse arise,
And heave the fomy swelling waves up to the starry skies,
So that the broosed barke in cruell seas betost,
Dispayreth of the happy haven in daunger to be lost.
The pylate bold a helme, cryes, mates strike now your sayle
And turnes her stemme into the waves, that strongly her assayle,
Then, driven hard upon the bare and wrackfull shore,
In greater daunger to be wract, then he had been before
He seeth his ship full right against the rocke to ronne,
But yet he dooth what lyeth in him the perilous rocke to
    shonne.   1370
Sometimes the beaten boate, by cunning government,
The ancors lost, the cables broke, and all the tackle spent,
The roder smitten of, and over boord the mast,
Doth win the long desyred porte, the stormy daunger past.
But if the master dread, and overprest with woe,
Begin to wring his handes, and lets the gyding rodder goe
The ship rents on the rocke, or sinketh in the deepe,
And eke the coward drenched is. So, if thou still beweepe
And seke not how to helpe the chaunges that do chaunce,
Thy cause of sorow shall increase, thou cause of thy
    mischaunce.   1380
Other account thee wise, proove not thy selfe a foole,
Now put in practise lessons learnd, of old in wisdomes schoole.
The wise man saith, beware thou double not thy payne,
For one perhaps thou mayst abyde, but hardly suffer twayne.
As well we ought to seeke thinges hurtfull to decrease,
As to endevor helping thinges by study to increase.
The prayse of trew fredom, in wisdomes bondage lyes,
He winneth blame whose deedes be fonde, although his woords be
    wise.
Sickenes the bodies gaole, greefe, gaole is of the mynd:

21—S.N.D. I

If thou canst scape from heavy greefe, true fredome shalt thou
  finde. 1390
Fortune can fill nothing, so full of hearty greefe,
But in the same a constant mynd, finds solace and releefe.
Vertue is alwayes thrall, to troubles and annoye,
But wisdome in adversitie, findes cause of quiet joye,
And they most wretched are, that know no wretchednes
And after great extremity, mishaps ay waxen lesse.
Like as there is no weale, but wastes away somtime,
So every kind of wayled woe, will weare away in time.
If thou wilt master quite, the troubles that thee spill,
Endevor first by reasons help, to master witles will. 1400
A sondry medson hath, eche sondry faynt disease,
But pacience, a common salve, to every wound geves ease.
The world is alway full of chaunces and of chaunge,
Wherfore the chaunge of chaunce must not seeme to a wise man
  straunge.
For tickel Fortune doth, in chaunging but her kind,
But all her chaunges cannot chaunge a steady constant minde.
Though wavering Fortune toorne from thee her smyling face,
And sorow seeke to set him selfe, in banishd pleasures place,
Yet may thy marred state, be mended in a while,
And she eftsones that frowneth now, with pleasant cheere shall
  smyle. 1410
For as her happy state, no long whyle standeth sure,
Even so the heavy plight she brings, not alwayes doth endure.
What nede so many woordes to thee that art so wyse?
Thou better canst advise thy selfe, then I can thee advyse.
Wisdome, I see, is vayne, if thus in time of neede
A wise mans wit unpractised, doth stand him in no steede.
I know thou hast some cause, of sorow and of care
But well I wot thou hast no cause thus frantikly to fare.
Affections foggy mist, thy febled sight doth blynde
But if that reasons beames agayne might shine into thy
  mynde, 1420
If thou wouldst view thy state with an indifferent eye,
I thinke thou wouldst condemne thy plaint, thy sighing, and thy
  crye.
With valiant hand thou madest thy foe yeld up his breth,
Thou hast escapd his swerd, and eke the lawes that threatten
  death.
By thy escape thy frendes are fraughted full of joy,
And by his death thy deadly foes are laden with annoy.

Wilt thou, with trusty frendes, of pleasure take some part?
Or els to please thy hatefull foes, be partner of theyr smart?
Why cryest thou out on love, why doest thou blame thy fate?
Why dost thou so crye after death, thy life why dost thou
    hate?   1430
Dost thou repent the choyce, that thou so late didst choose?
Love is thy Lord, thou oughtst obay and not thy prince accuse,
For thou hast found (thou knowst) great favour in his sight:
He graunted thee, at thy request, thy onely hartes delight,
So that the Gods envyde the blisse thou livedst in;
To geve to such unthankefull men, is folly and a sin.
Me thinkes I heare thee say the cruell banishment
Is onely cause of thy unrest, onely thou dost lament
That from thy natife land and frendes thou must depart,
Enforsd to flye from her that hath the keping of thy hart,   1440
And so opprest with waight of smart that thou dost feele,
Thou dost complaine of Cupides brand, and Fortunes turning
    wheele.
Unto a valiant hart there is no banishment,
All countreys are his native soyle beneath the firmament.
As to the fishe the sea: as to the fowle the ayre:
So is like pleasant to the wise, eche place of his repayre.
Though froward Fortune chase thee hence into exyle,
With doubled honor shall she call thee home within a whyle.
Admyt thou shouldst abyde abrode a yere or twayne,
Should so short absence cause so long and eke so greevous
    payne?   1450
Though thou ne mayst thy frendes, here in Verona see,
They are not banishd Mantua, where safely thou mast be.
Thether they may resort, though thou resort not hether,
And there in suretie may you talke of your affayres together.
Yea, but this whyle (alas) thy Juliet must thou misse,
The onely piller of thy helth, and ancor of thy blisse.
Thy hart thou leavest with her, when thou dost hence depart,
And in thy brest inclosed bearst, her tender frendly hart.
But if thou rew so much, to leave the rest behinde,
With thought of passed joyes, content thy uncontented
    mynde;   1460
So shall the moane decrease, wherwith thy mynd doth melt,
Compared to the heavenly joyes which thou hast often felt,
He is too nyse a weakeling, that shrinketh at a showre,
And he unworthy of the sweete, that tasteth not the sowre.
Call now againe to mynde, thy first consuming flame,

How didst thou vainely burne in love of an unloving dame?
Hadst thou not welnigh wept, quite out thy swelling eyne?
Did not thy parts, fordoon with payne, languishe away and pyne?
Those greefes and others like were happly overpast
And thou in haight of Fortunes wheele well placed at the
    last,   1470
From whence thou art now falne, that, raysed up agayne,
With greater joy a greater while in pleasure mayst thou raygne.
Compare the present while, with times ypast before,
And thinke that Fortune hath for thee, great pleasure yet in store.
The whilst, this little wrong, receive thou paciently,
And what of force must nedes be done, that doe thou willingly.
Foly it is to feare that thou canst not avoyde,
And madnes to desire it much that can not be enjoyde.
To geve to Fortune place, not ay deserveth blame,
But skill it is, according to the times, thy selfe to frame.   1480
    Whilst to this skilfull lore, he lent his listning eares,
His sighes are stopt, and stopped are the conduits of his teares.
As blackest cloudes are chaced, by winters nimble winde,
So have his reasons chaced care out of his carefull mynde.
As of a morning foule, ensues an evening fayre,
So banisht hope returneth home to banish his despayre.
Now is affections veile, removed from his eyes,
He seeth the path that he must walke, and reson makes him wise.
For very shame, the blood doth flashe in both his cheekes,
He thankes the father for his lore, and farther ayde he
    seekes.   1490
He sayth, that skilles youth, for counsell is unfitte,
And anger oft with hastines are joind to want of witte;
But sound advise aboundes in heddes with ho[a]rishe haires,
For wisdom is by practise wonne, and perfect made by yeares.
But aye from this time forth, his ready bending will
Shalbe in awe and governed by fryer Lawrence skill.
The governor is nowe, right carefull of his charge,
To whom he doth wisely discourse, of his affaires at large.
He telles him how he shall, depart the towne unknowne,
Both mindfull of his frendes safetie, and carefull of his owne   1500
How he shall gyde him selfe, how he shall seeke to winne
The frendship of the better sort, how warely to crepe in
The favour of the Mantuan prince, and how he may
Appease the wrath of Escalus, and wipe the fault away;
The choller of his foes, by gentle meanes t'asswage,
Or els by force and practises to bridle quite theyr rage.

And last he chargeth him, at his appointed howre,
To goe with manly mery cheere, unto his ladies bowre,
And there with holesome woordes to salve her sorowes smart,
And to revive, (if nede require), her faint and dying hart.   1510
   The old mans woords have fild with joy our Romeus brest,
And eke the olde wives talke, hath set our Juliets hart at rest.
Whereto may I compare, (O lovers) this your day?
Like dayes the painefull mariners, are woonted to assay;
For, beat with tempest great, when they at length espye
Some little beame of Phoebus light, that perceth through the skie,
To cleare the shadowde earth, by clearenes of his face,
They hope that dreadles, they shall ronne the remnant of their
      race.
Yea they assure them selfe, and quite behynd theyr backe
They cast all doute, and thanke the Gods for scaping of the
      wracke.   1520
But straight the boysterous windes, with greater fury blowe,
And over boord the broken mast the stormy blastes doe throwe.
The heavens large, are clad with cloudes, as darke as hell,
And twise as hye, the striving waves begin to roare and swell.
With greater daungers dred, the men are vexed more:
In greater perill of their lyfe, then they had been before.
   The golden sonne was gonne to lodge him in the west:
The full moone eke in yonder South had sent most men to rest
When restles Romeus, and restles Juliet,
In woonted sort, by woonted meane, in Juliets chaumber
      met,   1530
And from the windowes top, downe had he leaped scarce,
When she with armes outstretched wide, so hard did him embrace,
That welnigh had the sprite (not forced by dedly force)
Flowne unto death, before the time abandoning the corce.
Thus muet stoode they both, the eight part of an howre,
And both woulde speake, but neither had of speaking any powre.
But on his brest her hed doth joylesse Juliet lay,
And on her slender necke, his chyn doth ruthfull Romeus stay.
Their scalding sighes ascende, and by their cheekes downe fall,
Their trickling teares, as christall cleare, but bitterer farre then
      gall.   1540
Then he, to end the greefe, which both they lived in,
Did kysse his love, and wisely thus hys tale he dyd begin:
   My Juliet, my love, my onely hope and care,
To you I purpose not as now, with length of woords declare,
The diversenes, and eke the accidents so straunge,

Of frayle unconstant Fortune, that delyteth still in chaunge,
Who, in a moment, heaves her frendes up to the height
Of her swift turning slippery wheele, then fleetes her frendship
    straight.
O wondrous chaunge, even with the twinkling of an eye,
Whom erst her selfe had rashly set, in pleasant place so hye,   1550
The same in great despyte, downe hedlong doth she throwe,
And while she treades and spurneth at the lofty state laid lowe,
More sorow doth she shape, within an howers space,
Then pleasure in an hundred yeres: so geyson[1] is her grace.
The proofe wherof in me (alas) too plaine apperes,
Whom tenderly my carefull frendes have fostered with my feers,
In prosperous high degree, mayntayned so by fate,
That (as your selfe did see) my foes envyde my noble state.
One thing there was I did above the rest desire,
To which, as to the soveraigne good, by hope I would
    aspyre:
                                        1560
That by our mariage meane we might within a while,
(To woorke our perfect happines) our parentes reconsile,
That safely so we might (not stopt by sturdy strife)
Unto the boundes that God hath set, gyde forth our pleasant lyfe.
But now (alacke) too soone my blisse is overblowne,
And upside downe my purpose and my enterprise are throwne,
And driven from my frendes, of straungers must I crave,
(O graunt it God) from daungers dread, that I may suertie have.
For loe, henceforth I must, wander in landes unknowne:
(So hard I finde the princes doome,) exyled from mine
    owne.
                                        1570
Which thing I have thought good, to set before your eyes:
And to exhort you, now to prove your selfe a woman wise,
That paciently you beare my absent long abod,
For, what above by fatall doomes decreed is that God—
And more then this, to say it seemed, he was bent,
But Juliet, in dedly greefe, with brackish teares besprent,
Brake of his tale begonne, and whilst his speche he stayde,
These selfe same wordes, or like to these, with dreery chere she
    sayde.
Why Romeus, can it be, thou hast so hard a hart?
So farre removed from ruth? so farre from thinking on my
    smart?
                                        1580
To leave me thus alone, (thou cause of my distresse)
Beseged with so great a campe, of mortall wretchednesse,

---

[1] scanty.

That every hower now, and moment in a day,
A thousand times, death bragges, as he would reave my life away?
Yet such is my mishap, (O cruell destenye)
That still I live, and wish for death, but yet can never dye.
So that just cause I have, to thinke (as seemeth me)
That froward Fortune did of late, with cruell death agree
To lengthen lothed life, to pleasure in my payne,
And tryumph in my harme, as in the greatest hoped gayne. 1590
And thou, the instrument of Fortunes cruell will,
Without whose ayde she can no way, her tyrans lust fulfill,
Art not a whit ashamde, (as farre as I can see)
To cast me of, when thou hast culd the better part of me.
Wherby (alas) to soone, I seely wretch do prove,
That all the auncient sacred lawes, of frendship and of love,
Are quelde and quenched quite, since he on whom alway,
My cheefe hope, and my steady trust, was wonted still to stay,
For whom I am becomme, unto my selfe a foe,
Disdayneth me, his stedfast frend, and scornes my frendship
   so. 1600
Nay Romeus, nay, thou mayst of two thinges choose the one:
Either to see thy castaway, as soone as thou art gone,
Hedlong to throw her selfe downe from the windowes haight,
And so to breake her slender necke, with all the bodies waight,
Or suffer her to be companion of thy payne,
Where so thou goe (Fortune thee gyde) till thou retoorne agayne.
So wholy into thine, transformed is my hart,
That even as oft as I do thinke that thou and I shall part,
So oft (me thinkes) my life withdrawes it selfe awaye,
Which I retayne to no end els, but to the end I may 1610
In spite of all thy foes, thy present partes enjoye,
And in distres to beare with thee, the halfe of thine annoye.
Wherfore, in humble sort (Romeus) I make request,
If ever tender pity yet, were lodgde in gentle brest,
O let it now have place, to rest within thy hart;
Receave me as thy servant, and the fellow of thy smart:
Thy absence is my death, thy sight shall geve me life.
But if perhaps thou stand in dred, to leade me as a wyfe,
Art thou all counsellesse, canst thou no shift devise?
What letteth, but in other weede I may my selfe disguyse? 1620
What, shall I be the first? hath none done so ere this?
To scape the bondage of theyr frendes? thy selfe can aunswer yes.
Or dost thou stand in doute, that I thy wife ne can
By service pleasure thee as much, as may thy hyred man?

Or is my loyalte of both accompted lesse?
Perhaps thou fearst lest I for gayne, forsake thee in distresse?
What, hath my bewty now, no powre at all on you,
Whose brightnes, force, and praise somtime, up to the skyes you
    blew?
My teares, my frendship and my pleasures donne of olde,
Shall they be quite forgote in dede? When Romeus dyd
    behold   1630
The wildnes of her looke, her cooler pale and ded,
The woorst of all that might betyde to her, he gan to dred,
And once agayne he dyd in armes his Juliet take,
And kist her with a loving kysse. And thus to her he spake.
   Ah Juliet (quoth he) the mistres of my hart,
For whom (even now) thy servant doth abyde in dedly smart,
Even for the happy dayes which thou desyrest to see,
And for the fervent frendships sake that thou dost owe to me,
At once these fansies vayne, out of thy mynd roote out,
Except perhaps unto thy blame, thou fondly go about   1640
To hasten forth my death, and to thine owne to ronne,
Which Natures law, and wisdoms lore teache every wight to
    shonne.
For, but thou chaunge thy mynde, (I do foretell the ende)
Thou shalt undoo thy selfe for ay, and me thy trusty frende.
For why, thy absence knowne, thy father wilbe wroth,
And in his rage so narowly he will pursue us both:
That we shall trye in vayne, to scape away by flight,
And vainely seeke a loorking place, to hyde us from his sight,
Then we found out, and caught, quite voyde of strong defence
Shall cruelly be punished, for thy departure hence.   1650
I, as a ravishor, thou, as a careles childe,
I, as a man who doth defile, thou, as a mayde defilde,
Thinking to leade in ease, a long contented life,
Shall short our dayes by shamefull death: but, if (my loving wife)
Thou banish from thy mynde, two foes that counsell hath,
(That wont to hinder sound advise) rashe hastines and wrath;
If thou be bent tobay the lore of reasons skill,
And wisely by her princely powre suppresse rebelling will,
If thou our safetie seeke, more then thine owne delight,
Since suerty standes in parting, and thy pleasures growe of
    sight,
        1660
Forbeare the cause of joy, and suffer for a while,
So shall I safely live abrode, and safe turne from exile,
So shall no slaunders blot, thy spotles life destayne,

So shall thy kinsmen be unstyrd, and I exempt from payne.
And thinke thou not that aye, the cause of care shall last;
These stormy broyles shall overblow, much like a winters blast.
For Fortune chaungeth more, then fickel fantasie;
In nothing Fortune constant is, save in unconstancie.
Her hasty ronning wheele, is of a restles coorse,
That turnes the clymers hedlong downe, from better to the
    woorse,   1670
And those that are beneth, she heaveth up agayne,
So we shall rise to pleasures mount, out of the pit of payne.
Ere fowre monthes overpasse, such order will I take,
And by my letters, and my frendes, such meanes I mynd to make,
That of my wandring race, ended shalbe the toyle,
And I cald home with honor great, unto my native soyle,
But if I be condemd to wander still in thrall,
I will returne to you (mine owne) befall what may befall.
And then by strength of frendes, and with a mighty hand,
From Verone will I cary thee, into a forein lande,   1680
Not in mans weede disguisd, or as one scarcely knowne,
But as my wife and onely feere, in garment of thyne owne.
Wherfore represse at once, the passions of thy hart,
And where there is no cause of greefe, cause hope to heale thy
    smart.
For of this one thing thou mayst well assured bee;
That nothing els but onely death shall sunder me from thee.
The reasons that he made, did seeme of so great waight,
And had with her such force, that she to him gan aunswer straight.
Deere syr, nought els wish I, but to obay your will;
But sure where so you go, your hart with me shall tary still,   1690
As signe and certaine pledge, tyll here I shall you see,
Of all the powre that over you your selfe did graunt to me;
And in his stead take myne, the gage of my good will—
One promesse crave I at your hand, that graunt me to fulfill;
Fayle not to let me have at fryer Lawrence hand,
The tydinges of your health, and how your doutfull case shall
    stand
And all the wery while that you shall spend abrode,
Cause me from time to time to knowe the place of your abode.
His eyes did gushe out teares, a sigh brake from his brest,
When he did graunt, and with an othe did vowe to kepe the
    hest.   1700
    Thus these two lovers passe away the wery night,
In payne and plaint, not (as they wont) in pleasure and delight.

But now (somewhat too soone) in farthest East arose
Fayre Lucifer, the golden starre that Lady Venus chose,
Whose course appoynted is, with spedy race to ronne,
A messenger of dawning daye, and of the rysing sonne.
Then freshe Aurora, with her pale and silver glade,
Did clear the skyes, and from the earth, had chased ougly shade.
When thou ne lookest wide, ne closely dost thou winke,
When Phoebus from our hemysphere, in westerne wave doth
 sinke.   1710
What cooller then the heavens do shew unto thine eyes,
The same, (or like) saw Romeus in farthest Esterne skyes.
As yet, he saw no day, he could he call it night,
With equall force, decreasing darke, fought with increasing light.
Then Romeus in armes his lady gan to folde,
With frendly kisse, and ruthfully she gan her knight beholde.
With solemne othe they both theyr sorowfull leave do take;
They sweare no stormy troubles shall theyr steady frendship shake.
Then carefull Romeus, agayne to cell retoornes,
And in her chamber secretly our joyles Juliet moornes.   1720
Now hugy cloudes of care, of sorow, and of dread,
The clearnes of their gladsome harts hath wholy overspread.
When golden crested Phoebus bosteth him in skye,
And under earth, to scape revenge, his dedly foe doth flye,
Then hath these lovers day an ende, their night begonne,
For eche of them to other is, as to the world the sunne.
The dawning they shall see, ne sommer any more,
But blackfaced night with winter rough, (ah) beaten over sore.
 The wery watch discharged, did hye them home to slepe,
The warders, and the skowtes were chargde theyr place and
 coorse to keepe,   1730
And Verone gates awyde, the porters had set open.
When Romeus had of hys affayres with frier Lawrence spoken,
Warely he walked forth, unknowne of frend or foe,
Clad like a merchant venterer, from top even to the toe.
He spurd apace, and came withouten stop or stay,
To Mantua gates, where lighted downe, he sent his man away
With woords of comfort, to his olde afflicted syre:
And straight in mynd to sojorne there, a lodgeing doth he hyre,
And with the nobler sort he doth himselfe acquaint,
And of his open wrong receaved, the Duke doth heare his
 plaint.   1740
He practiseth by frendes, for pardon of exyle,
The whilst, he seeketh every way, his sorowes to begyle.

But who forgets the cole that burneth in his brest?
Alas his cares denye his hart, the sweete desyred rest;
No time findes he of myrth, he findes no place of joye,
But every thing occasion geves of sorow and annoye.
For when in toorning skyes, the heavens lampes are light,
And from the other hemysphere, fayre Phoebus chaceth night,
When every man and beast, hath rest from painfull toyle,
Then in the brest of Romeus, his passions gyn to boyle;   1750
Then doth he wet with teares, the cowche wheron he lyes,
And then his sighes the chamber fill, and out aloude he cryes
Against the restles starres, in rolling skyes that raunge,
Against the fatall sisters three, and Fortune full of chaunge.
Eche night a thousand times he calleth for the day,
He thinketh Titans restles stedes, of restines do stay,
Or that at length they have some bayting place found out,
Or (gyded yll) have lost theyr way and wandred farre about.
Whyle thus in ydel thoughts, the wery time he spendeth,
The night hath end, but not with night the plaint of
        night he endeth.   1760
Is he accompanied, is he in place alone?
In cumpany he wayles his harme, apart he maketh mone.
For if his feeres rejoyce, what cause hath he to joy,
That wanteth still his cheefe delight, while they theyr loves enjoy?
But if with heavy cheere, they shewe their inward greefe,
He wayleth most his wretchednes, that is of wretches cheefe.
When he doth heare abrode, the praise of ladies blowne,
Within his thought he scorneth them, and doth preferre his
        owne;
When pleasant songes he heares while others do rejoyce
The melody of Musike doth styrre up his mourning voyce.   1770
But if in secret place he walke some where alone,
The place it selfe, and secretnes redoubleth all his mone.
Then speakes he to the beastes to fethered fowles, and trees,
Unto the earth, the cloudes, and to what so beside he sees.
To them he shewth his smart, as though they reason had,
Eche thing may cause his heavines, but nought may make him
        glad,
And (wery of the day) agayne he calleth night,
The sunne he curseth, and the howre, when fyrst his eyes saw
        light.
And as the night, and day, their course do enterchaunge,
So doth our Romeus nightly cares, for cares of day
        exchaunge.   1780

In absence of her knight, the lady no way could
Kepe trewce betwene her greefes and her, though nere so fayne
    she would;
And though with greater payne she cloked sorowes smart,
Yet did her paled face disclose the passions of her hart.
Her sighing every howre, her weping every where,
Her recheles heede of meate, of slepe, and wearing of her geare,
The carefull mother markes; then of her health afrayde,
Because the greefes increased still, thus to her child she sayde.
Deere daughter, if you shoulde long languishe in this sort,
I stand in doute that over soone your sorowes will make
    short   1790
Your loving fathers life, and myne, that love you more
Then our owne propre breth, and life. Brydel hence forth therfore
Your greefe, and payne, your selfe on joy your thought to set,
For time it is that now you should our Tybalts death forget,
Of whom, since God hath claymd the lyfe that was but lent,
He is in blisse, ne is there cause why you should thus lament.
You can not call him backe with teares, and shrikinges shrill:
It is a falt thus still to grudge at Gods appoynted will.
The seely soule had now no longer powre to fayne,
Ne longer could she hyde her harme, but aunswered thus
    agayne,   1800
With heavy broken sighes, with visage pale and ded.
Madame, the last of Tybalts teares, a great while since I shed,
Whose spring hath been ere this so laded out by me,
That empty quite, and moystureles, I gesse it now to be,
So that my payned hart by conduites of the eyne,
No more henceforth (as wont it was) shall gush forth dropping
    bryne.
The wofull mother knew not, what her daughter ment,
And loth to vexe her childe by woordes, her peace she warely
    hent,
But when from howre to howre, from morow to the morow,
Still more and more she saw increast her daughters wonted
    sorow,   1810
All meanes she sought of her, and howshold folke, to know
The certaine roote, whereon her greefe, and booteless mone doth
    growe.
But lo, she hath in vayne, her time and labor lore,
Wherfore without all measures, is her hart tormented sore,
And sith her selfe could not fynd out the cause of care,
She thought it good to tell the syre, how yll his childe did fare.

And when she saw her time, thus to her feere she sayde:
Syr, if you marke our daughter well, the countenance of the
    mayde,
And how she fareth, since that Tybalt unto death,
(Before his time, forst by his foe) dyd yeld his living breath,   1820
Her face shall seeme so chaunged, her doynges eke so straunge,
That you will greatly wonder at, so great and sodain chaunge.
Not onely she forbeares, her meate, her drinke, and sleepe,
But now she tendeth nothing els but to lament and weepe;
No greater joy hath she, nothing contentes her hart
So much, as in the chaumber, close to shut her selfe apart,
Where she doth so torment her poore afflicted mynde,
That much in daunger standes her lyfe, except somme helpe we
    fynde.
But (out alas) I see not how it may be founde,
Unlesse that fyrst, we might fynd whence her sorowes thus
    abounde,   1830
For though with busy care, I have employde my wit,
And used all the wayes I knew, to learne the truth of it,
Neither extremitie, ne gentle meanes could boote;
She hydeth close within her brest, her secret sorowes roote.
This was my fyrst conceite, that all her ruth arose
Out of her cousin Tybalts death, late slayne of dedly foes,
But now my hart doth hold a new repugnant thought;
Some greater thing, not Tybalts death, this chaunge in her hath
    wrought.
Her selfe assured me, that many dayes a goe,
She shed the last of Tybalts teares, which woord amasd me
    so,   1840
That I then could not gesse what thing els might her greeve,
But now at length I have bethought me, And I doe beleve
The onely crop and roote of all my daughters payne,
Is grudgeing envies faynt disease: perhaps she doth disdayne
To see in wedlocke yoke the most part of her feeres,
Whilst onely she unmaried, doth lose so many yeres.
And more perchaunce she thinkes you mynd to kepe her so,
Wherfore dispayring doth she weare her selfe away with woe.
Therfore (deere syr) in time, take on your daughter ruth;
For why, a brickel thing is glasse, and frayle is frayllesse
    youth.   1850
Joyne her at once to somme, in linke of mariage,
That may be meete for our degree, and much about her age.
So shall you banish care out of your daughters brest:

So we her parentes in our age, shall live in quiet rest.
Wherto gan easely her husband to agree,
And to the mothers skilfull talke, thus straight way aunswerd he,
Oft have I thought (deere wife) of all these thinges ere this,
But evermore my mynd me gave, it should not be amisse,
By farther leysure had, a husband to provyde;
Scarce saw she yet full xvi. yeres: too yong to be a bryde.   1860
But since her state doth stande on termes so perilous,
And that a mayden daughter is a treasour daungerous,
With so great speede I will endevour to procure
A husband for our daughter yong, her sickenes faynt to cure.
That you shall rest content, (so warely will I choose)
And she recover soone enough the time she seemes to loose.
The whilst, seeke you to learne, if she in any part
Already hath (unware to us) fixed her frendly hart,
Lest we have more respect to honor and to welth,
Then to our daughters quiet life, and to her happy helth: 1870
Whom I do hold as deere, as thapple of myne eye,
And rather wish in poore estate, and daughterles to dye,
Then leave my goodes and her ythrald to such a one,
Whose chorlish dealing (I once dead) should be her cause of
     mone.
   This pleasant aunswere heard, the lady partes agayne,
And Capilet the maydens sire, within a day or twayne,
Conferreth with his frendes, for mariage of his daughter,
And many gentlemen there were, with busy care that sought her;
Both, for the mayden was well shaped, yong, and fayre,
As also well brought up, and wise, her fathers onely heyre.   1880
Emong the rest was one inflamde with her desire,
Who County Paris cliped was, an Earle he had to syre.
Of all the suters, him the father liketh best,
And easely unto the Earle he maketh his behest,
Both of his owne good will, and of his frendly ayde,
To win his wife unto his will, and to perswade the mayde.
The wife dyd joy to heare the joyfull husband say,
How happy hap, how meete a match, he had found out that day,
Ne did she seeke to hyde her joyes within her hart,
But straight she hyeth to Juliet; to her she telles apart,   1890
What happy talke (by meane of her) was past no rather
Betwene the woing Paris, and her carefull loving father.
The person of the man, the fewters[1] of his face,
His youthfull yeres, his fayrenes, and his port and semely grace,

---

[1] features.

With curious wordes she payntes before her daughters eyes,
And then with store of vertues prayse she heaves him to the skyes.
She vauntes his race, and gyftes, that Fortune did him geve,
Wherby (she saith) both she and hers, in great delight shall live.
When Juliet conceived her parentes whole entent,
Wherto, both love, and reasons right, forbod her to assent,   1900
Within her selfe she thought, rather then be forsworne,
With horses wilde, her tender partes asonder should be torne.
Not now with bashfull brow (in wonted wise) she spake,
But with unwonted boldnes, straight into these woordes she brake.
    Madame, I marvell much, that you so lavasse[1] are
Of me your childe, (your jewel once, your onely joy and care,)
As thus to yelde me up, at pleasure of another,
Before you know if I doe like, or els mislike my lover.
Doo what you list, but yet of this assure you still,
If you do as you say you will, I yelde not there untill.   1910
For had I choyse of twayne, farre rather would I choose,
My part of all your goodes, and eke my breath and lyfe to lose,
Then graunt that he possesse of me the smallest part;
First, weary of my painefull life, my cares shall kill my hart,
Els will I perce my brest, with sharpe and bloody knife,
And you my mother shall becomme the murdresse of my life,
In geving me to him, whom I ne can ne may,
Ne ought to love. Wherfore on knees, deere mother I you pray
To let me live henceforth, as I have lived tofore:
Cease all your troubles for my sake, and care for me no
        more,   1920
But suffer Fortune feerce, to worke on me her will,
In her it lyeth to doe me boote, in her it lyeth to spill.
For whilst you for the best desyre to place me so,
You hast away my lingring death, and double all my woe.
    So deepe this aunswere made the sorowes downe to sinke
Into the mothers brest, that she ne knoweth what to thinke
Of these her daughters woords, but all appalde she standes,
And up unto the heavens she throwes her wondring head and
        handes,
And nigh besyde her selfe her husband hath she sought.
She telles him all; she doth forget ne yet she hydeth ought.   1930
The testy old man, wroth, disdainfull without measure,
Sendes forth his folke in haste for her, and byds them take no
        leysure:
Ne on her teares or plaint, at all to have remorse,
But (if they can not with her will,) to bring the mayde perforce.

[1] O. F. Lavasse, lavish.

The message heard, they part, to fetch that they must fet,
And willingly with them walkes forth obedient Juliet.
Arrived in the place, when she her father saw,
Of whom (as much as duety would) the daughter stoode in awe,
The servauntes sent away, (the mother thought it meete),
The wofull daughter all bewept, fell groveling at his feete,   1940
Which she doth washe with teares as she thus groveling lyes:
So fast, and eke so plenteously distill they from her eyes.
When she to call for grace her mouth doth think to open,
Muet she is; for sighes and sobs her fearefull talke have broken.
      The syre, whose swelling wroth her teares could not asswage,
With fiery eyen, and skarlet cheekes, thus spake her in his rage,
Whilst ruthfully stood by the maydens mother mylde,
Listen (quoth he) unthankfull and thou disobedient childe;
Hast thou so soone let slip out of thy mynde the woord,
That thou so often times hast heard rehearsed at my boord?   1950
How much the Romayne youth of parentes stood in awe,
And eke what powre upon theyr seede the fathers had by lawe?
Whom they not onely might pledge, alienate, and sell,
(When so they stoode in neede) but more, if children did rebell,
The parentes had the power, of lyfe and sodayn death.
What if those goodmen should agayne receave the livyng breth,
In how straight bondes would they thy stubberne body bynde?
What weapons would they seeke for thee? what tormentes would
      they fynde?
To chasten (if they saw) the lewdnes of thy lyfe,
Thy great unthankfulnes to me, and shamefull sturdy
      strife?   1960
Such care thy mother had, so deere thou wert to me,
That I with long and earnest sute provided have for thee
One of the greatest lordes, that wonnes about this towne,
And for his many vertues sake, a man of great renowne.
Of whom, both thou and I, unworthy are too much,
So riche ere long he shalbe left, his fathers welth is such.
Such is the noblenes, and honor of the race,
From whence his father came, and yet thou playest in this case,
The dainty foole, and stubberne gyrle; for want of skill,
Thou dost refuse thy offred weale, and disobay my will.   1970
Even by his strength I sweare, that fyrst did geve me lyfe
And gave me in my youth the strength, to get thee on my wyfe,
Onlesse by Wensday next, thou bende as I am bent,
And at our castle cald Free towne, thou freely doe assent
To Counte Paris sute, and promise to agree

To whatsoever then shall passe, twixt him, my wife, and me,
Not onely will I geve all that I have away
From thee, to those that shall me love, me honor, and obay,
But also too so close, and to so hard a gaole,
I shall thee wed, for all thy life, that sure thou shalt not
    fayle   1980
A thousand times a day to wishe for sodayn death,
And curse the day, and howre when first thy lunges did geve thee
    breath.
Advise thee well, and say that thou art warned now,
And thinke not that I speake in sport, or mynd to breake my
    vowe.
For were it not that I to Counte Paris gave
My fayth, which I must kepe unfalst, my honor so to save,
Ere thou go hence, my selfe would see thee chastned so,
That thou shouldst once for all be taught, thy duetie how to
    knowe;
And what revenge of olde, the angry syres did finde
Against theyr children that rebeld, and shewd them selfe
    unkinde.   1990
   These sayd, the olde man straight, is gone in hast away:
Ne for his daughters aunswere would the testy father stay.
And after him, his wife doth follow out of doore,
And there they leave theyr chidden chylde kneeling upon the
    floore.
Then she that oft had seene the fury of her syre,
Dreading what might come of his rage, nould farther styrre his yre.
Unto her chamber she withdrew her selfe aparte,
Where she was wonted to unlode, the sorowes of her hart.
There did she not so much busy her eyes in sleping,
As, overprest with restles thoughts, in piteous booteless
    weping.   2000
The fast falling of teares make not her teares decrease,
Ne by the powring forth of plaint, the cause of plaint doth cease.
So that to thend the mone and sorow may decaye,
The best is that she seeke some meane to take the cause away.
Her wery bed betime the wofull wight forsakes,
And to sainct Frauncis church to masse her way devoutly takes.
The fryer forth is calde, she prayes him heare her shrift:
Devocion is in so yong yeres, a rare and precious gyft.
When on her tender knees the dainty lady kneeles,
In minde to powre forth all the greefe, that inwardly she
    feeles,   2010

With sighes and salted teares her shryving doth beginne,
For she of heaped sorowes hath to speake, and not of sinne.
Her voyce with piteous plaint was made already horce,
And hasty sobs, when she would speake, brake of her woordes
    parforce.
But as she may peece meale, she powreth in his lappe,
The mariage newes, a mischief newe, prepared by mishappe,
Her parentes promisse erst to Counte Paris past,
Her fathers threats she telleth him, and thus concludes at last.
Once was I wedded well, ne will I wed agayne,
For since I know I may not be the wedded wyfe of twayne,   2020
For I am bound to have one God, one fayth, one make,
My purpose is as soone as I shall hence my jorney take,
With these two handes which joynde unto the heavens I stretch,
The hasty death which I desire unto my selfe to reache.
This day (O Romeus) this day, thy wofull wife
Will bring the end of all her cares by ending carefull lyfe.
So my departed sprite shall witnes to the skye,
And eke my blood unto the earth beare record how that I
Have kept my fayth unbroke, stedfast unto my frende.
    When this her heavy tale was tolde, her vowe eke at an
      ende,   2030
Her gasing here and there, her feerce and staring looke,
Did witnes that some lewd attempt, her hart had undertooke.
Whereat, the fryer astonde, and gastfully afrayde,
Lest she by dede perfourme her woord, thus much to her he
    sayde.
Ah lady Juliet, what nede the wordes you spake?
I pray you graunt me one request for blessed Maries sake.
Measure somewhat your greefe, holde here a while your peace,
Whilst I bethinke me of your case, your plaint and sorowes cease.
Such comfort will I geve you ere you part from hence,
And for thassaltes of Fortunes yre prepare so sure defence,   2040
So holesome salve will I for your afflictions finde,
That you shall hence depart agayne with well contented mynde.
His wordes have chased straight out of her hart despayre,
Her blacke and ougly dredfull thoughts by hope are waxen fayre.
So fryer Lawrence now hath left her there alone,
And he out of the church in hast is to his chaumber gone,
Where sundry thoughtes within his carefull head arise;
The old mans foresight divers doutes hath set before his eyes.
His conscience one while condems it for a sinne,
To let her take Paris to spouse, since he himselfe had byn   2050

The chefest cause, that she, unknowne to father or mother,
Not five monthes past in that selfe place was wedded to another.
An other while an hugy heape of daungers dred,
His restles thought hath heaped up, within his troubled hed.
Even of it selfe thattempt he judgeth perilous,
The execucion eke he demes so much more daungerous,
That to a womans grace he must himselfe commit,
That yong is, simple, and unware, for waighty affaires unfit,
For if she fayle in ought, the matter published,
Both she and Romeus were undonne, himselfe eke punished.   2060
When too and fro in mynde he dyvers thoughts had cast,
With tender pity and with ruth his hart was wonne at last.
He thought he rather would in hasard set his fame,
Then suffer such adultery. Resolving on the same,
Out of his closet straight, he tooke a litele glasse,
And then with double hast retornde where wofull Juliet was;
Whom he hath found welnigh in traunce, scarce drawing breath,
Attending still to heare the newes of lyfe or els of death.
Of whom he did enquire of the appointed day.
On Wensday next, (quod Juliet) so doth my father say: 2070
I must geve my consent, but (as I do remember)
The solemne day of mariage is, the tenth day of September.
Deere daughter, quoth the fryer, of good chere see thou be,
For loe, sainct Frauncis of his grace hath shewde a way to me,
By which I may both thee, and Romeus together,
Out of the bondage which you feare assuredly deliver.
Even from the holy font thy husband have I knowne,
And, since he grew in yeres, have kept his counsels as myne owne.
For from his youth he would unfold to me his hart,
And often have I cured him, of anguish and of smart;   2080
I know that by desert his frendship I have wonne,
And I him holde as dere, as if he were my propre sonne,
Wherfore my frendly hart, can not abyde that he
Should wrongfully in ought be harmde, if that it lay in me
To right or to revenge the wrong by my advise,
Or timely to prevent the same in any other wise.
And sith thou art his wife, thee am I bound to love,
For Romeus frindships sake, and seeke thy anguishe to remove,
And dreadfull torments which thy hart besegen rounde,
Wherfore, my daughter, geve good eare, unto my counsels
     sounde.   2090
Forget not what I say, ne tell it any wight,
Not to the nurce thou trustest so, as Romeus is thy knight,

For on this threed doth hang thy death and eke thy life,
My fame or shame, his weale or woe that chose thee to his wyfe.
Thou art not ignorant (because of such renowne
As every where is spred of me, but chefely in this towne,)
That in my youthfull dayes abrode I travayled
Through every lande found out by men, by men inhabited.
So twenty yeres from home, in landes unknowne a gest,
I never gave my weary limmes long time of quiet rest,   2100
But in the desert woodes, to beastes of cruell kinde,
Or on the seas to drenching waves, at pleasure of the winde,
I have committed them to ruth of rovers hand,
And to a thousand daungers more by water and by lande.
But not, in vayne (my childe) hath all my wandring byn,
Beside the great contentednes my sprite abydeth in,
That by the pleasant thought of passed thinges doth grow,
One private frute more have I pluckd which thou shalt shortly
    know:
What force the stones, the plants, and metals have to woorke,
And divers other thinges that in the bowels of earth do
    loorke,   2110
With care I have sought out, with payne I did them prove,
With them eke can I helpe my selfe, at times of my behove,
(Although the science be against the lawes of men)
When sodain daunger forceth me, but yet most cheefly when
The worke to doe is least displeasing unto God,
Not helping to do any sinne that wrekefull Jove forbode.
For since in lyfe no hope of long abode I have,
But now am comme unto the brinke of my appointed grave,
And that my death drawes nere, whose stripe I may not shonne,
But shalbe calde to make account of all that I have donne,   2120
Now ought I from hence forth more depely print in mynde
The judgement of the lord, then when youthes folly made me
    blynde,
When love and fond desyre were boyling in my brest,
Whence hope and dred by striving thoughts had banishd frendly
    rest.
Knowe therfore (daughter) that with other gyftes which I
Have well attained to by grace and favour of the skye,
Long since I did finde out, and yet the way I knowe,
Of certain rootes and savory herbes, to make a kinde of dowe,
Which baked hard, and bet into a powder fine,
And dronke with conduite water, or with any kynd of wine,   2130
It doth in halfe an howre astonne the taker so,

And mastreth all his sences, that he feeleth weale nor woe,
And so it burieth up the sprite and living breath,
That even the skilfull leche would say, that he is slayne by death.
One vertue more it hath, as mervelous as this;
The taker by receiving it, at all not greeved is;
But painlesse as a man that thinketh nought at all,
Into a swete and quiet slepe immediately doth fall;
From which, (according to the quantitie he taketh,)
Longer or shorter is the time before the sleper waketh.   2140
And thence (theffect once wrought) agayne it doth restore
Him that receaved unto the state, wherin he was before.
Wherfore, marke well the ende, of this my tale begonne,
And therby learne what is by thee hereafter to be donne.
Cast of from thee at once, the weede of womannish dread,
With manly courage arme thy selfe, from heele unto the head;
For onely on the feare or boldnes of thy brest,
The happy happe, or yll mishappe of thy affayre doth rest.
Receive this vyoll small, and keepe it as thine eye,
And on thy mariage day before the sunne doe cleare the
     skye,   2150
Fill it with water full, up to the very brim,
Then drinke it of, and thou shalt feele, throughout eche vayne
     and lim
A pleasant slumber slide, and quite dispred at length,
On all thy partes, from every part reve all thy kindly strength.
Withouten moving thus thy ydle parts shall rest,
No pulse shall goe, ne hart once beate within thy hollow brest,
But thou shalt lye as she that dyeth in a traunce:
Thy kinsmen, and thy trusty frendes shall wayle the sodain
     chaunce:
Thy corps then will they bring to grave in this church yarde,
Where thy forefathers long agoe a costly tombe preparde,   2160
Both for him selfe, and eke for those that should come after,
Both deepe it is, and long and large, where thou shall rest my
     daughter,
Till I to Mantua sende for Romeus, thy knight.
Out of the tombe both he and I will take thee forth that night.
And when out of thy slepe thou shalt awake agayne,
Then mayst thou goe with him from hence, and healed of thy
     payne,
In Mantua lead with him unknowne a pleasant life,
And yet perhaps in time to comme, when cease shall all the strife,
And that the peace is made twixt Romeus and his foes,

My selfe may finde so fit a time these secretes to dysclose,   2170
Both to my prayse, and to thy tender parentes joy,
That daungerles, without reproche, thou shalt thy love enjoy.
    When of his skilfull tale, the fryer had made an ende,
To which our Juliet so well her eare and wits dyd bend,
That she hath heard it all, and hath forgotten nought,
Her fainting hart was comforted, with hope and pleasant thought,
And then to him she said, Doubte not but that I will
With stoute and unappauled hart, your happy hest fulfill.
Yea, if I wist it were a venemous dedly drinke,
Rather would I that through my throte the certaine bane
        should sinke,   2180
Then I (not drinking it) into his handes should fall,
That hath no part of me as yet, ne ought to have at all.
Much more I ought with bold and with a willing hart,
To greatest daunger yelde my selfe and to the dedly smart,
To comme to him, on whome my life doth wholy stay,
That is my onely hartes delight, and so he shalbe aye.
Then goe (quoth he) my childe, I pray that God on hye
Direct thy foote, and by thy hand upon the way thee gye[1]:
God graunt he so confirme in thee thy present will,
That no inconstant toy thee let, thy promesse to fulfill.   2190
    A thousand thankes and more, our Juliet gave the fryer,
And homeward to her fathers house joyfull she doth retyre.
And as with stately gate she passed through the streete,
She saw her mother in the doore, that with her there would meete,
In mynd to ask if she her purpose yet did holde,
In mynd also, a part twixt them, her duety to have tolde:
Wherfore with pleasant face, and with unwonted chere,
As soone as she was unto her approched sumwhat nere,
Before the mother spake, thus did she fyrst begin.
Madame, at sainct Frauncis churche have I this morning
        byn,   2200
Where I did make abode, a longer while (percase)
Then dewty would, yet have I not been absent from this place,
So long a while, whithout a great and just cause why;
This frute have I receaved there; my hart erst lyke to dye,
Is now revived agayne, and my afflicted brest,
Released from affliction, restored is to rest.
For lo, my troubled gost (alas too sore diseasde,)
By gostly counsell and advise, hath fryer Lawrence easde,
To whome I did at large discourse my former lyfe,

----

[1] guide.

And in confession did I tell of all our passed strife,   2210
Of Counte Paris sute, and how my lord, my syre,
By my ungrate and stubborne stryfe, I styrred unto yre.
But lo, the holy fryer hath by his gostly lore,
Made me another woman now, then I had been before.
By strength of argumentes he charged so my mynde,
That (though I sought) no sure defence my serching thought could
          finde.
So forced I was at length to yelde up witles will,
And promist to be orderd by the friers praysed skill.
Wherfore, albeit I had rashely long before,
The bed and rytes of mariage, for many yeres forswore,   2220
Yet mother now behold your daughter at your will,
Ready (if you commaunde her ought) your pleasure to fulfill.
Wherfore in humble wise dere madam I you pray,
To goe unto my lord and syre, withouten long delay;
Of him fyrst pardon crave of faultes already past,
And shew him (if it pleaseth you) his child is now at last
Obedient to his just and to his skilfull hest.
And that I will (god lending life) on Wensday next be prest
To wayte on him and you, unto thappoynted place,
Where I will, in your hearing, and before my fathers face,   2230
Unto the Counte geve my fayth and whole assent,
To take him for my lord and spouse; thus fully am I bent.
And that out of your mynde I may remove all doute,
Unto my closet fare I now, to searche and to choose out
The bravest garmentes and the richest jewels there,
Which (better him to please) I mynd on Wensday next to weare;
For if I did excell the famous Grecian rape,
Yet might attyre helpe to amende my bewty and my shape.
The simple mother was, rapt in to great delight,
Not halfe a word could she bring forth, but in this joyfull
          plight,   2240
With nimble foote she ran and with unwonted pace,
Unto her pensive husband, and to him with pleasant face
She tolde what she had heard, and prayseth much the fryer,
And joyfull teares ranne downe the cheekes of this gray-berded
          sire.
With handes and eyes heaved up, he thankes God in his hart,
And then he sayth. This is not (wife) the friers first desart;
Oft hath he shewde to us, great frendship heretofore,
By helping us at nedefull times, with wisdomes pretious lore.
In all our common weale, scarce one is to be founde,

But is for somme good torne unto this holy father bounde.　2250
Oh that the thyrd part of my goods (I doe not fayne)
But twenty of his passed yeres might purchase him agayne
So much in recompence of frendship would I geve,
So much (in faith) his extreme age my frendly hart doth greve.
　These said, the glad old man, from home goeth straight
　　abrode,
And to the stately palace hyeth, where Paris made abode,
Whom he desyres to be on Wensday next his geast,
At Freetowne, where he myndes to make for him a costly feast.
But loe, the Earle saith such feasting were but lost,
And counsels him till mariage time to spare so great a cost,　2260
For then he knoweth well the charges wilbe great,
The whilst his hart desyreth still her sight, and not his meate.
He craves of Capilet, that he may straight go see
Fayre Juliet, wher to he doth right willingly agree.
The mother warnde before, her daughter doth prepare.
She warneth and she chargeth her that in no wyse she spare
Her curteous speche, her pleasant lookes, and commely grace,
But liberally to geve them forth when Paris commes in place:
Which she as cunningly could set forth to the shewe,
As cunning craftesmen to the sale do set their wares on row,　2270
That ere the County did out of her sight depart,
So secretly unwares to him, she stale away his hart,
That of his lyfe and death the wyly wench hath powre.
And now his longing hart thinkes long for theyr appoynted
　　howre,
And with importune sute, the parentes doth he pray,
The wedlocke knot to knit soone up, and hast the mariage day.
　The woer hath past forth the first day in this sort,
And many other more then this, in pleasure and disport.
At length the wished time of long hoped delight,
(As Paris thought) drew nere, but nere approched heavy
　　plight.　2280
Against the bridall day the parentes did prepare
Such rich attyre, such furniture, such store of dainty fare,
That they which did behold the same the night before
Did thinke and say, a man could scarcely wishe for any more.
Nothing did seeme to deere, the deerest thinges were bought,
And (as the written story saith) in dede there wanted nought,
That longd to his degree and honor of his stocke.
But Juliet, the whilst, her thoughts within her brest did locke;
Even from the trusty nurce, whose secretnes was tryde,

The secret counsell of her hart the nurce childe seekes to
    hide.   2290
For sith, to mocke her dame, she dyd not sticke to lye,
She thought no sinne with shew of truth, to bleare her nurces eye.
In chamber secretly the tale she gan renew,
That at the doore she tolde her dame, as though it had been trew.
The flattring nurce did prayse the fryer for his skill,
And said that she had done right well by wit to order will.
She setteth foorth at large the fathers furious rage,
And eke she prayseth much to her, the second mariage;
And County Paris now she praiseth ten times more,
By wrong, then she her selfe by right, had Romeus praysde
    before.   2300
Paris shall dwell there still, Romeus shall not retourne,
What shall it boote her life, to languish still and mourne.
The pleasures past before, she must account as gayne,
But if he doe retorne, what then? for one she shall have twayne.
The one shall use her as his lawfull wedded wyfe,
In wanton love, with equall joy the other leade his lyfe.
And best shall she be sped of any townish dame,
Of husband and of paramour, to fynde her chaunge of game.
These wordes and like, the nurse did speake, in hope to please,
But greatly did these wicked wordes the ladies mynde
    disease,   2310
But ay she hid her wrath, and seemed well content,
When dayly dyd the naughty nurse new argumentes invent.
But when the bryde perceved her howre approched nere,
She sought (the best she could) to fayne, and temperd so her
    cheere,
That by her outward looke, no living wight could gesse
Her inward woe, and yet anew renewde is her distresse.
Unto her chaumber doth the pensive wight repayre,
And in her hand a percher light[1] the nurse beares up the stayre.
In Juliets chamber was her wonted use to lye,
Wherfore her mistres, dreading that she should her work
    descrye,   2320
As sone as she began her pallet to unfold,
Thinking to lye that night, where she was wont to lye of olde,
Doth gently pray her seeke her lodgeing some where els;
And lest she crafty should suspect, a ready reason telles.
Dere frend (quoth she) you knowe, to morow is the day
Of new contract, wherfore this night, my purpose is to pray

---

[1] tall candle.

Unto the heavenly myndes, that dwell above the skyes,
And order all the course of thinges, as they can best devyse,
That they so smyle upon the doynges of to morow,
That all the remnant of my lyfe, may be exempt from
          sorow.   2330
Wherfore I pray you leave me here alone this night,
But see that you to morow comme before the dawning light,
For you must curle my heare, and set on my attyre.
And easely the loving nurse, dyd yelde to her desire,
For she within her hed dyd cast before no doute;
She little knew the close attempt, her nurce childe went about.
    The nurce departed once, the chamber doore shut close,
Assured that no living wight, her doing myght disclose,
She powred forth into the vyole of the fryer,
Water, out of a silver ewer, that on the boord stoode by
          her.   2340
The slepy mixture made, fayre Juliet doth it hyde,
Under her bolster soft, and so unto her bed she hyed:
Where divers novel thoughts arise within her hed,
And she is so invironed about with deadly dred,
That what before she had resolved undoutedly,
That same she calleth into doute, and lying doutfully
Whilst honest love did strive with dred of dedly payne,
With handes ywrong, and weping eyes, thus gan she to complaine.
What, is there any one beneth the heavens hye,
So much unfortunate as I? so much past hope as I?   2350
What, am not I my selfe, of all that yet were borne,
The depest drenched in dispayre, and most in Fortunes skorne?
For loe the world for me, hath nothing els to finde,
Beside mishap and wretchednes, and anguish of the mynde,
Since that the cruel cause of my unhappines
Hath put me to this sodaine plonge, and brought to such distres,
As (to the end I may my name and conscience save)
I must devowre the mixed drinke, that by me here I have,
Whose woorking and whose force as yet I doe not know.
And of this piteous plaint began another doute to growe: 2360
What doe I knowe (quoth she) if that this powder shall
Sooner or later then it should or els not woorke at all?
And then my craft descride as open as the day,
The peoples tale and laughing stocke shall I remayne for aye.
And what know I (quoth she) if serpentes odious,
And other beastes and wormes that are of nature venemous,
That wonted are to lurke, in darke caves under grounde,

And commonly, as I have heard, in dead mens tombes are found,
Shall harme me, yea or nay, where I shall lye as ded.
Or how shall I, that alway have in so freshe ayre been bred,   2370
Endure the lothsome stinke of such an heaped store
Of carkases, not yet consumde, and bones that long before
Intombed were, where I my sleping place shall have,
Where all my auncesters doe rest, my kindreds common grave?
Shall not the fryer and my Romeus, when they come,
Fynd me (if I awake before) ystifled in the tombe?

    And whilst she in these thoughtes doth dwell somwhat to long,
The force of her ymagining, anon dyd waxe so strong,
That she surmysde she saw out of the hollow vaulte,
(A griesly thing to looke upon), the carkas of Tybalt,   2380
Right in the selfe same sort, that she few dayes before
Had seene him in his blood embrewde, to death eke wounded sore.
And then, when she agayne within her selfe had wayde
That quicke she should be buried there, and by his side be layde,
All comfortles, for she shall living feere have none,
But many a rotten carkas, and full many a naked bone,
Her dainty tender partes gan shever all for dred,
Her golden heares did stand upright, upon her chillish hed.
Then pressed with the feare that she there lived in,
A sweat as colde as mountaine yse, pearst through her tender
    skin,   2390
That with the moysture hath wet every part of hers,
And more besides, she vainely thinkes, whilst vainely thus she
    feares,
A thousand bodies dead have compast her about,
And lest they will dismember her, she greatly standes in dout.
But when she felt her strength began to weare away,
By little and little, and in her hart her feare increased ay,
Dreading that weakenes might, or foolish cowardise,
Hinder the execution of the purposde enterprise,
As she had frantike been, in hast the glasse she caught,
And up she dranke the mixture quite, withouten farther
    thought.   2400
Then on her brest she crost her armes long and small,
And so, her senses fayling her, into a traunce did fall.

    And when that Phoebus bright heaved up his seemely hed,
And from the East in open skies his glistring rayes dispred,
The nurce unshut the doore, for she the key did keepe,
And douting she had slept to long, she thought to breake her
    slepe.

Fyrst, softly dyd she call, then lowder thus did crye,
Lady, you slepe to long, (the Earle) will rayse you by and by,
But wele away, in vayne unto the deafe she calles,
She thinkes to speake to Juliet, but speaketh to the walles.   2410
If all the dredfull noyse, that might on earth be found,
Or on the roaring seas, or if the dredfull thunders sound
Had blowne into her eares, I thinke they could not make,
The sleping wight before the time by any meanes awake:
So were the sprites of lyfe shut up, and senses thrald,
Wherwith the seely carefull nurce was wondrously apalde.
She thought to daw her now as she had donne of olde,
But loe, she found her parts were stiffe, and more then marble
  colde,
Neither at mouth nor nose, found she recourse of breth;
Two certaine argumentes were these, of her untimely death.   2420
Wherfore as one distraught, she to her mother ranne,
With scratched face, and heare betorne, but no woord speake she
  can.
At last (with much a doe) dead (quoth she) is my childe.
Now, out alas (the mother cryde) and as a Tyger wilde,
Whose whelpes whilst she is gonne out of her denne to prey,
The hunter gredy of his game, doth kill or cary away:
So, rageing forth she ranne, unto her Juliets bed,
And there she found her derling, and her onely comfort ded.
Then shriked she out as lowde, as serve her would her breth,
And then (that pity was to heare) thus cryde she out on
  death.   2430
Ah cruell death (quoth she) that thus against all right
Hast ended my felicitie, and robde my hartes delight,
Do now thy worst to me, once wreake thy wrath for all,
Even in despite I crye to thee thy vengeance let thou fall.
Wherto stay I (alas) since Juliet is gone?
Wherto live I since she is dead, except to wayle and mone?
Alacke, dere chyld, my teares for thee shall never cease;
Even as my dayes of life increase, so shall my plaint increase.
Such store of sorow shall afflict my tender hart,
That dedly panges when they assayle, shall not augment my
  smart.   2440
Then gan she so to sobbe, it seemde her hart would brast,
And while she crieth thus, behold the father at the last,
The County Paris, and of gentilmen a route,
And ladies of Verona towne, and country round about,
Both kindreds and alies, thether apace have preast,

For by theyr presence there they sought to honor so the feast.
But when the heavy newes the bydden geastes did heare,
So much they mournd, that who had seene theyr countnance and
    theyr cheere,
Might easely have judgde, by that that they had seene,
That day the day of wrath, and eke of pity to have beene.   2450
But more then all the rest the fathers hart was so
Smit with the heavy newes, and so shut up with sodain woe,
That he ne had the powre his daughter to bewepe,
Ne yet to speake, but long is forsd, his teares and plaint to kepe.
In all the hast he hath for skilfull leaches sent,
And, hearyng of her passed life, they judge with one assent,
The cause of this her death was inward care and thought,
And then with double force againe the doubled sorowes wrought.
If ever there hath been a lamentable day,
A day, ruthfull, unfortunate, and fatall, then I say,   2460
The same was it in which, through Veron towne was spred
The wofull newes how Juliet was sterved in her bed.
For so she was bemonde, both of the yong and olde,
That it might seeme to him that would the commen plaint
    behold,
That all the commen welth did stand in jeopardy,
So universall was the plaint, so piteous was the crye.
For lo, beside her shape, and native bewties hewe,
With which, like as she grew in age, her vertues prayses grewe,
She was also so wise, so lowly, and so mylde,
That, even from the hory head unto the witles childe,   2470
She wan the hartes of all, so that there was not one,
Ne great, ne small, but dyd that day her wretched state bemone.
    Whilst Juliet slept, and whilst the other wepen thus,
Our fryer Lawrence hath by this, sent one to Romeus,
A frier of his house, there never was a better,
He trusted him even as himselfe, to whom he gave a letter,
In which, he written had, of every thing at length,
That past twixt Juliet and him, and of the powders strength;
The next night after that, he willeth him to comme
To helpe to take his Juliet out of the hollow toombe,   2480
For by that time, the drinke, he saith, will cease to woorke,
And for one night his wife and he within his cell shall loorke.
Then shall he cary her to Mantua away,
(Till fickell Fortune favour him) disguisde in mans aray.
    Thys letter closde he sendes to Romeus by his brother:
He chargeth him that in no case he geve it any other.

Apace our frier John to Mantua him hies,
And, for because in Italy it is a wonted guise,
That friers in the towne should seeldome walke alone,
But of theyr covent ay should be accompanide with one　　　2490
Of his profession, straight a house he fyndeth out,
In mynde to take some frier with him, to walke the towne about.
But entred once, he might not issue out agayne,
For that a brother of the house, a day before or twayne,
Dyed of the plague (a sickenes which they greatly feare and hate)
So were the brethren charged to kepe within theyr covent gate,
Bar[r']d of theyr felowship, that in the towne do wonne;
The towne folke eke commaunded are, the fryers house to shonne,
Tyll they that had the care of health, theyr fredome should renew.
Wherof, as you shall shortly heare, a mischeefe great there
　　　　grewe.　　　　2500
The fryer by this restraint, beset with dred and sorow,
Not knowing what the letters held, differd untill the morowe,
And then he thought in tyme to send to Romeus.
But whilst at Mantua where he was, these dooinges framed thus,
The towne of Juliets byrth was wholy busied,
About her obsequies, to see theyr darlyng buried.
Now is the parentes myrth quite chaunged into mone,
And now to sorow is retornde the joy of every one.
And now the wedding weedes for mourning weedes they chaunge,
And Hymene into a Dyrge, alas it seemeth straunge.　　　2510
In steade of mariage gloves, now funerall gloves they have,
And whom they should see maried, they follow to the grave.
The feast that should have been of pleasure and of joy,
Hath every dish, and cup, fild full of sorow and annoye.
　　Now throughout Italy this common use they have,
That all the best of every stocke are earthed in one grave;
For every houshold, if it be of any fame,
Doth bylde a tombe, or digge a vault that beares the housholdes
　　　　name;
Wherein (if any of that kindred hap to dye)
They are bestowde, els in the same no other corps may lye.　　2520
The Capilets her corps in such a one dyd lay,
Where Tybalt slayne of Romeus was layde the other day.
An other use there is, that whosoever dyes,
Borne to their church with open face, upon the beere he lyes
In wonted weede attyrde, not wrapt in winding sheete.
So, as by chaunce he walked abrode, our Romeus man dyd meete
His maisters wyfe; the sight with sorow straight dyd wounde

His honest hart; with teares he sawe her lodged under ground.
And, for he had been sent to Verone for a spye,
The doynges of the Capilets by wisdome to descrye, 2530
And for he knew her death dyd tooch his maister most,
(Alas) too soone, with heavy newes he hyed away in post,
And in his house he found his maister Romeus,
Where he, besprent with many teares, began to speake him thus.
Syr, unto you of late is chaunced so great a harme,
That sure, except with constancy you seeke your selfe to arme,
I feare that strayght you will brethe out your latter breath,
And I, most wretched wight, shalbe thoccasion of your death.
Know syr that yesterday my lady and your wyfe,
I wot not by what sodain grefe, hath made exchaunge of
        life, 2540
And for because on earth, she found nought but unrest,
In heaven hath she sought to fynde a place of quiet rest.
And with these weping eyes my selfe have seene her layde
Within the tombe of Capilets: and here withall he stayde.
This sodayne message sounde sent forth with sighes and teares,
Our Romeus receaved too soone with open listening eares,
And therby hath sonke in such sorow in his hart,
That loe, his sprite annoyed sore with torment and with smart,
Was like to breake out of his prison house perforce,
And that he might flye after hers, would leave the massy
        corse. 2550
But earnest love that will not fayle him till his ende,
This fond and sodain fantasy into his head dyd sende:
That if nere unto her he offred up his breath,
That then an hundred thousand parts more glorious were his
        death;
Eke should his painfull hart a great deale more be eased,
And more also (he vainely thought) his lady better pleased.
Wherfore, when he his face hath washt with water cleene,
Lest that the staynes of dryed teares might on his cheekes be
        seene,
And so his sorow should of every one be spyde,
Which he with all his care dyd seeke from every one to
        hyde, 2560
Straight, wery of the house, he walketh forth abrode:
His servaunt, at the maisters hest, in chamber styll abode.
And then fro streate to streate, he wandreth up and downe,
To see if he in any place may fynde, in all the towne,
A salve meete for his sore, an oyle fitte for his wounde,

And seeking long (alack too soone) the thing he sought, he founde.
An Apothecary sate unbusied at his doore,
Whom by his heavy countenaunce he gessed to be poore,
And in his shop he saw his boxes were but fewe,
And in his window (of his wares) there was so small a
    shew,   2570
Wherfore our Romeus assuredly hath thought,
What by no frendship could be got, with money should be bought;
For nedy lacke is lyke the poore man to compell
To sell that which the cities lawe forbiddeth him to sell.
Then by the hand he drew the nedy man apart,
And with the sight of glittring gold inflamed hath his hart:
Take fiftie crownes of gold (quoth he) I geve them thee,
So that, before I part from hence, thou straight deliver me
Somme poyson strong, that may, in lesse then halfe an howre,
Kill him whose wretched hap shalbe the potion to devowre.   2580
The wretch by covetise is wonne, and doth assent
To sell the thing, whose sale ere long, too late, he doth repent.
In hast he poyson sought, and closely he it bounde,
And then began with whispering voyce thus in his eare to rounde:
Fayre syr (quoth he) be sure, this is the speeding gere,
And more there is then you shall nede, for halfe of that is there
Will serve, I under take, in lesse then half an howre,
To kill the strongest man alive; such is the poysons power.
   Then Romeus somwhat easd of one part of his care,
Within his bosome putteth up his dere unthrifty ware.   2590
Retorning home agayne, he sent his man away,
To Verone towne, and chargeth him, that he, without delay,
Provyde both instruments, to open wyde the toombe,
And lightes to shew him Juliet, and stay (till he shall comme,)
Nere to the place whereas his loving wyfe doth rest,
And chargeth him not to bewray the dolours of his brest.
Peter, these heard, his leave doth of his maister take;
Betyme he commes to towne, such hast the paynfull man did
    make:
And then with busy care he seeketh to fulfill,
But doth dysclose unto no wight his wofull maisters will.   2600
Would God he had herein broken his maisters hest!
Would God that to the fryer he had dysclosed all hys brest!
But Romeus, the whyle, with many a dedly thought,
Provoked much, hath caused ynke and paper to be brought,
And in few lynes he dyd of all his love dyscoorse,
How by the fryers helpe, and by the knowledge of the noorse,

The wedlocke knot was knyt, and by what meane that night
And many moe he dyd enjoy, his happy hartes delight;
Where he the poyson bought, and how his lyfe should ende;
And so his wailefull tragedy the wretched man hath pend.   2610
 The letters closd and seald, directed to his syre,
He locketh in his purse, and then, a post hors doth he hyre.
When he approched nere, he warely lighted downe,
And even with the shade of night he entred Verone towne,
Where he hath found his man, wayting when he should comme,
With lanterne, and with instruments, to open Juliets toomme.
Helpe Peter, helpe, quod he, helpe to remove the stone,
And straight when I am gone fro thee, my Juliet to bemone,
See that thou get thee hence, and on the payne of death,
I charge thee that thou comme not nere, whyle I abyde
       beneath,   2620
Ne seeke thou not to let thy masters enterprise,
Which he hath fully purposed to doe, in any wise.
Take there a letter, which, as soone as he shall ryse,
Present it in the morning to my loving fathers eyes;
Which unto him perhaps farre pleasanter shall seeme,
Than eyther I do mynd to say, or thy gros[s]e head can deeme.
 Now Peter, that knew not the purpose of his hart,
Obediently a little way withdrew himselfe apart,
And then our Romeus, (the vault stone set upright)
Descended downe, and in his hand he bare the candle light.   2630
And then with piteous eye, the body of his wyfe
He gan beholde, who surely was the organ of his lyfe;
For whom unhappy now he is, but erst was blyst.
He watred her with teares, and then an hundred times her kyst,
And in his folded armes, full straightly he her plight,
But no way could his greedy eyes be filled with her sight.
His fearfull handes he layd upon her stomacke colde,
And them on divers parts besyde, the wofull wight did hold.
But when he could not fynd the signes of lyfe he sought,
Out of his cursed box he drewe the poyson that he bought;   2640
Wherof he gredely devowrde the greater part,
And then he cryde with dedly sigh, fetcht from his mourning hart:
Oh Juliet, of whom the world unwoorthy was,
From which, for worldes unworthines thy worthy gost dyd passe,
What death more pleasant could my hart wish to abyde,
Then that which here it suffreth now, so nere thy frendly syde?
Or els so glorious tombe, how could my youth have craved,
As in one selfe same vaulte with thee haply to be ingraved?

23—S.N.D. I

What Epitaph more worth, or halfe so excellent,
To consecrate my memorye, could any man invente,   2650
As this, our mutuell, and our piteous sacrifice
Of lyfe, set light for love.—But while he talketh in this wise,
And thought as yet a while his dolors to enforce,
His tender hart began to faynt, prest with the venoms force,
Which little and little gan to overcomme hys hart,
And whilst his busy eyne he threwe about to every part,
He saw hard by the corce of sleping Juliet,
Bold Tybalts carkas dead, which was not all consumed yet.
To whom (as having life) in this sort speaketh he:
Ah cosin dere Tybalt whereso thy restles sprite now be,   2660
With stretched handes to thee for mercy now I crye,
For that before thy kindly howre I forced thee to dye.
But if with quenched lyfe, not quenched be thine yre,
But with revengeing lust as yet thy hart be set on fyre,
What more amendes, or cruell wreke desyrest thou
To see on me, then this which here is shewd forth to thee now?
Who reft by force of armes from thee thy living breath,
The same with his owne hand (thou seest) doth poyson himselfe
        to death.
And for he caused thee in tombe too soone to lye,
Too soone also, yonger then thou, himselfe he layeth by.   2670
These said, when he gan feele the poysons force prevayle,
And little and little mastred lyfe, for aye beganne to fayle,
Kneeling upon his knees, he said with voyce full lowe.
Lord Christ, that so to raunsome me descendedst long agoe
Out of thy fathers bosome, and in the virgins wombe
Didst put on fleshe, Oh let my plaint out of this hollow toombe,
Perce through the ayre, and graunt my sute may favour finde;
Take pity on my sinnefull and my poore afflicted mynde.
For well enough I know, this body is but clay,
Nought but a masse of sinne, to frayle, and subject to decay.   2680
Then pressed with extreme greefe, he threw with so great force,
His overpressed parts upon his ladies wayled corps,
That now his wekened hart, weakened with tormentes past,
Unable to abyde this pang, the sharpest and the last,
Remayned quite deprived, of sense and kindly strength,
And so the long imprisond soule hath freedome wonne at length.
Ah cruell death, too soone, too soone was this devorce,
Twixt youthfull Romeus heavenly sprite, and his fayre earthy
        corse.
    The fryer that knew what time the powder had been taken,

Knew eke the very instant when the sleper should awaken,   2690
But wondring that he could no kind of aunswer heare,
Of letters, which to Romeus his fellow fryer did beare,
Out of sainct Frauncis church hymselfe alone dyd fare,
And for the opening of the tombe, meete instrumentes he bare.
Approching nigh the place, and seeing there the lyght,
Great horror felt he in his hart, by straunge and sodaine sight
Tyll Peter (Romeus man) his coward hart made bolde,
When of his masters being there, the certain newes he tolde.
There hath he been (quoth he) this halfe howre at the least,
And in this time I dare well say his plaint hath still increast.   2700
Then both they entred in, where they (alas) dyd fynde,
The bretheles corps of Romeus, forsaken of the mynde;
Where they have made such mone, as they may best conceve,
That have with perfect frendship loved, whose frend, feerce death
      dyd reve.
But whilst with piteous playnt, they Romeus fate bewepe,
An howre too late fayre Juliet awaked out of slepe,
And much amasde to see in tombe so great a light,
She wist not if she saw a dreame, or sprite that walkd by night.
But cumming to her selfe, she knew them, and said thus:
What, fryer Lawrence, is it you? where is my Romeus?   2710
And then the auncient frier, that greatly stoode in feare,
Lest if they lingred over long, they should be taken there,
In few plaine woordes, the whole that was betyde he tolde,
And with his fingar shewd his corps out stretched, stiffe, and colde,
And then perswaded her with pacience to abyde
This sodain great mischaunce, and sayth that he will soone
      provyde
In somme religious house for her a quiet place,
Where she may spend the rest of lyfe, and where in time percase
She may with wisdomes meane, measure her mourning brest,
And unto her tormented soule call backe exiled rest.   2720
But loe, as soone as she had cast her ruthfull eye
On Romeus face, that pale and wan, fast by her side dyd lye,
Straight way she dyd unstop the conduites of her teares,
And out they gushe; with cruell hand she tare her golden heares.
But when she neither could her swelling sorow swage,
Ne yet her tender hart abyde her sickenes furious rage,
Falne on his corps, she lay long panting on his face,
And then with all her force and strength, the ded corps dyd
      embrace,
As though with sighes, with sobs, with force and busy payne,

She would him rayse, and him restore from death to lyfe
    agayne. 2730
A thousand times she kist his mouth as cold as stone,
And it unkist agayne as oft, then gan she thus to mone.
Ah pleasant prop of all my thoughtes, ah onely ground
Of all the sweete delightes, that yet in all my lyfe I found,
Did such assured trust within thy hart repose,
That in this place, and at this time, thy churchyarde thou hast
    chose,
Betwixt the armes of me, thy perfect loving make?
And thus by meanes of me to ende thy lyfe, and for my sake?
Even in the flowring of thy youth, when unto thee,
Thy lyfe most deare (as to the most) and pleasant ought to
    be, 2740
How could this tender corps withstand the cruell fight
Of furious death, that wonts to fray the stoutest with his sight?
How could thy dainty youth agree with willing hart,
In this so fowle infected place, (to dwell) where now thou art
Where spitefull Fortune hath appoynted thee to be,
The dainty foode of greedy wormes, unworthy sure of thee?
Alas, alas, alas, what neded now anew,
My wonted sorowes doubled twise agayne thus to renewe?
Which both the tyme and eke my patient long abode,
Should now at length have quenched quite, and under foote
    have trode. 2750
Ah wretch and caytive that I am, even when I thought
To find my painefull passions salve, I myst the thing I sought,
And to my mortall harme, the fatall knyfe I grounde,
That gave to me so deepe, so wyde, so cruell dedly wounde.
Ah thou most fortunate and most unhappy tombe,
For thou shalt beare from age to age, witnes in time to comme,
Of the most perfect leag[u]e, betwixt a payre of lovers,
That were the most unfortunate, and fortunate of others.
Receave the latter sigh, receave the latter pang,
Of the most cruell of cruell slaves, that wrath and death ay
    wrang. 2760
And when our Juliet would continue still her mone,
The fryer and the servant fled, and left her there alone,
For they a sodayne noyse, fast by the place did heare,
And lest they might be taken there, greatly they stoode in feare.
When Juliet saw her selfe left in the vaulte alone,
That freely she might worke her will, for let or stay was none,
Then once for all, she tooke the cause of all her harmes,

The body dead of Romeus, and claspd it in her armes.
Then she with earnest kisse, sufficiently did prove,
That more then by the feare of death she was attaint by
    love.   2770
And then past deadly feare, for lyfe ne had she care,
With hasty hand she did draw out the dagger that he ware.
O welcome death (quoth she) end of unhappines,
That also art beginning of assured happines;
Feare not to darte me nowe, thy stripe no longer stay,
Prolong no longer now my lyfe, I hate this long delaye,
For straight my parting sprite, out of this carkas fled,
At ease shall finde my Romeus sprite, among so many ded.
And thou my loving lord, Romeus my trusty feer,
If knowledge yet doe rest in thee, if thou these woordes dost
    heer,   2780
Receve thou her, whom thou didst love so lawfully,
That causd (alas) thy violent death although unwillingly;
And therfore willingly offers to thee her gost,
To thend that no wight els but thou, might have just cause to
    boste
Thinjoying of my love, which ay I have reserved,
Free from the rest, bound unto thee, that hast it well deserved:
That so our parted sprites, from light that we see here,
In place of endlesse light and blisse, may ever live yfere.
These said, her ruthlesse hand through gyrt her valiant hart.
Ah, Ladies, helpe with teares to wayle the ladies dedly
    smart.   2790
She grones, she stretcheth out her limmes, she shuttes her eyes,
And from her corps the sprite doth flye. what should I say? she
    dyes.
The watchemen of the towne, the whilst are passed by,
And through the gates the candel light within the tombe they
    spye:
Wherby they did suppose, inchaunters to be comme,
That with prepared instrumentes had opend wide the tombe,
In purpose to abuse the bodies of the ded,
Which by theyr science ayde abusde, do stand them oft in sted.
Theyr curious harts desire the trueth herof to know,
Then they by certaine steppes descend, where they do fynd
    below,   2800
In clasped armes ywrapt the husband and the wyfe,
In whom as yet they seemd to see somme certaine markes of lyfe.
But when more curiously with leysure they did vew,

The certainty of both theyr deathes, assuredly they knew.
Then here and there so long with carefull eye they sought,
That at the length hidden they found the murthrers so they
  thought.
In dongeon depe that night they lodgde them under grounde,
The next day do they tell the prince the mischefe that they
  found.
  The newes was by and by throughout the towne dyspred,
Both of the takyng of the fryer, and of the two found ded.   2810
Thether might you have seene whole housholdes forth to ronne,
For to the tombe where they did heare this wonder straunge was
  donne,
The great, the small, the riche, the poore, the yong, the olde,
With hasty pace do ronne to see, but rew when they beholde,
And that the murtherers to all men might be knowne,
Like as the murders brute abrode through all the towne was
  blowne,
The prince did straight ordaine, the corses that wer founde
Should be set forth upon a stage, hye raysed from the grounde,
Right in the selfe same fourme, (shewde forth to all mens sight)
That in the hollow valt they had been found that other
  night,   2820
And eke that Romeus man, and fryer Lawrence should
Be openly examined, for els the people would
Have murmured, or faynd there were some wayghty cause,
Why openly they were not calde, and so convict by lawes.
  The holy fryer now, and reverent by his age,
In great reproche set to the shew upon the open stage,
(A thing that ill beseemde a man of silver heares)
His beard as whyte as mylke he bathes, with great fast-falling
  teares:
Whom straight the dredfull Judge commaundeth to declare
Both how this murther hath been donne, and who the
  murthrers are,   2830
For that he nere the tombe was found at howres unfitte,
And had with hym those yron tooles, for such a purpose fitte.
The frier was of lively sprite, and free of speche,
The Judges woordes appald him not, ne were his wittes to seeche.
But with advised heed, a while fyrst did he stay,
And then with bold assured voyce, aloude thus gan he say.
My lordes, there is not one emong you, set togyther,
So that (affection set aside) by wisdome he consider
My former passed lyfe, and this my extreme age,

And eke this heavy sight, the wreke of frantike Fortunes
    rage,   2840
But that, amased much, doth wonder at this chaunge,
So great, so sodainly befalne, unlooked for, and straunge.
For I, that in the space of lx. yeres and tenne,
Since first I did begin, to soone, to leade my lyfe with men,
And with the worldes vaine thinges, my selfe I did acquaint,
Was never yet, in open place, at any time attaynt
With any cryme, in waight, as heavy as a rushe,
Ne is there any stander by, can make me gylty blushe,
(Although before the face of God, I doe confesse,
My selfe to be the sinfulst wretch of all this mighty presse.)   2850
When readiest I am, and likeliest to make
My great accompt, which no man els for me shall undertake;
When wormes, the earth, and death doe cite me every howre,
Tappeare before the judgement seate of everlasting powre,
And falling ripe I steppe upon my graves brinke,
Even then, am I, most wretched wight, (as eche of you doth
    thinke)
Through my most haynous deede, with hedlong sway throwne
    downe,
In greatest daunger of my lyfe, and domage of renowne.
The spring, whence in your head, this new conceite doth ryse,
And in your hart increaseth still your vayne and wrong
    surmise,   2860
May be the hugenes of these teares of myne (percase),
That so aboundantly downe fall, by eyther syde my face.
As though the memory in scriptures were not kept,
That Christ our saviour himselfe for ruth and pittie wept.
And more, whoso will reade, ywritten shall he fynde,
That teares are as true messengers of mans ungyltie mynde.
Or els, (a liker proofe) that I am in the cryme,
You say these present yrons are, and the suspected tyme;
As though all howres alike had not been made above!
Did Christ not say the day had twelve? whereby he sought to
    prove,   2870
That no respect of howres, ought justly to be had,
But at all times men have the choyce of dooing good or bad;
Even as the sprite of God the hartes of men doth guyde,
Or as it leaveth them to stray from Vertues path asyde.
As for the yrons that were taken in my hand,
As now I deeme, I neede not seeke, to make ye understande
To what use yron first was made, when it began:

How of it selfe it helpeth not, ne yet can helpe a man.
The thing that hurteth, is the malice of his will,
That such indifferent thinges is wont to use and order yll.   2880
Thus much I thought to say, to cause you so to know,
That neither these my piteous teares, though nere so fast they
    flowe,
Ne yet these yron tooles, nor the suspected time,
Can justly prove the murther donne, or damne me of the cryme.
No one of these hath powre, ne powre have all the three,
To make me other then I am, how so I seeme to be.
But sure my conscience (if so my gylt deserve)
For an appeacher, witnesse, and a hangman eke should serve,
For through mine age, whose heares, of long time since were hore,
And credyt greate that I was in, with you in time tofore,   2890
And eke the sojorne short that I on earth must make,
That every day and howre do loke my journey hence to take,
My conscience inwardly, should more torment me thrise,
Then all the outward deadly payne that all you could devyse.
But (God I prayse) I feele no worme that gnaweth me,
And from remorses pricking sting, I joy that I am free.
I meane, as touching this, wherwith you troubled are,
Wherwith you should be troubled still if I my speche should
    spare.
But to the end I may set all your hartes at rest,
And plucke out all the scrupuls that are rooted in your
    brest,   2900
Which might perhappes henceforth increasing more and more
Within your conscience also, increase your curelesse sore,
I sweare by yonder heavens, whither I hope to clym,
And for a witness of my woordes, my hart attesteth him,
Whose mighty hand doth welde them in their vyolent sway,
And on the rolling stormy seas the heavy earth doth stay:
That I will make a short and eke a true dyscourse
Of this most wofull Tragedy, and shew both thend and sourse
Of theyr unhappy death, which you perchaunce no lesse
Will wonder at, then they (alas) poore lovers in distresse,   2910
Tormented much in mynd not forcing lively breath,
With strong and patient hart dyd yelde themselfe to cruell death.
Such was the mutuall love, wherin they burned both,
And of their promyst frendshippes fayth, so stedy was the troth.
    And then the auncient frier began to make dyscourse,
Even from the first of Romeus, and Juliets amours.
How first by sodayn sight, the one the other chose,

And twixt them selfe dyd knitte the knotte, which onely death
    might lose,
And how within a while, with hotter love opprest,
Under confessions cloke, to him them selfe they have adrest, 2920
And how with solemne othes they have protested both,
That they in hart are maried by promise and by othe;
And that except he graunt the rytes of church to geve,
They shalbe forst by earnest love in sinnefull state to live:
Which thing when he had wayde, and when he understoode,
That the agreement twixt them twayn was lawfull, honest, good,
And all thinges peysed well, it seemed meete to bee,
For lyke they were of noblenesse, age, riches, and degree;
Hoping that so at length, ended myght be the stryfe,
Of Montagewes and Capelets, that led in hate theyr lyfe, 2930
Thinking to woorke a woorke well pleasing in Gods sight,
In secret shrift he wedded them, and they the selfe same night
Made up the mariage in house of Capelet,
As well doth know (if she be askt) the nurce of Juliet.
He told how Romeus fled, for reving Tybalts lyfe,
And how the whilst, Paris the Earle was offred to hys wyfe;
And how the lady dyd, so great a wrong dysdayne,
And how to shrift unto his church she came to him agayne;
And how she fell flat downe before his feete aground,
And how she sware her hand, and blody knife should
    wound 2940
Her harmeles hart, except, that he some meane dyd fynde
To dysappoynt the Earles attempt, and spotles save her mynde.
Wherfore he doth conclude, (although that long before)
By thought of death and age, he had refusde for evermore
The hidden artes which he delighted in, in youth,
Yet wonne by her importunenes, and by his inward ruth,
And fearing lest she would her cruell vowe dyscharge,
His closed conscience he had opened and set at large.
And rather did he choose to suffer for one tyme,
His soule to be spotted somdeale with small and easy cryme, 2950
Then that the lady should, (wery of living breath)
Murther her selfe, and daunger much her seely soule by death.
Wherfore, his auncient artes agayne he puttes in ure,
A certaine powder gave he her that made her slepe so sure,
That they her held for dead, and how that frier John
With letters sent to Romeus, to Mantua is gone,
Of whom he knoweth not as yet, what is becomme,
And how that dead he found his frend within her kindreds tombe.

He thinkes with poyson strong, for care the yong man sterved,
Supposing Juliet dead, and how that Juliet hath carved,   2960
With Romeus dagger drawne, her hart and yelded breath,
Desyrous to accompany her lover after death.
And how they could not save her, so they were afeard,
And hidde them selfe, dreding the noyse of watchmen that they
          heard.
And for the proofe of thys his tale, he doth desyer
The Judge, to send forthwith to Mantua for the fryer,
To learne his cause of stay, and eke to reade his letter,
And more beside, to thend that they might judge his cause the
          better,
He prayeth them depose the nurce of Juliet,
And Romeus man, whom at unwares besyde the tombe he
          met.   2970
     Then Peter not so much as erst he was, dysmayd:
My lordes (quoth he) too true is all, that fryer Laurence sayd.
And when my maister went into my mystres grave,
This letter that I offer you, unto me then he gave,
Which he himselfe dyd write as I do understand,
And charged me to offer them unto his fathers hand.
The opened packet doth conteyne in it the same,
That erst the skilfull frier said, and eke the wretches name
That had at his request, the dedly poyson sold,
The price of it, and why he bought, his letters playne have
          tolde.   2980
The case unfolded so, and open now it lyes,
That they could wish no better proofe, save seeing it with theyr
          eyes.
So orderly all thinges were tolde and tryed out,
That in the prease there was not one, that stoode at all in doute.
     The wyser sort to councell called by Escalus,
Have geven advyse, and Escalus sagely decreeth thus.
The nurse of Juliet, is banisht in her age,
Because that from the parentes she dyd hyde the mariage,
Which might have wrought much good, had it in time been
          knowne,
Where now by her concealing it, a mischeefe great is growne; 2990
And Peter, for he dyd obey his masters hest,
In woonted freedome had good leave to lead his lyfe in rest:
Thapothecary, high is hanged by the throte,
And for the paynes he tooke with him, the hangman had his cote.
But now what shall betyde of this gray-bearded syre?

Of fryer Lawrence thus araynde, that good barefooted fryre?
Because that many times he woorthely did serve
The commen welth, and in his lyfe was never found to swerve,
He was discharged quyte, and no marke of defame
Did seeme to blot, or touch at all, the honor of his name.   3000
But of him selfe he went into an Hermitage,
Two myles from Veron towne, where he in prayers past forth his
        age,
Tyll that from earth to heaven, his heavenly sprite dyd flye.
Fyve yeres he lived an Hermite, and an Hermite dyd he dye.
The straungenes of the chaunce, when tryed was the truth
The Montagewes and Capelets hath moved so to ruth,
That with their emptyed teares, theyr choler and theyr rage,
Was emptied quite, and they whose wrath no wisdom could
        asswage,
Nor threatning of the prince, ne mynd of murthers donne,
At length, (so mighty Jove it would) by pitye they are
        wonne.   3010
   And lest that length of time might from our myndes remove
The memory of so perfect, sound, and so approved love,
The bodies dead removed from vaulte where they did dye,
In stately tombe, on pillers great, of marble rayse they hye.
On every syde above, were set and eke beneath,
Great store of cunning Epitaphes, in honor of theyr death.
And even at this day the tombe is to be seene,
So that among the monumentes that in Verona been,
There is no monument more worthy of the sight,
Then is the tombe of Juliet, and Romeus her knight.   3020

¶ Imprinted at London in
Flete strete within Temble barre, at
the signe of the hand and starre, by
Richard Tottill the xix day of
November, An. do. 1562.

A MIDSUMMER NIGHT'S DREAM

INTRODUCTION

ENTERED IN THE STATIONERS' Register on 8 October, 1600, *A Midsummer Night's Dream* was first printed for Thomas Fisher in that year (Q1). A second Quarto, printed in 1619 but dated 1600, was taken from Q1. F1 was printed from a copy of Q2. The date of composition has been much disputed. The play was certainly written before September 1598, for it is mentioned in the *Palladis Tamia* of Francis Meres, fifth among the Comedies. The emphasis on weddings suggests that it was originally written for the marriage of some noble (cf. Chambers *W.Sh.* I.358–63). Several names have been proposed inconclusively. Internal evidence, including style, points to composition between *Titus Andronicus* and *The Merchant of Venice*. The thin characterization of the young lovers puts it early; but the plot demands that they be no more than puppets. The humorous attitude to them and their passion links *A Dream* with *Love's Labour's Lost* and the early scenes of *Romeo and Juliet* rather than with *Two Gentlemen of Verona*. It was probably written in 1594 or 1595, though additions may have been made later, possibly for another wedding. Did it originally include Titania's lengthy account of the bad summer of 1594 (II.1.88)? Lines 88–118 might well have been inserted later. In keeping with the hymeneal occasion Shakespeare treats the play as a merry prank, exercising great ingenuity to unify a hotch-potch of material. Surely it was written for a summer wedding in view of the title and the theme of midsummer madness or enchantment. The action takes place on the night before May-day; for when Theseus finds the lovers he says 'No doubt they rose up early to observe The rite of May'. In this Night of Errors Plautine realism is discarded, the mistakes are not mistakes of identity so much as of emotional direction. The comic 'errors' of physical resemblance are replaced by those of magic, itself sometimes erroneously used.

Shakespeare's main ingredients are: 1. The marriage of Theseus and Hippolyta; 2. The courtship and difficulties of the four young lovers; 3. The fairy world with its spells and quarrels; 4. The misadventures of Bottom; 5. The play of *Pyramus and Thisbe*.

No known source combines these elements. Probably Shakespeare combined them himself; Quiller-Couch (*Camb.* 1924, xiv–xvii) brilliantly imagines how the poet's mind may have worked; but there are many possibilities.

THESEUS AND HIPPOLYTA

The choice of these legendary figures to provide a setting and a resolution to the action must be significant. Theseus was greatly admired as a conqueror in love and war; his marriage to Antiopa or Hippolyta ended the war against the Amazons. These warrior-women were interesting to the Elizabethans; and there were jocular—sometimes scurrilous—references in *Gesta Grayorum* to the Prince of Purpoole's campaign against them. Shakespeare would recall the warrior-heroine in Montemayor's *Diana* whose heroism he diminished to make Julia in *Two Gentlemen of Verona*; his main sources however were Chaucer's *Knightes Tale* [Text I] and North's Plutarch [II]. Chaucer gave a contrast between the wedding and married happiness of a couple already mature and experienced, and the loves of two young men unhappily situated and divided by their passion for the same woman. The 'Marriage of Theseus' might well have been a theme for a short entertainment more serious than *Pyramus and Thisbe*; Shakespeare chose it to start and finish his comedy of absurd lovers, maybe because he was celebrating the marriage of older people than usual. They might be Sir Thomas Heneage, the Queen's Vice-Chamberlain (aged about 60) and Mary, Countess of Southampton, widowed mother of Shakespeare's friend, who married on 2 May, 1594.

Plutarch's *Life of Theseus* probably helped Shakespeare, since it gives stability and poise to its portrait of Theseus by historical verisimilitude and archaeological details. Moreover its ethical material coloured Shakespeare's attitude. In Plutarch Theseus was a lawgiver, who gave order and social hierarchy to the state and founded the Isthmian Games. Also he did what Shakespeare admired Henry V for doing; he moved freely among the people to ascertain their needs and qualities. His kindness and tolerance towards the craftsmen in our play is noteworthy:

> I will hear that play;
> For never anything can be amiss,
> When simpleness and duty tender it. . . . (*MND* V.1.81–105)

If Shakespeare intended a compliment to someone at court he did it very pleasantly. But Theseus, a man of many love-affairs, married again after Hippolyta had brought him a son, Hippolytus, and his next wife Phaedra was the cause of hideous woe. This would never do; so Shakespeare attributed to Theseus staid and steadfast qualities taken from Plutarch's parallel picture of Romulus, a monogamous character. Thus North's translation is used to expand the sketch in Chaucer, where Theseus and his wife live 'in joye and honour'.

There may be other connections with Chaucer's Tale, where two young men fall in love with the same lady and quarrel about her. By adding another lady (Helena) who pursues one of the young men, Shakespeare increases the comedy, particularly when the Fairies cast their spells and all goes topsy-turvy. The comedy itself may be in part a whimsical revulsion against the sentimental love and friendship which colour the *Knightes Tale* as well as *Two Gentlemen of Verona*. None of the four lovers behaves with chivalric grace, but the princely behaviour of Theseus in Shakespeare reminds one of Chaucer, and his entry to initiate the festivities in Act V recalls the beginning of Part IV of the *Knightes Tale*, though the settings differ, for the Athens of Shakespeare is Tudor-Greek, not medieval. Philostrate the Master of Revels in the *Dream* (V.1.38ff) gets his name from Arcite, who in *KT* Pt. II disguised himself and became

> Page of the chambre of Emelye the brighte,
> And Philostrate he seyde that he highte. (1427–8)

Chaucer got it, not from the *Teseide*, but from the title of Boccaccio's other long poem, *Filostrato*, the original of *Troilus and Criseyde*.

24—S.N.D. I

THE FAIRIES

Fairies were almost essential in a Midsummer play, and Shakespeare has used them to enforce the view of love as an enchantment which alienates the minds of its victims with a sudden, ridiculous madness. In love, as Puck exclaims, 'Lord, what fools these mortals be!'—whether under a fairy spell or not. Putting into operation Lyly's dramatic parallelism, Shakespeare sets over against the degrees of mankind the different ranks and kinds of fairy according to folklore and literature. Incidentally Lyly in *Endimion* IV.3 has fairies who kiss the sleeping hero and pinch Corsites, thus illustrating the two sides of fairy behaviour. The theme of marriage is associated with fairy monarchs in Chaucer's *Merchant's Tale*—which treats of the marriage of an elderly man, Januarius, who marries the young May. She falls in love with the squire Damian, who finally possesses her in a pear tree after her husband has gone blind. There is much discussion of the ethics of marriage and the relations between the sexes in this tale, and towards the climax the King and Queen of the Fairies, Pluto and Proserpina, sit in the garden and discuss the infidelity and wiles of the female sex; thus paralleling in their way the previous discussions between mortals. Pluto restores January's sight in time for him to see his wife *in flagrante delicto*, but Proserpina gives her wit to persuade her husband that he did not see straight. Chaucer took this story from Boccaccio (*Decameron*, Day 7, Nov. 9). The idea of fairy monarchs commenting on human life and taking sides for and against mortals while quarrelling between themselves probably came to Shakespeare from Chaucer when he was thinking about the marriage of the mature Theseus (and maybe of the bridegroom for whom the play was written). Shakespeare's brilliant and mocking invention made the King and Queen suffer from the same passions as men and women, know desire, anger, jealousy, like the ancient gods. Instead of Pluto and Proserpina he introduced Oberon, Titania, and Puck or Robin Goodfellow.

Oberon comes from the romance *Huon of Bordeaux*, translated by Lord Berners before 1533 [III], and maybe from Greene's *James IV* where he appears in the introductory dialogue and later brings in 'rounds of fairies'. According to

Philip Henslowe's Diary a play 'hewen of burdoche' was performed by Sussex's men three times during the Christmas season of 1593–4, probably at the Rose Theatre. In Shakespeare, as in *Huon*, Oberon is an Eastern fairy from the farthest steep of India (II.1.124 etc.); he has power over nature and haunts a wood where he works enchantments. The claim that Shakespeare knew the romance is supported by the references in *MND* II.1.232 to the griffin and at III.1.31 to the 'fearful wild fowl', which, as H. Cuningham asserted (*Arden*, p. xxxix), allude to *Huon*, II ch. xxx.

Titania comes directly from Ovid, *Met*. iii.173, which refers to Diana ('dumque ibi perluitur solita Titania lympha'); Golding did not use the word 'Titania' in his translation— evidence that Shakespeare read Ovid in the original. Puck, the Old Norse 'puki', Cornish 'pukka' or 'pixy', was originally an earth demon, as probably was the dwarf Oberon (Alberich). Shakespeare identifies him with Robin Goodfellow, who seems to have been a different sort of fairy, a house-fairy.[1] He would need no books to define Robin Goodfellow's qualities, which were well known in the countryside, but he had certainly read Reginald Scot's *The Discoverie of Witchcraft* (1584) which described belief in Robin Goodfellow as declining, and gave much information about witches, fairies and transformations while denying most of the stories about them in a tone of stern protestant reproof for the popish beliefs of Bodin and other writers [IV]. Shakespeare must have been amused at the earnestness of both parties, and though it might be argued that he sided more with Bodin since he actually shows fairies, Robin, and spells as operating in the greenwood, he makes them ridiculous and charming, not bugbears or demoniac creatures. The very 'human' passions of the fairy King and Queen are the more amusing because Scot denied that spirits could have lusts like ours (Bk. IV.x). Shakespeare may well have been the inventor of the fairy-cult which appears in late Elizabethan and Jacobean poetry—and to which Jonson and Drayton contributed. Most of the fairy songs collected by Halliwell and W. C. Hazlitt seem to be of later date, as is the

---

[1] M. C. Latham in *The Elizabethan Fairies* (1930) has amassed much material on the various attributes of the fairies, whom Shakespeare made less sinister than his predecessors.

lively tract *Robin Goodfellow; his mad prankes and merry Jests* (1628).[1]

There is no need to seek a literary source for the love-juice, but there were many analogues, besides that in Montemayor's *Diana* where a magic water changes the direction of Felix's love (cp. Var 284). Scot attacked all love-potions, classing them under poisonous drugs (Veneficia), and asserting that they were more likely to bring madness or death than lasting affection.

BOTTOM AND THE ASS'S HEAD

Like Sly the 'rude mechanicals' are drawn from life, but with a stylization derived no doubt from Lyly, who however was too literary and classical in inspiration to make the most of plebeian comicality. By making Bottom have a love-affair with Titania Shakespeare not only obtains a parallel in the fairy and guildsmen's world to what is happening among the young courtiers, but can also poke fun at the romantic supernatural of such stories as *Thomas of Erceldoun*. This lay tells how Thomas saw a lovely lady and thought her the Queen of Heaven till she replied:

> Thomas, let such wordis be,
> For quen of heven am I noght,
> I toke never so hye degre.
> But I am a lady of another cuntre.

Though she urged him not to do so he fell in love with her and lay with her, after which he had to accompany her to fairyland where he stayed for what seemed to him three days but really seven years and more. The setting of an ass's head on Bottom recalls Circe's charms. It is a piece of poetic justice like the well-known story of Phoebus's revenge on King Midas which I give from Cooper's *Thesaurus Linguae* [V]. Note that Bottom too pretends to 'have a reasonable good ear in music' with a preference for 'the tongs and the bones' (IV.1.30). Midas has only his ears changed. Bottom's assification is more like that of the amorous Apuleius in *The Golden Asse*, translated by Adlington in 1566 [VI], but nearer still to Shakespeare is a version of this story of witches' spells found in Scot [VII], who disbelieves

---

[1] This and other useful material is printed in *Fairy Tales, Legends and Romances Illustrating Shakespeare and other Early English Writers*, ed. W. C. Hazlitt (1875).

it, but also refers to Pope Benedict IX, condemned after death to walk the earth in a bear skin and an ass's head '*in such sort as he lived*'. Later Scot gives a recipe to make people smeared with a certain ointment look as if they had asses' or horses' heads. Such solemn nonsense must have amused the poet, who laughingly answers Scot by showing transformations happening. As Scot declares (Bk. VII.ii) Robin Goodfellow was no longer as terrible and credible as he used to be. Shakespeare presents a somewhat obsolescent bugbear and shows him as more genial than tradition made him.

THE ENTERTAINMENT

The themes offered to Theseus by Philostrato (*MND* V.1.44–60) comprise three from mythology and one of allegory. 'The battle with the Centaurs' would be a lay or ode, since it would be sung 'By an Athenian eunuch to the harp'. Theseus himself fought the Centaurs when they invaded the wedding feast of Pirithous and Hippodamia (cf. Ovid *Met.* xii.210–360) —so Philostrato's suggestion was apt. Hercules took part in the fight, and later he exterminated the Centaurs when, going to hunt the Eurymanthian boar, he was attacked by them and slew his old tutor Chiron. Hercules also rescued Theseus from Hell, where he was tied to a stone. The piece would be a compliment to his kinsman, Theseus declares, as well as to himself.

'The riot of the tipsy Bacchanals' refers to the revenge of the Thracian women who, offended by the coldness of Orpheus towards them, attacked him in a Dionysian frenzy, and threw his head into the Hebrus; and the head still cried 'Eurydice, Eurydice', as it floated down to the sea. This piece in praise of love and fidelity might be thought suitable for the Amazon Hippolyta.

The allegory of the nine 'Muses mourning for the death/ of Learning late deceased in beggary' may have had topical reference, e.g. to Robert Greene, whose books were still appearing in 1594, or it might be a general reference to the well-known fate of learned men. This would be, as Theseus said, a satire, doubtless accompanied by an appeal for money or patronage by those who gave it.

The 'tedious brief scene' of Pyramus and Thisbe might seem no more suited to a wedding feast, being a tragedy, but it was a well-known story of true love. In *The Petite Pallace of Pettie his Pleasure* (1576), George Pettie regarded it as a parallel with the Romeo and Juliet story: 'such presiness [oppressiveness] of parents brought Pyramus and Thisbe to a woful end, Romeo and Julietta to untimely death' (1908 ed. I.168). The playlet would have special relevance because the love of Hermia and Lysander was forbidden by Egeus, the girl's stern father, and because the pair arranged to meet in the wood 'a league without the town' (I.1.165). (Perhaps this situation was originally suggested to Shakespeare by the Pyramus-Thisbe theme.) Since it becomes riotously funny as performed, the piece does not cloud the proceedings with any suggestion of what Arthur Golding called in dedicating his *Ovid* to the Earl of Leicester, 'The headie force of frantike love whose end is wo and payne.' It is indeed a manifold skit. It laughs at the entertainments and the amateur acting presented by humble subjects to the Queen in her Progresses or to her Lords on their estates. It burlesques the theme of young love in the main action; and it mocks the bad literary habits, the technical tricks and extravagant emotions of contemporary writers who told mythological and legendary tales. This particular story had been told many times. Chaucer included it in *The Legende of Good Women* (ll. 706–923) and a few parallel phrases may be seen in Shakespeare (cp. the 'lyme' and 'stoon' of *LGW* 765 with *MND* 'lime and hair' (V.1.191); Chaucer's 'wikked walle', 756, with *MND ibid.* 180; *LGW* 750–1, with *MND* 'right and sinister', *ibid.* 163; *LGW* 760–1 and *MND ibid.* 200; Chaucer mentions the moon twice; Shakespeare makes great play with the Moon). A poem *Perymus and Thesbye* was entered to William Griffith in 1562. Golding's translation of Ovid's version in *Metamorphoses* (IV.55ff) is given below [IX]. The English players who went to Germany in Lord Spencer's train may have taken plays called *Romeo and Juliet* and *Pyramus and Thisbe* (Chambers, *ElSt.* II.283). Clement Robinson's *Handefull of Pleasant Delites* (1584) included a 'New Sonet of Pyramus and Thisbe' by I. Thomson [X] which may have given Shakespeare the stanza-form for the dying moans of his lovers, and material for parody such as the references to the Fates and the use of some words such as 'certaine' with the accent on the second syllable, and 'make moan'. Professor Kenneth Muir discussed many parallels in this and other versions of the tale in an article on 'Pyramus and Thisbe' in *Shakespeare Quarterly* 1954, (141–53). Undoubtedly Shakespeare drew mainly on Golding, who gave him words like 'cranny', 'mantle', 'courteous' (of the wall), and the parody of 'the excessive use as padding of the auxiliary "did"' (Muir). From a Pyramus story in *A Gorgeous Gallery of Gallant Inventions* may possibly come 'The pap of Pyramus', for there Thisbe takes the sword 'Wherwith beneath her pap (alas) into her brest she strake.' Most of these versions had something ridiculous in them, and perhaps the worst was Thomas Mouffet's, inserted into his didactic poem *The Silke-wormes and their Flies* (pubd. 1599) because the food of silk-worms, mulberry leaves, got their colour from the lovers' blood. But I am not convinced by Muir's argument that Mouf-fet's poem preceded *MND* and that Shakespeare parodied it, that he got Bottom's name from Mouffet's unconsciously am-biguous use of the word 'bottom' when describing the silk cocoons. (A 'bottom' might be any clew on which any thread was wound before the weaver got it.) Nor was it necessary to go to Mouffet for the fairies' names Cobweb and Moth, for Theseus' first speech in Act V, or for Bottom's transformation.

An amusing dramatic parallel to Shakespeare's play is pro-vided by the hitherto unprinted *Tragedy of Pyramus and Thisbe* in B.M. Add. MSS 15,227, here given [XI]. E. K. Chambers believed that this was a seventeenth-century production, per-haps by Nathaniel Richards (fl. 1630–54), a Cambridge poet, author of *The Tragedy of Messalina* (1640) and *The Celestiall Publican, A Sacred Poem* (1635). The style is strangely archaic for a Cambridge poet of the thirties, and might possibly be of the sixteenth century. Richards was master of St Albans School, and the piece is a stilted academic attempt to dramatize Ovid's story into a short classical play keeping as close as pos-sible to the original, and giving references to the Latin in mar-ginal notes (here given as footnotes). Feeble as it is, the Tra-gedy shows the sort of thing which Shakespeare was laughing at. Note the stiff exclamatory rhetoric:

> What shall I doe? I know not what to doe.
> Where shall I runne, O runne? I can not goe.
> Where shall I goe, oh goe? I cannot stirre;

the pedantic scientific and mythological references. There is alliteration, but not the type found in Shakespeare's play, which is nearer to Gascoigne. The conflict between Love and Duty is so clearcut as to suggest a seventeenth-century origin. The name Lysander is mentioned (Sc. i.6).

It is impossible to be sure of the chronological relationship between *A Midsummer Night's Dream* and *Romeo and Juliet*. It is tempting to think that soon after completing his tragedy Shakespeare wrote *Pyramus* in self-mockery, as a relief, like a horse kicking up his heels when let into pasture. But he would be quite capable of writing *Romeo and Juliet* after *Pyramus*, for the latter was composed to fit into the context of its own play and its mockery of romantic love does not represent a lasting mood. *Romeo* itself contains some pleasant mockery of love and lovers, before the hero becomes fast-bound to Juliet and the fatal stars.

CANTERBURY TALES
THE KNIGHT'S TALE
by Geoffrey Chaucer

Lines 859–930; 1056–1181; 2483–2532; 2565–2604

(text as edited by A. W. Pollard, etc., (1898))

[TALES OF THE FIRST DAY]

KNIGHT'S TALE

Heere bigynneth The Knyghtes Tale

Whilom, as olde stories tellen us,
Ther was a duc that highte Theseus;   860
Of Atthenes he was lord and governour,
And in his tyme swich a conquerour,
That gretter was ther noon under the sonne.
Ful many a riche cóntree hadde he wonne;
That with his wysdom and his chivalrie
He conquered al the regne of Femenye,[1]
That whilom was y-cleped Scithia;
And weddede the queene Ypolita,
And broghte hire hoom with hym in his contrée
With muchel glorie and greet solempnytee,
And eek hir faire suster Emelye.   871
And thus with victorie and with melodye
Lete I this noble duc to Atthenes ryde,
And al his hoost in armes hym bisyde.

And certes, if it nere to long to heere,
I wolde han told yow fully the manere
How wonnen was the regne of Femenye
By Theseus and by his chivalrye;
And of the grete bataille for the nones

[1] the realm of the Amazons.

Bitwixen Atthenes and Amazones;   880
And how asseged was Ypolita,
The faire, hardy queene of Scithia,
And of the feste that was at hir weddynge,
And of the tempest at hir hoom-comynge;
But al that thyng I moot as now forbere.
I have, God woot, a large feeld to ere,[1]
And wayke been the oxen in my plough.
The remenant of the tale is long ynough,
I wol nat letten eek noon of this route.
Lat every felawe telle his tale aboute,   890
And lat se now who shal the soper wynne;
And ther I lefte I wil ageyn bigynne.
    This duc, of whom I make mencioun,
Whan he was come almost unto the toun,
In al his wele, and in his mooste pride,
He was war, as he caste his eye aside,
Where that ther kneled in the hye weye
A compaignye of ladyes, tweye and tweye,
Ech after oother, clad in clothes blake;
But swich a cry and swich a wo they make
That in this world nys creature lyvynge
That herde swich another waymentynge[2]:
And of this cry they nolde nevere stenten,
Til they the reynes of his brydel henten,[3]
    'What folk been ye, that at myn hom-comynge
Perturben so my feste with criynge?'
Quod Theseus. 'Have ye so greet envye
Of myn honour, that thus compleyne and crye?
Or who hath yow mysboden[4] or offended?
And telleth me if it may be amended,
And why that ye been clothed thus in blak?'   911
    The eldeste lady of hem alle spak
Whan she hadde swowned with a deedly cheere,
That it was routhe for to seen and heere,
And seyde, 'Lord, to whom fortune hath yeven
Victorie, and as a conqueror to lyven,
Nat greveth us youre glorie and youre honour,
But we biseken mercy and socour.
Have mercy on oure wo and oure distresse:
Som drope of pitee, thurgh thy gentillesse,
Upon us wrecched wommen lat thou falle:

---

[1] plough.   [2] lamenting.   [3] seize.   [4] injured.

For certes, lord, ther is noon of us alle
That she ne hath been a duchesse or a queene.
Now be we caytyves,[1] as it is wel seene:
Thanked be Fortune and hire false wheel,
That noon estat assureth to be weel.
And certes, lord, to abyden youre presence,
Heere in the temple of the goddesse Clemence
We han ben waitynge al this fourtenyght;
Now help us, lord, sith it is in thy myght . . .   930

The grete tour, that was so thikke and stroong,   1056
Which of the castel was the chief dongeoun
(Ther as the knyghtes weren in prisoun,
Of whiche I tolde yow and tellen shal),
Was evene joynant to the gardyn wal,
Ther as this Emelye hadde hir pleyynge.
Bright was the sonne, and cleer that morwenynge,
And Palamon, this woful prisoner,
As was his wone, bi leve of his gayler,
Was risen, and romed in a chambre on heigh,   1065
In which he al the noble citee seigh,
And eek the gardyn, ful of braunches grene,
Ther as this fresshe Emelye the sheene
Was in hire walk and romed up and doun.
This sorweful prisoner, this Palamoun,
Goth in the chambre romynge to and fro,
And to hymself compleynynge of his wo;
That he was born, ful ofte he seyde, 'allas!'
And so bifel, by aventure or cas,
That thurgh a wyndow, thikke of many a barre   1075
Of iren, greet and square as any sparre,
He cast his eyen upon Emelya,
And therwithal he bleynte[2] and cride, 'A!'
As though he stongen were unto the herte.
And with that cry Arcite anon up sterte,
And seyde, 'Cosyn myn, what eyleth thee,
That art so pale and deedly on to see?
Why cridestow? who hath thee doon offence?
For Goddes love, taak al in pacience
Oure prisoun, for it may noon oother be;
Fortune hath yeven us this adversitee.

---

[1] captives.   [2] went pale.

Som wikke aspect or disposicioun
Of Saturne, by sum constellacioun,
Hath yeven us this, although we hadde it sworn;
So stood the hevene whan that we were born;   1090
We moste endure: this is the short and playn.'
    This Palamon answerde, and seyde agayn,
'Cosyn, for sothe of this opinioun
Thow hast a veyn ymaginacioun;
This prison caused me nat for to crye,
But I was hurt right now thurghout myn eye
Into myn herte, that wol my bane be.
The fairnesse of that lady that I see
Yond in the gardyn romen to and fro,
Is cause of al my criyng and my wo.   1100
I noot wher she be womman or goddesse,
But Venus is it, soothly, as I gesse.'
And therwithal on knees doun he fil,
And seyde: 'Venus, if it be thy wil
Yow in this gardyn thus to transfigure
Bifore me, sorweful, wrecche creature,
Out of this prisoun helpe that we may scapen.
And if so be my destynee be shapen,
By eterne word, to dyen in prisoun,
Of our lynage have som compassioun,   1110
That is so lowe y-broght by tirannye.'
    And with that word Arcite gan espye
Wher as this lady romed to and fro,
And with that sighte hir beautee hurte hym so,
That if that Palamon was wounded sore,
Arcite is hurt as moche as he, or moore;
And with a sigh he seyde pitously:
'The fresshe beautee sleeth me sodeynly
Of hire that rometh in the yonder place,
And but I have hir mercy and hir grace,
That I may seen hire atte leeste weye,   1121
I nam but deed; ther is namoore to seye.'
    This Palamon, whan he tho worde herde,
Dispitously he looked, and answerde,
'Wheither seistow this in ernest or in play?
    'Nay,' quod Arcite, 'in ernest, by my fey!
God helpe me so, me list ful yvele pleye.'
    This Palamon gan knytte his browes tweye,
'It nere,' quod he, 'to thee no greet honour,

For to be fals, ne for to be traitour 1130
To me, that am thy cosyn and thy brother
Y-sworn ful depe, and ech of us til oother,
That never, for to dyen in the peyne,
Til that deeth departe shal us tweyne,
Neither of us in love to hyndre oother,
Ne in noon oother cas, my leeve brother,
But that thou sholdest trewely forthren me
In every cas, as I shal forthren thee.
This was thyn ooth, and myn also certeyn;
I woot right wel thou darst it nat withseyn.
Thus artow of my conseil, out of doute:
And now thow woldest falsly been aboute
To love my lady, whom I love and serve.
And ever shal, til that myn herte sterve.
Nay certes, false Arcite, thow shalt nat so;
I loved hire first, and tolde thee my wo
As to my cosyn, and my brother sworn
To forthre[1] me, as I have toold biforn.
For which thou art y-bounden as a knyght
To helpen me, if it lay in thy myght; 1150
Or elles artow fals, I dar wel seyn.'

This Arcite ful proudly spak ageyn;
'Thou shalt,' quod he, 'be rather fals than I;
And thou art fals, I telle thee, outrely,
For *par amour* I loved hire first er thow.
What wiltow seyn? thou wistest nat yet now
Wheither she be a womman or goddesse!
Thyn is affeccióun of hoolynesse,
And myn is love as to a creature;
For which I tolde thee myn aventure 1160
As to my cosyn and my brother sworn.
I pose that thow lovedest hire biforn,
Wostow nat wel the olde clerkes sawe,[2]
That *who shal yeve a lovere any lawe;*
Love is a gretter lawe, by my pan,[3]
Than may be yeve of any erthely man?
And therfore positif lawe and swich decree
Is broken al day for love, in ech degree.
A man moot nedes love, maugree his heed;
He may nat flee it, thogh he sholde be deed, 1170

---

[1] further, help.
[2] Found in Boethius, *De Consolatione Philosophiae*, lib. iii. met. 12.
[3] brain-pan, head.

Al be she mayde, or wydwe, or elles wyf;
And eek it is nat likly, al thy lyf,
To stonden in hir grace; namoore shal I;
For wel thou woost thyselven, verraily,
That thou and I be dampned to prisoun
Perpetuelly; us gayneth no raunsoun.
We stryven as dide the houndes for the boon,
They foughte al day, and yet hir part was noon;
Ther cam a kyte, whil that they weren so wrothe,
And baar awey the boon bitwixe hem bothe; 1180
And therfore, at the kynges court, my brother,
Ech man for hymself, ther is noon oother.
Love, if thee list, for I love and ay shal,
And soothly, leeve brother, this is al. . . .

· · · · · · · · · · ·

PART IV

Greet was the feeste in Atthenes that day, 2483
And eek the lusty seson of that May
Made every wight to been in such plesaunce,
That al that Monday justen they and daunce,
And spenten it in Venus heigh servyse;
But, by the cause that they sholde ryse
Eerly, for to seen the grete fight,
Unto hir reste wenten they at nyght. 2490
And on the morwe, whan that day gan sprynge,
Of hors and harneys noyse and claterynge
Ther was in hostelryes al aboute,
And to the paleys rood ther many a route
Of lordes, upon steedes and palfreys.
Ther maystow seen divisynge of harneys
So unkouth and so riche, and wroght so weel
Of goldsmythrye, of browdynge, and of steel,
The sheeldes brighte, testeres,[1] and trappures;
Gold-hewen helmes, hauberkes, cote armures; 2500
Lordes in paramentz[2] on hir courseres;
Knyghtes of retenue, and eek squieres,
Nailynge the speres, and helmes bokelynge,
Giggynge of sheeldes, with layneres lacynge;
There, as nede is, they weren no thyng ydel.
The fomy steedes on the golden brydel

---

[1] headpieces.   [2] rich array.

Gnawynge, and faste the armurers also,
With fyle and hamer, prikynge to and fro;
Yemen on foote, and communes many oon
With shorte staves, thikke as they may goon;   2510
Pýpes, trompes, nakers, clariounes,
That in the bataille blowen blody sounes;
The paleys ful of peples up and doun,—
Heere, thre, ther ten, holdynge hir questioun,
Dyvynynge of thise Thebane knyghtes two.
Somme seyden thus, somme seyde it shal be so,
Somme helden with hym with the blake berd,
Somme with the balled, somme with the thikke herd,
Some seyde he looked grymme and he wolde fighte,
He hath a sparth[1] of twenty pound of wighte,—   2520
Thus was the halle ful of divynynge
Longe after that the sonne gan to sprynge.

The grete Theseus, that of his sleepe awaked
With mynstralcie and noyse that was maked,
Heeld yet the chambre of his paleys riche,
Til that the Thebane knyghtes, bothe y-liche
Honured, were into the paleys fet.
Duc Theseus was at a wyndow set,
Arrayed right as he were a god in trone.
The peple preesseth thiderward ful soone
Hym for to seen, and doon heigh reverence,   2531
And eek to herkne his heste and his sentence . . .

. . . .

Up goon the trompes and the melodye   2565
And to the lystes rit the compaignye
By ordinance, thurgh-out the citee large,
Hanged with clooth of gold, and nat with sarge.
Ful lik a lord this noble duc gan ryde,
Thise two Thebanes upon either side;   2570
And after rood the queene and Emelye,
And after that another compaignye
Of oon and oother, after hir degre;
And thus they passen thurgh-out the citee,
And to the lystes come they by tyme.
It nas not of the day yet fully pryme
Whan set was Theseus ful riche and hye,
Ypolita the queene and Emelye,

[1] halberd.

And othere ladys in degrees aboute.
Unto the seattes preesseth al the route,
And westward, thurgh the gates under Marte,   2581
Arcite, and eek the hondred of his parte,
With baner reed is entred right anon.
And in that selve moment Palamon
Is under Venus, estward in the place,
With baner whyt, and hardy chiere and face.
In al the world to seken up and doun
So evene, withouten variacioun,
Ther nere swiche compaignyes tweye;
For ther was noon so wys that koude seye
That any hadde of oother avauntage   2591
Of worthynesse, ne of estaat, ne age,
So evene were they chosen, for to gesse;
And in two renges faire they hem dresse.
   Whan that hir names rad were everichon,
That in hir nombre gyle were ther noon,
Tho were the gates shet, and cried was loude,
'Do now youre devoir, yonge knyghtes proude!
   The heraudes lefte hir prikyng up and doun;   2599
Now ryngen trompes loude and clarioun;
Ther is namoore to seyn, but west and est
In goon the speres ful sadly in arrest;
In gooth the sharpe spore into the syde.

II. Probable Source

From THE LIFE OF THESEUS
in Plutarch's Lives of the Noble Grecians and Romans
translated by Sir Thomas North

The Lives of the Noble Grecians and Romanes compared together by that grave learned philosopher and historiographer Plutarke of Chaeronea, translated out of Greeke

into French by James Amyot . . . and out of French into
Englishe by Thomas North. 1579.

. . . [Theseus] brought all the inhabitantes of the whole province
of Attica, to be within the citie of Athens, and made them all one
corporation, which were before dispersed into diverse villages, and
by reason thereof were very hard to be assembled together, when
occasion was offered to establish any order concerning the common state.   Many times also they were at variance together, and
by the eares, making warres one upon an other.   But Theseus tooke
the paines to goe from village to village, and from family, to familie,
to let them understand the reasons why they should consent unto
it.   So he found the poore people and private men, ready to obey
and followe his will: but the riche, and such as had authorytye in
every village, all against it.   Nevertheles he wanne them, promising that it should be a common wealth, and not subject to the power
of any sole prince, but rather a populer state.   In which he woulde
only reserve to him selfe the charge of the warres, and the preservation of the lawes: for the rest, he was content that every citizen in
all and for all should beare a like swaye and authorytye . . . Yet for
all that, he suffered not the great multitude that came thither tagge
and ragge, to be without distinction of degrees and orders.[1]   For he
first divided the noble men, from husbandmen and artificers,
appointing the noblemen as judges and magistrates to judge upon
matters of Religion, and touching the service of the godds: and of
them also he dyd chuse rulers, to beare civill office in the common
weale, to determine the lawe, and to tell all holy and divine things.
By this meanes he made the noble men and the two other estates
equall in voyce.   And as the noblemen dyd passe the other in
honour: even so the artificers exceeded them in number, and the
husbandmen them in profit.   Nowe that Theseus was the first
who of all others yelded to have a common weale or popular estate
(as Aristotle sayeth) and dyd geve over his regall power[2]: Homer self
semeth to testifie it, in numbring the shippes which were in the
Graecians armie before the cittie of Troia.   For amongest all the
Graecians, he only calleth the Athenians people.   Moreover
Theseus coyned money, which he marked with the stampe of an oxe,
in memorye of the bulle of Marathon, or of Taurus the captaine of
Minos, or els to provoke his citizens to geve them selves to labour . . .

[1] In margin: Theseus maketh difference of states and degrees in his common
weale.
[2] In margin: Theseus the first that gave over regall power, and framed a popular
state.

. . . It was he also which made the games called Isthmia, after the imitation of Hercules, to the ende that as the Grecians dyd celebrate the feast of games called Olympia, in the honour of Jupiter, by Hercules ordinance: so, that they should also celebrate the games called Isthmia, by his order and institution, in the honour of Neptune. . . .

Touching the voyage he made by the sea Major, Philochorus, and some other holde opinion, that he went thither with Hercules against the Amazones: and that to honour his valiantnes, Hercules gave him Antiopa the Amazone. But the more parte of the other Historiographers, namely Hellanicus, Pherecides, and Herodotus, doe write, that Theseus went thither alone, after Hercules voyage, and that he tooke this Amazone prisoner, which is likeliest to be true.[1] For we doe not finde that any other who went this jorney with him, had taken any Amazone prisoner besides him selfe. Bion also the Historiographer, this notwithstanding sayeth, that he brought her away by deceit and stealth. For the Amazones (sayeth he) naturally loving men, dyd not flie at all when they sawe them lande in their countrye, but sente them presents, and that Theseus entised her to come into his shippe, who brought him a present: and so sone as she was aborde, he hoysed his sayle, and so caried her away. . . . Now heare what was the occasion of the warres of the Amazones, which me thinckes was not a matter of small moment, nor an enterprise of a woman.[2] For they had not placed their campe within the very cittie of Athens, nor had not fought in the very place it selfe (called Pnyce) adjoyning to the temple of the Muses, if they had not first conquered or subdued all the countrye thereabouts: neither had they all comen at the first, so valiantly to assaile the cittie of Athens. Now, whether they came by lande from so farre a countrye, or that they passed over an arme of the sea, which is called Bosphorus Cimmericus, being frosen as Hellanicus sayeth: it is hardely to be credited. But that they camped within the precinct of the very cittie it selfe, the names of the places which continewe yet to this present daye doe witnesse it, and the graves also of the women which dyed there. But so it is, that both armies laye a great time one in the face of the other, ere they came to battell. Howbeit at the length Theseus having first made sacrifice unto Feare the goddesse, according to the counsaill of a prophecie he had receyved, he gave them battell[3] in the moneth of August, on the same daye, in the which the Athenians doe even

---

[1] In margin: Antiopa the Amazone ravished by Theseus.

[2] In margin: The cause of the warres of the Amazones against the Athenians.

[3] In margin: Theseus fighteth a battell with the Amazones.

at this present solemnise the feast, which they call Boedromia. But Clidemus the Historiographer, desirous particularly to write all the circumstances of this encownter, sayeth that the left poynte of their battell bent towards the place which they call Amazonion: and that the right poynte marched by the side of Chrysa, even to the place which is called Pnyce, upon which, the Athenians comming towards the temple of the Muses, did first geve their charge. And for proofe that this is true, the graves of the women which dyed in this first encounter, are founde yet in the great streete, which goeth towards the gate Piraica, neere unto the chappell of the litle god Chalcodus. And the Athenians (sayeth he) were in this place repulsed by the Amazones, even to the place where the images of Eumenides are, that is to saye, of the furies. But on thother side also, the Athenians comming towards the quarters of Palladium, Ardettus, and Lucium, drave backe their right poynte even to within their campe, and slewe a great number of them. Afterwards, at the ende of foure moneths, peace was taken betwene them by meanes of one of the women called Hyppolita. For this Historiographer calleth the Amazone which Theseus maried, Hyppolita, and not Antiopa.[1] Nevertheles, some saye that she was slayne (fighting on Theseus side) with a darte, by another called Molpadia. In memorie whereof, the piller which is joyning to the temple of the Olympian ground, was set up in her honour. We are not to marvell, if the historie of things so auncient, be founde so diversely written. For there are also that write, that Queene Antiopa sent those secretly which were hurte then into the cittie of Calcide, where some of them recovered, and were healed: and others also dyed, which were buried neere to the place called Amazonion. Howsoever it was, it is most certain that this warre was ended by agreement. For a place adjoyning to the temple of Theseus, dothe beare recorde of it, being called Orcomosium: bicause the peace was there by solemne othe concluded. And the sacrifice also dothe truely verifie it, which they have made to the Amazones, before the feast of Theseus, long time out of minde. They of Megara also doe shewe a tumbe of the Amazones in their cittie, which is as they goe from the market place, to the place they call Rhus: where they finde an auncient tumbe, cut in facion and forme of a losenge. They saye that there died other of the Amazones also, neere unto the cittie of Chaeronea, which were buried all alongest the litle br[o]oke passing by the same, which in the olde time, (in mine opinion) was called Thermodon, and is nowe named Haemon, as we have in other places written in the life of

---

[1] In margin: Peace concluded at foure moneths ende by meanes of Hypolita.

Demosthenes. And it semeth also, that they dyd not passe through Thessalie, without fighting: for there are seene yet of their tumbes all about the cittie of Scotusa, hard by the rocks, which be called the doggs head. And this is that which is worthy memorie (in mine opinion) touching the warres of these Amazones. How the Poet telleth that the Amazones made warres with Theseus to revenge the injurie he dyd to their Queene Antiopa, refusing her, to marye with Phaedra: and as for the murder which he telleth that Hercules dyd, that me thinckes is altogether but devise of Poets. It is very true, that after the death of Antiopa, Theseus maried Phaedra, having had before of Antiopa a sonne called Hippolytus, or as the Poet Pindarus writeth, Demophon. And for that the Historiographers doe not in any thing speake against the tragicall Poets, in that which concerneth the ill happe that chaunced to him, in the persons of this his wife and of his sonne: we must needes take it to be so, as we finde it written in the tragedies. And yet we finde many other reportes touching the mariages of Theseus, whose beginnings had no great good honest ground, neither fell out their endes very fortunate: and yet for all that they have made no tragedies of them, neither have they bene played in the Theaters. . . .

From THE COMPARISON OF THESEUS WITH ROMULUS

. . . Theseus' faults touching women and ravishements, of the twaine, had the lesse shadowe and culler of honestie. Bicause Theseus dyd attempt it very often: for he stale awaye Ariadne, Antiope, and Anaxo the Troezenian. Againe being stepped in yeres, and at later age, and past mariage: he stale awaye Helen in her minoritie, being nothing neere to consent to marye. Then his taking of the daughters of the Troezenians, of the Lacedaemonians, and the Amazones (neither contracted to him, nor comparable to the birthe and linadge of his owne countrie which were at Athens, and descended of the noble race and progenie of Erichtheus, and of Cecrops) dyd geve men occasion to suspect that his wommanishenes was rather to satisfie lust, then of any great love. Romulus[1] nowe in a contrarie manner, when his people had taken eight hundred, or thereabouts, of the Sabyne women to ravishe them: kept but

[1] In margin: Romulus ravishement of women excused.

onely one for him selfe that was called Hersilia, as they saye, and delivered the reste to his best and most honest cittizens. Afterwardes by the honour, love, and good entertainment that he caused them to have and receyve of their husbands, he chaunged this violent force of ravishement, into a most perfect bonde and league of amitie: which dyd so knyt and joyne in one these two nations, that it was the beginning of the great mutuall love which grewe afterwards betwext those two people, and consequently of the joyning of their powers together. Furthermore, time hath geven a good testimonie of the love, reverence, constancie, kyndenes, and all matrimoniall offices that he established by that meanes, betwext man and wife. For in two hundred and thirtie yeres afterwards, there was never man that durst forsake or put awaye his wife, nor the wife her husband.[1] And as among the Grecians, the best learned men, and most curious observers of antiquities doe knowe his name, that was the first murderer of his father or mother: even so all the Romaines knewe what he was, which first durst put away his wife. It was one called Spurius Carvilius, bicause his wife was barren and had no children. The effects also doe agree with the testimonie of the time. For the Realme was common unto Kings of both nations, and through the alliance of these mariages that beganne first of ravishements, both nations lived peaciblie, and in equalitie, under one civill policie, and well governed common weale. The Athenians contrariewise, by Theseus mariages, dyd get neither love nor kynred of any one persone, but rather they procured warres, enmities, and the slaughter of their cittizens, with the losse in the ende of the cittie of Aphidnes.

III. Probable Source

From HUON OF BOURDEAUX
translated by Lord Berners (1601 edn.)[2]

The Ancient Honorable, Famous, and delightfull Historie of Huon of Bourdeaux, one of the Peeres of Fraunce,

[1] In margin: No divorce made in Rome for 230 yeres space. Val. Max. sayeth 520.

[2] For text of first edition (1533-42), which is less readable, see E.E.T.S. Extra Series XL, 1882, ed. S. L. Lee.

and Duke of Guyenne. Enterlaced with the love of many Ladies, as also the fortunes and adventures of Knights errant, their amorous Servants. Being now the Third time imprinted, and the rude English corrected and amended. London. Printed by Thomas Purfoot, and are to be sould by Edward White, at his shop at the little North dore of Poules, at the signe of the Gunne. 1601.

[Chap. XX]

How Huon of Bourdeaux . . . found Gerames, and of their conference

When Huon had heard the Knight's tale, he had great joy, and embraced him and saide, Howe often times he had seene Guyre his Brother the Provost weepe for him, and when I departed from *Bourdeaux,* (quoth he) I delivered unto him all my Lands to governe: wherefore I require you shewe mee your name. Sir, (quoth he) I am called Gerames, and now I pray you shew me your name. Sir, (quoth he) I am named Huon, and my younger Brother is called Gerard. But, sir, I pray you shew me how you have so long lived heere, and what sustenance you have had. Sir, (quoth Gerames) I have eaten none other thing but rootes and fruites that I have found in the wood. Then Huon demaunded of him if he could speake the language Sarazin. Yes, sir, (quoth he) as well or better then any Sarazin in the Countrey, nor there is no way but that I know it.

When Huon had heard Gerames, then he demaunded further of him if he could goe to *Babilon.* Yes, sir, (quoth Gerames) I can goe thether by two wayes; the most surest way is hence about fortie dayes journey, and the other is but fifteene dayes journey: but I councell you to take the longe way, for if you take the shorter way, you must passe thorow a wood about sixteene leagues of length, but the way is so full of the Fayryes and strang[e] things, that such as passe that way are lost, for in that wood abideth a King of the Fayryes named Oberon; he is of height but of three foote, and crooked shouldered, but yet he hath an Angell-like visage, so that there is no mortal man that seeth him, but that taketh great pleasure to behold his face; and you shall no sooner be entred into that wood, if you go that way, but he wil find the meanes to speake with you, and if you speake unto him, you are lost for ever, and you shall ever find him before you, so that it shall be in manner impossible that you can scape from him without speaking to him, for his words be so pleasant to heare, that there is no mortall man that can well scape without speaking unto him. And if he see that you will not speake a word unto him, then he will be sore displeased with you, and before you can get out of the wood, he will cause raine and wind, hayle and snowe, and will make marvelous tempests, with thunder and lightenings, so that it shall seeme unto you that all the world should perish, and he will make to seeme before you a great running River blacke and deepe: but you may passe it at your ease, and it shall not wet the feet of your horse, for all is but fantasie and enchauntments that the Dwarfe shall make, to the entent to have you with him, and if you can keepe yourselfe without speaking unto him, you may then well escape. But, Sir, to eschew all perils, I councell you to take the longer way, for I thinke you cannot escape from him: and then you be lost for ever.

When Huon had well heard Gerames, he had great marvaile, and he had great desire in himselfe to see that Dwarfe King of the Fayryes, and the strang adventures that were in that wood. Then he said unto Gerames, that for feare of any death hee would not leave to passe that way, seeinge hee might come to *Babilon* in fifteene dayes, for in taking the longer way hee might perchaunce find more adventures, and since he was advertised that with keeping his tongue from speaking he might abridge his journey, he sayd that surely he would take that way whatsoever chaunce befell. Sir, (quoth Gerames) you shall doe your own pleasure, for which way soever you take, it shall not be without me; I shall bring you to *Babilon* to the Admirall Gaudise; I knowe him right well, and when you bee come thether, you shall see there a Damsell, (as I have heard say) the most fairest creature in all *Inde*, and the onely and most sweetest and most courteous that ever was borne, and it is shee that you seeke, for shee is daughter to the admirall Gaudise.

[Chap. XXI]

How Gerames went with Huon and his companie, and so came into the wood, whereas they found King Oberon, who conjured them to speake unto him

When Huon had well heard Gerames, how he was minded to goe along with him, hee was thereof right joyfull, and thanked him of his courtesy and service, and gave him a goodly horse, whereon he mounted, and so road foorth together so long that they came into the wood whereas King Oberon haunted most. Then Huon, who was wearie of travaile, and what for famine and for heate, the which he and his companie had endured two dayes without bread

or meat, so that he was so feeble that he could ride no further, and
then he began pityously to weepe, and complayned of the great
wronge that Kinge Charlemaine had done unto him; and then
Garyn and Gerames comforted him, and had great pitie of him,
and they knew well by the reason of his youth, hunger oppressed
him more than it did to them of greater age.   Then they alighted
under a great Oake, to the entent to search for some fruit to eate.
They glad thereof let their horses goe to pasture.

When they were thus alighted, the Dwarfe of the Fayry Kinge
Oberon came ryding by, and had on a Gowne so rich that it were
marvaile to recount the riches and fashion thereof, and it was so
garnished with precious stones, that the clearnesse of them shined
like the Sonne.   Also he had a goodlie bow in his hand, so rich
that it could not be esteemed, and his arrowes after the same sort;
and they were of such a nature or qualitie, that any beast in the
world that he would wish for, the arrowe would arrest him. Also
he had about his necke a rich Horne hanging by two Laces of gold.
The Horne was so rich and faire, that there never was seene any
such. It was made by foure Ladies of the Fayries in the Isle of
Chafalone; one of them gave to the horne such a propertie, that
whosoever heard the sound thereof, if he were in the greatest sickenesse in the world, he should incontinent be whole and sound: the
Ladie that gave this gift to the Horne was named *Glorianda*. The
second ladie was named *Translyna*; she gave to this Horne another
propertie, and that was, whosoever heard this horne, if he were in
the greatest famine of the worlde, he should be satisfied as well as
though he had eaten al that he woulde wishe for, and so likewise
for drinke as well, as though he had droonke his fil of the best wine
in al the world. The third Ladie named *Margala* gave to this Horne
yet a greater gift, and that was, whosoever heard this Horne, though
he were never so poore or feeble by sicknesse, he should have such
joy in his heart, that he should singe and daunce. The fourth Ladie
named *Lempatrix* gave to this Horne such a gift that whosoever
heard it, if he were an hundred dayes journeys of[f], he should come
at the pleasure of him that blew it farre or neare.

Then King Oberon, who knew well and had seene the fourteene
Companions, he set his Horne to his mouth, and blew so melodious
a blast, that the fourteene Companions, being under the Tree, had
so perfit a joy at their hearts, that they al rose up and began to
sing and daunce. Ah, good Lord, (quoth Huon) what fortune is
come unto us? Me thinke we be in *Paradise*; right now I could not
sustaine myselfe for lacke of meat and drinke, and nowe I feele
myselfe neither hungrie nor thirstie; from whence may this come?

Sir, (quoth Gerames) knowe for troth, this is done by the Dwarfe
of the Fayrye, whome you shall soone see passe by you. But, Sir,
I require you on jeopardie of loosing of your life, that you speake
to him no word, without you purpose to abide ever with him. Sir,
(quoth Huon) have no doubt of me, seeing I know the jeopardie.
Therewith the Dwarfe began to crie aloude and saide: Yee fourteene
men that passe by my wood, God keepe you all! and I desire you
speake with mee, and I conjure you thereto by God almightie, and
by the christendome that you have received, and by all that God
hath made, answeare mee!

[Chap. XXII]

*How King Oberon was right sorrowfull and sore displeased, in that
Huon would not speake: and of the great feare that he put Huon and
his companie in*

When that Huon and his companie heard the Dwarfe speake,
they mounted on their Horses, and road away as fast as they might,
without speaking of any word; and the Dwarfe seeing how that they
road away and would not speake, hee was sorrowfull and angrie.
Then hee set one of his fingers on his Horne, out of the which
yssued such a winde and tempest so horrible to heare, that it bare
downe Trees, and therewith came such a raine and hayle, that it
seemed that heaven and the earth had fought together, and that
the world should have ended; the beasts in the woods brayed and
cryed, and the foules of the ayre fell down dead for the feare that
they were in; there was no creature but he would have been afrayd
of that tempest. Then suddainly appeared before them a great
River that ran swifter then the birds did flye, and the water was
so blacke and so perilous, and made such a noyse that it might be
heard ten leagues of. Alas! (quoth Huon) I see well now we be all
lost; wee shall heere be oppressed without God have pitie of us. I
repent me that ever I entred into this wood. I had been better to
have travailed a whole yeere, then to have come hether. Sir, (quoth
Gerames) dismay you not, for all this is done by the Dwarfe of the
Fayrye. Well, (quoth Huon) I thinke it best to alight from our
horses, for I thinke we shall never escape from hence, but that we
shalbe all oppressed. Then Garyn and the other Companions had
great marvaile, and were in great feare. Ah! Gerames, (quoth
Huon) you shewed mee well that it was great perill to passe this
wood. I repent mee now that I had not beleeved you.

Then they sawe on the other side of the River a faire Castell,
envyroned with fourteene great Towers, and on everie Tower a

clocher[1] of fine gould by seeming, the which they long regarded, and by that time they had gone a little by the River side, they lost the sight of the Castle; it was cleane vanished away: whereof Huon and his companie were sore abashed. Huon, (quoth Gerames) of all this that you see dismay you not, for all this is done by the crooked Dwarfe of the Fayrye, and all to beguile you, but he cannot greeve you so you speake no word: howbeit ere we depart from him, he will make us all abashed, for anone he will come after us like a mad man, bicause you will not speake unto him: but, sir, I require you as in God's name, be nothing afrayd, but ride foorth surely, and ever beware that you speake unto him no word. Sir, (quoth Huon) have no doubt thereof, for I had rather he were destroyed, then I should speake one word unto him. Then they road to passe the River, and they founde there nothing to let them, and so road about five Leagues. Sir, (quoth Huon) wee may well thanke God that wee bee thus escaped this Dwarfe, who thought to have deceived us; I was never in such feare during my life, God confound him. Thus they road, devising of the little Dwarfe, who had done them so much trouble.

[In Chapters XXIII–V Oberon pursues them, and, after forcing Huon to speak, shows him many marvels, and gives him a magic Horn and a Cup.]

IV. Probable Source

THE DISCOVERIE OF WITCHCRAFT
by Reginald Scot (1584)

The discoverie of witchcraft, Wherein the lewde dealing of witches and witchmongers is notablie detected, the knaverie of conjurors, the impietie of inchantors, the follie of soothsaiers, the impudent falshood of cousenors . . . the vertue and power of naturall magike, and all the conveiances of Legerdemaine and juggling are deciphered. . . . Heereunto is added a treatise upon the

---

[1] bell.

nature and substance of spirits and divels. By Reginald
Scot. W. Brome. London. 1584.

Booke IV. Chapter X

[Discussing Incubus and denying its existence Scot rejects stories of
'carnall societie with women' because a spirit cannot engender,
since it does not feed or live materially as we do.]

But to use few words herein, I hope you understand that they
affirme and saie, that *Incubus* is a spirit; and I trust you know that
a spirit hath no flesh nor bones, &c: and that he neither dooth eate
nor drinke. In deede your grandams maides were woont to set a
boll of milke before him and his cousine Robin goodfellow, for
grinding of malt or mustard, and sweeping the house at midnight:
and you have also heard that he would chafe exceedingly, if the maid
or goodwife of the house, having compassion of his nakednes, laid
anie clothes for him, beesides his messe of white bread and milke,
which was his standing fee. For in that case he saith; 'What have
we here? Hemton hamten, here will I never more tread nor
stampen.'

But to proceed to this confutation. Where there is no meate
eaten, there can be no seed which thereof is ingendred: although
it be granted, that Robin could both eate and drinke, as being a
cousening idle frier, or some such rog[u]e, that wanted nothing
either belonging to lecherie or knaverie, &c. Item, where the
genitall members want, there can be no lust of the flesh: neither
dooth nature give anie desire of generation, where there is no
propagation or succession required. And as spirits cannot be greeved
with hunger, so can they not be inflamed with lustes. And if men
should live ever, what needed succession or heires? For that is but
an ordinance of God, to supplie the place, the number, the world,
the time, and speciallie to accomplish his will. But the power of
generation consisteth not onlie in members, but chieflie of vitall
spirits, and of the hart: which spirits are never in such a bodie as
Incubus hath, being but a bodie assumed, as they themselves saie.
And yet the most part of writers herein affirme, that it is a palpable
and visible bodie; though all be phansies and fables that are written
hereupon.

Book VII. Chapter II

[Robin Goodfellow is not now much believed in.]

And know you this by the waie, that heretofore Robin goodfellow,
and Hob gobblin were as terrible, and also as credible to the people,

as hags and witches be now: and in time to come, a witch will be as much derided and contemned, and as plainlie perceived, as the illusion and knaverie of Robin goodfellow. And in truth, they that mainteine walking spirits, with their transformation, &c: have no reason to denie Robin goodfellow, upon whom there hath gone as manie and as credible tales, as upon witches; saving that it hath not pleased the translators of the Bible, to call spirits by the name of Robin goodfellow, as they have termed divinors, soothsaiers, poisoners, and couseners by the name of witches.

Booke VII. Chapter XV

Of vaine apparitions, how people have beene brought to feare bugges,
which is partlie reformed by preaching of the gospell, the true effect
of Christes miracles

But certeinlie, some one knave in a white sheete hath cousened and abused manie thousands that waie; speciallie when Robin good-fellow kept such a coile in the countrie. But you shall under-stand, that these bugs speciallie are spied and feared of sicke folke, children, women, and cowards, which through weaknesse of mind and bodie, are shaken with vaine dreames and continuall feare. The *Scythians*, being a stout and a warlike nation (as divers writers report) never see anie vaine sights or spirits. It is a common saieng; A lion feareth no bugs. But in our childhood our mothers maids have so terrified us with an ouglie divell having hornes on his head, fier in his mouth, and a taile in his breech, eies like a bason, fanges like a dog, clawes like a beare, a skin like a Niger, and a voice roring like a lion, whereby we start and are afraid when we heare one crie Bough: and they have so fraied us with bull beggers, spirits, witches, urchens, elves, hags, fairies, satyrs, pans, faunes, sylens, kit with the cansticke, tritons, centaurs, dwarfes, giants, imps, calcars, con-jurors, nymphes, changlings, *Incubus*, Robin good-fellowe, the spoorne, the mare, the man in the oke, the hell waine, the fierdrake, the puckle, Tom thombe, hob gobblin, Tom tumbler, boneles, and such other bugs, that we are afraid of our owne shadowes: in so much as some never feare the divell, but in a darke night; and then a polled sheepe is a perillous beast, and manie times is taken for our fathers soule, speciallie in a churchyard, where a right hardie man heretofore scant durst passe by night, but his haire would stand upright. For right grave writers report, that spirits most often and speciallie take the shape of women appearing to monks, &c: and of beasts, dogs, swine, horsses, gotes, cats, hairs; of fowles, as crowes, night owles, and shreeke owles; but they delight most in the likenes of snakes and dragons. Well, thanks be to God, this wretched and cowardlie infidelitie, since the preaching of the gospell, is in part forgotten: and doubtles, the rest of those illusions will in short time (by Gods grace) be detected and vanish awaie.

V. Analogue

From THESAURUS LINGUAE ROMANAE ET BRITANNICAE
by Thomas Cooper (1573 edition)[1]

MIDAS

Midas, The riche king of Phrygia, who, for his friendly intertainement of the God Bacchus, beeing willed to wishe what hee woulde, with promise presently to obteyne the same, desired that what soever hee touched might forthwith become golde. By which wishe graunted, hee tourned castels and towers into golde. But when he came to eate his meate, and sawe that it also was made golde, beeing almost famished, hee besought Bacchus agayne to take from him the graunt that hee had given him. Bacchus therefore willed him to goe washe himselfe in the ryver Pactolus: whereby the covetous king washed away his golden wishe, and the ryver ever after had small shardes of golde appearing in it. Afterwarde when the rusticall God Pan, chalenged to contend in musicke with Apollo, and Tmolus the judge appointed of that controversie had given sentence on Apollos side: All other that were present did alowe his judgement as good and true, onely king Midas reprooved it, and in his estimation preferred Pan with his screaking pypes. Wherewith Apollo being verie wroth, in reproche of his grosse judgement, made him to have long eares like an Asse. But Midas kept them so secrete, that never man knewe it, saving onely hys Barber. Who not able to conceale so uncouthe and straunge a thing, and yet not so bolde to publishe it for feare of the kings displeasure, went into the fielde, and digging an hole in the grounde, cryed out *Aures asininas habet rex Midas*, that is, true it is that king Midas hath long eares lyke an Asse. In processe of tyme reedes did growe in that place: which,

---

[1] First published 1565.

when they were blowne with the winde, did yeelde the same voyce
that Midas his Barber had there uttered, and so (say poetes) became it first knowne, that Midas had an Asses eares. By this devise
poets signifie that Midas as a tyranne, had many harkeners and
tale bearers, by whome he understood all that was done or spoken
of him in all parts of his dominion, as if hee had had long eares to
heare what every man had sayde.

VI. Possible Source

From THE XI BOOKES OF THE GOLDEN ASSE, CONTEININGE THE METAMORPHOSIE OF LUCIUS APULEIUS
translated by William Adlington (1566)[1]

Book III. Chapter XVII

[Apuleius, hoping to be turned into a bird like the witch Pamphiles,
is given ointment by her servant Fotis.]

After that I had well rubbed every part and member of my body,
I hovered with myne armes, and moved my selfe, looking still when
I should bee changed into a Bird as Pamphiles was, and behold
neither feathers nor appearance of feathers did burgen out, but verily
my haire did turne in ruggednesse, and my tender skin waxed
tough and hard, my fingers and toes losing the number of five,
changed into hoofes, and out of myne arse grew a great taile, now
my face became monstrous, my nosthrils wide, my lips hanging
downe, and myne eares rugged with haire: neither could I see any
comfort of my transformation, for my members encreased likewise,
and so without all helpe (viewing every part of my poore body) I
perceived that I was no bird, but a plaine Asse.

Then I thought to blame Fotis, but being deprived as wel of
language as humane shape, I looked upon her with my hanging lips
and watery eyes. Who as soone as shee espied me in such sort,
cried out, Alas poore wretch that I am, I am utterly cast away. The

---

[1] The text here is from the 1639 edition.

feare I was in, and my haste hath beguiled me, but especially the
mistaking of the boxe, hath deceived me. But it forceth not much,
in regard a sooner medicine may be gotten for this than for any other
thing. For if thou couldst get a Rose and eat it, thou shouldst be
delivered from the shape of an Asse, and become my Lucius againe.
And would to God I had gathered some garlands this evening past,
according to my custome, then thou shouldst not continue an Asse
one nights space, but in the morning I will seeke some remedy.
Thus Fotis lamented in pittifull sort, but I that was now a perfect
asse, and for Lucius a brute beast, did yet retaine the sence and
understanding of a man. And did devise a good space with my selfe,
whether it were best for me to teare this mischievous and wicked
harlot with my mouth, or to kicke and kill her with my heels. But
a better thought reduced me from so rash a purpose: for I feared
lest by the death of Fotis I should be deprived of all remedy and help.
Then shaking myne head, and dissembling myne ire, and taking my
adversity in good part, I went into the stable to my own horse,
where I found another Asse of Miloes, somtime my host, and I
did verily think that mine owne horse (if there were any natural
conscience or knowledge in brute beasts) would take pitty upon me,
and profer me lodging for that night: but it chanced far otherwise.
For see, my horse and the asse as it were consented together to work
my harm, and fearing lest I should eat up their provender, would
in no wise suffer me to come nigh the manger, but kicked me with
their heeles from their meat, which I my self gave them the night
before. Then I being thus handled by them, and driven away, got
me into a corner of the stable, where while I remembred their
uncurtesie, and how on the morrow I should return to Lucius by
the help of a Rose, when as I thought to revenge my self of myne
owne horse, I fortuned to espy in the middle of a pillar sustaining
the rafters of the stable the image of the goddesse Hippone, which
was garnished and decked round about with faire and fresh roses:
then in hope of present remedy, I leaped up with my fore feet as
high as I could, stretching out my neck, and with my lips coveting
to snatch some roses. But in an evill houre I did go about that
enterprise, for behold the boy to whom I gave charge of my horse
came presently in, and finding mee climbing upon the pillar, ranne
fretting towards me and said, How long shall wee suffer this wild
Asse, that doth not onely eat up his fellowes meat, but also would
spoyle the images of the gods? Why doe not I kill this lame theefe
and weake wretch? And therewithall looking about for some cudgel,
hee espied where lay a fagot of wood, and chusing out a crabbed
truncheon of the biggest hee could finde, did never cease beating

of me poore wretch, untill such time as by great noyse and rumbling hee heard the doores of the house burst open, and the neighbours crying in most lamentable sort, which inforced him being stricken in feare, to fly his way. And by and by a troup of theeves entred in, and kept every part and corner of the house with weapons. And as men resorted to aid and help them which were within the doores, the theeves resisted and kept them back, for every man was armed with a sword and target in his hand, the glimpses whereof did yeeld out such light as if it had bin day. Then they brake open a great chest with double locks and bolts, wherein was layd all the treasure of Milo, and ransackt the same: which when they had done they packed it up and gave every one a portion to carry: but when they had more than they could beare away, yet were they loth to leave any behind, but came into the stable, and took us two poore asses and my horse, and laded us with greater trusses than wee were able to beare. And when we were out of the house they followed us with great staves, and willed one of their fellows to tarry behind, and bring them tydings what was done concerning the robbery: and so they beat us forward over great hils out of the way. But I, what with my heavy burden and long journy, did nothing differ from a dead asse: wherfore I determined with my self to seek some civil remedy, and by invocation of the name of the prince of the country to be delivered from so many miseries: and on a time I passed through a great faire, I came among a multitude of Greeks, and I thought to call upon the renowned name of the Emperor, and to say, O Cesar, and cried out aloud, O, but Cesar I could in no wise pronounce. The Theeves little regarding my crying, did lay mee on and beate my wretched skinne in such sort, that after it was neither apt nor meet to make Sives or Sarces. Howbeit at last Jupiter administred unto me an unhoped remedy. For when we had passed through many townes and villages, I fortuned to espy a pleasant garden, wherein beside many other flowers of delectable hiew, were new and fresh roses: and being very joyful, and desirous to catch some as I passed by, I drew neerer and neerer: and while my lips watered upon them, I thought of a better advice more profitable for me, lest if from an Asse I should become a man, I might fall into the hands of the theeves, and either by suspition that I were some witch, or for feare that I should utter their theft, I should be slaine, wherefore I abstained for that time from eating of Roses, and enduring my present adversity, I eat hay as other Asses did.

VII. Probable Source

THE DISCOVERIE OF WITCHCRAFT
by Reginald Scot (1584)

Booke V. Chapter III

*Of a man turned into an asse, and returned againe into a man by
one of Bodins witches: S. Augustines opinion thereof*

It happened in the city of *Salamin*, in the kingdome of *Cyprus*
(wherein is a good haven) that a ship loaden with merchandize
staied there for a short space. In the meane time many of the
souldiers and mariners went to shoare, to provide fresh victuals.
Among which number, a certaine English man[1] being a sturdie
yoong fellowe, went to a womans house, a little waie out of the
citie, and not farre from the sea side, to see whether she had anie
egs to sell. Who perceiving him to be a lustie yoong fellowe, a
stranger, and farre from his countrie (so as upon the losse of him
there would be the lesse misse or inquirie) she considered with hir
selfe how to destroie him; and willed him to staie there awhile,
whilest she went to fetch a few egs for him. But she tarried long, so
as the yoong man called unto hir, desiring hir to make hast: for
he told hir that the tide would be spent, and by that meanes his
ship would be gone, and leave him behind. Howbeit, after some
detracting of time, she brought him a few egs, willing him to returne
to hir, if his ship were gone when he came. The young fellowe
returned towards his ship; but before he went aboord, hee would
needs eate an egg or twaine to satisfie his hunger, and within short
space he became dumb and out of his wits (as he afterwards said).[2]
When he would have entred into the ship, the mariners beat him
backe with a cudgell, saieng; What a murren lacks the asse? Whither
the divell will this asse? The asse or yoong man (I cannot tell by
which name I should terme him) being many times repelled, and
understanding their words that called him asse, considering that
he could speake never a word, and yet could understand everie
bodie; he thought that he was bewitched by the woman, at whose

---

[1] In margin: What the divel shuld the witch meane to make chois of the
English man?

[2] In margin: A strange metamorphosis of bodie, but not of mind.

house he was. And therefore, when by no means he could get into the boate, but was driven to tarrie and see hir departure; being also beaten from place to place, as an asse; he remembred the witches words, and the words of his owne fellowes that called him asse, and returned to the witches house, in whose service hee remained by the space of three yeares, dooing nothing with his hands all that while, but carried such burthens as she laied on his backe; having onelie this comfort, that although he were reputed an asse among strangers and beasts, yet that both this witch, and all other witches knew him to be a man.

After three yeares were passed over, in a morning betimes he went to towne before his dame; who upon some occasion (of like to make water) staied a little behind. In the meane time being neere to a churche, he heard a little saccaring bell ring to the elevation of a morrowe masse, and not daring to go into the church, least he should have beene beaten and driven out with cudgels, in great devotion he fell downe in the churchyard, upon the knees of his hinder legs, and did lift his forefeet over his head, as the preest doth hold the sacrament at the elevation.[1] Which prodigious sight when certeine merchants of Genua espied, and with woonder beheld; anon commeth the witch with a cudgell in hir hand, beating foorth the asse. And bicause (as it hath beene said) such kinds of witchcrafts are verie usuall in those parts; the merchants aforesaid made such meanes, as both the asse and the witch were attached by the judge. And she being examined and set upon the racke, confessed the whole matter, and promised, that if she might have libertie to go home, she would restore him to his old shape; and being dismissed, she did accordinglie. So as notwithstanding they apprehended hir againe, and burned hir: and the young man returned into his countrie with a joifull and merrie hart.

Upon the advantage of this storie *M. Mal. Bodin,* and the residue of the witchmongers triumph; and speciallie bicause S. *Augustine* subscribeth thereunto; or at the least to the verie like. Which I must confesse I find too common in his books, insomuch as I judge them rather to be foisted in by some fond papist or witchmonger, than so learned a mans dooings. The best is, that he himselfe is no eie-witnesse to any of those his tales; but speaketh onelie by report; wherein he uttereth these words: to wit, that It were a point of great incivilitie, &c: to discredit so manie and so certeine reports. And in that respect he justifieth the corporall transfigurations of *Ullysses* his mates, throgh the witchcraft of *Circes*: and that foolish fable of *Praestantius* his father, who (he saith) did eate pro-

---

[1] In margin: Note the devotion of the asse.

vender and haie among other horsses, being himselfe turned into an
horsse. Yea he verifieth the starkest lie that ever was invented, of
the two alewives that used to transforme all their ghests into horsses,
and to sell them awaie at markets and faires. And therefore I saie
with *Cardanus*, that how much *Augustin* saith he hath seen with his
eies, so much I am content to beleeve. Howbeit S. *Augustin* conclud-
eth against *Bodin*. For he affirmeth these transubstantiations to be
but fantasticall, and that they are not according to the veritie, but
according to the appearance. And yet I cannot allow of such appearances made by witches, or yet by divels: for I find no such power
given by God to any creature. And I would wit of S. *Augustine*, where
they became, whom *Bodins* transformed woolves devoured. But

o quam

Credula mens hominis, & erectae fabulis aures!

> *Good Lord! how light of credit is*
> *the wavering mind of man!*
> *How unto tales and lies his eares*
> *attentive all they can?*

Generall councels, and the popes canons, which *Bodin* so regard-
eth, doo condemne and pronounce his opinions in this behalf to
be absurd; and the residue of the witchmongers, with himselfe in
the number, to be woorsse than infidels. And these are the verie
words of the canons, which else-where I have more largelie repeated; Whosoever beleeveth, that anie creature can be made or
changed into better or woorsse, or transformed into anie other
shape, or into anie other similitude, by anie other than by God
himselfe the creator of all things, without all doubt is an infidell,
and woorsse than a pagan. And therewithall this reason is rendered,
to wit: bicause they attribute that to a creature, which onelie
belongeth to God the creator of all things.

Booke XIII. Chapter XIX

... Of divers woonderfull experiments, and of strange conclusions
in glasses, of the art perspective, &c.

Howbeit, these are but trifles in respect of other experiments to
this effect; speciallie when great princes mainteine & give countenance to students in those magicall arts, which in these countries and
in this age is rather prohibited than allowed, by reason of the abuse
commonlie coupled therewith; which in truth is it that mooveth
admiration and estimation of miraculous workings. As for example.
If I affirme, that with certeine charmes and popish praiers I can
set an horsse or an asses head upon a mans shoulders, I shall not

be beleeved; or if I doo it, I shall be thought a witch. And yet if *J. Bap. Neap.* experiments be true, it is no difficult matter to make it seeme so[1]: and the charme of a witch or papist joined with the experiment, will also make the woonder seeme to proceed thereof. The words used in such case are uncerteine, and to be recited at the pleasure of the witch or cousener. But the conclusion is this: Cut off the head of a horsse or an asse (before they be dead) otherwise the vertue or strength thereof will be the lesse effectuall, and make an earthern vessell of fit capacitie to conteine the same, and let it be filled with the oile and fat thereof; cover it close, and dawbe it over with lome: let it boile over a soft fier three daies continuallie, that the flesh boiled may run into oile, so as the bare bones may be seene: beate the haire into powder, and mingle the same with the oile; and annoint the heads of the standers by, and they shall seeme to have horsses or asses heads. If beasts heads be annointed with the like oile made of a mans head, they shall seeme to have mens faces, as diverse authors soberlie affirme. If a lampe be annointed heerewith, everie thing shall seeme most monstrous. It is also written, that if that which is called *Sperma* in anie beast be burned, and anie bodies face therewithall annointed, he shall seeme to have the like face as the beast had. But if you beate arsenicke verie fine, and boile it with a little sulphur in a covered pot, and kindle it with a new candle, the standers by will seeme to be hedlesse. . . . But I thinke not but *Pharaos* magicians had better experience than I for those and such like devises. And (as *Pompanacius* saith) it is most true, that some for these feats have been accounted saints, some other witches. And therefore I saie, that the pope maketh rich witches, saints; and burneth the poore witches.

VIII. Analogue

From THESAURUS LINGUAE LATINAE ET BRITANNICAE
by T. Cooper (1573 edition)

PYRAMUS AND THISBE

Pyramus, A yong man of Babilon, betweene whome and a mayden named *Thysbe*, was passing great love, contrarie to the willes of

[1] In margin: Wonderfull experiments.

their parentes: by whome they were so diligently kept, that not-withstanding their houses joyned togither, they could not eche enjoy others companie. Wherefore by an hole in a wall they agreed both in the night to steale out of their fathers houses, and meete at a certaine place in the field. Thither came first *Thysbe*, who, being in great feare of a Lionesse that she espyed by the Moone light, ranne into a cave thereby, and for haste did let fall hir upper garment, which the beast did rent and teare in pieces. Not long after (while *Thysbe* was yet in the Cave) Pyramus comming to the place appointed, and seeing his loves garment torne and blouddie, thinking she had beene destroyed by some wilde beast, for sorrow drew out his sworde, and slue himselfe. *Thysbe*, when hir feare was past, comming from the place, where as she hid hirselfe, and espying Pyramus in such maner slain, and the life not yet cleane out of his body, surmysing how the matter came to passe, with many teares pitifully bewayling both their fortunes, with the same sworde ended hir lyfe, wherewith not long before he had killed himselfe, for whose love shee came thither.

IX. Source

OVID: METAMORPHOSES
translated by Arthur Golding (1567)
Book IV. 67–201

PYRAMUS AND THISBE

Within the towne (of whose huge walles so monstrous high and
    thicke
The fame is given *Semyramis* for making them of bricke)
Dwelt hard together two yong folke in houses joynde so nere
That under all one roofe well nie both twaine conveyed were.
The name of him was *Pyramus*, and *Thisbe* calde was she.
So faire a man in all the East was none alive as he,
Nor nere a woman maide nor wife in beautie like to hir.
This neighbrod bred acquaintance first, this neyghbrod first did
    stirre
The secret sparkes, this neighbrod first an entrance in did showe,

For love to come to that to which it afterward did growe.
And if that right had taken place, they had bene man and wife,
But still their Parents went about to let which (for their life)
They could not let. For both their hearts with equall flame did
  burne.
No man was privie to their thoughts. And for to serve their turne
In steade of talke they used signes: the closelier they supprest
The fire of love, the fiercer still it raged in their brest.
The wall that parted house from house had riven therein a crany
Which shronke at making of the wall. This fault not markt of any
Of many hundred yeares before (what doth not love espie?)
These lovers first of all found out, and made a way whereby
To talke togither secretly, and through the same did goe
Their loving whisprings verie light and safely to and fro.
Now as at oneside *Pyramus* and *Thisbe* on the tother
Stoode often drawing one of them the pleasant breath from other,
O thou envious wall (they sayd), why letst thou lovers thus?
What matter were it if that thou permitted both of us
In armes eche other to embrace? Or if thou thinke that this
Were overmuch, yet mightest thou at least make roume to kisse.
And yet thou shalt not finde us churles: we thinke our selves in det
For the same piece of courtesie, in vouching safe to let
Our sayings to our friendly eares thus freely come and goe.
Thus having where they stoode in vaine complayned of their woe,
When night drew nere, they bade adew and eche gave kisses sweete
Unto the parget on their side, the which did never meete.
Next morning with hir cherefull light had driven the starres asyde
And *Phebus* with his burning beames the dewie grasse had dride.
These lovers at their wonted place by foreappointment met.
Where after much complaint and mone they covenanted to get
Away from such as watched them, and in the Evening late
To steale out of their fathers house and eke the Citie gate.
And to thentent that in the feeldes they strayde not up and downe,
They did agree at *Ninus* Tumb to meete without the towne,
And tarie underneath a tree that by the same did grow
Which was a faire high Mulberie with fruite as white as snow,
Hard by a coole and trickling spring. This bargaine pleasde them
  both,
And so daylight (which to their thought away but slowly goth)
Did in the Ocean fall to rest: and night from thence doth rise.
Assoone as darkenesse once was come, straight *Thisbe* did devise
A shift to wind hir out of doores, that none that were within
Perceyved hir: And muffling hir with clothes about hir chin,

That no man might discerne hir face, to *Ninus* Tumb she came
Unto the tree, and sat hir downe there underneath the same.
Love made hir bold. But see the chaunce, there comes besmerde with
    blood,
About the chappes a Lionesse all foming from the wood,
From slaughter lately made of kine, to staunch hir bloudie thurst
With water of the foresaid spring. Whome *Thisbe* spying furst
Afarre by moonelight, thereupon with fearfull steppes gan flie,
And in a darke and yrksome cave did hide hirselfe thereby.
And as she fled away for hast she let hir mantle fall
The whych for feare she left behind not looking backe at all.
Now when the cruell Lionesse hir thurst had stanched well,
In going to the Wood she found the slender weede that fell
From *Thisbe*, which with bloudie teeth in pieces she did teare.
The night was somewhat further spent ere *Pyramus* came there:
Who seeing in this suttle sande the print of Lions paw,
Waxt pale for feare. But when also the bloudie cloke he saw
All rent and torne, one night (he sayd) shall lovers two confounde,
Of which long life deserved she of all that live on ground.
My soule deserves of this mischaunce the perill for to beare.
I wretch have bene the death of thee, which to this place of feare
Did cause thee in the night to come, and came not here before.
My wicked limmes and wretched guttes with cruell teeth therfore
Devour ye O ye Lions all that in this rocke doe dwell.
But Cowardes use to wish for death. The slender weede that fell
From *Thisbe* up he takes, and streight doth beare it to the tree,
Which was appointed erst the place of meeting for to bee.
And when he had bewept and kist the garment which he knew,
Receyve thou my bloud too (quoth he) and therewithall he drew,
His sworde, the which among his guttes he thrust, and by and by ⎫
Did draw it from the bleeding wound beginning for to die   ⎬
And caste himselfe upon his backe. The bloud did spin on hie ⎭
As when a Conduite pipe is crackt, the water bursting out
Doth shote itselfe a great way off and pierce the Ayre about.
The leaves that were upon the tree besprincled with his blood
Were dyed blacke. The roote also bestained as it stoode,
A deepe darke purple colour straight upon the Berries cast. ⎫
Anon scarce ridded of hir feare with which shee was agast, ⎬
For doubt of disapointing him commes *Thisbe* forth in hast, ⎭
And for hir lover lookes about, rejoycing for to tell
How hardly she had scapt that night the daunger that befell.
And as she knew right well the place and facion of the tree
(As whych she saw so late before:) even so when she did see

The colour of the Berries turnde, shee was uncertaine whither
It were the tree at which they both agreed to meete togither.
While in this doubtfull stounde she stood, shee cast hir eye aside
And there beweltred in his bloud hir lover she espide
Lie sprawling with his dying limmes: at which she started backe,
And looked pale as any Box, a shuddring through hir stracke,
Even like the Sea which sodenly with whissing noyse doth move, ⎫
When with a little blast of winde it is but toucht above. ⎬
But when approching nearer him she knew it was hir love, ⎭
She beate hir brest, she shricked out, she tare hir golden heares,
And taking him betweene hir armes did wash his wounds with
    teares.
She meynt hir weeping with his bloud, and kissing all his face
(Which now became as colde as yse) she cride in wofull case
Alas what chaunce my *Pyramus* hath parted thee and mee?
Make aunswere O my *Pyramus*: It is thy *Thisb*, even shee
Whome thou doste love most heartely that speaketh unto thee.
Give eare and rayse thy heavie heade. He hearing *Thisbes* name,
Lift up his dying eyes, and having seene hir closde the same.
But when she knew hir mantle there and saw his scabberd lie
Without the swoorde: Unhappy man thy love hath made thee die:
Thy love (she said) hath made thee slea thy selfe. This hand of mine
Is strong inough to doe the like. My love no lesse than thine
Shall give me force to worke my wound. I will pursue the dead.
And wretched woman as I am, it shall of me be sed
That like as of thy death I was the only cause and blame,
So am I thy companion eke and partner in the same.
For death which only coulde alas a sunder part us twaine,
Shall never so dissever us but we will meete againe.
And you the Parentes of us both, most wretched folke alyve,
Let this request that I shall make in both our names bylive,
Entreate you to permit that we whome chaste and stedfast love
And whome even death hath joynde in one, may as it doth behove
In one grave be together layd. And thou unhappie tree
Which shroudest now the corse of one, and shalt anon through mee
Shroude two, of this same slaughter holde the sicker signes for ⎫
    ay. ⎬
Blacke be the colour of thy fruite and mourninglike alway, ⎭
Such as the murder of us twaine may evermore bewray.
This said, she tooke the sword yet warme with slaughter of hir love
And setting it beneath hir brest, did too hir heart it shove.
Hir prayer with the Gods and with their Parentes tooke effect.
For when the frute is throughly ripe, the Berrie is bespect

With colour tending to a blacke. And that which after fire
Remained, rested in one Tumbe as *Thisbe* did desire.

> [Ovid, Bk. IV, 55–166]

X. Possible Source

From A HANDEFULL OF PLEASANT DELITES
by Clement Robinson and divers others (1584)

A NEW SONET OF PYRAMUS AND THISBE

To the [tune of] 'Downe right Squier.'

You Dames (I say) that climbe the mount
    of Helicon,
Come on with me, and give account
    what hath been don:
Come tell the chaunce, ye Muses all,
    and dolefull newes,
Which on these Lovers did befall,
    which I accuse.
In Babilon, not long agone,
    a noble Prince did dwell,
whose daughter bright, dimd ech ones sight,
    so farre she did excel.

An other Lord of high renowne,
    who had a sonne;
And dwelling there within the towne,
    great love begunne:
Pyramus, this noble Knight,
    (I tel you true)
Who with the love of Thisbie bright,
    did cares renue.
It came to passe, their secrets was
    beknowne unto them both:
And then in minde, they place do finde,
    where they their love unclothe.

This love they use long tract of time;
    till it befell,
At last they promised to meet at prime,
    by Minus Well;
Where they might lovingly imbrace,
    in loves delight:
That he might see his Thisbies face,
    and she his sight.
In joyful case, she approcht the place
    where she her Pyramus
Had thought to viewd; but was renewd
    to them most dolorous.

Thus, while she staies for Pyramus
    there did proceed
Out of the wood a Lion fierce,
    made Thisbie dreed:
And, as in haste she fled awaie,
    her mantle fine
The Lion tare, in stead of praie;
    till that the time
That Pyramus proceeded thus,
    and see how Lion tare
The mantle this, of Thisbie his
    he desperately doth fare.

For why? he thought the Lion had
    faire Thisbie slaine:
And then the beast, with his bright blade,
    he slew certaine.
Then made he mone, and said, 'Alas!
    O wretched wight!
Now art thou in a woful case
    for Thisbie bright:
Oh! gods above, my faithfull love
    shal never faile this need;
For this my breath, by fatall death,
    shal weave Atropos threed.'

Then from his sheathe he drew his blade,
    and to his hart
He thrust the point, and life did vade,
    with painfull smart:

Then Thisbie she from cabin came,
    with pleasure great;
And to the Well apase she ran,
    there for to treat,
And to discusse to Pyramus,
    of al her former feares;
And when slaine she found him, truly,
    she shed foorth bitter teares.

When sorrow great that she had made,
    she took in hand
The bloudie knife, to end her life
    by fatall hand.
You Ladies, all, peruse and see
    the faithfulnesse,
How these two Lovers did agree
    to die in distresse.
You Muses waile, and do not faile,
    but still do you lament
These lovers twaine, who with such paine
    did die so well content.

                I. TOMSON

XI. Analogue

THE TRAGEDY OF PYRAMUS AND THISBE

(from B.M. Add. MS 15,227)

Tragoedia miserrima Pyrami & Thisbes fata enuncians.
Historia ex Publio Ovidio
Authore. N: R:

PROLOGUS

In stately Babylon, that triumphant place
Where once Semiramis o're Assyrians raign'd

Two goodly lovers dwelt,[1] one Pyramus
By name was call'd, the other Thisbe
Hee of [all] men the fairest, whilst shee was
'mongst all those Easterne Dames the sprusest lasse.
But churlish Parents so their Loves did crosse
That they poore wights could only through a wall
Their amorous soules breath out, where twas agreed
That to a shadie tree by Ninus tombe   10
They should repayre, and at midnight houre
Solace themselves under its pleasant bower.

But ah what immaturely Parents did begin
Unhappy Fates did second. They the Prologue
These the Epilogue were of this short Tragedy,
For Thisbe thither, beeing first approacht
A Liones shee spied which made her thence
With nimble legs to runne for her defence

When not long after Pyramus hee came
Unto the place appointed, where missing Thisbe deare   20
Her vaile he found sprinckled with goarie blood
Whence her devoured thinking, hee his word
Within his bowels sheaths/ him Thisbe finding so
Her Soule shee woundeth with a fatall blow.

This tragick story, who will reade or heare
These sequent lines, will it to him declare.   26

Actus Primus & Ultimus

Scena 1ᵃ

Enter Iphidius Pyrami pater, & Labetrus Thisbes pater

IPH.   I heare my deare Labetrus that my sonne
Your daughter loves, and that her amorous mind
Reciprocally doth place her soule on him.
     LAB.   True good Ihpidius. thus did Olympio
A freind of mine certify mee of late,

---

[1] In margin:
    Contiguas habuere domos ubi dicʳ altam
    Coctilibus muris cinxisse Semiramis urbem.
    Pyramus & Thisbe juvenum pulcherrimus alter,
    Altera quas Oriens habuit praelata puellis.
                        [i.e. Ovid IV. 57–8, 55, 6]

When through the streets wee with Lysander pass'd.
  IPH.   But the erraticall motions in childrens notions
Must to a regular forme by parents be reduced.
Wee are the Sunne; from whence as lesser starrs
Their light they borrow, and must therefore looke   10
That none of their designes doe any time eclipse
Our glorious splendour.—
  LAB.   Indeed this Lecture Nature teacheth all
But once affection plac'd, for to remove
     Is hard & dangerous, this events doe show
Reason demonstrates this. The Carthaginian Queene
Her inauspicious Love to great Anchises sonne
Could not but with Death dis[en]throne—
  IPH.   Yet not to try is Cowardice. Hee scarce
Will scatch the hare, who dares not give the chase.   20
Time and diswasion will worke much; Jason left
His Medea, and Theseus his Ariadne; moreover,
The inconstancy of women promiseth noe litle
To our future hopes.
  LAB.   Since then you'le have it so, my dear Iphidius
Bee you the Oracle to pronounce, what's fitting
To doe in such an action, for at your sacred shrine
My genious' thoughts consult, and what your wisdome shall
Dictate to mee, my selfe will execute.
  IPH.   Keepe then your daughter from her lovers sight   30
Immure her within your owne domestick walls
Whilst I my sonne endeavour to restraine
From's wonted libertie, and detaine him from
His dearest consorts company; my eyes
Shall bee his sentinels, and my walled house
His prison, his fetters my commaunds shall proove
So shall hee live, untill hee leaves to love.
  LAB.   Farewell it shall bee done.   *[Exeunt* 38

Scena 2ᵃ

Enter Thisbe sola

Ah mee poore soule my Father knowes I love,
But hence my woe hee will not let mee love
Mee doth hee cloyster in his uncoth house
And from my tendrest object doth debarre.
Water oftimes exasperates the fire

So love in mee restrain'd[1] doth burne the more
Ah Pyramus knewst thou thy Thisbes miserie
Pitty thou wouldst her great perplexitie.   [*Exit*

Enter Pyramus solus

Like as the harmles harte with dreadfull wound
Infested, rangeth o're the spatious plaines,
So doth my hearte by Cupid wounded wander   10
Whilst Center-like my body standeth still,
For heere my Father hath mee close pent up.
Within his strongest walls, hee mee imprisons.
What shall I doe? I know not what to doe,
Where shall I runne, Oh runne? I cannot goe,
Where shall I goe, oh goe? I cannot stirre

Bound is poore Pyramus with a twofold band
Of Love and Duety by 2 different hands
Love binds my soule, my Body duety binds,
The chaines of Love, will not my soule let goe,   20
The chaines of duety will my bodie owe,
Yet chaines of Love would have my bodie free
But Chaines of duety will not my soule let woe.   [sic]
Deformed Vulcan could faire Venus winne
Whilst I my Thisbe lose, crook-back'd Endimion
Could sport in Lunaes lap, and joy in her,
Happy was Vulcan; Happy Endimion
But I, but I——   [*Exit*
Enter Thisbe sola

Let woods and mountaines Eccho out my woe,   30
But woe is mee, nor woods nor mountaines view
Can my poore soule, nor can they heare the sound
Of these my aerie blasts. Thisbe loves Pyramus,
But pitteous wretch, Pyramus shee can't enjoy.
Io Jupiter, Helena could Paris get,
But Pyramus cannot wretched Thisbe see,
Thus like the Turtle I with teares bemoane
Him whom my soule is forc'd to leave alone.

Enter Casina Ancilla

Your dolefull sighes, your fearefull ecchoing groanes
Sounded Deare M^ris have my eares and heart,   40

---

[1] In margin:
    Quoque magis tegitur, tectus magis aestuat ignis.
        [*ibid.* 64]

Whence quick repayre, unto this place of sorrow
With speede I made, for as the adamant
Attracteth iron, or the Amber straw,
So doth your presence mine.

THISBE.   I love (Casina), but my love is gone
This love breeds greife within my dismall soule
This greife produced hath a threefold progenie
Of sighs, of teares, and of lamenting words.
I cannot greive, but that my heart will sigh,
I cannot sigh, but that mine eyes will weepe,   50
I cannot weepe, but that my tongue breakes foorth
Into expressions of great passion.
I love, I greive, I sigh, I weepe, I speake,
The sound of which hath brought Casina hither.

CAS.   Love is a passion alwaies in extremes,
It is the author of our life or death,
I love, I die, I love, I die, sayth hee,
But die you shall not, you shall live and love,
Our fathers old have often sayd, that love
Through stone walls breaks, now now that proverbs true,   60
For in our wall, a rime[1] I lately found
In which your soule may joy, and through which hole
You may have private conference with your Pyramus.
To him I'll runne, and certify I will
Him of this new-invented project——

THISBE.   Methinkes some little influence I now feele
Of future happines; oh how my soule revives
At these thy words Casina, and my spirrits
In these dry veines, now caper. Goe: goe, and tell
My Pyramus, that in thy destind place,   70
Anon I'll meete him by the houre of seven.   [*Exit Casina*
Propitious powers favour my designes,
And graunt you heav'ns that this same petty rime
To greater blisse, may ope a greater gate.
Prosper this image, Venus of thine owne,
And make thy Cupid happy in our Loves.
When that thou wert inaumoured on Mars
Successe thou didst implore as well as I.

Enter Casina

----

[1] In margin:
   Fissus erat tenui rima, quam duxerat olim,
   Cum fieret, paries domui communis utrique,
           [*ib.* 65, 6] rime, chink.

CASI. Goe, Goe my Thisbe, to thy Pyramus.
And with thy presence heale his wounded heart   80
Thy person hee attends in that same place
Wheer last I left him, and where thou must goe,
There vent your loves, your soules oh comfort there,
With pleasing murmure[1] pleasing words outsend
And each his frozen'st(?) breath to other lend   85

[*Exeunt*

Scena 3^{tia}

*Enter Pyramus, and Thisbe, speaking through the cranye of
the wall*

PYR. Were I great Ninus the Assyrian King,
Or heere did Orpheus tune his sweetest harpe
Were the whole world, a table for my dish,
Or did mee Tagus golden sands environ;
These were but shadows to that mightie joy
Which in thee Thisbe now my soule conceives.

THISBE Were I Semiramis the Assyrian Queene,
Were I the object of Appolloe's love,
Did I drinke Nectar and Ambrosia,
They were but as the litle, least pinshead,   10
Unto a mountaine great, or as this globe of earth,
Unto the highest shining spheare in heaven,
Compared with that happiness which in thee
My soule receives, and as the tender dew
Before the Sunne, so at thy presence great
They melt, and Vanish would.

PYR. My heart Sweet soule is like a ship at Sea
Which long hath tattered beene with blustring blasts
Of furious Aeolus, who hath oft gainst rockes
Of drearie feare, and sad despayre it dasht,   20
But now at last some happie gale of wind
Hath brought it safe unto the harbouring haven,
But Land I cannot, I can not but see
My Thisbe deare, latera, fata negant.

THISB. My soule sweetheart is like the she-palmetree,
Which angry winds have often torne and rent.

---

[1] In margin:

tutaeque per illud
Murmure blanditiae minimo transire solebant . . .
In que vicem fuerat captatus anhelitus oris.
[*ib*. 70, 72]

Its strength decay'd hath, its naturall force
Is spent and gone, till now at last conjoyn'd
To thee its mate it doth recover and live.
    PYRA.   Noe joyning, Thisbe, by embraces sweet   30
Doe yet attend our blessed wished hopes.
O Envious stones[1] why doe you hinder thus
Two wretched Lovers, what were it for you
To suffer now these bodies for to joyne?
Or were that happines[2] too much to graunt
Let but our lips each others to salute:
Ingratefull soules[3] wee are not, what wee have
From you wee confesse given, but did you more
Affoord, more thankes you should receive.
    THISB.   Oh that with Salmacis I were conjoyn'd   40
Unto thy lovely corpse, as once shee was
To her Hermaphrodite, and that wee both were one.
But since that blisse this place to us denyes,
Another shall it graunt,[4] by silent night
Let's strive to breake foorth from our Keepers hands
And them deceive, as once the piping boy
Did Junoe's Argus, and his hundred eyes.
    PYR.   I am content[5] but least our devious steps
Should wander too much in the spatious feilds,
Let Ninus tombe, the place appointed bee   50
Of our intended meeting, there a Tree [6]
With scattered boughs stands, ready to receive

---

[1] In margin:
    Invide, dicebant, paries, quid amantibus obstas
    Quantum erat, ut sineres nos toto corpore jungi?
[2] In margin:
    Aut, hoc si nimium, vel ad oscula danda pateres!
                    [*ibid.* 73–5]
[3] In margin:
    Nec sumus ingrati. Tibi nos debere fatemur,
    Quod datus est verbis ad amicas transitus aures
                    [*ibid.* 76–7]
[4] In margin:
                statuunt ut nocti silenti
    Fallere custodes, foribusque excedere tentent.
                    [*ibid.* 84–5]
[5] In margin:
    Neve sit errandum lato spatiantibus arvo
                    [*ibid.* 87]
[6] In margin:
    Conveniant ad busta Nini: lateantque sub umbra
    Arboris   [*ibid.* 88–9]

Our lovely Soules, there let our persons meete,
There let us both each others kindly greete.   54

[*Exeunt*

Scena 4ta

Enter Labetrus, & Iphidius

LAB.   Your worthy councel Sir, I have observd
My daughter is mew'd up in her fathers house,
But there with Niobe shee spends the time
In feareful sighs, in tragick dolefull straines.
Pyramus, Pyramus, her voice alwaies sounds
As Hercules did Hylas, Hylas faire.

IPH.   As doth thy Thisbe, so my Pyramus
Hee weeps and moanes, his fortune hee laments,
But time I hope will heale his wounds of Love
And from his cheekes wipe off all brinie teares   10
Our naturalists observe it as an axiome,
That violent motions least perpetuall are.

Enter Straton Servus

STRAT.   Mr Labretus, Thisbe is escap'd;
The doores are shut but her wee cannot find.

LAB.   This my Iphidius is the end of all,
This, this I feard, this, this is come to passe.
Goe range thou Babels streets, go narrowly
Search out my daughter, lest her ranging mind
Her feete shall also cause to runne and shee
Away from mee may steale——   20

[*Exit Straton*

Enter Clitipho Servus

CLITIPH.   Mr Iphidius, Pyramus is gone
But whether none knows, neither know they when.

IPH.   Both gone and flowne! have both escap'd our hand?
Tis strange, unles some stupid negligence,
The keepers hath oretaken, or that fates
With us full angry, our designes to crosse,
Have sworne and vow'd, and now gone who knowes
What may befall them in their dismall fright?
But may I find my sonne, with stricter eye
I will observe him least hee from mee fly.   30

[*Exeunt*

Scena 5ᵗᵃ

Enter Thisbe sola

Descended[1] now hath golden Phoebus bright
The westerne climates, where his glorious rayes,
That Hemisphaere enlighten, Dame Diana now
The sable world salutes, whilst lesser starrs
By brightsome splendor, shine on darksome earth,
When now I Thisbe wayte by Ninus tombe[2]
Of fairest Pyramus the kind approach
Heere does I hope to meete my tender love,
Whose Love did promise, for to meete mee heere.
Come, Come, my deare, why stayest thou so long   10
Doe Parents hinder, or to golden Love
Hast put on leaden feete, but ah my heart

                          [*Shee sees Liones*

Fayles at yon dreadfull, horrid fearefull sight,
Loe, loe a raging Liones[s][3] from ye woods
With full carrere makes hither nimble speed.
Oh Thisbe runne, or else thy flesh shee'le rend;
Fly with the wind, or else thy purple blood
Sheele sprinckle on insatiate earth, but loe
A Denne I see,[4] which shall my corpse receive,
Untill the danger is o'repast and I   20
May issue foorth, free from all feare to die.

                          [*Exit in antrum*

Enter Pyramus solus

Rejoyce o Pyramus in thy future hopes,
And Joy thou Thisbe in thy dearest Love,
My drowsy keepers have I now deceiv'd
And now I'me journeying to the appointed place,
Where mee should meete the image of my soule

                          [*He seeth the liones footsteps*

But sure these ominous steps portend noe good.

[1] In margin:
    Lux tarde discedere visa   [*ibid.* 91]
[2] In margin:
    Pervenit ad tumulum dictaque sub arbore sedit
                         [*ibid.* 95]
[3] In margin:
    Venit ecce . . . Leaena   [*ibid.* 96–7]
[4] In margin:
    obscurum timido pede fugit in **antrum**
                     [*ibid.* 100]

What fierce wild beast, hath heere its footsteps left
Where should my Thisbe tread; these o my deare
Are not the reliques of thy princely feete,　　　　　　　30
But ah whats this?

> [*Hee takes up Thisbe's vayle*[1] *which
> shee had left behind her and the Lyon
> had besmeared with blood*][2]

Now perish Pyramus, and let ne're thine eyes
Open to see another sunshine day.
This this one night two Lovers shall destroy[3]
And end that love, which nought but death can end
Oh that my soule would languish, and my blood
Forsake my tenderest heart, perish you veynes
To conquering death, let life now yeeld the feild.
Thou wert unworthy Thisbe of this end
And worthy wert to live a longer life.　　　　　　　40
Thy soule was spotles, mine was full of guilt.[4]
Twas I that sent thee to this fearefull place
And I now feareles man will follow thee,
But ah my death, will not to thee give life.
Oh that it would, that mightie kindnes then
Which once Orestes showed to Pylades,
Should now in me revive, but since th'art dead
This only can I doe, to dye with thee.
Oh savage beast why didst thou kill my love,
Could noe prey satisfie thee but her life.　　　　　　　50
Come then you rabid Lions, and take mine.[5]
These wicked bowels[6] teare with cruell teeth.

---

[1] In margin:
vestem quoque sanguine tinctam
Repperit——　　　　　　[*ibid.* 107]
[2] In margin:
　　　　　　　　　　Leoni
Ore cruentato tenues laniavit amictus.
　　　　　　　　　　[*ibid.* 104]
[3] In margin:
Una duos nox, inquit, perdet amantes.
　　　　　　　　　　[*ibid.* 108]
[4] In margin:
Nostra nocens anima est. Ego te miseranda, peremi,
In loca plena metus . . .　　[*ibid.* 110–11]
[5] In margin:
Nostrum divellite corpus　　[*ibid.* 112]
[6] In margin:
Et scelerata fero consumite viscera morsu
　　　　　　　　　　[*ibid.* 113]

Sed timidi est optare necem[1] ah pitteous vayle
Dyed with the tincture of my Thisbes blood.
Thee let mee kisse,[2] because thy mistress deare
I cannot now salute. Now Fatall knife
Receive my blood,[3] and let thou out my life.

[Hee kils himselfe

Enter Thisbe

The liones is gone, the coast is cleare
Come foorth now Thisbe to thy Pyramus.
Is this the tree,[4] under whose spreading bowre   60
My love and I should meete, but what spectacle
Presents it selfe to my amazed sight.

[Shee sees Pyramus

A man lies slaine, his membres beat the earth[5]
Oh how my blood mee fayles, oh how I feare
Lest yon dead man my Pyramus should proove.

[Shee views the corpse

Oh its my Pyramus.[6] Hee hee is slaine
Rend wretched armes now my disheveld hayre
Gush foorth mine eyes, fountaines of moornefull teares.
That I with Cristall waters may thy blood
Mixe. O my deare, oh let these hands embrace   70
Thy now inanimate body, let these lips

----

[1] In margin:
Tollit Velamina Thisbes
    [*ibid.* 115–6]
[2] In margin:
Utque dedit notae lachrymas dedit oscula vesti
    [*ibid.* 117]
[3] In margin:
Accipe nunc, inquit, nostri quoque sanguinis haustus
    [*ibid.* 118]
[4] In margin:
Haeret an haec sit   [*ibid.* 132]
[5] In margin:
tremebunda videt pulsare cruentum
Membra solum.   [*ibid.* 133–4]
[6] In margin:
Sed postquam remorata suos cognovit amores
Percutit indignos claro plangore lacertos
Et laniata comas amplexaque corpus amatum
Vulnera supplevit lacrymis; fletumque cruori
Miscuit: et gelidis in vultibus oscula figens
Pyrame clamavit quis te mihi casus ademit?
Pyrame, responde. Tua te charissime Thisbe
Nominat   [*ibid.* 137–44]

Salute thy tender cold, and paleshootne cheeks.
What cruel fate Pyramus thee tooke from me?
Answere O Pyramus, thee thy Thisbe calls.

                     [*Hee opens his eyes upon her, and*
                           shuts them

Ah never shut thou now thine opened eyes.[1]
Wilt thou but see thy Thisbe and then die?
Thy Love to mee reàcht out that fatall hand,
That fatall hand[2] drew out this mortall sword
This mortall sword, sent that immortall soule,
Out of this murthered body, and so shall   80
My Love, this hand,[3] that sword now doe to mee.
Thee will I follow in this tragick scene.
And in thyne end Ile thy companion bee.
O you that were the wretched Parents of us twaine
Graunt, that whom truest Love,[4] whom latest howre
Did joyne together, may not bee disjoyn'd
By a disunion in a severall tombe
And thou o tree[5] that with thy shadie boughs
This wretched corpse dost cover, shew that once
Two lovers, under thee did end their lives,   90
And let thy fruit bee coloured with our blood.
Now bloodie sword bee sheathed in my breast
And send my soule into eternal rest.   93

                                [*Shee dies*

     [1] In margin:
         oculos jam morte gravatos
         Pyramus erexit, visaque recondidit illa.
                         [*ibid.* 145–6]
     [2] In margin:
         Tua te manus, inquit, amorque
         Perdidit infelix   [*ibid.* 148–9]
     [3] In margin:
         Est et mihi fortis in unum ipsius
         Hoc manusque amor   [*ibid.* 149–50]
     [4] In margin:
         Ut quos certus amor, quos hora novissima junxit
         Componi tumulo non invideatis eodem.
                         [*ibid.* 156–7]
     [5] In margin:
         At tu quae ramis arbor miserabile corpus
         Nunc tegis—
         Signa tene caedis: pullosque et luctibus aptos
         Semper habe foetus, gemini monumenta cruoris
         . . . aptato pectus mucrone sum imum
         Incubuit ferro.—
                         [*ibid.* 158–163]

LOVE'S LABOUR'S LOST

INTRODUCTION

'A PLEASANT CONCEITED COMEDIE Called Loves Labors Lost. As it was presented before her Highnes this last Christmas. New Corrected and augmented by W. Shakespere', was printed at London by W.W. (William White) for Cutbert Burby in 1598. This Quarto contains many errors and repetitions, as well as variations in names (e.g. Braggart for Armado, Pedant for Holofernes, Curate for Nathaniel, Clown for Costard). The date of composition is much disputed. Till recently it was thought an early play, perhaps the first comedy, because of the slender plot and the presence of doggerel, elaborate puns and a wit in the underplot based on Lyly. Today few critics regard it with Hazlitt as perhaps Shakespeare's worst play, and those who argue that most of it is early recognize the splendour of some passages (e.g. Biron's speech, Act IV.3.287ff) and support their argument for revision with reference to the Quarto title-page. Revision there may have been before 1598, but I accept E. K. Chambers's view (in *W.Sh.*) that the play was mainly written in 1595 though some of the repetitions in the Q text suggest either 'false starts at the time of the original writing' (E.K.C.) or hasty revision in which 'alternative versions of an identical speech are retained side by side' (R. David, *New Arden*). There is confusion between Katharine and Rosaline in II.1 which H. B. Charlton (*The Library*, 8, p. 355) and Dover Wilson (*Camb.*, p. 125) have plausibly explained as due to transferring the comedy of mistaken identities from Act II to Act V.2, where it becomes the 'Muscovite' jest.

Usually it is assumed that the original version, whether written in 1589–90, 1592, or 1594–5, was by Shakespeare, and there is nothing to support J. M. Robertson's doubt: 'There is no good reason for believing either that Shakespeare origin-

425

ated it, or that he wrote all of it as it now stands'.[1] Of course
there may have been an earlier play, continental in origin and
affected by the *commedia dell'arte* tradition (hence the type-
names in *Q*). The doggerel lines point neither to early date nor
to an earlier play but to composition by Shakespeare in 1593–5;
for they are part of an extensive exercise in various kinds of
rhythm and rhyme which shows itself in long passages such as
I.1.49–177 and II.1.179–256. Experiments in rhyme were a
feature of court-drama under the influence of the Pembroke
circle (cf. Samuel Daniel and his remarks in *The Defence of
Ryme* (1603)). The play shows the same delight in rhetorical
dexterity and imagery as *Venus* and *Lucrece*, but has a new
lightness of touch with which the metrical gaiety is in complete
accord.

The source-hunter has little to offer. No one story has been
found to cover the plot. Thin though that is, it is neatly worked
out with a balance worthy of Lyly, whose influence is especially
potent in the witty teasing women, the interest in ideas, and
the underplot which parodies high life below stairs. From
Lyly spring the scholastic humour of its pedants, the comic
use of logic, rhetoric and grammar, as in I.2, (Armado and
Moth in logical dialectic); III.1 (Moth on love); and IV.1
(Armado's letter), but Shakespeare has developed his own
euphemistic style, and though the relationship between
Armado and Moth recalls that of Sir Tophas and Epiton in
Endimion, the situations and tone are different.

Foiled in their attempt to find one single source, scholars
have turned their attention to the following features: (1) the
young men's oaths of studious celibacy with the consequent
opposition between love and learning, and the breaking of the
oaths; (2) the diplomatic exchanges between France and
Navarre; (3) the use of a royal lady as an ambassador; (4) the
Muscovite Mask; (5) the actions and topicality of Armado and
his friends.

Concerning these last, it is easy to find in Latin comedy and
plays influenced by the Italian *commedia dell'arte* individual
scenes, speeches and tricks foreshadowing the behaviour of the
Braggart, the Pedant, &c. Holofernes for example is close to

---

[1] *The Genuine in Shakespeare.* 1930. p. 11.

the Doctor Gratiano of Italian plays,[1] as well as to characters like Rombus in *The Lady of May* by Sir Philip Sidney (1579?), and pedants in the Latin *Pedantius* (1581) and *Victoria* (1581–3) —the latter being a version by Abraham Fraunce of L. Pasqualigo's *Il Fedele* (1576).[2] But the relationship is generic rather than particular. This is not the place to discuss the topicality of the humour in the subplot, Moth's resemblance to Thomas Nashe, Armado's to Harvey (or Raleigh?), and the fascinating 'Schoole of Night' theories of Arthur Acheson, Miss M. C. Bradbrook and Miss F. A. Yates involving Shakespeare in a controversy about the superiority of action to contemplation between the Essex-Southampton and Raleigh-Northumberland groups. Such current references could be incorporated into the play just because the dramatic action is otherwise so scanty, and the piece becomes an intellectual fantasy, the nearest to a play of ideas that Shakespeare ever wrote, except perhaps *Troilus and Cressida.*

The idea, the topical reference, doubtless preceded the invention or organization of the plot. No precise literary source has been found for the story of the courtiers' oath, its breach, and the punishment inflicted by the ladies. Maybe none was needed, for Shakespeare (here and in *A Midsummer Night's Dream*) may have created his own plot out of miscellaneous reading and memories. In the controversy between commonsense practicality and pure theory, active life and scholarship, he usually took the popular side, as in *The Taming of the Shrew,* where Tranio counsels his master:

> Let's be no Stoics nor no stocks I pray,
> Or so devote to Aristotle's checks
> As Ovid be an outcast quite abjur'd (I.1.31–3)

For *Love's Labour's Lost* he may draw on a play or tale with a French setting such as is found in the *Académie Française* of P. de la Primaudaye (1577), one of the most popular ethical treatises of the time, translated into English in 1586. The Dedication (to Henry III of France) and the first pages of this book [Text I] show that the idea of a studious withdrawal of

---

[1] Cf. O. J. Campbell in *Studies in Shakespeare, Milton and Donne*; & K. M. Lea, *Italian Popular Comedy,* II, 393 ff.

[2] Cf. F. S. Boas, *University Drama in the Tudor Age,* pp. 140–47.

young men from the world of affairs and women was not new.[1] De la Primaudaye describes the nature and conduct of his Academy, and insists that study must be followed in moderation, that the courtier must learn to handle arms. He shows the world intruding harshly into the quiet of the hermitage when Civil War breaks out and the young men must go off to fight, returning only when peace has come. Shakespeare's 'academe' is an extreme instance of this sort of thing, maybe because he wished to mock at the Earl of Northumberland and Raleigh, maybe also because Essex himself would play the hermit on occasion, when in disgrace with fortune and the Queen, and Shakespeare wanted to laugh him out of such moods.

De la Primaudaye dedicated his work to Henry III; Shakespeare's hero was King Ferdinand of Navarre. Apart from any possible source in fiction there were good reasons for making the hero a King of Navarre (though one who never existed), and also for calling the nobles Berowne, Longaville and Dumain. Elizabeth was linked by loose alliance to Henry of Navarre whose chequered career before and after the Massacre of St Bartholomew excited great interest and at times admiration in England. In 1589 the Protestant hero had 4,000 English troops sent out to aid him under Lord Willoughby, who complained that Navarre treated them badly and three-quarters of them lost their lives. So Elizabeth sent no more even after the victory at Ivry (1590) until Spanish attacks on Picardy and Brittany seemed to endanger this country. Then in July 1591 Essex was sent out, besieged Rouen, and made contact with the Marshal de Biron, Navarre's 'liaison officer with the English'.[2] Though Essex was recalled and the siege was abandoned, Navarre had English sympathy until rumours spread that he was wooing Rome. Converted in July, 1593, he entered Paris in March, 1594. As an apostate Henry IV lost English esteem, and it is unlikely that *Love's Labour's Lost* would be written between July 1593 and the autumn of 1594, for his oath-breaking would not make the parallel between him and Ferdinand pleasing to the audience. But at the end of 1594 Henry IV was nearly assassinated by Jean Chastel, a

---

[1] Cf. F. A. Yates, *French Academies.* 1947.

[2] H. B. Charlton, 'The Date of Loves Labours Lost'. *MLR.* 1918. XIII pp. 257–266; 387–400.

pupil of the Jesuits. Soon he was at war with Spain (a sure way into English hearts), and Elizabeth, with whom he had concluded an alliance in 1593, occasionally supplied him with arms, money and troops. By June 1595 most of Burgundy rebelled against the Spaniards and welcomed young Biron, son of the old Marshal (who died in 1592). One of Henry's chief opponents, Charles, Duc de Mayenne, whom he had defeated at Ivry, now made a truce, followed by peace on 23 September, henceforth proving a valuable supporter. It seems likely that Dumain was named after de Mayenne rather than after the Maréchal D'Aumont, who fought on Henry's side. If so either Shakespeare misunderstood de Mayenne's earlier allegiance, or wrote the play after he had made his truce with the King. Longueville was a firm supporter of Navarre. Boyet and Marcadé also appear in contemporary French records.

Henry of Navarre emulated his brother-in-law Henry III in patronizing a literary circle, but there does not seem to be any special reference to this in *Love's Labour's Lost*. Possibly some source used by the dramatist had another Navarre-France antithesis, for the alleged father of King Ferdinand, Charles of Navarre (*LLL*. II.1.162) had a dispute in 1425 about a debt of 200,000 crowns owed him by the King of France. A brief account of this is given later [II]. It bears a certain resemblance to the diplomatic exchange between the King and Princess in II.1.129–168. The political meeting of a king of Navarre with a royal lady was however probably suggested by more recent events. In 1578 Marguerite de Valois, who had been unwillingly married to Henry of Navarre and separated from him, went with her mother (Catherine dei Medici) and 'l'escadron volant' of her ladies-in-waiting to meet the King at Nérac, where they discussed her dowry, which included Aquitaine.[1] (This may explain the reference to Aquitaine in *LLL* II.1.129ff). In her *Memoirs* Marguerite describes an earlier journey into Flanders in 1577 with about fourteen ladies: 'This sprightly company made such a favourable impression upon the foreigners who foregathered with it, that their admiration for France was thereby greatly increased.' At Nérac 'our court was so brilliant that we had no cause to regret that of

[1] Cf. A. Lefranc, *Sous le Masque de William Shakespeare*. 1918.

France.' She used to attend Mass while her husband went to Sermon, and then 'we were wont to reassemble and walk together, either in a beautiful garden which had long alleys planted with laurel and cypress, or in a park which I had had laid out in avenues three thousand paces long, by the side of the river, the remainder of the day being generally passed in all kinds of innocent amusements, and the afternoons and evenings in dancing.'[1] (Compare *LLL* IV.3.371–377.)

For a time she and her husband came close together, only to part again. Her *Memoirs* were not published till 1628, but many Englishmen in London had been in France, and Shakespeare may have got information from them about Navarre's habits as huntsman, letter-writer and lover, as well as about Marguerite and her mother. The latter often acted as plenipotentiary for her son Henry III, and in 1586 met Navarre at St. Bris in an attempt to end the Civil War and to arrange that (if he divorced Marguerite) he should marry the Princess of Lorraine. I give Davila's account of this meeting, without suggesting that Shakespeare had St. Bris in mind [III]. *Love's Labour's Lost* is more likely to have been based on some entertainment given at Nérac than on the abortive negotiations of 1586.

Love's Labour's Lost is not a play of political allegory, but in writing his delicate comedy against studious seclusion and other extravagances of learning Shakespeare was doubtless pleased by the sidelong glances at modern France and Navarre provided by his plot. Henry IV, though no great scholar, was a patron of learning; he had forsworn himself for power when he turned Catholic, so it would not surprise an English audience to find a fictitious King of Navarre forswearing himself more innocently for love. He had also had to endure a period of waiting before the Church accepted his conversion and gave him absolution. The parallel would not be lost when Ferdinand must become a real hermit for a year before being forgiven by his Princess (*LLL* V.2.780–97). The notion that the King of Navarre was unwilling to meet the ladies would be ludicrous in itself, since Henry was notorious for his love-affairs.

Before the play was performed for Queen Elizabeth at Christmas 1596–7, Henry IV had won victories in alliance with

---

[1] *Memoirs of Marguerite de Valois* ... translated by Violet Fane. 1892. p. 241 &c.

England and the States-General against Spain. Though he was negotiating peace with France by the end of 1597, it was not agreed till May, but the twists and turns of his policy were topical, and there must have been even more irony in Shakespeare's comedy than he had intended. The Edict of Nantes in April, 1598, however, consolidated Protestant privileges of worship and gave them civil rights, proving that some good had come of the King's forswearing.

The suspicion that the play as we have it was mainly written in 1595 is increased by the Muscovite mask in V.2 and Berowne's remark:

> here was a consent,
> Knowing aforehand of our merriment,
> To dash it like a Christmas comedy (V.2.461).

Shakespeare had reason to remember the Christmas Revels of 1594–5 held by the lawyers of Gray's Inn, at which an 'ambassador' from the Temple was received with mock-solemnity at the Court of the Prince of Purpoole. On 28 December the proceedings were marred by the spectators' unruly behaviour and the Temple Ambassador withdrew; perhaps he was 'ragged'. Consequently it 'was thought good not to offer any thing of Account (says *Gesta Grayorum* from which extracts are given below [IV]) saving Dancing and Revelling with Gentlewomen, and after such Sports, a Comedy of Errors (like to *Plautus* his *Menechmus*) was played by the Players.' This performance of little account was probably by the Lord Chamberlain's company, which had given the same play before the Queen at Greenwich that afternoon. Did Shakespeare take part in this 'Night of Errors'?

Next night it was jestingly complained that some Conjuror 'had foisted a Company of base and common Fellows, to make up our Disorders with a Play of Errors and Confusions.' A mock trial was held in which the prisoner was acquitted and the lawyers sent to the Tower. On another evening there were six speeches (probably written by Francis Bacon) suggesting ways of advancing the Honour and Happiness of the State. Those recommended were the exercise of War, the study of Philosophy, eternizement and fame by Buildings and Foundations, the increase of Authority or Revenue, Virtue and gracious

Government, Pastimes and Sports. Love was not praised, though on January 3 they had an altar to the Goddess of Amity at which classical pairs of friends burned incense. Next day there was a Progress through the City.

On Twelfth Night was held an entertainment in which an 'Ambassador' from 'the mighty Emperor of Russia and Muscovy' came 'in attire of Russia, accompanied with two or three of his own Country, in like Habit', who praised the behaviour of English knights said to have defeated the Bigarian and Negro-Tartars. The Russian joke was continued for some time, although at the beginning of term the authorities took down the scaffolding from the Hall and refused further facilities to the law-students. But the Prince 'returned' from an alleged expedition in Russia and was actually invited to visit Queen Elizabeth at Shrove-tide, when a Mask of Proteus was played before her. So that (the writer of *Gesta Grayorum* concludes) 'Our *Christmas* would not leave us till such time as *Lent* was ready to entertaine us.'

Too much stress must not be laid on this revel, but it seems likely that Shakespeare remembered it in writing or revising his comedy of Learning, and that his Muscovite mask is a reminiscence of the Gray's Inn entertainment. Very probably too, when wishing to make his courtly lovers comic, and to parody the diplomatic embassage in his main plot, he bethought himself of the somewhat ridiculous behaviour of a Russian ambassador sent by Ivan the Terrible, who after paying court to the Queen, determined to woo Lady Mary Hastings. The *Relacion or Memoriall* of Sir Jerome Horsey was not published till 1856[1], but the fact that Lady Mary was henceforth nicknamed 'the Empress of Muscovia' shows that the ambassador's gaucherie was not forgotten [V].

Interest in Russia was intermittent in the eighties and nineties when attempts at trade were made and reports on the country and its government were brought home by men such as Horsey, who had lived there from 1575 to 1591, and the Queen's Ambassador Giles Fletcher, whose book *Of the Russe Commonwealth* was published in 1591. Fletcher described the uncouthness of Russian manners, their 'bringing up, voide of

---

[1] Printed with Fletcher's book in *Russia at the Close of the Sixteenth Century*, ed. E. A. Bond. (Hakluyt Society.) 1856.

all good learning and civill behaviour' (p. 150). 'As for the truth of his word, the Russe for the most part maketh small regard of it, so he may gaine by a lie and breeche of his promise' (p. 152). 'They are for the most part of a large size and of very fleshly bodies, accounting it grace to be somewhat gross and burly'; and 'for the most part they are unwieldy and inactive withal' (cf. *LLL* V.2.114 and 269). On the other hand the Russians loved formality of address, and Fletcher got into trouble when he had audience with Ivan I for abridging him of some of his many titles. Queen Elizabeth herself had to apologize in 1591 for the same error, and did so in a delightfully ironic letter.[1] Russian pomposity as well as unskilful courtiership may have been in Shakespeare's mind, as they certainly were in the Gray's Inn revellers' and this may explain why Berowne, at V.2.402 declares first that he will 'never more in Russian habit wait' and then that he forswears the 'maggot ostentation' of 'Three-pil'd hyperboles, spruce affectation/ Figures pedantical.' We see again how Shakespeare's imagination, in selecting his material and organizing it, is directed by one or two ideas which govern his choice and tone and enable him to unite the most heterogeneous and farbrought stuff by the operation of his playful fancy. In this case Oath-making and breaking; Ambassadors female and male; the affectations of courts and schools in poetry and prose; Civil War between Navarre and France; the antithesis between French courtliness (with Boyet as its extreme (V.2.316–335) and Russian awkwardness; between courtly virtù and Armado's braggart baseness, with the pseudo-heroism of the Nine Worthies presented by 'the pedant, the braggart, the hedge-priest, the fool and the boy'; the whole interlinked to make a delicate comedy of manners, particularly suited to the well-informed and cosmopolitan minds, the mocking humour, the well-schooled but anti-academic taste, of the intellectuals in the Essex circle and the Inns of Court.

[1] Cf. Charlton, *op. cit.*, pp. 388–9.

I. Analogue

From THE FRENCH ACADEMIE
newly translated by T. B[owes] (1586)[1]

[The Dedication to Henry III of France declares:]

... The din[n]er of that prince of famous memorie (Francis your grandfather) was a second table of *Salomon*, unto which resorted from everie nation such as were best learned, that they might reape profit and instruction. Yours, Sir, being compassed about with those, who in your presence daily discourse of, and heare discoursed, many grave and goodly matters, seemeth to be a schoole erected to teach men that are borne to vertue. And for my selfe, having so good hap during the assemblie of your Estates at Blois. as to be made partaker of the fruit gathered thereof, it came in my mind to offer unto your Majestie a dish of divers fruits, which I gathered in a Platonicall garden or orchard, otherwise called an ACADEMIE where I was not long since with certaine young Gentlemen of Anjou my companions, discoursing together of the institution in good manners, and of the means how all estates and conditions may live well and happily. . . .

[In 'the first day's work' of the Academy the author describes how four young gentlemen of Anjou were taken into the house of an old nobleman who put them under the care of a good and learned man to be educated. Their master taught them Latin and some Greek, &c.]

He propounded for the chiefe part and portion of their studies the morall philosophie of ancient Sages and wise men, together with the understanding and searching out of histories, which are the light of life: therein following the intent and will of him that set him on worke, and also of the parents of this Nobilitie, who desired to see their children, not great Orators, suttle Logicians, learned Lawyers, or curious Mathematicians, but onely sufficiently taught in the doctrine of good living, following the traces and steps of

[1] A version of Pierre de La Primaudaye: *L'Académie française* (1577).

434

vertue, by the knowledge of things past from the first ages untill this present; that they might refer all to the glorie of the divine majestie, and to the profit and utilitie as well of themselves as of their country. And yet in the meane while these noble and toward youths were not deprived of other exercises meete for them, which (as the divine Plato saith) are very profitable for this age, and helpe much to quicken the spirits of young men, and to make their bodies which are weake by nature, more strong and apt to sustaine travel, as namely, to ride horses, to run at the ring, to fight at barriers, to applie themselves to all kind of weapons, and to followe the chace of beasts. . . .

[Their fathers came to visit them and heard their sons discoursing for two hours each morning and as much after dinner, but they enjoyed it so much that they usually gave six to eight hours a day to discussion.]

In this commendable maner of passing their time they continued certaine daies. But the sudden and sorrowful newes of the last frantike returne of France into civill war brake up the happie assemblie, to the end that these noble youths, betaking themselves to the service due to their prince, and to the welfare and safetie of their countrye, might make triall of their first feates of armes, wherein they wanted neither readiness, nor valure of hart, which being naturally in them was also increased by the knowledge of philosophie.

[After the war they all met again at the old man's house.]

Taking up their first order, and conferring anew of the same matters, [they] daily met in a walking place covered over in the midst with a goodly green Arbour, alotting for this exercise from eight to ten in the morning, and from two to fower in the afternoone. Thus they continued this exercise for the space of three whole weekes, which makes eighteen daies works, besides the three Sabboth daies, set apart by them, that they might rest, and cease from their studies, and attend the better to the chiefe point of the holie daies institution, which is to the contemplation, and consideration of the works of God, of his law, and of his praise. During which time it was my goodhap to be one of the companie when they began their discourses, at which I so greatly wondered, that I thought them worthie to be published abroad. . . .

II. Historical Parallel

From THE CHRONICLES OF ENGUERRAND DE MONSTRELET
translated by T. Johnes (1810)

. . . Charles King of Navarre came to Paris to wait on the King. He negotiated so successfully with the King and Privy Council that he obtained a gift of the castle of Nemours, with some of its dependent castle-wicks, which territory was made a duchy. He instantly did homage for it, and at the same time surrendered to the King the castle of Cherburgh, the county of Evreux, and all other lordships he possessed within the kingdom of France, renouncing all claims or profits in them to the King and to his successors, on condition that with the Duchy of Nemours the King of France engaged to pay him two hundred thousand gold crowns of the coin of the King our Lord.

(Compare *Love's Labour's Lost*, II.1.128–167.)

III. Historical Parallel

From THE HISTORY OF THE CIVIL WARS OF FRANCE

The History of the Civil Wars of France; Written in Italian by H. C. Davila. Translated out of the Original. The Second Impression, . . . Printed by T. N. for Henry Herringman. 1678.

Book VIII

[Henry of Navarre & the Queen-Mother at St. Bris.]

. . . the Queen-Mother (the place of interview with the King of *Navarre* being appointed) was come to Cognac, attended by *Ludovico*

Gonzaga Duke of Nevers ... by the Maréchal *de Retz*, the Sieurs *d'Abin*, and *de Rambouillet*, by the Abbot *Guadagni*, Secretary *Pinart*, Monsieur *de Lansac*, and divers other personages, who for quality and wisdom were of great esteem.

On the other side, the King of *Navarre* was come to *Jarnac*, with the Viscount *de Turenne*, the Sieur *de la Force*, and *Monguidon*, the Baron *de Salignac*, and many other Lords of his party; but with so great strength, (having with him eight hundred Horse, and few less than two thousand Foot) as at the first notice of them, put the Queen-Mother into very great suspicion, there not wanting those who doubted, and spread abroad a report, that he was come with an intention to take her and carry her away by force to *Rochel*. But after it was known that the King of *Navarre* was come in that manner for his own security, as one who by reason of his own weakness, and the usage he had received at other times, was in doubt of being deceived; and that the ingenuity of his nature, and the absurdity of that business had taken away all jealousies, they met at last upon the eighteenth of *October* at *St Bris*, equally distant from the places whence they came, there being on the Queen's part besides her ordinary Court, only the Captain of her Guard with fifty Horse, and on the King of *Navarre's* Captain *Lomelle* with as many. The Gates were guarded by two Companies of Foot, one of one party, and the other of the other, and in the field the Cavalry of both sides, in two several Squadrons; the King of *Navarre's* commanded by the Count *de la Vall*, and Monsieur *de la Noue*; and the Queen-Mother's by the Sieur *de Malicorne* and other Gentlemen of the Country.

Their publick discourses passed in complaints on both sides; the King lamenting that the King of Navarre's obstinacy not to change his Religion, and to keep so far from Court, put the King upon a necessity of making War: and on the other side, the King of *Navarre* complained that while he stood still obedient to the King's commands, and most observant of the Edicts, he to satisfie the Lords of *Guise*, and other Enemies to quietness, had broken the Peace. But being come to secret conference, the Queen laid open the conditions which the King propounded of the divorce of Queen *Margaret*, and of the Marriage with the Princess of *Lorain*, who was there present, and being of an age already marriageable, shewed tokens of most noble education and discreet modesty. To this Match, the Queen told him, that a Manifest should be added to declare him first Prince of the Blood, and lawful Successor to the Crown; and alledged, that from thence, would necessarily result the disuniting of the Duke of *Lorain*, Father to the Princess, from the League, and from the Lords of *Guise*, who losing so principal a foundation, either would become quiet of their own accord, or if they did not submit themselves freely to the King's will, they might with help of the German Army, which was upon the point of entring the Confines, be easily ruined and suppressed. That to attain so great a good, nothing else was required from the King of *Navarre*, but only his conversion to the Catholick Religion, and his return to Court; for as concerning the Excommunication of *Rome*, and the Popes Declaration of his incapacity to succeed to the Crown, as soon as he should be a real Catholick, the persecution of the *Guises* being taken away, and the League destroyed, the revocation of it would without difficulty be obtained. . . .

[The King of Navarre mistrusted the promises made him, and did not want to change his religion, and when the Duke of Nevers was admitted to the third conference on the Queen's side, this increased his disinclination;]

. . . for the Duke of *Nevers*, desiring to shew his Eloquence and Learning as he was wont to do, wrought greater doubts in the mind of the King of *Navarre*, to whom the Italian arts were suspected . . . whereby his jealousie increasing, not thinking it safe to trust either to the Kings inconstancy, or the Queen's too much cunning, he resolved in the end to follow the fortune of the Hugonots, and not to trust the Court; neither would he come to the Conference any more himself in person, but continued to send the Viscount of *Turenne* who treating very dexterously with the Queen, would never come to any conclusion at all.

With these negotiations began the year 1587. . . .

IV. Analogue

From GESTA GRAYORUM

Gesta Grayorum: or The History of the High and Mighty Prince Henry, Prince of Purpoole . . . who Reigned and Died, A.D. 1594. *For W. Canning.* (1688.)[1]

[The Grays Inn revels of 1594/5 included the election of a 'Prince of Purpoole' who held Court and received an Ambassador from the

[1] Text from edition by W. W. Greg (*Malone Society*, 1914).

Temple, who on one day made a Progress with him through the City, dining in state with the Lord Mayor.]

Shortly after this Shew, there came Letters to our State from *Frederick Templarius*; wherein he desired, that his Ambassador might be dispatched with Answer to those Things which he came to treat of. So he was very honourably dismissed, and accompanied homeward with the Nobles of *Purpoole*: Which Departure was before the next grand Day. The next grand Night was upon *Twelfth-day* at Night; at which time the wonted honourable and worshipful Company of Lords, Ladies and Knights were, as at other times, assembled; and every one of them placed conveniently, according to their Condition. And when the Prince was ascended his Chair of State, and the Trumpets sounded, there was presently a Shew which concerned His Highness's State and Government: The Invention was taken out of the Prince's Arms, as they are blazon'd in the beginning of his Reign, by the King at Arms.

First, There came six Knights of the Helmet, with three that they led as Prisoners, and were attired like Monsters and Miscreants. The Knights gave the Prince to understand, that as they were returning from their Adventures out of *Russia*, wherein they aided the Emperor of *Russia*, against the *Tartars*, they surprized these three Persons, which were conspiring against His Highness and Dignity: and that being apprehended by them, they could not urge them to disclose what they were: By which they resting very doubtful, there entred in the two Goddesses, *Arety* and *Amity*; and they said, that they would disclose to the Prince who these suspected Persons were; and thereupon shewed, that they were *Envy*, *Malecontent* and *Folly*: Which three had much mis-liked His Highness's Proceedings, and had attempted many things against his State; and but for them two, *Vertue* and *United Friendship*, all their Inventions had been disappointed. Then willed they the Knights to depart, and to carry away the Offenders; and that they themselves should come in more pleasing sort, and better befitting the present. So the Knights departed, and *Vertue* and *Amity* promised, that they two would support His Excellency against all his Foes whatsoever, and then departed with most pleasant Musick. After their Departure, entred the six Knights, in a very stately Mask, and danced a new devised Measure; and after that, they took to them Ladies and Gentlewomen, and danced with them their *Galliards*, and so departed with Musick. Which being done, the Trumpets were commaunded to sound, and then the King at Arms came in before the Prince, and told His Honour, that there was arrived an Ambassador from the mighty Emperor of *Russia* and *Moscovy*, that had some Matters of Weight to make known to His Highness. So the Prince willed that he should be admitted into his Presence; who came in Attire of *Russia*, accompanied with two of his own Country, in like Habit. When they were come in presence of the Prince, the Ambassador made his Obeysance, and took out Letters of Credence, and humbly delivered them to the Prince, who gave them to the King at Arms, to be read publickly, as followeth.

[The letter parodies the longwinded titles of the Russian emperor, who had not long before complained that Queen Elizabeth's letters to him omitted many of them (cf. J. Horsey, *A Relacion or Memoriall abstracted owt of Sir Jerome Horsey His Travells*, etc., p. 375 ff).]

When the King at Arms had read this Letter, the Ambassador made this Speech to the Prince.

Most Excellent Prince,

Fame seemed to the Emperor, my Sovereign, to do your Highness Right, by filling the World with the Renown of your Princely Vertues, and Valour of your brave Court; till of late, the gallant Behaviour, and heroical Prowess of divers your Knights of the *Helmet*, whom the good Fortune of *Russia*, addressed to your cold Climate, discovered that Fame to be either envious in suppressing a great part of your Valour, or unable to set forth so admirable Vertues to their full Merits: For by these five Knights (whose greatest Vaunts were, that they were your Excellency's Servants) an exceeding number of *Bigarian Tartars*, whose vagabond In-roads, and inhumane Fierceness infested his Borders, captivated his People, burnt his Cities, and spoiled whole Provinces, was by a most wonderful Victory, repulsed, and beaten back. And withal, by their brave Conduct, they surprized another Army of *Ne-gro-Tartars*; whose wretched Devices ceased not to work the Confusion and Combustion of our whole Country, and diverted their barbarous Cruelty where it might do us most damage. These same worthy Knights, before they could receive that Honour wherewith my Soveraign intended to adorn their Vertues, did withdraw themselves, and are retired, as His Majesty is informed, to your Court. Whereupon, he sent me, partly to congratulate your Happiness, who deserve to command over such a number of gallant Gentlemen; but especially, to conjure your Excellency (according to the ancient League and Amity continued betwixt you) that you would send him these six Knights, accompanied with an hundred other of the same Order; for he doubteth not, but by their Vertues, accompanied and attended with his own Forces, who are, in largeness of Dominion, and number of People, and all other Warlike

Furniture and Provision, inferiour to no Earthly Potentate, that these Runagate *Tartars* shall be again confined to their Deserts, with their memorable Slaughter, and your common Glory and Profit: ...

[The Russian Ambassador was feasted, and after many jests the Prince made a speech ending as follows:]

Our Self, with Our chosen Knights, with an Army Royal, will make towards our Brother of Russia, *with my Lord here, his Ambassador, presently to join with him against his Enemies, the* Negarian Tartars; *more dreadful, the* Barbarian Tartars: *And if* Fortune *will not grace Our good Attempt, as I am rightful Prince, and true Sovereign of the honourable Order of the* Helmet, *and by all those Ladies whom, in Knightly Honour, I love and serve, I will make the Name of a* Grayan *Knight more dreadful to the* Barbarian Tartars, *than the* Macedonian *to the wearied* Persians, *the* Roman *to the dispersed* Britains, *or the* Castalian *to the weakned* Indians. *Gentle Ladies, be now benign and gracious to your Knights, that never pleased themselves, but when their Service pleased you; that for your sakes shall undertake hard Adventures, that will make your Names and Beauties most famous, even in Foreign Regions; let your Favour kindle the Vigour of their Spirits, wherewith they abound; for they are the Men, by whom your Fame, your Honour, your Vertue shall be for ever advanced, protected and admired.*

When the Prince had concluded, for his Farewel, he took a Lady to dance withal, and so did the rest of the Knights and Courtiers; and after some time spent in Revelling, the Prince took his way to his Lodging, and so the Company dissolved, and made an end of this Night's Work.

On the next Morning His Highness took his Journey towards *Russia*, with the Ambassador, and there he remained until *Candlemas*; at which time, after his glorious Conquests abroad, His Excellency returned home again; ...

V. Historical Parallel

From TRAVELS OF SIR JEROME HORSEY in RUSSIA AT THE CLOSE OF THE SIXTEENTH CENTURY
ed. E. A. Bond (Hakluyt Society) 1856[1]

[A Russian Ambassador woos an English Court-lady in 1582.]

... Now was the Emperowr more ernest to send into England about this longe conceated match and marriage then ever: adressed one Feother Pissempscoie, a noble, grave, wise and trustie gentilman, to conferr and desier of the Queen the Lady Marye Hastings, daughter to that noble Henry lord Hastings, Errell of Huntington, whome he haerd was her kyndsweoman, and of the bloud royall, as he termed it; and that yt would please her Majesty to send som noble ambassodor to treat with him aboute it. His ambassador went forward; toke shippinge at St. Nicholas; arived in England; magnificently receaved; had audience of the Quen; delivered his letters comendatory. Her Majesty caused that lady to be atended on, with divers great ladies and maieds of honnor and yonge noblemen, the nomber of each apointed, to be seen by the said ambassodor in Yorcke Howse garden. She put on a staetly countenance accordinglie. The ambassodor, atended with divers other noblemen and others, was brought before her Ladyship; cast down his countenance; fell prostrate to her feett, rise, ranne backe from her, his face still towards her, she and the rest admiringe at his manner. Said by an interpritor yt did suffice him to behold the angell he hoped should be his masters espouse; comended her angellicall countenance, state and admirable bewty. She after was called by her famillier frends in court the Emporis of Muscovia. (p. 195, 6).

[When Horsey returned from Russia in 1587 the Queen showed great interest in the Russian language and its writing.]

Said she: 'I could quicklie lern it'—Preyed my Lord of Essex to lern the famoust and most copious language in the world; after which commendacion his honor did much affect it and delight in it, if he might ateyn therunto without paiens-takinge and spendinge more time then he had to spare. (p. 233).

[1] Entitled in the MS 'A Relacion or Memoriall abstracted owt of Sir Jerome Horsey his Travells, Imploiments, Services & Negociations ...'

THE MERCHANT OF VENICE

INTRODUCTION

THE MERCHANT OF VENICE was entered in S.R. to James Roberts on 22 July, 1598, and again on 28 October, 1600, to Thomas Heyes 'by Consent of Master Robertes', who printed Q1 for Heyes in that year. Q2, though dated 1600, was printed in 1619. F1 (1623) came from Q1, probably a playhouse text including act-divisions and directions for musical effects.

Francis Meres mentioned the play, so it must have been performed before 7 September, 1598. An allusion to Robert Cecil the hunchback as St. Gobbo in a letter of 1596 may have no significance, since 'Gobbo' was Italian for 'hunchback', and Q1, F1 and F3 call Gobbo 'Iobbe', i.e. Job, which would suit his catalogue of sufferings in Shylock's household (II.2). Similarly the reference to the 'Wolf, . . . hang'd for human slaughter' may not be to Roderigo Lopez, executed on 7 June, 1594, after being accused by Essex of trying to poison Queen Elizabeth and the Pretender to the throne of Portugal (cf. Brown, *Arden* 1955, p. xxiii). But Antonio may get his name from the Pretender, Antonio Perez. The allusion to the 'wealthy Andrew' (I.i.27) may date the play by referring to the Spanish vessel the *St. Andrew* captured at Cadiz in 1596. The style certainly suggests 1596 rather than 1594. Nothing is known of 'the Venesyon comedey' entered in Henslowe's Diary on 15 August, 1594.

AN EARLIER PLAY?

Consideration of sources is complicated by the probability that there was a play (now lost) on the subject, for Stephen Gosson in his *Schoole of Abuse* (1578), referring to some exceptions to the general rule of corruption in the drama wrote:

'The *Iew* and *Ptolome*, showne at the Bull, the one representing the greedinesse of worldly chusers, and bloody mindes of

445

Usurers: The other very liuely discrybing howe seditious estates, with their owne deuises, false friendes, with their own swoordes, and rebellious commons in their owne snares are ouerthrowne: neither with Amorous gesture wounding the eye: nor with slouenly talke hurting the eares of the chast hearers.' (Ed. Arber, p. 40.)

Since *The Merchant of Venice* includes features which might be meant by 'the bloody mindes of usurers' (the Bond Story) and 'the greedinesse of worldly chusers' (the Casket Story), *The Jew* may have been Shakespeare's source. S. A. Small has tried to reconstruct this old play (*MLR* XXVI, 1931, 281–7). Other critics such as C. Knight and T. M. Parrott have declared that no dramatist of 1579 could have combined two such plots. The defeated suitors, writes the latter, are not really guilty of greediness. But they may have been greedy in *The Jew*, and Gosson might well have thought so anyway, because they were 'worldly chusers'. The two plots may not have been united as in Shakespeare but given as separate examples of money-love (cf. *The Three Ladies of London, infra*). Honigmann regards the two phrases as repetitious (*MLR* XLIX, 1954, 293–307), since usurers are greedy and 'worldly chusers' and often described as 'bloody' even when they seek no pound of flesh. Brown (*Arden* 1955) considers the theory that *The Jew* was the source-play as 'most insecure'. Unproven it certainly is, but the possibility remains. The passages given below may be no more than analogues, but as Brown declares 'it remains at least a strong probability that Shakespeare himself adapted the story as found in *Il Pecorone*. Shakespeare often used more than one source for a single play, and there is no reason why he should not have done so for *The Merchant*.'

THE FLESH-BOND

The story of the giving of a pound of flesh probably begins in India, for the *Mahabharata* has a tale about King Usinara who saves a dove from a hawk by giving its weight from his own flesh instead. The Talmud attributes a similar sacrifice to Moses who, after scolding an eagle for stealing a lamb, offers his breast to the bird. According to the Twelve Tables of Roman Law, creditors might as a last resort claim the body of a defaulting debtor and divide it among themselves.[1] Arising out of this no doubt, by the twelfth century A.D. the story began to take its modern shape, as in *The King and the Seven Sages* by Johannes de Alta Sylva. Here a Knight makes a bond with his former slave who then seeks his life in revenge for previous injuries, and is prevented from taking the flesh by a horseman who advises the King in court and proves to be the Knight's lady in disguise.[2]

The tale of a wicked merchant who made a bond with a trusting debtor by which the latter must lose part of his body if he could not repay on the proper day has many variations in the later Middle Ages. In some MSS of the *Gesta Romanorum* (13th century) the bond is associated with a romantic love-story.[3] The hero falls in love with the Emperor's daughter, who lets him go to bed with her, but he falls asleep and thereby forfeits 'a hundred mark of florins'. This occurs again. Before the third attempt he goes to a far country and a city where there are many merchants and wise men ('among the which was Master Virgile the philosopher'). The hero offers his lands to a great merchant in bond for the money. The merchant however refuses them, demanding:

> that thou make to me a charter of thine own blood, on con-
> dition that if thou keep not thy day of judgement, it shal be
> lawful for me to draw away all the flesh of thy body from
> the bone, with a sharp sword.

Becoming afraid, the Knight asks advice of Virgil, who tells him that the covenant must stand, 'for as a man bindeth him-self with his wil, right so he shal be served, by law of the Emperor'. In order to stay awake when next with the lady, he should feel between the sheet and coverlet of the bed for a hidden letter which has previously cast a spell on him. The young man finds the letter, possesses the Princess, and forgets his bond till fourteen days after it is due. Then he hastens home, followed by the Princess dressed as a knight. When the

---

[1] Cf. Joseph Kohler, *Shakespeare vor dem Forum der Jurisprudenz* (Wurzburg, 1883).

[2] Cf. H. Sinsheimer, *Shylock*, 1947, pp. 71–2.

[3] Cf. *Early English Versions of the Gesta Romanorum*, ed. S. J. H. Herrtage. *EETS*. Extra S. 53, 1879. (Story XL.)

hero gives himself up, the merchant refuses to free him, 'for without doubt I will have the law, since he bound himself so freely; and therefore shall have no other grace than the law wills; for he came to me and I not to him; I desired him not thereto against his will.' The disguised lady pleads in vain; then she makes her counterstroke: 'Ye know well that the knight bound him never by letter but that the merchant should have power to cut his flesh from the bones, but there was no covenant made of shedding bloode; thereof was nothing spoken. And therefore let him set hand on him anon, and if he shed any blood with his shaving of the flesh, for sooth then shall the King have good law upon him.' And when the merchant heard this, he said, 'Give me my money, and I forgive my action.' 'Forsooth,' quoth she, 'thou shalt not have one penny.' The merchant goes away, the Knight returns home, and his wife reveals herself by dressing up again in her male costume.

Here we see several features of Shakespeare's plot: the bond, a triple love test, the disguising of the hero's bride, her casuistry about flesh and blood,[1] and her subsequent revelation of her identity.

This story was not included in Wynkyn de Worde's version of forty-three tales from *Gesta Romanorum* printed 1510–15; nor is it in Richard Robinson's collection (1577, revised 1595) which contains a Caskets story. The merchant in *Gesta Romanorum* is not a Jew, but other stories in the collection show anti-Jewish feeling; e.g. Story LXI relates a miracle which happened when a Canon had sinned with a Jew's daughter on a Good Friday; the father and other Jews came to accuse him publicly in Church, but the Canon begged Christ to forgive him, and the Jews suddenly lost their power of speech and could not accuse him.

The first mention of the story in English seems to occur in the late thirteenth-century poem *Cursor Mundi* in which a Christian goldsmith at the court of Helena, mother of Constantine the Great, makes a bond with a Jew to repay either the money borrowed or the weight of it in his own flesh. In court

---

[1] The separation of flesh and blood is less of a quibble than critics have thought, when the usurer becomes a Jew. For the Mosaic Law made such a distinction in daily life, forbidding as unclean the eating of blood and of flesh not drained of blood. (*Leviticus* 17.10–6; cf. *Exodus* 21.28; 22.31).

the Jew says that he will do the worst he legally can to his enemy. 'I shall first put out his eyes, then have his hands that he works with, his tongue and nose and so on, till I have my covenant.' When told that he must shed no blood he curses his judges, and is condemned by Queen Helena to lose his goods and his tongue. Whereupon he cries 'I would rather tell you where your Lord's Rood-Tree lies than be thus condemned.' He earns forgiveness by showing the Queen where the true Cross is hidden.

In *Il Pecorone* (The Dunce) of Ser Giovanni Fiorentino, a late fourteenth-century collection of prose stories not published in Italian until 1558 and not Englished in Shakespeare's time, the villain is a Jew, the setting is Venice and the bond is made not by the hero but by a friend on his behalf. The hero journeys to find the lady, not, as in *Gesta Romanorum*, to find a money-lender, and the identification of the lawyer-wife is made by means of her ring. This delightful narrative (here translated [Text I]) with its gay tone and many parallels, was probably known to Shakespeare, and may have been his main source, even if he used *The Jew*.

There were many allusions to the Bond-story in Elizabethan England. A ballad 'Shewing the crueltie of *Gernutus* a Jew' is probably pre-Shakespearian. Here the Venetian Jew is a miser who makes his wife practise moneylending too. A 'merchant of great fame' borrows a hundred crowns and the Jew gives him a year to pay, making 'a merry jeast' of a bond (the pound of flesh), which he demands when 'The merchant's ships were all at sea,/The money came not in'. The merchant's friends offer ten thousand crowns, in vain. 'The bloudie Jew now ready is/ With whetted blade in hand, / To spoyle the bloud of innocent, / By forfeit of his bond', when the judge bids him beware of shedding blood or of cutting 'either more or lesse' than his due. The Jew raves and says he will take the ten thousand crowns instead, but this is not allowed by the judge, nor any diminution of the sum:

> Either take your pound of flesh, quoth he,
> Or cancell me your bond.
> O cruel judge, then quoth the Jew,
> That doth against me stand!

29—S.N.D. I.

Here there is no love-story, no woman in disguise, no Giannetto-Ansaldo relationship. Shakespeare may have known the ballad, which shows the Jew with 'whetted knife', but he cannot have taken much from it.

The Jew's name, Gernutus, however, may be significant and inclines me to think that the ballad may be derived from the plot of the old play *The Jew*. Evidence is scanty, but it is possible that in *The Three Ladies of London* by R. W. (Robert Wilson?), played by Leicester's men, and printed in 1584, we have, not (as Fleay argued) *The Jew* itself, but a rival play, indeed an answer to *The Jew*. *The Three Ladies of London*, though highly edifying, is unlikely to be the play praised by Gosson, for although it contains a Jew who lends money he has anything but a 'bloody mind'; he is indeed an entirely virtuous moneylender, who behaves better than his Christian debtor. His name is Gerontus.

The play suggests what *The Jew* may well have been, a piece combining allegorical with realistic characters, the latter appearing in episodes illustrating the moral lessons of the drama. *The Three Ladies* is a play about money, about the conquest of the world, and England in particular, by Lady Lucar (Lucre) and her minions, Fraud, Usury, Dissimulation, etc. Love and Conscience, the two other Ladies, are ruined by Lucar, who spots the face of Conscience with 'abhominations' and reduces Love to lust. Simplicitie is tricked into association with thieves and is arrested by the Constable Serviceable Diligence. Four scenes tell the story of an Italian merchant Mercadorus who is ruining England by taking its valuable exports to Turkey in exchange for gewgaws and trinkets which demoralize the people. The Jew Gerontus dwells in Turkey, and has lent Mercadorus money, being cheated when the merchant left the country. Meeting him again Gerontus asks for repayment and goes to law only when Mercadorus refuses. A remarkable twist in the story now occurs, for Mercadorus tries to take advantage of a Turkish law which frees any convert to the Muslim faith from all previous obligations. The Jew, horrified that a Christian should apostatize, reduces his demands in order to persuade Mercadorus not to forswear his faith, finally giving up his legal rights altogether. At this the merchant refuses to turn Muslim, and goes off rejoicing to have tricked the Jew, who warns him to pay his debts in future.

In this interesting variant on the theme the audience, like the Judge, sympathizes with the virtuous Jew against the Merchant, who is made ridiculous by speaking in a broken English not far from that of the music-hall Italian today. The play contains one casket, for Lucar sends Usury to bring 'the box of all abhominations that standes in the window. / It is little and round, painted with divers colours and is prettie to the show.' Into this she dips to spot the face of Conscience.

Shakespeare did not use this play for *The Merchant of Venice*, but with its treatment of Usury and Lucar, its references to current economic problems, it forms part of the background against which he wrote, and should be especially enlightening to critics who consider *The Merchant* too occupied with money-matters. I give the scenes in which Mercadorus takes part [II].

Against the crudity of the Gernutus ballad and the exemplary gravity of *The Three Ladies* may be set the rhetorical refinement of the French Alexandre Sylvain's *Epitomes de cent histoires, partie extraictes des Actes des Romains et autres, de l'invention de l'Autheur, avecq' les demandes, accusations, et deffences sur la matiere d'icelles'* (Paris, 1581). This was translated (by Anthony Munday?) in 1596 as '*The Orator: Handling a hundred severall Discourses in forme of Declamations* . . . by L. P.' [Lazarus Piot]. Each 'histoire' consists of an anecdote followed by a speech and a reply thereto dealing with some strange point of ethics, law or custom. No. 95, 'Of a Jew, who would for his debt have a pound of the flesh of a Christian' is a good example of the whole [III].

Shakespeare may have seen this translation or the original. His Court Scene has similar arguments; he too stresses the importance of keeping covenants (III.3.27–31) as Shylock insists (IV.1.38, 9) but whereas Shylock declares

> You'll ask me why I rather choose to have
> A weight of carrion flesh, than to receive
> Three thousand ducats; I'll not answer that!
> But say it is my humour! . . .

Sylvain's Jew lists many reasons which he might allege before concluding, like the merchant in *Gesta Romanorum*, that he merely insists on his legal right. A more important divergence is that in *The Orator* the Jew asserts that the debtor's duty is 'to *give* me a pound of flesh'—the creditor need not cut it off. This avoids the difficulty about shedding blood, which is not introduced by his opponent, who speaks of having 'to satisfie the crueltie of this mischeevous man with the price of my flesh and blood'. Like the author of *The Three Ladies* Sylvain sets his scene in Turkey.

A note in an MS in Trinity College, Cambridge (*The Doctrine of the Heart*, MS Trin. Coll. B. 14.15/301) which belonged to Stephen Batman, author of a treatise against Usury (1575) and *Batman upon Bartholome His Book De proprietatibus Rerum* (1582), shows that he regarded the flesh-blood antithesis as a legal problem of some interest: 'The note of a Jew wch for the interest of his money required a *li* of the mans flesh to whome he lent the money, the bonde forfeit and yet the Jew went wthoute his purpose / the parti notwithstanding condemn'd by Lawe / the question whether he coulde cut the flesh wthoute spilling of blood . . .'[1]

Not to be ignored is a variant of the story in Anthony Munday's *Zelauto or The Fountaine of Fame* (1580)[2] in which the moneylender is no Jew but 'an extorting Usurer' of Verona named Truculento. He falls in love with Cornelia, sister to Rodolfo, who helps his friend Strabino to win her by buying a jewel for her father with money borrowed from Truculento. The latter's bond includes both Rodolfo and Strabino, for, after Rodolfo has told him that he is the right man for his sister to marry, and that Strabino is willing, should his promise to repay fail, 'to forfayte his patrimony, and besydes the best lym of his body', Truculento declares that he could take no pleasure 'to maime or mangle this Gentleman for mine owne: truly I had rather if I could well spare so much, to give it him outright, so should I sustayne no reproch my selfe; nor he be endamaged in the distresse of the law'. But he demands that Rodolfo be bound with Strabino, the forfeit to be that 'eache of your Lands shall stand to the endamagement, besides the losse of bothe your right eyes.' Strabino fears the bond from the

---

[1] I quote this from the valuable M.A. thesis now in the Goldsmith's Library, Univ. of London, by Miss E. J. Brockhurst on *The Life and Works of Stephen Batman*. P. 434. She believes the note to be in Batman's own hand.

[2] Extracts are given by J. R. Brown, *MV Arden* 1955, Appendix III.

first. 'Is not our landes sufficient to glut up his greedinesse? But that each of our eyes must stand to the hazard? Oh miserable miser, oh egregious cormorant. . . . Well cease (quoth *Rodolfo*) no more woordes, *Lupus est in fabula*, little sayd is soone amended'.

Here as in Shakespeare the usurer pretends not to regard the bond seriously, but there is no jest, no *merry* bond, and the misgivings of the victims are deeper. Truculento has a daughter whom he allows to marry Rodolfo when he expects to marry the young man's sister himself. Discovering that Cornelia has married Strabino he summons the two bridegrooms to appear before the Judge where he makes a long speech demanding his rights very much in the manner of Sylvain. The two brides disguise themselves; 'Cornelia apparalleth herselfe all in blacke like a Scholler and Brisana attyreth her selfe in the same sorte', and go to court, where they hear the arguments and bide their time. As the extract given below shows [IV] this version has in common with Shakespeare's the Judge's appeal for mercy, which Truculento rejects. There are some close parallels in *The Merchant of Venice*, IV.1, e.g. the suggestion that in God's sight we are all sinners and

> That in the course of justice, none of us
> Should see salvation. . . . (197, 8)

the allusion to 'stubborn Turks' (32); and the usurer's insistence on the letter of the law throughout the scene. (This last is not peculiar to Munday). The novel gives other arguments not in Shakespeare, but there is enough likeness between the to-fro-movement of the debate in *Zelauto* and in our play to make it seem possible that Shakespeare remembered *Zelauto* in drafting his Court Scene. Incidentally, the father of Strabino is Vincentio who has sent his son to Verona 'there to be trayned up in such vertuous educations as was meete for one of his tender time.' This recalls *The Taming of the Shrew*, where Vincentio is father to Lucentio who has been sent to Padua to study 'Virtue and that part of philosophy . . . that treats of happiness', etc. (*T.Sh.* I.1.19). Had Shakespeare read Munday's tale some years before writing *The Merchant* and already taken a hint from it? Nothing was lost in Shakespeare's experience. Traces of his reading remained below the surface of his mind, waiting for an opportunity to float up as images or names or incidents or ideas maybe years later. It has been suggested that *Zelauto*, Book III, may be based on the old play; but if so, why is not Truculento a Jew? Munday's story goes back to the other version of the story which persisted side by side with the anti-Semitic one.

THE JESSICA-SHYLOCK-LORENZO THEME

The love-story between Lorenzo and Shylock's daughter has something in common with Munday's Rodolfo and Brisana, between whom 'there was hot loove on bothe sides, and each of them so farre in that it was unpossible for eyther to gette out'. Shylock's rage is increased, like Truculento's, by the loss of his daughter. But Shakespeare probably owed much more to Marlowe's *Jew of Malta*, and above all to a story in *Il Novellino* of Masuccio. *The Jew of Malta* would seem to be one of Shakespeare's major sources in developing the character of the Jew beyond the thin outline given in Ser Giovanni. Marlowe obviously knew something about Jewish life and habits, and his Barabas, in the first two Acts, is a real person as well as a figure of horror. He is presented, if not sympathetically, at least objectively as having a case against the Christians whose profession is 'policy', 'And not simplicity as they suggest'. The presentation of Shylock by Shakespeare as a villain with a point of view, not just a monster, owes much to Marlowe's Jew, and Shakespeare touches (though differently) on several topics introduced by his predecessor. Thus both Jews discuss the multiplying of money; Shylock in prosperity (*MV* I.3.66–92), Barabas in total deprivation:

> Christians, what or how can I multiply?
> Of naught's nothing made. . . .

In the same scene Barabas declares:

> What, bring you Scripture to confirm your wrongs?
> Preach me not out of my possessions,
> Some Jews are wicked, as all Christians are . . .

In Shakespeare the idea is turned against the Jew when Antonio says, 'The Devil can cite Scripture for his purpose'. Shylock's cry on losing all his money, 'Nay, take my life and all . . .'

(*MV* IV.1.373) was anticipated by Barabas when the officers said that they would not kill him:

> Why I esteem the injury far less,
> To take the lives of miserable men
> Than be the causers of their misery . . .
> You have my wealth, the labour of my life,
> The comfort of mine age, my children's hope . . . (I.379ff.)

Similarly Barabas's 'Sufferance breeds ease' in hope of an occasion for vengeance, becomes Shylock's sinister 'patient shrug / For suff'rance is the badge of all our tribe' (I.3.108–9). This occurs in Shylock's complaint to Antonio of how he has been ill-treated, which clearly goes back to Barabas's more virulent soliloquy. Shylock's later outburst, 'Hath not a Jew eyes? . . .' (III.1.53–66) was also suggested by Marlowe's daring division of blame between both races, and like him Shakespeare was not so much seeking sympathy for his Jew as explaining the depth of his hatred. Shylock is at once less and more than Barabas. The latter is the total Machiavellian, skilled in every murderous art, who kills 'sick people groaning under walls', poisons wells (and his daughter), and engineers casualties for both sides in war. Usury is only one of his methods when

> with extorting, cozening, forfeiting,
> And tricks belonging unto brokery,
> I fill'd the gaols with bankrupts in a year
> And with young orphans planted hospitals (II.956ff.)

Shylock is less violent, less many-sided, and he does not degenerate into a bloody automaton; for Shakespeare has selected from the incoherence of *The Jew of Malta* just enough facets to make his villain credible throughout and suited to a romantic tragi-comedy. The passages cited below [V] should suffice to suggest his indebtedness and originality.

Marlowe's Jew uses his daughter Abigail to obtain his wealth from its hiding-place in the convent and also to lure Mathias and Lodowick into quarrelling over her. Shakespeare's Jessica neither saves her father's gold nor aids his revenge; she steals his property and elopes with Lorenzo to happiness at Belmont. Abigail falls in love with Mathias, and when he is killed by Lodowick in a duel she enters the Convent again and is poisoned by her father along with the nuns. Shakespeare's comic taste in handling the situation is better than Marlowe's tragic taste. It is noteworthy that Shakespeare has taken over from Marlowe the Jew's confusion between love for money and of his daughter; compare Barabas's delight when Abigail has thrown his treasure-bags down to him from the convent-window:

> O my girl,
> My gold, my fortune, my felicity . . .
> O girl! O gold! O beauty! O my bliss!

and Shylock's reported outcry after his daughter has escaped with his treasure from her window: 'My daughter! O my jewels! O my daughter!' (*MV* II.8.15). Both fathers are equally affected by the apostasy, and Marlowe's savage epitaph:

> I grieve because she liv'd so long,
> An Hebrew born, and would become a Christian (IV.1526)

produced Shylock's 'Fled with a Christian!'; 'I would my daughter were dead at my foot, and the jewels in her ear', and the definite reference to Marlowe's play:

> Would any of the stock of Barabas
> Had been her husband, rather than a Christian!
>
> (IV.1.295-6)

For much of the atmosphere of his Jewish theme Shakespeare was thus indebted to Marlowe; but the elopement of Jessica came directly or indirectly from the fifteenth century Italian *Novellino* of Masuccio, which, so far as we know, had not been translated into English. Masuccio's fourteenth tale [VI] is about a young cavalier of Messina who falls in love with the daughter of a miser in Naples. After ingratiating himself with the old man the young one borrows money from him and gives as security a slave who, once in the house, helps the daughter to plunder her father and elope with her lover. The father deplores the loss of daughter and jewels but finally has to accept the situation. Obvious points of resemblance between this story and Ser Giovanni's explain why they came together in the dramatist's mind to enrich the Bond-story and increase the Jew's desire for vengeance. It is a story of avarice overreached, of a creditor tricked by the nature of the bond made. It has a rebellious daughter, like Marlowe's play, but one who can be used in the comic castigation of the miser. With its cunning slave the plot is almost Plautine—though the slave is a woman. Whether Shakespeare found it in a source-play or himself interwove it with the rest we cannot be sure; but he certainly gave it his own romantic tone. Broached suddenly *in medias res* so that we know Jessica is about to elope before we see how tyrannical (like Masuccio's miser) Shylock is towards her, the little subplot serves to keep the erotic action moving and, being interpolated between the arrival of Morocco and his Casket-Scene, it keeps up suspense and gives the contrast of a different kind of lovemaking. Moreover, Jessica elopes in boy's dress. The substitution of Launcelot Gobbo for Masuccio's female slave is also valuable, since he is not only humorous but illuminating about the unhappiness of Shylock's household, thus removing all suspicion of filial ingratitude from Jessica. We do not lose sight of the couple afterwards; for they are present when Bassanio receives Antonio's appeal for help (III.2); Lorenzo is given charge of Belmont while Portia goes to Venice (III.4.24); Jessica and he bandy words playfully with Gobbo (III.5); and in the Trial Scene they are mentioned when Antonio generously provides for them out of Shylock's forfeited wealth (IV.1.383). Lastly they prepare with poetic conversation the atmosphere of love, music and sweet humour suited to the revealing of Portia's disguise and the ending of the play. Rarely did Shakespeare use so effectively figures with so little part in the main story.

THE CASKETS

In Ser Giovanni Giannetto starts off on three voyages to the Eastern Mediterranean from which he is deflected by his desire for the Lady of Belmont. On each occasion he is tested by being given the chance of sleeping with her, but he is twice deceived and drugged, losing all his wealth. On the third occasion he is warned by a friendly maid and wins the lady and all her lands. Whoever first combined this tale with the Pound of Flesh story was doubtless encouraged to do so because it too is a Bond story, since the hero pledges himself to lose his vessel if he cannot win the lady, and she pledges herself too. This is a covenant of fairytale kind, with no moral weight: Giannetto undergoes the Custom of the Country, and having won the lady marries her with universal applause. The bedroom scenes, apart from their repetitiveness, made the climactic situation unsuitable for the stage. Hence either Shakespeare or the author of *The Jew* sought another means of testing the hero, and found it in a story almost as widely known as the Flesh-Bond story, and in many variants. In the story of Barlaam the hermit written in Greek by the Greek monk Joannes Damascenus in the ninth century and translated into Latin before the thirteenth, a king is reproved by his courtiers for stopping to talk to two apparently poor and squalidly dressed men. He thereupon 'commanded four chests to be made, two of which were covered with gold and secured with golden locks, but filled with rotten bones of human carcases. The other two were overlaid with pitch and bound with rough cords; but filled with precious stones and exquisite gems, and ointments of the richest odour.' (Warton's *History of English Poetry*, III.xlix, ed. 1781.) When asked to choose, the nobles chose the best-looking chests. 'Then said the king, I presumed that would be your determination; for ye look with the eyes of sense. But to discern baseness or value, which are hid within we must look with the eyes of the mind.' This story was used by Vincent of Beauvais in the *Speculum Historiale* (Lib. XV, Cap. x) (1290) in the *Golden Legend*, by Boccaccio in his *Decameron*, Day X, Story 1, in *Gesta Romanorum*, and in the *Confessio Amantis* of John Gower.

In Boccaccio the chooser is a Florentine knight named Ruggieri de' Figiovanni, who after serving Alfonso of Spain becomes dissatisfied at the way in which the King gives away castles, cities and baronies to the undeserving, and nothing to deserving people like himself. He asks leave to return home and sets off accompanied by a servant who is to discover his true opinion of Alfonso and then order him to return to the Spanish court. The only critical remark made by Ruggieri came after a mule which the King had given him staled at an inconvenient time and place; whereupon he said that the King was like his mule. Ordered back to court and asked to explain, the knight said that he meant that the King gave when and where he should not and failed to give when he should. Alfonso replied that this was just Ruggieri's ill-fortune, as he would prove:

'The King then led him into one of his great halls, where, as he had previously arranged, there stood two large locked coffers; and in the presence of many of his lords he said: "Sir Ruggieri, in one of these coffers is my crown, the royal sceptre and orb, and many of my finest belts, clasps, rings, and other precious objects. The other is full of soil. Choose one of the two, and the one you choose shall be yours. Thus you will see which has been ungrateful to you, myself, or malicious Fortune."

'Sir Ruggieri, obeying the royal will, chose one of the coffers, which the King ordered to be opened; and he found it was the one filled with soil. Whereupon the King said, laughing: "You can well see, Sir Ruggieri, that what I told you about Fortune was true. But indeed your worth is such that I must oppose her on your behalf. I know that you do not want to become a Spaniard, so I do not propose to give you either a castle or a town, but that chest which Fortune took from you shall be yours in spite of her. Carry it home to your own country therefore, and you can boast of your honour among your friends with this proof of my bounty."

'Sir Ruggieri took it, and having given due thanks to the King for such a gift, departed with it joyfully into Tuscany.'

In Boccaccio the tale is told as an example of magnanimity. In Gower's *Confessio Amantis*, Book V, two versions are given to show the evils of Covetousness (particularly vicious among courtiers) and the need for every man to 'take his chance / Or of richesse or of poverte' [VII]. The idea behind both stories is that Good or Ill Fortune rules over much in material life, and the only wise procedure is to trust in God, like the second beggar. These stories differ from *Barlaam and Josophat* in that the objects to be chosen are alike in appearance. More akin to *Barlaam* and nearer also to Shakespeare is the tale in *Gesta Romanorum* [VIII] one form of which was Englished as No. XXXII of Wynkyn de Worde's collection, and 'bettered' by Richard Robinson. Here the test is made on a woman to find whether she is worthy to become the wife of the Emperor's son. She has to choose between three vessels, one gold, one silver, and one lead. Each vessel has a superscription; and it has been noted that Robinson's word 'insculpt' used of the posy on the leaden vessel occurs in Shakespeare when Morocco is making his choice (II.7.57)—the poet's only use of the word. The heroine's choice is dictated by religious faith and self-knowledge. Like Boccaccio's knight she has no rivals.

In taking over this tale and substituting it for the threefold test of Giannetto Shakespeare may be following *The Jew*, but we can be sure that he used it very differently. If Gosson approved of the old play, its morality must have been extremely obvious and perhaps allegorical. Maybe *The Jew* introduced two or three male suitors into the *Gesta Romanorum* story. These showed the greediness of 'worldly chusers'.

The posies on the caskets (*MV* II.7.14–37) differ somewhat from those in *Gesta Romanorum*. The golden offers 'what many men desire', the silver 'as much as he deserves', and the lead offers no such obvious lure as 'what God hath disposed', but starkly declares 'Who chooseth me must give and hazard all he hath.' This is what Giannetto did each time he went to Belmont, and by choosing lead Bassanio is doing for love of Portia what Antonio in his different way has done for him. And note the severe conditions accepted by the suitors: they must swear if they fail, 'Never to speak to lady afterward / In way of marriage' [II.1.41, 42]. Thus the idea of a Bond recurs in this part of the story.

Portia speaks of 'the lott'ry of my destiny' [II.1.15], and it may appear that chance plays a large part in the plot, since Antonio's argosies are delayed unexpectedly, and the Casket-choice may seem a matter of luck (or faith), as it certainly was in medieval stories where the containers were alike. But chance does not reign in *The Merchant of Venice*. Antonio is saved, despite bad fortune, by the gratitude and skill of his friends. And the differentiation of the Caskets, as in *Gesta Romanorum*, at once brings in character and ethical choice. Shakespeare's Morocco is consciously princely: 'A golden mind stoops not to shows of dross', he says [II.7.20] and shows a wish to have 'what many men desire', the glory of possessing the unique; he is a 'collector' like Soames Forsyte. Arragon more subtly rejects the gold because 'I will not jump with common spirits', and takes the silver because 'I will assume desert'; his is the Coriolanian pride of the aristocrat. Both are egoists, but Shakespeare has diminished the greediness of these worldly choosers so that their failure, besides being a proof of presumption to be contrasted with Bassanio's humility and search for the truth behind appearances, is a tribute to Portia's excellence.

Bassanio does not choose by chance. Portia longs to tell him, but like her dead father she believes that the true lover will choose aright. Giannetto in Ser Giovanni was helped on the third occasion by his Lady's maid; here however the song 'Tell me where is Fancy bred' cannot be intended as a clue laid by Portia, though it prepares the audience for what follows, and it may be said to assist Bassanio by suggesting a distinction between outward appearances, the shortlived Fancy bred by them, and Truth. The sweet solemnity of this scene, with Portia's trepidation and her lovely self-surrender, has no precursor. But the making of Bassanio Lord of the house, and Nerissa's cry 'Good joy', recall the festivities which followed Giannetto's success.

The giving of the ring to Giannetto by his lady is not described in Ser Giovanni, though we learn later that he has sworn to wear it for love of her. Shakespeare introduces the theme as the climax of the Casket scene [III.2.172]. The ring is the token of the marriage bond between Bassanio and Portia, the very symbol of their union, and this lends force to Bassanio's reluctance to surrender it to the lawyer until requested to do so by Antonio.

The betrothal of Nerissa and Gratiano, a pleasant act of symmetry, also increases the comedy of the ring by a typical piece of Shakespearian duplication so that the later doubts cast on the husbands' fidelity may begin with Nerissa and Gratiano and so increase Bassanio's confusion when he is cited by Portia as sure to have kept her gift. By the clever sustaining of this situation the women dominate the final scene not only as practical jokers but also as generous lovers and friends. 'Sweet lady, you have given me life and living,' says Antonio, a sentiment echoed by Lorenzo.

This insistence on generosity, on giving, is significant. Shakespeare has taken over themes long associated with greed and avarice—the flesh-bond, the Jewish usurer, the choice of caskets, and has made of them not just a morality play, a piece of didacticism, a savage play of poetic justice—the biter bit—but an ethical comedy in which the base, vengeful greed of Shylock and the loftier egoism of the princely suitors are overcome by the simple wisdom of good principles and adventurous unspoiled youth. Some critics have thought the play materialistic and shallow; but wealth is here put into its rightful place in worldly life, as a necessary good, a commodity to be used. We are delighted both to learn that Jessica has spent in one night in Genoa four-score ducats of her father's ill-gotten gains, and to leave all the Christians comfortably off at the end of the play. But the lesson (if there be one) of the piece is that money is a trifle as compared with love and friendship, though it may be serviceable to both; and that generosity whether it take the form of openhandedness, mercy, or surrender to love's demands, is a fitting counterpoise to hate and greed and narrow legality.

I. Translation of Probable Source

IL PECORONE
by Ser Giovanni Fiorentino (1558)
Day 4　Story 1
translated by the editor

Day 4　Story 1

There lived at Florence, in the house of the Scali, a merchant named Bindo, who had been several times to Tana, and Alexandria, and had made all the other long voyages usually taken with merchandise. This Bindo was very rich, and had three grown-up sons. When he neared his end, he called for the two eldest, and in their presence made his will, leaving these two heirs of everything he had in the world; to the youngest he left nothing. After the will had been made this youngest son, whose name was Giannetto, hearing what had been done, went to his father's bedside, and said to him, 'Father, I am amazed at what you have done—not remembering me in your will.' The father replied, 'My dear Giannetto, there is no creature on earth whom I love better than you; so I want you to leave this city after my death, and go to Venice to your godfather, whose name is Ansaldo. He has no child, and has often written asking me to send you to him; and I can tell you, he is the richest Christian merchant there. Therefore it is my desire that as soon as I am dead, you go to him bearing this letter; if you behave well you will certainly become rich. The son answered, 'Father, I am ready to do whatever you command.' Whereupon his father gave him his blessing, and in a few days died, and the sons made great grief and paid his body every fitting honour.

Some days afterwards, his two brothers sent for Giannetto and told him, 'Brother, it is true that our father made a will, and left us his heirs, without mentioning you; nevertheless, you are our brother, and you shall not want for anything while we have it. Giannetto replied, 'My dear brothers, I thank you heartily for your offer, but I mean to seek my fortune in some other place. This I am determined to do, while you enjoy the inheritance legally left you.'

463

Seeing his resolution his brothers gave him a horse, and money for
his expenses. Giannetto took leave of them, and went to Venice, to
Ansaldo's counting house, and presented the letter given him by
his father before his death. Reading the letter, Ansaldo knew that
this youth was the son of his dearest friend Bindo, and when he had
finished it he embraced him, saying 'Welcome, my dear godson,
whom I have so long wished to see.' Straightway he asked about
Bindo, and when Giannetto replied that he was dead, he embraced
the young man again with tears and kissed him. 'I am very grieved,'
said Ansaldo, 'at Bindo's death, for he helped me to gain the
greatest part of what I own; but the joy I feel in seeing you mitigates
my sorrow.' He conducted him to his home, and instructed his
stewards and attendants, his grooms, servants, and everyone in the
house, that Giannetto should be obeyed and served better than
himself. He then gave him the keys of his cash-box, and told him,
'My boy, spend whatever you find here on clothes and shoes as
you like best; keep open house for the people in the city and get
yourself known. I leave this idea with you; and remember, that the
more you gain the goodwill of others, the more I shall like it.'

So Giannetto began to frequent the noblemen of Venice and to
pay visits, dine out and give dinners. He kept servants, and bought
good horses, and took part in tiltings and tournaments, in which he
excelled, being adroit, expert, magnanimous, and courteous in
everything. He knew well how to pay honourable and courtly
respects where they were due, and particularly to Ansaldo he was
more obedient and courteous than if the former had been a hundred
times his father. He behaved so discreetly towards all sorts of people
that almost everybody in Venice thought well of him, seeing him
to be so prudent, agreeable and unusually courteous. All the ladies
and gentlemen appeared in love with him, while Messer Ansaldo
could think of nobody but him, so pleased he was with his good
manners and behaviour. There was scarcely a festivity in Venice to
which Giannetto was not invited, so much was he esteemed by all.

Now it happened that two of his intimate friends planned to go
with two ships, laden with merchandise, to Alexandria, as they did
every year. They spoke to Giannetto about it, saying, 'You ought
to take a pleasure-trip by sea with us, to see the world, and especially Damascus and the country thereabouts.' 'Indeed,' replied
Giannetto, 'I would come willingly if my father Messer Ansaldo
would give me leave.' 'We shall see that he gives you leave,' they
said, 'and that he is quite happy about it.' And they went at once to
Messer Ansaldo and said, 'We want to beg you please to give permission for Giannetto to come with us this spring to Alexandria,

and to furnish a ship of some kind for him so that he may see a little of the world.' Said Ansaldo, 'I am willing if he wishes it.' They replied, 'Sir, he does.' So Ansaldo at once provided a fine ship, and had it laden with much merchandise, and equipped with banners and the necessary arms. As soon as it was prepared he gave orders to the captain and others on board to do everything Giannetto commanded and to care for him in every way; 'For I do not send him,' said he, 'for the sake of the profit I want him to make, but for his own pleasure in seeing the world.' And when Giannetto was on board, all Venice was gathered to see him, since it was a long time since so fine and well-equipped a ship had sailed from that port; and everyone was sorry to see him go away. So he took leave of Ansaldo and all his acquaintance; and putting out to sea, they hoisted their sails and stood for Alexandria in the name of God and good fortune.

The three friends in their three ships had sailed in company for several days when one morning, before it was fully light, Giannetto saw a sea-gulf with a fine port, and asked the captain what the port was called. He answered, 'Sir, that place belongs to a widow lady, who has ruined many gentlemen.' 'How is that?' asked Giannetto. The other replied, 'Sir, she is a beautiful and capricious woman, and makes this law, that anyone who arrives must sleep with her, and if he possesses her he can take her for his wife and become lord of the port and all that country. But if he fails, he loses everything that he has.' After a little reflection Giannetto said, 'Find any way you can to get me into that port.' Said the captain, 'Sir, consider well what you are saying, for many gentlemen have gone in who have been stripped of everything.' 'Do not trouble yourself on that score,' said Giannetto, 'do what I tell you.' It was done; in an instant they turned the ship, and slid into the port so that those on the other ships perceived nothing.

In the morning the news spread that this fine ship had put into port, and all the people ran to see it. The lady, being soon informed of it, sent for Giannetto, who went to her without delay and saluted her with great respect. Taking him by the hand, she asked him who he was, where he came from, and if he knew the custom of the country. Giannetto replied that he did, and that he had come for no other reason. 'You are a hundred times welcome,' said the lady, and all that day paid him great honour, and invited the barons, counts, and knights in great number who were her subjects, to keep him company. These nobles were highly delighted with Giannetto's bearing, his social graces, pleasantness and agreeable discourse. Everyone fell in love with him; the whole day was spent in

dancing, singing and feasting at court in his honour; and all would
have been pleased to have him for their lord.

When night came, the lady took him by the hand, and leading
him into her chamber, said, 'It seems to be time to go to bed.'
'Madam,' said Giannetto, 'I am at your service.' And immediately
two damsels entered, one with wine, the other with sweetmeats.
The lady said, 'I am sure that you are thirsty; please drink.' Giannetto took some sweetmeats and drank some of the wine, which was
drugged to make him sleep. Unaware of this he drank half the cup,
for he found it excellent. He undressed at once and got into bed;
and as soon as his head touched the pillow, he fell asleep. The lady
lay down by his side, but he never woke till past nine in the morning.
She however rose with the sun and gave orders to unload the vessel,
which she found full of fine and costly merchandise.

When it was past nine o'clock, the chambermaids went to Giannetto's bed and made him get up, and told him to depart, for he
had lost the ship and all that was in it. He was much ashamed,
perceiving that he had behaved with great folly. The lady gave
him a horse and money for his needs, and he left the place very
sorrowful and melancholy, and returned towards Venice. When he
arrived he dared not return home for shame, but at night went to
the house of a friend, who marvelled much, and exclaimed, 'Alas,
Giannetto, what has happened?' He answered, 'My ship struck a
rock in the night, and was broken in pieces, and everything smashed
and scattered. I held fast to a piece of wood, which cast me ashore,
so I have come back by land, and here I am.'

Giannetto stayed some days in the house of his friend, who,
going one day to visit Ansaldo, found him very disconsolate. 'I so
greatly fear,' said Ansaldo, 'that this son of mine is dead, or harmed
by the sea, that I cannot rest, and am not well: I love him so much.'
The young man said, 'I can give you news of him; he has been shipwrecked, and has lost everything, but he himself is safe.' 'God be
praised!' cried Ansaldo. 'If he is alive, I am satisfied. I care nothing
for the wealth that is lost. Where is he?' The young man replied,
'At my house.' Ansaldo instantly got up and went off to find him,
and when he saw him, ran to embrace him, saying, 'My dear son,
you need not be ashamed for what has happened, for it is a common
accident for ships to be lost at sea. Trouble yourself no further;
since you have received no hurt, I am happy.' And he took him
home, comforting him all the way.

The news quickly spread all over Venice, and everyone regretted
the loss Giannetto had sustained. Soon afterwards his companions
arrived from Alexandria, very rich, and on landing asked about

Giannetto. Having heard the story, they ran to see and embrace him, saying, 'How did you leave us, and where did you go, so that we lost all trace of you? We turned back for a whole day, but could not see or learn where you had gone. We were so grieved at it that we could not be merry for the rest of the voyage, believing that you were dead.' Giannetto told them 'A contrary wind got up in an arm of the sea and drove my ship plumb against a rock near shore, so that I escaped with difficulty, while everything else was overwhelmed.' This excuse Giannetto made in order not to reveal his fault.

Together they made a great feast, and returned thanks to God for his safety, telling him, 'Next spring, with God's grace, we shall make up all that you have lost this time; meanwhile let us have a good time, and not be melancholy.' And they amused and diverted themselves as they had done before. But Giannetto had no thought other than how he might return to the lady. 'Surely I must have her for my wife or die!' he said to himself, and could hardly be cheerful; wherefore Messer Ansaldo said to him frequently, 'Do not be cast down, fearing that we have not enough left to live on very comfortably.' Giannetto replied, 'Sir, I shall never be happy if I do not make that voyage again.'

Realising his desire, Ansaldo when the time came provided another ship of more value, and with more merchandise than the first; indeed he put into it the greater part of his whole wealth. His companions, when they had furnished their vessels with trading goods, put to sea with Giannetto and hoisted sail and started their voyage. After sailing along with them several days, Giannetto was all agog to discover once more the port of the lady, which was called, 'The port of the lady of Belmonte'. Coming one night to the mouth of it, which was in a gulf of the sea, he knew it to be the same, and, shifting sails and rudder, he entered so secretly that his companions in the other ships did not realise it.

On getting up the next morning, and looking down on the port, the lady saw the pennants of the ship playing in the wind and at once recognised it. She called one of her maids and said to her, 'Do you know those pennants?' Said the maid, 'Madam, it looks like the ship of that young man who came last year, and left so much riches behind with his cargo.' 'What you say is true,' said the lady, 'and he must surely be deeply in love with me, for I have never known any one return here a second time.' The maid said, 'I never saw a more courteous or charming man than he.' The lady sent many maidens and men-at-arms, who served Giannetto joyously, and he treated them all gaily and graciously, and went up to the castle and into the presence of the lady. When she saw him she embraced him with delight, and he embraced her with great respect, and the whole day was passed in joy and revels; for the lady sent for nobles and ladies who came to feast at court for love of Giannetto, and almost all the nobles were troubled, for with his pleasantness and courtesy they would willingly have had him as their lord. The ladies were enamoured of him for the way in which he led the dancing; while the beauty of his countenance made them all consider him the son of some great man. Bedtime being come, the lady took Giannetto by the hand, saying, 'Let us retire now,' and they went into the chamber. When they were seated, two damsels came with wine and sweetmeats, and having eaten and drunk of them they went to bed, and immediately Giannetto fell asleep. The lady undressed and lay by his side, but, in short, he waked not the whole night. In the morning the lady rose and gave orders to unload the ship. After nine o'clock Giannetto awoke, reached for the lady and could not find her. He raised his head and saw that it was fully day; he got up and began to feel full of shame. He was given a horse and money and was told to begone, and went off at once in his shame, sad and melancholy, and never rested for many days till he got to Venice, where he went by night to the house of his friend, who, when he saw him with great wonder asked him, 'Alas, what is wrong?' 'Everything is wrong!' answered Giannetto, 'Curses on my fate which brought me to this land!' His friend said, 'You may well curse your fate, since you have ruined Messer Ansaldo who was the greatest and richest of the Christian merchants. The shame of this is greater than the loss!'

Giannetto lived hidden many days in the house of his friend, not knowing what to do or say, and almost resolved to return to Florence without sending word to Ansaldo; but at last he determined to go and see him, and did so. When Messer Ansaldo saw him he rose and ran to embrace him, saying, 'Welcome, my son!' And Giannetto, embracing him, wept. When Ansaldo had heard his tale, 'You know how things are, Giannetto,' he said; 'do not make yourself melancholy for a moment. Since I have you back, I am content. We have still enough to live on quietly. The sea gives some men riches, from others takes away.'

All Venice heard the story, spoke of Ansaldo, and grieved sorely for the loss he had suffered, which obliged him to sell many of his possessions to pay the creditors who had supplied the goods. The companions of Giannetto, returning from Alexandria very rich, were informed how Giannetto had come back having been shipwrecked and lost everything. At this they marvelled, saying, 'This is the most

extraordinary thing that ever happened!' They called on Messer
Ansaldo and Giannetto and consoled them cordially, saying, 'Do
not be discouraged; we propose to make next year a voyage on your
account. We have been the cause of this your loss, since it was we
who first induced Giannetto to come with us. So fear nothing; while
we have anything, it is at your disposal.' Messer Ansaldo thanked
them and said that he still had enough to suffice for their needs.

Now Giannetto brooded day and night on these things, and he
could not regain his old cheerfulness. When Ansaldo asked what was
the matter, he replied, 'I shall never be satisfied till I have got back
what I have lost.' Said Ansaldo, 'My son, I do not wish you to go
again; better stay quietly here, content with the little we have
left, than risk another voyage.' Giannetto answered, 'I am determined to do all that I can: I should think it most shameful to live
always in that way.' When Ansaldo found him resolved, he decided
to sell everything he had in the world, to equip another ship; and
so he did. He disposed of everything, leaving himself with nothing,
to furnish a fine ship with merchandise; and since he still required
ten thousand ducats, he went to a Jew at Mestri, and borrowed
them on these terms:—that if he had not repaid the debt by the
feast of St. John in the following June, the Jew might take a pound
of flesh from any part of his body he pleased. Ansaldo agreed to this,
and the Jew had a formal bond drawn up and witnessed, with all
due form and ceremony. Then he counted out ten thousand ducats
of gold, with which Ansaldo supplied the vessel's needs. And if
the other two ships had been fine, this third was much richer and
better equipped. Meanwhile the friends furnished out their own,
with the intention that whatever they gained should be for Giannetto. When it was time to depart, before they left Ansaldo said to
Giannetto. 'My son, you are going and you see the bond under
which I stand. I ask of you one promise, that should any misfortune
occur, you will please come back to me, so that I may see you before
I die, and with that die content.' 'Messer Ansaldo,' replied Giannetto, 'I will do anything to please you.' Ansaldo gave him his
blessing, and so they took their leave, and set off on their voyage.

His two companions kept careful watch over Giannetto's ship,
while he for his part was always planning how to give them the slip
into the port of Belmont. He prevailed on one of the sailors to guide
the vessel there in the night. When morning brought clear daylight,
the others looked about and could see nothing of Giannetto's ship.
'Giannetto certainly has bad luck!' they said, and decided to
continue on their course, marvelling greatly. His ship meanwhile
having reached the port, all the people ran from the castle, hearing

that Giannetto had returned, and were amazed at it, saying, 'He must be the son of some great man, since he comes every year with such rich merchandise and fine ships. Would to God he were our master!'

He was visited by all the principal men of the country, barons and knights, and the lady was told that Giannetto had returned to her port. She went to the castle windows, saw this noble ship, and recognised his banners, whereupon she crossed herself, saying, 'This is indeed a great stroke of luck! It is the man who left such riches behind him!' And she sent for him.

Giannetto went to her with many embracings. They greeted each other and paid respects, and all the day was spent in joy and feasting. A fine jousting was held in his honour, and many barons and knights jousted that day, and Giannetto also took part and did wonders; he was so good with horse and lance. He pleased the nobles so much that again all wished he were their lord.

In the evening when it was bedtime the lady took him by the hand and said, 'Let us go to rest!' And as they were at the chamber door one of the lady's maids, being sorry for Giannetto, bent towards his ear and whispered softly 'Pretend to drink, but do not drink tonight.' Giannetto understood the words and went in. The lady said, 'I know that you must be thirsty, so I must have you drink before you go to bed.' And immediately two damsels came in, innocent as angels, with the usual wine and sweetmeats, and presented the drink. 'Who can refuse wine from two such beautiful damsels?' cried Giannetto, and the lady laughed. So Giannetto took the cup and pretended to drink the wine, but poured it into his bosom. The lady thought that he had drunk, and said to herself, 'You must bring another ship, young man; you have lost this one!'

Giannetto went to bed, and finding himself brisk and in good spirits he thought it a thousand years till the lady came to him. He said to himself, 'I have tricked her; this time the case is altered!' And to entice her soon to bed, he began to snore as if asleep. At which, 'This is excellent!' said the lady, and, quickly undressing, she got into bed with Giannetto, who lost no time, but as soon as she was in, turned towards her, embraced her, and saying, 'Now I have what I have desired so long!' bestowed on her the bliss of holy matrimony, and all night long she did not leave his arms. The lady was highly delighted, and got up before dawn next day, summoned all her nobles and other citizens, and told them, 'Giannetto is your lord; prepare to make holiday'. Immediately the news was spread through the land, the people shouting, 'Long live our new lord! Long live our new lord!', the bells and musical instruments inviting all to festivity. The nobles who were not at the castle were sent for saying: 'Come to see your overlord', and so a great and wonderful feasting began. When Giannetto came from his room he was knighted and placed on the throne; the sceptre was put in his hand and he was proclaimed sovereign of the country with great pomp and splendour. And when all the lords and ladies had come to court, he married the lady with great feasting and such joy as could not be told or imagined, while all the barons and other lords of the land came to rejoice, to joust, to tourney, to dance, to sing, to play, and all else belonging to so festive an occasion.

The generous Giannetto gave away silken stuffs and other rich things that he had brought with him. He showed himself a strong ruler, and made himself respected by administering right and justice to all sorts of people. He thus dwelt some time in joy and gladness, and never cared nor gave a thought for poor Messer Ansaldo who had given his bond to the Jew for ten thousand ducats. But one day, as he stood at the window of the palace with his bride, he saw a company of men passing through the square with lighted torches in their hands, going to make their offerings. 'What is the meaning of this?' asked Messer Giannetto. His lady replied, 'That is a company of guildsmen on their way to St. John's Church to make their offerings, for today is the feast of St. John.' Giannetto instantly remembered Ansaldo. Leaving the window, he gave a great sigh, turned pale, and paced about the room pondering the matter. His lady inquired what was wrong. 'Nothing,' he replied. She continued to press him saying, 'There is certainly something wrong, but you do not want to tell me.' And she said so much that Giannetto told her how Ansaldo had stood bond for ten thousand ducats. 'And the term expires today,' he said, 'and I greatly fear that my father will die for me, since if he cannot repay it today, he must lose a pound of his flesh.' The lady said, 'Take a horse at once, and go by land, for it is quicker than by sea; take what attendants you like, carry a hundred thousand ducats, and do not rest till you reach Venice. If he is not dead, bring him back here.' So Giannetto at once had the trumpet sounded. On horseback with twenty companions and carrying much money, he made for Venice.

Now the time being expired, the Jew had Ansaldo arrested, and insisted on having his pound of flesh. Ansaldo begged him to delay his death a few days only, so that, if his dear Giannetto arrived, he might at least see him once more. Said the Jew, 'I am willing to grant you the delay, but if he comes a hundred times I intend to take from you a pound of your flesh, according to our agreement.' Messer Ansaldo replied that he was content. All Venice talked about the affair; everyone was grieved at it, and many merchants joined together in offering to pay the money, but the Jew would not have it, for he wished to commit this homicide in order to be able to say that he had put to death the greatest of the Christian merchants.

While Giannetto was speeding towards Venice, his lady followed him dressed like a lawyer, with two servants. When he arrived Giannetto went to the Jew's house where he joyfully embraced Ansaldo, and told the Jew that he was willing to pay him his money and as much more in addition as he might demand. The Jew answered that he would take no money, since he had not received it at the proper time; he would have the pound of flesh.

The question was much debated, and everyone said that the Jew was in the wrong, but since Venice had a reputation as a place of strict justice, and the Jew's case was legal and formally made out, nobody dared to deny him, but only to plead with him. When the merchants of Venice one and all came and begged him to be merciful, he was more inflexible than ever. Giannetto offered him twenty thousand, which he refused; then thirty thousand, afterwards forty, fifty, and at last a hundred thousand ducats, whereupon the Jew said, 'I tell you frankly; if you offered me more ducats than this city is worth, I would not be satisfied and take them. I wish to act according to the letter of the agreement.'

When matters stood thus, the lady arrived in Venice dressed like a lawyer and alighted at an inn. The landlord asked a servant, 'Who is this gentleman?' The servant, who had already been told by her what to reply when questioned about her, answered, 'He is a gentleman of the law who has just finished his studies at Bologna, and is going back home.' The landlord thereupon showed his guest great civility. During dinner the lawyer asked him 'How is the law administered in this city?' 'Too strictly, sir,' replied the host. 'What makes you say that?' said the lawyer. 'Well, I will tell you,' said the landlord. 'There came here from Florence a young man named Giannetto who was commended to the care of an elderly relative, Messer Ansaldo. He was so agreeable and polished that both our men and our women fell in love with him; indeed there never came to this city anyone more popular than he was. Now this Ansaldo furnished him three times with ships of great value; each time he suffered shipwreck, so to equip the last Ansaldo borrowed ten thousand ducats from a Jew, on condition that if he did not repay them in June, at the feast of St. John, the Jew might take a pound of flesh from any part of his body he should choose. This excellent young man is now returned, and instead of the ten thousand ducats offers to pay a hundred thousand, but the wicked Jew won't take them. All the best men in the city have appealed to him, but to no purpose'. 'This matter,' said the lawyer, 'is easy to settle.' 'If you will take the trouble to settle it,' replied the host, 'so as to save the good man's life, you will win the esteem and love of the most virtuous young man who was ever born, and of all the best men in this country.'

So the lawyer caused a proclamation to be made that whosoever had any legal problem to solve might apply to him. Giannetto was told that a famous lawyer had come from Bologna who could decide all cases in law. He said to the Jew, 'Let us go to this lawyer.' 'Very well,' said the Jew, 'but no matter who comes, I intend to do what my bond says is my right.' When they came before the lawyer and saluted him duly, the lawyer knew Giannetto but Giannetto did not know him, for he had disguised his face with the juice of certain herbs. Giannetto and the Jew each stated his own case to the judge, who took the bond and read it. Then he said to the Jew, 'My opinion is that you should take the hundred thousand ducats, and release this honest man, who will always be grateful to you.' The Jew replied, 'I shall do no such thing.' 'It is your best course,' said the lawyer, but the Jew was determined to yield nothing.

They agreed to go to the tribunal appointed for such cases, and the lawyer spoke for Messer Ansaldo and said, 'Let the other come forward.' When the Jew had come, the lawyer said to him, 'Now take a pound of his flesh from wherever you like, and settle your claim.' The Jew ordered Ansaldo to be stripped naked, and took in his hand a razor which had been made ready. Messer Giannetto turned to the lawyer and said, 'Sir, this is not what I asked you to do.' 'Wait a while,' the latter replied. 'He has not yet cut off the pound of flesh.' Meanwhile the Jew went towards his victim. Then said the lawyer, 'Take care what you do. If you take more or less than a pound, I shall have your head struck off, and I tell you besides, that if you shed one drop of blood, I shall have you put to death. Your bond makes no mention of the shedding of blood, but says that you may take a pound of flesh, neither more nor less. If you are wise you will take great care what you do and how you do it.' And thereupon he sent for the executioner to bring the block and the axe, and said, 'If I see one drop of blood spilt, off goes your head.'

The Jew began to be afraid, and Messer Giannetto to feel more cheerful. At length the Jew after much arguing said, 'Judge, you are more cunning than I. Give me the hundred thousand ducats, and I shall be satisfied.' Said the lawyer, 'I grant you a pound of flesh, according to your bond, but I shall not give you a farthing. You should have taken them when I offered you them.' The Jew came down to ninety thousand, and then to eighty, but the judge was firm. 'Give him what he wants,' said Giannetto to the lawyer, 'so long as he gives up Ansaldo.' 'Leave him to me, I say,' said the lawyer. Then the Jew said, 'Give me fifty thousand.' 'I would not give you one miserable farthing,' said the judge. The Jew then said, 'Give me at least my ten thousand ducats, and a curse be on you all.' 'Did you not understand me?' said the judge, 'I'll give you nothing. If you want your pound of flesh, take it. If not, I shall declare your bond null and void.' Everyone present was delighted and they all mocked at the Jew, saying, 'He who lays snares for others is caught himself.' The Jew, seeing that he could not do what he had wished, took his bond and tore it in pieces in a rage. So Ansaldo was released and Giannetto conducted him home with great joy. The young man then speedily took the hundred thousand ducats to the lawyer whom he found in his room making preparations to depart.

Giannetto said to him, 'Sir, you have done me the most important service anyone could perform, so I hope that you will take this money away with you, for I am sure you have earned it well.' 'Thank you, Messer Giannetto,' replied the judge, 'but I do not need it. Keep it, so that your lady may not say that you have squandered it.' 'Indeed, she is so kind and generous,' said Giannetto, 'that if I spent four times as much as this, she would not mind. She wished me to bring much more with me than this.' 'Are you happy with her?' added the judge. 'I love her better than anything else in the world,' said Giannetto. 'She is as beautiful and wise as anyone Nature ever made. If you will do me the favour to come and see her you will be astonished at the honour she will do you, and you will see if she is as I say she is or not.' 'I cannot go with you,' said the lawyer, 'since I have other engagements, but since you speak so well of her I desire you, when you see her, to salute her on my behalf.' 'It shall be done,' said Giannetto, 'but now I entreat you to accept some of this money.' While he was saying these words, the lawyer saw a ring on his finger and said, 'I will take that ring, and no other payment.' 'Very well,' replied Giannetto, 'but I give it you with reluctance since my lady gave it me, and told me to wear it always for love of her. If she fails to see it on me she will believe that I have given it to some other woman, and quarrel with me, and believe that I have fallen in love elsewhere, though I love her better than I love myself.' The lawyer said, 'I am sure that she must love you well enough to believe you when you tell her that you gave it me.

But perhaps you wanted to give it to one of your old loves here?'
'Such is the love and faith I bear her,' answered Giannetto, 'that I
would not change her for any other woman in the world; she is so
absolutely perfect in every way.'

He took the ring from his finger and gave it to the lawyer, and
they embraced each other with respect. 'Do me a favour,' said the
lawyer. 'It shall be granted,' said Giannetto. 'Do not stay here,'
said the other, 'but go as soon as possible back to your lady.' 'It
will seem like a hundred thousand years till I see her again,' replied
Giannetto; and thus they took leave of each other. The lawyer found
a ship and went off, and Giannetto, after holding banquets and
dinners and giving horses and money to his friends, and making
merry, and holding court, took leave of the Venetians, and set off
home, together with Ansaldo and many of his old companions. Most
of the Venetian men and women shed tears of tenderness at his
departure; so amiably had he behaved to everyone while there. In
this manner he departed and returned to Belmont.

The lady arrived some days before him, pretending that she had
been to a health resort. She resumed her feminine dress, and gave
orders for great preparations, the streets to be hung with tapestries,
and many companies of men gathered for the tilting. When Giannetto and Ansaldo landed all the nobles of the Court went out to
meet them, crying, 'Long live our lord! Long live our lord!' And
when they dismounted, the lady ran to embrace Messer Ansaldo,
but pretended to be a little displeased with Messer Giannetto,
though she loved him better than herself. A great festival of jousting,
tilting, dancing and singing was held for all the noblemen and ladies.

But Giannetto, seeing that his wife did not receive him as sweetly
as usual, went to her room, called her, and asked, 'What is the
matter?' and would have embraced her. Said she, 'You do not need
to invent these caresses, when I know well that you met your old
sweethearts in Venice.' Giannetto began to expostulate, whereat
she said, 'Where is the ring which I gave you?' Giannetto replied,
'What I expected has happened; and I was right to say you would
think ill of me for it. But I swear by my love of God and you, that
I gave the ring to the lawyer who won our case for us.' 'And I can
swear,' said the lady, 'that you gave the ring to a woman. I know
it, so do not shame yourself by false-swearing!' Giannetto answered,
'May God destroy me if I am not speaking the truth, and if I did
not tell the lawyer this would happen, when he asked for the ring.'
His wife said, 'You would have done better to stay in Venice, and
to have sent Ansaldo here; then you could have enjoyed yourself
with your mistresses, who I hear all wept when you left them.'

Giannetto began to weep and show great sorrow, saying, 'You are swearing what is not true and never could be.'

The lady, seeing him weep, felt it like a dagger in her heart, and quickly ran to embrace him, laughing heartily. She showed him the ring, and told him everything that he had said to the lawyer, and how the lawyer had been herself, and how he had given her the ring. At this Giannetto was greatly astonished, and perceiving the truth of it all began to enjoy the jest hugely. When they left the chamber, he told each of his lords and companions, and these events increased and multiplied the love between him and his lady. Giannetto then called the damsel who had warned him not to drink that evening, and gave her as wife to Ansaldo; and they spent the rest of their lives in great joy and happiness.

II. Analogue

From THE THREE LADIES OF LONDON
by R[obert] W[ilson] (1584)

A right excellent and famous Comoedy called the three Ladies of London. Wherein is notablie declared and set foorth, how by the meanes of Lucar, Love and Conscience is so corrupted, that the one is married to Dissimulation, the other fraught with all abhomination. . . . Written by R. W. as it hath been publiquely played. At London, Printed by Roger Warde. . . . 1584.

[i] *Enter Mercadore* [f. Ciii v.]

MERCA. Ah my good friend a maister Userie, be my trot you be very well mette:

Me be muche beholding unto you for your good will, me be in your debt.

But a me take a your part so much against a scalde olde churle called Hospitalitie:

Did speake against you, and sayes you bring good honest men to
  beggerie.

   USURY   I thanke Sir, did he speake suche evill of me as you now
  say?

I doubt not but to reward him for his trecherie one day.

   MERCA.   But I pray tell a me how fare a my Ladie all dis while?

   USURY   Marie verie Sir, and here she comes if my selfe I do not
  beguile.

Enter Lucar

   LUCAR   What Señor Mercadore I have not seene you many a
  day,

I marvel what is the cause you kept so long away?

   MERCA.   Shall me say to you Madama dat me have had much
  businesse for you in hand,

For send away good commodities out of dis little Countrey England:

Me have nowe sent ouer Brasse, Copper, Pewter, and many oder
  ting:

And for dat me shall ha for Gentlewomans fine trifles, that great
  profite will bring.

   LUCAR   I perceave you have bene mindefull of me for whiche I
  thanke yee:

But Userie tell me, how have you spedde in that you went about?

   USURY   Indifferently Lady, you neede not to doubt,

I have taken possession, and because they were destitute:

I have lent it for a quarter my tale to conclude.

Marry I have a little raised the rent, but it is but after forty pound
  by the yeare:

But if it were to let now, I would let it more deare.

   LUCAR   Indeede tis but a trifle, it makes no matter,

I force it not greatly, being but for a quarter.

   MERCA.   Madona me tell ye vat you shall doe, let dem to
  straunger dat are content

To dwell in a little roome, and to pay muche rent:

For you know da french mans and fleminges in dis countrey be
  many,

So dat they make shift to dwell ten houses in one very gladly:

And be content a for pay fiftie or three score pound a yeare,

For dat whiche da English mans say twenty marke is to deare.

   LUCAR   Why senior Mercadore thinke you not that I

Have infinite numbers in London that my want doth supply.

Beside in Bristow, Northhampton, Norwich, Weschester, Caunter-
  bury,

Dover, Sandwich, Rie, Porchmouth, Plimmoth, and many moe,

That great rentes upon little roome doe bestow.
Yes I warrant you, and truely I may thanke the straungers for this,
That they have made houses so deare, whereby I live in blisse.
But senior Mercadore, dare you to travell undertake:
And goe amongest the Moores, Turkes, and Pagans for my sake?

    MERCA.　Madona, me dare a goe to de Turkes, Moores, Paganes and more too.
What doe me care and me goe to da great devill for you—
Commaund a me Maddam, and you shall see plaine,
Data for your sake me refuse a no paine.

    LUCAR　Then senior Mercadore I am forthwith to send ye
From hence, to search for some new toyes in Barbary or Turky,
Such trifles as you thinke will please wantons best:
For you know in this Countrey tis their chiefest request.

    MERCA.　Indeede de Gentlewomans here buy so much vaine toyes,
Dat me straungers laugh a to tinke wherein day have their Joyes:
Fayt Madona me will searche all da straunge countreys me can tell,
But me will have such tinges dat please dese Gentlewomans vell.

    LUCAR　Why then let us provide thinges readie to haste you away.

    MERCA.　A voutre commaundamento Madona me obay.

                                        [Exeunt

．　．　．　．　．　．　．　．　．　．　．　．

[*ii*]　*Enter Mercadorus the Merchaunt and Gerontus a Jewe*
[f. Diii v.]

    GERON.　But senior Mercadorus tell me, did ye serve me well or no?
That having gotten my money would seeme the countrey to forgoe:
You know I sent you two thousand duckets for three monthes space,
And ere the time came you got an other thousand by flatterie and your smooth face.
So when the time came that I should have receaved my money,
You were not to be found but was fled out of the countrey:
Surely if we that be Jewes should deale so one with an other,
We should not be trusted againe of our owne brother:
But many of you Christians make no conscience to falsifie your fayth and breake your day.
I should have bene paide at the monthes end, and now it is two yeare you have bene away.

Well I am glad you be come againe to Turky, now I trust I shall
receive the interest of you so well as the principall.

MERCA. A good a maister Geronto pray hartly beare a me a
little while,
And me shall pay ye all without any deceite or guile:
Me have a much businesse for by prety knackes to send to England,
Good a sir bare a me foure or five daies, me'll dispatch your money
out of [   ]

GERON. Senior Mercadore, I know no reason why, because you
have dealt with me so ill,
Sure you did it not for neede, but of set purpose and will:
And I tell ye to beare with ye foure or five dayes goes sore against
my minde,
Least you should steale away and forget to leave my money behinde.

MERCA. Pray hartly doe tink a no such ting my good friend a me,
Be me trot and fayt me'll pay you all every peny.

GERON. Well Ile take your faith and troth once more, ile trust
to your honesty
In hope that for my long tarying you will deale well with me:
Tell me what ware you would buy for England, such necessaries as
they lacke.

MERCA. O no lack some prettie fine toy or some fantastike new
knack,
For da Gentlewomans in England buy much tinges for fantasie:
You pleasure a me sir what me meane a dare buy.

GERON. I understand you sir, but keepe touch with me, and
I'le bring you to great store,
Such as I perceave you came to this countrey for:
As Muske, Amber, sweete Powders, fine Odors, pleasaunt perfumes,
and many such toys:
Wherein I perceave consisteth that country gentlewomans Joyes.
Besides I have Diamondes, Rubyes, Emerodes, Safiors, Smaradines,
Opalles, Onacles, Jasinkes, Aggattes, Turkasir, and almost of
all kinde of precious stones:
And many moe fit thinges to sucke away mony from such greene
headed wantons.

MERCA. Fatta my good frend me tanke you most hartly alway,
Me shall a content your debt within dis two or tree day.

GERON. Well looke you doe keepe your promise, and an other
time you shall commaund me:
Come, goe we home where our commodities you may at pleasure
see.

· · · · · · · ·

[*iii*]   *Enter Mercadorus reading a letter to himselfe, and let Gerontus the Jewe followe him, and speake as followeth*   [f. Eiii]

GERON.   Senior Mercadore, why doe you not pay mee? thinke you I will bee mockt in this sorte?

This is three times you have flowted mee, it seemes you make thereat a sporte.

Trulie pay me my money, and that even nowe presently,

Or by mightie Mahomet I sweare, I will forthwith arrest yee.

MERCA.   Ha pray a bare wit me tre or foure daies, mee have much businesse in hand:

Me be troubled with letters you see heere, dat comes from England.

GERON.   Tush this is not my matter, I have nothing therewith to do,

Pay me my money or I'le make you, before to your lodging you go.

I have Officers stand watching for you, so that you cannot passe by,

Therefore you were best to pay me, or els in prison you shall lie.

MERCA.   Arrest me dou skal knave, mary do and if thou dare,

Me will not pay de one peny, arrest me, doo, me do not care.

Me will be a Turke, me came hedar for dat cause,

Darefore me care not for de so mush as two strawes.

GERON.   This is but your wordes, because you would defeate me,

I cannot thinke you will forsake your faith so lightly.

But seeing you drive me to doubt, I'le trie your honestie:

Therefore be sure of this, I'le go about it presently.   [*Exit*

MERCA.   Mary farewell and be hangd, sitten scald drunken Jew,

I warrant yee me shalbe able very vell to pay you.

My Lady Lucar have sent me heere dis letter,

Praying me to coossen[1] de Jewe for love a her.

Darefore me'll go to get a some Turks apparell,

Dat me may coossen da Jewe, and end dis quarrell.   [*Exit*

. . . .

[*iv*]   *Enter the Judge of Turkie, with Gerontus and Mercadorus*

[f. Eiv v]

JUDGE   Sir Gerontus, because you are the plaintife, you first your minde shall say,

Declare the cause you did arrest this Merchant yesterday.

GERON.   Then learned Judge attende. This Mercadorus whome you see in place,

Did borrowe two thousand Duckets of mee, but for a five weeks space.

[1] cozen, cheat.

Then Sir, before the day came, by his flatterie he obtained one
thousand more,
And promist mee at two monthes ende I should receive my store:
But before the time exspired, he was closly[1] fled away,
So that I never heard of him at least this two yeeres day:
Till at the last I met with him, and my money did demande,
Who sware to me at five daies end, he would pay me out of
hand.
The five daies came, and three daies more, then one day he
requested,
I perceiving that he flouted me, have got him thus arrested:
And now he comes in Turkish weedes to defeat me of my mony,
But I trow he wil not forsake his faith, I deeme he hath more
honestie.

JUDGE   Sir Gerontus you knowe, if any man forsake his faith,
king, countrie, and become a Mahomet,
All debtes are paide, tis the lawe of our Realme, and you may not
gainesay it.

GERON.   Most true (reverent Judge) we may not, nor I will not
against our Lawes grudge.

JUDGE   Senior Mercadorus is this true that Gerontus doth tell?

MERCA.   My Lord Judge, de matter, and de circumstance be
true me know well.
But me will be a Turke, and for dat cause me came heere.

JUDGE   Then it is but a follie to make many wordes. Senior
Mercadorus draw neere.
Lay your hand upon this booke, and say after mee,

MERCA.   With a good will my Lord Judge, me be all readie.
Not for any devotion, but for Lucars sake of my monie.[2]

JUDGE & MERCA.   Say I Mercadorus, do utterly renounce before
all the world, my dutie to my Prince, my honour to my parents,
and my good wil to my cuntry:
Furthermore I protest and sweare to be true to this country during
life, and thereupon I forsake my Christian faith.

GERON.   Stay there most puissant Judge. Senior Mercadorus,
consider what you doo,
Pay me the principall, as for the interest, I forgive it you:
And yet the interest is allowed amongst you Christians, as well as
in Turky,
Therefore respect your faith, and do not seeme to deceive me.

MERCA.   No point da interest, no point da principall.

GERON.   Then pay me the one halfe, if you will not pay me all.

---

[1] secretly.   [2] This to the audience, aside.

31—S.N.D.

MERCA.   No point da halfe, no point den[i]ere,[1] me will be a
Turke I say,
Me be wearie of my Christes religion, and for dat me come away.

GERON.   Well seeing it is so, I would be loth to heare the people
say, it was long of me
Thou forsakest thy faith, wherefore I forgive thee franke and free:
Protesting before the Judge, and all the world, never to demaund
peny nor halfepeny.

MERCA.   O Sir Gerontus, me take a your proffer, and tanke you
most hartily.

JUDGE   But Señor Mercadorus, I trow ye will be a Turke for all
this.

MERCA.   Señor no, not for all da good in da world, me forsake a
my Christ.

JUDGE   Why then it is as Sir Gerontus saide, you did more for
the greedines of the mony,
Then for any zeale or good will you bare to Turky.

MERCA.   Oh Sir, you make a great offence,
You must not judge a my conscience.

JUDGE   One may judge and speake truth, as appeeres by this,
Jewes seeke to excell in Christianitie, and Christians in Jewisnes.

[*Exit*

MERCA.   Vell vell, but me tanke you Sir Gerontus with all my
very hart.

GERON.   Much good may it do you sir, I repent it not for my
part.
But yet I would not have this bolden you to serve an other so,
Seeke to pay, & keepe day with men, so a good name on you wil go.

[*Exit*

III. Analogue

From THE ORATOR
by Alexander Silvayn
translated by L. P. (1596)

THE ORATOR. Handling a hundred severall Discourses,
in forme of declamations; some of the arguments being

[1] A French coin, $\frac{1}{12}$ of a sou.

drawne from T. Livius and other ancient writers, the rest of the authors owne invention. . . . Written in French by A. Silvayn and Englished by L[azarus] P[iot]. A. Islip. London. 1596.

Declamation 95

Of a Jew, who would for his debt have a pound of the flesh of a Christian

A Jew unto whom a Christian Marchant ought nine hundred crownes, would have summoned him for the same in Turckie: the Merchant because he would not be discredited, promised to pay the said summe within the tearme of three months, and if he paied it not, he was bound to give him a pound of the flesh of his bodie. The tearme being past some fifteene daies, the Jew refused to take his money, and demaunded the pound of flesh: the ordinarie Judge of that place appointed him to cut a just pound of the Christians flesh, and if he cut either more or lesse, then his owne head should be smitten off: the Jew appealed from this sentence, unto the chief judge, saying:

Impossible is it to breake the credite of trafficke amongst men without great detriment unto the Commonwealth: wherfore no man ought to bind himselfe unto such covenants which hee cannot or wil not accomplish, for by that means should no man feare to be deceaved, and credit being maintained, every man might be assured of his owne; but since deceit hath taken place, never wonder if obligations are made more rigorous & strict then they were wont, seeing that although the bonds are made never so strong, yet can no man be very certaine that he shal not be a loser. It seemeth at the first sight, that it is a thing no lesse strange then cruel, to bind a man to pay a pound of the flesh of his bodie, for want of money: Surely, in that it is a thing not usuall, it appeareth to be somewhat the more admirable, but there are divers others that are more cruell, which because they are in use seeme nothing terrible at all: as to bind al the bodie unto a most lothsome prison, or unto an intoller-able slaverie, where not only the whole bodie but also al the sences and spirits are tormented, the which is commonly practised, not only betwixt those which are either in sect or Nation contrary, but also even amongst those that are all of one sect and nation, yea amongst neighbours and kindred, & even amongst Christians it hath ben seene, that the son hath imprisoned the father for monie. Likewise, in the Roman Commonwealth, so famous for laws and armes, it was lawfull for debt, to imprison, beat, and afflict with torments the free Cittizens: How manie of them (do you thinke) would have thought themselves happie, if for a small debt they might have ben excused with the paiment of a pound of their flesh? Who ought then to marvile if a Jew requireth so small a thing of a Christian, to discharge him of a good round summe?   A man may aske why I would not rather take silver of this man, then his flesh: I might alleage many reasons, for I might say that none but my selfe can tell what the breach of his promise hath cost me, and what I have thereby paied for want of money unto my creditors, of that which I have lost in my credit: for the miserie o[f] those men which esteeme their reputation, is so great, that oftentimes they had rather indure any thing secretlie then to have their discredit blazed abroad, because they would not be both shamed and harmed. Neverthelesse, I doe freely confesse, that I had rather lose a pound of my flesh, then my credit should be in any sort cracked: I might also say that I have need of this flesh to cure a friend of mine of a certaine maladie, which is otherwise incurable, or that I would have it to terrifie thereby the Christians for ever abusing the Jewes anie more hereafter: but I will onelie say, that by his obligation he oweth it me. It is lawfull to kill a souldior if he come unto the warres but an houre too late, and also to hang a theefe though he steale never so little: is it then such a great matter to cause such a one to pay a pound of his flesh, that hath broken his promise manie times, or that putteth another in danger to lose both credit & reputation, yea and it may be life and al for greife? were it not better for him to lose that which I demand, then his soule, alreadie bound by his faith? Neither am I to take that which he oweth me, but he is to deliver it me: And especiallie because no man knoweth better then he where the same may be spared to the least hurt of his person, for I might take it in such a place as hee might thereby happen to lose his life: what a matter were it then, if I should cut of his privie members, supposing that the same would altogether weigh a just pound? Or els his head, should I be suffered to cut it off, although it were with the danger of mine owne life? I beleeve I should not; because there were as little reason therein, as there could be in the amends whereunto I should be bound: or els if I would cut off his nose, his lips, his eares, and pull out his eies, to make of them altogether a pound, should I be suffered? Surely I thinke not, because the obligation dooth not specifie that I ought either to chuse, cut, or take the same, but that he ought to give me a pound of his flesh. Of every thing that is sold, he which delivereth the same is to make waight, and he which receiveth, taketh heed that it be just: seeing then that neither the obligation, custome, nor law doth bind me to cut, or weigh, much lesse unto the above mentioned satisfaction,

I refuse it all, and require that the same which is due should bee delivered unto mee.

The Christians Answere

It is no strange matter to here those dispute of equitie which are themselves most unjust; and such as have no faith at all, desirous that others should observe the same inviolable, the which were yet the more tollerable, if such men would bee contented with reasonable things, or at the least not altogether unreasonable: but what reason is there that one man should unto his own prejudice desire the hurt of another? as this Jew is content to lose nine hundred crownes to have a pound of my flesh, whereby is manifestly seene the antient and cruell hate which he beareth not only unto Christians, but unto all others which are not of his sect: yea, even unto the Turkes, who overkindly doe suffer such vermine to dwell amongst them, seeing that this presumptuous wretch dare not onely doubt, but appeale from the judgement of a good and just Judge, & afterwards he would by sophisticall reasons proove that his abhomination is equitie: trulie I confesse that I have suffered fifteene daies of the tearme to passe, yet who can tell whether he or I is the cause thereof, as for me I thinke that by secret meanes he hath caused the money to bee delaied, which from sundry places ought to have come unto me before the tearm which I promised unto him; Otherwise, I would never have been so rash as to bind my selfe so strictly: but although he were not the cause of the fault, is it therefore said, that he ought to bee so impudent as to goe about to proove it no strange matter that he should be willing to be paied with mans flesh, which is a thing more natural for Tigres, then men, the which also was never heard of: but this divell in shape of a man, seeing me oppressed with necessitie propounded this accursed obligation unto me. Whereas hee alleageth the Romanes for an example, why doth he not as well tell on how for that crueltie in afflicting debtors over greevously, the Commonwealth was almost overthrowne, and that shortly after it was forbidden to imprison men any more for debt. To breake promise is, when a man sweareth or promiseth a thing, the which he hath no desire to performe, which yet upon an extreame necessitie is somewhat excusable; as for me, I have promised, and accomplished my promise, yet not so soone as I would; and although I knew the danger wherein I was to satisfie the crueltie of this mischeevous man with the price of my flesh and blood, yet did I not flie away, but submitted my selfe unto the discretion of the Judge who hath justly repressed his beastlinesse. Wherein then have I falsefied my promise, is it in that I would not, (like him) disobey the judgement of the Judge? Behold I will present a part of my bodie unto him, that he may pay himselfe, according to the contents of the judgement, where is then my promise broken? But it is no marvaile if this race be so obstinat and cruell against us, for they doe it of set purpose to offend our God whom they have crucified: and wherefore? Because he was holie, as he is yet so reputed of this worthy Turkish nation: but what shal I say? Their own bible is full of their rebellion against God, against their Priests, Judges, & leaders. What did not the verie Patriarks themselves, from whom they have their beginning? They sold their brother, and had it not been for one amongst them, they had slaine him even for verie envie. How manie adulteries and abhominations were committed amonst them? How manie murthers? *Absalon* did not he cause his brother to be murthered? Did he not persecute his father? Is it not for their iniquitie that God hath dispersed them, without leaving them one onlie foot of ground? If then, when they had newlie received their law from God, when they saw his wonderous works with their eies, and had yet their Judges amongst them, they were so wicked, What may one hope of them now, when they have neither faith nor law, but their rapines and usuries? And that they beleeve they do a charitable work, when they do some great wrong unto anie that is not a Jew? It may please you then most righteous Judge to consider all these circumstances, having pittie of him who doth wholy submit himselfe unto your just clemencie: hoping thereby to be delivered from this monsters crueltie.

IV. Possible Source

From ZELAUTO OR THE FOUNTAIN OF FAME
by Anthony Munday (1580)
Book III

[When the young men Rodolfo and Strabino admit that they are two days late in paying their debt the Judge tells Truculento that he should accept Strabino's money. Truculento replies:]

No, the money is none of mine, ne will I have it, his Landes I respect not, ne care I for them, and now his submission I way not, ne will I accept of it. You my Lord shall rather reape reproche by pleading on his part: then gayne any credite in maintayning so careless a creature. I drive my whole action to this issue, I plead my priviledge unto this poynt, & to this clause I am severely bent: I will have the due which breach of promise dooth deserve, I will exempt all courtesie: and accoumpt of cruelty. I wyll be pleased with no ritch reward whatsoever, no pitty shall prevayle, rigor shall rule, and on them bothe I will have Lawe to the uttermost.

Why *Truculento* (quoth the Judge) respect you cruelty: more then Christian civillitie, regard you rigor more then reason? Should the God above all Gods, the Judge above all Judges, administer desert, which your sinnes hath deserved? If his fatherly affection, if his mercifull myldnesse, if his righteous regard, dyd not consider the frayltie of your fleshe, your promptnes unto peryll, and your aptness unto evyll: how mightie were the myserie, which should justly fall upon you? Howe sharpe the sentence that should be pronounced against you, and howe rigorous the revenge, which should rightly reward you? Is this the loove you beare to your brother? Is this the care you have of a Christian? The Turke, whose tyranny is not to be talked of: could but exact to the uttermost of his crueltie. And you a braunche of that blessed body, which bare the burden of our mani- folde sinnes: howe can you seeme to deale so sharply with your selfe? seeing you should use to all men: as you would be dealt withall. Yet to let you have the lybertie of your demaund in Lawe, and you to stand to the Justice which heere I shall pronounce, let first your right eye be put foorth in theyr presence: and then shall they bothe abide lyke punishment.

For since neyther the restoring of your debt wyll suffice you, nor yet the lyberall amendes they are content to make you: I deeme it expedient you should be pertaker of theyr paynes, so shall you knowe if you demaund a reasonable request. Howe say you, will you stand to the verdict pronounced: or take the rewarde which they have promised.

My Lord (quoth *Truculento*) neyther doo I deserve to abide any such doome, nor they woorthy to be favoured with any such freend- shippe. I may lawfully alleadge that you permit partiality: & that you devide not each cause indifferently, for to what ende should you seeme to satisfie me with their woordes: when your selfe perceyves how they are found faultie? And what urgeth you to use such gentle perswasions: when you see your selfe they deserve no such dealing? If I had wylfully offended in any such cause, and wyttingly broken in such sort my bonde: I would be contented you should deliver me my deserts, so that you dyd minister nothing but Justice. And wherefore should you seeme to demaund the losse of my eye who have not offended: for savegarde of their eyes that have so trecherously trespassed? I am sure I go not beyond the breache of my bande[1], nor I desire no more then they have deserved. Wherefore object no more matters, whereby to delude me, nor impute no occasions to hinder my pretence, I crave Justice to be uprightly used, and I crave no more, wherefore I will have it.

Indeede my freends (quoth the Judge) who seeketh the extremitie, & urgeth so much as his wilfull minde dooth commaund him: his commission is very large, & his request not to be refused. Wherfore, since neither pittie can prevaile, nor freendly counsayle perswade: you must render the raunsome that he dooth require, for we cannot debarre him in these his dealings, nor we can not chuse but give our consentes. Therfore if you have any that will pleade your case in Law: let them speake & they shall be heard, to further your safety as much as we may. . . .

. . . Then *Brisana* (*Truculentos* Daughter) began in this order to pleade for her avayle. Admit my Lord (quoth she) that I come to such a person as this partie, to borrow the lyke sum of money, binding me in the selfe same band, to restore the money to the same party of whome I had it. Well, the time expyred, I come to deliver the due to the owner, he being not at home, nor in the Citty, but ridden foorth, and uncertaine of his comming: I returne home to my house, and he him selfe comes out of the Countrey as yesterday. Now he upon some severall spight or malicious intent: sueth me in the Lawe, not demaunding his due, nor I knowing of his arivall. Am I to be condempned for breaking the Lawe: when the partie him selfe hath deferred the day?

How lyke you this geere *Truculento*? you have now an other Pigeon to pull, and heere is one wiser then you were beware. Can you condempne this partie, not demaunding your due, nor beeing at home when it might have beene discharged? And making the bande to be restored to your selfe?

My Lord (quoth *Truculento*) though I was not at home: my house was not emptie, and though I was away, if it had beene restored: it stoode in as good effect as if it had beene payd to me. Wherefore it is but follie to frame such an allegation: for my Receyver in my absence dooth represent my selfe.

Well (quoth *Brisana*) admit your servaunt in your absence, standeth in as full effect as your selfe, and admit the debt had beene discharged to him, if wylfulnesse had allured your servaunt to wandering, and that he had departed with the debt he receyved:

---

[1] bond.

you returne and finde it styll in your booke, neither marked nor crossed, as if payment had not beene made, you wyll let your servaunt slyp with his offence: but you wyll demaund the debt agayne of me.

Tush (quoth *Truculento*) this is but a tryfle, and your woordes are now to be esteemed as winde, you should have restored the summe to my servaunt: and I would not have troubled you in any such sort, for there is no man that useth such follie: but he will see the booke crossed before he depart. Therefore you doo but trouble tyme with mentioning such matters: for your redemption is never the neere.

Well then Syr (quoth she) you will thus much allow, that at the delivery: the bande should be restored, and if I had delyvered the money to your servaunt: I should have respected my bande tyll yesterday, for your servaunt had it not to delyver: and I would not pay it before I had my bande. Ah *Signor Truculento* (quoth the Judge) he toucheth you to the quick now, how can you reply to this his demaund? In deede I confesse (quoth he) my Cubborde kept the bande tyll I returned, but yet noting the receyt in the booke, would have been sufficient tyll my comming home.

With that *Cornelia* stepped up, saying, Since (*Signor Truculento*) you will neyther allowe the reasonable aunsweres he hath made, nor be content to abide my Lord the Judges verdict: receyve the raunsome you so much require, and take both their eyes, so shall the matter be ended. But thus much (under verdict of my Lord his lycence) I give you in charge, and also especially notifie, that no man but your selfe shall execute the deede, ne shall you crave any counsayle of any the standers by. If in pulling foorth their eyes, you diminishe the least quantitie of blood out of their heads, over and besides their only eyes, or spyll one drop in taking them out: before you styrre your foote, you shall stand to the losse of bothe your owne eyes. For that the bande maketh mention of nothing but their eyes, and so if you take more then you should, and lesse then you ought: you shall abide the punishment heere in place pronounced. Nowe take when you will, but beware of the bargayne.

Truly (quoth the Judge) this matter hath beene excellently handled, it is no reason if you have your bargayne: that you should hinder them with the losse of one droppe of blood, wherefore I pronounce, no other Judgement shall at this tyme be ministred.

Now was *Truculento* more mad that he could not have his hearts desire, for that he knewe he must needes spyll some blood, it could not be otherwyse chosen, wherefore he desired he might have his money, and so let all other matters alone. Nay (quoth the Judge) since you would not accept of it when it was offered, nor would be contented with so large a promise: the money shall serve to make them amendes, for the great wrong which you would have offered. Thus in my opinion is Judgement equally used, and neyther partie I hope will be miscontented.

Truculento seeing there was no remedy, and that all the people praysed the Judgement so woorthily: accepted *Rodolfo* for his lawfull sonne, and put him in possession of all his lyvinges after his disease. Thus were they on all partes verie well pleased, and everie one accoumpted him selfe well contented.

V. Source

From THE JEW OF MALTA
by Christopher Marlowe (1633)

ACT ONE
(lines 141–177)

JEW   Thus trowles our fortune in by land and Sea,
And thus are wee on every side inrich'd:
These are the Blessings promis'd to the Jewes,
And herein was old *Abrams* happinesse:
What more may Heaven doe for earthly man
Then thus to powre out plenty in their laps,
Ripping the bowels of the earth for them,
Making the Sea their servants, and the winds
To drive their substance with successefull blasts?
Who hateth me but for my happinesse?
Or who is honour'd now but for his wealth?
Rather had I a Jew be hated thus,
Then pittied in a Christian poverty:
For I can see no fruits in all their faith,
But malice, falshood, and excessive pride,
Which me thinkes fits not their profession.
Happily some haplesse man hath conscience,
And for his conscience lives in beggery.
They say we are a scatter'd Nation:
I cannot tell, but we have scrambled up

More wealth by farre then those that brag of faith.
There's *Kirriah Jairim*, the great Jew of *Greece*,
Obed in Bairseth, *Nones* in *Portugall*,
My selfe in *Malta*, some in *Italy*,
Many in *France*, and wealthy every one:
I, wealthier farre then any Christian.
I must confesse we come not to be Kings:
That's not our fault: Alas, our number's few,
And Crownes come either by succession,
Or urg'd by force; and nothing violent,
Oft have I heard tell, can be permanent.
Give us a peacefull rule, make Christians Kings,
That thirst so much for Principality.
I have no charge, nor many children,
But one sole Daughter, whom I hold as deare
As *Agamemnon* did his *Iphigen*:
And all I have is hers. But who comes here?

. . . .

ACT ONE

(lines 333–364; 493–520)

[Barabas's goods are confiscated by the Christians, and the
Governor says:]

Yet *Barrabas* we will not banish thee,
But here in *Malta*, where thou gotst thy wealth,
Live still; and if thou canst, get more.
     BAR.   Christians; what, or how can I multiply?
Of nought is nothing made.
     I KNIGHT   From nought at first thou camst to little welth,
From little unto more, from more to most:
If your first curse fall heavy on thy head,
And make thee poore and scornd of all the world,
'Tis not our fault, but thy inherent sinne.
     BAR.   What? bring you Scripture to confirm your wrongs?
Preach me not out of my possessions.
Some Jewes are wicked, as all Christians are:
But say the Tribe that I descended of
Were all in generall cast away for sinne,
Shall I be tryed by their transgression?
The man that dealeth righteously shall live:
And which of you can charge me otherwise? . . .

1 KNI.　Grave Governor, list not to his exclames:
Convert his mansion to a Nunnery,　　　　　　　　*[Enter Officers*
His house will harbour many holy Nuns.
　　GOV.　It shall be so: . . .

[Soon Barabas learns from his daughter that this has been done and
that he cannot get into his house to remove the treasure he has
hidden.]

　　BAR.　My gold, my gold, and all my wealth is gone.
You partiall heavens, have I deserv'd this plague?
What will you thus oppose me, lucklesse Starres,
To make me desperate in my poverty?
And knowing me impatient in distresse
Thinke me so mad as I wil hang myselfe.
That I may vanish ore the earth in ayre,
And leave no memory that e're I was.
No, I will live; nor loath I this my life:
And since you leave me in the Ocean thus
To sinke or swim, and put me to my shifts,
I'le rouse my senses, and awake my selfe.
Daughter, I have it: thou perceiv'st the plight
Wherein these Christians have oppressed me:
Be rul'd by me, for in extremitie
We ought to make barre of no policie.
　　ABIG.　Father, what e're it be to injure them
That have so manifestly wronged us,
What will not *Abigall* attempt?
　　BAR.　Why so;
Then thus, thou toldst me they have turn'd my house
Into a Nunnery, and some Nuns are there.
　　ABIG.　I did.
　　BAR.　Then *Abigall*, there must my girle
Intreat the Abbasse to be entertain'd.
　　ABIG.　How, as a Nunne?
　　BAR.　I, Daughter, for Religion
Hides many mischiefes from suspition. . . .

ACT TWO
(lines 640–705)

Enter Barabas with a light

　　BAR.　Thus like the sad presaging Raven that tolls
The sicke mans passeport in her hollow beake,
And in the shadow of the silent night

Doth shake contagion from her sable wings;
Vex'd and tormented runnes poore *Barabas*
With fatall curses towards these Christians.
The incertaine pleasures of swift-footed time
Have tane their flight, and left me in despaire;
And of my former riches rests no more
But bare remembrance; like a souldiers skarre,
That has no further comfort for his maime.
Oh thou that with a fiery piller led'st
The sonnes of *Israel* through the dismall shades,
Light *Abrahams* off-spring; and direct the hand
Of *Abigall* this night; or let the day
Turne to eternall darkenesse after this:
No sleepe can fasten on my watchfull eyes,
Nor quiet enter my distemper'd thoughts,
Till I have answer of my *Abigall*.

Enter Abigall above

ABIG.   Now have I happily espy'd a time
To search the plancke my father did appoint;
And here behold (unseene) where I have found
The gold, the perles, and Jewels which he hid.

BAR.   Now I remember those old womens words,
Who in my wealth wud tell me winters tales,
And speake of spirits and ghosts that glide by night
About the place where Treasure hath bin hid:
And now me thinkes that I am one of those:
For whilst I live, here lives my soules sole hope,
And when I dye, here shall my spirit walke.

ABIG.   Now that my fathers fortune were so good
As but to be about this happy place;
'Tis not so happy: yet when we parted last,
He said he wud attend me in the morne.
Then, gentle sleepe, where e're his bodie rests,
Give charge to *Morpheus* that he may dreame
A golden dreame, and of the sudden walke,
Come and receive the Treasure I have found.

BAR.   *Bueno para todos mi ganado no era:*
As good goe on, as sit so sadly thus.
But stay, what starre shines yonder in the *East*?
The Loadstarre of my life, if *Abigall*.
Who's there?

ABIG.   Who's that?

BAR.   Peace, *Abigal*, 'tis I.

ABIG.   Then father here receive thy happinesse.

BAR.   Hast thou't?   [*Throwes downe bags*

ABIG.   Here, Hast thou't? There's more, and more, and more.

BAR.   Oh my girle,

My gold, my fortune, my felicity;

Strength to my soule, death to mine enemy;

Welcome the first beginner of my blisse:

Oh A[b]igal, Abigal, that I had thee here too,

Then my desires were fully satisfied,

But I will practise thy enlargement thence:

Oh girle, oh gold, oh beauty, oh my blisse!   [*Hugs his bags*

ABIG.   Father, it draweth towards midnight now,

And 'bout this time the Nuns begin to wake;

To shun suspition, therefore, let us part.

BAR.   Farewell my joy, and by my fingers take

A kisse from him that sends it from his soule.

Now *Phoebus* ope the eye-lids of the day,

And for the Raven wake the morning Larke,

That I may hover with her in the Ayre,

Singing ore these, as she does ore her young.

Hermoso placer de los dineros.   [*Exeunt*

ACT TWO
(lines 768–792)

BAR.   In spite of these swine-eating Christians,

(Unchosen Nation, never circumciz'd;

Such as, poore villaines, were ne're thought upon

Till *Titus* and *Vespasian* conquer'd us,)

Am I become as wealthy as I was:

They hop'd my daughter would ha bin a Nun;

But she's at home, and I have bought a house

As great and faire as is the Governors;

And there in spite of *Malta* will I dwell:

Having *Fernezes* hand, whose heart I'le have;

I, and his sonnes too, or it shall goe hard.

I am not of the Tribe of *Levy*, I,

That can so soone forget an injury.

We Jewes can fawne like Spaniels when we please;

And when we grin we bite, yet are our lookes

As innocent and harmelesse as a Lambes.

I learn'd in *Florence* how to kisse my hand,

Heave up my shoulders when they call me dogge,

And ducke as low as any bare-foot Fryar,
Hoping to see them starve upon a stall,
Or else be gather'd for in our Synagogue;
That when the offering-Bason comes to me,
Even for charity I may spit intoo't.
Here comes Don *Lodowicke* the Governor's sonne,
One that I love for his good fathers sake.

. . . .

ACT TWO

(lines 983–1079)

Enter Lodowicke

LOD.   Oh *Barabas* well met;
Where is the Diamond you told me of?

BAR.   I have it for you, Sir; please you walke in with me:
What, ho, *Abigall*; open the doore I say.

Enter Abigall

ABIG.   In good time, father, here are letters come
From *Ormus*, and the Post stayes here within.

BAR.   Give me the letters, daughter, doe you heare?
Entertaine *Lodowicke* the Governors sonne
With all the curtesie you can affoord;
Provided, that you keepe your Maiden-head.
Use him as if he were a *Philistine*.   [*Aside*
Dissemble, sweare, protest, vow to love him,
He is not of the seed of Abraham.
I am a little busie, Sir, pray pardon me.
Abigall, bid him welcome for my sake.

ABIG.   For your sake and his own he's welcome hither.

BAR.   Daughter, a word more; kisse him, speake him faire,
And like a cunning Jew so cast about,
That ye be both made sure e're you come out.

ABIG.   Oh father, Don *Mathias* is my love.

BAR.   I know it: yet I say make love to him;
Doe, it is requisite it should be so.
Nay on my life it is my Factors hand,
But goe you in, I'le thinke upon the account:—
The account is made, for *Lodowicke* dyes.
My Factor sends me word a Merchant's fled
That owes me for a hundred Tun of Wine:
I weigh it thus much; I have wealth enough.

For now by this has he kist *Abigall*;
And she vowes love to him, and hee to her.
As sure as heaven rain'd *Manna* for the *Jewes*,
So sure shall he and Don *Mathias* dye:
His father was my chiefest enemie.—

Enter Mathias

Whither goes Don *Mathias*? stay a while.
    MATH.   Whither but to my faire love *Abigall*?
    BAR.   Thou know'st, and heaven can witnesse it is true,
That I intend my daughter shall be thine.
    MATH.   I, *Barabas*, or else thou wrong'st me much.
    BAR.   Oh, heaven forbid I should have such a thought.
Pardon me though I weepe; the Governors sonne
Will, whether I will or no, have *Abigall*:
He sends her letters, bracelets, jewels, rings.
    MATH.   Does she receive them?
    BAR.   Shee? No, *Mathias*, no, but sends them backe,
And when he comes, she lockes her selfe up fast;
Yet through the key-hole will he talke to her,
While she runs to the window looking out
When you should come and hale him from the doore.
    MATH.   Oh treacherous *Lodowicke*!
    BAR.   Even now as I came home, he slipt me in,
And I am sure he is with *Abigall*.
    MATH.   I'le rouze him thence.
    BAR.   Not for all *Malta*, therefore sheath your sword;
If you love me, no quarrels in my house;
But steale you in, and seeme to see him not;
I'le give him such a warning e're he goes
As he shall have small hopes of *Abigall*.
Away, for here they come.

Enter Lodowicke, Abigall

    MATH.   What, hand in hand, I cannot suffer this.
    BAR.   *Mathias*, as thou lov'st me, not a word.
    MATH.   Well, let it passe, another time shall serve.   [*Exit*
    LOD.   *Barabas*, is not that the widowes sonne?
    BAR.   I, and take heed, for he hath sworne your death.
    LOD.   My death? what, is the base borne peasant mad?
    BAR.   No, no, but happily he stands in feare
Of that which you, I thinke, ne're dreame upon,
My daughter here, a paltry silly girle.
    LOD.   Why, loves she Don *Mathias*?

BAR. Doth she not with her smiling answer you?
ABIG. He has my heart, I smile against my will. [*Aside*
LOD. *Barabas*, thou know'st I have lov'd thy daughter long.
BAR. And so has she done you, even from a child.
LOD. And now I can no longer hold my minde.
BAR. Nor I the affection that I beare to you.
LOD. This is thy Diamond, tell me, shall I have it?
BAR. Win it, and weare it, it is yet unsoyl'd.
Oh but I know your Lordship wud disdaine
To marry with the daughter of a Jew:
And yet I'le give her many a golden crosse
With Christian posies round about the ring.
LOD. 'Tis not thy wealth, but her that I esteeme,
Yet crave I thy consent.
BAR. And mine you have, yet let me talke to her;—
This off-spring of *Cain*, this *Jebusite*
That never tasted of the Passeover,
Nor e're shall see the land of *Canaan*,
Nor our *Messias* that is yet to come, [*Aside*
This gentle Magot *Lodowicke* I meane,
Must be deluded: let him have thy hand,
But keepe thy heart till Don *Mathias* comes.
ABIG. What shall I be betroth'd to *Lodowicke*?
BAR. It's no sinne to deceive a Christian;
For they themselves hold it a principle,
Faith is not to be held with Heretickes;
But all are Hereticks that are not Jewes;
This followes well, and therefore daughter feare not.—

[The two young men kill each other in their jealousy, and Abigall,
revolting against her father, enters the Convent in earnest.]

VI. Probable Source

IL NOVELLINO OF MASUCCIO
translated by W. G. Waters (1895)

The Fourteenth Story

Messer Tommaso Mariconda, my grandfather and a kinsman of
your own, was, as no doubt you know well, a very notable and

elegant cavalier[1], and one who in his time was held in no small repute and esteem in this our city. Now this gentleman, when he was aged and full of years, took vast delight, as is the habit of old men, in telling to his listeners great numbers of very remarkable stories, all of which he would set forth with the most distinguished eloquence, and with the most marvellous memory. And amongst others I well remember to have heard him tell, when I was a very young child, as a real and undoubted fact, how, after the death of King Charles III.,[2] there arose in our kingdom grave and pro-longed warfare provoked by the habitual tyranny of the house of Anjou. At this time there chanced to be in Naples a certain cavalier of the city of Messina, called by name Giuffredi Saccano, a man who was a vehement partisan of the house of Durazzo; and one day when, according to his habit, he was making a round of the city on horseback, he happened to espy at a window a very lovely young damsel, the daughter of an old man, a merchant, whose name at this moment I cannot rightly call to mind. Now, as he was beyond all measure delighted with her appearance, he found himself straightway inflamed with a violent passion for her, and, as the kindly fortune of both of them willed it, the young girl, whose name was Carmosina, perceived in her heart that she had found favour in the eyes of this gentleman. Although she had never before known what manner of thing love might be, and had scarcely ever set eyes on a man, the affair now came to a strange issue, and one almost unheard of before, inasmuch as one flame set those two hearts ablaze at one and the same moment. Indeed, they were both stricken therewith in such fashion that neither one nor the other could move from the spot. Nevertheless, after a certain time had passed, being drawn away by modesty and bashfulness, they parted one from another, though not without sorrow and regret on either side.

Whereupon Messer Giuffredi, being well assured how love had all on a sudden levelled two mortals to the earth with a single blow, and that nothing but the advent of some favourable opportunity was needed to allow them to satisfy their sympathetic desires, gave himself up entirely, as is the habit of lovers, to the task of searching out who the maiden might be, and what was her parentage. At last he discovered who her father was, and learned besides that he was an old man inordinately jealous and avaricious, inasmuch as he was

---

[1] The Mariconda were a noble family both in Naples and Salerno. [W.G.W.]

[2] Charles III. of Durazzo, who deposed and murdered Joanna I., and was the father of Ladislas and Joanna II. The wars referred to waged by Margaret, his widow, on behalf of her son, against Louis of Anjou. Charles died in 1386. [W.G.W.]

possessed by these vices even beyond the common measure of old
age. Furthermore he ascertained that the miser, in order to escape
the prayers of suitors to bestow his only daughter in marriage, was
accustomed to keep her always closely shut up in the house, treating
her the while worse than the meanest servant.

Now the cavalier, having thoroughly informed himself concerning
the things written above, began to feign to be enamoured, now with
one and now with another of the young women who dwelt near to
the damsel's abode, so that he might be able to advance some colour-
able reason for betaking himself into that quarter, and at least
gladdening his eyes with the sight of the walls which contained her,
if he might not see her in person. When this became known he was
set down by many of his friends as nothing better than one who
fills himself with wind,[1] and his cunning sagacity was made a mock
of by all the fools of the place. But he, caring naught for all this, and
following resolutely the purpose he had framed, contrived to contract a close and intimate friendship with the damsel's father, who
was engaged in the traffic of merchandise, purchasing very often
from the old man divers wares at a monstrous price, for which
things he had no need whatever; and over and beyond this, in
order to inveigle the miser still more, he would not fail to bring
other clients every day into the warehouse, so that the old man made
fresh profits without ceasing.

Seeing that the old merchant drew very great advantage from his
traffic with the cavalier and his friends, he let grow up between
himself and the young man so close a friendship and intimacy that
all those who knew him were mightily astonished thereat. However,
after a time the cavalier, being seized with the desire to bring his
scheme to the end he had designed, found opportunity one day to
shut himself up with the old merchant in the warehouse, whereupon he began to address him in the following words: 'For the
reason that I stand in need of counsel and help in my affairs, I feel
that I cannot do better than have recourse to you, whom, on account
of your goodness, I love and reverence as my own father. Wherefore
I will not hold back from laying bare all my secrets to you, and I
will first let you know that, at a season now many years past, I left
my father's house, and since that time I have been detained in this
city on account of the love I bear to your king and of the circumstances of the war. And things have fared with me in such wise that,
up to this present time, no chance has been offered to me of going
back to my country. But now for several days past I have been
urged by my father, who has sent many letters and messengers to

[1] Orig., *non altro che per un pascivento giudicato.*

me concerning this matter, that I should forthwith betake myself to see him once again before the season of his old age shall be sped. As I cannot refuse to hearken to these commands of his or to the voice of filial love, I have made up my mind to go to him straightway, and, after having tarried with him some short period, I intend at once to return hither, and to take up again my service under my lord the king. Now as I know of no one to whom I can more conveniently entrust my confidence on such an occasion than to you, I come to ask you whether you would be willing to take under your charge certain possessions of mine, and to keep the same for me till the time of my return. And above all this, the chief concern I feel is on account of a certain female slave of mine, one whom I am most unwilling and aggrieved to sell by reason of her worth and goodness. But, on the other hand, finding myself sorely beset by the lack of thirty ducats, and being kept back by my honour from requesting any friend of mine to make me a loan so trifling, I have determined, finding myself placed in this doubtful position, rather to take security of you alone in this business, and to give you the trouble to advance the sum aforesaid, leaving in your hands the slave as a pledge for the same. If at any time before I shall return you may find an opportunity of selling her for the price of seventy ducats, which is the sum I gave for her, I will beg you to deal with her as if she were your own.'

The old man, who in sooth was far more of a miser than of a sage, began to busy his brains in canvassing and considering what possible profit might come to him if he should consent to do the cavalier the service that was demanded, and, without detecting aught therein of the nature of fraud or debating the affair further with himself, made answer in these words: 'See here, Messer Giuffredi, the love which I bear towards you is so great, that I assuredly could never bring myself to answer no to any request you might make of me, supposing that the thing demanded lay within my power to perform, and for this reason I am strongly disposed to accommodate you with whatever sum of money you may want for your purposes. And besides this, I will keep the slave on your behalf, in order that you may not suffer ill through having to sell her. Then, when you shall have come back here safe and sound—supposing always that the slave should have done what was needed of her—I will settle my account with you in such fashion that you will find you could not have been better treated even if you had been my own son.'

The cavalier, rejoicing greatly at the answer he received from the old man, then replied to him saying, 'In sooth I did not expect any other answer from you, and it seems to me that to render you thanks therefor would be superfluous, but may our Lord God grant that I may be able to lay before you clearly the product of this our friendship to our common profit and advantage.' And after he had thus brought his discourse to an end he took leave of the old man, and having mounted his horse according to his wont, he made his way along the street in which was the lodging of his lady-love; and, as he passed along, by the working of the fate which ruled the lives of the one and the other, he espied by chance the form of the damsel partially revealed at the casement of her chamber—a boon granted perchance for the satisfaction of both of them. Then drawing herself back from the window like one bewildered, she cast down upon him a sweet and piteous glance; whereupon he, looking cautiously around him and observing no one in the neighbourhood, and conscious that he had no time to spare for the making of long speeches, said to her, 'My Carmosina, be comforted, forasmuch as I have at last found a means by which I shall be able to deliver you from your prison.' And having thus spoken he went his way, God speeding him.

Meantime the young damsel, who had understood quite clearly the purport of her lover's words, was in no small measure comforted therewith, and although it did not enter her head to hope that from such a speech could ensue any working which might make for her advantage, nevertheless the bare hope roused in her breast thereby gave her heart, though she knew not wherefore. The cavalier, when he had returned to his house, called his slave into his presence and said, 'My good Anna, the business which we discussed and arranged is already set in order, wherefore see that you prove wary and prudent in the affair which you will have to bring to pass.' And although the slave was already well instructed in all the arts and methods she would be called upon to employ, nevertheless the cavalier caused her to rehearse several times afresh the concerted plan of their subtle stratagem.

When a few days had elapsed, and when he had set everything duly in order, the cavalier went once more to the old merchant and addressed him in the following words: 'Alas! how irksome it is to me to withdraw myself for ever so limited a time from your friendship, which has been so precious and so profitable to me. Of this he who truly knows all our secrets will be a witness. Nevertheless, as it is convenient for my purpose that I should take my departure this very night, for the reason that all preparations for my passage are now complete, I have come hither to take my leave of you, and besides this to fetch the money which I begged you to advance me as a loan. Also I am come to bid you send for the chattel you wot of.' The old man, who could have prayed God for nothing better, was overjoyed at this news, seeing that he had begun to feel some apprehension lest the cavalier might have repented him of his proposal. Whereupon, without further delay he counted out the thirty ducats, and, having done this, he sent to fetch the slave, who forthwith went to his house, taking with her certain small and delicate things which were the property of the cavalier.

Now when the evening was at last come, Messer Giuffredi, accompanied by the old merchant and certain others of his friends, betook himself to the seashore, and then, having embraced them all and bidden them farewell, he embarked on board a light galley which was about to set sail for Messina. But when the aforesaid ship had fared a short distance from the port of Naples, he made the shipmen place at his service a small boat (which matter in sooth he had already arranged with the captain), and in this he had himself conveyed to Procida.[1] Having come there, he found lodging in the house of a certain friend of his, and there he tarried until three days had passed. On the night of the third day, when the hour had come which he had appointed with the slave and with other associates of his, Sicilian fellows keen to act and well set towards any deed of dangerous adventure, he returned to Naples and made his way into the city in very cautious wise. Having come there, he took secret lodging, together with his associates, in a certain house hard by that of the old merchant—a dwelling which, through the ill times brought about by the wars, was at that period quite void of occupants, and there they all abode hidden and silent until the following day came.

In the meantime the cunning and quick-witted slave had gone to the merchant's house, and had there met with most friendly and joyful reception from Carmosina. The last-named, knowing full well from whom the woman had come, in a brief space of time became on very intimate terms with her; whereupon the slave, spurred on by remembering how short was the time in which her purpose would have to be accomplished, laid bare to the damsel point by point the reasons for which she had come thither, using the while the most consummate arts and the most skilful discourse, and furthermore telling her exactly what her master had settled with her concerning the matter in question, and heartening the damsel little by little by the arguments she brought forward to carry out in daring fashion the enterprise to its issue, so as to secure for herself and her lover a lasting time of peace and happiness.

---

[1] An island between Ischia and the mainland.

The young girl, who for many reasons was even more strongly minded than the cavalier towards this end, did not suffer the slave to waste more time in adding one lengthy argument to another, but told her straightway that she was fully prepared to consent to every one of the proposals just made by her, and likewise to follow all the directions laid down by the cavalier, whom she herself loved as she loved her own life.

To these words the slave replied: 'My daughter, if it should happen that you have a few little things of your own which you would like to carry away with you, I would counsel you to get the same in order at once, seeing that our plan will have to be put in execution this very night. You must know also that my master and his servant and certain other companions of his are now concealed in the house next door to us. This fact I have learnt from a signal which I have this day seen displayed from the house in question, and, as you well know, it would be an easy task to get into it from our paved courtyard.' When the young girl heard how short was the time before her flight, she gave the slave a hundred kisses, and told her that she possessed nothing of her own, either great or small, which she could take away with her, but that she had made up her mind to abstract from the store of her avaricious old father a much greater sum of money than anyone could have reckoned sufficient for her dowry.

When they had brought the matter to this conclusion, and when the midnight hour had come, and the old man and everyone else in the house were fast asleep, Carmosina and the slave broke open a chest and took out therefrom jewels and money of a value exceeding one thousand five hundred ducats, and, having bestowed these safely away, they silently crossed over the courtyard and came to the spot where the cavalier was awaiting them. He, with the greatest joy, took the young girl in his arms and covered her lips with ardent kisses. Further pleasure they did not enjoy, seeing how precarious was their present abiding-place; wherefore the whole company set out on their way, and took the road which led to the seashore. Having cautiously issued from the city through a breach in the wall behind the slaughter-houses, they found their bark ready armed and fully equipped for a swift passage, and ready to cast off at a moment's notice. Whereupon they all went on board the same, and, having dipped their oars in the water, they found themselves at Ischia before many hours had elapsed. Then the cavalier and all those accompanying him presented themselves before the lord of that place, who chanced to be a particular friend of Messer Giuffredi, and one indeed who had been made privy to the whole affair. From this gentleman they all received most kindly and hospitable reception, and while they were abiding there the lovers, deeming that they were now upon safe ground, partook of the first and sweetest delights of their reciprocal love, and rejoiced the one as well as the other with no less joy over the circumstances of their flight.

In the meantime the old father, when the daylight came, first found that neither his daughter nor the slave whom he had taken in pledge were in the house, and then became aware that he had been robbed of his money and of his jewels to boot, and for the last-named loss he felt no less grief than for the first; indeed, how sore were his tears and lamentations each one may judge for himself. Moreover, no one need wonder to hear that he found his affliction so sharp and cruel that he was over and over again fain to hang himself by the neck therefor. And thus, overcome by his losses and the shame that had been put upon him, he spent his days in continual weeping shut up in his house.

Meantime the enamoured couple in Ischia lived their lives in the greatest delight, and by reason of their constant intercourse it came to pass that the fair damsel became with child. Which thing, when the cavalier came to know it, caused him the greatest delight, and he forthwith made a resolve to treat her with a worthy spirit of generosity, and at the same time to give full satisfaction to God, to the world, and to himself. Wherefore, having despatched a message through the intervention of the lord of Ischia to the father of Carmosina and to divers of his own kinsfolk, these aforesaid all came to Ischia, and, when they were all there assembled, and after certain contracts had been duly signed, the cavalier by the favour of the king and with the universal approval and general rejoicing of the people of Naples, took Carmosina for his lawful wife. Thus, having exchanged the secret sport of Venus for the career of married folk, they went back to their Neapolitan home and passed their days in great happiness as long as they both lived. In this manner it may be seen how the jealous, miserly, and foolish old man atoned for the deed after all the damage had been done.

MASUCCIO

The fortunate ending which I have let ensue to the story I have just completed will, I make little doubt, give cause to many of those who may read the same to hold up for approbation with unbounded praises the great foresight and sagacity of the young girl, who, marking how she was thus kept in this wretched plight and held to be meaner than the meanest hireling, contrived to procure for herself so seemly and valiant a lover; and, besides this, to obtain out of the hoard of her miserly old father a greater sum of money than would have been given to her as a dower, becoming in the end the wife of her lover with honour and happiness. Now the things above written, although in sooth they may be laid less to her charge than to that of Love, who awakened her slumbering wits and thereby taught her how to bring to an issue with the greatest courage those lessons which he himself had taught her, I for my part do not intend to praise, nor do I intend to advise any woman, however lavish may be the promises of her lover, to imitate Carmosina in this matter, and suffer herself to be carried away in such fashion. For, admitting that the issue of the affair was a fortunate one for our Carmosina, it must nevertheless be borne in mind that the tempers of men are not all of the same quality and inclination, and that the course of action which the cavalier followed, urged thereto by his innate goodness and uncommon virtue, may perchance be censured as faulty and poor-spirited by others, who are so minded that, if they should find themselves in a similar case, would plume themselves upon having done a valiant deed of prowess when they should have robbed their sweethearts of the flower of their virginity and afterwards left them in scorn to their disgrace. And even though each individual girl should feel well assured that in her own case the end must needs be a fortunate one, I still judge that she would be taking the wiser part who might follow a course opposite to that adopted by Carmosina, forasmuch as it is by far better never to put oneself in peril of meeting ruin at the hands of another, than to escape the danger though running near the precipice.

And furthermore I am persuaded that it is a fact to be controverted by no one that the inordinate suspicion combined with the senile avarice of the old merchant were the real causes of the flout that was put upon him, and of the heavy loss which accompanied it. If afterwards there followed a reparation of the same in the creditable issue of the matter, it was assuredly not because the execrable vices of the old man did not exhibit their poisonous results, which results seem to me so monstrous and horrible that I am driven, out of sheer confusion, to cease to talk of them.

VII. Analogue

From CONFESSIO AMANTIS
by John Gower
Book V[1]

[In Book V the Confessor warns his pupil Amans (with the aid of exemplary stories) against Covetousness, which is particularly odious when it occurs among courtiers.]

... The man, whiche hath his londe tilled,
Awaiteth nought more redely
The harvest, than they gredily   2240
Ne maken thanne warde and wacche
Where they the profit mighten cacche.
And yet full oft it falleth so,
As men may sene among hem tho,
That he which most coveiteth fast
Hath leest avauntage atte last.
For whan fortune is there ayein,[2]
Though he coveite, it is in vaine;
The happes ben nought alle liche,[3]
One is made pouer, an other riche,   2250
The court to some it doth profite,
And some ben ever in o[4] plite.
And yet they both aliche sore
Coveite, but fortune is more
Unto that o part favourable;
And though it be nought resonable,
This thing a man may sene al day,
Wherof that I thee telle may
After ensample in remembrance,
How every man may take his chaunce   2260
Or of richesse or of pouerte,
How so it stonde of the deserte.[5]
Here is nought every thing acquit,

---

[1] Text from Henry Morley's edition (1889).
[2] against, contrary.   [3] chances ... alike.
[4] one.   [5] Whatever his deserts may be.

For oft a man may se this yit
That who best doth lest thank shal have;
It helpeth nought, the world to crave,
Whiche out of reule and of mesure
Hath ever stonde in aventure
Als well in court as elles where;
And how in olde daies there   2270
It stood so as the thinges felle,
I thenke[1] a tale for to telle.
　　In a cronique this I rede:
About a kinge as it must nede
There was of knightes and squiers
Great route and eke of officers.
Some of long time him hadden served
And thoughten that they have deserved
Avauncement and gone withoute;
And some also ben of the route   2280
That comen but a while agone,
And they avaunced were anone.
These olde men upon this thing
So as they durst ayein the king
Among hem self compleignen ofte:
But there is nothing said so softe,
That it ne cometh out at last.
The king it wist anone als fast
As he which was of high prudence.
He schope therfore an evidence   2290
Of hem[2] that pleignen in that cas,
To knowe in whose default it was.
And all within his owne entent,
That no man wiste what it ment
Anone he let two cofres make
Of one semblaunce and of o make,
So lich that no life thilke throwe
That one may fro that other knowe.
They were into his chambre brought,
But no man wot why they be wrought.   2300
And netheles the king hath bede,
That they be set in prive stede,
As he that was of wisdom sligh.[3]
Whan he therto his time sigh[4]

---

[1] intend.　　　　[2] arranged . . . an illustration for them.
[3] cunning.　　　[4] saw.

All privelich, that none it wist,
His owne hondes that o kist
Of fine golde and of fine perrie.[1]
The which out of his tresorie
Was take, anone he filde full,
That other cofre of strawe and mull[2]   2310
With stones meind[3] he filde also.
Thus be they fulle bothe two.
So that erliche upon a day
He bad withinne where he lay
There shoulde be to-fore his bedde
A borde up set and faire spredde.
And than he let the cofres fet,
Upon the borde and did hem set.[4]
He knew the names well of tho,
The whiche ayein him grucche[5] so   2320
Both of his chambre and of his halle,
Anone and sende for hem alle
And saide to hem in this wise:
      'There shall no man his hap despise;
I wot well ye have longe served,
And God wot what ye have deserved.
But if it is along on[6] me
Of that ye unavaunced be
Or elles it belonge on you,
The sothe shall be proved now   2330
To stoppe with your evil worde.
Lo here two cofres on the borde,
Chese which you list of bothe two
And witeth well, that one of tho
Is with tresor so full begon
That if ye happe therupon
Ye shal be riche men for ever.
Now chese and take whiche you is lever.[7]
But be well ware, er that ye take,
For of that one I undertake   2340
There is no maner good therinne
Whereof ye mighten profit winne.
Now goth to-gider of one assent
And taketh your advisement,[8]

[1] precious stones.   [2] dirt, rubbish.
[3] mingled.   [4] And had them set upon the board.
[5] grumbled.   [6] because of.
[7] dearer.   [8] take due consideration.

For but I you this day avaunce
It stant upon your owne chaunce
All only in default of grace:
So shall be shewed in this place
Upon you alle well and fine,
That no defaulte shall be mine.'   2350
    They knelen all and with one vois
The king they thonken of this chois.
And after that they up arise
And gon aside and hem avise
And atte laste they accorde,
Wherof her tale to recorde
To what issue they be falle
A knight shall speke for hem alle.
He kneleth down unto the king
And saith, that they upon this thing   2360
Or for to winne or for to lese
Ben all avised for to chese.
    Tho toke this knight a yerd[1] on hond
And goth there as the cofres stond
And with th'assent of everychone
He laith his yerde upon one
And saith the king how thilke same
They chese in reguerdon[2] by name,
And preith him that they might it have.
The king, which wold his honour save,   2370
When he hath herd the comun vois,
Hath graunted hem her owne chois
And toke hem therupon the key.
But for he wolde it were seie[3]
What good they have as they suppose,
He bad anone the cofre unclose,—
Which was fulfilled with straw and stones,
Thus be they served all at ones.
This king than in the same stede
Anone that other cofre undede,   2380
Where as they sighen great richesse
Wel more than they couthen gesse.
'Lo,' saith the king, 'now may ye see,
That there is no defaulte in me,
Forthy my self I woll acquite
And bereth ye your owne wite[4]

---

[1] stick.   [2] reward.   [3] might be seen.   [4] blame.

Of that fortune hath you refused.'
Thus was this wise king excused,
And they lefte of her evil speche
And mercy of her king beseche.   2390
         Somdele to this matere like
I finde a tale, how Frederike,
Of Rome that time emperour,
Herde, as he went, a great clamour
Of two beggers upon the way,
That one of hem began to say:
'Ha lord, wel may the man be riche,
Whom that a king list for to riche.'
That other said: 'No thinge so,
But he is riche and well bego,   2400
To whom that God wol sende wele.'
And thus they maden wordes fele,
Wherof this lord hath hede nome
And did hem bothe for to come
To the paleis where he shall ete,
And bad ordeigne for her mete
Two pastees which he let do make;
A capon in that one was bake,
And in that other, for to winne,
Of floreins all that may withinne   2410
He let do put a great richesse,
And even aliche as man may gesse
Outward they were bothe two.
This begger was commaunded tho,
He that which held him to the king,
That he first chese upon this thing.
He sigh[1] hem, but he felt hem nought,
So that upon his owne thought
He chese the capon and forsoke
That other, which his felaw toke.   2420
But whan he wist how that it ferde,
He said aloud, that men it herde:
'Now have I certainly conceived,
That he may lightly be deceived
That tristeth unto mannes helpe.
But wel is him, that God wol helpe,
For he stant on the siker[2] side,
Whiche elles shulde go beside.

---

[1] saw.   [2] sure.

I se my felaw wel recouer,
And I mot dwelle stille pouer.'   2430
Thus spake the begger his entent,
And pouer he cam and pouer he went,
Of that he hath richesse sought
His infortune[1] it wolde nought.
So may it shew in sondry wise
Betwene Fortune and Covetise
The chaunce is cast upon a dee,[2]
But yet full oft a man may see
Inough of suche netheles
Which ever put hem self in pres   2440
To get hem good, and yet they faile.

VIII. Probable Source

From GESTA ROMANORUM

The Old English Versions of the Gesta Romanorum: ed. Sir F. Madden (Roxburghe Club) London (1838).[3]

Story LXVI

ANCELMUS THE EMPEROUR

ANCELMUS regnyd Emperour in the cite of Rome, and he weddid to wife the kynges doghter of Jerusalem, the whiche was a faire woman, and long dwelte in his company; but she never conceyvid, ne brought forthe frute, and therof were lordis gretly heveid and sory. Happinge in a certeyne evenynge, as he walkide after his soper in a faire greene, and thoghte of alle the worlde, and specially that he had noon heyr, and howe that the kynge of Naplis strongly therfore noyed him eche yere; and so, whenne it was nyght, he went to bedde, and tooke a slep, and dremyd this. He sawe the firmament in his most clernesse, and moore cler than it was wonyd to be, and the mone was more pale; and on a party of the mone was a faire colourid brid, and beside hire stoode too bestis, the whiche

---

[1] ill fortune.   [2] dice.
[3] Also, re-edited, in *Early English Versions of the Gesta Romanorum*, ed. S. J. H. Herrtage, *EETS*.Extra S. 33, 1879.

norisshid the brid with hire heete and brethe. After this come
diverse bestis and briddis fleynge, and thei song so swetly, that the
Emperour was with the songe awakid. Thenne on the morowe the
Emperour hadde gret merveile of this swevene, and callid to him
divinours, and lordis of alle the empire, and said to hem, 'Deere
frendis, tellithe me what is the interpretacione of my swevene, and
I shall wel rewarde you; and but if ye do, ye shulle be dede.' And
then thai saide, 'Lord, shew to us thi dreme, and we shulle telle the
the interpretacione of it.' And then the Emperour tolde hem as is
said before, from bigynnynge to endynge. And then thei were glad,
and with a gret gladnesse spake to him, and saide, 'Ser, this was a
goode swevene; for the firmament that thou sawe so clere is the
empire, the which hens forwarde shalle be in prosperitie; the paale
mone is the empresse, the whiche hath conceivid, and for hire con-
ceivinge is the more discolourid; the litille bryd is the faire sone
whom the emperesse shalle brynge forthe, when tyme comithe; the
too bestis ben riche men and wise men, that shulle be obedient to thi
childe; the other bestis ben other folke, that never made homage,
and nowe shulle be subiet to thi sone; the briddis, that songe so
swetly, is the empire of Rome, that shalle joy of thi childis burthe;
and, sir, this is the interpretacione of your drem.' When the empresse
hurde this, she was glad y-nowe; and soone she bare a faire sone, and
therof was maade moche joy. And when the kynge of Naplis hurde
that, he thowte to him selfe, 'I have long tyme holdyne werre ayenst
the Emperour, and it may not be but that it wol be tolde to his sone,
when that he comythe to his fulle age, howe that I have foght alle
my lyfe ayenst his fadir. Ye,' thowte he, 'he is nowe a childe, and it is
goode that I procour for pese, that I may have rest of him, when he
is in his best, and I in my worste.' So he wrote letteres to the Emperour, for pese to be had; and the Emperour seynge that he dude
that more for cause of drede than of love, he sent him worde ayen,
and saide, that he would make him surte of pese, with condicione
that he wolde be in his servitute, and yelde him homage alle his
life, eche yer. Thenne the kynge callid his conseil, and askid of hem
what was best to do; and the lordis of his kyngdome saide, that it
was goode to folowe the Emperour in his wille. 'In the first ye aske
of him surte of pese; to that we say thus, thou hast a doughter, and
he hathe a sone; let matrimony be maad bytwene hem, and so
ther shalle be good sikirnesse; also it is goode to make him homage,
and yelde him rentes.' Thenne the kynge sent worde to the Emperour, and saide, that he wolde fulfille his wille in all poyntys,
and yive his doghter to his sone in wife, yf that it were plesing to
him. This answere likid wele the Emperor, but he sent worde ayen,

that he wolde not assent to matrimony, but if that his doghter hadde
bene a virgine fro hire nativite. The kinge was herewith hiely glad,
for his doghter was suche a cleene virgyn. So letteres were maade of
this covenaunt; and he maade a shippe to be ordeyned, to lede his
doghter with a certayne of knyghtis and ladeys to the Emperour,
to be mareyd with his sone. And whenne thei were in the shippe,
and hadde far passid fro the londe, ther rose up a great horribille
tempest, and draynt alle that were in the ship, except the mayde.
Thenne the mayde sette all hire hope strongly in God; and at the
laste, the tempest sesid; but their folowide strongly a gret whale, to
devowre this maide. And whenne she sawe that, she moche dradde;
and whan the nyght com, the maide dredynge that the whale
wolde have swolewide the ship, smot fire at a stone, and hadde gret
plente of fire; and as longe as the fire laste, the whale dorst come no
nere, but abowte cockis crowe the mayde, for gret vexacione that
she hadde with the tempest; felle on slepe, and in hire slep the fire
went out; and when it was out, the whale com nye, and swolewid
bothe the ship and the mayde. And when the mayde felte that she
was in the wombe of a whale, she smot, and maade gret fire, and
grevously woundid the whale with a litille knyfe, in so moche that
he drowe to the londe, and deyde; for that is the kynde, to drawe
to the londe when he shall dye. And in this tyme there was an erle
namyd Pirius, and he walkid in his disport by the see, and afore
him he sawe the whale come towarde the lond. He gaderid gret
helpe and strenght of men; [and] with diverse instrementis thei
smote the whale in every party of hym. And when the dameselle
hurde the gret strokys, she cryde with an hye voys, and saide,
'Gentille siris, havithe pite of me, for I am the dowter of a kynge,
and a mayde have y-ben sithe I was borne.' Whenne the erle hurde
this, he merveilid gretly, and openyd the whale, and tooke out the
dameselle. Thenne the maide told by ordre how that she was a
kyngys dowter, and howe she loste hire goodis in the see, and how
she sholde be mareyd to the sone of the Emperour. And when the
erle hurde theise wordis, he was glad, and helde the maide with
him a gret while, till tyme that she was wele confortide; and thenne
he sent hire solemply to the Emperour. And whenne he sawe hire
comynge, and hurde that she had tribulacions in the see, he hadde
gret compassione for hire in his herte, and said to hire, 'Goode
dameselle, thou hast sufferid moche angre for the love of my soone,
neverthelesse, if that thou be worthi to have him, I shalle sone
preve.' The Emperour let make iii. vesselles, and the first was of
clene goolde, and full of precious stonys owtewarde, and withinne
fulle of deede bonys; and it hade a superscripcione in theise wordis,

Thei that chese me shulle fynde in me that thei servyde. The secunde vesselle was alle of cleene silver, and fulle of precious stonys; and outwarde it had this superscripsione, *Thei that chesithe me, shulle fynde in me that nature and kynde desirithe.* And the third vesselle was of leed, and with inne was fulle of precious stonys; and with oute was sette[1] this scripture, *Thei that chese me, shulle fynde [in] me that God hathe disposid.* Theise iii. vessellys tooke the Emperour, and shewid the maide, seyinge, 'Lo! deere dameselle, here ben thre worthi vessellys, and thou chese on of theise, wherein is profit, and owithe to be chosyne, thenne thou shalt have my sone to husbonde; and if thou chese that that is not profitable to the, ne to noone othir, forsothe thenne thou shalt not have hym.' Whenne the dowter hurde this, and sawe the thre vessellys, she lifte up hire yene to God, and saide, 'Thowe, Lord, that knowist alle thinges, graunt me thy grace nowe in the nede of this tyme, *scil.* that I may chese at this tyme, wherthorowe I may joy the sone of the Emperour, and have him to husbond.' Thenne she byhelde the first vesselle, that was so sotilly maad, and radde the superscripcione; and then she thowte, what have I deservid for to have so precious a vesselle, and thogh it be never so gay with oute, I not howe fowle it is with inne; so she tolde the Emperour that she wolde by no way chese that. Thenne she lokid to the secunde, that was of silver, and radde the super-scripcione; and thenne she saide, 'My nature and kynde askithe but dilectacions of the flessh; forsothe ser,' quod she, 'and I refuse this.' Then she lokid to the third, that was of leede, and radde the superscripcione; and then she saide, 'Sothely, God disposide never iville; forsothe that which God hathe disposid wolle I take and chese.' And whenne the Emperour sawe that, he saide, 'Goode dameselle, opyne nowe that vesselle, and see what thou fondyne.' And whenne it was openyd, it was fulle of golde and precious stoonys. And thenne the Emperour saide to hire ayen, 'Dameselle, thou hast wisely chosen, and wonne my sone to thyn husbonde.' So the day was sette of hire bredeale, and gret joy was maade; and the sone regnyde after the decese of the fadir, the whiche maad faire ende. Ad quod nos perducat! Amen.

[1] insculpt (Robinson) cf. *MV*.II.7.57.

BIBLIOGRAPHY

1. General Works relating to Sources and Analogues

A Companion to Shakespeare Studies. Cambridge, 1934.

ADAMS, J. Q. *A Life of William Shakespeare.* London, 1923.

ANDERS, H. R. D. *Shakespeare's Books.* Berlin, 1904.

ARBER, E. ed. *A Transcript of the Registers of the Company of Stationers of London 1554–1640,* 5 vols. London, 1875–94.

BAKER, E. A. *The History of the English Novel: The Elizabethan Age and After.* London, 1929.

BALDWIN, T. W. *William Shakspere's Petty School.* Urbana, 1943.

— *William Shakespeare's Small Latine and Lesse Greeke.* Urbana, 1944.

— *William Shakespeare's Five-Act Structure.* Urbana, 1947.

Bibliographical Society Publications. London, 1902–

BOAS, F. S. *University Drama in the Tudor Age.* Oxford, 1914.

BOND, R. W. ed. *John Lyly, the Complete Works.* 3 vols. Oxford, 1902.

— ed. *Early Plays from the Italian.* Oxford, 1911.

BRADBROOK, M. C. *Themes and Conventions of Elizabethan Tragedy.* Cambridge, 1935.

BROOKE, C. F. T. *The Works of Christopher Marlowe.* Oxford, 1910.

— *Essays on Shakespeare and other Elizabethans.* London, 1949.

BUSH, D. *Mythology and the Renaissance Tradition in English Poetry.* Minneapolis and London, 1932.

BYRNE, M. ST CLARE. *Anthony Munday and his Books,* in Bibliog. Soc. Trans. N.S. I.4. 1921; and *Library* 4th Ser. I. 1921.

CHAMBERS, E. K. *The Elizabethan Stage.* 4 vols. Oxford, 1923.

— *The Medieval Stage.* 2 vols. Oxford, 1903.

— *William Shakespeare.* 2 vols. Oxford, 1930.

CHARLTON, H. B. *Shakespearian Comedy.* London, 1938.

— *Shakespearian Tragedy.* Cambridge, 1948.

— *The Senecan Tradition in Renaissance Tragedy.* Manchester, 1946. (Also in *Poetical Works of Sir W. Alexander,* ed. Kastner and Charlton. 2 vols. Manchester, 1921.)

COLLIER, J. P. *Shakespeare's Library.* 2 vols. 1843 (texts).

— and HAZLITT, W. C. *Shakespeare's Library.* 2nd edn. 6 vols. 1875 (texts).

COLLINS, J. C. *Studies in Shakespeare.* London, 1904.

COLLISON-MORLEY, L. *Shakespeare in Italy.* Stratford, 1916.

CRAIG, HARDIN. *The Enchanted Glass.* Oxford, 1950.

— *An Interpretation of Shakespeare.* New York, 1948.

CREIZENACH, W. *The English Drama in the Age of Shakespeare.* London, 1916.

DOWDEN, E. Introductory studies of plays and poems in the Oxford edition of Shakespeare. 3 vols. 1936–40.

— *Essays Modern and Elizabethan.* London, 1910.

EBISCH, W., and SCHÜCKING, L. L. *A Shakespeare Bibliography.* Oxford, 1931. *Supplement,* 1937.

ESDAILE, A. *A List of English Tales and Prose Romances printed before 1740.* London, Bibliog. Soc., 1912.

FARNHAM, W. *The Medieval Heritage of Elizabethan Tragedy.* 1936.

FEUILLERAT, A. *John Lyly.* Cambridge, 1910.

FRIPP. E. I. *Master Richard Quyny, bailiff of Stratford and friend of William Shakespeare.* Oxford, 1924.

— *Shakespeare, Man and Artist.* London, 1938.

— 'Shakespeare's Use of Ovid's *Metamorphoses*' in *Shakespeare Studies, Biographical and Literary.* London, 1930.

GREG, W. W. *Pastoral Poetry and Pastoral Drama.* London, 1906.

— *Henslowe's Diary.* 2 parts. London, 1904, 1908.

— *The Editorial Problem in Shakespeare.* London, 1942.

GRILLO, E. N. G. *Shakespeare and Italy.* Glasgow, 1949.

GUTTMANN, S. *The Foreign Sources of Shakespeare's Works: An Annotated Bibliography of the Commentary written on this subject between 1904 and 1940, together with Lists of certain Translations available to Shakespeare.* New York, 1947.

HARBAGE, A. *Shakespeare and the Rival Traditions.* New York, 1951

HAZLITT, W. C. ed. R. Dodsley's *Select Collection of Old English Plays.* 15 vols. London, 1874–6.

— *Shakespeare's Jest Books.* 2nd edn. 3 vols. London, 1881.

HERFORD, C. H. *Studies in the Literary Relations of England and Germany in the Sixteenth Century.* Cambridge, 1886.

HIGHET, G. *The Classical Tradition.* Oxford, 1951.

JUSSERAND, J. J. *The English Novel in the time of Shakespeare.* 1890.

KELSO, RUTH. *The Doctrine of the English Gentleman in the Sixteenth Century*. Urbana, 1929.

LAWRENCE, W. J. *Shakespeare's Workshop*. Oxford, 1928.

LAWRENCE, W. W. *Shakespeare's Problem Comedies*. New York, 1931.

LEE, SIR S. *A Life of William Shakespeare*. London, 1904.

— *The French Renaissance in England*. Oxford, 1910.

— *Elizabethan and other Essays*. Oxford, 1929.

LEWIS, C. S. *English Literature in the Sixteenth Century, excluding Drama*. Oxford, 1954.

MACCALLUM, M. W. *Shakspeare's Roman Plays and their Background*. London, 1910.

MAGNUS, L. *English Literature in its Foreign Relations, 1300–1800.*

Malone Society Publications. Oxford, 1907–

MATTHEWS, B. *Shakespeare as a Playwright*. New York and London, 1913.

MANLY, J. M. *Specimens of the Pre-Shakespearean Drama*. 2 vols. Boston, 1897–8.

MATTHIESSEN, F. O. *Translation, an Elizabethan Art*. Boston, 1931.

OWEN, S. G. 'Ovid and Romance' in *English Literature and the Classics*, ed. G. S. Gordon. Oxford, 1912.

QUILLER-COUCH, SIR A. *Shakespeare's Workmanship*. London, 1927.

REBORA, P. *L'Italia nel dramma inglese, 1558–1642*. Milan and London, 1925.

ROBERTSON, J. M. *The Shakespeare Canon*. 4 parts. London, 1922–30.

— *The Genuine in Shakespeare*. London, 1930.

ROOT, A. K. *Classical Mythology in Shakespeare*. New York, 1903.

SCHELLING, F. E. *Elizabethan Drama (1558–1642)*. 2 vols. London, 1908, 1911.

SCHOELL, F. L. *L'Hellénisme français en Angleterre à la fin de la Renaissance. Rev. de Litt. Comp.* 1925. 193–238.

SCOTT, M. A. *Elizabethan Translations from the Italian. PMLA X* (N.S.3) 1895, 249–93; *XI* (N.S. 4) 1896, 377–484; *XIV* (N.S. 7) 1899, 465–571.

— *Elizabethan Translations from the Italian*. Boston, 1916.

Shakespeare's England. 2 vols. Oxford, 1917.

SIMONINI, R. C. *Italian Scholarship in Renaissance England*. Chapel Hill, 1951.

SIMPSON, P. *Studies in Elizabethan Drama*. Oxford, 1955.

SIMPSON, R. *The School of Shakespeare*. 2 vols. London, 1878.

SISSON, C. J. *The Lost Plays of Shakespeare's Age*. Cambridge, 1936.

SMITH, H. 'Pastoral Influence in the English Drama', *PMLA* 12 (N.S. 5) 1897, pp. 355ff.

STARNES, D. T. 'Shakespeare and Elyot's *Governour*'; in *Studies in English*. Univ. of Texas. 7. 1927, pp. 112–32.

STEVENSON, D. L. *The Love-Game Comedy*. New York, 1946.

STOLL, E. E. *Shakespeare Studies*. New York, 1927.

— *Art and Artifice in Shakespeare*. New York, 1933.

STOPES, C. C. *Shakespeare's Environment*. London, 1918.

— *The Life of Henry, Third Earl of Southampton*. Cambridge, 1922.

Studies in the First Folio written for the Shakespeare Association. London, 1924.

THEOBALD, W. *The Classical Element in Shakespeare's Plays*. London, 1909.

THOMAS, SIR H. *Shakespeare and Spain*. London, 1922.

THOMPSON, E. N. S. *Literary Bypaths of the Renaissance*. Newhaven and Oxford, 1924.

THOMSON, J. A. K. *Shakespeare and the Classics*. London, 1951.

TYNAN, J. L. 'The Influence of Greene on Shakespeare's early Romance', *PMLA* 27 (N.S. vol. 20), 1912, pp. 246–64.

TSCHERNJAJEW, P. 'Shakespeare und Terenz'. *Anglia*. 55. 1931, 282–95.

Tudor Fascimile Texts, ed. J. S. Farmer. 1907–14.

UNDERHILL, J. G. *Spanish Literature in the England of the Tudors*. New York, 1899.

UPHAM. A. H. *The French Influence in English Literature*. New York, 1906.

WHITAKER, V. K. *Shakspeare's Use of Learning*. San Marino, 1953.

WILSON, F. P. 'Shakespeare's Reading'; in *Shakespeare Survey*, 3. 1950.

WILSON, J. D. *The Essential Shakespeare*. Cambridge, 1932.

— Introductions to the *Cambridge edition*. 1921–

WOLF, S. L. *The Greek Romances in Elizabethan Prose Fiction*. New York, 1912.

WRIGHT, L. B. *Middle Class Culture in Elizabethan England*. Chapel Hill, 1935.

2. Editions and Criticism of Individual Works

THE COMEDY OF ERRORS

I. *Editions of (a) the Play, (b) Sources and Analogues*

(a) F1. 1623. *Modern Edns*. Cuningham H. Arden. London, 1906; French R. D. Yale. Newhaven, 1926; Quiller-Couch, A., & Wilson, J. D. Cambridge, 1922.

(*b*) PLAUTUS. *M. Accii Plauti Comoediae XX cura et studio J. Camerarii . . . editae*. Basileae. 1558.

WARNER, W. *Menaecmi. A pleasant and fine Conceited Comoedie; taken out of the most excellent wittie Poet Plautus . . . Written in English, by W. W*. London, 1595.

COLLIER, J. P., and HAZLITT, W. L. *Shakespeare's Library*. 2nd edn. 1875. Vol. V (text of Warner).

ROUSE, W. H. D. ed. *The Menaechmi, the original of Shakespeare's Comedy of Errors. The Latin text together with the Elizabethan translation*. (The Shakespeare Classics.) London, 1912.

SUGDEN, E. H. *Comedies of T. Maccius Plautus, translated in the original Metres*. London 1893. (*Amphitruo*.)

GOWER, J. *This booke is intituled confessio amantis*. W. Caxton. 1493. (Other edns. 1532, 1554.) Modern edns. by H. Morley, 1889; G. C. Macaulay, 1901.

II. *Critical Studies of Sources, etc.*

BALDWIN, T. W., *Shakespeare's Five-Act Structure*. Urbana, 1947, pp. 665–718

GAW, A. 'The Evolution of *The Comedy of Errors*', *PMLA* xli, 1926, pp. 620ff.

GILL, ERNA M. 'A Comparison of the characters in "The Comedy of Errors" with those in the *Menaechmi*.' Univ. of Texas Studies in English. 5. Austin, 1925.

— 'The plot-structure of *The Comedy of Errors* in relation to its sources.' Univ. of Texas Studies in English. 10. Austin, 1930, pp. 13–65.

ISAAC, H. 'Shakespeare's *Comedy of Errors* und die Menächmen des Plautus.' *Archiv*. lxx. 1883. 1ff.

ROEDER, K. *Menechmi und Amphitruo in Englischen Drama bis zur Restauration*. Dissertation. Leipzig, 1904.

THE TAMING OF THE SHREW

I. *Editions of* (*a*) *the Play*, (*b*) *Sources and Analogues*

(*a*) *The Shrew*. F1. 1623. *The Taming of the Shrew*. Modern edns.: Bond, R. W. Arden, 1904; Perry, H. T. E. Yale, 1921; Quiller-Couch, A., and Wilson, J. D. Cambridge, 1928.

(*b*) Q. *A Pleasant Conceited Historie, called The taming of a Shrew. As it was sundry times acted by the Right honorable the Earle of Pembrook his servants. . . .* London, 1594.

AMYOT, T. *The Old Taming of a Shrew*. London, 1844.

BOAS, F. S. ed. *The Taming of a Shrew*. (Shakespeare Classics.) London, 1908.

COLLIER, J. P., and HAZLITT, W. C. *Shakespeare's Library.* 2nd edn. 1875. Vol. VI.

FREY, A. R. Parallel text of both plays. 1888.

PRAETORIUS, C. *Shakespeare Quarto Facsimiles,* XV. ed. F. J. Furnivall. London, 1886.

ARIOSTO, L. *Comedia . . . intitolata li Suppositi.* Roma, 1524, etc.

— *La Comedie des Supposez . . . En Italien et Françoys.* (Tr. J. P. de Mesmes.) Paris, 1552.

— *Supposes and Jocasta,* ed. J. W. Cunliffe. 1906.

BURTON, R. *The Anatomy of Melancholy.* 1621.

COLLIER-HAZLITT. *Shakespeare's Library.* 2nd edn. 1875. Vol. IV (gives passages from Grimeston, *The Waking Man's Dreame*; and 'A Merry Jest of a Curst Wife Lapped in a Morel's Skin, for her Good Behaviour.')

DES PERIERS, B., *Nouvelles Récreations et Joyeux Devis* (1735) cf. *Fabliaux et Contes des 12me et 13me Siècles.* Paris, 1781

GASCOIGNE, G. *The Posies of George Gascoigne Esquire.* 2nd edn. 1575. (Contains *Supposes.*) Modern edn.: *The Complete Works.* Vol. I. (*Supposes,* etc.) Cambridge, 1907.

GOULART, S. *Histoires admirables et memorables de nostre temps . . . par S. Goulart.* (2nd edn.) Rouen, 1606.

— *Admirable and Memorable Histories containing the wonders of our time. . . .* (trans.) E. Grimston. London, 1607.

HEUTERUS, P. *De Rebus Burgundicis.* Lib. IV. 1584: and *Opera historica omnia . . .* Lovanii, 1643.

Jest-books. *A Hundred Mery Talys.* (c. 1525); *Tales and Quick Answers very Mery and Pleasant to Reade.* (c. 1535); *The first and best part of Scoggins Jests.* (1565?) 1626. Modern edn.: Hazlitt, W. C. *Shakespeare Jest-Books.* 3 vols. 1864.

PERCY, T. *Reliques of Ancient English Poetry.* Series 1, Bk II. 17. 'The Frolicsome Duke, or the Tinkers Good Fortune.' 4th edn. 1794.

II. *Critical Studies of Sources, etc.*

ALEXANDER, P. 'The Taming of *A* Shrew.' *TLS,* 16 Sept., 1926.

CRAIG, H. '*The Shrew* and *A Shrew*: Possible Settlement of an Old Debate' in *Presentation Volume to George F. Reynolds,* 1948.

DUTHIE, G. I. 'The Taming of A Shrew and The Taming of the Shrew.' *RES,* Oct. 1943.

HOUK, R. A. 'Strata in *The Taming of the Shrew.*' *S.Phil.* 39. 1942, pp. 291–302.

— *The Evolution of The Taming of the Shrew. PMLA,* Dec. 1942.

PARROTT, T. M. 'The Taming of A Shrew—A New Study of an Old Play' in *Elizabethan Studies &c. in honor of George F. Reynolds.* Boulder, Colorado, 1945.

TOLMAN, A. H. 'Shakespeare's Part in The Taming of the Shrew.' *PMLA* V, No. 4, 1890, and (separately) Strassburg, 1891.

VAN DAM, B. A. P. 'The Taming of A Shrew and The Taming of The Shrew.' *EngStud.* X. 97, 161. 1928.

WENTERSDORF, K. 'The Authenticity of the Taming of the Shrew.' *ShQ.* V. 1954. 11–21.

VENUS AND ADONIS

I. *Editions of (a) the Poem, (b) Sources and Analogues*

(a) Q1 *Venus and Adonis* . . . London, 1593.

> F1 1623. Modern edns.:—Wyndham, G. 1898; Dowden, E. 1903; Pooler, C. Knox. Arden, 1911, 1927; Feuillerat, A. Yale, 1927; Rollins, Hyder. Variorum, 1938. Facsimiles: W. Griggs (Q1) 1886; S. Lee (Q1) 1905.

(b) *The XV Bookes of P. Ovidius Naso, entytuled Metamorphosis, translated out of Latin into English meeter, by Arthur Golding Gentleman* . . . London, 1567.

> *The Pleasant Fable of Hermaphroditus and Salmacis.* Trans. Thomas Peend. London, 1565.

> *The Fable of Ovid treating of Narcissus, translated out of Latin into Englysh Mytre, with a moral therunto, very pleasante to rede.* London, MDLX.

> Modern edns.:—*Shakespeare's Ovid, being Arthur Golding's Translation of the Metamorphoses, edited by* W. H. D. Rouse. (The King's Library.) London, 1904.

> *Ovid: Selected Works,* ed. J. C. & M. J. Thornton. London, 1939, has selections from Golding.

II. *Critical Studies of Sources, etc.*

BALDWIN, T. W. *On the Literary Genetics of Shakespere's Poems and Sonnets.* Urbana, 1950.

BROWN, CARLETON. 'Shakespeare and the horse.' *Library,* Ser. 3. III. 1912. 152–220.

REARDON, J. P. 'Shakespeare's *Venus and Adonis* and Lodge's *Scillaes Metamorphosis.' Sh.Soc. Papers* iii. 1847. 143ff.

ROOT, R. K. *Classical Mythology in Shakespeare.* New York, 1903.

SARRAZIN, G. 'Die Abfassungszeit von *Venus and Adonis.' Eng. Studien.* xix. 1894. 352ff.

SPENCER, H. 'Shakespeare's Use of Golding in *Venus and Adonis.' MLN* 44. 1929. 435–7.

33*

THE RAPE OF LUCRECE

I. *Editions of (a) the Poem, (b) Sources and Analogues*

(*a*) Q. *Lucrece.* London, 1594. F1 1623.

Modern edns.: Wyndham, G. 1898; Pooler, C. K. Arden, 1911, 1927; Rollins, Hyder. Variorum, 1938.

Facsimiles: Praetorius, C. *Sh.Q.* Fac. xxxv. 1886; Lee, S. 1905.

(*b*) CHAUCER, G. *The Legende of Good Women* in *The Works of Geoffray Chaucer newly printed* . . . (ed. W. Thynne). 1532. Modern edn.: *The Works,* ed. A. W. Pollard, etc. London, 1898.

COOPER, T. *Thesaurus Linguae Latinae et Britannicae.* London, 1565, etc.

LIVIUS, T. *T Livii Patavini Romanae historiae principis libri omnes.* London, 1589.

OVID. *P. Ovidii Nasonis fastorum libri diligenti emendatione* . . . *commentatoribus Antonio Constantio fanensi: Paulo Marso piscinate.* Venetiis, 1520.

Ovid's festivalls, or Romane Calendar. Translated into English verse equinumerally by J. Gower, master of arts. Cambridge, 1640.

PAINTER, W. *The Palace of Pleasure.* (Vol. i) London, 1566. Modern edn.: ed. Joseph Jacobs, 3 vols. 1890.

II. *Critical Studies of Sources, etc.*

BALDWIN, T. W. *On the Literary Genetics of Shakespeare's Poems and Sonnets.* Urbana, 1950.

COLVIN, S. ' The sack of Troy in Shakespeare's *Lucrece* and in some 15th century drawings and tapestries.' In: *A Book of Homage to Shakespeare,* ed. I. Gollancz. London, 1916.

EWIG, E. 'Shakespeare's Lucrece.' Anglia xxii, 1899. 12ff.

GALINSKY, H. *Der Lucretia-Stoff in der Weltliteratur.* Dissertation. Breslau, 1932.

THE TWO GENTLEMEN OF VERONA

I. *Editions of (a) the Play, (b) Sources and Analogues*

(*a*) F1 1623. Modern edns. Bond, R. E. Arden, 1906 (includes summary of *Julio und Hyppolita* and extract from A. Munday's *Downfall of Robert Earl of Huntington,* III.2, from Dodsley-Hazlitt; Quiller-Couch, A., and Wilson, J. D. Cambridge, 1921; Young, K. Yale, 1924.

(*b*) BOCCACIO, G. *La Teseide.* Ferrara, 1475; and *La Theseide innamoramento piacevole e honesto di due Giovani Thebane, Arcita e Palemone* . . . *nuovamente ridotta in prosa per N. Granucci.* Lucca, 1579.

— *Il Decamerone . . . nuovamente corretto, historiato e stampato . . .* Venetia, 1540.

CHAUCER, G. *The workes of Geffray Chaucer newly printed, with dyvers workes never in print before.* (Ed. W. Thynne.) London, 1532. Modern (Globe) edn. by A. W. Pollard, etc., 1898.

ELYOT, SIR T. *The boke named The Governour.* London, 1531. Modern edn. ed. F. Watson. 1907.

LYLY, J. *Euphues, The Anatomy of Wit.* 1578? Modern edns:— E. Arber, 1868; R. W. Bond, *Complete Works*, 3 vols. 1902.

[LYLY, J.] *Sapho and Phao.* 1584. *Endimion, the man in the moone.* 1591. *Midas.* 1592. *Mother Bombie.* 1594. Modern edn.: Bond, *op. cit.*

MONTEMAYOR, J. DE. *Los siete libros de la Diana de Jorge de Montemayor.* Valencia, 1559, etc. (The Lisbon 1565 edn. has the poem *Piramo y Tisbe.*)

— *Diana of George of Montemayor. Translated out of Spanish into English by Bartholomew Yong of the Middle Temple Gentleman.* London, 1598. 3 parts.

COLLIER, J. P. *Shakespeare's Library*, 1843. Vol. 2; and Collier-Hazlitt, *Shakespeare's Library.* 2nd edn. 1875, Pt. I, Vol. I give part of 'The story of Filismena' from Yong.

SIDNEY, SIR P. *The Countess of Pembroke's Arcadia.* 1590. Modern edn.: A. Feuillerat. Cambridge, 1922.

Julio und Hyppolita from *Englische Comedien und Tragedien.* 1620; in Cohn, A. *Shakespeare in Germany.* 1865.

II. *Critical Studies*

CAMPBELL, O. J. 'The Two Gentlemen of Verona and Italian Comedy' in *Michigan Studies in Shakespeare, Milton and Donne.* New York, 1925.

HARRISON, T. P. 'Concerning *The Two Gentlemen of Verona* and Montemayor's Diana.' *MLN* xli 251 and Univ. of Texas Bull., 1926, pp. 72–120.

PARKS, G. B. 'The Development of *The Two Gentlemen of Verona.*' Huntington Library Bull., April 1937.

SARGENT, R. M. '*Sir T. Elyot & The Integrity of Two Gentlemen of Verona.*' *PMLA*, Dec. 1950.

SMALL, S. A. 'The ending of *The Two Gentlemen of Verona.*' *PMLA* 48, 1933, 767–76.

ROMEO AND JULIET

I. *Editions of (a) the Play, (b) Sources and Analogues*

(*a*) Q1. *An Excellent conceited Tragedie of Romeo and Juliet. As it hath been often (with great applause) plaid publiquely, by the right Honourable the L. of Hunsdon his Servants.* London, John Danter, 1597 (A 'bad' Quarto).

Q2. *The most Excellent and lamentable Tragedie of Romeo and Juliet.
Newly corrected, augmented, and amended: As it hath bene sundry
times publiquely acted, by the right Honourable the Lord Chamberlaine his servants.* Thomas Creede for Cuthbert Burby. 1599.
Q3 1609. Q4 n.d. Q4 1637.

F1. 1623. Modern edns.: Facsimile (Q2), C. Praetorius, *Sh.
Quartos.* 1886; Furness, H. H. Variorum, 1871, 1909;
Dowden, E. Arden, 1900; Durham, W. H. Yale, 1917;
Wilson, J. D. and Duthie, G. I. Cambridge, 1955.

(*b*) BANDELLO, M. *Le Novelle del Bandello.* (Pt. II. Nov. 9.) Lucca,
1554.

BOAISTUAU, P. *Histoires Tragiques extraictes des oeuvres italiens de
Bandel.* . . . Paris, 1559, 1561, etc.

BROOKE, A. *The Tragicall Historye of Romeus and Juliet.* London,
1562.

Modern edns.: P. A. Daniel, *Sh.Soc.* Ser. III. 1875; Collier-Hazlitt,
Shakespeare's Library. Vol. i. 1875; J. J. Munro, *Brooke's
Romeus and Juliet* (Shakespeare Classics). 1908.

CLIZIA. *L'infelice Amore di due fedelissimi Amanti*; in L. da Porto,
Giulietta e Romeo. Pisa, 1831.

GROTO, L. *La Hadriana, tragedia nova.* Venetia, [1578], 1583, 1599.

MASUCCIO (SALERNITANO). *Il Novellino* (Nov. xxxiii). 1476.
Modern edn.: in *Novelle del Quattrocento*, ed. Fatini,
Torino, 1929.

— *Il Novellino.* Translated by W. G. Waters. London, 1895.
Vol. II.

PAINTER, W. *The second Tome of the Palace of Pleasure conteyning
manifolde store of goodly Histories, Tragicall matters and other
Morall arguments . . . chosen and selected out of divers good and
commendable Authors by William Painter . . .* London, 1567.
Modern edns.: ed. Joseph Jacobs. 3 vols. London, 1890.
(Vol. iii); P. Haworth, *An Elizabethan Story-Book.* London,
1928.

PORTO, L. DA. *Istoria novellamente ritrovata di due Nobili Amanti
con la loro pietosa morte intervenuta nella Città di Verona nel Tempo
del S. Bartholomeo della Scala.* (1530?) Modern edns.: G.
Pace-Sanfelice, *The Original Story of Romeo & Juliet.* 1868
(with trans.); W. J. Rolfe, *Juliet & Romeo.* Boston, 1895
(trans.); *Romeo and Juliet: A Photographic reproduction of
Luigi da Porto's prose version of Romeo and Giulietta dated 1535
. . . With a literal translation into English from the Italian . . .*
by Maurice Jonas. London, 1921.

SEVIN, A. Dedication to *Le Philocope de Messire Jehan Boccace.*
Venetia, 1542, 1553. Reprinted A. Cohn, *ShJb* 24. 1889.
122–30.

VEGA, L. DA. *Los Castelvines y Manteses.* Trans. F. W. Cosens. 1869.

II. *Critical Studies of Sources, etc.*

ALLEN, N. B. 'Shakespeare and Arthur Brooke.' *Delaware Notes.* 17 Series, 1944.

CHARLTON, H. B. 'France as Chaperone of Romeo and Juliet' in *Studies in French Language and Medieval Literature presented to Professor M. K. Pope.* Manchester, 1939.

— 'Romeo and Juliet as an Experimental Tragedy.' *Brit. Acad. Lecture.* 1939.

COHN, A. On *Romio und Julietta*, in *Shakespeare in Germany.* 1865.

DELIUS, N. 'Brooke's episches und Shakespeare's dramatisches Gedicht von R.u.J.' *ShJb* XVI. 1881.

DOWDEN, E. In *Transcripts and Studies.* 1888.

DRAPER, J. W. 'Shakespeare's "Star-crossed Lovers".' *RES*, Jan. 1939.

ERSKINE, J. 'Romeo and Juliet' in *Shakespearian Studies*, ed. Matthews and Thorndike. New York, 1916.

LAW, R. E. 'On Shakespeare's changes of his source material in *Romeo and Juliet.*' *Texas.* No. 9. 1929. 87–102.

MOORE, O. H. 'Le rôle de Boaistuau dans le developpement de la légende de Romeo et Juliette.' *Litt. Comp.* ix. 1929.

— 'The origins of the Legend of Romeo and Juliet in Italy.' *Speculum* v. 1930.

— 'Shakespeare's Deviations from *Romeus and Juliet.*' *PMLA* 52. N.S. 45. 1937.

— *The Legend of Romeo & Juliet.* Columbus, Ohio, 1950.

SMITH, W. 'A Comic Version of Romeo and Juliet.' *MPhil.* VII. 1909–10. 217–20.

A MIDSUMMER NIGHT'S DREAM

I. *Editions of (a) the Play, (b) its Sources and Analogues*

(a) Q1. *A Midsommer nights dreame. As it hath beene sundry times publickely acted, by the Right honourable, the Lord Chamberlaine his servants. Written by William Shakespeare.* For T. Fisher. London, 1600.

Q2 dated 1600 but actually printed 1619. F1 1623.

Modern edns.: Furness, H. H. Variorum, 1895; Cuningham H. Arden, 1905; Durham, W. H. Yale, 1918; Quiller-Couch, A., and Wilson, J. W. Cambridge, 1924.

(b) APULEIUS. *The XI Bookes of the Golden Asse, conteininge the Metamorphoses of Lucius Apuleius.* Trans. William Adlington, 1566, 1571, 1596; 1639: Mod. edn. C. Whibley, 1893.

BERNERS, LORD, trans. *The ancient historie of Huon of Bordeaux* (1534 Wynkyn de Worde?; 1570 R. Copland?) 1601. Mod. edn.: S. L. Lee, *EETS* xl, xliii. 1883–5.

CHAUCER, G. *The Knightes Tale* in *The Works of Geoffrey Chaucer* newly printed . . . [ed. W. Thynne] 1532. Mod. edn.: *The Works*, ed. A. W. Pollard, etc. 1898.

COOPER, T. *Thesaurus Linguae Romanae et Britannicae.* 1565, 1573, 1578, 1587.

HAZLITT, W. C. *Fairy Tales, Legends and Romances illustrating Shakespeare and other early English writers.* London, 1875. (Includes *Huon of Bordeaux; Robin Goodfellow* (1628); etc.)

MS *The Tragedie of Pyramus and Thisbe.* (*c.* 1630?) Brit. Mus. Add. MS 15,227. f. 56v ff.

OVID. *The XV bookes of P. Ovidius Naso entytuled Metamorphosis.* *Trans. into English meeter by A. Golding.* 1567, 1575, 1584, 1587, 1593. Mod. edn.: W. H. D. Rouse (The King's Library). 1904.

PLUTARCH. *The Lives of the noble Grecians and Romanes.* Trans. out of the French by T. North. 1579. Mod. edn.: G. Wyndham. 6 vols. 1895.

ROBINSON, C. *A handefull of pleasant delites by C. Robinson and divers others.* 1584. Mod. edn.: A. Kershaw. 1926; H. Rollins. 1924.

SCOT, R. *The Discoverie of Witchcraft.* B.L. 1584. Mod. edn.: M. Summers. London, 1930.

SIDGWICK, F. *Sources and Analogues of A Midsummer Night's Dream.* (King's Classics.) 1908.

II. *Critical Studies of Sources, etc.*

BETHURUM, D. 'Sh's Comment on Med. Romance' *MLN*, Feb. 1945.

FLUGEL, E. 'Pyramys und Tysbe.' *Anglia* 12. 1889. 13–20.

DAVENPORT, A. 'Weever, Ovid and Shakespeare.' *N. & Q.* 1949. Nov. 26.

HALLIWELL-PHILLIPS, J. O. Illustrations of the Fairy Mythology of *Midsummer Night's Dream. Sh.Soc.* 1845.

HART, G. *Die Pyramus-und-Thisbe Saga.* 1889–91.

HEMINGWAY, S. B. 'The Relation of *MND* to Romeo and Juliet.' *MLN* xxvi. 1911. 78.

LAW, R. A. 'The Pre-Conceived Pattern of *MND*.' Univ. of Texas Studies in English. 1943.

POIRIER, R. 'Sidney's Influence upon *MND.*' *SPhil.* July, 1947.

SARRAZIN, G. 'Die Abfassungszeit des *Sommernachtstraums.*' *Arch.* 95. 1895; and 104. 1900.

TOBLER, R. 'Shakespeare's *MND* und Montemayor's *Diana.*' *ShJb* xxxiv. 1898. 358ff.

LOVE'S LABOUR'S LOST

I. *Editions of (a) the Play, (b) Sources and Analogues*

(a) Q1 *A Pleasant Conceited Comedie called, Loves Labours Lost. As it was presented before her Highnes this last Christmas. Newly corrected and augmented by W. Shakespere.* London. W. W. for Cutbert Burby, 1598.

F1 1623. Modern edns.: Furness, H. H. Variorum, 1904; Hart, H. C. Arden, 1906; Charlton, H. B. 1917; Quiller-Couch, A., and Wilson, J. D. Cambridge, 1923; Cross, W. L., and Brooke, C. F. T. Yale, 1925; David, R. New Arden, 1951.

(b) BOND, E. A. *Travels of Sir Jerome Horsey* in *Russia at the Close of the Sixteenth Century.* Hakluyt Society. London, 1856.

DAVILA, H. C. *The History of the Civil Wars of France.* Trans. C. Cottrell, 1678.

GREG, W. W. ed. *Gesta Grayorum (1688).* Mal. Soc. Reprint, 1915.

MARGUÉRITE DE VALOIS. *Mémoires,* ed. A. de Mauléon. Paris, 1628. Trans. Violet Fane, 1892.

MONSTRELET, E. DE. *Les Chroniques.* (c.1500). Trans. T. Johnes, 1810.

LA PRIMAUDAYE, P. DE. *L'Académie française.* 1577. Trans. T. B[owes]. *The French Academie.* London, 1586, 1589, 1594, etc.

II. *Critical Studies of Sources, etc.*

CAMPBELL, O. J. 'Love's Labour's Lost Re-studied.' Michigan Studies, 1925.

CHARLTON, H. B. 'The Date of Love's Labour's Lost.' *MLR* xiii. 1918. 257ff, 387ff.

DRAPER, J. W. 'Shakespeare and Muscovy.' *Slavonic Review.* xxxiii. 80. 1955.

GRAY, H. D. *The Original Version of Love's Labour's Lost.* Stanford, 1918.

LEE, S. 'A new Study of Love's Labour's Lost.' *Gent. Mag.,* Oct. 1880, and *Sh.Soc. Trans.* Pt. iii. 80.

LEFRANC, A. *Sous le Masque de Shakespeare.* 1918.

STRATHMANN, E. A. 'The Textual Evidence for "The School of Night".' *MLN.* March, 1941.

YATES, F. A. *A Study of Love's Labour's Lost.* Cambridge, 1934.

— *French Academies of the Sixteenth Century.* London, 1947.

THE MERCHANT OF VENICE

I. *Editions of (a) the Play, (b) Sources and Analogues*

(*a*) Q1. *The most excellent Historie of the Merchant of Venice. With the extreame crueltie of Shylocke the Jewe towards the sayd Merchant, in cutting a just pound of his flesh: and the obtayning of Portia by the choyce of three chests. As it hath beene divers times acted by the Lord Chamberlaine his Servants. Written by William Shakespeare.* London, I. R. for Thomas Heyes, 1600.

Q2 dated 1600 but actually printed 1619. Q3 1637. Q4 1652. F1 1623.

Modern edns.: Q1 Fascimile: C. Praetorius, *Sh. Quartos.* 1887. Furness, H. H. Variorum, 1888; Pooler, C. K. Arden, 1905, 1927; Phelps, W. L. Yale, 1923; Quiller-Couch, A., and Wilson, J. D. Cambridge, 1926; Brown, J. R. New Arden, 1955.

(*b*) (Anon.) 'A new Song: Shewing the crueltie of Gernutus a Jew . . . Printed at London by E.P. for I. Wright.' n.d. Mod. edn.: in *The Pepys Ballads*, ed. H. E. Rollins. 1929. I. 16–17.

Cursor Mundi, ed. R. Morris, *EETS.* 1874–93; L. Toulmin Smith, *Sh.Soc. Trans.* 1875–6, pp. 181–9.

GIOVANNI SER, FIORENTINO. *Il Pecorone . . . nel quale si contengono cinquanta novelle antiche . . .* Milano, 1558, etc. Trans. of Day IV, Nov. 1, in Collier-Hazlitt. *Sh.Lib.* I. 1875. Variorum and New Arden.

Gesta Romanorum, trans. R. Robinson. 1577, 1595. Mod. edns.: Madden, Sir F., *The Old English Versions of the Gesta Romanorum*. Roxburghe Club. 1838; re-ed. J. H. Herrtage, *EETS.*, Ex.S.33, 1879.

GOWER, J. *This booke is intituled confessio amantis.* W. Caxton. 1493, 1532, 1554. Mod. edns.: H. Morley, 1889; G. C. Macaulay, 1901.

MARLOWE, C. *The Famous Tragedy of the Rich Jew of Malta . . . Written by Christopher Marlo.* 1633. Mod. edns.: Tucker Brooke, *Works*, 1910; H. S. Bennett, 1931.

MASUCCIO OF SALERNO. *Il Novellino.* 1476. Trans. W. G. Waters. 2 vols. 1895. (Nov. 14.)

MUNDAY, A. *Zelauto or the Fountaine of Fame.* 3 pts. 1580.

SILVAYN, A. *The Orator*, by Alexandre Silvayn (Alex. van den Busche), trans. L. P[iot]. 1596.

W[ILSON] R[OBERT]. *A right excellent & famous Comoedy called The three Ladies of London.* Written by R. W. London, 1584. Modern edn.: J. S. Farmer (Tudor Facs. Texts) 1911.

II. *Critical Studies of Sources, etc.*

BROWN, B. D. 'Medieval Prototypes of Lorenzo and Jessica.' *MLN* xliv, 1929, pp. 227–32.

CARDOZO, J. L. 'The background of Shakespeare's *Merchant of Venice.' Eng. St.* xiv, 1932, pp. 177–86.

DIMOCK, I. F. 'The Conspiracy of Dr Lopez.' *EHR*, ix, 1894, 440ff.

ELZE, K. 'Zum Kaufmann von Venedig.' *ShJb* VI, 1871, pp. 129–68.

GRÄTZ, H. *Shylock in der Sage, um Drama und in der Geschichte*, Krotoschin. 1880, 1888.

KOHLER, J. *Shakespeare vor dem Forum der Jurisprudenz.* Berlin, 1883–4, 1919.

LEE, S. *Elizabethan England and the Jews. New Sh.Soc.* 1888, 143ff.

ROTH, C. 'The background of Shylock.' *RES.* ix. 1933.

SCHLAUCH, M. 'The pound of flesh story in the north.' *JEGP* xxx, 1931, pp. 348–80.

SINSHEIMER, H. *Shylock: The History of a Character, or the Myth of the Jew.* London, 1947.

SMALL, S. A. 'The Jew.' *MLR* xxvi, 1931, pp. 281–7.

STOLL, E. E. *Shylock. JEGP* x, 1911, 236–79; and in *Shakespeare Studies.* New York, 1927.

STONEX, A. B. 'The Usurer in Elizabethan Drama.' *PMLA* 31 (N.S. xxiv), 1916, 190ff.

TOULMIN SMITH. 'On the Bond-story in *MV* and a version of it in *Cursor Mundi.' New Sh.Soc.* 1875, pp. 181–9.

INDEX TO THE INTRODUCTIONS